Dr. Arun Kumar R.

MW00523083

Oracle®
Database 10g

SAMS   800 East 96th Street, Indianapolis, Indiana 46240 USA

Oracle Database 10g Insider Solutions

Copyright © 2006 by Sams Publishing

International Standard Book Number: 0-672-32791-0

Library of Congress Catalog Card Number: 2005902434

Printed in the United States of America

First Printing: September 2005

08   07   4 3 2

Trademarks

All terms mentioned in this book that are known to be trademarks or service marks have been appropriately capitalized. Sams Publishing cannot attest to the accuracy of this information. Use of a term in this book should not be regarded as affecting the validity of any trademark or service mark.

Warning and Disclaimer

Every effort has been made to make this book as complete and as accurate as possible, but no warranty or fitness is implied. The information provided is on an "as is" basis. The authors and the publisher shall have neither liability nor responsibility to any person or entity with respect to any loss or damages arising from the information contained in this book.

Bulk Sales

Sams Publishing offers excellent discounts on this book when ordered in quantity for bulk purchases or special sales. For more information, please contact

U.S. Corporate and Government Sales
1-800-382-3419
corpsales@pearsontechgroup.com

For sales outside of the U.S., please contact

International Sales
international@pearsoned.com

Publisher
Paul Boger

Acquisitions Editor
Loretta Yates

Development Editor
Songlin Qiu

Managing Editor
Charlotte Clapp

Project Editor
George Nedeff

Copy Editor
Kate Shoup Welsh

Indexer
Erika Millen

Proofreader
Leslie Joseph

Technical Editor
K. Gopalakrishnan

Designer
Gary Adair

Publishing Coordinator
Cindy Teeters

Contents at a Glance

Introduction 1

Part I **Getting Started with Oracle Database 10g**

1 Exploring Oracle Database 10g Architecture 7

2 Installing Oracle Database 10g 23

3 Customizing Installation Options 53

4 Setting Up Automatic Storage Management 73

Part II **Quick Wins Using Oracle Database 10g**

5 Using Automatic Memory Management 93

6 Monitoring with Automatic Statistics Collection 105

7 Managing Automatic Undo 131

8 Leveraging Automatic Segment Management 141

9 Implementing Recovery Manager 153

Part III **Tuning Oracle Database 10g**

10 Adopting a New Approach to Tuning 175

11 Effectively Using the Automatic Workload Repository 207

12 Effectively Using the Automatic Database Diagnostic Monitor ... 239

13 Effectively Using the SQL Advisors 263

14 Influencing the Cost Based Optimizer 287

Part IV **Scaling and Availability with Oracle Database 10g**

15 Utilizing Oracle Database 10g Real Applications Clusters 313

16 Utilizing 10g Physical and Logical Standby with Data Guard 339

17 Effectively Using Flashback Technologies 369

18 Leveraging Grid Technology Features 413

Part V **Using Oracle Database 10g Utilities and Other Advanced Features**

19 Maximizing Data Movement with Oracle Data Pump 425

20 Using 10g SQL*Plus and iSQL*Plus 447

21 Making the Most of Oracle Database 10g 455

Index 469

Table of Contents

Introduction 1

Who Should Read This Book 1

What You Need to Use This Book 1

How This Book Is Organized 2

About the Book's Sample Code 3

Conventions Used in This Book 3

Part I   Getting Started with Oracle Database 10g

1   Exploring Oracle Database 10g Architecture 7

Overview of New Features 7

SYSAUX Tablespace 8

Rename Tablespace Option 8

Automatic Storage Management 9

Temporary Tablespace Group 9

BigFile Tablespace 9

Cross-Platform Transportable Tablespaces 10

Performance Management Using AWR 11

Automatic Database Diagnostic Monitor (ADDM) 12

DROP DATABASE Command 13

Data Pump Utilities 13

Processes Beneath the Hood 14

Classification of Database Processes 14

Memory Architecture 16

System Global Area (SGA) 17

Program Global Area (PGA) 18

Memory Manager (MMAN) 18

Automatic Undo Management 18

SQL Advisors 19

Oracle's Suite of Other Advisors 19

Flash Recovery Area 19

Flashback Operations 20

Flashback Database 20

Improved Oracle Enterprise Manager 20

Grid Technology Unveiled 21

Summary 21

2   Installing Oracle Database 10g   23

Installation Decisions 23

Prerequisites 24

    Overview of Silent Installation 25

Installing 10g on UNIX/Linux 25

    Installation Steps 27

    Platform-Independent Database Installation Questions 27

    Optimal Flexible Architecture (OFA) 29

    Common Steps for Installation 30

    Components to Access Other Databases and Applications 32

Oracle Database 10g DBCA Overview 32

    Tracing the Database Configuration Assistant (DBCA) 33

Installing 10g on Windows 34

Companion CD Installation and Patches (All Platforms) 35

    Manual Database Installation Steps 36

Installation Checklists 36

Database and Binary Cloning 36

Using Enterprise Manager for Cloning 38

Migrating a Database from 8i or 9i 39

Overview of Database Upgrade Assistant 40

    Upgrade Path for Standby Environments 41

    Database Upgrade Assistant in Silent Mode 42

    Using DBUA with Oracle 9i Physical Standby Configuration 42

    Using DBUA with Oracle 9i Logical Standby Configuration 44

Applying Patches to Database Installations 46

Uninstalling from a Failed Install 47

    Step 1: Identify All Database Instances 48

    Step 2: Remove the Database(s) 48

    Step 3: Remove the Oracle Software 50

Summary 52

3   Customizing Installation Options   53

OEM and Automatic Alerts 53

    OEM Preinstallation Requirements 54

    OEM Installation Process 55

    Control for Oracle Management Agents 58

    Automatic Alerts and Management 58

    Metric-Thresholds Management 59

    Mobile Management Using EM2Go 60

XML DB for XML Data Processing 61
    Installing XML DB 61
ConText and Other Options 63
    Manual Installation of Oracle Text 64
    Installation of Oracle Spatial 65
    Operations with Oracle UltraSearch 65
Setting Up RAC 66
    Manual Installation of RAC Instance 66
    Installation of RAC Instance Using Data Guard 68
Managing Backups with RMAN 68
    Important Points on RMAN During Database Upgrade 70
    Unregister a Target Database 71
    Glimpse of Oracle Database 10g Release 2 71
Summary 72

4 Setting Up Automatic Storage Management   73
Automatic Storage Management (ASM) 73
Prerequisites for Using ASM 74
    ASM Architecture in a Nutshell 75
Configuration Options 76
    Initialization Parameters for ASM Instances 78
    StartUp/Shutdown Commands on an ASM Instance 79
Performing ASM Operations 79
    The CREATE DISK GROUP Command 79
    Other Operations on a Disk Group 80
Avoiding ASM Pitfalls 85
    Unable to Connect to ASM Instance 85
    Non-ASM and ASM Database Migrations 86
    Discovering ASM Instances in a RAC Environment 88
    VIP Timeouts and VIP Failure on RAC 88
When and Where to Use ASM 89
    ASM Improvements in Oracle Database 10g Release 2 89
Summary 90

Part II Quick Wins Using Oracle Database 10g

5 Using Automatic Memory Management   93
Introduction to Quick Wins 93
What Is Automatic Shared Memory Management? 94
    SGA Sizing Considerations 96

Understanding Memory Advisor 97
    Memory Advisors Through OEM 97
Automated Maintenance Tasks 100
Memory Management Tips 100
    Converting a Manual Memory–Managed Database to ASMM 101
    Tuning SGA_TARGET and SGA_MAX_SIZE 102
Scaling for Database Expansion 103
ASMM Improvements in 10g Release 2 104
Summary 104

6   Monitoring with Automatic Statistics Collection   105

Automatic Statistics Collection Fundamentals 105
    Types of Database Statistics 106
    Database Metrics Revisited 108
    Statistics Levels and AWR Snapshots 108
Collecting and Analyzing Statistics 111
    Preventing the Time Out of GATHER_STATS_JOB 112
    Cross-Checking Your Statistics and Ratios 112
    AWR Reports Generation 113
Metrics Monitoring and Customization 125
Using Database Alerts with Metrics 126
Making the Most of Metrics and Statistics Collection 127
    Statistics Collection During Database Upgrades 128
New Features in Oracle Database 10g Release 2 128
Summary 130

7   Managing Automatic Undo   131

Using Automatic Undo Management 131
    How Undo Data Helps the Database 132
    The Significance of the UNDO_RETENTION Parameter 133
    Resumable Space Allocation 133
    Undo Management in Real Application Clusters 134
Redo Log File Sizings 134
Using Undo Advisor 134
    Undo Management Using OEM 135
    Making the Most of Undo Advisor 136
Guaranteeing Undo Availability 137
Undo Tips from the Trenches 138
Automatic Undo Management Improvements in Release 2 139
Summary 139

8   **Leveraging Automatic Segment Management**   **141**

    Segment Management in Oracle Database 10g.............................141
        Data, Index, and Temporary Segments..............................142
    Making Segment Management Work for You................................143
    Using Segment Advisor...143
        Invoking Segment Advisor from Enterprise Manager.................144
        Invoking Segment Advisor from PL/SQL.............................145
        Reviewing Segment Advisor Results................................146
    Intelligent Segment Resource Estimation...............................147
    Space-Management Tips and Tricks......................................148
        Limitations for Online Segment-Shrink Operations................150
        For Dictionary-Managed Tablespaces..............................150
    ASSM Improvements in Release 2..150
    Summary...151

9   **Implementing Recovery Manager**   **153**

    RMAN Basics...153
        Difference Between RMAN and Hot Backup..........................154
        Advantages of RMAN over Hot Backup..............................154
        A Sample RMAN Backup Session....................................156
        RMAN Documentation..160
        Accessing RMAN..161
    New Features of RMAN..161
        Use of Flash Recovery Area......................................162
        Fast Incremental Backups..163
        Incrementally Updated Backups...................................164
        Recovery Through RESETLOGS......................................166
        RMAN Tuning...167
        Other RMAN Improvements...167
    Recovery Without Hurdles..168
        Backup Strategies...168
        Recovery Scenarios..169
    New Features in Oracle Database 10g Release 2.........................170
    Summary...171

Part III   Tuning Oracle Database 10g

10 **Adopting a New Approach to Tuning**   **175**

    A New Performance Philosophy..175
        Performance-Management Tools....................................177
        STATSPACK Shortfalls..177

New and Improved Views 180
    V$METRIC, V$METRIC_HISTORY, V$METRICNAME, and
        V$METRICGROUP 181
    V$SERVICES, V$SERVICEMETRIC, and
        V$SERVICEMETRIC_HISTORY 182
    V$SERVICE_STATS 182
    V$SERVICE_EVENT 183
    V$EVENTMETRIC 184
    V$EVENT_HISTOGRAM 184
    V$FILEMETRIC and V$FILEMETRIC_HISTORY 186
    V$FILE_HISTOGRAM 186
    V$TEMP_HISTOGRAM 188
    V$ENQUEUE_STATISTICS 188
    V$OSSTAT 189
    Changes in Existing Views 189
    Changes in Other Views 190
Time and Wait Model 191
OEM and Tuning 194
    Navigating OEM Database Control 195
    Alerts and Metrics 203
    Advisors 205
New Features in Oracle Database 10g Release 2 205
Summary 206

11 Effectively Using the Automatic Workload Repository   207
Introducing the AWR 207
    AWR Collection 208
    Comparison to STATSPACK 209
    AWR Storage and Reporting 210
    Accessing the AWR Snapshots 213
Customizing the AWR 215
    AWR Dependencies 215
    Using the OEM to Customize the AWR 216
    Using the SQL Interface to AWR 217
Performing Baselining 220
    Capturing Baselines 220
    Dropping Baselines 221
Active Session History 222
    Session-State Information 222
    Using Session-State Information 223

The Connection to Active Session History 225

Size of Active Session History Buffers 229

An Example of Spot Analysis Using ASH 229

Using OEM to Obtain Active Session History 233

Dumping ASH Buffer Contents 234

The Downside of ASH 236

New Features in Oracle Database 10g Release 2 236

Summary 237

12 **Effectively Using the Automatic Database Diagnostic Monitor**   239

Introduction to ADDM 239

The Goal of ADDM 240

Problem Areas Handled by ADDM 241

Using ADDM with ASH 242

Nonproblematic Areas 242

Helpful ADDM Views 243

Interfacing to ADDM 244

Using OEM for ADDM 244

Using SQL to Get to ADDM 250

Making Sense of ADDM Data 254

Finding 1: SQL Statements Consuming Significant Time 254

Finding 2: SQL Statements Waiting for Locks 257

Finding 3: Session Management 258

Other Findings 259

Expected I/O Response Time 261

Cross-Verification from the Advisor Views 261

New Features in Oracle Database 10g Release 2 262

Summary 262

13 **Effectively Using the SQL Advisors**   263

Automating the SQL Advisors 263

The SQL Tuning Advisor 263

The SQL Access Advisor 267

Using the Advisors for Tuning 268

OEM Interface to the SQL Tuning Advisor 268

OEM Interface to the SQL Access Advisor 271

APIs to the SQL Tuning Advisor 275

Avoiding Advisor Pitfalls 284

New Features in Oracle Database 10g Release 2 285

Summary 285

14   Influencing the Cost Based Optimizer   287

New Optimizer Improvements 287

    RBO and CBO: A Comparison 288

    What the Optimizer Does 289

    The Relevance of Object Statistics 291

    The Relevance of System Statistics 293

    The Relevance of Dictionary Statistics 295

    Dynamic Sampling 295

    Table and Index Monitoring 296

    Parameters Influencing the Optimizer 297

    Cardinality, Selectivity, and Column Usage 302

    Tracing the Optimizer 303

SQL Profiles 304

Effective Use of Histograms 307

New Features in Oracle Database 10g Release 2 309

Summary 310

Part IV   Scaling and Availability with Oracle Database 10g

15   Utilizing Oracle Database 10g Real Applications Clusters   313

Oracle 10g RAC Overview 313

Cluster Ready Services 314

    Cluster Ready Services Architecture 315

    Installing Cluster Ready Services 316

    Troubleshooting the CRS Install 322

Service Workload Management 323

10g RAC Installation and Migration Enhancements 324

    Local Versus Shared Install 324

    Installing the 10g ORACLE_HOME 324

    Adding a Node to or Removing a Node from an Existing
       ORACLE_HOME 325

    Migrating from a Previous Release 326

10g RAC Manageability Enhancements 326

    Oracle Cluster Registry 326

    New Support for 10g Utilities 327

    Managing RAC with 10g Enterprise Manager 330

Automatic Storage Management for Cluster Management 331

    Managing ASM with 10g RAC 331

    ASM Maximum File Size Limitation with 10g RAC 332

Third-Party Cluster Management Support 333

Limited Rolling Upgrade with OPATCH 334

10g RAC Tips for Better Use 335

    Cluster Interconnect 335

    SGA Components 335

    Tablespaces 336

    Tables and Indexes 336

    Function-Dependent Routing 336

    Object Partitioning 336

    Running 10g RAC with 9i RAC in Same Environment 336

    CRS and ASM 337

Advanced RAC Features in Oracle Database 10g Release 2 337

Summary 338

16 Utilizing 10g Physical and Logical Standby with Data Guard   339

Oracle 10g Data Guard Overview 339

General Improvements with Oracle 10g Data Guard 340

    Real Time Apply 340

    Flashback Database Support 342

    Redo Transmission Authentication and Encryption 343

    Role-Based Destinations 343

    Improved Data Guard Configuration Management 345

    Improved Data Guard STARTUP Command 345

    Improved Data Guard Archiving 345

Logical Standby Improvements 346

    Zero Outage for Instantiation 346

    Support for Redo Log Files 348

    The PREPARE TO SWITCHOVER Command 348

    Support for SQL Apply Services 349

    Rolling Database Upgrades with SQL Apply 349

    Enhanced Logical Standby Commands and Views 349

Data Guard Broker Improvements 351

    Broker Support for RAC Databases 351

    Enhancements to the Enterprise Manager Data Guard GUI 351

    New 10g Broker Commands 358

Applying Patch Sets with Data Guard in Place 361

    Patching a Physical Database 361

    Patching a Logical Database 363

New Features in Oracle Database 10g Release 2 367

    Automatic Failover 367

    Faster Redo Apply Failover 367

Flashback Database Across Switchovers 367
Asynchronous Redo Transmission 367
SQL Apply 368
Summary 368

17 **Effectively Using Flashback Technologies**   **369**

Brief Overview of Flashback Technology 369
Flashback Database 370
  Flashback Database Architecture 371
  Configuring Flashback Database 372
  Managing Flashback Database 373
  Flashback Database in Action 375
  Using Flashback Database with Data Guard 380
  Troubleshooting Flashback Database 384
Flashback Table 385
  Configuring Flashback Table 385
  Flashback Table in Action 386
  Troubleshooting Flashback Table 390
Flashback Drop with Recycle Bin 392
  Oracle Recycle Bin 392
  Flashback Drop in Action 393
  Troubleshooting Flashback Drop 398
  Disabling Flashback Drop 399
Flashback Versions Query 399
  Flashback Versions Query in Action 400
  Troubleshooting Flashback Versions Query 404
Flashback Transaction Query 405
  Flashback Transaction Query in Action 406
Advanced Flashback Features in Oracle Database 10g Release 2 409
  Flashback Restore Points 410
  Flashback Across Global Database Changes 410
  Additional 10g R2 Views 411
Summary 411

18 **Leveraging Grid Technology Features**   **413**

What Exactly Is the Grid? 413
  A Familiar Example: The Electricity Grid 414
  Similarities in the Computing Grid 415
  Grid Computing: A Little History 417

Oracle's Version of the Grid 418

Managing the Grid 420

Summary 422

Part V   Using Oracle Database 10g Utilities and Other Advanced Features

19   Maximizing Data Movement with Oracle Data Pump   425

Oracle 10g Data Pump Enhancements 425

    Oracle 10g Data Pump Concepts 425

    Data Pump Architecture 426

    Data Pump Process Flow 429

    Data Pump Export and Import Utilities 430

    Diagnosing Data Pump Issues with TRACE 441

    Managing Data Pump Jobs 442

External Table Enhancements 443

Advanced Data Pump Features in Oracle Database 10g Release 2 444

Summary 445

20   Using 10g SQL*Plus and iSQL*Plus   447

10g SQL*Plus Enhancements 447

    DEFINE Enhancements 447

    SPOOL Enhancements 449

10g iSQL*Plus Enhancements 450

    iSQL*Plus Environment 450

    iSQL*Plus Workspace 450

Advanced iSQL*Plus and SQL*Plus Features in Oracle Database 10g
Release 2 453

Summary 454

21   Making the Most of Oracle Database 10g   455

A Collection of Useful Features 455

DML/DDL Features 455

Network Features 456

    New Features in Oracle Database 10g Release 2 457

Security Features 458

    Access Control Features 459

Resource Manager and Scheduler 459

    Job Management Using the Scheduler 460

    Overview of the Resource Manager 460

New Database Initialization Parameters 461
Oracle Streams Enhancements 462
    Streams Architecture 462
    Streams Administrator 462
    Streams Downstream Capture 464
    Streams-Enhanced RAC Support 464
    Other Streams Enhancements 465
MetaLink Integration with Oracle Database 10g 465
Oracle Database 10g EM Patch Cache 466
Oracle Applications 11i with Oracle Database 10g 467
Summary 467

Index   469

Preface

Oracle databases have a significant market share in the enterprise database market. Oracle Database 10g has made a major breakthrough in the database world, surpassing all previous hurdles with its ease of installation, administration, and performance. Oracle Corporation has brought this premier database product to the mass market to benefit organizations of all sizes. DBAs can now easily set up and administer their databases on traditional UNIX and Windows platforms as well as on the cheaper and robust Linux, making it appealing across all user platforms.

With more than 160 manuals in the Oracle Database 10g Documentation Library and more than 50 books from major publishers, novice database developers as well as experienced database administrators find it difficult and confusing to find a reliable, single source of information on this subject. The sheer volume of material presented in these books and manuals makes it tedious for any user to obtain the essential knowledge and get familiar with the database features. Also, small businesses as well as large IT organizations find that there is no single source of knowledge to judge how easily and reliably they could install or upgrade their databases to Oracle Database 10g. This book is the culmination of dedicated efforts by the authors to address all the major challenges and help the Oracle reader with a one-stop resource guide.

This book is conveniently divided into multiple parts, organized by topics of interest. Part I deals with getting started, while Part II moves quickly into how you use Oracle Database 10g for some quick wins. Part III deals with tuning, and Part IV deals with topics related to scaling and availability. We wrap things up with Part V, which is devoted to utilities and other features not covered elsewhere. We hope that this book will serve you well and end up dog-eared and well-thumbed!

About the Authors

Dr. Arun Kumar R., Systems Architect at Cingular Wireless in Dallas, has a decade of experience in Oracle database technologies and multiple relational database systems in telecommunications, retail, and health-care industries. He serves as the Executive Editor for *IOUG SELECT Journal* and as a columnist on Oracle data strategies for *Database Trends and Applications Journal*. He has published in many technical journals and has spoken at various national and international conferences. In addition to *Oracle Database 10g Insider Solutions*, he is the author of *Easy Oracle Automation*. He is a senior member of the IEEE and was chosen for the IEEE Young Engineer of the Year award in 2005. He has a Ph.D. in Business Administration and an M.S. in Computer Science (Louisiana State University). Arun is an adjunct faculty member in the Database Technologies (B.S./M.S.) and E-Business (M.B.A. program) at the University of Phoenix. He can be reached via his Web page at www.dbatrends.com or at arunkumar@dbatrends.com.

John Kanagaraj is a principal consultant with DB Soft Inc. and resides in the Bay Area in sunny California. He has been working with various flavors of UNIX since 1984 and with Oracle since 1988, mostly as a Developer/DBA/Apps DBA and System Administrator. Prior to joining DB Soft, he led small teams of DBAs and UNIX/NT sys admins at Shell Petroleum companies in Brunei and Oman. He started his troubleshooting career as a member (and later became head) of the Database SWAT/Benchmarking team at Wipro Infotech, India. His specialization is UNIX/Oracle performance management, backup/recovery, and system availability, and he has put out many fires in these areas during his career! John is also a Contributing Editor for *IOUG SELECT Journal*. He can be reached via his Web page at http://www.appsdba.biz or via email at ora_apps_dba_y@yahoo.com.

Richard Stroupe is president of TRS Consulting Inc., a northern Virginia–based consulting firm that specializes in Oracle development, administration, and training for the federal government. He has more than 10 years of experience in analysis, design, development, integration, and engineering of large-scale Oracle systems using both core and apps DBA technologies on both NT and UNIX/Solaris platforms. Along with his consulting experience, he has also taught Oracle courses for the past five years at various local universities and corporations and is a member of the review board for *IOUG SELECT Journal*. Richard holds OCP credentials for Oracle 8i/9i/10g, an M.S. degree from the George Washington University, and a B.S. degree from Appalachian State University. He can be reached at richard@trsconsulting.com.

Dedications

Arun: I dedicate this book to my loving wife Karthika Devi and daughter Anjitha for their relentless support making this book possible; to my parents; to all my teachers; and to the almighty GOD.

John: To my Lord and Saviour Jesus Christ who gives freely to all who ask; to my family—Sharmila, Samantha, Jerry, and my parents and in-laws—Jeya, Saro, Chakravarthi, and Chandra. Thanks!

Richard: I dedicate this book to the ones that were most affected by this effort: my beautiful wife, Tina, and my wonderful children, Trey and Audrey.

Acknowledgments

We would like to express our sincere thanks to Sams Publishing for giving us an opportunity to work with a team of well-known industry experts in producing this book. In particular, our thanks go to Loretta Yates for initiating and nurturing the project and providing direction when needed; Songlin Qiu for helping us develop the book and keeping us on track; George Nedeff for the production management, including the coordination of the cover art, page proofing, printing, and distribution; Kate Welsh for her eagle eye and gentle correction of our text; Sean Dixon for initial evaluation of the proposal, guidance, and approval of the topics and contents; and K. Gopalakrishnan, for his expert technical review of the content and his encyclopedic knowledge of all things Oracle.

We would also like to thank Sheila Cepero, Cathy Szen, Donna Cooksey, Lynn Snyder, and Victoria Lira of Oracle; the Beta Team at Oracle Corporation; and Tony Jedlinski and other *SELECT Journal* team members for their appropriate support. A highly technical book such as this requires the dedicated efforts of many people and an excellent technical review team. Our sincere thanks to the editorial team for their reviews, timely suggestions, and corrections. The authors played a modest role in the development of this book, and we need to thank and acknowledge everyone who helped bring this book to fruition.

Arun: I wish to acknowledge the tremendous amount of support I received from my wife Karthika; my daughter Anjitha; our parents, Prof. R. K. Nair and Prof. Anandavally, UnniKrishnaPilla and Krishnamma; and other family members during the six months that this authoring venture was paralleling a very busy career and life. All of them provided great encouragement, offered support, and shared in the excitement of seeing a major piece of work become a reality. I am really grateful to Karthika for letting me work on the book for several weekends and for taking care of all my responsibilities, and for her consistent love, support, and sacrifice of family time. I would like to offer this work at the Lotus Feet of GOD, who has been instrumental in providing my family, in all our successes, and in helping us sail over the rough seas of life.

I would also like to express my sincere appreciation to Cingular Wireless, including my management team (Stan, Thaddeus, Victor, Noni, Joe, Dan, and Greg) and colleagues (Amy, Roma, and PDBA and ADBA teams) for all their support for this book. I would like to express my thanks to Elliot, Elizabeth, and the *DBTA* magazine team for their help in promoting the book through my column. Thanks are also due to all my family friends, and friends at IEEE Dallas section and Engineers' Association. I am really grate-ful to all my friends for all their encouragement while preparing this book.

A book such as this would not have seen the light of day without the dedicated efforts of all the Sams Publishing staff who helped us. I would like to express my sincere thanks to Tony Jedlinski and Sheila Cepero for introducing us to SAMS Publishing and Loretta, Sean, Songlin, Kate, and George for help with the book from initial conception until publishing. Special mention is due to the Oracle Beta Team and OTN for their support for this book.

I wish to profusely thank my co-authors John and Richard, who put in the greatest efforts and teamwork to make this book a reality. I have been really amazed at the wisdom of my co-authors and their practical knowledge in Oracle. Without them, this book would not have materialized. My special thanks to Gopal for his excellent techni-cal editing and valuable insights for making our book more complete.

John: There have been many who have helped me become who I currently am, and who have directly or indirectly participated in this project. I must start with my grati-tude to God, the source of all wisdom, knowledge, and ever-present help. On earth, I acknowledge the consistent support from my wife Sharmila, my daughter Samantha, and my son Jerry. They patiently put up with my absences as I sat at the PC, typing away late in the night and on weekends, missing family time together. A great big thanks! I love you all and promise to make it up to you! Our parents and siblings have always supported us in everything that we do and they deserve my gratitude. My dad instilled a sense of curiosity and the "get to the bottom of it" attitude that is the hall-mark of a true techie, and my mom gave me the persistence to go after and hold on to something I love. Thank you both! And Peter, you are a real bro!

I have known Gopalakrishnan for almost nine years now. X$KG, as he is known, is a good friend and a true Oracle guru. He has been a great inspiration to me personally and has validated all that we said in this book—my sincere thanks! Gaja Vaidyanatha, Kirti Deshpande, Steve Adams, Jared Still, and many others from the Oracle-l DBA list-serv also deserve a big thank you for teaching me many things I would never have known otherwise. My thanks go out to my colleagues at work and to Suresh Kumar, who is both a friend and my employer at the same time!

A book such as this would not have seen the light of day without the dedicated efforts of all the SAMS Publishing staff who helped us. My sincere thanks to Loretta, Songlin, Kate, and George. Last but not least, I thank my co-authors Arun and Richard. You guys are the greatest and once again proved that together we win!

Richard: First and foremost, I would like to thank my co-authors Arun Kumar and John Kanagaraj for their tireless dedication and many sacrifices to help make this project a reality. It has been a real honor to work with you both. I especially would like to thank Arun for providing me the initial opportunity to work on this effort. You are a true friend Arun! I would also like to thank the wonderful staff of Sams Publishing—in particular, Loretta Yates, Songlin Qiu, Kate Welsh, George Nedeff, and Sean Dixon. Without their tremendous amount of hard work and support, this book would not have been possible.

In addition to my co-authors and the SAMs Publishing staff, I would also like to express my sincerest gratitude to the following people who also assisted with this effort: K. Gopalakrishnan for his outstanding contributions as our technical editor; Lynn Snyder; Sheila Cepero and Wendy Delmolino for their efforts with the 10g beta program; Tammy Hensley and Tom Knoerzer for providing me the flexibility to work on this effort during the week instead of only late at night and on weekends; Don McKinley and Brian Jackson for holding down the fort during my many absences from work; Cindy "AP" Murabito; Steve "IB" Donnelly; Doug Muhlbauer and Tom Sheys for providing the environment on which much of the 10g RAC work is based; my father, Tom Stroupe Sr., for not only assisting me with the day-to-day needs of TRS Consulting in my absence, but also for instilling in me his work ethic and professionalism; Richard Niemiec for his invaluable advice, friendship, and encouragement; Pat Sack, John Franklin, Bill Maroulis, and Chuck Adams for their copious advice, support, and friendship, which began several years ago during our times with Oracle APG; and Nick Hoppler, Bill Eisner, Mike Pippen, and Jerald Pike for their efforts with our previous 11i Apps project.

Last but not least, to my wife Tina, son Trey (age 3), and daughter Audrey (age 1), thanks for your enduring level of patience, love, encouragement, support, and sacrifice during the past six months. Without Tina, none of this would have been possible. She is not only a wonderful mother but also my true love and best friend. I thank God every day for her presence in my life and for the opportunity to raise our children together in a strong Christian environment. Finally, acknowledging the contributions and efforts of my family would not be complete without also acknowledging my parents—Dad and Cindy, Mom and Chap—for their love, support, and encouragement throughout the years; Tony and Jean DiPalo and Tom, Noele, Chas, and Lucia Simmons for their continued love and support—especially Jean and Noele for their help with the kids during the past six months.

We Want to Hear from You!

As the reader of this book, *you* are our most important critic and commentator. We value your opinion and want to know what we're doing right, what we could do better, what areas you'd like to see us publish in, and any other words of wisdom you're willing to pass our way.

As a publisher for Sams Publishing, I welcome your comments. You can email or write me directly to let me know what you did or didn't like about this book—as well as what we can do to make our books better.

Please note that I cannot help you with technical problems related to the topic of this book. We do have a User Services group, however, where I will forward specific technical questions related to the book.

When you write, please be sure to include this book's title and author as well as your name, email address, and phone number. I will carefully review your comments and share them with the author and editors who worked on the book.

Email: feedback@samspublishing.com

Mail: Paul Boger
          Publisher
          Sams Publishing
          800 East 96th Street
          Indianapolis, IN 46240 USA

For more information about this book or another Sams Publishing title, visit our website at www.samspublishing.com. Type the ISBN (excluding hyphens) or the title of a book in the Search field to find the page you're looking for.

Introduction

Oracle Corporation released its flagship Oracle Database 10g relational database management system in February of 2004. This new version not only arrived with a slew of features, it fundamentally changed the way certain functions and operations are done in the database. When combined with the comprehensive but voluminous documentation set, it is no wonder that first-time users and even experienced Oracle technicians stumble during implementation of this new version. They want to get the best of Oracle Database 10g, but are faced with plowing through the thousands of pages in the 150-odd manuals, searching for nuggets to implement and exploit.

If this describes you, a solution to this problem is now in your hands. This book has been written by a trio of experienced Oracle professionals who have faced and overcome the very same issues you face. Having worked in the trenches with previous versions of Oracle products, and now with this new version, they have distilled their combined real-life experiences into this tome. We hope you enjoy reading this book and discovering the nuggets that the authors have laid out for you in the subsequent pages!

Who Should Read This Book

This book is for anyone who has to work with Oracle Database 10g. Primarily written for database administrators, it caters to database architects as well as developers who would like to know how this new version affects their enterprise and their applications. The chapters are replete with examples and code that the authors themselves have used and tested so you can apply them confidently in a real-life situation.

This book, however, is not designed to act as an introductory book or even a comprehensive reference of new features in Oracle Database 10g. Only those features that are useful and have the most bang-for-the-buck in practical terms are listed and discussed. Such topics are covered in depth and, where warranted, additional sources for reading from manuals and MetaLink notes are recommended.

What You Need to Use This Book

This book covers Oracle Database 10g Release 1 as well as Release 2 of the product, making specific reference to the latter where necessary. Hence, you need to use a supported version of Oracle Database 10g Release 1 at the least. By default, the features and code listed would work for installations that use Oracle Database Release 1 on any operating-system platform unless specifically mentioned otherwise. All SQL code listed is operating-system neutral unless UNIX-style directories are referred to within the code. In certain cases, UNIX-based shell scripts have been used as wrappers around SQL code to demonstrate a few features in principle. These scripts can easily be adapted to Windows and should work without change if they are executed under an emulator such as CygWin or MKS Toolkit. Please note that some of the database features are available only when licensed separately. These are specifically indicated.

Throughout the text, we refer to a number of manuals and MetaLink notes. Although the manuals are available both online at `http://tahiti.oracle.com` and with the software distribution, all readers may not have access to MetaLink. If you do not have a MetaLink account that can be used to access these notes, you can easily create one at `http://metalink.oracle.com` using your Customer Support Identifier (CSI). This should be available from whomever administers your Oracle Support Contract.

How This Book Is Organized

This book is divided into five logical parts. Chapters within these sections deal with specific topics related to that area. The parts are as follows:

- **Part I, "Getting Started with Oracle Database 10g."** This part provides an introduction to the architecture of this version as well practical tips on installing and customizing your installation. If you are new to Oracle Database 10g or are installing it for the first time, you may find this section helpful when you get started. If you are currently using ASM or plan to use it later, Chapter 4 in this part, "Setting Up Automatic Storage Management," can provide some insider tips!

- **Part II, "Quick Wins Using Oracle Database 10g."** This part launches straight away into a number of administrative tools and options that you can configure quickly and easily in Oracle Database 10g. This includes using Automatic Memory Management, Automatic Statistics Collection, Automatic Undo, Automatic Segment Management, as well as RMAN. This part shows how you can use these features that are already present in Oracle Database 10g to generate "quick wins."

- **Part III, "Tuning Oracle Database 10g."** This part deals exclusively with topics related to tuning. Starting with a new approach to tuning, we deal with the workload repository and various tuning-related advisors in this part. The part is rounded off with a chapter on the Cost Based Optimizer.

- **Part IV, "Scaling and Availability with Oracle Database 10g."** This part discusses products and options related to this topic. Oracle RAC (Real Application Clusters), Data Guard, and Flashback technologies are discussed in detail. We also introduce the concept and application of grid technologies now made possible with Oracle Database 10g.

- **Part V, "Using Oracle Database 10g Utilities and Other Advanced Features."** This part discusses the new utilities provided by Oracle Database 10g. We wrap it up with a separate chapter listing a collection of interesting new features that are worth pursuing further.

About the Book's Sample Code

All sample code for this book can be downloaded on the Sams website at `http://www.samspublishing.com`. To access it, type this book's ISBN (without the hyphens) in the Search box and click Search. When the book's title is displayed, click the title to go to a page where you can download the code.

Conventions Used in This Book

The following typographic conventions are used in this book:

- Code lines, commands, and programming-related language appears in a `monospace` typeface.

- Placeholders in syntax descriptions appear in an *`italic monospace`* typeface.

- The ➥ icon is used before a line of code that signifies to readers that the author meant for the continued code to appear on the same line.

In addition, this book contains the following special elements.

> Notes show how you can further explore the topic in question, or provide additional information about a particular topic being described.

> Tips highlight shortcuts, convenient techniques, or tools that can make a task easier.

> **Sidebars**
> A large number of sidebar topics add value without distracting from the main flow.

> Cautions alert you to common pitfalls you should avoid.

PART I

Getting Started with Oracle Database 10g

1 Exploring Oracle Database 10g Architecture

2 Installing Oracle Database 10g

3 Customizing Installation Options

4 Setting Up Automatic Storage Management

1

Exploring Oracle Database 10g Architecture

IN THIS CHAPTER

Overview of New Features	7
Processes Beneath the Hood	14
Memory Architecture	16
Automatic Undo Management	18
SQL Advisors	19
Oracle's Suite of Other Advisors	19
Flash Recovery Area	19
Flashback Operations	20
Improved Oracle Enterprise Manager	20
Grid Technology Unveiled	21

Overview of New Features

Welcome to the first chapter of this book, which includes a quick overview of Oracle Database 10g's new features and underlying architecture. This is the first relational database ever made to automate the traditional database administrative functions, support enterprise grid computing, and reduce the cost of owning a truly scalable and high-availability database.

Oracle Database 10g has a long list of impressive architecture enhancements over its previous versions. Oracle has made this database very sophisticated and powerful, and has automated many of the traditional and mundane administrative functions. Oracle has tried to automate as much database functionality as possible and made it more scalable. Several changes have been made to improve memory structures, resource management, storage handling, SQL tuning, data movement, recovery speed, and globalization. This chapter will go over the most notable revisions to the database architecture for releases 1 and 2 of the Oracle Database 10g and any significant improvements for Release 2 is specifically mentioned in this and all chapters.

Here is a quick overview of the major feature upgrades in Oracle Database 10g.

SYSAUX Tablespace

The SYSAUX tablespace is an auxiliary tablespace that provides storage for all non sys-related tables and indexes that would have been placed in the SYSTEM tablespace. SYSAUX is required for all Oracle Database 10g installations and should be created along with new installs or upgrades. Many database components use SYSAUX as their default tablespace to store data. The SYSAUX tablespace also reduces the number of tablespaces created by default in the seed database and user-defined database. For a RAC implementation with raw devices, a raw device is created for every tablespace, which complicates raw-device management. By consolidating these tablespaces into the SYSAUX tablespace, you can reduce the number of raw devices. The SYSAUX and SYSTEM tablespaces share the same security attributes.

Creating and Using SYSAUX Tablespace

You need SYSDBA privileges to create a SYSAUX tablespace. Before you create this tablespace, however, you must ensure that there is enough space for it. Any attempts to alter the mandatory attributes of the SYSAUX tablespace are prohibited and will result in an error. The DBA can monitor the space usage by each occupant in SYSAUX tablespace by querying the v$sysaux_occupants table. This view will give the occupant name, occupant description, schema name, move procedure, and current space usage. Enterprise Manager has a GUI interface to relocate any occupant using too much space in the SYSAUX tablespace. Also, the wksys.move_wk procedure can be used to manually move occupants in and out of the tablespace.

When the CREATE DATABASE command is executed, the SYSAUX tablespace and its occupants are created. When a database is upgraded to 10g, the CREATE TABLESPACE command is explicitly used. CREATE TABLESPACE SYSAUX is called only in a database-migration mode.

Rename Tablespace Option

Oracle Database 10g has implemented the provision to rename tablespaces. To accomplish this in older versions, you had to create a new tablespace, copy the contents from the old tablespace to the new tablespace, and drop the old tablespace. The Rename Tablespace feature enables simplified processing of tablespace migrations within a database and ease of transporting a tablespace between two databases. The rename tablespace feature applies only to database versions 10.0.1 and higher. An offline tablespace, a tablespace with offline data files, and tablespaces owned by SYSTEM or SYSAUX cannot be renamed using this option. As an example, the syntax to rename a tablespace from REPORTS to REPORTS_HISTORY is as follows.

```
SQL> ALTER TABLESPACE REPORTS RENAME TO REPORTS_HISTORY;
```

Automatic Storage Management

Automatic Storage Management (ASM) is a new database feature for efficient management of storage with round-the-clock availability. It helps prevent the DBA from managing thousands of database files across multiple database instances by using disk groups. These disk groups are comprised of disks and resident files on the disks. ASM does not eliminate any existing database functionalities with file systems or raw devices, or Oracle Managed Files (OMFs). ASM also supports RAC configurations. ASM is discussed further in Chapter 4, "Setting Up Automatic Storage Management."

In Oracle Database 10g Release 2, the ASM command-line interface (ASMCMD) has been improved to access files and directories within ASM disk groups. Other enhancements include uploading and extracting of files into an ASM-managed storage pool, a WAIT option on disk rebalance operations, and the facility to perform batch operations on multiple disks.

Now it's time to take a deeper look into the new storage structures in Oracle Database 10g—temporary tablespace groups and BigFile tablespaces. These will help you to better utilize the database space and to manage space more easily.

Temporary Tablespace Group

A temporary tablespace is used by the database for storing temporary data, which is not accounted for in recovery operations. A *temporary tablespace group* (*TTG*) is a group of temporary tablespaces. A TTG contains at least one temporary tablespace, with a different name from the tablespace. Multiple temporary tablespaces can be specified at the database level and used in different sessions at the same time. Similarly, if TTG is used, a database user with multiple sessions can have different temporary tablespaces for the sessions. More than one default temporary tablespace can be assigned to a database. A single database operation can use multiple temporary tablespaces in sorting operations, thereby speeding up the process. This prevents large tablespace operations from running out of space.

In Oracle Database 10g, each database user will have a permanent tablespace for storing permanent data and a temporary tablespace for storing temporary data. In previous versions of Oracle, if a user was created without specifying a default tablespace, SYSTEM tablespace would have become the default tablespace. For Oracle Database 10g, a default permanent tablespace can be defined to be used for all new users without a specific permanent tablespace. By creating a default permanent tablespace, nonsystem user objects can be prevented from being created in the SYSTEM tablespace. Consider the many benefits of adding users in a large database environment by a simple command and not having to worry about them placing their objects in the wrong tablespaces!

BigFile Tablespace

We have gotten past the days of tablespaces in the range of a few megabytes. These days, database tables hold a lot of data and are always hungry for storage. To address this craving, Oracle has come up with the Bigfile tablespace concept. A *BigFile tablespace* (*BFT*) is a tablespace containing a single, very large data file. With the new addressing scheme in 10g, four billion blocks are permitted in a single data file and file sizes can be from 8TB to 128TB, depending on the block size. To differentiate a regular tablespace from a BFT, a regular tablespace is called a *small file tablespace*. Oracle Database 10g can be a mixture of small file and BigFile tablespaces.

BFTs are supported only for locally managed tablespaces with ASM segments and locally managed undo and temporary tablespaces. When BFTs are used with Oracle Managed Files, data files become completely transparent to the DBA and no reference is needed for them. BFT makes a tablespace logically equivalent to data files (allowing tablespace operations) of earlier releases. BFTs should be used only with logical volume manager or ASM supporting dynamically extensible logical volumes and with systems that support striping to prevent negative consequences on RMAN backup parallelization and parallel query execution. BFT should not be used when there is limited free disk space available.

Prior to Oracle Database 10g, K and M were used to specify data file sizes. Because the newer version introduces larger file sizes up to 128TB using BFTs, the sizes can be specified using G and T for gigabytes and terabytes, respectively. Almost all the data warehouse implementations with older versions of Oracle database utilize data files sized from 16GB to 32GB. With the advent of the BigFile tablespaces, however, DBAs can build larger data warehouses without getting intimidated by the sheer number of smaller data files. Table 1.1 illustrates BFTs.

TABLE 1.1

Relationship Between Oracle Block Size and Maximum File Size

Oracle block size	Maximum file size
2KB	8TB
4KB	16TB
8KB	32TB
16KB	64TB
32KB	128TB

For using BFT, the underlying operating system should support Large Files. In other words the file system should have Large File Support (LFS).

Cross-Platform Transportable Tablespaces

In Oracle 8i database, the transportable tablespace feature enabled a tablespace to be moved across different Oracle databases using the same operating system. Oracle Database 10g has significantly improved this functionality to permit the movement of data across different platforms. This will help transportable tablespaces to move data from one environment to another on selected heterogeneous platforms (operating systems). Using cross-platform transportable tablespaces, a database can be migrated from one platform to another by rebuilding the database catalog and transporting the user tablespaces. By default, the converted files are placed in the flash recovery area (also new to Oracle Database 10g), which is discussed later in this chapter. A list of fully supported platforms can be found in v$transportable_platform.

A new data dictionary view, v$transportable_platform, lists all supported platforms, along with the platform ID and endian format information. The v$database dictionary view has two new columns (PLATFORM_ID, PLATFORM_NAME) to support it.

The table v$transportable_platform has three fields: PLATFORM_ID (number), PLATFORM_NAME (varchar2(101)), and ENDIAN_FORMAT (varchar2(14)). *Endianness* is the pattern (big endian or little endian) for byte ordering of data files in native types. In big-endian format, the most significant byte comes first; in little-endian format, the least significant byte comes first.

The source and target databases must have the same character set and national character set in order for transportable tablespaces to work. If the platforms are of different endianness, an additional step will be needed on either the source or target database to match the target's endianness format. Here is the information from v$transportable_platform on a typical server.

PLATFORM_ID	PLATFORM_NAME	ENDIAN_FORMAT
1	Solaris[tm] OE (32-bit)	Big
2	Solaris[tm] OE (64-bit)	Big
7	Microsoft Windows IA (32-bit)	Little
10	Linux IA (32-bit)	Little
6	AIX-Based Systems (64-bit)	Big
3	HP-UX (64-bit)	Big
5	HP Tru64 UNIX	Little
4	HP-UX IA (64-bit)	Big
11	Linux IA (64-bit)	Little
15	HP Open VMS	Little
8	Microsoft Windows IA (64-bit)	Little
9	IBM zSeries Based Linux	Big
13	Linux 64-bit for AMD	Little
16	Apple Mac OS	Big
12	Microsoft Windows 64-bit for A	Little

In Oracle Database 10g Release 2, transportable tablespaces to the database have been enhanced to generate a tablespace set from the source database and they have been plugged in to the target database, facilitating data movement and export/import operations. Also, you can transport a tablespace from backup, without making the tablespace read-only.

Performance Management Using AWR

Automatic Workload Repository (AWR) is the most important feature among the new Oracle Database 10g manageability infrastructure components. AWR provides the background services to collect, maintain, and utilize the statistics for problem detection and self-tuning. The AWR collects system-performance data at frequent intervals and stores them as historical system workload information for analysis. These metrics are stored in the memory for performance reasons. These statistics are regularly written from memory to disk by a new background process called Memory Monitor (MMON). This data will later be used for analysis of performance problems that occurred in a certain time period and to do trend analysis. Oracle does all this without any DBA intervention. Automatic Database Diagnostic Monitor (ADDM), which is discussed in the next section, analyzes the information collected by the AWR for database-performance problems.

By default, the data-collection interval is 60 minutes, and this data is stored for seven days, after which it is purged. This interval and data-retention period can be altered.

This captured data can be used for system-level and user-level analysis. This data is optimized to minimize any database overhead. In a nutshell, AWR is the basis for all self-management functionalities of the database. It helps the database with the historical perspective on its usage, enabling it to make accurate decisions quickly.

The AWR infrastructure has two major components:

- **In-memory statistics collection.** The in-memory statistics collection facility is used by 10g components to collect statistics and store them in memory. These statistics can be read using v$performance views. The memory version of the statistics is written to disk regularly by a new background process called Memory Monitor or Memory Manageability Monitor (MMON). We will review MMON in background processes as well.

- **AWR snapshots.** The AWR snapshots form the persistent portion of the Oracle Database 10g manageability infrastructure. They can be viewed through data dictionary views. These statistics retained in persistent storage will be safe even in database instance crashes and provide historical data for baseline comparisons.

AWR collects many statistics, such as time model statistics (time spent by the various activities), object statistics (access and usage statistics of database segments), some session and system statistics in v$sesstat and v$sysstat, some optimizer statistics for self-learning and tuning, and Active Session History (ASH). We will review this in greater detail in later chapters.

Automatic Database Diagnostic Monitor (ADDM)

Automatic Database Diagnostic Monitor (ADDM) is the best resource for database tuning. Introduced in 10g, ADDM provides proactive and reactive monitoring instead of the tedious tuning process found in earlier Oracle versions. Proactive monitoring is done by ADDM and Server Generated Alerts (SGAs). Reactive monitoring is done by the DBA, who does manual tuning through Oracle Enterprise Manager or SQL scripts.

Statistical information captured from SGAs is stored inside the workload repository in the form of snapshots every 60 minutes. These detailed snapshots (similar to STATSPACK snapshots) are then written to disk. The ADDM initiates the MMON process to automatically run on every database instance and proactively find problems.

Whenever a snapshot is taken, the ADDM triggers an analysis of the period corresponding to the last two snapshots. Thus it proactively monitors the instances and detects problems before they become severe. The analysis results stored in the workload repository are accessible through the Oracle Enterprise Manager. In Oracle Database 10g, the new wait and time model statistics help the ADDM to identify the top performance issues and concentrate its analysis on those problems. In Oracle Database 10g Release 2, ADDM spans more server components like Streams, RMAN, and RAC.

DROP DATABASE **Command**

Oracle Database 10g has introduced a means to drop the entire database with a single command: DROP DATABASE. The DROP DATABASE command deletes all database files, online log files, control files, and the server parameter (spfile) file. The archive logs and backups, however, have to be deleted manually.

Data Pump Utilities

Data Pump is the new high-speed infrastructure for data and metadata movement in Oracle Database 10g. The Data Pump commands are similar to the traditional export and import commands, but they are separate products. Data Pump provides a remarkable performance improvement over the original export and import utilities. It also provides faster data load and unload capability to existing tables. Using Data Pump, platform-independent flat files can be moved between multiple servers. You can use the new network mode to transfer data using database links.

Export and import operations in Data Pump can detach from a long-running job and reattach to it later with out affecting the job. You can also remap data during export and import processes. The names of data files, schema names, and tablespaces from the source can be altered to different names on the target system. It also supports fine-grained object selection using the EXCLUDE, INCLUDE, and CONTENT parameters.

Data Pump Export (dpexp) is the utility for unloading data and metadata from the source database to a set of operating system files (dump file sets). Data Pump Import (dpimp) is used to load data and metadata stored in these export dump file sets to a target database.

The advantages of using Data Pump utilities are as follows.

- You can detach from a long-running job and reattach to it later without affecting the job. The DBA can monitor jobs from multiple locations, stop the jobs, and restart them later from where they were left.

- Data Pump supports fine-grained object selection using the EXCLUDE, INCLUDE, and CONTENT parameters. This will help in exporting and importing a subset of data from a large database to development databases or from data warehouses to datamarts, and so on.

- You can control the number of threads working for the Data Pump job and control the speed (only in the Enterprise version of the database).

- You can remap data during the export and import processes.

In Oracle Database 10g Release 2, a default DATA_PUMP_DIR directory object and additional DBMS_DATAPUMP API calls have been added, along with provisions for compression of metadata in dump files, and the capability to control the dump file size with the FILESIZE parameter.

This section has reviewed the significant new features introduced in Oracle Database 10g. Let us now go over the new processes introduced in Oracle Database 10g to support these features.

Processes Beneath the Hood

This section begins with an introduction to Oracle processes and discusses the new processes introduced in Oracle Database 10g. Some of the new processes are dedicated to the advanced manageability features of Oracle Database 10g.

Classification of Database Processes

An Oracle database utilizes processes and memory structures to access the database. The memory structures reside in the memory of the machines that host the database. *Processes* are jobs that operate within the memory.

An Oracle database server has two types of processes:

- **User processes.** User processes, also called *client processes*, are generated to run Oracle tools (like Enterprise Manager) or application programs (like OCI), and manage the communication with the server processes.

- **Oracle processes.** To perform their functions and services, some user processes invoke Oracle processes, which can be broken down into server processes and background processes.

Oracle can adjust the number of server processes to support the user processes depending on the server configuration. In a shared server configuration, many user processes share a smaller number of server processes, while in a dedicated server configuration, each user process has its own server process. The user and server processes are separate in shared server configuration and client/server systems running on separate machines.

Each Oracle database instance has its own set of background processes, which performs the functions for the user processes. These background processes monitor other Oracle processes for improving the performance and availability of the database for multiple users.

Background Processes Revisited

An Oracle database instance can have many background processes, but all of them are not always needed. When the database instance is started, these background processes are automatically created. The important background processes are given next, with brief explanations of each:

> More details on the background processes are available in the following Oracle manuals on the Oracle website: *Oracle Database Concepts, Oracle Database 2 Day DBA*, and *Oracle Database Administrator's Guide.*

- **Database Writer process (DBW*n*).** The database writer process (DBWn) is responsible for writing modified (dirty) buffers in the database buffer cache to disk. Although one process (DBW0) is sufficient for most systems, you can have additional processes up to a maximum of 20 processes (DBW1 through DBW9 and DBWa through DBWj) to improve the write performance on heavy online transaction processing (OLTP) systems. By moving the data in dirty buffers to disk, DBW*n* improves the performance of finding free buffers for new transactions, while retaining the recently used buffers in the memory.

- **Log Writer process (LGWR).** The log writer process (LGWR) manages the redo log buffers by writing the redo log buffer to a redo log file on disk in a circular fashion. After the LGWR moves the redo entries from the redo log buffer to a redo log file, server processes can overwrite new entries in to the redo log buffer. It writes fast enough to disk to have space available in the buffer for new entries.

- **Checkpoint process (CKPT).** Checkpoint is the database event to synchronize the modified data blocks in memory with the data files on disk. It helps to establish data consistency and allows faster database recovery. When a checkpoint occurs, Oracle updates the headers of all data files using the CKPT process and records the details of the checkpoint. The dirtied blocks are written to disk by the DBW*n* process.

- **System Monitor process (SMON).** SMON coalesces the contiguous free extents within dictionary managed tablespaces, cleans up the unused temporary segments, and does the database recovery at instance startup (as needed). During the instance recovery, SMON also recovers any skipped transactions. SMON checks periodically to see if the instance or other processes need its service.

- **Process Monitor process (PMON).** When a user process fails, the process monitor (PMON) does process recovery by cleaning up the database buffer cache and releasing the resources held by that user process. It also periodically checks the status of dispatcher and server processes, and restarts the stopped process. PMON conveys the status of instance and dispatcher processes to the network listener and is activated (like SMON) whenever its service is needed.

- **Job Queue processes (J*nnn*).** Job queue processes run user jobs for batch processing like a scheduler service. When a start date and a time interval are assigned, the job queue processes run the job at the next occurrence of the interval. These processes are dynamically managed, allowing the job queue clients to demand more job queue processes (J000–J999) when needed. The job queue processes are spawned as required by the coordinator process (CJQ0 or CJQ*nn*) for completion of scheduled jobs.

- **Archiver processes (ARC*n*).** The archiver processes (ARCn) copy the redo log files to an assigned destination after the log switch. These processes are present only in databases in ARCHIVELOG mode. An Oracle instance can have up to 10 ARCn processes (ARC0–ARC9). Whenever the current number of ARCn processes becomes insufficient for the workload, the LGWR process invokes additional ARCn processes, which are recorded in the alert file. The number of archiver processes is set with the initialization parameter LOG_ARCHIVE_MAX_PROCESSES and changed with the ALTER SYSTEM command.

- **Queue Monitor processes (QMN*n*).** The queue monitor process is an optional background process that monitors the message queues for Oracle Advanced Queuing in Streams.

- **Memory Monitor process (MMON).** MMON is the acronym for Memory Monitor, a new process introduced in Oracle Database 10g associated with the Automatic Workload

Repository (AWR). AWR gets the necessary statistics for automatic problem detection and tuning with the help of MMON. MMON writes out the required statistics for AWR to disk on a regularly scheduled basis.

- **Memory Monitor Light process (MMNL).** Memory Monitor Light (MMNL) is another new process in Oracle Database 10g; it assists the AWR with writing the full statistics buffers to disk on an as-needed basis.

Other Background Processes

The following background processes are not directly related to the processes in the preceding list, but are given here for an overview:

- **Recovery Writer process (RVWR).** Recovery Writer (RVWR) is a new background process introduced in Oracle Database 10g to write flashback logs with pre-images of data blocks to disk. The location for writing the logs can be specified by DB_RECOVERY_FILE_DEST parameter.

- **ASMB process.** *ASM* stands for "Automatic Storage Management." ASMB is the background process used to pass the necessary information to and from the Cluster Synchronization Services to manage the disk resources used by ASM. ASMB also updates statistics and maintains the heartbeat mechanism for storage management. You'll find more details on ASM in Chapter 4.

- **RBAL process.** RBAL is an ASM-related process to perform the rebalancing of disks controlled by ASM. You will learn more about rebalancing operations in Chapter 4.

- **ORB*n* process.** ORB*n* processes are used by the RBAL process to do the actual rebalancing operations on ASM-controlled disk recources. The total number of ORBn processes started is controlled by the ASM_POWER_LIMIT parameter, also explained in Chapter 4.

- **Change Tracking Writer process (CTWR).** Change Tracking Writer (CTWR) is a new process that works with the new block changed tracking features in Oracle Database 10g. CTWR assists in fast RMAN incremental backups.

Now that you have learned about the background processes, we will go over the memory architecture.

Memory Architecture

The important memory structures associated with an Oracle database instance are the System Global Area (SGA) and the Program Global Area (PGA). As you know, an Oracle instance is made up of SGA and Oracle processes. Oracle allocates memory for the SGA on database startup and returns the memory when the instance is shut down. The size of the SGA is controlled by the sga_max_size initialization parameter in the initInstance.ora file or the server parameter (SPFILE) file.

System Global Area (SGA)

The System Global Area (SGA) is a group of shared memory structures in the Oracle database instance that has the data and control information for the instance. When multiple users are connected to the same database instance, the SGA information is shared by all of them. The SGA is also called "Shared Global Area" for this reason.

The SGA has the following data structures:

- **Database buffer cache.** The portion of System Global Area that holds copies of data blocks read from data files. All concurrent user processes share access to the database buffer cache, the size of which is set by the initialization parameter file `db_block_size` (2KB to 32KB). This size determines a cache hit or miss. Oracle database supports multiple block sizes, whose sizes and numbers are specified by the following parameters: `DB_2K_CACHE_SIZE`, `DB_4K_CACHE_SIZE`, `DB_8K_CACHE_SIZE`, `DB_16K_CACHE_SIZE`, and `DB_32K_CACHE_SIZE`. If the cache size is sufficiently large, a request for data is very likely to find the required information, resulting in a cache hit.

- **Redo log buffer.** A circular buffer in the SGA that holds information on changes made to the database in the form of redo entries. The LGWR process writes the redo log buffer to the active redo log file (or redo group on disk).

- **Shared pool.** Contains the library cache, the dictionary cache, buffers for parallel execution, and control structures. The shared pool size is determined by the `shared_pool_size` parameter.

- **Java pool.** Used in memory for all session-specific java code and data within the Java Virtual Machine (JVM). The Java pool advisor has the information on Java pool size, which can affect the parse rate.

- **Large pool.** A large optional memory area used to provide memory allocations for memory requests larger than the size of the shared pool. Memory management of the large pool is not subject to normal LRU algorithms as with shared pool. The sessions themselves deallocate the memory chunks after usage. A large pool can only hold certain types of memory components like RMAN, PQ slaves, and UGA memory if MTS/shared server is used.

- **Data dictionary cache (or row cache).** A special location in memory to hold data dictionary data. It is a collection of database tables and views containing reference information about the database, database structures, and database users. Row cache holds the definitions of the tables, views, and related dictionary objects and those definitions are protected by row cache latches. Contrary to normal buffer cache algorithms, the dictionary cache caches in rows, where as buffer cache caches in blocks. This is the major difference between buffer cache and dictionary cache. Hence we call database dictionary cache as row cache.

- **Streams pool.** Controls the Streams memory.

How Does SGA Handle the Memory?

The part of SGA that has information about the database and its instance is called *fixed SGA*. All SGA components allocate and deallocate memory in units called *granules*. The size of a granule is determined by the total SGA size and its operating system. The size of the SGA is determined by the following initialization parameters, given in the order of relevance:

- **DB_CACHE_SIZE**. Size of the cache of standard blocks.

- **LOG_BUFFER**. Number of bytes allocated for the redo log buffer.

- **SHARED_POOL_SIZE**. Size in bytes of the area for shared SQL and PL/SQL.

- **LARGE_POOL_SIZE**. Size of the large pool. The default is 0.

- **JAVA_POOL_SIZE**. Size of the Java pool.

- **DB_*n*K_CACHE_SIZE**. Size of nondefault block size cache.

Before Oracle Database 10g, DBAs had to manually specify different SGA component sizes by setting the preceding parameters. In Oracle Database 10g, you can dynamically set these values using the Automatic Shared Memory Management feature (see Chapter 5, "Using Automatic Memory Management," for more details).

Program Global Area (PGA)

Program global area (PGA) is that part of memory that has data and control information for a server process. PGA access is exclusive to the server processes and its application code. The PGA memory can be classified into Private SQL Area, Cursors, and Session Memory.

Memory Manager (MMAN)

MMAN stands for Memory Manager, the new background process used by the Automatic Shared Memory Management feature. MMAN acts as the SGA memory broker and coordinates the size of various memory components within the allowable limits. It also tracks the sizes of the memory components and tracks pending resize operations. You will learn more about the Automatic Shared Memory Management feature in Chapter 5.

Automatic Undo Management

Oracle has completely deprecated the use of rollback segments for storing rollback data. It replaced rollbacks with automatic undo management using an undo tablespace. For enabling automatic undo management, you should set the init.ora parameter UNDO_MANAGEMENT to AUTO. You can define any name for undo tablespace by using the UNDO TABLESPACE clause at database-creation time. If the UNDO TABLESPACE clause was omitted during database creation and automatic undo management is enabled, then the database creates a default undo tablespace called SYS_UNDOTBS.

SQL Advisors

For SQL tuning, Oracle Database 10g has two advisors: SQL Tuning Advisor and SQL Access Advisor. SQL Tuning Advisor provides tuning advice for SQL statements without modifying any SQL statements. SQL Access Advisor provides tuning advice on indexes, materialized views, and materialized view logs for larger reports or work load. Both advisors are available through OEM. Rule Based Optimizers are completely de-supported in Oracle Database 10g, and these SQL advisors could help to a certain extent in rewriting your old RBO queries and taking advantage of Cost Based Optimization (CBO).

SQL Tuning Advisor takes one or more SQL statements as its input and invokes the automatic tuning optimizer to perform SQL tuning. The output is a series of advice or recommendations along with the rationale behind each one, as well as their expected benefits. The recommendations prompt the user to collect statistics on the affected objects, create new indexes, restructure the statements, or create new profiles. The user can accept the recommendations or reject them. The various inputs to SQL Tuning Advisor come from a variety of sources including ADDM, top SQL statements from AWR, the cursor cache, the SQL tuning set, and SQL statements given by users.

SQL Access Advisor is used for applications with complex queries on large sets of data. It usually recommends a combination of indexes, materialized views, materialized view logs, and benefits from general query rewrites. It also recommends the use of bitmap and B-tree indexes.

> For those who prefer the hands-on approach, these advisors have separate procedures to be run from a command window.

Oracle's Suite of Other Advisors

Oracle Database 10g has a suite of advisors that provide feedback about resource utilization and performance. You have already reviewed the ADDM and SQL Advisors. The other important advisors are SGA Advisor (tuning SGA), PGA Advisor (tuning PGA), Buffer Cache Advisor (buffer cache), Library Cache Advisor (different library cache sizes), Segment Advisor (object space issues and growth trends), and Undo Advisor (flashback support).

All these database advisors have some common attributes. For example, each advisor can be launched in one of two modes—limited mode or comprehensive mode—depending on the time available for completing the advisory task. When an advisor is launched to investigate a problem, it performs an in-depth analysis of the statistics to generate the advice. In limited mode, the advisor does a relatively shallow (quick) analysis, while in comprehensive mode, the advisor does an in-depth analysis, taking a much longer time.

Flash Recovery Area

Oracle Database 10g stores and manages files related to its backup and recovery operations in a different nondatabase location called the *flash recovery area*. A flash recovery area is specified by the init.ora parameters DB_RECOVERY_FILE_DEST (location) and DB_RECOVERY_FILE_DEST_SIZE (size). For a RAC environment, these two parameters should be the same on all instances. Use of the flash recovery area will ease your burden on backup and recovery operations.

The flash recovery area can be an Oracle-managed directory or a file system, or an ASM disk group. (ASM disk groups are discussed in Chapter 4.) The flash recovery area is used by Oracle for its archive logs and by RMAN for its backups.

Flashback Operations

The flashback query feature was introduced in Oracle 9i. In Oracle Database 10g, this functionality has been expanded to include several powerful options, and for use with the entire database. All flashback features rely on the database undo information to re-create a state in the past. Flashback transaction query, flashback versions query, Flashback Table, and Flashback Database are the major flashback operations. A more detailed explanation of flashback operations is given in Chapter 17, "Effectively Using Flashback Technologies."

Flashback Database

Flashback Database is a new feature introduced in Oracle Database 10g. This feature helps the DBA to quickly revert an entire Oracle database to a former state at any past point in time. It is different from the traditional point-in-time recovery used from Oracle 7.x version until 9i.

You can use Flashback Database to back out of changes to the database that are caused by user errors and that have resulted in logical data corruptions. It is not useful for recovering the database in case of media (disk) failures.

The actual time needed to flashback a database to a point in the past is directly proportional to the number of changes made to the database during that duration and not dependent on the actual size of the database.

Using this fetaure is faster than point-in-time recovery using backups and redo log files. The database must be mounted in an exclusive state to perform the flashback operation. We will review this in detail in Chapter 17.

Improved Oracle Enterprise Manager

Oracle Corporation has significantly improved the Oracle Enterprise Manager (OEM) to manage almost every feature of your hardware and software environment, including the Grid Control. The Oracle Enterprise Manager console can be invoked from a Web browser, from a client installation, or from the database server itself.

OEM Database Control is installed along with every Oracle Database 10g installation. You can monitor and administer single or multiple database instances from the Database Control. It monitors the entire Oracle environment and provides detailed system-monitoring information for timely detection and notification of problems.

OEM makes use of metrics and thresholds to monitor each parameter and uses alerts to provide information on them. *Metrics* are defined as units of measurement to assess the health of the system. Each target will have a set of predefined metrics with thresholds associated with them. Thresholds are the boundary values against which the metric values are compared. An alert is generated when a parameter value reaches its threshold. Alerts are also generated when there is a change in availability of a monitored service, when a specific error condition occurs or database action takes place, or when a significant change is noted by the clearing of a previous alert, or what have you.

For a more detailed explanation of all Enterprise Manager features and setup, refer to the *Enterprise Manager Concepts Guide* and *Enterprise Manager Advanced Configuration Guide.*

Grid Technology Unveiled

Grid technology is built on the idea that computing can be considered as a utility, like the electric power grid or the telephone network. These utilities are meant to be unbreakable and highly available for consumers. Likewise, the primary initiative for grid computing at organizations is improving affordability and availability of enterprise systems. Organizations are looking at different ways to improve the system availability and process efficiencies at lower expenses. This forms the client-side view on utility computing. From a server-side view, grid computing achieves this goal by consolidating islands of hardware and using centralized tools to allocate and manage resources more effectively. Looking at the utilization perspective, computing resources are not sitting idle, and all requests for resources are answered promptly. Grid computing began with ideas developed in the academic and research communities.

Oracle Corporation has been working on grid technology for several years to provide seamless availability solutions with its database products. Oracle 9i has technologies for building the grid, such as Oracle Streams, Oracle transportable tablespaces, and Oracle Real Application clusters. Oracle has matured this technology in Oracle Database 10g. The availability of cheaper, faster, and affordable hardware; better operating systems; and newer, cheaper open source software like Linux has supplemented the path for grid-technology development. Grid computing has become one of the best means to save money on hardware and software, enjoy resource optimization, and receive better results on investments.

You will learn more about grid technology and the Grid Control in Chapter 18, "Leveraging Grid Technology Features."

Summary

This chapter reviewed the important new features of Oracle Database 10g (Releases 1 and 2) and the processes that support these features. The major architectural changes include performance improvement, storage management, system resources, application tuning, and recovery management. ADDM and AWR are the key improvements to this Oracle version; they support the automatic diagnosis and correction of performance problems. Now that you have an overview of all the new features of Oracle Database 10g, we will proceed to the various installation processes for a database.

2

Installing Oracle Database 10g

Installation Decisions

Now that you have decided to try out the new features of Oracle Database 10g, let's focus on a few preliminary steps in the installation process. The Oracle Database 10g software is available online for downloads from the Oracle Technology Network (OTN) website (`http://otn.oracle.com`, specifically from `http://www.oracle.com/technology/software/products/database/oracle10g/index.html`) or on discs (CD or DVD formats). If your company has a valid support agreement with Oracle Support, you can log an iTAR asking Oracle to send the installation CDs to you. The database usually comes in a single (Enterprise/Standard Edition) downloadable file or CD along with a companion CD or file. The installation process itself is an easier and quicker one than for the Oracle 9i database.

IN THIS CHAPTER

Installation Decisions	23
Prerequisites	24
Installing 10g on UNIX/Linux	25
Oracle Database 10g DBCA Overview	32
Installing 10g on Windows	34
Companion CD Installation and Patches (All Platforms)	35
Installation Checklists	36
Database and Binary Cloning	36
Using Enterprise Manager for Cloning	38
Migrating a Database from 8i or 9i	39
Overview of Database Upgrade Assistant	40
Applying Patches to Database Installations	46
Uninstalling from a Failed Install	47

This chapter discusses the several methods available to facilitate the installation process. It goes over the installation process from the media discs, downloadable files, and directly from the hard disk. You will also learn about the different installation options available with the product, some easy hacks to get the database working on your personal computer, and other useful tips.

Prerequisites

Regardless of the platform being used for your Oracle Database 10g deployment, the following minimum system requirements should be met. The difference in requirements for UNIX and Windows platforms is discussed later in this chapter.

- The system should have a minimum memory of 512MB.

- The system should have sufficient paging space and disk space.

- The operating system should be up to date with service packs or patches.

- The system should have the correct file system format.

Backdoor Installation Techniques

Although Oracle Database 10g is certified to run on the supported platforms with appropriate patches installed, there are a few backdoor methods to get it running on comparable Linux desktop systems and some UNIX systems without appropriate patch levels. We tested the Enterprise edition of the database on RedHat Linux 9.*x* personal computers and on Solaris servers. Be forewarned that this is not a recommended method for any critical application deployments, but should be used only for development purposes while the supported platforms are being built. For RedHat Linux 9.1 desktop installation (instead of the supported RedHat Enterprise Linux AS 2.1), we commented out the entry on Linux under [Certified Versions] in the oraparam.ini; the installation checklist bypassed the OS version, and didn't even recognize it. All the major database features were satisfactorily tested on this server. For Solaris, we got the database running fine even after installing it with commented-out entries on some Sun patches in the oraparam.ini. We will give pointers to similar installation tricks from other published resources in appropriate sections.

Oracle Universal Installer (OUI) checks the environment to verify that it meets the minimum requirements for a successful installation. This early analysis by OUI reduces the chances of any problems during the installation process.

OUI performs all the prerequisite checks in the installation process before actually installing any software. These checks include OUI-specific verifications and those defined for a specific product for the particular operating system on which it runs. All prerequisite check parameters are defined in the oraparam.ini file or should be mentioned in another user-defined .ini file. The prerequisite check results are written to the installActions*timestamp*.log file.

The Oracle Universal Installer does the prerequisite checks in one of the following ways:

- Automatically when the user runs the OUI executable during the installation process

- In silent mode when the checks are run and managed from the command line (during a silent install)

- Standalone when the checks are run without actually completing any installation

For the silent mode, the OUI will perform as many prerequisite checks as possible, record the alerts on errors, and provide the location of the `installActionstimestamp.log` file before exiting the installation.

Overview of Silent Installation

Let us have a quick overview of the silent installation process. A silent mode installation runs in the background without any inputs from the user. The interactive dialog boxes found in a traditional graphical user interface installation process are not displayed. Instead of relying on user prompts to choose from a series of installation options, the OUI installs the software using a predefined set of options stored in a response file or passed on from the command line. A *response file* is a specifications file with necessary database-installation information from the user. For every variable in the response file, an answer is stored as its value. The response file template for the silent installation is found in the stage directory (on the CD-ROM) under the `<root of CD>`/Response directory, as in `<Products.xml_Location>`/Response/`<product>`.`<installtype>`.rsp.

> For the review of installation prerequisites, necessary inputs are listed in the `prerequisite.xml` file located in the `oraInventory/logs` directory. After the prerequisite checks are run, the results, along with the prerequisite checks' predefined inputs, are written to the `prerequisite_results.xml` file in the `oraInventory/logs` directory. The `prerequisite_results.xml` file can be reused as an input file for future executions of the checker process.

If you need a new response file for silent installs based on your installation options, use the record mode of OUI to write the installation session into a response file. The response file is written immediately after the Summary page (which you will see in the section titled "Common Steps for Installation"). Use this response file for future identical installation sessions on multiple servers.

> **When Should You Use Silent Installation?**
> Silent installations are helpful if you have to install the same Oracle product several times on different computers. If you are choosing the same options and doing identical installations, silent mode can help you to save time choosing the various installation options with each install. This will also help to coordinate multiple installations by different users on different servers and having a uniform approach to applying patches and planning database upgrades.

The silent installation method is valid only for the base release of the database software. It cannot be used for already patched software. Silent installation is not recommended for installations using ASM disks because it is a little complex for that.

Installing 10g on UNIX/Linux

Oracle Database 10g is supported on Linux, Solaris, HP-UX, hp Tru64 UNIX, and AIX-based systems. For more details on the supported UNIX platforms, operating system versions, and appropriate patch levels, please refer to *Oracle Database Installation Guide for UNIX Systems*. If you are installing Oracle for the first time on your UNIX or Linux servers, please review the appropriate OS-specific documentation to make sure that you have applied the appropriate patches and have set appropriate values for shared memory and semaphore-related parameters.

The UNIX server where you are planning to do the database installation must meet at least the following hardware requirements:

- A minimum physical memory (RAM) of 512MB.

- A minimum swap space of 1GB (or twice the size of available RAM). On larger systems with 2GB or more of memory, the swap space can be up to twice the size of RAM.

- A minimum disk space of 400MB in the /temp directory.

- A minimum disk space of 1.5GB to 3GB for the Oracle software, depending on the installation type and platform.

- 1.2GB of disk space for file system storage if you are installing the preconfigured database.

> The flash recovery area can be used as a disk cache for tape and also to store RMAN backups. RMAN can use these backups for restoring files during media recovery.

You will also need additional disk space for the flash recovery area to configure automated backups. In the case of ASM (Automatic Storage Management) deployments, additional ASM disks will be needed as well.

For installations on UNIX or Linux platforms, use one of the following methods to make the software accessible on the server:

- Download the software files from the OTN website (mentioned previously) to separate directories on your server. Uncompress and extract the downloaded files as follows:

  ```
  $gunzip filename_db.cpio.gz
  ```

  This will create a file called *filename*_db.cpio, where *filename* varies depending on operating system.

  ```
  $cpio - imdv < filename_db.cpio
  ```

  This step will create a subdirectory called Disk*N*, where *N* denotes the disk number in the filename.

- Mount the CDs or DVD on your server and copy the contents to separate directories on the hard disk. You can also install directly from the CD or DVD, but the copied files will help you avoid mount/unmount processes if any re-install or updates must be made. Please refer to the installation manual for the necessary steps.

Installation Steps

This section discusses the actual installation process of Oracle Database 10g. Although we primarily focus on the installation process on UNIX/Linux servers, we will also look at the Windows installation later in this chapter. You will be guided through a step-by-step interactive installation procedure in the following pages.

The installer adjusts any operating system variables needed for the Oracle database server. It also provides guidance through a series of questions and accepts feedback from the users on software installation and database creation.

Platform-Independent Database Installation Questions

The following questions apply to all database installations, regardless of platform:

1. What type of database installation (as shown in Figure 2.1) do you want?

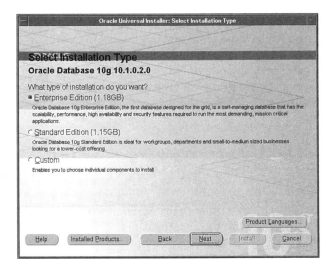

FIGURE 2.1
Oracle Universal Installer: the Select Installation Type screen.

- ■ **Oracle Enterprise Edition.** This is Oracle's full-fledged database product with all the bells and whistles for high-end applications that require scalability, performance, and availability.

- ■ **Oracle Standard Edition.** A scaled-down, lower-cost offering of the Enterprise edition for departmental-level applications.

- ■ **Custom.** Allows for customization by enabling users to choose to install or prevent installation of certain components.

2. What database configuration and starter database (as shown in Figure 2.2) do you wish to use?

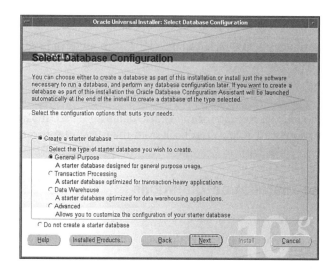

FIGURE 2.2
OUI: the Select Database Configuration screen.

If you choose to select a starter database, you will be prompted to pick one of the following options: General Purpose, Transaction Processing, Data Warehouse, or Advanced. For Oracle to create a preconfigured database, select among the first three choices. If you choose Advanced, the installer will automatically launch the Database Configuration Assistant (DBCA) at the end of installation process. For creating a custom database, choose this option.

Installing a database at this stage is not necessary. The Database Configuration Assistant (DBCA) can be invoked later in the installation process for this purpose. We will discuss the use of DBCA later in this chapter.

The database configuration options are Global Database Name, Oracle System Identifier (SID), and sample schemas. The global database name is the full name of the database, which distinguishes it from other databases, as in Q00R10G.US.ACME.COM. In this example, the database name is Q00R10G and the database domain name is US.ACME.COM. The database name and database domain name, when combined together, become the global database name.

During the installation process, you will be prompted for passwords for SYS, SYSTEM, and so on, which enable administration of the database.

What Are the Database Storage Options?

A typical Oracle database installation consists of datafiles, control files, logfiles, and so on. In Oracle Database 10g, you have three choices for setting up the storage as shown in Figure 2.3:

- File system for database files managed by the operating system. Oracle will create and manage these files in the directories specified by the DBA during the installation.

- Raw devices, which is the preferred choice for Oracle real application clusters. This choice enables management of storage devices outside the operating system.

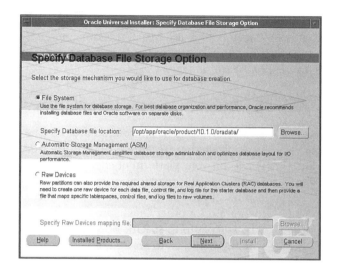

FIGURE 2.3
OUI: the Specify Database File Storage
Option screen.

- Automatic Storage Management (ASM), where Oracle Database 10g automatically manages database file placements and naming. ASM simplifies file management and database administration, and improves performance in large environments. For a detailed review of ASM, see Chapter 4, "Setting Up Automatic Storage Management."

> **Choose Among File System or ASM-Managed Files**
>
> For the basic installation, the default selection is File System. ASM-managed files can be added to such a database at a later stage. If you are experimenting with the use of ASM files, make sure that you are comfortable with executing disk-management commands as root or can get help from a UNIX administrator to complete those tasks. Almost every organization using Oracle Database 10g is likely to have both file system–managed and ASM-managed files in their databases for quite some time.

Database Management Options

Oracle will ask you if databases are to be managed centrally or locally. The central deployment mode allows for management of multiple databases and application servers from a single console by using a special agent on the database machine. The local deployment mode manages only a single database instance.

Optimal Flexible Architecture (OFA)

The Optimal Flexible Architecture (OFA) standard has been established by Oracle as a set of configuration guidelines to ensure reliable Oracle installations with a little maintenance.

Oracle's recommended `ORACLE_HOME` path (per OFA guidelines) was similar to `/u01/app/oracle/product/9.2.0` for earlier releases of Oracle databases. With Oracle Database 10g, the OFA-recommended `ORACLE_HOME` path has changed to `/u01/app/oracle/product/10.2.0/type_n`, where `type` is the type of Oracle home—Oracle database (`db`)or Oracle client (`client`) and *n* is an optional counter.

This improved OFA syntax helps you to install different products (db_1, client_1, http_1) with the same release number in the same ORACLE_BASE directory and also install the same product more than once in the same ORACLE_BASE directory (db_1, db_2, and so on). For more details on OFA, please refer to your platform-specific *Oracle Database Installation Guide.*

Enabling Tracing for OUI Installations

When you are using OUI (espicially in RAC installations) and you get an error, debugging will be quite complex without any tracing. So from Oracle database versions 9.2.0.5.0 and later, you can turn on tracing for OUI by invoking the installer with the –DTRACING.ENABLED option.

```
$ ./runInstaller -J-DTRACING.ENABLED=true
-J-DTRACING.LEVEL=2
```

This tracing will generate more details on what the installer is doing behind the screens and give lots of information on the internal operations. You can use the following sample script to capture the output:

```
% script /tmp/oui_tracing.txt
% ./runInstaller -J-DTRACING.ENABLED=true
-J-DTRACING.LEVEL=2
...............<script truncated>..................
  % exit
```

In addition to the OUI trace file, you can also review the logs created by OUI in the oraInventory/logs directory and $ORACLE_HOME/install/make.log for analysis of the installation process.

Common Steps for Installation

The following steps are common for all database installations regardless of platform. For details on your platform of choice, please refer to specific operating system installation manuals from Oracle. Also review the documentation for other Oracle products and add-ons. The platform-specific documentation will also help you to set up users, groups, and privileges for Oracle installation accounts. You will need system administrator (root) privileges for most of these task.

1. Log on to the server as a member of the administrative group who has permission to run the Oracle software.

2. Insert the distribution CD for the database into the CD drive. Mount the CD in non-Windows environments and set the DISPLAY variable correctly. If you are using downloaded software (as mentioned earlier in the section "Installing 10g on UNIX/Linux"), go to the appropriate install directory under Disk1 and click or run the installer (runInstaller.sh) program.

3. The Oracle Universal Installer (OUI) Welcome page appears. Select Next to begin installation.

If you are installing Oracle for the first time on your UNIX or Linux server, verify that appropriate patches are applied and that appropriate values for shared memory and semaphore-related parameters are set. The following additional steps are also required:

a) Specify Inventory Directory. This is different from ORACLE_HOME, discussed later. Select Next to continue

b) A dialog box appears asking that oraInst.sh be run as root in a separate window. Run this and return to the OUI page. Select Continue.

4. The Specify File Locations page appears, where you enter the Oracle Home name and directory path to install the software. Choose a different name and path for additional new installations on the server. Select Continue.

5. Choose the type of database installation. The options are Enterprise Edition, Standard Edition, and Custom, as discussed earlier. Select Continue.

6. Choose the type of preconfigured database to be installed. The options are General Purpose, Transaction Processing, Data Warehouse, and Advanced. Do not choose Advanced unless you have prior experience performing a custom database installation. Select Continue.

7. Specify whether you need a starter database or would prefer to run DBCA after the installation is completed.

8. If you have chosen a starter database, select a global database name and SID, a database character set (choose Default for the language of the operating system), and various other database-management options.

9. Under Database Management, choose Use Database Control for Database Management.

10. Make your choice of database storage as discussed previously.

11. Choose recovery configuration options—flash recovery area and so forth.

12. Choose passwords for SYS and SYSTEM accounts.

13. A summary page appears. Click *Install* to start the installation. A progress bar will be displayed to help you track the progress of the installation process.

14. On UNIX and Linux platforms, a dialog box appears asking you to run root.sh in a separate window. You need root privileges for this step, as well as for some of the preliminary steps. When the script finishes, choose Continue in OUI.

15. Toward the end of the installation process, the Configuration page appears. Allow the various tools to install and start configuring the network and netservice listener process, and create the database and management tools. Click Next.

16. As the database is created, an information page presents the details of your database. Review the list. Click Password Management to unlock or change passwords of database accounts.

17. The End of Installation page appears with relevant information on Web application port numbers. You may want to note this information for future use.

The database installation is now complete. You can use the Enterprise Manager or a Web browser to connect to the database. When you are prompted for a user name and password, enter SYS and the password you selected.

Install the Companion CD for your platform after the first database disk has been succesfully installed. Apply the patches (if any) specific to your database version and operating systems.

Besides Oracle documentations, there is a good website with lot of tips for Oracle installations on Linux platforms at `http://www.puschitz.com/InstallingOracle10g.shtml`.

Components to Access Other Databases and Applications

Please review component-specific installation guidelines for other Oracle products and for add-ons like third-party database (transparent) gateways. Oracle provides software and documentation for accessing the Oracle Procedural Gateway for APPC-enabled systems (like IBM mainframe data and services), and Oracle Transparent Gateways to access data in IBM DB2, Microsoft SQL Server, Teradata databases, iWay Server databases, and so on.

Oracle Database 10g DBCA Overview

If you decided not to choose the default database install, or if additional databases are desired, use the DBCA option. DBCA can also be used to delete an existing database, add options to an existing database, or manage database templates. We discuss using DBCA to remove a failed database installation toward the end of this chapter.

> ### Choosing the File System Option with DBCA
>
> With the file system option, DBCA will create the database files in a directory on a file system on the server. This file system should be separate from the OS file systems and the Oracle software, if possible. You can use a file system on a physically attached disk or on a logical volume manager (LVM) disk or a RAID device. If you are using disks that are not logical volumes or RAID devices, Oracle advises on the use of Optimal Flexible Architecture (OFA) recommendations. For disks in an LVM or RAID configuration, Oracle recommends using stripe-and-mirror-everything (SAME) methodology for better performance and reliability. With Custom installation or advanced database creation options, you can select Oracle-managed files, where you just specify the database object name for creating or deleting database files.

DBCA is typically found in `$ORACLE_HOME/bin`. To use DBCA in a UNIX/Linux environment, type `dbca` at the command prompt. To use DBCA in a Windows environment, choose Programs, select Oracle-Home *Name*, choose Configuration and Migration Tools, and select Database Configuration Assistant.

Database Configuration Assistant provides a series of options for creating a database, deleting a database, and so on. Choose `Create a Database` to start the wizard to create and configure the database. It will step through a series of prompts for the database as follows:

- **Database Templates.** This prompt enables the selection of the type of database to be created. By default, there are Data Warehouse, General Purpose, and Transaction Processing templates. For complex environments, select the Custom Database option.

- **Database Identification.** This prompt enables you to select the global database name, Oracle System Identifier (SID), and sample schemas.

- **Management Options.** This prompt enables the management of the database with Oracle Enterprise Manager (OEM). To use OEM, select Configure the Database with Enterprise

Manager. Choose Grid Control for Database Management or Database Control for Database Management.

- **Database Credentials.** Specify passwords for accounts like SYS and SYSTEM, DBSNMP, and SYSMAN. It is not recommended to choose the Use the Same Password for All Accounts option.

- **Storage Options.** Choose among File System, Raw Devices, or Automatic Storage Management (ASM).

- **Database File Options.** Select Oracle Home and a directory path on which to install the Oracle software.

- **Recovery Configuration.** Choose the Flash Recovery Area and Enable Archiving options.

- **Database Content.** Select the Sample Schemas option on the Sample Schemas screen, and mark the Run the Following Scripts check box on the Custom Scripts screen.

- **Initialization Parameters.** Use the Memory screen to set the initialization parameters that control the memory usage of the database. Under Sizing, specify the smallest block size (8K is recommended) and the maximum number of operating system user processes that can connect simultaneously to the database (150 by default). Under Character Sets, select a character set that determines what languages can be represented in the database. Use Unicode (AL32UTF8) to support multiple languages for database users and applications. Select the National Character Set here or choose the default. Opt for the default values under Default Language and Default Data Format according to location.

- **Database Storage.** This shows the storage structure of the database, where objects can be created or deleted. If one of the preconfigured templates is chosen, control files, datafiles, and rollback segments cannot be added or removed.

- **Creation Options.** Save the database definition to a template, create the database, or select both.

Many of these prompts have a default setting. To accept all default parameters, click Finish at any step during the navigation process. Figure 2.4 shows the Confirmation screen.

Tracing the Database Configuration Assistant (DBCA)

Sometimes, the DBCA will exit without giving you adequate warnings or hints on what went wrong with the configuration process. For addressing this scenario, tracing can be turned on to provide additional output. To enable tracing with DBCA on UNIX/Linux platforms, do the following:

1. Edit the DBCA file in the $ORACLE_HOME/bin directory using the vi editor.

2. Find the following line at the end of the file:

```
# Run DBCA
$JRE_DIR/bin/java -Dsun.java2d.font.DisableAlgorithmicStyles=true -DORACLE_HOME=$OH -
DDISPLAY=$DISPLAY -DJDBC_PROTOCOL=thin -mx64m -classpath $CLASSPATH oracle.sysman.
assistants.dbca.Dbca $ARGUMENTS
```

3. Add the following words just before -classpath on the $JRE_DIR/bin/JRE line:

```
-DTRACING.ENABLED=true -DTRACING.LEVEL=2
```

4. When you run the DBCA, use one of the following commands. The output file will be
    dbca_trace.log.

```
$ORACLE_HOME/bin> dbca > dbca_trace.log &
```

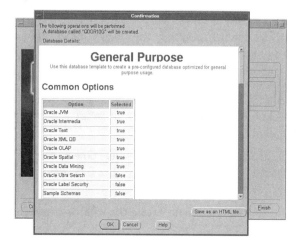

FIGURE 2.4
Database Configuration Assistant: the
Confirmation screen.

In a Windows environment, use Notepad or any other editing tool to open dbca.bat in the
$ORACLE_HOME\bin directory and add -DTRACING.ENABLED=true -DTRACING.LEVEL=2 just before
-ORACLE_HOME="%OH%". Invoke DBCA from the command line using the following syntax:

```
ORACLE_HOME\bin\dbca.bat > D:\oracle\logs\dbcatrace.log
```

When DBCA is run, the file dbcatrace.log will be generated in the D:\oracle\logs directory.

Installing 10g on Windows

For installing Oracle Database 10g on a Windows computer (server), choose the different
options like CD, shared drives, copied software on disk, OTN downloads, and the like to make
the installation disks available on the computer. Refer to *Oracle Database Installation Guide for
Windows* to get more details on these.

Once you have made the software available on the computer, log on as a member of the Administrators group and select `setup.exe` or `autorun.exe` to invoke the Oracle Universal Installer. You can also do silent installations using a response file. The installation steps are similar to those of the UNIX environment.

When you try the Oracle Database 10g instal-lation on Windows XP or 2000 servers using Dynamic Host Configuration Protocol (DHCP), you will get an error saying that the IP address cannot be determined. Similarly, if the installation is done on your laptop or any machine not on the network, you must configure the Microsoft loopback adapter as the primary network interface to make it work on its network. This is a known bug and is mentioned in Oracle documentation as well as MetaLink (#277780.1). After installing the adapter on the DHCP computer, assign a nonroutable IP. Add an entry with *<new IP>* *<fully qualified machine name> <machine alias>* to the `System32\drivers\etc\hosts`. See installation notes for more details.

> **Installation on Your PC with Low Memory**
>
> You can install Oracle Database 10g on computers with 256MB of RAM and 500MB of virtual memory, but you will not be able to run Oracle Database Upgrade Assistant, Database Configuration Assistant, or Oracle Net Services Configuration Assistant during the OUI installation session. Stop all other applications running on the computer, increase the paging file size, and use the smallest SGA for your installation. Choose Basic or Advanced Installation and do not select the Create Starter Database option. After the software has been installed, choose the right `ORACLE_HOME` and start the Database Configuration Assistant. Use DBCA to create your database.

Companion CD Installation and Patches (All Platforms)

The Oracle Database 10g companion CD has additional products that are not in the primary CD or download file. You can down-load this disk as mentioned before or use available media from Oracle. The products in this disk should be installed into a different `ORACLE_HOME` from the one used for the data-base.

> For more details on installation requirements for Oracle HTTP Server, Oracle HTML DB, Operating System, and Service Pack, please refer to the platform-specific *Oracle Database Companion CD Installation Guide*.

The Oracle Database 10g companion CD offers two types of installations: Oracle Database 10g Products and Oracle Database 10g Companion Products. If you install Oracle Database 10g Products, OUI will install all available products with it. Follow the instructions in the *Oracle Database Companion CD Installation Guide* for your choice of installation.

Oracle Corporation highly recommends applying the latest patch-set release (if any) after installing the Oracle Companion CD products. Oracle has started a quarterly schedule for patches since January 2005; register and use Oracle MetaLink (`http://metalink.oracle.com`) to get patches.

Manual Database Installation Steps

The manual database-creation process has a few steps similar to database cloning, which is discussed in the next section:

1. Create an init<*SID*>.ora in your $ORACLE_HOME/dbs directory in UNIX or in your $ORACLE_HOME\database directory for Windows. You can make a copy of the sample init.ora to init<*SID*>.ora and alter the copied file to have new database parameters, filenames, and sizes.

2. Log in to the database as SYS and start up the database in NOMOUNT mode.

3. Create the database using the database creation script (similar to clone_db.sql). Run additional scripts to create SYSAUX, temporary tablespaces, users, and so on.

4. Run the necessary scripts (catalog.sql and catproc.sql) to build views, synonyms, and so on.

Installation Checklists

When you create an Oracle Database 10g instance, make it a point to create a default permanent tablespace along with it at the database level. Oracle will assign any nonsystem users and objects to this tablespace. Whenever the DBA creates a new user or object, it will use this default permanent tablespace unless the default tablespace is mentioned for the user/object. (Similarly the default temporary tablespace created along with the database will be used as the temporary tablespace for users without an assigned temporary tablespace.) The init.ora parameter compatible>=10.0 should be set to utilize this feature.

Why Should You Prefer Locally Managed Tablespaces?

A locally managed tablespace manages its own extents by maintaining a bitmap in each datafile to keep track of the free or used status of blocks in that datafile. Each bit in the bitmap corresponds to a block or a group of blocks in the data file. Whenever the extents are allocated or released for reuse, Oracle changes the bitmap values to reflect the new status for the blocks. These changes do not update tables in the data dictionary like the default method of dictionary-managed tablespaces. These changes do not generate rollback and reduce the contention on datadictionary tables and fragmentation.

This default permanent tablespace as well as default temporary tablespaces can only be locally managed. If the SYSTEM tablespace is created as locally managed, no tablespaces within the database can be dictionary managed, including the default tablespace. Once a default tablespace has been assigned at the database level, it cannot be dropped, but its name can be changed.

Database and Binary Cloning

Most organizations need at least two identical databases for testing and production deployments. Cloning refers to creating an identical copy of a database. After you have successfully installed a database, it can be cloned to create an identical database for testing or training purposes.

A database can be cloned or re-created from another database by several methods, the most notable ones being hot or cold backups, copying the datafiles, and export/import processes. When you clone a database, do not keep it in mounted stage during the copy process because it will cause database corruption. Recovery Manager (RMAN) can be used as well for making a duplicate copy of the database. For more details on using RMAN for cloning a database, refer to *Oracle Database Backup and Recovery Advanced User's Guide*.

Can Database Block Size Be Different in a Clone?

One of the important points to be remembered in any database cloning effort is to have an identical db_block_size value in the cloned database as in the original database. If you use a different block size than that of the database being cloned, you will get ORA-600 errors. Remember to specifically set this value, or the database will assume the default block size of 2,048 bytes and the database copy will fail.

The following are the common steps for cloning any database, regardless of its data content and platform:

1. Perform a full backup of the database.

2. Back up the control file to trace. The trace file will be created in user_dump_dest:

   ```
   SQL> alter database backup controlfile to trace resetlogs;
   SQL> select name, value from v$parameter where name='user_dump_dest';
   ```

3. Find the latest trace file (with the extension.trc) and rename it clone_db.sql.

4. Get a list of all data files and redo log files to be copied over to the new database:

   ```
   SQL> select name from v$datafile;
   SQL> select member from v$logfile;
   ```

5. Perform a clean shutdown of the database.

6. Create directories on the target server to hold the cloned database file. Copy all data and redo log files from step 4 to the newly created directories.

7. If you are planning to use the init.ora parameter file for the cloned database, make a copy of the host's file and rename it to init<clone>.ora file. Edit the init<clone>.ora file to have new values (paths) for the target database. This step will include paths for control_files, user_dump_dest, background_dump_dest, and so on.

8. Make a copy of the trace file (clone_db.sql) on the target machine. This file has the commands for creating the control file for the original database.

9. Delete the header information and the comments in the copied file on the target machine.

10. Modify the startup command statement to include the new initclone.ora parameter file:

    ```
    SQL> startup nomount pfile= <new location/initclone.ora>
    ```

Installing Oracle Database 10g

11. Modify the control file command statement as follows:

```
SQL> create controlfile set database "clone_db" resetlogs noarchivelog;
```

12. Modify the data and redo filenames to point to the names of the appropriate files on the new server.

13. Remove the lines containing the RECOVER DATABASE command and its associated comments.

14. Set the Oracle environments (ORACLE_HOME and ORACLE_SID) to the new database.

15. Edit tnsnames.ora and listener.ora to include the new database instance information.

16. Stop and restart the listener.

17. In UNIX systems, add an entry for the cloned database in the oratab file.

18. Run the script on the target database server. Mount and open the database.

19. Change the global name of the new cloned database as follows:

```
SQL> alter database rename global_name to
<clone_db_name>;
```

Can Databases Be Cloned Independent of Platforms?

Nowadays Linux servers are very affordable; hence, some organizations may want to keep their training environments in Linux or Windows platforms instead of the costly production environments on UNIX platforms. For cloning databases independent of platforms, export/import of the source database to its lower-end clone is the best option. Before you take the export of the source database, remember to perform a Shutdown Immediate operation followed by Startup Restrict command to keep all user activities out of the database. The actual modus operandi of the export/import process will be explained later in this section.

Using Enterprise Manager for Cloning

Oracle Enterprise Manager has a cloning wizard to automate the cloning of Oracle homes, databases, and application server (9.0.4 and up) installations to the same host or multiple hosts. Oracle Enterprise Manager provides a Clone Oracle Home tool that will help you to clone an Oracle home to one or more hosts. Similarly, the Clone Database tool helps in cloning a database to one or more hosts. By default, it clones the database instance to an existing Oracle home. If you want to clone the database instance under a new Oracle home, create a new Oracle home using the Clone Oracle Home tool and then clone the instance to that home using the Clone Database tool.

When you use Oracle Database 10g on a host with a lower level of Enterprise Manager Agent (9.2) on it, the cloning of ORACLE_HOME will fail. (This is reported as bug #3164441.) If this happens to you, stop the agent and attempt the cloning again. If you are attempting the database cloning in a RAC cluster–enabled installation of Oracle Database 10g Release 1, it will also fail (bug #3319121). Before you clone a database using Oracle Enterprise Manager Release 1, change the ownership of extjob to Oracle user to avoid errors. Cloning of cluster-enabled ORACLE_HOME installations is available only in Oracle Database 10g Release 2.

In a Windows installation, when you use Oracle Enterprise Manager to clone an Oracle home or database, you may get password errors with your OS user account. To resolve this, make sure that the user has Log On as Batch Job privileges. Using Windows administrative tools, under Local Security Policy, Local Policies, User Rights Assignment, add the OS user to Log On as Batch Job (see Figure 2.5).

Notes on Binary Cloning

Binary cloning is the process of copying the installed database binaries from one server or vtier location to another server having the same layout or file structure with identical naming conventions. After copying the Oracle binary file systems using the UNIX commands, the binaries are recompiled and database files can be copied to the new location. Many organizations use vtiers instead of dedicated servers for database installations. A vtier can be considered as an area assigned with its own IP address on a very large server sharing a storage network. Because the vtier file systems are named differently from traditional servers, copied binaries will not work properly.

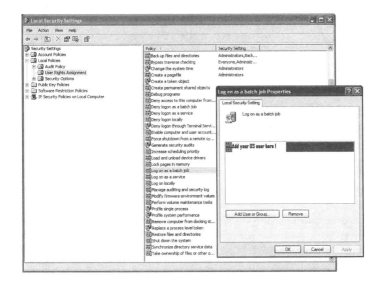

FIGURE 2.5
Adding privileges to an OS user for cloning on Windows.

Migrating a Database from 8i or 9i

You have several options to upgrade your existing databases in Oracle 8i or 9i to Oracle Database 10g. We will skim over the various steps used for the manual migration process as well as direct migration steps for the different versions. Before you plan for any upgrade process, make sure that you have the latest backup of your database on media and keep a database copy on another identical machine. This copy database will be there for you to point your applications to in the event something goes wrong during the upgrade process and you experience significant downtime.

> ### Is Export/Import a Good Option?
>
> The traditional export/import process can be used for migrating data from any prior supported Oracle database versions if their data types are still supported in Oracle Database 10g. The export/import process is advisable only for smaller databases (maximum of a few tens of gigabytes in database size) and for databases with relatively few indexes or constraints. In the case of database upgrades with a large number of indexes, it is advisable to import the data with the indexes option turned off (INDEXES=N) and to run a separate script to re-create the indexes after data load. Make sure that the data in the migrating database is clean and that indexes are consistent before you start the export/import process.

More details of the upgrade processes are mentioned in *Oracle Database Upgrade Guide 10g*.

If your old database is Oracle 7.3.4 or earlier, you have to upgrade it to Oracle 8.0.6 or 8.1.7. If the old database is version 8.0.5 or earlier, then upgrade it to 8.0.6. From 8.0.6, you can upgrade it to Oracle Database 10g. For 8.1.5 and 8.1.6 databases, upgrade to 8.1.7 and from there to 10g. For all Oracle 9i databases, direct upgrade is available.

For a direct upgrade from Oracle 8.0.6 to 10g, use the script u0800060.sql in the $ORACLE_HOME/rdbms/admin directory. From Oracle 8.1.7 to 10g, use the script u0801070.sql; from Oracle 9.0.1 to 10g, use the script u0900010.sql; and from Oracle 9.2 to 10g, use the script u0902000.sql. All these scripts are in the $ORACLE_HOME/rdbms/admin directory.

There are several steps to be done after the migration, such as collecting baseline statistics, tuning the database and SQL statements for Cost Based Optimizer (CBO), managing objects, adding new features, and so on, which are discussed in specific MetaLink documentation and in the upgrade guide. The steps would easily run over several pages if completely listed here, and as such have been omitted.

Overview of Database Upgrade Assistant

In case you are planning to upgrade an existing database, Oracle provides a tool called Database Upgrade Assistant (DBUA). It interactively steps you through the upgrade process and configures the database for the new Oracle Database 10g release.

It can be invoked by the dbua command from the UNIX/Linux prompts or from Database Migration Assistant under Configuration and Migration Tools in a Windows environment. The DBUA shows a list of databases and prompts you to choose. After you choose a database for upgrade, it gathers database details (see Figure 2.6). DBUA will also interactively verify whether the database is backed up and start the upgrade process. Please see *Oracle Database Upgrade Guide* for more details.

Because upgrading a single standalone database to 10g is much simpler than upgrading an environment where there is a primary database and one or more standby databases, we will focus our discussion on standby databases. Most organizations run Oracle 9i Data Guard environment for standby environments (logical or physical). If there are multiple standby databases in your

(Data Guard) environment, you have to do the upgrade process discussed next for each standby database.

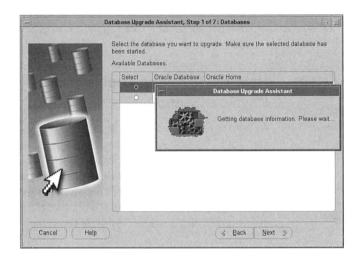

FIGURE 2.6
Choosing a database for upgrade with DBUA.

Upgrade Path for Standby Environments

The preliminary things to be done before any upgrade are checking for nologging operations on standby databases and the recovery of tablespaces or datafiles brought offline.

The common steps in any database-upgrade process for standby configuration are as follows:

1. Install the new Oracle database release on production (primary) site(s), apply redo logs to standby databases, and complete the upgrade on primary database as per instructions.

2. After upgrading the primary, switch log files to archive any remaining redo logs.

3. Copy archive logs on the upgraded primary site to the archive destination on the standby host.

4. Shut down the standby database and related processes (listener and so on).

5. Start and mount the standby database.

6. Keep the standby database in managed recovery mode. Apply the archive logs created during the upgrade process.

7. Ensure that the standby database has recovered up to the last (copied) log from primary. Update archive log gaps between the primary and the standby.

8. Restart remote archiving on the primary database.

9. Place the standby database back into the recovery state.

The following sections look at more details of upgrading a physical standby and a logical standby configuration.

Database Upgrade Assistant in Silent Mode

Database Upgrade Assistant (DBUA) can be invoked in silent mode similar to in silent installation. For this, use the `-silent` option along with `dbua` command from the command line. In silent mode, you will not see any user interface; check for the upgrade status (messages, alerts, errors, and so on) from the log file. See the *Oracle Database Upgrade Guide* for more details.

A Word on the Oracle Companion CD and Patches

For any Oracle Database 10g installation during upgrade process, install the software into a new `ORACLE_HOME` using Oracle Universal Installer as explained earlier in this chapter. Download the companion CD, extract it, and do a similar installation using OUI. Do not forget to apply any available patches for the version of the Oracle software and platform you are working with.

Using DBUA with Oracle 9i Physical Standby Configuration

Now that you have learned about the Database Upgrade Assistant, we will briefly discuss the upgrade path from an Oracle 9i database in a Data Guard configuration. For more details and SQL commands involved in each step, refer to *Oracle Data Guard Broker 10g Guide*, *Oracle Database Upgrade Guide10g*, and MetaLink Note #278521.1.

1. Log in to the primary and standby databases in separate windows as `oracle` or as the owner of the Oracle software directory. Set the environment to the existing 9.2.0 installation.

2. On the primary database, stop all user activity. If you are using RAC, shut down (normal or immediate) every instance except the primary database instance.

3. On the active database instance, archive the current log file:

   ```
   SQL> alter system archive log current;
   ```

4. On the active primary database instance, note the current log thread number and sequence number:

   ```
   SQL> select thread#, sequence# from v$log where status='CURRENT';
   ```

5. Archive the current log:

   ```
   SQL> alter system archive log current;
   ```

6. Shut down the active primary database instance cleanly (normal or immediate). Stop the Oracle processes running against the `ORACLE_HOME`.

7. Place the standby database instance in managed recovery mode. If you are using RAC on standby, shut down all other instances cleanly (normal or immediate) except this standby database instance.

8. Verify that each log file archived in the primary has been applied by querying the v$log_history:

   ```
   SQL> select max(sequence#) from v$log_history;
   ```

9. After all logs have been applied to this standby database, stop managed recovery, shut down the standby database, and stop all agents/listeners against the 9i installation:

```
SQL> alter database recover managed standby database cancel;
SQL> shutdown immediate;
```

10. On the standby host, install 10.1.0.2 into a new ORACLE_HOME using OUI as explained earlier in this chapter. Don't forget to install the Oracle companion CD.

   Copy the initialization parameter file (spfile), password file, and networking files from the 9i ORACLE_HOME/dbs directory into the new 10g ORACLE_HOME/dbs directory. Make sure that this standby database has remote_login_exclusive = shared (or exclusive), that a password file exists, and that the SYS password is the same as the SYS password on the primary.

11. On the primary host, install 10.1.0.2 into its own ORACLE_HOME using OUI and install the (platform-specific) Oracle companion CD. Add the Oracle Net Service name in the tnsnames.ora file that resides in the 10g ORACLE_HOME. After 10g is installed, with the environment still set to the 9.2 installation, start up the primary database:

```
SQL> startup migrate;
```

12. Keep the archive log mode set to true during the upgrade process to validate the standby after upgrade. Then set DisableArchiveLogMode="false" in $ORACLE_HOME/rdbms/admin/utlu101x.sql.

13. From the 10.1.0.2 ORACLE_HOME, start the Database Upgrade Assistant and upgrade the primary database. Ignore the errors in the alert log noting that the primary database is unable to connect to the standby.

14. When the upgrade process has started on the primary database, start the standby listener on the standby database (10g).

15. Set the ORACLE_HOME to 10g environment and bring the standby to the nomount state. Check to verify that STANDBY_FILE_MANAGEMENT, FAL_SERVER, and FAL_CLIENT are set properly as in the upgrade guide:

```
SQL> startup nomount;
SQL> alter system set standby_file_management=auto scope=both;
SQL> alter system set fal_server=<OracleNet_ServiceName_of_Standby database> scope=both;
SQL> alter system set fal_client=<OracleNet_ServiceName_of_Primary database>_scope=both;
```

16. Mount the standby database and start managed recovery:

```
SQL> alter database mount standby database;
SQL> recover managed standby database disconnect;
```

17. When the Database Upgrade Assistant has completed on the primary, set the ORACLE_HOME to the new 10g home and connect to the primary database. Identify and record the current log thread and sequence number. Then, archive the current log:

```
SQL> select thread#, sequence# from v$log where status='CURRENT';
SQL> alter system archive log current;
```

18. On the standby database instance, verify that each log file archived in the primary has applied by querying the v$log_history:

    ```
    SQL> select max(sequence#) from v$log_history;
    ```

19. Start using the primary database on Oracle Database 10g.

Using DBUA with Oracle 9i Logical Standby Configuration

This section discusses the upgrade path from Oracle 9i database in a logical standby Data Guard configuration. For more details and SQL commands involved, refer to *Oracle Data Guard Broker 10g Guide*, *Oracle Database Upgrade Guide10g*, and MetaLink Note #278108.1. Please note that only important SQL commands are given here; we assume that you are familiar with common database-administration tasks.

1. Log in to the primary and standby databases on separate windows as oracle or as the owner of the Oracle software directory. Set the environment to the existing 9.2.0 installation.

2. On the primary database, stop all user activity. If you are using RAC, shut down (normal or immediate) every instance except the primary database instance.

3. On the active database instance, archive the current log file:

    ```
    SQL> alter system archive log current;
    ```

4. On the active primary database instance, note the current log thread number and sequence number:

    ```
    SQL> select thread#, sequence# from v$log where status='CURRENT';
    ```

5. Archive the current log:

    ```
    SQL> alter system archive log current;
    ```

6. If you are using RAC, shut down all other instances cleanly (normal or immediate) except this standby database instance.

7. Verify that each log file archived in the primary has applied by querying dba_logstdby_log (get *x* and *y* from the primary database):

    ```
    SQL> select file_name from dba_logstdby_log where thread#=x and sequence#=y;
    ```

8. Stop the SQL apply operations on this standby database:

    ```
    SQL> alter database stop logical standby apply;
    ```

9. Shut down the standby database and stop all agents and listeners against the 9i installation.

10. Shut down the active primary database instance cleanly (normal or immediate). Stop the Oracle processes running against the `ORACLE_HOME`.

11. On the primary host, install 10.1.0.2 into a new `ORACLE_HOME` using OUI as explained earlier in this chapter. Don't forget to install Oracle companion CD and patches, if any.

12. After 10g is installed, with the environment still set to the 9.2 installation, start up the primary database and disable remote archiving:

```
SQL> startup migrate;
SQL> alter system set log_archive_dest_state_2=defer scope=both;
```

13. From the 10.1.0.2 `ORACLE_HOME`, start the Database Upgrade Assistant and upgrade the primary database.

14. When the upgrade process has been completed on the primary database, point your environment to the new 10g installation, shut down the primary database instance, and restart the agent and listener.

15. Start the primary database instance and enable restricted session. Open the primary database and build the logminer dictionary:

```
SQL> alter system enable restricted session;

SQL> alter database open;

SQL> execute dbms_logstdby.build;
```

16. Disable the restricted session and archive the current log file:

```
SQL> alter system disable restricted session;
SQL> alter system archive log current;
```

17. Execute the following scripts to get the name of the latest dictionary build log file (*file_name.arc*). Note the name of the log file for later reference.

```
SQL> select name from v$archived_log where (sequence#=(select max(sequence#) from
v$archived_log where dictionary_begin = 'YES' and standby_dest= 'NO'));
```

18. On the standby host, install 10.1.0.2 into a new `ORACLE_HOME` home. With the environment still set to Oracle 9i, start up the logical standby database, activate it, and disable remote archiving:

```
SQL> startup migrate;
SQL> alter database activate logical standby database;
SQL> alter system set log_archive_dest_state_2=defer scope=both;
```

19. From the 10g `ORACLE_HOME`, start the Database Upgrade Assistant and upgrade the logical standby database. After upgrading the logical standby database, shut down the instance and restart the agent and listener.

20. Copy the latest dictionary build log file from the primary system to the standby system. Start the logical standby database instance. Turn on the database guard to prevent all users from updating any objects:

    ```
    SQL> startup mount;
    SQL> alter database guard all;
    SQL> alter database open;
    ```

21. Register the copied log file on the logical standby:

    ```
    SQL> alter database register logical logfile 'file_name.arc';
    ```

22. Begin SQL apply operations on the standby database. On a RAC setup, you can start the remaining standby database instances:

    ```
    SQL> alter database start logical standby apply initial;
    ```

23. Begin remote archiving on the primary database. On a RAC setup, you can start the remaining primary database instances:

    ```
    SQL> alter system set log_archive_dest_state_2=enable;
    ```

24. Start using the primary database on Oracle Database 10g.

Applying Patches to Database Installations

After you have installed a database, you may find that it needs periodic patching as per scheduled patch releases by Oracle Corporation. If you are not sure about the latest patch release applied to your database, use the `OPatch` utility (located in `$ORACLE_HOME/OPatch`) to get a list of installed software components as well as the installed patches. Use the command `opatch lsinventory` to get a list from your database installation. A sample output for an Oracle Database 10g Release 2 installation is given here.

```
$ opatch lsinventory


Oracle interim Patch Installer version 10.2.0.0.0
Copyright (c) 2004, Oracle Corporation.  All rights reserved..



Oracle Home       : /opt/app/oracle10g/oracle/product/10.2.0/db_1
Central Inventory : /opt/app/ora10g/oracle/oraInventory
   from           : /opt/app/oracle10g/oracle/product/10.2.0/db_1/oraInst.loc
OPatch version    : 10.2.0.0.0
```

```
OUI version      : 10.2.0.0.0
OUI location     : /opt/app/oracle10g/oracle/product/10.2.0/db_1/oui
Log file location : /opt/app/oracle10g/oracle/product/10.2.0/db_1/cfgtoollogs/opatch/opatch-
2005_Apr_26_18-37-14-EDT_Tue.log


-------------------------------------------------------------------------
Installed Top-level Products (1):

Oracle Database 10g                                      10.2.0.0.0
There are 1 products installed in this Oracle Home.


There are no Intermin patches installed in this Oracle Home.


-------------------------------------------------------------------------


OPatch succeeded.
```

An `interim patch` (formerly known as a *one-off patch*) is a patch set made available by Oracle other than scheduled patch releases to rectify any immediate bugs to the database installation. Interim patches should not be applied on any versions other than for which it is intended. The interim patch installer is the aforementioned `OPatch tool` supplied by Oracle. `OPatch` utilizes the same inventory used by Oracle Universal Installer. Refer to the notes that come with the interim patch for more details and bug fixes.

Uninstalling from a Failed Install

Of course, no DBA is perfect, and chances are that at some point you may want to remove one of your Oracle databases and its binaries and do a fresh installation. We discuss the major points to be noted for such an operation here. For operating system–specific instructions, please refer to the appropriate *Oracle Database Installation Guide*. The point to be noted for all platforms is that you should remove all related Oracle homes, Oracle files, and daemons by using DBCA or a series of steps from the command line for a fool-proof cleanup process. The following sections focus primarily on UNIX/Linux-based systems, and cover Windows-based systems at the end.

Get a Backup Before the Uninstall Process

Before you start any unistall process, make sure that you do not have any useful data in the database. If you feel that there may be any worthwhile data for you to keep, make a complete backup of the database (assuming that the database is in an operable state). If the database has very little data and you are sure of the schema owner information, do an export of that schema or schemas so that the data can be salvaged. If the database installation didn't complete successfully, then you shouldn't have second thoughts on removing it.

The major steps for any uninstall process are to identify all database instances associated with the Oracle home, remove database and ASM instances (if any), stop all the processes/daemons, and completely remove the software. You may also need to reconfigure the Oracle Cluster Synchronization Services (CSS) daemon, depending on your installation. More details on cluster services are given in Chapter 15, "Utilizing Oracle Database 10g Real Applications Clusters."

Step 1: Identify All Database Instances

To begin the uninstall process, you must mark all database instances associated with the Oracle home. The Oracle instances are noted in the oratab file, which is located in the /var/opt/oracle directory for Solaris systems and in the /etc directory for other UNIX- and Linux-based systems. Use cat or more to read the oratab file. You will see an output like the following:

```
+ASM:/u01/app/oracle/product/10.1.0/ASMDB:Y
Q0OR10G:/u01/app/oracle/product/10.1.0/Q0OR10G:Y
```

These entries show that the +ASM Automatic Storage Manager instance and the Q0OR10G Oracle database instance are associated with the /u01/app/oracle/product/10.1.0/Q0OR10G Oracle home directory.

Step 2: Remove the Database(s)

Log in to the database server where you want to do the database operation as oracle. Using oraenv or coraenv (under /usr/local/bin/), set your environment to point to the database you will be working on. Specify your database instance name (SID) at the prompt and you will be connected to the appropriate one. The steps in this process are as follows:

1. Start the Database Configuration Assistant (DBCA) by typing dbca at the UNIX prompt.

2. The Welcome screen appears. Click Next to continue to the Operations screen.

3. Select Delete a Database, and then click Next.

4. Select the name of the database to be deleted and click Finish.

5. In the Confirmation screen, confirm that you want to delete the database.

File Deletion After a DROP DATABASE **Command**

When you issue a DROP DATABASE command, it does not remove archived log files and back up copies of the database. You should use RMAN to delete these files. If the database is on raw disks, the actual raw disk files will not be deleted by the DROP DATABASE command. If you have used DBCA to create the database, you can use it to drop the database and remove the files, as well.

After the DBCA has removed the database, you will be asked if you want to perform another operation. Click Yes to get back to the Operations screen or click No to exit from the DBCA. For removing multiple databases, click Yes and repeat the preceding steps.

Removing ASM Database(s)

If you have started experimenting with ASM installations and would like to remove an ASM database, you must remove any associated ASM instances running in the Oracle home.

Follow the steps mentioned in the preceding section until the SID selection at the oraenv/coraenv prompt. Here you specify the SID for the ASM instance to be removed. When you have chosen the correct instance, connect to it as the SYS user:

```
$ sqlplus "SYS/password AS SYSDBA"
```

Check to see if any Oracle database instance is using this ASM instance by using the following SQL command:

```
SQL> select instance_name from v$asm_client;
```

You will see a list of all database instances that are running and are associated with this ASM instance under the Oracle home. If you have a database instance using this ASM instance, but using another Oracle home, do not remove this ASM instance or the Oracle home.

If the preceding query doesn't return any rows, then there are no associated database instances and you can proceed to clean up the ASM disk groups. (You will learn more about ASM and ASM disk groups in Chapter 4.) This is accomplished by dropping the ASM disk group, which relieves the disk device for use with another ASM instance.

Identify the disk groups associated with the ASM instance by using the following SQL command:

```
SQL> select name from from v$asm_diskgroup;
```

For every disk group to be deleted, use the following command. Shut down the ASM instance on successful removal of disk groups.

```
SQL> drop diskgroup diskgroup_name including contents;
SQL> shutdown immediate;
```

When the ASM instance is shut down, clean up the oratab files by deleting or commenting out the appropriate ASM instance entries.

Configuring Oracle Cluster Synchronization Services

When you install Oracle Database 10g for the first time, root.sh configures a daemon process called Oracle Cluster Synchronization Services (CSS). This CSS daemon, which starts at the time of system boot, is required for synchronization between Oracle ASM and database instances.

On cluster systems with Oracle Real Application Clusters (RAC) installations, the CSS daemon is configured during the Oracle Cluster Ready Services (CRS) installation. A discussion on Oracle CRS and RAC will be done in Chapter 15. For more details, refer to the *Oracle Real Application Clusters Installation and Configuration Guide*.

Before you remove an Oracle home, check to see whether the CSS daemon is running from that Oracle home and whether any other Oracle Database 10g Oracle homes exist on the system. If the Oracle home to be removed is the the only Oracle Database 10g installation on the system, you can delete the CSS daemon. If there are other Oracle databases on this system, you have to reconfigure the CSS daemon to run from another Oracle home.

In step 1, if you found only one Oracle home directory that contains Oracle Database 10g, follow the action items given here:

Remove all Oracle databases and ASM instances associated with this Oracle home.

As root, go to the Oracle home directory that you are removing and set the ORACLE_HOME environment variable:

```
$ cd $ORACLE_HOME
$ export ORACLE_HOME=<environment variable>
```

Delete the CSS daemon configuration from this Oracle home. The last command stops the Oracle CSS daemon and deletes its configuration. When the system reboots, the CSS daemon will not start.

```
$ cd $ORACLE_HOME/bin
$ localconfig delete
```

In step 1, if you found any other Oracle databases, reconfigure the CSS daemon as follows:

Switch to each Oracle home directory identified on the system. Stop all Oracle ASM instances and any associated Oracle databases.

Login as root. Identify the Oracle home directory being used to run the CSS daemon. This information can be found in the ocr.loc file under /etc/oracle (for Linux/AIX) or /var/opt/oracle (for all other UNIX-based systems). The ocrconfig_loc parameter in the ocr.loc file gives the location of the Oracle Cluster Registry (OCR) used by the CSS daemon. The path until the cdata directory gives the ORACLE_HOME directory hosting the CSS daemon. If this ORACLE_HOME is not the one that you want to remove, go to step 3.

If you want to reset the ORACLE_HOME, change this directory (in ocr.loc) to the ORACLE_HOME of an Oracle Database 10g installation that you are planning to keep. Then reconfigure the CSS daemon to run from this new Oracle home as follows:

```
$ $ORACLE_HOME/bin/localconfig reset $ORACLE_HOME
```

This script stops the Oracle CSS daemon, reconfigures it, and restarts it from the new home. From the next system reboot, the CSS daemon will start automatically from the new ORACLE_HOME.

Step 3: Remove the Oracle Software

This section discusses how to use the Oracle Universal Installer (OUI) to remove Oracle software from an Oracle home. Many DBAs (especially on Windows platforms) attempt to delete Oracle home directories to remove the software, which leaves unwanted registry entries and creates chaos with the next installation. As a rule of thumb, it is preferable to use the Oracle Universal Installer to remove the software and then delete any unwanted Oracle home directories.

1. Assuming that you are still logged in as `oracle` user, set the `ORACLE_HOME` environment variable to the path of the Oracle home directory to be removed.

2. With Bourne or Korn shell, run the following:

   ```
   $ ORACLE_HOME=/u01/app/oracle/product/10.1.0/Q0OR10G
   $ export ORACLE_HOME
   ```

   With C shell, run the following:

   ```
   $ setenv ORACLE_HOME /u01/app/oracle/product/10.1.0/Q0OR10G
   ```

3. You should have already deleted any database or ASM instance associated with this `ORACLE_HOME`. The next step is to stop all remaining processes running on this `ORACLE_HOME`. The following commands are for iSQL*Plus, database console, Oracle listener, and Ultra Search options:

   ```
   $ORACLE_HOME/bin/isqlplusctl stop
   $ORACLE_HOME/bin/emctl stop dbconsole
   $ORACLE_HOME/bin/lsnrctl stop
   $ORACLE_HOME/bin/searchctl stop
   ```

4. Set the `DISPLAY` variable correctly on your screen and start the installer (`runInstaller.sh`) program with tracing on:

   ```
   $ cd $ORACLE_HOME/oui/bin
   $ ./.runInstaller  -D-JTRACING.ENABLED=TRUE -D-JTRACING.LEVEL=2
   ```

5. In the Welcome screen, click Deinstall Products.

6. The Inventory screen appears, listing all available Oracle homes on the server. Choose the Oracle home and the products to be removed, and then click Remove. If you select Oracle JVM, the OUI will remove all installed products including Oracle databases (which depend on Oracle JVM).

7. The Confirmation screen appears, asking you to verify your choice to deinstall the products and dependant components. Click Yes.

8. The OUI will show a progress bar while it removes the software. After all the selected products have been deleted, click Cancel to exit from the Oracle Universal Installer and then click Yes to confirm.

Summary

This chapter reviewed the important database installation procedures, including installation prerequisites, installation steps on UNIX- and Windows-based systems, and using Database Configuration Assistant to create a database. The section on database and binary cloning will help you to create development and testing database instances from a production database instance. Many of these tasks can be accomplished using the improved Enterprise Manager or manually from the command line. You also learned the database upgrade procedures for an Oracle 9i physical and logical standby configuration. The final section, on backing out from a failed installation, will guide you in the event of any installation hiccups. The next chapter covers the various customization options available with Oracle Database 10g, and how you can optimize your database configuration.

3

Customizing Installation Options

IN THIS CHAPTER

OEM and Automatic Alerts	53
XML DB for XML Data Processing	61
ConText and Other Options	63
Setting Up RAC	66
Managing Backups with RMAN	68

OEM and Automatic Alerts

Oracle has greatly improved the Oracle Enterprise Manager (OEM), giving it more tools for you to manage all components of the software and hardware framework in the corporate environment. The OEM has extended its level of control to manage Oracle databases, Oracle Application Server, Oracle Collaboration Suite, Oracle Ebusiness Suite, different hosts or servers in the environment, and application groups.

With the updated Enterprise Manager, you can perform all the database-administration activities as well as monitor and administer the different targets and applications in the corporate ecosystem. This will afford you a higher level of flexibility and functionality to centrally manage all the applications on a Web-based Grid Control Console over the

Oracle uses two names, `Oracle Enterprise Manager` and `Enterprise Manager`, and two acronyms, `OEM` and `EM`, interchangeably in its documentation to represent the same product.

Internet or an intranet. Using the Software Development Kit from Oracle, you can also add new targets in your environment as you expand the infrastructure.

A typical Enterprise Manager framework consists of the following components:

- An Oracle Management Agent is added to each monitored host to monitor all targets on that host. It transmits the information to the middle-tier management service for management and maintenance. The managed targets can be anything from databases, application servers, or listeners to vendor applications or software.

- The Oracle Management Service is a J2EE Web-based application that provides a user interface for the Grid Control Console. It also works with the management agents to process job information, and stores related data in the Management Repository.

- An Oracle Management Repository consists of two tablespaces in the Oracle database with information about administrators, targets, and applications managed by the Enterprise Manager. This repository organizes the stored data for easy access by the Management Service and display on the Grid Control Console.

- Oracle Enterprise Manager 10g Grid Control uses various technologies to look up, monitor, and administer the environment.

- Oracle Enterprise Manager 10g Grid Control Console is another Web-based interface for managing the corporate computing environment from a single location, as if the environment were a single unit.

For more details on setting up and monitoring the grid environment, see Chapter 18, "Leveraging Grid Technology Features." In this chapter, we will go over the major steps involved in the setup and utilization of OEM for database-monitoring functions.

OEM Preinstallation Requirements

Let us review the preinstallation requirements for Oracle Enterprise Manager for use with an Oracle database. We will discuss the requirements for the basic components of a small as well as a large environment. For more details, refer to *Oracle Enterprise Manager Grid Control Installation and Basic Configuration 10g*.

The management repository needs 1GB of hard disk and 512MB of memory for small environments with fewer than 25 managed targets. For a large organization with around 500 targets, the recommended memory is 2GB and 24–48GB of hard disk space depending on your installation and database requirements. The repository is created within two tablespaces, `MGMT_ TABLESPACE` and `MGMT_ECM_DEPOT_TS`, requiring around 120MB of disk space for the smallest default installation.

The management service needs a minimum of 500MB for a Windows installation and around 1.5GB for UNIX, with a minimum memory of 1GB and a processor speed of 1GHz for the host.

The management agent needs a minimum of 400MB of initial disk space for Solaris (350MB for Windows) to do all logging and tracing activities, and around 25MB of operating memory per database or application server. You will need proportionately higher numbers for the service and agent for larger installations.

The management repository requires Oracle9i Database (or RAC) Enterprise Edition Release 2 (9.2.0.4 or higher), or Oracle Database 10g Database (or RAC) Release 1 (10.1.0.3 or higher). Regardless of whether you choose to create a new database or use an existing database for the repository, the intended repository database must have fine-grained access control turned on with satisfactory software, patch, and tuning requirements met as per the installation guide.

OEM Installation Process

Oracle Enterprise Manager is installed with a default super administrator account called SYSMAN. During the database installation process, you will install the OEM 10g database control. The Enterprise Manager directories and files are installed into each Oracle Database 10g home directory and database control commands are installed into ORACLE_HOME/bin directory. The database control has the necessary tools to help you manage the database. As for the management agent and management service support files, those files common to all database instances are stored in the ORACLE_HOME/sysman directory. Files unique to each database instance are stored under the ORACLE_HOME/*hostname_sid* directory. The presence of the *hostname_sid* directory indicates that the OEM database control was configured for that instance.

During the database-installation process, you will be prompted to provide a password for SYSMAN. This password is needed for the initial login to OEM. The SYSMAN account cannot be deleted or renamed. Oracle also recommends creating an administrator account using the SYSMAN account for each database administrator (DBA) using the system. This will help you to control access for every DBA working on the system in various roles and responsibilities.

> **Options for Setting Up Database Control**
>
> There are several methods to configure OEM database control for a database. You can configure your database to be managed by OEM during the database-installation process (from the Select Database Management Option screen). You can configure an existing database for database control using DBCA through the Configure Database Options screen. For the database control configuration from a command line, use emca as explained in this section.

The Enterprise Manager Configuration Assistant (EMCA) installation script (emca) for Oracle Enterprise Manager is located in the $ORACLE_HOME/bin directory in UNIX and Linux. When executed, the script will present a series of questions with regard to the host name, instance name, and so on, as given in Listing 3.1. Your screen may vary depending on the operating system being used. You should set the appropriate environment variables (ORACLE_HOME and ORACLE_SID) for the database to be managed before you run EMCA. The complete list of EMCA command-line arguments is given in the *Oracle Enterprise Manager Grid Control Installation and Basic Configuration 10g* guide. For Oracle Real Application Clusters (discussed later in this chapter), create the instances first and then configure the database control for each instance in the cluster using EMCA.

LISTING 3.1   Running the EMCA Installation Script

```
STARTED EMCA at Fri Mar 18 08:24:06 CST 2005
Enter the following information about the database to be configured
Listener port number: 1521
Database SID: Q0OR10G
Service name: Q0OR10G
Email address for notification:
Email gateway for notification:
Password for dbsnmp:
Password for sysman:
Password for sys:
Password for sys:
----------------------------------------------------------------
You have specified the following settings
Database ORACLE_HOME ............/opt/app/oracle/product/10.1.0/
Enterprise Manager ORACLE_HOME ........../opt/app/oracle/product/10.1.0/OEM
Database host name ................QLAB10G.US.ACME.COM
Listener port number ................ 1521
Database SID ................ Q0OR10G
Service name ................ Q0OR10G
Email address for notification ...............
Email gateway for notification ...............
----------------------------------------------------------------
Do you wish to continue? [yes/no]: yes
..........
..........
.........
..........
```

Using an Input File for EMCA

If you would like to use an input file for EMCA instead of answering the prompts, you can use the `emca -f` *file_path/file_name* option to supply appropriate values. The input file for our installation example will be as follows:

```
ORACLE_HOME = /opt/app/oracle/
product/10.1.0/
EM_HOME =
/opt/app/oracle/product/10.1.0/OEM
PORT = 1521
SID = Q0OR10G
HOST = QLAB10G.US.ACME.COM
DBSNMP_PWD = dbsnpass
SYSMAN_PWD = sysmpass
```

When you do your OEM installation, you may see slightly different screens depending on your operating system. The dotted lines denote the execution of various scripts in the process.

The URL to access the Enterprise Manager from a Web browser for the preceding installation is
`http://QLAB10G.US.ACME.COM:5500/em`.

You can now check the status of the OEM control using the command as shown in Listing 3.2.

LISTING 3.2   Checking the Status of OEM Control

```
QLAB10G:/opt/app/oracle10g/product/10.1.0/bin> emctl status dbconsole
Oracle Enterprise Manager 10g Database Control Release 10.1.0.2.0
Copyright (c) 1996, 2004 Oracle Corporation.  All rights reserved.
http://QLAB10G.US.ACME.COM:5500/em/console/aboutApplication
Oracle Enterprise Manager 10g is running.
------------------------------------------------------------------
Logs are generated in directory /opt/app/oracle10g/product/10.1.0/
[ic:ccc]QLAB10G.US.ACME.COM_Q0OR10G/sysman/log
```

If you are not sure of the various command options for *emctl*, type `emctl` at the command line and Oracle will provide all available options for the command. Listing 3.3 shows the result of this operation.

LISTING 3.3   Command Options for `emctl`

```
QLAB10G:/opt/app/oracle10g/product/10.1.0/bin>emctl
Oracle Enterprise Manager 10g Database Control Release 10.1.0.2.0
Copyright (c) 1996, 2004 Oracle Corporation.  All rights reserved.
Invalid arguments
Unknown command option
Usage::
   Oracle Enterprise Manager 10g Database Control commands:
       emctl start¦ stop¦ status dbconsole
       emctl secure <options>

       emctl set ssl test¦off¦on em
       emctl set ldap <host> <port> <user dn> <user pwd> <context dn>
emctl blackout options can be listed by typing "emctl blackout"
emctl config options can be listed by typing "emctl config"
emctl secure options can be listed by typing "emctl secure"
emctl ilint  options can be listed by typing "emctl ilint"
emctl deploy  options can be listed by typing "emctl deploy"
```

Once the installation is completed, use the appropriate URL to log in to OEM. For those who are using the Web browser version of OEM, type in the following address: `http://localhost:port_number/em`. The port number can be changed by modifying `$ORACLE_HOME/install/portlist.ini`. You can also use the OEM interface in Windows by choosing Start, Programs, Oracle Enterprise Manager Console Environment.

After you enter the user name and password, the Web interface will change into the instance summary display, which provides guidance through the rest of the instance administration tasks. The new look and feel of OEM provides a feature-rich display that allows a DBA to drill down to detailed reports on any metric.

Control for Oracle Management Agents

If you installed the Oracle management agent as part of Grid Control or Application Server, it would have its own home (AGENT_HOME), like ORACLE_HOME. We will discuss briefly the process of controlling the management agent using emctl located in the AGENT_HOME/bin directory. You can use the emctl command to start, stop, or check the status of an agent. The syntax for the appropriate command on UNIX systems is emctl <start/stop/status> agent. For Windows-based systems, the agent is listed under Services (likely found in Control Panel). When you find the appropriate service, you can start or stop it using the Services control panel. You can also switch to the AGENT_HOME/bin directory using the DOS prompt on Windows and run the emctl commands.

Automatic Alerts and Management

Before diving into alert management using OEM, let's review some preliminary information on database metrics and alerts. Metrics are units of measurement to assess the health of your system with predefined thresholds for each unit. Oracle has thresholds for most of the metrics. When a metric reaches a threshold, an alert is generated. The alert also indicates that a particular condition has been encountered—for example, a threshold has been reached or an alert has been cleared. You can use OEM to set up alerts to send a notification to the DBA, start another job, and so on. The vast majority of the OEM metric-based alerts are polled by the management agent at intervals. As soon as the condition or conditions that triggered the alert are resolved and the metric's value is within its predefined boundary, Oracle clears the alert.

You can review the metrics on the All Metrics page under Related Links on the OEM Database Home page. Refer to Figure 3.1 for details. An online help feature is available in OEM to give you a description of each metric. Alerts are displayed on the Database Home page under the Alerts section. Nondatabase alerts are displayed under Related Alerts.

FIGURE 3.1
OEM: Alerts.

EM2Go uses HTTPS communications and has the security model with administrator privileges and roles. You can connect your PDA desktop browser to the EM2Go URL and view targets assigned to you with proper privileges. No data is stored on the hand-held device; hence, a lost or stolen device poses no security risk.

> Refer to the *Oracle Enterprise Manager Concepts 10g* and *Oracle Enterprise Manager Advanced Configuration 10g* guides for more details on setting up the EM2Go application through firewalls.

XML DB for XML Data Processing

Oracle XML DB is ideal for any application that processes or accesses XML data. Oracle XML DB is suitable for Internet applications, high-performance search applications (such as

> A good place to learn more about using XML DB is *Oracle XML DB Developer's Guide 10g*.

online libraries), business-to-business (B2B) applications, content management applications, and for interoperability with any other databases. The database user XDB owns all the metadata for managing the Oracle XML DB repository in the database. Oracle XML DB includes DBMS_XDB, a PL/SQL package, to allow resources to be created, modified, and deleted programmatically.

Installing XML DB

Oracle XML DB can be installed with or without Database Configuration Assistant (DBCA). It is a part of the default seed database installed by DBCA.

Using DBCA to Install XML DB

As part of the default installation, DBCA creates an Oracle XML DB tablespace for the XML DB repository, enables all needed protocols (FTP, HTTP, and WebDAV), and configures FTP at port 2100 and HTTP/WebDAV at port 8080. The Oracle XML DB repository is set up inside the Oracle XML DB tablespace. (You should not drop the Oracle XML DB tablespace; doing so will make all your repository data inaccessible). If you select the Advanced Database Configuration option in DBCA, you can change the Oracle XML DB tablespace and FTP, HTTP, and WebDAV port numbers to your requirements.

Oracle XML DB installation has a dynamic protocol registration feature that registers FTP and HTTP services with the local listener. You can change the FTP or HTTP port numbers by altering the <ftp-port> and <http-port> tags in the xdbconfig.xml file in the Oracle XML DB repository. After you have changed the port numbers, dynamic protocol registration will automatically stop the FTP/HTTP service on old port numbers and restart them on new port numbers, provided the local listener is up and running. If the local listener is not up, restart the listener after updating the port numbers. Use lsnrctl <start/stop/status> commands for these operations.

> **Listener Configuration on a Nonstandard Port**
>
> If your database listener is running on a nonstandard port (that is, a port other than 1521), then your init*SID*.ora file should contain a local_listener entry for the protocols to register accurately with the correct listener. After you edit the init*SID*.ora parameter file, regenerate the SPFILE using the CREATE SPFILE command.

If your application allows unauthenticated HTTP access to the Oracle XML DB repository data (as in an online content-management application), then you must unlock the ANONYMOUS user account.

Manual Installation of XML DB

To manually install Oracle XML DB without using DBCA, perform the following steps:

1. After the database installation, connect as SYS and create a new tablespace for the Oracle XML DB repository. Run the catqm.sql script in the ORACLE_HOME/rdbms/admin directory to create the tables and views needed for XML DB:

   ```
   catqm.sql <XDB_password> <XDB_Tablespace_Name> <TEMP_Tablespace_Name>
   ```

   If you get ORA-22973 error during this step, make sure your NLS_LENGTH_SEMANTICS variable is set to CHAR. It should be set to BYTE (using ALTER SYSTEM SET NLS_LENGTH_SEMANTICS = BYTE;) as a workaround. NLS_LENGTH_SEMANTICS does not apply to data dictionary tables because they use BYTE semantics.

2. Reconnect as SYS and run catxdbj.sql in the ORACLE_HOME/rdbms/admin directory to load the XDB Java library. The database should be set up with a compatibility of 9.2.0 or higher, and Java Virtual Machine (JVM) should be installed.

3. Once you have completed the manual installation, add the following dispatcher entry to the init*SID*.ora file:

   ```
   dispatchers="(PROTOCOL=TCP) (SERVICE=<sid>XDB)"
   ```

4. Restart the database and listener. If your application allows unauthenticated HTTP access to the Oracle XML DB repository data, unlock the ANONYMOUS user account.

Manual Removal of Oracle XML DB

To manually remove the XML DB, remove the XML DB dispatcher entry from the init*SID*.ora file. If SPFILE is used, run the following command as SYS while the instance is up:

```
ALTER SYSTEM RESET dispatchers scope=spfile sid='<XML_SID>';
```

Run catnoqm.sql and the following steps to drop the user XDB and tablespace XDB:

```
@ORACLE_HOME/rdbms/admin/catnoqm.sql
alter tablespace <XDB_Tablespace_Name> offline;
drop tablespace <XDB_Tablespace_Name> including contents;
```

If you need to reinstall XML DB, you may want to shut down and restart the database to have a clean database for the installation. Use the steps described in the section titled "Manual

Installation of XML DB" for the installation process. For more details on reinstalling or upgrading an existing XML DB, please refer to *Oracle XML DB Developer's Guide 10g*.

XQuery Support in Oracle Database 10g R2

In Oracle Database 10g Release 2, XQuery support is introduced in the database server through a SQL-centric approach using XMLTable by breaking the XQuery values into XML and relational values. The SQL * Plus command XQUERY is provided to use XQuery expressions directly with the Oracle XML DB.

To initialize XQuery support in the database, run `initxqry.sql` as SYSDBA. After running this script, enable XQuery support for your database instance and provide the required Java pool size (40MB).

> **Changing the Timeout Levels**
>
> As a DBA, you may have to adjust the timeout levels for accessing large XML files over a Web browser and/or FTP server. Timeout is expressed in centiseconds (1/100 of a second). `Call-TimeOut` is the amount of time allowed to load an XML document using `DBUri`. `Session-TimeOut` is the amount of time allowed for a session to be connected before being disconnected. All these times can be altered using the `dbms_xdb.cfg_update` procedure. To manually edit these values, get the `xdbconfig.xml` file via FTP from the XML DB repository, edit the values for the timeouts, save the file, and reload it into the XML DB repository. After reloading the changed `xsd` file, refresh the `xdbconfig.xml` file using the `exec dbms_xdb.cfg_refresh;` command. For more details on the `DBUri` and `dbms_xdb` package, refer to *Oracle XML DB Developer's Guide 10g*.

```
SQL> $ORACLE_HOME/rdbms/admin/initxqry.sql
SQL> ALTER SYSTEM SET EVENT = '19119 trace
name context forever, level 1' scope=SPFILE;
SQL> ALTER SYSTEM SET java_pool_size = 41943040 scope=both;
```

The database instance has to be restarted for the changes to take effect. After restarting the database instance, verify that XQuery has been enabled as follows:

```
SQL> set long 8000
SQL> ALTER SYSTEM SET java_pool_size = 41943040 scope=both;
SQL> xquery for $q in <xmlquery>4</xmlquery> return $q
/
Result Sequence
----------------------------------------
< xmlquery>4</xmlquery>
```

These details have been provided to give an overview of the updates available in Release 2 of the database.

ConText and Other Options

Oracle Database 10g can handle data types such as relational data, object-relational data, XML, text, audio, images, video, and spatial data. These data types are stored as native types in the database, making the data searchable using SQL, even when different types are combined.

XML is treated as a native data type in the database. Oracle XML DB provides new capabilities for both content-oriented and data-oriented access.

Oracle introduced ConText and *inter*Media Text in versions prior to Oracle 9i, where data from tables, files, or URLs could be searched on. Starting with Oracle 9i, the whole concept was renamed "Oracle Text." Oracle Text leverages scalability features such as replication and supports a local partitioned index. Oracle Text is set up in the SYSAUX tablespace (with CTXSYS as schema owner) by default unless you create a separate tablespace and do a manual installation of Oracle Text in that tablespace.

Oracle UltraSearch is another way to index and search database tables, websites, files, Oracle Application Server portals, and other data sources. Oracle Ultra Search uses a *crawler* to index documents and builds an index in the designated Oracle database. It allows concept searching and theme analysis, and supports full globalization including Unicode. Oracle provides complete APIs to work with Oracle Text, UltraSearch, *inter*Media, and Oracle Spatial options.

Oracle *inter*Media helps to develop and deploy traditional, online, and wireless applications with multimedia content (images, audio, and video). These kinds of multimedia data can be stored and managed directly in or outside Oracle. Oracle *inter*Media allows access to multimedia content from within the database web as well as external locations (the Internet).

> Oracle Database 10g also enables you to perform XML searches in documents using the Oracle Text, the Oracle XML DB framework, and a combination of Oracle Text features with Oracle XML DB features. For more details on Oracle Text, refer to the *Oracle Text Reference 10g* guide.

Oracle Spatial allows users to store, index, and manage location content (buildings, roads, and so on, as in online map portals) and query location relationships (driving directions and what have you) using the database. It also supports linear reference and coordinate systems for geographic mapping. Oracle Spatial has its own spatial indexing mechanism.

The next section will discuss the manual installation process for Oracle Text.

Manual Installation of Oracle Text

If you have done a database upgrade from Oracle 9i, Oracle Text would have been automatically upgraded along with it. Similar to the manual installation of XML DB, however, you can set up Oracle Text manually. Please refer to Oracle's platform-specific installation guides for more details. For manual installation, do the following steps:

1. Change the library path environment variables for your platform to include the `ORACLE_HOME/ctx/lib` directory.

2. Login as `SYS` and create default and temporary tablespaces for Oracle Text.

3. Run the `ORACLE_HOME/ctx/admin/dr0csys.sql` script to create the `CTXSYS` user.

4. Connect as the `CTXSYS` user and run `ORACLE_HOME/ctx/admin/dr0inst.sql` to create and populate the required data dictionary tables.

5. Choose the language-specific script (`drdefXX.sql`, where *XX* is the language code) from the `ORACLE_HOME/ctx/admin/defaults` directory. This completes the required steps; exit the SQLPlus session.

You can de-install Oracle Text manually by running `catnoctx.sql` from the same directory as the installation script.

Installation of Oracle Spatial

With the installation of Oracle Enterprise Edition, all Oracle Spatial configuration tasks are completed automatically. For custom installation of Oracle Spatial and Oracle Database together with Enterprise or Standard Edition software, the `DBCA` will start at the end of installation. For custom installation with the Create New Database option, `DBCA` will ask you if Oracle Spatial should be configured automatically.

> **Search Issues with Oracle Text**
>
> If you are experiencing problems with the search operation on PDF documents, make sure that you are not working with password-protected documents or with documents containing custom fonts. To unset the password, open the PDF file, display the File menu, select Document Properties, and click the Security tab. You should have no password assigned, and the Security Method should be set to None. To determine whether custom fonts are used, open the File menu, choose Document Properties, and click the Fonts tab, and see whether the Encoding option is set to Custom; if so, that could be the cause (if the font is not supported). Also, zipped files cannot be searched.

For a separate installation of Oracle Spatial, you must use Database Configuration Assistant and select Configure Database Options in a database or configure Oracle Spatial manually. For manual configuration, log in to the database as SYS using SQLPlus and run `ordinst.sql` under the `ORACLE_HOME/ord/admin` directory. Then connect as SYSTEM and run `ordinst.sql` in the `ORACLE_HOME/ord/admin` directory. The Spatial option is owned by MDSYS. Use platform-specific guides for more information on these steps.

Operations with Oracle UltraSearch

For manual installation of the UltraSearch option, perform the following steps (refer to MetaLink documents #280713.1 and #283292.1 for more details):

1. Ensure that Oracle Text and JVM are set up correctly. Switch to the `ORACLE_HOME/ultrasearch/admin` directory, depending on your platform of installation (operating system).

2. Use SQLPlus and log in as SYS with SYSDBA privileges.

3. Run the `wk0install.sql` script. It will prompt for a few responses with regard to passwords (including SYS), WKSYS schema owner, temporary tablespace, and the like. If you do not get any errors from running `wk0install.sql`, then the installation is successful.

4. Confirm the following object count totals after running `wk0install.sql`:

```
SQL> select count(*) from dba_objects  where owner = 'WKSYS';
SQL> select count(*) from dba_objects where owner = 'WKSYS' and status = 'INVALID';
```

The second SQL should return a `ZERO(0)` value.

For de-installing UltraSearch, make sure that the WKSYS user does not have any open sessions, and then run the `wk0deinst.sql` script from the same directory as `wk0install.sql`. If there are no errors running the script, you have successfully removed WKSYS.

Setting Up RAC

> A detailed explanation of CRS is given in *Oracle Database Real Application Clusters Administrator's Guide 10g* and *Oracle Real Application Clusters Deployment and Performance Guide 10g*.

Cluster Ready Services (CRS) has been introduced in Oracle 10g Real Application Clusters (RAC) to provide a standard cluster interface on all platforms, enabling improved high-availability operations. CRS should be installed prior to installing 10g RAC in a HOME other than ORACLE_HOME.

There are several combinations with regard to installing RAC in your environment. To name but a few of the most common scenarios: You can do a fresh installation, convert a standby database on Data Guard to RAC, and upgrade existing RAC instances. Oracle recommends the use of DBCA to create new databases, which was covered in Chapter 2, "Installing Oracle Database 10g." Hence, we will focus here on performing a new manual installation of RAC.

Manual Installation of RAC Instance

For a manual installation of a RAC instance, follow these steps:

1. Start the installation process by making a copy of init*SID*.ora in your $ORACLE_HOME/dbs directory on UNIX platforms or in $ORACLE_HOME\database on Windows platforms. If you are using an SPFILE, create an init*SID*.ora file, edit it, and point your SPFILE to it or use `alter system set…` commands to change the instance-specific parameters. Make sure that your control file is pointing to an existing raw device or cluster file system location. For the entire example, we will call our database as Q0RAC and call our instances Q0RAC1 and Q0RAC2 on nodes 1 and 2.

2. Make changes to the path, filenames, and sizes as needed to suit your installation. Cluster-wide parameters for the Q0RAC database would be as follows:

```
db_block_size=8192
db_cache_size=104857600
background_dump_dest=/opt/app/oracle/product/10.0.1/rdbms/log
core_dump_dest=/opt/app/oracle/product/10.0.1/rdbms/log
user_dump_dest=/opt/app/oracle/product/10.0.1/rdbms/log
timed_statistics=TRUE
control_files=("/dev/Q0RAC/control_01.ctl", "/dev/Q0RAC/control_02.ctl")
db_name=RAC
shared_pool_size=104857600
sort_area_size=1638400
undo_management=AUTO
```

```
cluster_database=true
cluster_database_instances=2
remote_listener=LISTENERS_Q0RAC
```

3. For the Q0RAC1, instance-specific parameters will be as follows. Add the listener address to your tnsanames.ora file for the local_listener parameter on node 1 and 2:

```
instance_name=Q0RAC1
instance_number=1
local_listener=LISTENER_Q0RAC1
thread=1
undo_tablespace=UNDOTBS
```

4. Connect to the database using SYS (as SYSDBA) and execute the following SQLPlus command:

```
SQL> startup nomount
```

5. Create the database using pre-created raw devices:

```
create database Q0RAC
controlfile reuse
maxdatafiles 250
maxinstances 32
maxloghistory 100
maxlogmembers 5
maxlogfiles 128
datafile '/dev/q0rac/system_01.dbf' size 900m segment space management auto
reuse autoextend on next 10240k maxsize unlimited
undo tablespace "undotbs" datafile
'/dev/q0rac/undotbs_01.dbf' size 200m reuse
default tablespace user_default datafile
'/opt/app/oracle/racdb1/user_default_1.dbf' size 2000m reuse segment space management
auto
sysaux datafile '/opt/app/oracle/racdb1/sysaux_1.dbf' size 500m reuse segment space
management auto
character set us7ascii
logfile group 1 ('/dev/q0rac/redo1_01.dbf') size 100m reuse,
group 2 ('/dev/q0rac/redo1_02.dbf') size 100m reuse;
```

6. Create temporary tablespace:

```
create temporary tablespace "temp_q0rac" tempfile  '/dev/q0rac/temp_01.dbf' size 40m
reuse;
```

7. Create a second UNDO tablespace as follows:

```
create undo tablespace "undotbs2" datafile  '/dev/q0rac/undotbs_02.dbf' size 200m reuse
next  5120k maxsize unlimited;
```

8. Run the catalog.sql, catproc.sql, and catparr.sql scripts in the
   ORACLE_HOME/rdbms/admin directory to build the necessary views, synonyms, and packages.

9. Edit initSID.ora and set appropriate values for the second instance on node 2.

```
instance_name= Q0RAC2
instance_number=2
local_listener=LISTENER_Q0RAC2
thread=2
undo_tablespace=UNDOTBS2
```

10. From Q0RAC1 (the first instance), run the following command:

```
alter database add logfile thread 2
group 3 ('/dev/Q0RAC/redo2_01.dbf') size 100M,
group 4 ('/dev/Q0RAC/redo2_02.dbf') size 100M;
alter database enable public thread 2;
```

11. Check whether your cluster configuration is up and running. Use the ps -ef ¦ grep crs
    command or run crs_stat from the $ORA_CRS_HOME/bin directory. The crs_stat
    command will provide status information for resources on cluster nodes throughout the
    cluster.

12. Start the second instance, Q0RAC2. Now your RAC environment is ready for use.

Installation of RAC Instance Using Data Guard

You can also install a RAC instance using Data Guard, but it will be more complicated than the
manual installation. The steps are too elaborate to be discussed within the limited scope of this
chapter. Refer to *Oracle Data Guard Concepts and Administration 10g* and MetaLink Note
#273015.1 for more details.

Managing Backups with RMAN

Recovery Manager (RMAN) is a client application that performs backup and recovery operations
on databases. The RMAN environment may consist of components like a target database, RMAN
client, recovery catalog, recovery catalog schema, standby database, media management application, media management catalog, and the OEM. Of these components, the target database and
RMAN client are necessary for RMAN operation.

The RMAN client application uses database server sessions to perform all backup and recovery
tasks. When you connect the RMAN client to a target database, RMAN gets server sessions on

the target instance to perform the necessary operations. The RMAN client uses internal PL/SQL packages to communicate with the target database and recovery catalog.

1. Start RMAN from the (UNIX) command prompt and then type the following commands at the RMAN command line:

   ```
   >rman Target_DB SYS/oracle@Target CATALOG rman/cat@catalogdb
   ```

2. After the RMAN prompt is displayed, enter the following command:

   ```
   RMAN> BACKUP DATABASE;
   ```

   You can also run a command file (BackUpCmds.rcv) with a list of commands and get the output into the log file (BckUpLog.log) as follows:

   ```
   >rman Target_DB SYS/oracle@Target CATALOG rman/cat@catalogdb
   [ic:ccc]CMDFILE BackUpCmds.rcv LOG BckUpLog.log
   ```

When you run RMAN in command-line mode, the output will be sent to the terminal if the LOG option is not specified. The output from currently executing RMAN jobs is also written to the V$RMAN_OUTPUT view.

The RMAN repository has the metadata on target databases. RMAN always stores this information in records in the control file. You can create a recovery catalog in an external Oracle database to store this information. The advantage of an external recovery catalog is longer history retention for metadata compared to the smaller size of control file.

For Oracle Database 10g Release 2, the FLASHBACK DATABASE command has been improved to quickly return a database to a prior time without restoring data files and performing media recovery. Also the reporting on RMAN through OEM has been improved.

RMAN creates database backups, which could be stored as image copies or backup sets. Image copies are exact byte-for-byte copies of the files, while backup sets are logical entities consisting of several physical files called *backup pieces*.

> Oracle recommends the use of a flash recovery area and that you run your production databases in ARCHIVELOG mode for RMAN backups. Always use the flash recovery area as an archive log destination on a separate disk to prevent a single point of failure for the entire database. The size of the flash recovery area depends on the size and activity levels of the database and recovery objectives. The DBID and the DB_UNIQUE_NAME should be noted to help with scenarios like recovery of a lost database control file.

When you create image copy backups through RMAN or OEM, RMAN will create a record of those image copies in the RMAN repository. RMAN uses these copies during database restore and recovery. RMAN will only use those files in the RMAN repository for restore operations.

Backup pieces use an Oracle proprietary format to store the file contents. They can be accessed only as part of backup sets and not individually.

When you back up data files into backup sets, free data blocks (with no data) are not written into the backup pieces in order to save space. This process is known as *unused block compression*.

These backup sets can be compressed using an additional binary data compression algorithm during the writing stage to save some more space. The additional compression will affect the CPU and database performance and should be used if disk space is preferred over backup speed.

> **More details on RMAN, channels, and parallelism are available in** `Oracle Database Backup and Recovery Basics 10g` **and** `Oracle Database Backup and Recovery Advanced User's Guide.`

RMAN uses server sessions to perform backup and restore tasks. It supports parallelism, and you can have multiple channels and sessions to speed up the backup process.

You can set up the device properties, parallelism, backup type, and location from OEM under Database Home page > Maintenance property > Backup/Recovery.

Important Points on RMAN During Database Upgrade

Refer to the RMAN compatibility matrix before you do a database upgrade. Each component in the RMAN environment has a release number associated with it. The following components are usually present: RMAN executable, recovery catalog database, recovery catalog schema in the recovery catalog database, target database, and auxiliary database (duplicate or standby database).

When you upgrade a database, make sure that the RMAN catalog schema version is greater than or equal to the catalog database version. The catalog schema version is the version of `dbms_rcvcat`, `dbms_rcvman` packages, and catalog tables and views in the schema. The RMAN executable version should be the same as the target database version. The RMAN catalog is backward-compatible with target databases from earlier releases.

RMAN will give the following errors when components are not compatible as per the matrix:

- RMAN-6186: PL/SQL package %s.%s version %s in %s database is too old

- RMAN-6429: %s database is not compatible with this version of RMAN

If your recovery catalog is older than that required by the RMAN client, then you must upgrade it. You will get an error if the recovery catalog version is higher than the RMAN client requirements.

To upgrade the recovery catalog, do the following:

1. Grant `TYPE` privilege to RMAN:

   ```
   sqlplus> connect sys/oracle@catdb as sysdba;
   sqlplus> grant TYPE to rman;
   ```

2. Connect to the target and recovery catalog databases using RMAN.

3. Once connected, issue the `UPGRADE CATALOG;` command. You'll be prompted to enter the `UPGRADE CATALOG;` command again to confirm; do so. Oracle will process the command and show the results as follows, where *XX* is the new version number:

```
recovery catalog upgraded to version XX
DBMS_RCVMAN package upgraded to version
XX
DBMS_RCVCAT package upgraded to version
XX
```

> Please refer to Oracle Database Recovery
> Manager Reference and Oracle Database
> Upgrade Guide for more information on
> RMAN and upgrade processes.

Unregister a Target Database

Beginning with Oracle Database 10g, you can unregister a target database from the recovery catalog by using a new RMAN command (unregister) in one of the following ways (where <database_name> is the name of the target database to be unregistered and noprompt implies that RMAN should not prompt for confirmation before unregistering):

```
rman> unregister database <database_name>;
```

```
rman> unregister database <database_name> noprompt;
```

If RMAN is connected to the target database where it is registered, you need not specify this name. If the database name is unique, provide the database_name argument to identify the database to unregister. If RMAN is not connected to the target database and the database_name is not unique in the recovery catalog, use SET DBID to identify the database.

Glimpse of Oracle Database 10g Release 2

This section includes a quick summary of the feature improvements in Oracle Database 10g Release 2.

- Oracle Database 10g Release 2 has improved the JDBC standards support and the dynamic load balancing of connections in RAC and grid environments, and enhanced the HTML DB user interface, PL/SQL gateway, and SQL.

- For XML application development, the Enterprise Developer's Kit supports XMLType in Java, C++, and C, and offers XPATH Rewrite feature of XML DB.

- The Data Guard provides a Fast-Start failover feature to rapidly failover to the standby database, automatically convert the primary to standby database on failover, and offers improved redo transmission to standby databases.

- For RAC and grid support, you can have as many as 1,055 instances in a control file, although practically you may not encounter such a scenario.

- Oracle Backup is tightly integrated with RMAN, providing media management and avoiding any need for third-party backup software.

- Release 2 also has improved ASM to support multiple Oracle database versions, offering the functionality of the lowest database version as well as OS level file system manipulation commands.

■   The Database Upgrade Assistant will ease the upgrade process to 10.2 from older versions and from 10.1.

Summary

This chapter discussed setting up Oracle Enterprise Manager and using automatic alerts to notify the DBA of database issues. It also reviewed the installation of XML DB, Oracle Text, and other related multimedia storage options. The introduction to RAC setup will help you undesrtand the the concepts better in Chapter 15 "Utilizing Oracle Database 10g Real Applications Clusters." Finally, it reviewed RMAN and important components in registering a database for backup. The installation of the database and the many components alone would take over 1,000 pages for all the supported platforms; please refer to the appropriate platform-specific Oracle Installation manuals for details relevant to yours.

Now that you have completed all the major database installation processes and related options, you can proceed to discussing the new database features of Oracle Database 10g and how you can make the most of them. We will start with a discussion of Automatic Storage Management(ASM) in the next chapter.

4

Setting Up Automatic Storage Management

IN THIS CHAPTER

Automatic Storage Management (ASM)   73

Prerequisites for Using ASM   74

Configuration Options   76

Performing ASM Operations   79

Avoiding ASM Pitfalls   85

When and Where to Use ASM   89

Automatic Storage Management (ASM)

This chapter covers the Automatic Storage Management (ASM) feature introduced in Oracle Database 10g, for efficient management of disk drives with round-the-clock (24×7) availability. ASM simplifies disk-space management by creating disk groups, which are comprised of disks and the files that reside on them. Using ASM, the DBA needs to manage a smaller number of disk groups. All you have to do for disk management is to allocate disks to Oracle with your preferences for striping and mirroring using templates and let the database handle the storage-management issues.

ASM helps resolve the routine disk-management problems of large Oracle databases. It also manages disks across multiple nodes of a cluster in RAC as in standalone

Multiple Oracle Instances Using ASM on a Single Server

If you have more than one Oracle Database 10g instance on a single system using ASM for database file storage, you should set up different Oracle homes for the database instances and run the CSS daemon and the ASM instance from the same `ORACLE_HOME` directory. The `oracle` user for each database instance should be a member of the `dba` group for the ASM instance and the disks must have read/write permission to the ASM `dba` group. The ASM `oracle` user does not need to be in the `dba` group as users of other database instances.

Stop all Oracle ASM instances and any Oracle database instances that use ASM for database file storage under all `ORACLE_HOME`s. As root, identify the `ORACLE_HOME` directory used to run the CSS daemon. It will be `/etc/oracle/ocr.loc` for AIX and Linux, `/var/opt/oracle/ocr.loc` for other UNIX operating systems, and `\oracle\ocr.loc` for Windows. The `ocrconfig_loc` parameter (located in `ORACLE_HOME/cdata/localhost/local.ocr`) specifies the location of the Oracle Cluster Registry (OCR) used by the CSS daemon. Change the `ORACLE_HOME` to the `new_ORACLE_HOME` directory of the Oracle Database 10g installation from which you want the CSS daemon to run. Reconfigure the CSS daemon to run from this Oracle home as follows:

```
$ORACLE_HOME/bin/localconfig reset
$new_ORACLE_HOME
```

This will stop the Oracle CSS daemon, reconfigure it in the new Oracle home, and then restart it. When the system reboots, the CSS daemon starts automatically from the new Oracle home. When you configure the CSS daemon to run from `new_ORACLE_HOME`, the ASM instance can be started in this new Oracle home. The other database instances running should be able to access this ASM instance and the underlying disks with appropriate permissions.

servers. ASM prevents hot spots and improves performance by load-balancing across available disk drives and prevents fragmentation of disks. ASM allows for incremental addition and removal of disks and reduces DBA or system administrator intervention in database file management.

ASM integrates the file system and volume manager functionalities for Oracle database files. It removes the need for manual I/O tuning and extends the concept of stripe-and-mirror-everything (SAME) for better performance.

Prerequisites for Using ASM

This section looks at the prerequisites for using ASM and how it works in the database. Oracle Database 10g needs a separate smaller database instance (in a separate ORACLE_HOME) for ASM administration. This is created during the database setup and is known as an *ASM instance*. This instance manages the metadata needed to make ASM files available to regular database instances. ASM instances and database instances have access to a common set of disks called *disk groups*. Database instances communicate with the ASM instance to get information about the layout of ASM files and access its contents directly.

The ASM instance should be started first to create a database that will use ASM. An ASM instance can be shared by several database instances for using ASM files. In a RAC environment, only one ASM instance is needed per node regardless of the number of database instances on that node. The ASM instances communicate with each other on a peer-to-peer basis across the nodes.

When you install Oracle Database 10g on a system for the first time, the installation configures and starts a single-node version of the CSS daemon. The CSS daemon is needed for synchronization between the ASM instance and the database instances that depend on it for database file storage. It is configured and started regardless of your choice of ASM for storage. The CSS daemon must be running before you start any ASM instance or before a database instance starts, so it is configured to start automatically when the system boots.

For setting up multiple Oracle databases on a single server, you should run the CSS service and the Automatic Storage Management instance from the same ORACLE_HOME and use different homes for the database instances. With Oracle RAC installations, the CSS service is installed with Oracle Cluster Ready Services (CRS) in a separate ORACLE_HOME (called the CRS_HOME directory). For single-node installations, the CSS service is installed in the same ORACLE_HOME. So before you remove an ORACLE_HOME with an Oracle database, you must delete the CSS service configuration, or reconfigure the CSS service to run from another Oracle home directory.

ASM Architecture in a Nutshell

The basic component of Automatic Storage Management is the disk group. Oracle provides SQL statements to create and manage disk groups, their contents, and their metadata. A *disk group* is a group of (ASM) disks managed together as a unit. On UNIX/Linux systems, an ASM disk can be a block device, a network attached file (SAN), a logical unit number (LUN), or a LUN partition; on Windows-based systems, an ASM disk is always a disk partition. A disk group has its own file directory, disk directory, and other directories.

Inside a disk group, I/Os are balanced across all the disks. Dissimilar disks should be partitioned into separate disk groups for better performance. The redundancy characteristics (EXTERNAL, NORMAL, or HIGH REDUNDANCY) are set up when a disk group is defined. NORMAL REDUNDANCY is the default and prompts the disk group to tolerate the loss of a single failure without data loss. EXTERNAL REDUNDANCY means that ASM does not provide any redundancy for the disk group, while HIGH REDUNDANCY provides a greater degree of protection (three-way mirroring).

> **How Do We Group Disks on a System?**
> When you use more than one disk in a disk group, the disks should have similar size and performance characteristics. Group the disks according to their size and usage type (database files, control files, flash recovery areas, and so on). For storage array disks, do not divide the physical volumes into logical volumes. To the ASM instance, any type of disk division will hide the physical disk boundaries and hinder operational performance.

When you start the ASM instance, it will automatically discover all available ASM disks. ASM discovers disks in the appropriate paths that are listed in an initialization parameter or in an operating system–dependent default path (if the initialization parameter is NULL).

ASM uses failure groups to identify the disks (for normal and high-redundancy disk groups) that share a common potential failure mechanism, such as a set of SCSI disks using

> You need to define the failure groups in a disk group whenever you create or alter the disk group.

the same controller. *Failure groups* determine which ASM disks are to be used for storing redundant copies of data.

Files written on ASM disks are known as *ASM files*. A data file can be stored as an ASM file, a file system file, or as a raw device. ASM files can be created for redo log files, temporary files, RMAN files, parameter files, and data pump dump files.

> ### How Do We Name an ASM File?
>
> The ASM filename format depends on the context of file usage, such as referencing an existing file, creating a single file, or creating multiple files. You can use fully qualified filenames with a disk-group name, a database name, a file type, a type-specific tag, a file number, and an incarnation number. The fully qualified name is generated for every ASM file on its creation. Numeric names can be derived from fully qualified names. The DBA can also specify user-friendly alias names for existing as well as new ASM files. Incomplete filenames with disk-group names are used only for ASM file-creation operations. Refer to *Oracle Database Administrator's Guide 10g* for more details.

Each ASM file will belong to only a single disk group. A disk group may contain files belonging to several databases, and a single database may form multiple disk groups. ASM files are always spread across all the disks in the disk group. When an ASM file is created, certain file attributes such as a protection policy (mirroring or none) or a striping policy are set. These files are visible to RMAN and other Oracle-supplied tools. In Oracle Database 10g Release 2, new features have been added to make them visible to the operating system and its file-movement utilities.

Oracle uses templates to simplify database file creation by mapping complex file attribute specifications about ASM files (in ASM disk groups) to a single name. A *disk-group template* is a collection of attributes that are applied to all files created within the disk group. Oracle provides a set of initial default templates for use by ASM. The v$asm_template view has a list of all templates identifiable by the ASM instance. You can add new templates to a disk group, modify existing ones, or even drop existing ones using the ALTER DISKGROUP statement.

Configuration Options

This section reviews the various ways to set up and configure a database using ASM files, manage the ASM instance, and so on, which will be useful in the forthcoming section on ASM operations titled "Performing ASM Operations."

Automatic Storage Management is integrated into the database server. It is available in both the Enterprise Edition and Standard Edition installations. When you use Oracle Universal Installer, it will prompt you to install and configure a database using ASM or to install and configure an ASM instance without creating a database instance. When you create a database, Database Configuration Assistance (DBCA) searches for an existing ASM instance; if it does not find one, you have the option of creating and configuring one during the installation process. To configure the ASM instance using DBCA, choose the ASM disk(s) and create the disk group(s) on it by choosing available disk(s). (See the section titled "Performing ASM Operations" for more information on configuring disk groups.) The DBCA creates a separate instance called *+ASM* in the nomount stage, which controls your ASM installations. Choose all your data files, control files, redo logs, and SPFILEs for your ASM volumes. A typical ASM instance needs around 100MB of disk space.

You cannot use the silent installation method for database installation (in UNIX) and create a database using ASM, because `root.sh` script has to be run before the database-creation step.

For the most part, an ASM instance is started and managed like any other database instance, except that the initialization parameter file contains the parameter `INSTANCE_TYPE=ASM`. Similarly, the ASM instance can be shut down like any other database instance using similar commands. For ASM instances, the `mount` option tries to mount only the disk groups that are specified by the `ASM_DISKGROUPS` initialization parameter and not the database. ASM instances require a much smaller SGA (typically 64MB). An ASM instance should be running at all times and should be brought up automatically on server reboots.

An ASM instance does not have a data dictionary, so you have to be SYSDBA or SYSOPER to connect to an ASM instance. Use the password file to connect remotely to an ASM instance. Those who connect with SYSDBA privilege will have complete administrative access to all disk groups in the system.

The SYSOPER privilege is limited to the following SQL commands: STARTUP and SHUTDOWN, ALTER DISKGROUP MOUNT/DISMOUNT/REPAIR, ALTER DISKGROUP ONLINE/OFFLINE DISK, ALTER DISKGROUP REBALANCE/CHECK, and access to all V$ASM_* views.

Automatic Storage Management has the following operational limits:

- Maximum storage of 4 petabytes (4,000 terabytes) for each ASM disk and a maximum of 2.4 terabyte storage for each file

- Maximum of 63 disk groups and a maximum of 1,000,000 files per disk group

---

ASM Installations on Linux

Those of you who are trying to install ASM on Linux systems should review the MetaLink Note #275315.1 and http://www.oracle.com/technology/tech/linux/asmlib/install.html to learn about the issues with setting up ASM files and about ASMLib. ASMLib is a support library for the ASM feature of Oracle Database 10g. This library will enable ASM I/O to Linux disks without standard UNIX I/O API limitations. This provides an alternative interface for the ASM-enabled kernel to identify and access block devices. It is not required to run ASM. The preceding documents describe the steps required to install the Linux-specific ASM library and its associated drivers on a Linux system. If you encounter issues with free space on disks, you can use MetaLink Note #266028.1 to use files instead of raw devices.

Refer to platform-specific release notes available on Oracle Technology Network (OTN) (http://www.oracle.com/technology/documentation/database10g.html) to get more details.

The storage measurement units vary in definition according to the user's context. Although many storage vendors and disk manufacturers consider 1,000 bytes to be 1KB, 1,000,000 bytes to be 1MB, and so on, Oracle considers 1,024 bytes to be 1KB and 1,048,576 bytes to be 1MB. So the actual values for these file sizes will vary depending on which calculations you use.

- Maximum of 10,000 ASM disks for a storage system

- Storage of 40 exabytes (40×1,000,000 terabytes) per storage system

We will review the initialization parameters for an ASM instance in the next section, which will help you understand ASM operations.

Initialization Parameters for ASM Instances

The ASM instance has very few initialization parameters when compared with a database instance. The important parameters, along with their default values in parentheses, are given here:

- **INSTANCE_TYPE (ASM).** This is the only required parameter. All other parameters have default values suited for most environments.

- **DB_UNIQUE_NAME (+ASM).** This is the unique name for ASM (or group of instances) within the cluster or on the node.

- **ASM_DISKSTRING (NULL).** This parameter limits the set of disks that ASM considers for recovery.

- **ASM_DISKGROUPS (NULL).** This gives the list of names for disk groups mounted by the ASM instance at startup or when ALTER DISKGROUP ALL MOUNT is used. With SPFILE, you may rarely need to alter this dynamic value.

- **ASM_POWER_LIMIT (1).** This parameter controls the maximum power on an ASM instance for disk rebalancing. Possible values range from 1 to 11, with 11 being the fastest and 1 the slowest. We discuss this parameter in detail later in this chapter in the section titled "RESIZE and REBALANCE Operations."

- **LARGE_POOL_SIZE (8MB or higher).** The large pool is used by ASM internal packages. For other buffer parameters, you can use the default values.

The initialization parameters that start with ASM can be used only for ASM instances. If you use any other database initialization parameter in an ASM initialization parameter file, it will cause one of the following scenarios:

- For an invalid initialization parameter, the ASM instance will produce an ORA-15021 error.

- For parameters related to buffer cache and dump destinations valid for ASM instance, those values will be accepted.

- If you specify an ASM-specific parameter in a database instance, it will produce an ORA-15021 error.

StartUp/Shutdown Commands on an ASM Instance

When you connect to an ASM instance and issue the STARTUP command in SQL*Plus, it will try to mount the disk groups specified in ASM_DISKGROUPS instead of the database. Similarly, when you issue the command SHUTDOWN NORMAL, the ASM instance goes down like any other normal database. Other extensions to the STARTUP and SHUTDOWN commands on an ASM instance are interpreted as follows:

- STARTUP MOUNT mounts the disk groups specified by ASM_DISKGROUPS.

- STARTUP NOMOUNT does not mount any disk groups, but starts up the instance.

- STARTUP OPEN is not valid for an ASM instance.

- STARTUP FORCE issues the command SHUTDOWN ABORT to the ASM instance and restarts it.

- SHUTDOWN NORMAL causes the ASM instance to wait for the connected ASM instances and other active ASM SQL sessions to exit before shutting down.

- SHUTDOWN IMMEDIATE causes the ASM to wait for SQL sessions in progress to finish before shutting down. All database instances need not be disconnected to shut down the instance.

- SHUTDOWN ABORT will immediately shut down the ASM instance.

- SHUTDOWN TRANSACTIONAL is similar to the IMMEDIATE operation.

Performing ASM Operations

This section discusses the important ASM commands that will help you deploy databases using ASM files.

The CREATE DISK GROUP Command

The CREATE DISK GROUP command is used to create a disk group. The ASM instance will verify that the disk in a disk group is addressable and usable before it does any operations on it. It reads the first block of the disk to determine whether it belongs to a group and writes a header to disks not in any group.

When you issue the CREATE DISKGROUP command, ASM mounts the disk group for the first time and adds the disk-group name to the ASM_DISKGROUPS initialization parameter in SPFILE. If you are using the initSID.ora file and need the disk group to be automatically mounted at startup, you have to manually add the disk-group name to the ASM_DISKGROUPS entry in the init file.

Let's use the previous Q00R10G database as an example throughout this section. ASM_DISKSTRING is set to /dev/*. The following disks are in /dev: /dsk_qa_a01, /dsk_qa_a02, /dsk_qa_b01, /dsk_qa_b02. /dsk_qa_a01 and /dsk_qa_a02 are on separate SCSI controllers from other disks on the server: The following code will create the disk group dskgrp10g01 using two failgroups:

```
CREATE DISKGROUP dskgrp10g01 NORMAL REDUNDANCY
FAILGROUP fgctl_qa01 DISK '/dev/dsk_qa_a01', '/dev/dsk_qa_a02',
FAILGROUP fgctl_qa02 DISK '/dev/dsk_qa_b01', '/dev/dsk_qa_b02' ;
```

dskgrp10g01 has four disks belonging to the failure group, fgctl_qa01 or fgctl_qa02. With the NORMAL REDUNDANCY option, ASM provides redundancy for all files in dskgrp10g01 and dskgrp10g02 subject to the attributes given in the disk-group templates, as explained later in this chapter in the section "Using Disk-Group Templates."

Because no names were given to the disks using the NAME clause, the disks will be named dskgrp10g01_0001, dskgrp10g01_0002, dskgrp10g01_0003, and dskgrp10g01_0004 by default.

Other Operations on a Disk Group

Use the ALTER DISKGROUP command to add, drop, or resize any disk(s). This command can be used simultaneously on multiple disks in a single statement. After issuing an ALTER DISKGROUP statement, ASM rebalances the file extents automatically to suit the new disk-group configuration. The rebalancing operation continues even after the ALTER DISKGROUP command completes successfully. The status of this rebalancing task can be viewed from V$ASM_OPERATION.

ADD DISK
If you want to add a disk—for example, /dsk_qa_a03—to the dskgrp10g01 disk group, use the ADD DISK clause as follows:

```
ALTER DISKGROUP dskgrp10g01 ADD DISK '/dev/dsk_qa_a03';
```

This will add the disk and assign dsk_qa_a03 to its own failgroup, as no other failgroup was specifically mentioned in the command.

If you want to add a few disks (for example, /dsk_qa_c01, /dsk_qa_c02, and /dsk_qa_c03) under another failure group (fgctl_qa03), issue the following command:

```
ALTER DISKGROUP dskgrp10g01 NORMAL REDUNDANCY
FAILGROUP fgctl_qa03 DISK '/dev/dsk_qa_c*' ;
```

DROP DISK
If you want to drop a disk from a disk group, use the DROP DISK command. To drop all disks in a failure group, use the DROP DISKS IN FAILUREGROUP clause of the ALTER DISKGROUP command. When you drop a disk, the files in the dropped disk are moved to other disks in the disk group, and the header entry on the dropped disk is cleared. The disk can be dropped without waiting for the ASM to read or write to the disk through the use of the FORCE clause of the DROP commands (for disk groups made under NORMAL or HIGH REDUNDANCY options).

To drop the disk /dsk_qa_a03 from the dskgrp10g01 disk group, issue this command:

```
ALTER DISKGROUP dskgrp10g01 DROP DISK '/dev/dsk_qa_a03' ;
```

You can do simultaneous `ADD` and `DROP` operations on disk groups. In the next example, we will drop a disk from and add another one to `dskgrp10g01` in a single command:

```
ALTER DISKGROUP dskgrp10g01 DROP DISK '/dev/dsk_qa_a03'
ADD FAILGROUP fgctl_qa04 DISK '/dev/dskd01', '/dev/dskd02';
```

If you change your mind and wish to cancel a `DROP` operation of all disks in a disk group, use the `UNDROP DISKS` clause of the `ALTER DISKGROUP` command. This will cancel all pending `DROP DISK` operations within a disk group unless the `DROP` statement has completely finished. `UNDROP DISKS` will also restore the disks that were being dropped as part of the `DROP DISKGROUP` or `FORCE` commands:

```
ALTER DISKGROUP dskgrp10g01 UNDROP DISKS;
```

RESIZE and REBALANCE Operations

You use the `RESIZE` clause of `ALTER DISKGROUP` command to resize a disk or all disks in a disk group or a failure group. The `RESIZE` option needs a `SIZE` parameter to complete its operation, or it will resize to the size of the disk as returned by the operating system. The new size from the `RESIZE` operation is written to the ASM disk header record.

When you resize the disk to a higher size, it is immediately available for utilization. Resizing the disk to a lower size will require the completion of the `REBALANCE` operation. This operation attempts to reallocate the files among other disks. The `RESIZE` command will fail if the data extents cannot be successfully transferred and rebalanced. Similarly, the `RESIZE` command will fail when you try to resize a disk to values higher than the disk capacity.

Suppose that the disks in previous examples were sized at 128GB. To reduce the size of dsk_qa_a01 to 96GB, you would issue the following command:

```
ALTER DISKGROUP dskgrp10g01 RESIZE DISK '/dev/dsk_qa_a01' SIZE 96G;
```

This command can be modified to reduce the size of all disks under a failgroup—say, fgctl_qa01:

```
ALTER DISKGROUP dskgrp10g01 RESIZE DISKS IN FAILGROUP fgctl_qa01 SIZE 96G;
```

Manual rebalancing of disks can be done with the `REBALANCE` clause of the `ALTER DISKGROUP` command. A manual rebalance is seldom needed unless the DBA feels that the `REBALANCE` operation is not fast enough.

> **REBALANCE** is an expensive operation and could sometimes crash the ASM instance.

We discussed the `ASM_POWER_LIMIT` initialization parameter earlier in this chapter. `ASM_POWER_LIMIT` controls the degree of parallelism for `REBALANCE` operations. This parameter has a significant impact on the `REBALANCE` operation of disks.

The `POWER` clause used along with the `REBALANCE` operation specifies the parallelism and speed of the `REBALANCE` operation. To alter the speed of an ongoing `REBALANCE` operation, change the

POWER to a new level. With a POWER value of 0, the REBALANCE operation is stopped until the value is changed.

With a POWER value of 10 and ASM_POWER_LIMIT of 1, the degree of parallelism will not exceed the value of ASM_POWER_LIMIT (1). So the REBALANCE operation is limited by the ASM_POWER_LIMIT initialization parameter. ASM_POWER_LIMIT can be found in the V$ASM_OPERATION view.

An example of a REBALANCE operation with ASM_POWER_LIMIT of 10 and POWER of 5 is given here:

```
ALTER DISKGROUP dskgrp10g01 REBALANCE POWER 5;
```

In Oracle Database 10g Release 2, the ALTER DISKGROUP REBALANCE operation has an option to use WAIT in the command to halt the REBALANCE operation until a later time. The WAIT option allows a user script to be run to add or remove disks.

Mounting Disk Groups

The disk groups in the ASM_DISKGROUPS initialization parameter are automatically mounted at the ASM instance startup and unmounted when the ASM instance is shut down. ASM will mount the disk group when you create it, and unmount it when you drop it.

The ALTER DISKGROUP...MOUNT (UNMOUNT) command is used for manual operations on disk groups by name or using ALL. For dismounting a disk group with open files, use the FORCE clause of the DISMOUNT operation. See the following examples to dismount a disk group and mount it back:

```
ALTER DISKGROUP dskgrp10g01 dismount;
```

```
ALTER DISKGROUP dskgrp10g01 mount;
```

To dismount all the disk groups in our examples (dskgrp10g01 and dskgrp10g02), use the ALL clause as follows:

```
ALTER DISKGROUP ALL DISMOUNT;
```

Using Disk-Group Templates

A *disk-group template* is a collection of attributes that are applied to all files created within the disk group. Oracle provides a set of initial default templates for use by ASM, which is listed in v$asm_template view. You can add new templates to a disk group, modify existing ones, or drop existing ones using the ALTER DISKGROUP statement.

The default templates are ARCHIVELOG, AUTOBACKUP, BACKUPSET, CONTROL, DATAFILE, DATAGUARDCONFIG, DUMPSET, FLASHBACK, ONLINELOG, PARAMETERFILE, and TEMPFILE. Refer to *Oracle Database Administrators Guide 10g* for a detailed explanation of templates and file types.

If you want to add a new template (say, OLTP_DBF_T1) for a disk group, use the ADD TEMPLATE clause of the ALTER DISKGROUP command along with its attributes:

```
ALTER DISKGROUP dskgrp10g01 ADD TEMPLATE OLTP_DBF_T1 ATTRIBUTES (MIRROR FINE);
```

The ALTER TEMPLATE clause will help to modify existing templates on specified attributes. Unspecified attributes are not modified. When an existing template is modified, new files created using that template will get new attribute values, while existing files continue to retain their old attributes.

For example, if you wish to change the striping for the template OLTP_DBF_T1 from FINE to COARSE, issue the following command:

```
ALTER DISKGROUP dskgrp10g01 ALTER TEMPLATE OLTP_DBF_T1 ATTRIBUTES (COARSE);
```

Use the DROP TEMPLATE clause to drop an existing template or templates from a disk group. Only user-defined templates can be dropped.

```
ALTER DISKGROUP dskgrp10g01 DROP TEMPLATE OLTP_DBF_T1;
```

Directory Structure

A disk group uses a hierarchical directory structure with fully qualified filenames (system aliases) along with alias filenames. When you create a new file, the system alias is automatically created by ASM. For more user-friendly aliases, you have to create a directory structure that supports the new naming conventions. The directory path should always begin with a plus (+) sign, followed by subdirectory names separated by forward slash (/) characters.

Use the ADD DIRECTORY clause to create a new directory as follows:

```
ALTER DISKGROUP dskgrp10g01 ADD DIRECTORY '+dskgrp10g01/q0testdb';
```

If you want to add a new directory called qateam under q0testdb, use the following command with accurate relative paths:

```
ALTER DISKGROUP dskgrp10g01 ADD DIRECTORY '+dskgrp10g01/q0testdb/qateam';
```

To rename this directory, use the RENAME DIRECTORY clause of ALTER DISKGROUP command:

```
ALTER DISKGROUP dskgrp10g01 RENAME DIRECTORY '+dskgrp10g01/q0testdb/qateam' to
'+dskgrp10g01/q0testdb/qausers';
```

To drop any directory (other than system-created directories), use the DROP DIRECTORY clause. The FORCE clause will drop a directory along with its subdirectories and contents (as in q0testdb):

```
ALTER DISKGROUP dskgrp10g01 DROP DIRECTORY '+dskgrp10g01/q0testdb' FORCE;
```

With Oracle Database 10g Release 2, when using the ASMCMD utility, files can be accessed directly using a command-line interface.

Alias Names for ASM files

You can add alias names to provide more meaningful names to ASM files in the directories. Use the ADD ALIAS, RENAME ALIAS, or DELETE ALIAS clauses to add, rename, or delete alias names, except for the system alias. Every alias known to the ASM instance is listed in the `v$asm_alias` view. The system-generated aliases will be specified under the `SYSTEM_CREATED` column.

To add an alias name for an ASM filename, use the `ADD ALIAS` clause with full directory path and the new alias:

```
ALTER DISKGROUP dskgrp10g01 ADD ALIAS '+dskgrp10g01/q0testdb/RTLSALES_TBL01.dbf' FOR
''+dgroup1/qadata/testdb1/retail.472.1';
```

Use the `RENAME ALIAS` clause to give the alias another name:

```
ALTER DISKGROUP dskgrp10g01 RENAME ALIAS '+dskgrp10g01/RTLSALESDB/rtlsldata_1.dbf' FOR
''+dgroup1/qadata/testdb2/retail.472.1' ;
```

The `DELETE ALIAS` clause drops the alias name. Dropping an alias does not remove the underlying file on the file system. The following command will drop the alias, but will preserve the file on the system:

```
ALTER DISKGROUP dskgrp10g01 DELETE ALIAS '+dskgrp10g01/RTLSALESDB/rtlsldata_1.dbf';
```

To drop the files and associated alias names from a disk group, use the `DROP FILE` clause of the `ALTER DISKGROUP` command. You can also substitute the alias name with the system-generated alias.

```
ALTER DISKGROUP dskgrp10g01 DROP FILE  '+dskgrp10g01/RTLSALESDB/rtlsldata_1.dbf';
ALTER DISKGROUP dskgrp10g01 DROP FILE  '+dgroup1/qadata/testdb2/retail.472.1';
```

DROP DISKGROUP

You may want to drop an existing ASM disk group and its files for certain reasons. For this purpose, use the `DROP DISKGROUP` command for the disk group with the `INCLUDING CONTENTS` clause for its files. The default option for `DROP DISKGROUP` is `EXCLUDING CONTENTS`, which will prevent the accidental dropping of a disk group with its contents.

For a `DROP` operation to succeed, the ASM instance has to be up and running, the disk group has to be mounted, and no files in the disk group should be open. The `DROP DISKGROUP` command returns the user to the command prompt after the entire action is completed. When the server parameter file is used, the `DROP DISKGROUP` command will remove the disk-group name from the `ASM_DISKGROUPS` parameter as well. With `init<SID>.ora` files, you will have to manually remove the disk group from the `ASM_DISKGROUPS` parameter after the `DROP` operation and before the next shutdown of the ASM instance:

```
DROP DISKGROUP dskgrp10g01 INCLUDING CONTENTS;
```

Checking the Internal Consistency of Disk Groups

When you run any operations to a disk group, you should verify the internal consistency of the disk group metadata using the `ALTER DISKGROUP...CHECK` command. The only requirement for this consistency check is that the disk group has to be in the mounted state during the checks.

You can run the CHECK operation on specific files, on some or all disks in a disk group, or on specific failure groups in a disk group.

```
ALTER DISKGROUP dskgrp10g01 CHECK ALL;
```

During the CHECK operation, ASM attempts to correct any errors unless the user specifies a NOREPAIR clause. If there are any errors, they will be displayed and written to an alert log as well.

> **ASM Implementation in RAC Mode**
>
> ASM instances can also be implemented in RAC mode. This would eliminate ASM as a single point of failure. When implemented in RAC mode, failure of one ASM instance will not bring down the rest of the databases. The usual RAC benefits—load balancing, failover, and the like—are available to the ASM instance, along with improved storage management.

Avoiding ASM Pitfalls

This section discusses the common issues, challenges, and tips to overcome problems associated with setting up and using ASM for database storage.

Unable to Connect to ASM Instance

If you get errors like ORA-17203 or ORA-15055 when trying to connect from a database instance to an ASM instance, follow these steps to check and fix the error conditions.

1. Verify that the ASM instance is up and running:

   ```
   setenv ORACLE_SID +ASM
   ```

   or use

   ```
   export ORACLE_SID=+ASM
   sqlplus "/as sysdba"
   SQL> startup;
   ```

2. When the ASM instance starts up, export your session to point to the ORACLE_HOME of the database you had problems with. Follow the same steps as in the ASM instance:

   ```
   setenv ORACLE_SID = Q0OR10G
   ```

   or use

   ```
   export ORACLE_SID= Q0OR10G
   sqlplus "/as sysdba"
   SQL> startup;
   ```

Now that the ASM instance is up and running, you should be able to make your database connect to the ASM instance.

Non-ASM and ASM Database Migrations

This section provides tips to migrate a non-ASM database to an ASM database or vice versa. These steps are also mentioned in ASM MetaLink Notes.

Non-ASM to ASM Migration

You, the DBA, may encounter situations where storage requirements get unmanageable and will benefit from using ASM files. To address this, set up the ASM database instance as mentioned in the section titled "Configuration Options" in this chapter. This example assumes that you have four sets of redo log members:

1. Edit the init*SID*.ora of the current non-ASM database to point to the new control_file location:

   ```
   control_file="+dskgrp10g01"
   ```

2. Start the database to nomount state:

   ```
   SQL> Startup nomount;
   ```

3. Copy the control file from the old location to the new location, using RMAN:

   ```
   RMAN> RESTORE CONTROLFILE FROM 'opt/app/oracle/product/10.0.1/Q0OR10G/control01.ctl';
   ```

4. Mount the database:

   ```
   SQL> ALTER DATABASE MOUNT;
   ```

5. Using RMAN, copy the data file from the non-ASM location to the ASM location:

   ```
   RMAN>BACKUP AS COPY DATABASE FORMAT '+dskgrp10g01';
   ```

6. Rename the data file using RMAN:

   ```
   RMAN> SWITCH DATABASE TO COPY;
   ```

7. Open the database and reset the logs:

   ```
   SQL> ALTER DATABASE OPEN RESETLOGS;
   ```

8. Repeat the following commands for all the four log members:

   ```
   SQL> ALTER DATABASE DROP LOGFILE '<old_log_name1>';
   SQL> ALTER DATABASE ADD LOGFILE '+dskgrp10g01';
   SQL> ALTER DATABASE SWITCH LOGFILE;
   SQL> ALTER DATABASE DROP LOGFILE '< old_log_name2>';
   SQL> ALTER DATABASE ADD LOGFILE '+dskgrp10g01';
   SQL> ALTER DATABASE SWITCH LOGFILE;
   SQL> ALTER DATABASE DROP LOGFILE '< old_log_name3>';
   SQL> ALTER DATABASE ADD LOGFILE '+dskgrp10g01';
   ```

```
SQL> ALTER DATABASE SWITCH LOGFILE;
SQL> ALTER DATABASE DROP LOGFILE '< old_log_name4>';
SQL> ALTER DATABASE ADD LOGFILE '+dskgrp10g01';
SQL> ALTER DATABASE SWITCH LOGFILE;
```

9. If you want to multiplex your control files to more than one location over ASM disk groups, use the following command:

> Oracle has issued a whitepaper titled *Oracle Database 10g Migration to Automatic Storage Management* to give you an overview of different cold/hot migration strategies.

```
SQL> ALTER SYSTEM SET
control_files='+dskgrp10g01/
control1.ctl',
➡ '+dskgrp10g02/control2.ctl' SCOPE=SPFILE;
```

ASM to Non-ASM Migration

You may want to revert the database in the preceding section from using ASM files to using non-ASM files for certain reasons. Follow these steps if you have a change of mind and need to go back to using file-based databases:

1. Make sure that the database is up and running.

2. Create the PFILE from SPFILE and edit the PFILE so that the control file name is pointing to a file system location (the reverse of the step done in the preceding example of nonASM to ASM migration).

3. Start the database up to nomount stage:

```
SQL> Startup nomount;
```

4. Copy the control file from ASM to non-ASM using RMAN:

```
RMAN> RESTORE CONTROLFILE FROM '+dskgrp10g01/control1.ctl';
```

5. Mount the database:

```
SQL> alter database mount;
```

6. Copy the database from ASM to non-ASM using RMAN:

```
RMAN> BACKUP AS COPY DATABASE format ''opt/app/oracle/product/10.0.1/Q0OR10G/%U';
allocate channel c1 type disk;
allocate channel c2 type disk;
copy datafile ''+dskgrp10g01/q0testdb/datafile/system.471.1' to ''opt/app/oracle/
product/10.0.1/Q0OR10G/system.471.1';
copy datafile ''+dskgrp10g01/q0testdb/datafile/sysaux.474.1' to ''opt/app/oracle/
product/10.0.1/Q0OR10G/sysaux.474.1';
copy datafile ''+dskgrp10g01/q0testdb/datafile/undotbs1.473.1' to ''opt/app/oracle/
product/10.0.1/Q0OR10G/undotbs1.473.1';
```

```
copy datafile ''+dskgrp10g01/q0testdb/datafile/undotbs2.478.1' to ''opt/app/oracle/
product/10.0.1/Q0OR10G/undotbs2.478.1';
copy datafile ''+dskgrp10g01/q0testdb/datafile/users.476.1' to ''opt/app/oracle/
product/10.0.1/Q0OR10G/users.476.1';
copy datafile ''+dskgrp10g01/q0testdb/datafile/asm_ts.479.1' to ''opt/app/oracle/
product/10.0.1/Q0OR10G/asm_ts.479.1';
copy datafile ''+dskgrp10g01/q0testdb/rtlsldata_1.dbf' to ''opt/app/oracle/
product/10.0.1/Q0OR10G/rtlsldata_1.dbf';
RMAN> SWITCH DATABASE TO COPY;
```

7. Repeat the following commands for all four redo log members.

```
SQL> ALTER DATABASE DROP LOGFILE '+dskgrp10g01'
SQL> ALTER DATABASE ADD LOGFILE '<new_log_name1>';
```

Discovering ASM Instances in a RAC Environment

If an ASM instance is added to an existing RAC environment, it will not be discovered automatically by the Database Control. You will have to help RAC discover the new ASM target manually.

To do so, create an XML file with the instance details, and run `emctl config agent addtarget` *filename* to append the new target to the list of targets in `targets.xml`. Restart the agent to complete the steps. Refer to MetaLink Notes #266770.1 and #273561.1 for more details on UNIX and Windows platforms.

VIP Timeouts and VIP Failure on RAC

In an Oracle Database 10g RAC environment running Oracle CRS, the `crsd` daemon (in UNIX) or OracleCRService (on Windows) is responsible for monitoring the resources associated with the cluster. One of these monitored resources is the virtual IP address (VIP) associated with each node. CRS creates dependencies for the listener service, ASM instance, and each database instance on a given node on this VIP.

If for some reason this VIP fails and cannot be restarted, the CRS will bring down all dependent resources, including the listener, ASM instance, and database instance, gracefully using a `SHUTDOWN IMMEDIATE` command.

When this happens, check the trace file for the VIP found in the `ORA_CRS_HOME`/racg/dump directory (`ora.`*nodename*`.vip.trc`) . This could be due to known issues with timeouts of the VIP under a high load. This issue is logged as bug #3718601. Similarly, another bug, # 3677437, is reported on VIP. If you increase the `TIMEOUT` values for the VIP from 60 to 120 seconds, as given in MetaLink Note #277274.1, you could resolve the issue.

1. Log in as root and, from the `ORA_CRS_HOME`/bin directory, create the `.cap` file for each VIP resource (on every node):

```
./crs_stat -p ora.<name1>.vip > /tmp/ora.<name1>.vip.cap
```

2. Update the .cap file to have CHECK_INTERVAL and SCRIPT_TIMEOUT values of 120 seconds (where ci = CHECK_INTERVAL and st = SCRIPT_TIMEOUT):

```
./crs_profile -update ora.<name1>.vip -dir /tmp -o ci=120,st=120
```

3. Re-register the VIP file using the -u option:

```
./crs_register ora.<name1>.vip -dir /tmp -u
```

Please refer to abovementioned MetaLink Notes and to Chapter 15, "Utilizing Oracle Database 10g Real Applications Clusters" for more details on CRS and details of the bugs.

When and Where to Use ASM

Automatic Storage Management is useful in environments with large databases and frequent increases in data volumes. Some examples of constantly increasing data volumes would be credit-card and banking applications, retail environments, cellular and telephone carriers, travel reservations, security applications, and the like, where the data needs to be preserved for a longer time due to regulatory and other business reasons.

ASM provides a centralized storage-management solution for Oracle databases. The deployment of ASM will be a stepping-stone for grid deployment, lower manageability costs, and higher availability of disk resources. It also simplifies migration to new storage hardware, reduces the number of devices to be managed, and reduces the overall complexity. ASM eliminates the need for I/O tuning and also avoids hotspots at the file-system level.

ASM provides clustered volume manager and file system functionality directly to the database and bypasses the need for third-party clustering software. It also helps to protect against storage array failures.

As in any other new technology, your organization should test smaller databases on the ASM storage and gain experience before doing a full-fledged conversion of all systems to ASM. The technology will mature and be even simpler to use in years to come and with coming releases of Oracle products. In future, ASM could replace all vendor products for database storage management.

ASM Improvements in Oracle Database 10g Release 2

We have already reviewed the WAIT option in conjunction with our discussion of the REBALANCE operation. Oracle Database 10g Release 2 offers an ASM command-line interface (ASMCMD) utility to access and manage files from a command prompt. ASM/XDB FTP support is another new feature that allows the use of XDB and ASM with a user interface for getting files into and out of ASM-managed storage.

Release 2 also expands the ASM capabilities to support multiple Oracle database versions and multiple database-to-ASM connection types. When multiple Oracle database versions are used,

ASM utilizes the functionality of the lowest available version. For this purpose, two new columns—SOFTWARE_VERSION and COMPATIBLE_VERSION—have been added to V$ASM_CLIENT.

ASM allows batch selection of multiple disks for operations like check, delete, and resize. This prevents the unnecessary rebalancing that occurs when disks are deleted one by one and improves usability of the disks by the database.

Summary

This chapter reviewed Automatic Storage Management, which represents a breakthough in the way disks are accessed for data storage. It also covered the major topics relating to database installations involving ASM, migrations, common bugs, implementation issues, and fixes. As with every new technology, there will be a slight learning curve for novice as well as experienced DBAs while testing out ASM. ASM will make storage management easier in companies where there is a large number of databases as well as SANs (storage devices). ASM may introduce a new kind of DBA role exclusively dedicated for Oracle storage administration.

This chapter concludes the first section of this book, "Getting Started with Oracle Database 10g." Let us proceed to the second phase of this book, beginning with a discussion of automatic memory management techniques in the next chapter.

PART II

Quick Wins Using Oracle Database 10g

5 Using Automatic Memory Management

6 Monitoring with Automatic Statistics Collection

7 Managing Automatic Undo

8 Leveraging Automatic Segment Management

9 Implementing Recovery Manager

5

Using Automatic Memory Management

IN THIS CHAPTER

Introduction to Quick Wins   93

What Is Automatic Shared Memory
Management?   94

Understanding Memory Advisor   97

Automated Maintenance Tasks   100

Memory Management Tips   100

Scaling for Database Expansion   103

ASMM Improvements in 10g
Release 2   104

Introduction to Quick Wins

In Part II, "Quick Wins Using Oracle Database 10g," you will learn about Automatic Memory Management, Automatic Statistics Collection, Automatic Undo Management, Automatic Segment Management, and Automatic Backup Management. All these features could be collectively highlighted as some of the important feature improvements of Oracle Database 10g over previous versions. These features in Oracle Database 10g are ready to be turned on and used at no extra cost and with no major effort. When used, these features can help you quickly reap benefits in various areas of database administration. After you learn to use these features with the help of Chapters 5–9 in this book, you will be able to implement and benefit from these "quick wins with Oracle Database 10g." Let's start the second phase of our expedition with automatic memory management.

In previous database releases, the database administrator (DBA) sized different SGA components manually through initialization parameters like SHARED_POOL_SIZE, DB_CACHE_SIZE, JAVA_POOL_SIZE, and LARGE_POOL_SIZE. Oracle Database 10g has introduced the Automatic Shared Memory Management feature to simplify the SGA memory management burdens of the DBA. The DBA can specify the total amount of SGA memory available to an instance with the SGA_TARGET parameter. The Oracle Database 10g will automatically allocate the memory among its components, enabling the most effective memory utilization. Let us dive into the details.

What Is Automatic Shared Memory Management?

Until Oracle 9i, the Oracle server allotted the required memory for fixed SGA and other internal allocations. The common problems with improper SGA sizing are undersized memory, leading to poor performance and out-of-memory errors (ORA-4031); and oversized memory, leading to wasted memory and latch contention. This scenario has changed with the introduction of Automatic Shared Memory Management, which is described in the following paragraphs.

Automatic Shared Memory Management (ASMM) is the new manageability feature that enables Oracle Database 10g to automatically determine the appropriate values for SGA components within the total size limits of SGA. The commonly tuned SGA components are the database buffer cache, the shared pool, the large pool, and the Java pool. These initialization parameters are referred to as *auto-tuned SGA parameters*.

In Oracle Database 10g, the DBA can assign the total amount of SGA available to an instance with the SGA_TARGET initialization parameter. Oracle database automatically distributes this memory among its various subcomponents for the most effective memory utilization. The SGA_TARGET parameter includes all SGA memory, including automatically sized components, manually sized components, and internal allocations during the database startup. Log buffer, other buffer caches (for example, recycle and keep), fixed SGA, and internal allocations are considered manually sized components in Oracle Database 10g. The default value for SGA_TARGET parameter is 0, with ASMM being disabled.

The SGA is made up of pools of memory such as the shared pool, java pool, buffer cache, and so on. These SGA components allocate and deallocate space in measurement units of *granules*. The granule size is determined by the total SGA size. As a generalization, for most platforms with total SGA size equal to or less than 1GB, granule size is 4MB. Granule size is usually 16MB (8MB for Windows) for SGAs larger than 1GB. Some platform dependencies may arise. Refer to your operating system–specific documentation for more details. The granule size can be identified from the V$SGAINFO view. All dynamic components in the SGA have the same granule size.

If you specify the size of a SGA component at a value different from a multiple of its granule size, Oracle Database will round the specified size up to the nearest higher multiple. If the

granule size is 16MB and you specify
DB_CACHE_SIZE as 30MB, for example, the
database will actually allocate 32MB.

To use ASMM, STATISTICS_LEVEL must be set
to TYPICAL (default) or ALL. You can query the
V$STATISTICS_LEVEL view to get more infor-
mation on the status of the statistics
controlled by the STATISTICS_LEVEL
parameter.

When ASMM is enabled in the database, the
sizes of various SGA components are flexible.
They resize among themselves to adapt to the
workload needs without any additional DBA
intervention. The database will automatically
distribute the SGA among the various components as needed, maximizing the consumption of all available memory. If the manually
tuned parameters are set, they consume their
memory from SGA_TARGET, leaving remaining
memory for automatically tuned components
as listed in Table 5.1.

> **Significance of the STATISTICS_LEVEL Parameter**
>
> Oracle Database collects database-level statistics and operating-system statistics for various reasons, including for self-management decisions. STATISTICS_LEVEL is the initialization parameter that determines the level of collection of these statistics. It can accept TYPICAL, ALL, or BASIC as inputs. A value of TYPICAL collects all major statistics required for database self-management and provides the best overall performance for most environments. ALL collects additional statistics like timed operating system statistics and execution plan statistics. BASIC disables the collection of many important statistics including automatic SGA, shared pool, buffer cache, and PGA target advisory statistics, which are discussed in this chapter. This setting is not at all recommended for a self-tuned database.

TABLE 5.1

SGA Components and Corresponding Initialization Parameters

Type of Tuning	SGA Component	Initialization Parameter
Automatic	Fixed SGA and related internal allocations	Not applicable
Automatic	Buffer cache	DB_CACHE_SIZE
Automatic	Shared pool	SHARED_POOL_SIZE
Automatic	Large pool	LARGE_POOL_SIZE
Automatic	Java pool	JAVA_POOL_SIZE
Automatic	Streams pool	STREAMS_POOL_SIZE
Manual	Log buffer	LOG_BUFFER
Manual	Keep buffer cache	DB_KEEP_CACHE_SIZE
Manual	Recycle buffer cache	DB_RECYCLE_CACHE_SIZE
Manual	Nonstandard block size buffer caches	DB_nK_CACHE_SIZE where n= (2, 4, 8, 16, 32)

With automatic SGA management enabled, Oracle's internal tuning algorithm continuously monitors the workload performance and increases the shared pool as needed to reduce the number of parses. It increases the value in small chunks over time until the optimal size is

> **ASMM with Unsupported Initialization Parameters**
>
> If your database instance startup failed with ORA-00824, review this sidebar carefully. If you have upgraded a database but have not removed all deprecated and unsupported parameters in the init*SID*.ora file, you will get this error. On Oracle Database 10g, if you enable automatic SGA management by setting the SGA_TARGET parameter to a value greater than 0 and retain the DB_BLOCK_BUFFERS parameter in the init*SID*.ora file, you will encounter ORA-00824. You should carefully edit the initialization parameter file and get rid of all unsupported parameters. Use DB_CACHE_SIZE parameter instead of DB_BLOCK_BUFFERS parameter. If you are unable to fix the parameters, disable ASMM by setting SGA_TARGET=0.

reached, but does not shrink it back. The presence of open cursors, pinned PL/SQL packages, and other SQL execution states in the shared pool make it impossible to find granules that can be freed. With manual configuration, compiled SQL statements may frequently age out of the shared pool with inadequate size.

SGA Sizing Considerations

The DBA can control the size of the automatically tuned SGA components by specifying minimum values for the components. This is helpful when an application needs a minimum amount of memory in order for specific components to work properly. You can query the V$SGA_DYNAMIC_COMPONENTS and V$SGAINFO views to get the current actual size of each SGA component, or get this information from the OEM memory configuration page.

When SGA_TARGET is resized, automatically tuned components (without a set minimum value) are affected by the operation. All manually tuned components remain unaffected.

When enabling Automatic Shared Memory Management, it is best to set SGA_TARGET to the desired non-zero value before starting the database. Dynamically modifying SGA_TARGET from zero to a non-zero value may not achieve the desired results because the shared pool may not be able to shrink. After startup, you can dynamically tune SGA_TARGET up or down as required.

We discussed the new Memory Manager (MMAN) background process used by ASMM, in Chapter 1, "Exploring Oracle Database 10g Structure." The MMAN background process coordinates the sizing of the memory components and acts as a memory broker. It keeps track of all memory components and their pending resize operations.

You can use the following V$ views to get more information about SGA components and their dynamic resizing:

- V$SGA gives summary information about the system global area (SGA).

- V$SGAINFO gives information about SGA size, including the different SGA components, the granule size, and free memory.

- V$SGASTAT gives detailed information about the SGA in terms of memory/space distribution and usage.

- V$SGA_DYNAMIC_COMPONENTS gives information about the dynamic SGA components.

- V$SGA_DYNAMIC_FREE_MEMORY gives information on SGA memory available for future dynamic SGA resize operations.

- V$SGA_RESIZE_OPS gives information about the last 400 completed SGA resize operations.

- V$SGA_CURRENT_RESIZE_OPS gives information about SGA resize operations that are currently in progress.

- V$SGA_TARGET_ADVICE gives helpful information to tune SGA_TARGET.

Understanding Memory Advisor

The Memory Advisor helps you tune the size of your memory structures. You can use the Memory Advisor only when automatic memory tuning is disabled in the database. When ASMM is disabled, the Memory Advisor is responsible for optimizing system memory for the database instance. Using the Memory Advisor, you can let Oracle tune the memory according to the database needs or use the SGA Advisor or the PGA Advisor to set the total size of the SGA or PGA and optimal values for their components.

The Memory Advisor consists of three advisors to give you recommendations on shared pool (SGA), buffer cache (SGA), and PGA. The main components of the shared pool are the library cache and the dictionary cache. The library cache stores the compiled form of recently used SQL and PL/SQL code, while the dictionary cache stores data accessed from the data dictionary. Buffer cache is used to store blocks read from disk. The PGA region has data and control information for a server process.

Memory Advisors Through OEM

You can use OEM to invoke the Memory Advisors. On OEM, access the Advisor Central page and click Memory Advisor in the Advisors list. The Memory Parameters—SGA page appears, as shown in Figure 5.1. This shows all the details on memory usage of system global area.

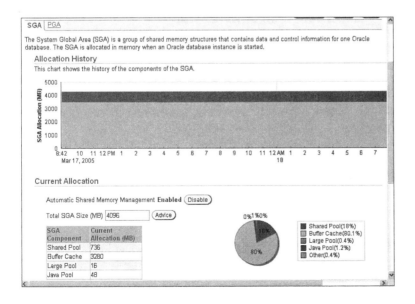

FIGURE 5.1
The Memory Parameters—SGA page in the OEM.

The shared pool and buffer cache are part of the SGA. If you need further information on any memory structure shown on this page, click Help. Click the Advice button to view a graphical representation of SGA size advice, as shown in Figure 5.2.

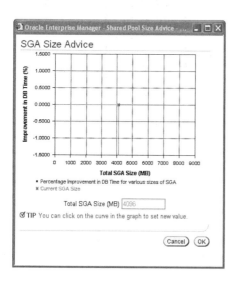

FIGURE 5.2   SGA size advice.

Assume for the sake of example that the Automatic Shared Memory Management is disabled on your database. If not, disable it on the SGA page. Then choose either Shared Pool or Buffer Cache from the list of SGA components and click the Advice button next to it (See Figure 5.3). You will get graphical representation of the memory and advice on its usage. (Note that all screenshots are not given here, as this description itself is self-explanatory.)

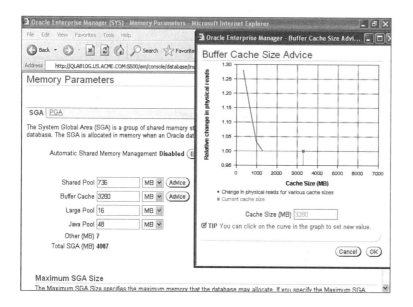

FIGURE 5.3
SGA—Buffer Cache Size
Advice.

To run the PGA Advisor, click on the PGA tab (see Figure 5.4). You can get advice on PGA usage in a similar manner as with the SGA (see Figure 5.5), by clicking the Advice button. To see a graphical representation of the PGA memory and its usage, click the PGA Memory Usage Details button (see Figure 5.6).

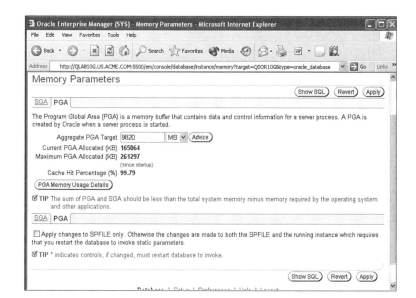

FIGURE 5.4
The Memory Parameters—PGA page in the OEM.

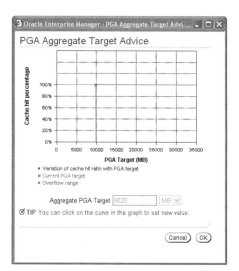

FIGURE 5.5   PGA aggregate target advice.

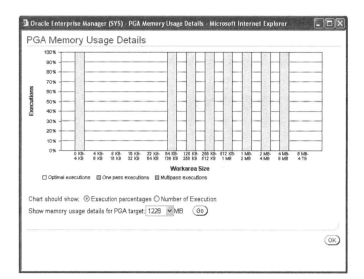

FIGURE 5.6
PGA memory usage.

Automated Maintenance Tasks

This section looks at the automated maintenance tasks in the realm of memory management. In earlier releases of Oracle, when you got an ORA-04031 error related to memory, you had to resort to several methods to find the true cause and rectify it. One of the methods was to create an event in the init*SID*.ora file to get a trace file with additional information about the problem. Starting with Oracle 9.2.0.5 and Oracle Database 10g releases, a trace file is created by default in the user_dump_dest directory whenever a memory error occurs. So if you still get errors, even with a sufficiently large memory and with automatic memory management turned on, Oracle has already created the trace files for you to be sent to Oracle support for analysis.

Some errors with ORA-04031 code may not be the result of insufficient SGA. If you run out of memory while compiling a Java code in an application (within loadjava or deployejb), you will get a SQL exception error with ORA-04031 code like this:

```
A SQL exception occurred while compiling: ORA-04031: unable to allocate bytes of
➥shared memory ("shared pool","unknown object","joxlod: init h",
➥"JOX: ioc_allocate_pal")
```

In this scenario, the error is not related to insufficient SGA, but is instead caused by a small value for JAVA_POOL_SIZE. When you get this error, the only solution is to shut down the database and increase the JAVA_POOL_SIZE setting to a larger value. Restart the database, and try the same command again.

Memory Management Tips

We discussed setting the STATISTICS_LEVEL parameter to TYPICAL or ALL to enable ASMM. For a more detailed understanding of various statistics levels, query the V$STATISTICS_LEVEL view.

You can use ALTER SESSION or ALTER SYSTEM to change the values if you decide to switch back and forth using ASMM. Use the following query to get your database session settings:

```
SQL> select STATISTICS_NAME, SESSION_STATUS, ACTIVATION_LEVEL from V$STATISTICS_LEVEL;
STATISTICS_NAME                     SESSION_ ACTIVAT
--------------------------------    -------- -------
Buffer Cache Advice                 ENABLED  TYPICAL
MTTR Advice                         ENABLED  TYPICAL
Timed Statistics                    ENABLED  TYPICAL
Timed OS Statistics                 DISABLED ALL
Segment Level Statistics            ENABLED  TYPICAL
PGA Advice                          ENABLED  TYPICAL
Plan Execution Statistics           DISABLED ALL
Shared Pool Advice                  ENABLED  TYPICAL
Modification Monitoring             ENABLED  TYPICAL
Longops Statistics                  ENABLED  TYPICAL
Bind Data Capture                   ENABLED  TYPICAL
Ultrafast Latch Statistics          ENABLED  TYPICAL
Threshold-based Alerts              ENABLED  TYPICAL
Global Cache Statistics             ENABLED  TYPICAL
Cache Stats Monitor                 ENABLED  TYPICAL
Active Session History              ENABLED  TYPICAL
Undo Advisor, Alerts and Fast Ramp up   ENABLED  TYPICAL
17 rows selected.
```

Converting a Manual Memory–Managed Database to ASMM

If you want to enable automatic shared-memory management in a manual memory–managed database, do the following:

1. Find the value for SGA_TARGET using the following SQL query:

   ```
   select ((select sum(value) from V$SGA)-
   ➥ (select current_size
   ➥from V$SGA_DYNAMIC_FREE_MEMORY))
   "SGA_TARGET_VALUE" from dual;
   ```

2. Alter the database to set the SGA_TARGET at the new value. This can be done by editing the initSID.ora file and restarting the database, or by using the following SQL command:

   ```
   alter system set SGA_TARGET=<SGA_TARGET_VALUE> [scope={spfile¦memory¦both}];
   ```

> **Error While Setting** STATISTICS_LEVEL
>
> If you wish to limit the amount of statistics collected in your database, you will have to alter the STATISTICS_LEVEL parameter to BASIC. When you issue the ALTER SESSION or ALTER SYSTEM command to make this change, you will encounter an ORA-00830 error on your database with auto-tuned SGA. The only workaround for this problem is to the disable SGA auto tuning so that the database can terminate the collection of any statistics. After you disable it, run the command to set STATISTICS_LEVEL to BASIC. Now you have a database with improved features over Oracle 9i, but with less sophistication than a self-managed 10g.

> **Is SGA Component Sizing a Good Practice?**
>
> If you specify the minimum size for an automatically tuned component, it reduces the total amount of memory available to Oracle for dynamic memory adjustment. This reduction in memory will hinder the system's ability to adapt to workload fluctuations. Do not specify minimum values for memory components unless you are absolutely sure of the nature of queries processed by the system. If you set the system to be managed by ASMM, it will help to improve system performance as well as optimize the utilization of available system resources.

SGA_TARGET_VALUE is either the value you got from step 1 or a number between the sum of all SGA component sizes and SGA_MAX_SIZE.

3. Enable complete automatic memory management by setting the values of the automatically sized SGA components listed in Table 5.1 to 0, as in step 2.

4. If you wish to set the minimum size of one or more automatically tuned SGA components, set those component sizes to the desired value and set the values of the other automatically tuned components to 0, as in step 2. Oracle will allocate memory among other components as needed, from the available memory.

Tuning SGA_TARGET and SGA_MAX_SIZE

Oracle Database 10g controls the virtual memory used by the SGA. It can start instances with minimal memory and allow the instance to use more memory up to SGA_MAX_SIZE by increasing the memory allocated for SGA components. If the value for SGA_MAX_SIZE in the init*SID*.ora file or SPFILE is less than the sum of the memory allocated for all memory components, then the database ignores the value for SGA_MAX_SIZE at instance startup.

SGA_MAX_SIZE cannot be dynamically resized. It is the maximum size of the SGA for the entire instance lifetime. When you set SGA_TARGET in an instance, the value of SGA_MAX_SIZE is automatically set to the new value for SGA_TARGET. But you cannot raise SGA_TARGET to a value higher than SGA_MAX_SIZE. So use the steps in the preceding section, "Converting a Manual Memory–Managed Database to ASMM," to find appropriate values for SGA_TARGET. The SGA_TARGET value should always be lower than SGA_MAX. You will get ORA-00823 if you try to raise SGA_TARGET above SGA_MAX as given in Listing 5.1.

LISTING 5.1   Tuning SGA_TARGET

```
SQL> show parameter sga ;
NAME                                 TYPE        VALUE
------------------------------------ ----------- ---------------------------
lock_sga                             boolean     FALSE
pre_page_sga                         boolean     FALSE
sga_max_size                         big integer 4G
sga_target                           big integer 0

SQL> alter system set sga_target=500M;
System altered.
```

LISTING 5.1   Continued

```
SQL>  show parameter sga ;
NAME                                 TYPE         VALUE
.................................... ............ .................................
lock_sga                             boolean      FALSE
pre_page_sga                         boolean      FALSE
sga_max_size                         big integer  4G
sga_target                           big integer  4G

SQL> alter system set sga_target=5000M;
alter system set sga_target=5000M
*
ERROR at line 1:
ORA-02097: parameter cannot be modified because specified value is invalid
ORA-00823: Specified value of sga_target greater than sga_max_size
```

Similarly, if you try to shrink SGA_TARGET to a value below the sum of individual components, you will get an ORA-00827 error. For resizing SGA to a lower value, reduce the size of individual components and try the shrink operation.

> Most of the database applications will run better if the underlying SQL code is tuned properly. If you get bad performance with an application on an Oracle Database 10g instance, check the memory values and see if they are sufficiently high. If the values look good, examine the underlying SQL code. Use various SQL tuning methods to improve the performance of the application code. Verify the performance improvements before you initiate memory increases.

Scaling for Database Expansion

When your large database application needs to allocate a large piece of contiguous memory in the shared pool for the batch job or updates, Oracle has to flush all unused objects from the memory pool and merge the resulting free memory chunks. The unavailability of a large piece of memory would result in ORA-04031 errors. This could still happen with Oracle Database 10g if the database cannot allocate enough free memory for the shared pool or large pool as needed. If you have sufficient physical memory on the server and enable automatic memory management, the database can get rid of most of the ORA-04031 errors.

In an ASMM-enabled database, when the database wants to allocate a large object into the shared pool but does not find enough contiguous space, it will automatically increase the shared pool size using free space from other SGA structures up to the maximum available limit. Oracle helps to reduce the DBA intervention for memory monitoring with automatic memory management. The current setting for ASMM can be obtained from the V$SGA_DYNAMIC_COMPONENTS view.

Allocating a large amount of memory for the system and enabling the ASMM will help the DBA to manage the database environment better than with a manually tuned environment. Consider any large retail database, which has OLTP jobs or a large number of concurrent transactions during the day and parallel batch jobs at night. In a manually tuned environment, the DBA would have to allocate large buffer caches for the OLTP jobs and a large pool for the nightly batch jobs.

You can use V$DB_CACHE_ADVICE view to get simulated miss rates for a range of potential buffer cache sizes. This view is populated when the DB_CACHE_ADVICE initialization parameter is set to ON. This is a dynamic parameter, which you can turn on and off dynamically to collect advisory data for a specific workload. When you turn on the advisory, there is a small increase in CPU usage for the sampling operation.

When you enable ASMM, all statistics are captured in the system and different memory advisors are invoked to get the best distribution for memory. MMAN coordinates the memory-resize operations to allocate different components with appropriate sizings as needed. With memory auto-tuning, the buffer cache gets more memory allocation during daily OLTP transactions. At night, the memory automatically shifts to the large pool to accommodate the parallel batch job runs. ASMM uses MMAN as the SGA memory broker to keep track of the component sizes and resize operations.

ASMM Improvements in 10g Release 2

Oracle has fixed the memory-related bugs in Oracle Database 10g Release 1.

In Oracle Database 10g Release 2, the Streams pool is automatically managed by the ASMM. The improved Oracle Streams can move data between databases and nodes and keep two or more databases synchronized when updates are made. Database objects can be shared between Oracle databases or between Oracle and non-Oracle databases through the use of Oracle Transparent Gateways.

When you use Streams in a single database, memory is allocated from a pool in the System Global Area (SGA) called the *Streams pool*. The Streams pool helps with the internal communication of the database during parallel capture and applies operations. The Streams pool is an automatically sized SGA component in Release 2, which improves the manageability. The Automatic Shared Memory Management feature automatically adjusts the size of the Streams pool based on workload requirements.

Summary

This chapter has covered the automatic shared-memory management feature of Oracle Database 10g. It reviewed how to turn ASMM on and off, and how to use the various memory advisors to get optimum size recommendations. Setting the appropriate statistics level is also important for utilizing the self-management features. In Chapter 6, "Monitoring with Automatic Statistics Collection," you will learn more about database metrics and statistics-collection processes, the basis for any well-managed database.

6

Monitoring with Automatic Statistics Collection

IN THIS CHAPTER

Automatic Statistics Collection Fundamentals	105
Collecting and Analyzing Statistics	111
Metrics Monitoring and Customization	125
Using Database Alerts with Metrics	126
Making the Most of Metrics and Statistics Collection	127
New Features in Oracle Database 10g Release 2	128

Automatic Statistics Collection Fundamentals

Automatic diagnosis and correction of existing and potential performance problems is an important feature in Oracle Database 10g. This is mostly accomplished by automatic statistics collection and retention and reporting using ADDM. The automatic statistics collection is done by the Automatic Workload Repository (AWR) as explained in Chapter 1, "Exploring Oracle Database 10g Architecture."

Database statistics are effective in diagnosing various performance problems within the database. When you analyze a performance problem, you look at the cumulative difference (delta) in statistics values between the starting point and the end. These cumulative statistics are available through dynamic performance views like V$SESSTAT and V$SYSSTAT, from the database starting time. When you shut down a database, these cumulative values in the dynamic views will be reset. The AWR automatically collects and retains these cumulative and delta values for most of the database statistics, except for the session level. AWR collects the performance data, processes it, and maintains performance statistics for use by ADDM and other advisors.

In order to learn more about the statistics collection and use of metrics for database performance improvement, let's review the fundamentals on metrics, base statistics, and statistics levels. We mentioned the use of metrics by the database in the section titled "Performance Management Using AWR" in Chapter 1.

Oracle Database 10g also collects another type of statistical data called sampled data using the Active Session History (ASH) sampling mechanism. ASH samples the current state of all active sessions into memory, which is viewed using V$ACTIVE_SESSION_HISTORY view. These samples are also written out of memory by AWR snapshot processing.

Types of Database Statistics

The important database statistics include the following:

- Wait events
- Time-model statistics
- System and session statistics
- Operating-system statistics

Wait Events

Wait events are statistics on server processes that wait for an event to complete before continuing processing. Examples of wait events include latch contention, buffer contention, and so on. The wait events are grouped into different classes (administrative, application, cluster, configuration, network, and so on) for easier analysis.

For analyzing wait-event statistics, use the following views:

- **V$ACTIVE_SESSION_HISTORY.** This shows active database session activity sampled every second.
- **V$SESSION_WAIT.** This shows resources or events for which active sessions are waiting.
- **V$SESSION.** This shows the same wait statistics as V$SESSION_WAIT along with session/connection information.
- **V$SESSION_EVENT.** This gives a summary of all the events the session has waited for since starting.
- **V$SESSION_WAIT_CLASS.** This gives the number of waits and the time spent in each class of wait events for every session.

- **V$SESSION_WAIT_HISTORY.** This shows the last 10 wait events for each active session.

- **V$SYSTEM_EVENT.** This gives a summary of all the event waits on the instance after start.

- **V$EVENT_HISTOGRAM.** This has a histogram of all waits, the maximum wait, and total wait time on an event basis.

- **V$FILE_HISTOGRAM.** This shows a histogram of times waited during single-block reads for each file.

- **V$TEMP_HISTOGRAM.** This has a histogram of wait times for single-block reads for each temporary file.

- **V$SYSTEM_WAIT_CLASS.** This gives time totals for the number of waits and the time spent in each class of wait events in the instance.

Time-Model Statistics

Each Oracle component has its own set of statistics. For analyzing the database as a whole, most Oracle advisors and reports compute statistics in reference to time as a common factor. The V$SESS_TIME_MODEL and V$SYS_TIME_MODEL views provide time-model statistics.

- **V$SESS_TIME_MODEL.** This contains time-model statistics including the total time spent in database calls at the session level. Time reported is microseconds.

- **V$SYS_TIME_MODEL.** This contains time-model statistics including the total time spent in database calls at the database level.

DB time is the most important statistic on the total time spent in database calls as a factor of instance workload. It is an aggregate of all CPU and wait times of all non-idle user sessions.

System and Session Statistics

Cumulative database statistics at the system and session level are available through the V$SYSSTAT and V$SESSTAT views. System statistics are available in the following views:

- **V$ACTIVE_SESSION_HISTORY.** This shows active database session activity sampled every second.

- **V$SYSSTAT.** This has overall statistics including rollback, physical I/O, logical I/O, and parse data.

- **V$FILESTAT.** This has detailed file I/O statistics for each file and average read time.

- **V$ROLLSTAT/V$UNDOSTAT.** These have details on rollback and undo segment statistics for each segment.

- **V$ENQUEUE_STAT.** This has enqueue-related statistics for each enqueue including the wait time and total number of waits.

- **V$LATCH.** This gives detailed latch usage statistics for each latch.

You will learn more about these views and their utilization with examples in Chapter 10, "Adopting a New Approach to Tuning."

Operating-System Statistics

Operating-system statistics give information about the usage and performance of hardware components and the operating system. OS statistics are comprised of CPU statistics, virtual-memory statistics, disk statistics, and network statistics. Using commonly available UNIX tools, you can measure the operating-system statistics as follows:

- CPU: `iostat, vmstat, mpstat, sar`

- Memory: `vmstat, sar`

- Disk: `iostat, sar`

- Network: `netstat`

Database Metrics Revisited

Base statistics represent the raw data that is collected from different database components. *Metrics* are the secondary statistical data, which are derived from base statistics. Oracle Database 10g has different metrics for session, system, file, and wait-event statistics.

Oracle defines metrics as a set of statistics for certain system attributes. These statistics are calculated and stored by the Automatic Workload Repository (AWR). Each metric has threshold values associated with them. *Thresholds* are the boundary values against which the metric values are compared. When a metric value reaches its threshold, an alert is generated. Alerts are also generated when a significant change is noted by the clearing of a previous alert, a change in availability of a monitored service, or when a specific error condition or database action occurs.

Most Oracle Database 10g metrics are used to track the rates of change of activities in the database, which in turn can be used for detailed performance analysis. They are used by the various internal components for monitoring system health, detecting problems, and self-tuning.

With metrics, the Oracle database has ready data availability for a component to compute the rate of change of activities. Until Oracle 9i, you had to run statistics before and after a database job to calculate the rate of change for base statistics. Using metrics, you can select these values directly after running the job.

> If you set values for any of the parameters—`DB_CACHE_ADVICE`, `TIMED_STATISTICS`, or `TIMED_OS_STATISTICS`—in the database initialization parameter file or by using `ALTER SYSTEM` or `ALTER SESSION` commands, the new value(s) will override any corresponding values derived from the `STATISTICS_LEVEL` parameter.

Statistics Levels and AWR Snapshots

You just learned that base statistics represent the raw data collected from different database components. The statistics levels are captured in the database by using the `STATISTICS_LEVEL` initialization parameter.

This parameter can take three values: BASIC, TYPICAL, or ALL. BASIC is the computation of AWR statistics; metrics are turned off. TYPICAL, which is the default value, collects only part of the statistics and represents values typically needed for Oracle Database 10g administration. Setting the STATISTICS_LEVEL parameter to ALL will collect all the database statistics.

We mentioned that Oracle database makes a snapshot of all its vital statistics and workload information and stores them in AWR. These snapshots are made every 60 minutes and stored in the AWR for a period of seven days by default. You can change the snapshot

> You will learn more details about the snapshots in the section "Customizing the AWR" in Chapter 11, "Effectively Using the Automatic Workload Repository."

frequency as well as data-retention period. The INTERVAL parameter determines the frequency of snapshot generation. The default interval is 60 minutes and the minimum value is 10 minutes. Setting the interval to 0 will disable the automatic capturing of snapshots and is therefore not recommended.

A *baseline* is uniquely defined on a pair of snapshots to tag data sets for important time periods. A baseline is usually identified by a user-created name or a system-generated identifier. You can also name a baseline manually by running the CREATE_BASELINE procedure with a name and a pair of snapshot identifiers. Each newly created baseline is assigned a baseline identifier, which is unique for the life of the database. Baselines are used to retain snapshot data for comparison with current system behavior and setting up threshold-based alerts. Creation and maintenance of baselines is discussed in Chapter 11 in the section titled "Performing Baselining."

We discussed in Chapter 1 that AWR gets the necessary statistics with the help of the MMON process. MMON writes the required statistics for AWR to disk on a regularly scheduled basis. MMON also purges all older snapshots (in chronological order) on a nightly basis to make room for new database statistics. All snapshots pertaining to baselines are retained until the baselines are removed. MMON performs this purge operation in the management window set by the DBA.

The MODIFY_SNAPSHOT_SETTINGS procedure is used to control the behavior of snapshots. The RETENTION parameter specifies the amount of AWR information retained by the database. The default data-retention period is

> More details on MODIFY_SNAPSHOT_SETTINGS procedure, AWR data retention, and AWR data purging are given in Chapter 11.

seven days (10080, for 24×7×60 minutes) and the minimum is one day. The space consumption depends mainly on the number of active sessions in the database. If the RETENTION parameter is set to 0, it will disable the automatic data purging. If AWR detects that the SYSAUX tablespace is out of space, it will automatically delete the oldest set of snapshots and reuse the space.

Creating and Dropping Snapshots and Baselines

The DBMS_WORKLOAD_REPOSITORY procedures are useful to manually create, drop, or modify the snapshots and baselines used by the ADDM. The database user should have DBA privileges to execute the procedures.

You can manually create a snapshot using the CREATE_SNAPSHOT option of the DBMS_WORKLOAD_REPOSITORY procedure. This procedure will capture statistics that are at times different from those from automatically generated snapshots. Similarly, you can drop a range of snapshots using the DROP_SNAPSHOT_RANGE procedure. This is discussed in greater detail in Chapter 11 under the sections "Accessing the AWR Snapshots" and "Using the SQL Interface to AWR."

You can also modify the interval, retention, and number of top SQL statements captured in a snapshot generation for a specified database. The INTERVAL parameter (in minutes) affects how often snapshots are automatically generated. The RETENTION parameter decides the tenure for snapshots in the workload repository.

TOPNSQL affects the number of top SQL to flush for every SQL criteria, such as elapsed time, CPU time, shareable memory, and so on. You can set this value to MAXIMUM and capture the complete set of SQL in the cursor cache at a higher operating cost of space and performance issues. A setting of MAXIMUM will usually collect a lot of data for a normally operating database. You can review the current settings on your database instance from the DBA_HIST_WR_CONTROL view.

The following code will set the snapshot retention period at 64800 minutes (45 days) with an interval at 60 minutes, and flushes the top 200 SQL.

```
BEGIN
DBMS_WORKLOAD_REPOSITORY.MODIFY_SNAPSHOT_SETTINGS(retention => 43200,  interval => 60,
 topnsql => 200, dbid => 2931102824);
END;
/
```

You will review the various operations with baselines now. You can create a baseline using the CREATE_BASELINE option of the DBMS_WORKLOAD_REPOSITORY procedure. A detailed discussion on baselines is given in Chapter 11 under "Capturing Baselines" and "Dropping Baselines." A list of existing snapshots can be found in the DBA_HIST_SNAPSHOT view. Choose the snap_id information and issue the following command to create a baseline.

```
BEGIN
    DBMS_WORKLOAD_REPOSITORY.CREATE_BASELINE (start_snap_id => 41, end_snap_id => 45,
        baseline_name => 'qa_test_bsln', dbid => 2931102824);
END;
/
```

The system will automatically assign a unique baseline_id to the new baseline created, which can be reviewed from the DBA_HIST_BASELINE.

```
select dbid, baseline_id, baseline_name, start_snap_id, end_snap_id
➥from dba_hist_baseline;
DBID            BASELINE_ID    BASELINE_NAME    START_SNAP_ID END_SNAP_ID
------------    -------------  ---------------- ------------- -----------
2931102824      1              qa_test_bsln     41            45
```

Similarly, you can drop the baseline along with or without its snapshots.

```
BEGIN
  DBMS_WORKLOAD_REPOSITORY.DROP_BASELINE (baseline_name => 'qa_test_bsln',
        cascade => TRUE, dbid => 2931102824);
END;
/
```

The value of TRUE for the cascade parameter indicates that the pair of snapshots associated with the baseline is also dropped. If you want to retain the snapshots, set the cascade parameter to FALSE. The dbid is for the optional database identifier.

Collecting and Analyzing Statistics

Until Oracle 9i, you could have used the COMPUTE STATISTICS option of the ANALYZE command to get faster statistics, especially for newly created indexes, which is not recommended in Oracle Database 10g. The COMPUTE and ESTIMATE clauses of the ANALYZE statement are still supported in Oracle Database 10g for backward compatibility. You may use the ANALYZE command to collect information on free list blocks and to list chained rows. From Oracle 8i, you also have the option of using the DBMS_STATS package to generate more accurate statistics than the legacy ANALYZE command. The DBMS_STATS package gathers statistics on tables, indexes, individual columns, and table partitions. You can even gather statistics on clustered tables with Oracle Database 10g Release 2, but not using Release 1. You can also use DBMS_STATS.GATHER_ DICTIONARY_STATS to gather statistics on system schemas.

In Oracle Database 10g, you can use optimizer statistics, which give details about the database and the objects in the database. These statistics are stored in several data dictionary views. You can query the following data dictionary views (DBA_*, USER_*, or ALL_*) to get more details on database objects:

- DBA_TABLES
- DBA_INDEXES
- DBA_OBJECT_TABLES
- DBA_TAB_STATISTICS
- DBA_IND_STATISTICS
- DBA_TAB_COL_STATISTICS
- DBA_TAB_HISTOGRAMS
- DBA_PART_HISTOGRAMS
- DBA_TAB_PARTITIONS
- DBA_TAB_SUBPARTITIONS
- DBA_IND_PARTITIONS

- DBA_IND_SUBPARTITIONS

- DBA_PART_COL_STATISTICS

- DBA_SUBPART_COL_STATISTICS

- DBA_SUBPART_HISTOGRAMS

- DBA_CLUSTERS

These optimizer statistics are automatically gathered with the GATHER_STATS_JOB job, created during database creation, on all objects in the database with missing statistics and stale statistics. This job is managed by the scheduler during the maintenance window. The default maintenance window runs from 10 p.m. to 6 a.m. every night and all day on weekends. The GATHER_STATS_JOB invokes the DBMS_STATS.GATHER_DATABASE_STATS_JOB_PROC procedure to collect statistics on database objects with no statistics or stale statistics.

> You will look at this topic in greater detail in Chapter 14 "Influencing the Cost Based Optimizer," and learn how these statistics affect the working of the optimizer.

Until Oracle 9i, you could automatically invoke DBMS_STATS to gather statistics for a table by using the MONITORING keyword with CREATE TABLE or ALTER TABLE statement. In Oracle Database 10g, MONITORING and NOMONITORING have been deprecated and table monitoring is controlled by the STATISTICS_LEVEL parameter. Monitoring is enabled when the parameter is set to TYPICAL and disabled with BASIC.

Preventing the Time Out of GATHER_STATS_JOB

Oracle Database 10g has a default maintenance window, where the optimizer statistics are automatically collected. If all the statistics have not been collected by the end of the maintenance window, the jobs can be cancelled or allowed to run until completion of the process. This is controlled by the STOP_ON_WINDOW_CLOSE parameter of the GATHER_STATS_JOB. The default setting for this paraneter is TRUE, which terminates the job not completed at the end of the maintenance window. A trace file is generated with an ORA-01013 error with a list of all objects that couldn't finish gathering statistics within the maintenance window. You can manually control this job using the catmwin.sql ($ORACLE_HOME/rdbms/admin/catmwin.sql) and editing the entry for DBMS_SCHEDULER.SET_ATTRIBUTE('GATHER_STATS_JOB'). You can also disable the automatic statistics collection using the following command.

```
EXECUTE DBMS_SCHEDULER.DISABLE('GATHER_STATS_JOB');
```

Cross-Checking Your Statistics and Ratios

Before you come to any conclusions by reviewing the performance data, you should cross-check it with other available evidence relating to the data. A classic example is the use of hit ratios like the buffer cache hit ratio and the latch hit ratio. These ratios should be used as indicators of database problems and not as final answers to solve your performance issues. You should look always for any other related evidence that causes deteriorating performance like increased number of users or running low on memory and so on. Also, when you are using computed statistics (rates or ratios), you should cross-check the computed statistic value with the actual statistic count.

When you use wait events with `TIMED_STATISTICS` set to `TRUE` at the instance level, you get data for comparing the total wait time for an event to the total elapsed time between the performance data collection periods. Look for how long the wait event occurred out of the total elapsed time and decide whether the wait time was a significant percentage of the total time. This methodology will help you to spend time on meaningful incidents rather than looking at all wait events. Also, the idle wait events are not useful and could be overlooked, because they indicate merely idle server processes.

AWR Reports Generation

The AWR has a reports-generation mechanism to produce summary reports based on database statistics stored in the AWR repository. This is very similar to `STATSPACK` in previous database versions. The analysis is done on statistics over a period of time. The reports are generated using the scripts (`awrrpt.sql`, `awrrpti.sql`, `awrsqrpt.sql`, and `awrsqrpi.sql`) in the `$ORACLE_HOME/rdbms/admin` directory. The database user should have DBA privileges to run these reports. All these reports can be generated as HTML pages or as text reports.

The `awrrpt.sql` shows all the AWR snapshots available and prompts you for options on how and where the reports are generated. The `awrrpti.sql` script displays the statistics for a range of snapshot IDs on a specified database and instance. The `awrddrpt.sql` script shows statistics of a particular SQL statement for a range of snapshot IDs. This report will help you to debug the performance of a SQL statement. The `awrddrpi.sql` script shows the statistics of a SQL statement for a range of snapshot IDs on a specified database and instance. We have used Oracle Database 10g Release 2 for the following four subsections involving AWR reports. The names of these scripts could change in future releases of Oracle.

Generating AWR Reports Using `awrrpt.sql`

The script `awrrpt.sql` produces two types of output: text format (like `STATSPACK` report, but from AWR repository) and the default HTML format (with hyperlinks). When you run the script, you will be prompted for the report format (text or HTML) as well as the report name. Entering the number of days will give the most recent snapshots for those days until the time the report was run. The output filename is the user-specified name given for the report.

In Listing 6.1 and in Figures 6.1 and 6.2, you will see how the `awrrpt.sql` is run and the report generated. If the report is created in HTML format, it can be viewed through any browser software. The code listing has been trimmed to conserve space.

LISTING 6.1   Running `awrrpt.sql`

```
Oracle Database 10g Enterprise Edition Release 10.2.0.0.0 - 64bit
With the Partitioning, OLAP and Data Mining options
```

Monitoring with Automatic Statistics Collection

LISTING 6.1 Continued
_____

```
SQL> @awrrpt.sql

Current Instance
~~~~~~~~~~~~~~~~~
   DB Id     DB Name     Inst Num Instance
 ..........  ...........  ........  ...........
  2931102824 Q0OR10G          1 Q0OR10G


Specify the Report Type
~~~~~~~~~~~~~~~~~~~~~~~~~
Would you like an HTML report, or a plain text report?
Enter 'html' for an HTML report, or 'text' for plain text
Defaults to 'html'
Type Specified:  html


Instances in this Workload Repository schema
~~~~~~~~~~~~~~~~~~~~~~~~~~~~~~~~~~~~~~~~~~~~~~

   DB Id     Inst Num DB Name     Instance     Host
 ..........  ........  ...........  ...........  ...........
* 2931102824      1 Q0OR10G      Q0OR10G      QLAB10G.US.ACME.COM


Using 2931102824 for database Id
Using           1 for instance number

Specify the number of days of snapshots to choose from
~~~~~~~~~~~~~~~~~~~~~~~~~~~~~~~~~~~~~~~~~~~~~~~~~~~~~~~~~~
Entering the number of days (n) will result in the most recent
(n) days of snapshots being listed.  Pressing <return> without
specifying a number lists all completed snapshots.


Enter value for num_days: 3
Listing the last 3 days of Completed Snapshots
                                                   Snap
Instance     DB Name      Snap Id   Snap Started    Level
...........  ...........  .........  ................  .....
Q0OR10G      Q0OR10G           8 21 Apr 2005 00:00     1
                               9 21 Apr 2005 01:00     1
                              10 21 Apr 2005 02:00     1
-----------------<Code Listing Truncated> ---------------
```

LISTING 6.1   Continued

```
                                29 21 Apr 2005 21:00      1
                                30 21 Apr 2005 22:00      1
------------------<Code Listing Truncated> ---------------

                                40 22 Apr 2005 08:00      1
                                41 22 Apr 2005 09:00      1
                                42 22 Apr 2005 10:00      1
                                43 22 Apr 2005 11:00      1
                                44 22 Apr 2005 12:00      1
                                45 22 Apr 2005 13:00      1
------------------<Code Listing Truncated> ---------------

                                68 23 Apr 2005 12:00      1
                                69 23 Apr 2005 13:00      1


Specify the Begin and End Snapshot Ids
~~~~~~~~~~~~~~~~~~~~~~~~~~~~~~~~~~~~~~~~~
Enter value for begin_snap: 41
Begin Snapshot Id specified: 41

Enter value for end_snap: 44
End    Snapshot Id specified: 44

Specify the Report Name
~~~~~~~~~~~~~~~~~~~~~~~~~
The default report file name is awrrpt_1_41_44.html.  To use this name,
press <return> to continue, otherwise enter an alternative.

Enter value for report_name: awrrpt_1_41_44_Q0.html

Using the report name awrrpt_1_41_44_Q0.html

-------<Pages of html code, truncated for saving space> -------
<P>
End of Report
</BODY></HTML>
Report written to awrrpt_1_41_44_Q0.html
SQL>
```

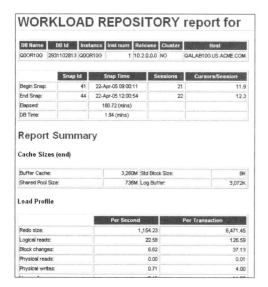

FIGURE 6.1 Summary page of the AWR report.

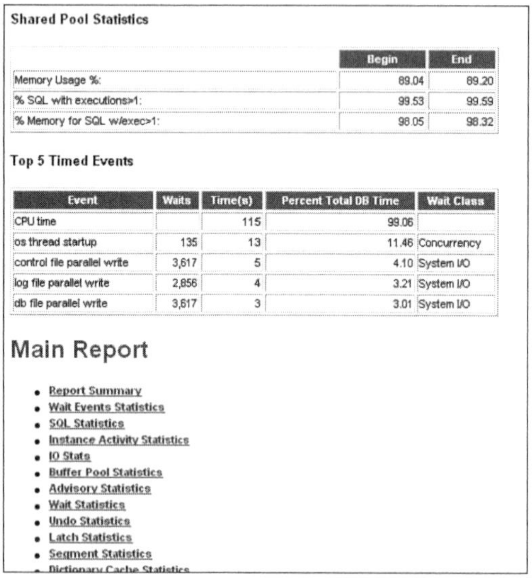

FIGURE 6.2 A sample list of statistics in an AWR report.

Listing 6.2 gives you the information on SNAP_ID and corresponding time spans for a 24-hour period. You can modify the query to include smaller or larger time frames and more details from the DBA_HIST_SNAPSHOT view.

LISTING 6.2 Selecting SNAP_IDs for a Time Period

```
SQL> select dbid, snap_id, begin_interval_time, end_interval_time from dba_hist_snapshot where
begin_interval_time > '22-APR-05 08:00' and end_interval_time < '23-APR-05 08:00';
```

LISTING 6.2   Continued

```
      DBID    SNAP_ID BEGIN_INTERVAL_TIME      END_INTERVAL_TIME
.......... .......... ........................ ........................
2931102824         42 22-APR-05 09.00.11.501 AM  22-APR-05 10.00.25.331 AM
2931102824         44 22-APR-05 11.00.41.051 AM  22-APR-05 12.00.54.901 PM
2931102824         47 22-APR-05 02.00.22.391 PM  22-APR-05 03.00.38.111 PM
2931102824         49 22-APR-05 04.00.51.951 PM  22-APR-05 05.01.05.811 PM
2931102824         50 22-APR-05 05.01.05.811 PM  22-APR-05 06.00.19.471 PM
2931102824         53 22-APR-05 08.00.49.071 PM  22-APR-05 09.01.02.901 PM
2931102824         59 23-APR-05 02.00.15.811 AM  23-APR-05 03.00.29.751 AM
2931102824         63 23-APR-05 06.00.13.201 AM  23-APR-05 07.00.27.101 AM
2931102824         43 22-APR-05 10.00.25.331 AM  22-APR-05 11.00.41.051 AM
2931102824         54 22-APR-05 09.01.02.901 PM  22-APR-05 10.00.18.451 PM
2931102824         58 23-APR-05 01.01.00.251 AM  23-APR-05 02.00.15.811 AM
2931102824         56 22-APR-05 11.00.32.441 PM  23-APR-05 12.00.46.331 AM
2931102824         62 23-APR-05 05.00.57.611 AM  23-APR-05 06.00.13.201 AM
2931102824         41 22-APR-05 08.00.57.851 AM  22-APR-05 09.00.11.501 AM
2931102824         45 22-APR-05 12.00.54.901 PM  22-APR-05 01.00.08.541 PM
2931102824         46 22-APR-05 01.00.08.541 PM  22-APR-05 02.00.22.391 PM
2931102824         48 22-APR-05 03.00.38.111 PM  22-APR-05 04.00.51.951 PM
2931102824         51 22-APR-05 06.00.19.471 PM  22-APR-05 07.00.35.211 PM
2931102824         52 22-APR-05 07.00.35.211 PM  22-APR-05 08.00.49.071 PM
2931102824         55 22-APR-05 10.00.18.451 PM  22-APR-05 11.00.32.441 PM
2931102824         57 23-APR-05 12.00.46.331 AM  23-APR-05 01.01.00.251 AM
2931102824         60 23-APR-05 03.00.29.751 AM  23-APR-05 04.00.43.691 AM
2931102824         61 23-APR-05 04.00.43.691 AM  23-APR-05 05.00.57.611 AM
```

23 rows selected.

Generating AWR Reports Using

`awrrpti.sql`

The `awrrpti.sql` script displays the statistics for a range of snapshot IDs on a specified database and instance, as shown in Listing 6.3 and in Figure 6.3. It produces two types of output: text format and the default HTML format (with hyperlinks).

Mapping `SNAP_ID` to Time for AWR Reports

If you prefer the hands-on approach, you can use the `DBA_HIST_SNAPSHOT` view to retrieve the mapping between `SNAP_ID` and the actual clock time. Query the `DBA_HIST_SNAPSHOT` against `begin_interval_time` and `end_interval_time` to determine which `SNAP_IDs` should be used. See Listing 6.2 for more details. You can also query the `SYS`-owned `WRM$SNAPSHOT` table to determine which `SNAP_IDs` to choose. The `begin_interval_time` and `end_interval_time` pair defines the time period over which the report is generated for both `DBA_HIST_SNAPSHOT` and `WRM$SNAPSHOT`.

LISTING 6.3 Using `awrrpti.sql`

```
SQL> @awrrpti.sql

Specify the Report Type
~~~~~~~~~~~~~~~~~~~~~~~~
Would you like an HTML report, or a plain text report?
Enter 'html' for an HTML report, or 'text' for plain text
Defaults to 'html'
Enter value for report_type: html
Type Specified:  html


Instances in this Workload Repository schema
~~~~~~~~~~~~~~~~~~~~~~~~~~~~~~~~~~~~~~~~~~~~~~~~~
   DB Id     Inst Num DB Name      Instance     Host
------------ -------- ------------ ------------ ------------
* 2931102824        1 Q00R10G      Q00R10G      QLAB10G.US.ACME.COM
Enter value for dbid: 2931102824
Using 2931102824 for database Id
Enter value for inst_num: 1
Using 1 for instance number


Specify the number of days of snapshots to choose from
~~~~~~~~~~~~~~~~~~~~~~~~~~~~~~~~~~~~~~~~~~~~~~~~~~~~~~~~~~~
Entering the number of days (n) will result in the most recent
(n) days of snapshots being listed.  Pressing <return> without
specifying a number lists all completed snapshots.


Enter value for num_days: 2
Listing the last 2 days of Completed Snapshots

                                                      Snap
Instance      DB Name      Snap Id   Snap Started     Level
------------ ------------ --------- ----------------- -----
Q00R10G      Q00R10G          128 26 Apr 2005 00:00      1
                              129 26 Apr 2005 01:00      1
------------------<Code Listing Truncated> ---------------
                              151 26 Apr 2005 23:00      1
                              152 27 Apr 2005 00:00      1
                              153 27 Apr 2005 01:00      1
                              154 27 Apr 2005 02:00      1
                              155 27 Apr 2005 03:00      1
                              156 27 Apr 2005 04:00      1
                              157 27 Apr 2005 05:00      1
                              158 27 Apr 2005 06:00      1
                              159 27 Apr 2005 07:00      1
```

LISTING 6.3   Continued

```
                           160 27 Apr 2005 08:00      1
                           161 27 Apr 2005 09:00      1
    -----------------<Code Listing Truncated> ----------------
                           172 27 Apr 2005 20:00      1


Specify the Begin and End Snapshot Ids
~~~~~~~~~~~~~~~~~~~~~~~~~~~~~~~~~~~~~~~~
Enter value for begin_snap: 152
Begin Snapshot Id specified: 152


Enter value for end_snap: 160
End   Snapshot Id specified: 160


Specify the Report Name
~~~~~~~~~~~~~~~~~~~~~~~~
The default report file name is awrrpt_1_152_160.html.  To use this name,
press <return> to continue, otherwise enter an alternative.


Enter value for report_name:awrrpt_1_152_160_Q0.html
Using the report awrrpt_1_152_160_Q0.html
....


</BODY></HTML>
Report written to awrrpt_1_152_160_Q0.html
SQL>
```

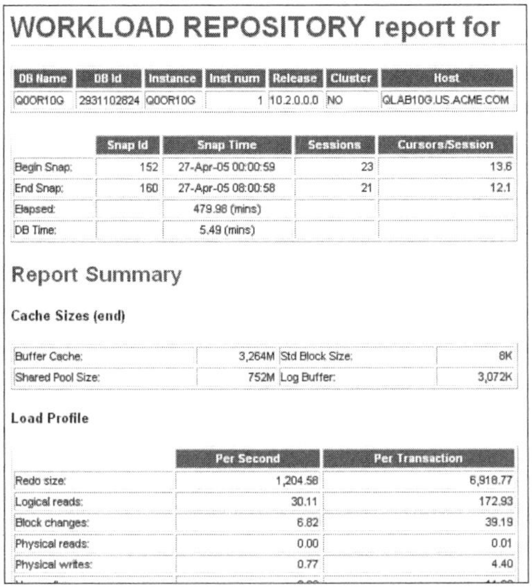

WORKLOAD REPOSITORY report for

DB Name	DB Id	Instance	Inst num	Release	Cluster	Host
QOOR10G	2931102824	QOOR10G	1	10.2.0.0.0	NO	QLAB10G.US.ACME.COM

	Snap Id	Snap Time	Sessions	Cursors/Session
Begin Snap:	152	27-Apr-05 00:00:59	23	13.6
End Snap:	160	27-Apr-05 08:00:58	21	12.1
Elapsed:		479.98 (mins)		
DB Time:		5.49 (mins)		

Report Summary

Cache Sizes (end)

Buffer Cache:		3,264M	Std Block Size:		8K
Shared Pool Size:		752M	Log Buffer:		3,072K

Load Profile

	Per Second	Per Transaction
Redo size:	1,204.58	6,918.77
Logical reads:	30.11	172.93
Block changes:	6.82	39.19
Physical reads:	0.00	0.01
Physical writes:	0.77	4.40

FIGURE 6.3   Summary page of the AWR
Snapshot Statistics report.

Monitoring with Automatic Statistics Collection

Generating AWR Reports Using awrddrpt.sql

The awrddrpt.sql displays the statistics of a particular SQL statement for a range of snap-shot IDs. This report (in text format and in the default HTML format) will help you to debug the performance of a SQL statement. In Listing 6.4 and in Figure 6.4, you will see how the awrddrpt.sql is run and the report that is generated.

LISTING 6.4   Using awrddrpt.sql

```
SQL> @awrddrpt.sql
Current Instance
~~~~~~~~~~~~~~~~


   DB Id       DB Id     DB Name     Inst Num Inst Num Instance
----------- ----------- ----------- -------- -------- -----------
 2931102824  2931102824 Q00R10G            1        1 Q00R10G


Specify the Report Type
~~~~~~~~~~~~~~~~~~~~~~~~~
Would you like an HTML report, or a plain text report?
Enter 'html' for an HTML report, or 'text' for plain text
Defaults to 'html'
Enter value for report_type: html


Type Specified:  html
Instances in this Workload Repository schema
~~~~~~~~~~~~~~~~~~~~~~~~~~~~~~~~~~~~~~~~~~~~~~~


   DB Id     Inst Num DB Name     Instance     Host
----------- -------- ----------- ----------- -----------
* 2931102824        1 Q00R10G      Q00R10G     QLAB10G.US.ACME.COM


Database Id and Instance Number for the First Pair of Snapshots
~~~~~~~~~~~~~~~~~~~~~~~~~~~~~~~~~~~~~~~~~~~~~~~~~~~~~~~~~~~~~~~~~~~
Using 2931102824 for Database Id for the first pair of snapshots
Using          1 for Instance Number for the first pair of snapshots
Specify the number of days of snapshots to choose from
~~~~~~~~~~~~~~~~~~~~~~~~~~~~~~~~~~~~~~~~~~~~~~~~~~~~~~~~~
Entering the number of days (n) will result in the most recent
(n) days of snapshots being listed.  Pressing <return> without
specifying a number lists all completed snapshots.


Enter value for num_days: 1
Listing the last day's Completed Snapshots
                                                     Snap
Instance     DB Name         Snap Id    Snap Started    Level
----------- ----------- --------- ------------------- ------
```

LISTING 6.4   Continued

```
Q0OR10G      Q0OR10G           152 27 Apr 2005 00:00      1
                               153 27 Apr 2005 01:00        1
          ------------------<Code Listing Truncated> ---------------
                               172 27 Apr 2005 20:00      1


Specify the First Pair of Begin and End Snapshot Ids
~~~~~~~~~~~~~~~~~~~~~~~~~~~~~~~~~~~~~~~~~~~~~~~~~~~~~~~
Enter value for begin_snap: 168
First Begin Snapshot Id specified: 168
Enter value for end_snap: 170
First End   Snapshot Id specified: 170
Instances in this Workload Repository schema
~~~~~~~~~~~~~~~~~~~~~~~~~~~~~~~~~~~~~~~~~~~~~~~~
   DB Id    Inst Num DB Name     Instance     Host
----------- -------- ----------- ------------ -----------
* 2931102824      1 Q0OR10G      Q0OR10G      QLAB10G.US.ACME.COM




Database Id and Instance Number for the Second Pair of Snapshots
~~~~~~~~~~~~~~~~~~~~~~~~~~~~~~~~~~~~~~~~~~~~~~~~~~~~~~~~~~~~~~~~~~~~

Using 2931102824 for Database Id for the second pair of snapshots
Using          1 for Instance Number for the second pair of snapshots

Specify the number of days of snapshots to choose from
~~~~~~~~~~~~~~~~~~~~~~~~~~~~~~~~~~~~~~~~~~~~~~~~~~~~~~~~~~
Entering the number of days (n) will result in the most recent
(n) days of snapshots being listed.  Pressing <return> without
specifying a number lists all completed snapshots.

Enter value for num_days2: 1
Listing the last day's Completed Snapshots
                                                   Snap
Instance     DB Name        Snap Id    Snap Started    Level
----------- ------------ --------- ---------------- -----
Q0OR10G      Q0OR10G           152 27 Apr 2005 00:00      1
                               153 27 Apr 2005 01:00        1

         ------------------<Code Listing Truncated> ---------------
                               172 27 Apr 2005 20:00      1
```

LISTING 6.4   Continued

```
Specify the Second Pair of Begin and End Snapshot Ids
~~~~~~~~~~~~~~~~~~~~~~~~~~~~~~~~~~~~~~~~~~~~~~~~~~~~~~~~
Enter value for begin_snap2: 152
Second Begin Snapshot Id specified: 152

Enter value for end_snap2: 154
Second End   Snapshot Id specified: 154

Specify the Report Name
~~~~~~~~~~~~~~~~~~~~~~~~~
The default report file name is awrdiff_1_168_1_152.html  To use this name,
press <return> to continue, otherwise enter an alternative.

Enter value for report_name:
press <return> to continue, otherwise enter an alternative.

Enter value for report_name: awrdiff_1_168_1_152.html

Using the report name awrdiff_1_168_1_152.html
------------------<Listing Truncated> ----------------
Report written to awrdiff_1_168_1_152.html
SQL>
```

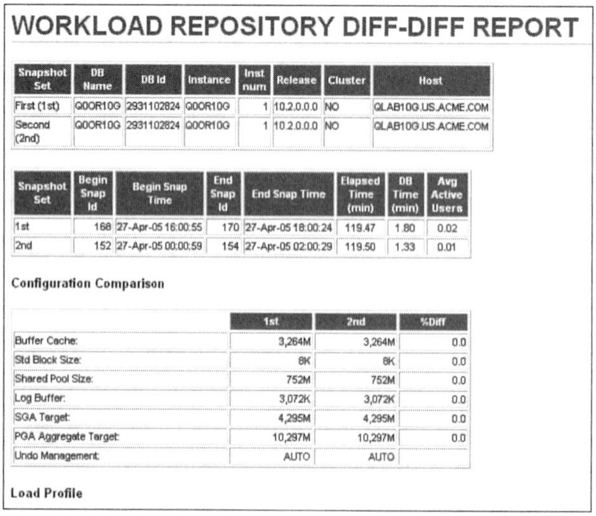

WORKLOAD REPOSITORY DIFF-DIFF REPORT

Snapshot Set	DB Name	DB Id	Instance	Inst num	Release	Cluster	Host
First (1st)	Q00R10G	2931102824	Q00R10G	1	10.2.0.0.0	NO	QLAB10G.US.ACME.COM
Second (2nd)	Q00R10G	2931102824	Q00R10G	1	10.2.0.0.0	NO	QLAB10G.US.ACME.COM

Snapshot Set	Begin Snap Id	Begin Snap Time	End Snap Id	End Snap Time	Elapsed Time (min)	DB Time (min)	Avg Active Users
1st	168	27-Apr-05 16:00:55	170	27-Apr-05 18:00:24	119.47	1.80	0.02
2nd	152	27-Apr-05 00:00:59	154	27-Apr-05 02:00:29	119.50	1.33	0.01

Configuration Comparison

	1st	2nd	%Diff
Buffer Cache:	3,264M	3,264M	0.0
Std Block Size:	8K	8K	0.0
Shared Pool Size:	752M	752M	0.0
Log Buffer:	3,072K	3,072K	0.0
SGA Target:	4,295M	4,295M	0.0
PGA Aggregate Target:	10,297M	10,297M	0.0
Undo Management:	AUTO	AUTO	

Load Profile

FIGURE 6.4
AWR report: awrddrpt.sql.

Generating AWR Reports Using awrddrpi.sql

The awrsqrpi.sql script shows the statistics of SQL statement execution for a range of snapshot IDs on a specified database and instance. This report also comes in both text format and HTML format. Execution is similar to awrddrpt.sql; for this reason, only the differences in code execution are shown in Listing 6.5. See Figure 6.5 for the opening page of the report, but realize that the report spans several pages because the other AWR scripts are displayed here completely. You could choose different databases to compare the same script execution, instead of the same database as in Listing 6.5.

LISTING 6.5   Using awrddrpi.sql

```
SQL> @awrddrpi.sql


------------------<Listing Truncated> ----------------
Instances in this Workload Repository schema
~~~~~~~~~~~~~~~~~~~~~~~~~~~~~~~~~~~~~~~~~~~~~~~


   DB Id     Inst Num DB Name     Instance     Host
----------- -------- ----------- ----------- -----------
* 2931102824       1 Q00R10G      Q00R10G      QLAB10G.US.ACME.COM


Database Id and Instance Number for the First Pair of Snapshots
~~~~~~~~~~~~~~~~~~~~~~~~~~~~~~~~~~~~~~~~~~~~~~~~~~~~~~~~~~~~~~~~~~~
Enter value for dbid: 2931102824
Using 2931102824 for Database Id for the first pair of snapshots
Enter value for inst_num: 1
Using 1 for Instance Number for the first pair of snapshots


Specify the number of days of snapshots to choose from
------------------<Listing Truncated> ----------------


Specify the First Pair of Begin and End Snapshot Ids
~~~~~~~~~~~~~~~~~~~~~~~~~~~~~~~~~~~~~~~~~~~~~~~~~~~~~~~
Enter value for begin_snap: 162
First Begin Snapshot Id specified: 162


Enter value for end_snap: 164
First End   Snapshot Id specified: 164


Instances in this Workload Repository schema
~~~~~~~~~~~~~~~~~~~~~~~~~~~~~~~~~~~~~~~~~~~~~~~
```

LISTING 6.5 Continued

```
    DB Id    Inst Num DB Name      Instance     Host
............ ........ ............ ............ ............
* 2931102824        1 Q00R10G      Q00R10G      QLAB10G.US.ACME.COM


Database Id and Instance Number for the Second Pair of Snapshots
~~~~~~~~~~~~~~~~~~~~~~~~~~~~~~~~~~~~~~~~~~~~~~~~~~~~~~~~~~~~~~~~~


Enter value for dbid2: 2931102824
Using 2931102824 for Database Id for the second pair of snapshots
Enter value for inst_num2: 1
Using 1 for Instance Number for the second pair of snapshots


Specify the number of days of snapshots to choose from
------------------<Listing Truncated> ----------------
Enter value for num_days2: 1
Listing the last day's Completed Snapshots

                                                    Snap
Instance     DB Name      Snap Id   Snap Started    Level
............ ............ ......... ................ ......
Q00R10G      Q00R10G          152 27 Apr 2005 00:00    1
------------------<Listing Truncated> ----------------
                              172 27 Apr 2005 20:00    1


Specify the Second Pair of Begin and End Snapshot Ids
Enter value for begin_snap2: 170
Second Begin Snapshot Id specified: 170
Enter value for end_snap2: 172


Specify the Report Name
~~~~~~~~~~~~~~~~~~~~~~~~
------------------<Listing Truncated> ----------------
Enter value for report_name: awrdiff_1_162_1_170.html


Report written to awrdiff_1_162_1_170.html
SQL>
```

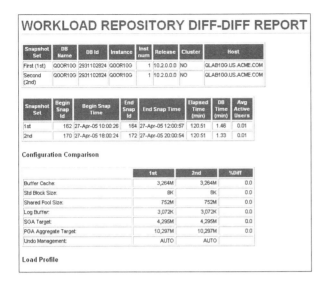

FIGURE 6.5
AWR report: `awrddrpi.sql`.

Metrics Monitoring and Customization

Oracle Database 10g metrics are tracked using AWR. Each metric has threshold values associated with them. Whenever a metric value reaches its threshold, an alert is generated. Alerts are also generated when a previous alert is cleared, when a change in the availability of a monitored service occurs, or when a specific error condition or database action occurs. MMON wakes up every minute to check the metric values. For metrics with thresholds, MMON verifies those values and generates alerts as needed.

The database-usage metrics are divided into two broad categories: database feature usage and high water–mark (HWM) value of certain database attributes. These metrics are useful for getting an idea of any resource usage within the database and for determining how often a particular feature is used. MMON tracks and records both these usage metrics on a weekly basis. The tracking is based on a sampling mechanism of the data dictionary. These statistics are recorded in AWR snapshots and can be viewed with queries on `DBA_FEATURE_USAGE_STATISTICS` and `DBA_HIGH_WATER_MARK_STATISTICS`. The OEM can also be used to view the recorded statistics. The following query is just a sample code for listing the currently used database features:

```
select  dbid,  name,  sample_interval, first_usage_date, last_usage_date from
dba_feature_usage_statistics where currently_used='TRUE';
```

Oracle Enterprise Manager can be used to view and customize the threshold values for metrics with the following steps:

1. Start Oracle Enterprise Manager and connect to the target database.

2. On the database Home page, click the Manage Metrics link at the bottom.

3. On the Thresholds page, click the Edit Thresholds link.

4. On the Edit Thresholds page, shown in Figure 6.6, select the metric to be customized and edit its values. Add entries in the Response Action field, if any.

5. Click OK to save the changes made to the metrics.

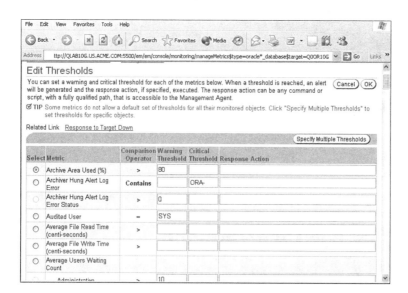

FIGURE 6.6
Using the OEM to customize threshold values for metrics.

Using Database Alerts with Metrics

Oracle Database 10g helps to reduce the time spent by the DBA on routine database-monitoring tasks by automatically sending messages with information about performance or resources-allocation issues and suggesting remedial actions.

A *server-generated alert* from the Oracle Database 10g server is a perfect example of a notification message about an impending problem. This message contains details about the error/alert condition and may contain recommendations for fixing the problem. Server-based alerts can also be based on threshold levels of different metrics, as explained earlier in this chapter.

MMON schedules the database-monitoring actions as explained earlier in this chapter. If the database detects any unusual conditions, it invokes the MMON to take immediate action and sends an alert. Along with the database alerts, many database components perform self-tuning on their own by using the history of metric values in the AWR. OEM used to collect many of these alerts in earlier editions. OEM alerts differ from server-generated alerts in that metrics computation and threshold validations are done by the Oracle Database 10g and not by the OEM agent.

There are two kinds of server generated alerts:

- **Threshold alerts.** These are database alerts based on threshold levels and can be triggered at warning and critical levels. These threshold levels can be set internally or by the customer, or can be customer-altered from preset values. These threshold alerts are also known as *stateful alerts*, which are automatically cleared when the alert condition is fixed. Stateful alerts are stored in DBA_OUTSTANDING_ALERTS and moved to DBA_ALERT_HISTORY when cleared. The DBA_ALERT_HISTORY view has the same structure as DBA_OUTSTANDING_ALERTS, except for the last column (RESOLUTION).

> There are 161 metrics with definable threshold values, such as physical reads per second, user commits per second, and so on in Oracle Database 10g Release 1. For Oracle Database 10g Release 2, the number of metrics with definable threshold values has increased to around 170.

- **Non-threshold alerts.** Also called *stateless alerts*, these are written directly to the DBA_ALERT_HISTORY. An example of a common non-threshold alert is "resumable session has been suspended." OEM stores these stateless alerts in its own repository; hence, clearing of these alerts makes sense only in the OEM environment.

Whenever an alert is generated, it is sent to a predefined persistence queue called alert_que (owned by SYS). OEM reads this queue and provides notifications on outstanding alerts along with suggestions for any corrective actions. These alerts are displayed on the OEM console. As discussed in Chapter 3, "Customizing Installation Options," in the section titled "Setup, Response, and Clearing of Alerts," OEM can send these messages to pager numbers or to email addresses. If the alert cannot be written to the alert_que, Oracle will record a message about the alert to the database alert log.

> **Sending Alerts to Third-Party Tools**
>
> You can get alerts pushed to a third-party tool or your own paging software by subscribing to alert_que with the DBMS_AQADM.ADD_SUBSCRIBER procedure. For this, associate a database user with the subscribing agent using the ENABLE_DB_ACCESS procedure. An asynchronous notification can also be received by enqueing alerts using alert_que. To get enqueue notifications through email or HTTP posts, you should configure the database server through dbms_aqelm with mail server or proxy server information. Subscribers have to denqueue the message metadata to get the alert content.

Making the Most of Metrics and Statistics Collection

> If your databases have weekly workload cycles, like major batch jobs during the weekend, you can use the default AWR retention period of seven days.

Your database should have enough data to provide accurate and valid results with Automatic Database Diagnostic Monitor, SQL Tuning Advisor, SQL Access Advisor, Undo Advisor, and Segment Advisor. So Oracle recommends that you set a larger AWR retention period to capture at least one complete workload cycle, which could be over a month for most companies.

You can also manually gather statistics depending on your application needs. For a read-only database with incremental table updates, you may elect to gather new statistics every week or fortnight or even once a month. You can use a script or job-scheduling tool to run the GATHER_SCHEMA_STATS and GATHER_DATABASE_STATS procedures.

For bulk-load OLTP applications where tables are updated in batch cycles, you should gather statistics as part of the batch job after the data load. For partitioned tables, you may choose to gather statistics only on affected partitions rather than on entire tables.

Oracle also recommends that automatic snapshot collection should not be turned off unless absolutely necessary under exceptional circumstances. You will not be able to manually create snapshots when the snapshot interval is set to 0. When the automatic snapshot collection is turned off, automatic collection of the workload and statistical data is stopped and the self-management functionality is mostly disabled.

The baselines will help you to compare database workloads when you have performance problems, so it is very important for the DBA to create baselines for typical performance periods.

Statistics Collection During Database Upgrades

See MetaLink Note #263809.1 for the scripts to collect statistics during database upgrades. Make sure that you test the scripts in a QA environment before trying them in production databases.

When you are upgrading an older version of an Oracle database to Oracle Database 10g, the optimizer statistics will be calculated for those dictionary tables that lack statistics. The statistics collection will be time-consuming and proportional to the number of dictionary tables whose statistics are lacking or have changed during the upgrade process. When you upgrade from Oracle 9i, you can decrease the database downtime by collecting statistics for the dictionary tables prior to the upgrade.

New Features in Oracle Database 10g Release 2

You can do online redefinition on clustered tables, MV logs, advanced queuing tables, and still preserve database statistics in Release 2. With this feature of preserving statistics, table analysis after reorganization is not needed, thereby improving the application availability. Also, the V$SQLSTATS view has been added to improve performance.

In previous Oracle releases, lock statistics would lock the statistics based on table usage in the application. This meant that you could not get to any statistics including table statistics, column statistics, histograms, and statistics on all the dependent indexes. Also, the database server provided the lock and unlock feature in the optimizer statistic area. In Oracle Database 10g Release 2, you can lock the statistics for a full volatile table and unlock for an empty table using the locking wizard.

You can restore the statistics of the database and related objects to a specified timestamp in the past within the AWR retention period using the OEM Restore Statistics wizard. (In the OEM, click Maintenance, and then click Manage Optimizer Statistics.) See the Operations section of Figure 6.7 for details.

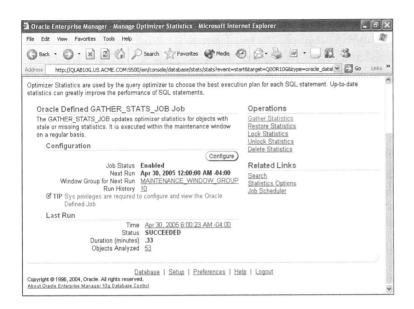

FIGURE 6.7
The Restore Statistics wizard in the OEM.

You can also gather statistics for fixed and dictionary objects in the optimizer statistic area using the OEM Gather Statistics wizard. (In the OEM, click Maintenance, and then click Manage Optimizer Statistics.) See Figure 6.8 for details.

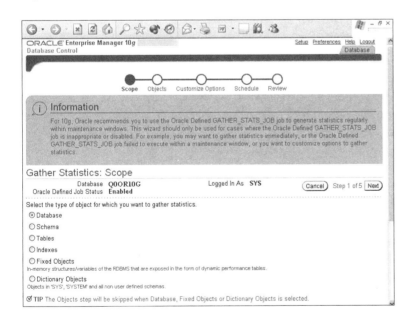

FIGURE 6.8
The Gather Statistics wizard in the OEM.

A time out feature has been introduced to flush SQL statistics every five seconds for a running SQL statement. When running, this feature will keep the SQL statistics current at all times.

For earlier releases of Oracle, DBAs using the OEM to check the status of the database would be running SQL calls to collect performance statistics. If the database was hung or running slowly, these SQL calls would further deteriorate the database performance. In Release 2, the OEM can collect key performance statistics of the database without making SQL queries. The OEM attaches to the SGA directly, reads statistics from the shared memory, and populates the database performance screens.

Summary

This chapter covered the automatic statistics collection feature of Oracle Database 10g. It also reviewed how to collect statistics for various database needs and how to use the various AWR reports for analysis. It discussed the statistics collection before and after database upgrades to Oracle Database 10g and the differences between database versions. The next chapter further explores using automatic undo management and the Undo Advisor.

7

Managing Automatic Undo

IN THIS CHAPTER

Using Automatic Undo Management	131
Redo Log File Sizings	134
Using Undo Advisor	134
Guaranteeing Undo Availability	137
Undo Tips from the Trenches	138
Automatic Undo Management Improvements in Release 2	139

Using Automatic Undo Management

Oracle introduced automatic undo management in Oracle 9i. This feature has been significantly improved in Oracle Database 10g; in addition, the Undo Advisor tool has been introduced. To run your database in automatic undo management mode, you should set the UNDO_MANAGEMENT initialization parameter to AUTO.

Oracle makes a copy of the original data in the database before modifying it. This is helpful if you ever wish to roll back any database changes. Oracle writes these change vectors to undo the operation. The original copy of the data before any modification is called the *undo data*. This undo data is stored in an undo tablespace. The automatic undo management feature automatically determines the retention period for undo data after committing a transaction, based on the queries against the database. Within this retention or preservation period, the undo data is in an unexpired state. Oracle retains the undo data in the unexpired state for as long as needed by currently running queries or by the undo retention threshold (whichever is the higher-value duration of the two). When Oracle crosses this time limit, the undo data changes its status to the expired state.

> AUTO EXTEND **should be turned on for undo tablespace, per Oracle recommendations. This is the best choice for undo sizing compared to manual sizing of the undo tablespace.**

> **Deprecated Oracle Initialization Parameters Related to Undo Management**
>
> Oracle 9i had a set of initialization parameters that are deprecated in the Oracle Database 10g. Some of these parameters related to undo (for example, MAX_ROLLBACK_SEGMENT, ROW_LOCKING, UNDO_SUPPRESS_ERRORS, SERIALIZABLE, and TRANSACTION_AUDITING) have been eliminated in Oracle Database 10g because they are automatically calculated instead of manually sized.

Under normal operations, undo data can be overwritten only when it is in the expired state. When the undo tablespace has inadequate free space (or expired space) to keep active undo data from current transactions, Oracle will be forced to overwrite the unexpired undo data. This could cause your queries to fail. For this reason, Oracle recommends that you either enable AUTO EXTEND ON for the undo tablespace or have a sufficiently large tablespace for any kind of transactions.

If you are unable to use auto extension to confine the undo tablespace size to certain limits, use the Undo Advisor provided by Oracle to get the optimal size. This is discussed later in this chapter in the section "Making the Most of Undo Advisor." In Oracle Database 10g Release 2, Undo Advisor calculates the optimum undo tablespace size as the maximum of the auto-tuned value of undo retention and the low threshold value.

How Undo Data Helps the Database

When you install Oracle Database 10g, Oracle automatically enables auto-tuning of the undo-retention period along with the database-creation process. This will help you to start building the database without tuning undo.

Undo data keeps changes made to the database by transactions for a certain time period or as long as the undo data remains in an unexpired state. Undo is used to reverse any uncommitted changes made to the database in the event you ever have to roll back an operation. It also provides read consistency for the database user while uncommitted changes could be occurring against the database records. Undo also helps to enable database flashback features (such as flashback query) to view or recover data from a prior time period.

The undo data has to be saved at least until the database transaction has been committed. This time is determined by the UNDO_RETENTION parameter. The undo tablespace should be large enough to hold the active undo data generated by the longest-running transactions in your database. Otherwise, your long-running transactions could fail. After the transaction has been committed, the undo data should not be immediately overwritten. This is important because flashback features rely on this data to work.

The Significance of the `UNDO_RETENTION` **Parameter**

With auto–undo tuning enabled, the `UNDO_RETENTION` parameter is set to 0. If the DBA wants to control this parameter and use a value other than 0, automatic-tuning functionality will not work.

Oracle Database 10g has an option to guarantee undo retention. When this option is enabled, the database never overwrites unexpired undo data (that is, undo data within the undo retention period). You can enable the guarantee option by specifying the `RETENTION GUARANTEE` clause for the undo tablespace when it is created (in the `CREATE DATABASE` or `CREATE UNDO TABLESPACE` statement) or at a later period using the `ALTER TABLESPACE` statement.

The `UNDO_RETENTION` parameter is valid only if the current undo tablespace has sufficient space. When an active transaction looks for undo space and cannot find enough space in the undo tablespace, the system will start reusing unexpired undo space as follows. It may even generate an error during SQL execution.

When more space is needed, Oracle allocates a new extent from the undo tablespace. If there are no free extents and the tablespace cannot autoextend, then Oracle tries to get an expired extent from another undo segment. If there are no extents with expired status, then Oracle will try to reuse an unexpired extent from the current undo segment. If that fails, it tries to get an unexpired extent from another undo segment. If all these attempts fail, Oracle reports an "out-of-space" error, causing queries to fail with ORA-01555.

Resumable Space Allocation

Oracle introduced a resumable space allocation feature in Oracle 9i to suspend and later restart the execution of large database operations during space-allocation failures. This enables you to take corrective action without the server returning an error to the database user. After the error condition is corrected, the suspended database operation automatically resumes. This feature can be used in tandem with automatic undo management.

Resumable space allocation was introduced in Oracle 9i for all database tablespaces at the session level. When the database encounters an out-of-space condition, all database operations are suspended. These suspended operations automatically resume after the error condition disappears or is cleared. In Oracle Database 10g, this feature can be enabled at the instance level. You can set up automatic alert notifications to be sent when an operation is suspended, as discussed in Chapter 6, "Monitoring with Automatic Statistics Collection," in the section "Using Database Alerts with Metrics."

When resumable space allocation mode is enabled, you can specify a timeout period using the `RESUMABLE_TIMEOUT` parameter, after which the suspended statement will error if no DBA intervention has taken place. The following code sets the timeout at 1,800 seconds, or 30 minutes.

```
SQL> ALTER SYSTEM SET RESUMABLE_TIMEOUT = 1800;
System altered.
```

The `RESUMABLE_TIMEOUT` parameter retains the value until it is changed by another `ALTER SESSION ENABLE RESUMABLE` statement or until the session ends. The default timeout interval is 7,200 seconds.

Undo Management in Real Application Clusters

In Oracle RAC, Oracle manages undo segments within a specific undo tablespace allotted to the instance. An instance can use segments assigned to its undo tablespace only. But all RAC instances can read all undo blocks in the cluster environment for consistent read purposes. Similarly, any instance can update any undo tablespace during transaction recovery not used by any other instance. All instances of a RAC database must operate in the same undo mode. That is, you cannot deploy automatic undo management and manual undo management in a RAC database.

Redo Log File Sizings

The size of the redo log files influences performance because the database writer and archiver processes depend on the redo log sizes. Larger redo log files tend to provide better performance along with appropriate expected recovery time. If the redo log files are small, they increase checkpoint activity and increase CPU usage. Smaller redo logs lessen the performance, because during log switching, all operations are frozen in the database and all sessions may wait for log switch completion.

Checkpoint frequency is influenced by log-file size and by the FAST_START_MTTR_TARGET parameter, among several factors. If the FAST_START_MTTR_TARGET parameter is set to limit the instance recovery time, Oracle automatically tries to checkpoint as frequently as necessary. Under this condition, the log files should be large enough to avoid additional checkpointing due to smaller log files.

The redo log file size can be tuned using recommendations mentioned in the OPTIMAL_LOGFILE_SIZE column of V$INSTANCE_RECOVERY. If the FAST_START_MTTR_TARGET has such a small value to do a recovery within its usual time frame, then the TARGET_MTTR field of V$INSTANCE_RECOVERY contains the effective MTTR target value, which is larger than FAST_START_MTTR_TARGET. If FAST_START_MTTR_TARGET is set to such a high value to make recovery possible in a very bad database crash, then TARGET_MTTR contains the estimated MTTR value for the worst-case scenarios.

Using Undo Advisor

Undo Advisor helps you to size the undo tablespace based on the workload history. By default, automatic undo retention tuning is enabled, and Oracle determines the optimal undo retention time depending on the undo tablespace size. Oracle Database 10g remembers these optimal undo settings and avoids any performance problems during instance restart, database migration, undo tablespace switching, and so on. After a database restart or undo tablespace switch, Oracle Database 10g determines the number of undo segments to be placed online based on data stored in the AWR. The Undo Advisor analyzes the undo usage over a period of time and suggests the optimal undo tablespace size to support the longest-running queries. Altering the collection interval and retention period for AWR statistics as explained in Chapter 6 can affect the precision and recommendations given by the Undo Advisor.

The V$UNDOSTAT view has the necessary statistics for monitoring and tuning undo space. Oracle utilizes these statistics to tune undo usage in the system. Using this view, you also can get a better estimate of the amount of undo space required for the current workload. The DBA_HIST_UNDOSTAT view contains statistical snapshots of V$UNDOSTAT information. The V$ROLLSTAT view has information about the behavior of undo segments in the undo tablespace. The V$TRANSACTION view has undo segment information, while the DBA_UNDO_EXTENTS gives the status and size of each extent in the undo tablespace.

You can use a fixed-size undo tablespace or a tablespace with auto-extensible on. If you choose a fixed-size undo tablespace, use the Undo Advisor to estimate the needed sizing. Undo Advisor can be invoked through Oracle Enterprise Manager or through the DBMS_ADVISOR PL/SQL package. OEM is the preferred method for accessing the Undo Advisor.

> Undo Advisor will not give any useful informa-
> tion unless the database has been up and
> running for a long enough time to gather
> sufficient statistics.

Undo Management Using OEM

To manage undo space using Oracle Enterprise Manager, click the Advisor Central link in the Database Instance page. Then click the Undo Management link in the Advisor Central page. See Figure 7.1 for details.

FIGURE 7.1
Undo management from the OEM.

In addition to an Undo Advisor button, which you can click to access the Undo Advisor, the Undo Management page includes the following sections:

- **Configuration.** The Configuration section displays details about the auto-tuned undo retention period, the minimum undo retention period, and the name and size of the undo tablespace. It also shows whether the undo tablespace has the auto-extensible feature enabled. With the auto-extensible feature enabled, Oracle automatically increases the size of the undo tablespace with space needs. Using the auto-extensible feature along with auto-tuned undo retention, the DBA can provide enough undo space for longest-running queries and ensure the successful completion of batch cycles. When the auto-extensible feature is disabled, you must manually extend the undo tablespace as needed. If you get an undo tablespace alert (warning or critical), or if you get alerts such as "query too long" or "snapshot too old," use the Undo Advisor to get recommendations and make changes to the sizing.

■ **Recommendations.** Using the Recommendations section, the DBA can choose a time period and ask Oracle for system-activity analysis. If there are any problems or any recommendations for the current undo configuration, they will be displayed here. You can update the analysis by clicking the Update Analysis button.

■ **System Activity and Tablespace Usage.** This section shows the longest-running query and a graphical depiction of both undo tablespace usage and undo generation rates.

Making the Most of Undo Advisor

Click the Undo Advisor button to get undo recommendations. Under the Advisor section, you can choose a new undo retention time and new undo retention periods. The Analysis section shows all the database-analysis results of your undo setup. The graph helps the DBA to visualize the undo tablespace size and the undo retention period. See Figure 7.2 for details.

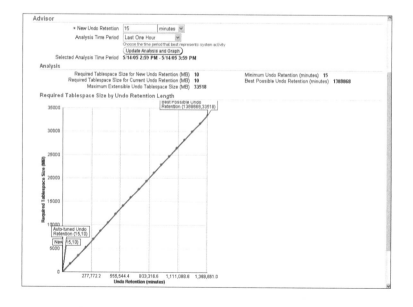

FIGURE 7.2
The Undo Advisor.

The maximum undo retention time corresponds to your longest-running query. The best possible undo retention time period should be longer than your longest-running query for the undo tablespace to be adequately configured.

> You should combine the length of your expected longest-running query and the longest interval needed for flashback operations to look up the required undo tablespace size on the Undo Advisor graph.

You can also use Undo Advisor to calculate undo retention time for flashback operations. For using flashback operations and to maintain an effective flashback recovery strategy, the DBA has to set the low threshold parameter optimally for automatic undo tuning.

> The database must be in archive log mode to enable flashback operations. Flashback logs are similar to redo logs and can be written to a file, a directory, or an ASM disk group.

Oracle always keeps the minimum undo retention time over this threshold parameter (expressed in minutes), so if your database requires a flashback recovery period of six hours, set the low threshold to six hours. On the Undo Advisor page, enter the threshold value in the New Undo Retention field and click OK.

You can also set the UNDO_RETENTION parameter from the Initialization Parameters page, as shown in Figure 7.3.

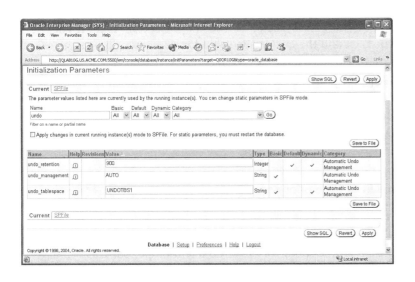

FIGURE 7.3
Changing the UNDO_RETENTION parameter

Guaranteeing Undo Availability

We discussed the option to guarantee undo retention in the section titled "The Significance of the UNDO_RETENTION Parameter" earlier in this chapter. You can enable the guarantee option by specifying the RETENTION GUARANTEE clause for the undo tablespace when it is created or at a later period using the ALTER TABLESPACE statement. The UNDO_RETENTION parameter is valid only if the current undo tablespace has sufficient space.

> **Errors During Undo Tablespace Switching**
>
> If the new tablespace (UNDOTBS2, as in the preceding code) does not exist, if the tablespace is not an undo tablespace, or if it is already being used by another instance (RAC environment only), an error will be generated and switching will not occur.

If you have more than one undo tablespace, you can switch from one tablespace to another for running longer batch jobs or for maintenance purposes. This is analogous to using larger rollback segments in Oracle 8i for long-running queries. Because the UNDO_TABLESPACE initialization parameter is dynamic, you can use the ALTER SYSTEM SET UNDO_TABLESPACE statement to switch to a new undo tablespace.

```
ALTER SYSTEM SET UNDO_TABLESPACE = UNDOTBS2;
```

The database has to be online and user transactions can be executed while the switch operation is executed. When the switch operation completes successfully, all new transactions started during and after the switch operation began are assigned to the new undo tablespace.

The switch operation does not wait for pending transactions in the old undo tablespace to commit. If there are any pending transactions, the old undo tablespace will enter PENDING OFFLINE mode. Existing transactions can continue there until committed and the undo tablespace automatically goes from the PENDING OFFLINE mode to the OFFLINE mode.

If you set the parameter value for UNDO TABLESPACE to '' (two single quotes), then the current undo tablespace will be switched out and the next available undo tablespace will be switched in. If there are no free undo tablespaces available, this operation will fail.

```
ALTER SYSTEM SET UNDO_TABLESPACE = '';
```

Undo Tips from the Trenches

For best practices and to control the retention of undo records, Oracle recommends that your database undo retention period be at least as long as your longest-running query. If you plan to use flashback features to recover your database from human errors, the undo retention period should be equal to or higher than the maximum time duration you want to go back in the past. You must judiciously compare the time needed for flashback operations as well as for longest-running queries and determine an optimal value for the undo retention period. This will in turn help you determine the undo tablespace sizing.

For certain databases, you may want to limit the undo space by establishing user quotas. You can use the Database Resource Manager directive UNDO_POOL to limit the amount of undo space consumed by a group of users (under Resource Consumer Group, using OEM or Oracle-supplied packages). More details on using the Database Resource Manager can be found in *Oracle Database Administrator's Guide 10g*. An undo pool will control the amount of total undo that can be generated by a consumer group (measured in kilobytes). When the total undo generated by the consumer group exceeds its limit, the current transaction generating the undo will be terminated. Members of the consumer group cannot perform any further updates until undo space is freed from this pool. The default value for UNDO_POOL size is UNLIMITED.

Automatic Undo Management Improvements in Release 2

Oracle Database 10g Release 2 has come up with feature improvements for undo management. Release 1 has the undo retention guarantee feature; in Release 2, you can enable and disable undo retention using Oracle Enterprise Manager.

When you enable the undo retention guarantee option, the database will never overwrite the unexpired undo data. This will cause the database to leave unexpired undo data even at the risk of failure of active DML operations. This option is disabled by default, so that the database can overwrite the unexpired undo data and prevent DML operations from failing due to lack of free space in undo tablespace.

> You must exercise caution when enabling the undo retention guarantee feature in Oracle Database 10g Release 2. Use this option only when you need to use flashback query in a controlled database environment, where you are sure of database transaction volumes and processing times.

The Undo Advisor interface has also received some enhancements in Release 2. Undo Advisor calculates the required undo tablespace size as the maximum of the auto-tuned value of undo retention and the low threshold value.

In the OEM, under System Activity and Tablespace Usage, you can track undos occurring within the previous seven days, instead of just one hour as is the case in Release 1.

Summary

This chapter reviewed the automatic undo management features of Oracle Database 10g. This chapter discussed how to enable and to disable undo, calculate the optimum value for undo tablespace, and set parameters that affect undo management. It also covered the changes made to undo management in Oracle Database 10g Release 2. In the next chapter, you will learn more about automatic segment management and space-management techniques.

8

Leveraging Automatic Segment Management

IN THIS CHAPTER

Segment Management in Oracle Database 10g	141
Making Segment Management Work for You	143
Using Segment Advisor	143
Intelligent Segment Resource Estimation	147
Space-Management Tips and Tricks	148
ASSM Improvements in Release 2	150

Segment Management in Oracle Database 10g

As a precursor to our discussion on segment management, this chapter starts with some preliminary information about data-storage principles in Oracle. Oracle databases use data files to hold data in the database. This data is written to the data files in a proprietary format read only by the database server. Oracle also uses temp files (a form of data files) exclusively with temporary tablespaces.

Data files are made up of segments and extents. There are different types of segments, specific to the database objects they hold—for example, data segments for tables and index segments for indexes. An *extent* is a contiguous set of data blocks within a segment, whose size is determined by the DBA either during or after creation of

Leveraging Automatic Segment Management

database objects. A *data block* (or *database block*) is the lowest unit for data transfer to database storage. The default database block size is determined at database creation by the DBA or chosen by default. The data block size cannot be altered after the database is created. But Oracle Database 10g supports the use of multiple data block sizes for tablespaces other than the default block size, as discussed in Chapter 1, "Exploring Oracle Database 10g Architecture," in the section "BigFile Tablespace."

Data, Index, and Temporary Segments

A single data segment in an Oracle database holds all the data for a table (clustered or not partitioned), a partition in a partitioned table, and a cluster of tables. The storage parameters determine how the extents for the data segment are allotted. Oracle also uses segments for materialized views and materialized view logs like tables and clusters. In a table or materialized view, LOB and varray column types are stored in LOB segments.

> As a best practice, you should not share the same tablespace for database application tables and indexes for any of your critical databases.

Oracle uses a single index segment for every nonpartitioned index and a single index segment per partition for partitioned indexes. The storage parameters are determined for index segments in a manner that is similar to table-creation methods.

Oracle uses a temporary workspace for intermediary stages of processing with SQL statement parsing and SQL query execution. The disk space for this purpose is called a *temporary segment*. If Oracle can do this sorting or processing in memory, or using indexes, it will not create a temporary segment. Oracle allocates temporary segments for temporary tables and indexes as well.

Examples of statements that utilize a temporary segment are CREATE INDEX, certain SELECT operations (SELECT ..ORDER BY, SELECT ..UNION, SELECT DISTINCT.., SELECT ..GROUP BY, and so on). Oracle may require more than one temporary segment if the query contains un-indexed joins and related subqueries.

> **Do Temporary Segments Always Reside in Temporary Tablespaces?**
>
> Temporary segments need not always be created in temporary tablespaces. For example, when you do a direct path load, index rebuild, or table move, temporary segments are initially created in the default tablespace or target tablespace. After the operation is complete, the temporary segment will be renamed as a permanent segment.

Oracle uses temporary segments for queries differently than for temporary tables. In a user session, Oracle uses temporary segments in the temporary tablespace of the user executing the statement. If the user does not have a temporary tablespace allotted, the default temporary tablespace will be the SYSTEM tablespace. Hence, it is very important that the DBA create a temporary tablespace during database creation itself to prevent using the SYSTEM tablespace. If the SYSTEM tablespace is locally managed, it cannot be used for default temporary storage. The data used for sorting purposes within temporary segments are not stored in the redo log.

When a temporary table is used for transaction processing, the segments are dropped by Oracle at the end of the transaction. Similarly, with a session-specific temporary table, Oracle drops the segments at the end of the session. If more than one transaction or session shares the same temporary table, Oracle will retain the segments containing their data in the table until operations are completed.

Making Segment Management Work for You

Oracle Database manages segment space in two ways—automatic and manual, in a locally managed tablespace. Automatic segment-space management (ASSM), which is the default for all new permanent locally managed tablespaces, is much more efficient than manual segment-space management.

> Using automatic segment-space management for tables and indexes eliminates the need to specify PCTFREE during object creation. Oracle supports setting a value for PCTFREE, but if you specify PCTUSED, it will be ignored.

The DBA can enable automatic segment-space management in a database using the SEGMENT SPACE MANAGEMENT AUTO clause, and can disable it with the SEGMENT SPACE MANAGEMENT MANUAL clause. The initialization parameter COMPATIBLE should be set to >=10.0 for ASSM to work. For Oracle Database 10g Release 1, you will have to enable ASSM; for Release 2, it is automatically enabled by default.

The segment-space management specified by the DBA at the time of tablespace creation applies to all new segments created in the tablespace. The segment space–management mode of a tablespace cannot be changed, unlike with the database. A locally managed tablespace utilizing automatic management can be created as a single file or a BigFile tablespace.

Automatic segment-space management is far superior to the manual process because it is scalable as the number of users or instances increases. This is true for a RAC environment as well.

Using Segment Advisor

The Segment Advisor is a database advisor that helps you identify database objects with space available for reclamation or with excessive row chaining. The Segment Advisor can be invoked from Oracle Enterprise Manager as well as from the command line. If it determines that a database object has a significant amount of free space below the high-water mark, Segment Advisor will recommend online segment shrink. Also, it will recommend online table redefinition for tables in a tablespace without automatic segment-space management. It also advises on objects with row chaining above a certain threshold.

Segment Advisor collects data from segments on segment growth trends and passes it to other advisors and AWR. AWR stores these persistent space usage statistics in the WR schema. The Segment Advisor uses the data in the Automatic Workload Repository (AWR) for segment analysis. The DBA can change the AWR data collection interval and retention period thereby improving the accuracy and historical perspective for recommendations made by the Segment Advisor.

The Segment Advisor can generate advice at the tablespace level and schema level. It can generate advice for every segment in the tablespace at the tablespace level and for objects at the object level by schemas. The Segment Advisor uses the growth-trend information to make recommendations based on space that can be released and future space requirements. The DBA can elect to implement or reject these recommendations.

Invoking Segment Advisor from Enterprise Manager

A task, also known as a *job* or a *process* in some operating systems, is a control mechanism that can run a series of steps with its own private memory area.

Oracle Enterprise Manager has a wizard that allows the DBA to create and schedule a Segment Advisor task. An advisor task is defined as an executable area in the AWR, which manages tuning efforts by all database users. (The task can be set to run immediately or can be set to run later through the use of scheduling features of the Oracle Database Scheduler.)

To invoke the Segment Advisor from OEM, go to the Database Home page and click Advisor Central under Related Links. On the Advisor Central page, under Advisors, click Segment Advisor. The Segment Advisor wizard launches, enabling you to go through a series of steps to set the scope of the advisor task—on individual schema objects or on entire tablespaces, as shown in Figure 8.1.

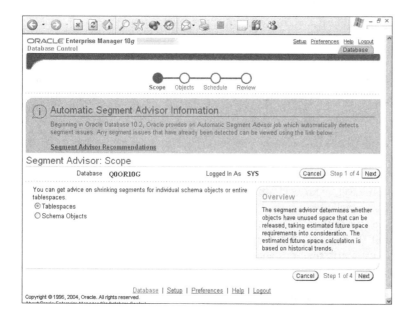

FIGURE 8.1
The Segment Advisor: Scope page in the OEM.

Complete the four steps and click Submit to schedule the Segment Advisor task. You can click the Refresh button until the task shows up as `Completed` under `Status`. Click on the View Result button to get Segment Advisor recommendations.

If you have scheduled multiple tasks to be run at a later time, select your task from the Results list and click on the View Result button to get recommendations. See Figure 8.2 for details on choosing the results of your task.

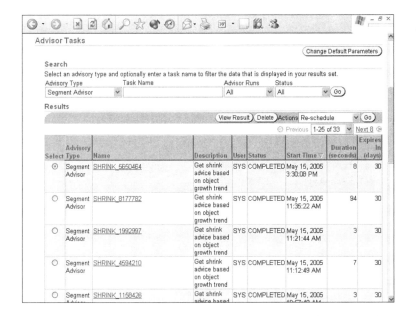

FIGURE 8.2
The Segment Advisor: Results page in the OEM.

Follow the advisor recommendations and perform the necessary remedial actions (online segment shrink, table redefinition, or whatever you have to do). You can also re-run or reschedule a task by selecting the task and choosing the Re-schedule option in the Actions drop-down list under Results.

Invoking Segment Advisor from PL/SQL

You can also invoke the segment advisor using the DBMS_ADVISOR package. Using the various package procedures, the DBA can create a Segment Advisor task, assign task arguments, and execute the task. Refer to *PL/SQL Packages and Types Reference Release 10.2* for more details on this package and all its options.

Listing 8.1 shows an example of the CREATE_TASK procedure used to create the Segment Advisor task. It uses Segment Advisor as the value for the ADVISOR_NAME parameter. The CREATE_OBJECT procedure identifies the target object for segment space advice. You use SET_TASK_PARAMETER to specify the time limit for the run and select all segments or affected segments. EXECUTE_TASK executes the task, and GET_TASK_REPORT gives the report from the task.

LISTING 8.1   Invoking the DBMS_ADVISOR Package

```
SQL> variable ID number;
SQL> begin
  2    declare
  3    TaskName varchar2(40);
  4    Comment varchar2(200);
  5    ObjectID number;
  6    begin
  7    TaskName:='Test Report for Sales 2005';
  8    Comment:='Segment Advisor Example';
  9    dbms_advisor.create_task('Segment Advisor', :ID, TaskName, Comment, NULL);
 10    dbms_advisor.create_object
 11       (TaskName, 'TABLE', 'OE', 'CUSTOMERS', NULL, NULL, ObjectID);
 12    dbms_advisor.set_task_parameter(TaskName, 'RECOMMEND_ALL', 'TRUE');
 13    dbms_advisor.execute_task(TaskName);
 14    end;
 15  end;
 16  /
```

PL/SQL procedure successfully completed.

Reviewing Segment Advisor Results

When you invoke the Segment Advisor from OEM or through the PL/SQL package, it will store
its results (including recommendations and remedial actions) in the database tables. You may
check the status of the Segment Advisor task from the STATUS column in DBA_ADVISOR_TASKS.

```
select task_name, status from dba_advisor_tasks where owner = 'OE' and
➥ advisor_name = 'Segment Advisor';
TASK_NAME                         STATUS
-------------------------------   ----------
Test Report for Sales 2005        COMPLETED
```

You can review all the task results from Enterprise Manager or from the following
DBA_ADVISOR_* views:

- DBA_ADVISOR_FINDINGS shows the space used and free space statistics for an analyzed
  segment. In the SET_TASK_PARAMETER procedure, if you specify TRUE for RECOMMEND_ALL, the
  advisor will generate a finding for every segment under analysis regardless of any recommendation.

- DBA_ADVISOR_OBJECTS has all findings, recommendations, and actions for the object.

- DBA_ADVISOR_RECOMMENDATIONS gives recommendations for the segment that will benefit from a segment shrink or reorganization.

- DBA_ADVISOR_ACTIONS provides the SQL to perform a segment shrink or a suggestion to reorganize the object.

Intelligent Segment Resource Estimation

The DBA can use the following dynamic performance queries to find performance problems associated with individual segments. Using segment-level statistics, you can identify top tables or indexes in the database instance and pinpoint the resource-intensive database objects. This information will help to allocate more resources to the database for various processing cycles or job schedules.

- V$SEGSTAT_NAM has the segment statistics being collected, along with properties of each statistic.

- V$SEGSTAT is a real-time view that shows the statistic value, statistic name, and other basic information on all segments including the top segments causing buffer busy waits.

- V$SEGMENT_STATISTICS has all the information from V$SEGSTAT and details on segment owner and tablespace name.

The following code selects the top 20 segments by statistic name from the V$SEGSTAT since the database instance was started:

```
select owner, object_name, object_type, statistic_name, value
from (select dbo.owner, dbo.object_name, dbo.object_type, vss.value,
vss.statistic_name, row_number () over (order by value desc)
from dba_objects dbo, v$segstat vss
where dbo.object_id = vss.obj#  ) where rownum <= 20 ;
```

The V$SEGMENT_STATISTICS view was introduced in Oracle 9.2. This dynamic performance view enables you to see many different statistics on the usage of segments since the database instance startup. You do not have to turn monitoring on or perform any extra steps to use it. Listing 8.2 shows many statistics available in Oracle Database 10g.

LISTING 8.2   Statistics in Oracle Database 10g

```
SQL>  select distinct statistic_name from v$segment_statistics;

STATISTIC_NAME
-----------------------------------
ITL waits
buffer busy waits
db block changes
gc buffer busy
```

LISTING 8.2 Continued

```
gc cr blocks received
gc current blocks received
logical reads
physical reads
physical reads direct
physical writes
physical writes direct
row lock waits
segment scans
space allocated
space used

15 rows selected.
```

Using the statistics from this view, you can identify which table has the highest physical I/O activity and whether an index has been used during a search. You can also customize the query by owner, object name, and statistic name.

```
select statistic_name, value from v$segment_statistics
where owner ='owner' and object_name ='objectname'
and statistic_name='statisticname';
```

Space-Management Tips and Tricks

Oracle recommends using automatic segment-space management for permanent tablespaces. These tablespaces are locally managed tablespaces and are also known as *bitmap tablespaces*. Locally managed tablespace (LMT) uses bitmaps at the extent level and ASSM uses bitmap at the segment level.

When you create database objects (tables and indexes), specify automatic segment-space management in the creation script itself. This helps Oracle to provide better performance for the database.

If, after using Segment Advisor, you find that there is space available in the object for reclamation, you should compact and shrink the segments. You may also deallocate free space at the end of a database segment. Segment shrink is available through the OEM as well as through the command-line interface.

The database will perform poorly during table scans and query operations when its segments have unused space above and below the high-water mark (HWM). When a segment is shrunk, the data is compacted and the HWM is pushed down to release unused space. This online operation does not take extra database space to run. With a shrink operation, row migration also could be reduced to a certain extent.

In ASSM, there are two types of high-water marks: Low High Water Mark (LHWM) and High High Water Mark (HHWM). Low High Water Mark is the one before which all the blocks are used. High High Water Mark is the other HWM where some unused blocks may be there before that. You can consider that from block 1 to LHWM, all the blocks are used and from LHWM to HHWM, some blocks may not be touched or utilized. This is because of the tree structure of the data blocks in ASSM where L1 blocks will have the actual data blocks and few of them may be unused, but still within HHWM.

> **Does the Shrink Operation Significantly Improve Database Performance?**
>
> Oracle Database 10g performs shrink operations to reclaim segment space. For the shrink operation to be successful, the segments must reside on automatic segment space–managed tablespaces. Even though the HWM is pushed to a lower limit for all shrunk segments, it may not touch all segment blocks. Hence, online shrink operations may not always result in significant performance improvements.

During the shrink operation, the database will compact the segment, adjust the high-water mark, and release the reclaimed space. You can optionally specify COMPACT or CASCADE clauses to control the shrink operation. The database actions associated with the COMPACT and CASCADE clauses are explained here:

- With the COMPACT clause, Oracle Database will defragment the segment space and compact the table rows. But it will postpone resetting of HWM and reallocation of the space to a future time. The defragmentation and compaction results are saved to disk. When you reissue the SHRINK SPACE clause without the COMPACT clause during maintenance hours, the database completes the resetting of the HWM and the reallocation of the space.

- With the CASCADE clause, the segment-shrink operation happens on all dependent segments of the object (like indexes for a table).

In the following code, substitute *TABLE*, *INDEX*, or *CLUSTER* for the *OBJECT* type and add the *Object_name*:

```
ALTER OBJECT Object_name SHRINK SPACE CASCADE;
```

Compact data will lead to better cache utilization and better performance. For full table scans, there will be fewer blocks to be scanned.

The DBA can deallocate unused space using the following command. Substitute *TABLE*, *INDEX*, or *CLUSTER* for *OBJECT*, and add an *Object_name* and a value for *integer*.

```
ALTER OBJECT Object_name DEALLOCATE UNUSED KEEP integer;
```

The optional KEEP clause can be used to specify the amount of retained space in the segment. Using the DBA_FREE_SPACE view to verify, you can check that the deallocated space is available for use by other objects.

You should run the UNUSED_SPACE procedure of the DBMS_SPACE package to get information about HWM and unused space in a segment. You can then deallocate unused space in that segment for other objects. For locally managed tablespaces using automatic segment-space management, run the DBMS_SPACE.SPACE_USAGE procedure to get information on unused space.

You can also set up database alerts to proactively manage the disk space used by tablespaces as discussed in Chapter 6, "Monitoring with Automatic Statistics Collection," under the heading "Metrics Monitoring and Customization." For temporary tablespaces, the threshold value should be set up as a limit on the used space. For read-only or offline tablespaces, you should not set up alerts because you cannot do any space reclamation on these tablespaces.

Limitations for Online Segment-Shrink Operations

You can only shrink segments in automatic segment space–managed tablespaces. Even in ASSM tablespaces, you cannot shrink the following objects:

- Tables in clusters
- Tables having long columns, or on-commit materialized views, or rowid-based materialized views
- LOB indexes

For Dictionary-Managed Tablespaces

If you are unable to use automatic segment-space management and still want to improve performance for segments, you will need to review the free lists or free list groups. A *free list* is a list of free data blocks whose free space has not reached the PCTFREE or whose used space is below PCTUSED. In other words, a free list is a linked list structure of data blocks associated with a segment that are eligible for accepting data when a new insert request comes.

The default value for the FREELISTS parameter is 1, while the maximum number depends on the block size. If you have to improve performance, increase the number of free lists or use the FREELIST GROUPS parameter. Increasing free lists will help only when there are too many concurrent sessions doing DMLs on that segment. For RAC, make sure that each instance has its own free list group.

ASSM Improvements in Release 2

Oracle Database 10g Release 2 has come up with feature improvements for automatic segment-space management. In Release 1, you had to turn on automatic segment-space management, whereas in Release 2, ASSM is set to AUTO. The advantage is that tablespaces have automatic segment-space management turned on by default, as soon as they are created.

Space-management features have been enhanced to identify empty data files and drop them. Segment Advisor can automatically identify tables and indexes that need to be compressed to reclaim free space. For Release 2, Segment Advisor is tightly integrated with segment findings to cover non-ASSM tablespaces and chained rows in them.

Summary

This chapter discussed the automatic segment-memory management feature of Oracle Database 10g. It covered using segment-management features to generate optimum segment-size recommendations. The next chapter will switch focus to Recovery Manager, RMAN features, RMAN tips, and better recovery techniques.

9

Implementing
Recovery
Manager

IN THIS CHAPTER

RMAN Basics   153

New Features of RMAN   161

Recovery Without Hurdles   168

New Features in Oracle Database 10g
Release 2   170

RMAN Basics

Oracle's Recovery Manager, also known as
RMAN, should be your tool of choice when
it comes to backing up Oracle databases.
RMAN was first introduced in Oracle 8.0
and has come a long way since then. This
chapter shows how RMAN has been
improved specifically in Oracle Database
10g. It also offers some practical tips that
you can use in configuring and using RMAN
for both backup as well as recovery. Before
we launch into the details, however, let's
look at some basics of RMAN and try to
understand why using RMAN is a good idea.
Especially if you are new to RMAN, you
might want to read this introduction.

Simply stated, RMAN is an excellent way to
provide a *physical* backup of your Oracle
database. This is in contrast to
export/import and Data Pump, which
provide *logical* backups. In all Oracle database versions, in addition to the Export and
Import utilities, Oracle has provided a way

> In Microsoft Windows platforms, you will need to use the OCOPY command rather than the COPY command because the former can be used to back up files that have been opened by another process. Note that when a database is open, the data file would have been held open by the oracle.exe process.

of backing up an open database that is currently being used, provided the database is in ARCHIVELOG mode. Such a backup, known as a *hot backup*, is performed by backing up database files using an operating system utility such as tar in UNIX or OCOPY in Microsoft Windows after placing the associated tablespaces in BACKUP mode. When a tablespace is placed in this mode, the redo information being written to logs is changed to write whole blocks rather than just the changed information, as is done normally. The redolog files are copied out to *archive logs* when they are full. A physical backup of the database files, along with a backup of the archive logs, can then be used to re-create the database to a specified point in time.

Difference Between RMAN and Hot Backup

The reason full-block logging occurs when a tablespace is in BACKUP mode is to compensate for the difference between operating-system blocksize (normally 512 bytes) and the database blocksize (anywhere from 2KB to 32KB). This is a crucial difference between RMAN and the hot backup method. Full-block logging avoids a phenomenon known as *fractured block read*. In other words, the database could be writing an 8KB block as a whole, while the operating-system backup utility could have backed up an older version of a *portion* of the block in an earlier read. The next read would then read a modified version of *another portion* of the same block. The operating-system backup would have otherwise been inconsistent, except for the fact that the whole block, which was previously logged in redo, is written back during recovery. This makes the block consistent *at recovery* and thus avoids the *fractured block read* phenomenon. RMAN, on the other hand, is *not* an operating-system utility but an Oracle Database–aware product. Hence, all reads by RMAN for the purpose of backup are performed using the block size of the database block itself, thus avoiding *fractured block reads*. When RMAN does encounter inconsistencies while reading blocks, RMAN notes these errors in the alert log and re-reads the block as may be required.

Although a few extra blocks of redo and ultimately more archive logs is normally not an issue in small, less-active databases, it quickly becomes a problem when the databases are large and more active. Larger databases usually mean tablespaces with a large number of large files that have to be kept for long periods in BACKUP mode, increasing the chances of extra redo related to backup. Large databases also normally support a large, active user community, and the amount of redo increases with activity. If you have this combination in a database, you should consider using RMAN to back up that database in order to avoid this extra overhead for redo during backups.

Advantages of RMAN over Hot Backup

RMAN also has other major advantages that are listed here. These advantages apply even if you are considering RMAN for versions below Oracle Database 10g.

- RMAN provides for centralized management using an RMAN recovery catalog. Optionally, you can use RMAN in a NOCATALOG mode. When used with a recovery catalog, RMAN is quickly able to provide you with the names, locations, and versions of all the files backed up at any level—whole database, tablespace, or data-file level. This information is also recorded in the control files in both cases. When operated in the NOCATALOG mode, the CONTROL_FILE_RECORD_KEEP_TIME initialization parameter determines the amount of time backup information is retained in the database's control files. This defaults to seven days and means that you cannot obtain backup information prior to this date when operating in the NOCATALOG mode.

■ RMAN backup and recovery actions can be scripted, so you can script all actions and prepare ahead of time for various recovery scenarios. These scripts work in a standard way across all platforms and servers, so you don't have to modify them for different operating systems and servers. RMAN scripts can be stored in a central RMAN catalog or on individual clients as operating-system files.

■ RMAN can be used from both the command line as well as from OEM, so it caters to beginners as well as advanced users.

■ RMAN supports incremental backups in the sense that only changed blocks are backed up. This can save an incredible amount of time and space for backup operations.

■ RMAN performs corrupt block detection for both database blocks and logs as it backs up. That way, you can be fore-warned and take steps to fix the corruption before it affects recovery at a later date.

■ RMAN can perform backup of external but related files such as the initialization parameter file, password file, control files, and so on. You may have to script them separately using the other methods.

■ RMAN provides a media management layer (MML) that can be used to inte-grate RMAN backups to your tape backup systems such as ones by Legato or Tivoli. This prevents confusion and enables division of labor and responsi-bilities with the operations and system administration teams. Database adminis-trators can, using the RMAN catalog, locate and request restoration of required files automatically, avoiding interfacing to another usually separate

CATALOG Versus NOCATALOG

The issue of using RMAN with CATALOG and NOCATALOG is quite simple. The only down side of using an RMAN catalog is that you will need an instance for the catalog itself, either shared with another application or dedicated for just the RMAN catalog. When you manage only one or two databases and are using RMAN to back them up, it is proba-bly not a good idea to use a catalog. If, however, you have a reasonably large number of databases being backed up via RMAN, it is probably a good idea to use a dedicated catalog database. If you are also implement-ing an OEM repository, then we recommend that you add the RMAN catalog into this data-base as well and make that database highly available, effectively killing two birds with one stone.

Although RMAN is designed to work without a recovery catalog, if you choose not to use a recovery catalog, you must perform some additional administrative tasks. In any case, the backup-related information is retained in the database control files. The length of time this is retained is determined by CONTROL_FILE_RECORD_TIME_KEEP, which defaults to seven days. When a catalog is not being used, this value should be changed to reflect the length of time backups should be retained.

team. Optionally, RMAN can also write to a disk backup area and stage the backup and recovery operations from this location.

■ RMAN parallelizes backup using a concept known as *channels*. Backups can be produced in evenly sized packages known as *backup sets*.

■ RMAN does not back up unused portions of a data file. In other words, when you create a data file but haven't allocated blocks within it yet, the empty space will not be backed up, saving time and backup resources.

These reasons should be enough to convince you to move all your Oracle backups to RMAN, or at least consider using it in a few databases to begin with.

> Note that Oracle Database 10g supports the
> ALTER DATABASE BEGIN BACKUP and ALTER
> DATABASE END BACKUP commands to place
> the entire database in backup mode all at
> once. You will not have to code BEGIN
> BACKUP and END BACKUP per tablespace in
> this case.

The only time we would recommend using hot backups is when using SAN (Storage Area Network) disk mirror technology such as EMC's BCV (Business Continuity Volume) or Hitachi Data Systems' ShadowImage to offload backup I/O onto the mirror copy rather than the production volumes. In this case, the whole database is placed in hot-backup mode and the mirror image is broken to produce a database image copy that can then be mounted back and backed up separately. This operation takes place in a matter of a few seconds, after which the tablespaces are again placed in normal mode. The amount of full-block redo is minimal in this case. This technique is well suited for large, active databases hosted on SANs that support such disk mirroring; you want to offload the backup I/O to the mirror copy.

For offline backups, RMAN needs a database to be mounted but not open. In the case of operating-system backups, an offline backup, also known as a *cold backup*, needs the database to be shut down and offline.

A Sample RMAN Backup Session

Running an RMAN backup is as simple as issuing a BACKUP DATABASE command, as shown in Listing 9.1. Commands entered by the user is shown in bold.

LISTING 9.1   A Simple RMAN Backup

```
$ rman

Recovery Manager: Release 10.1.0.2.0 - 64bit Production

Copyright (c) 1995, 2004, Oracle.  All rights reserved.

RMAN> connect target;
```

LISTING 9.1   Continued

```
connected to target database: TS10G (DBID=845721274)
using target database controlfile instead of recovery catalog

RMAN> backup database;

Starting backup at 07-MAY-05
using channel ORA_DISK_1
channel ORA_DISK_1: starting full datafile backupset
channel ORA_DISK_1: specifying datafile(s) in backupset
input datafile fno=00003 name=/u04/app/oracle/product/10.1.0/db_1/oradata/TS10G/
➥sysaux01.dbf
input datafile fno=00001 name=/u04/app/oracle/product/10.1.0/db_1/oradata/TS10G/
➥system01.dbf
input datafile fno=00005 name=/u04/app/oracle/product/10.1.0/db_1/oradata/TS10G/
➥example01.dbf
input datafile fno=00002 name=/u04/app/oracle/product/10.1.0/db_1/oradata/TS10G/
➥undotbs01.dbf
input datafile fno=00004 name=/u04/app/oracle/product/10.1.0/db_1/oradata/TS10G/
➥users01.dbf
channel ORA_DISK_1: starting piece 1 at 07-MAY-05
channel ORA_DISK_1: finished piece 1 at 07-MAY-05
piece handle=/u04/app/oracle/product/10.1.0/db_1/flash_recovery_area/TS10G/backu
➥pset/2005_05_07/o1_mf_nnndf_TAG20050507T154504_17t6p13k_.bkp comment=NONE
channel ORA_DISK_1: backup set complete, elapsed time: 00:05:55
channel ORA_DISK_1: starting full datafile backupset
channel ORA_DISK_1: specifying datafile(s) in backupset
including current controlfile in backupset
including current SPFILE in backupset
channel ORA_DISK_1: starting piece 1 at 07-MAY-05
channel ORA_DISK_1: finished piece 1 at 07-MAY-05
piece handle=/u04/app/oracle/product/10.1.0/db_1/flash_recovery_area/TS10G/backu
➥pset/2005_05_07/o1_mf_ncsnf_TAG20050507T154504_17t714dq_.bkp comment=NONE
channel ORA_DISK_1: backup set complete, elapsed time: 00:00:01
Finished backup at 07-MAY-05

RMAN> list backup;

List of Backup Sets
===================

BS Key  Type LV Size       Device Type Elapsed Time Completion Time
------- ---- -- ---------- ----------- ------------ ---------------
```

LISTING 9.1   Continued

```
28    Full    3G        DISK        00:05:46    07-MAY-05
        BP Key: 28   Status: AVAILABLE  Compressed: NO  Tag: TAG20050507T154504
        Piece Name: /u04/app/oracle/product/10.1.0/db_1/flash_recovery_area/TS10
➥G/backupset/2005_05_07/o1_mf_nnndf_TAG20050507T154504_17t6p13k_.bkp
  List of Datafiles in backup set 28
  File LV Type Ckp SCN    Ckp Time  Name
  ---- -- ---- ---------- --------- ----
    1       Full 13802579   07-MAY-05 /u04/app/oracle/product/10.1.0/db_1/oradata/
➥TS10G/system01.dbf
    2       Full 13802579   07-MAY-05 /u04/app/oracle/product/10.1.0/db_1/oradata/
➥TS10G/undotbs01.dbf
    3       Full 13802579   07-MAY-05 /u04/app/oracle/product/10.1.0/db_1/oradata/
➥TS10G/sysaux01.dbf
    4       Full 13802579   07-MAY-05 /u04/app/oracle/product/10.1.0/db_1/oradata/
➥TS10G/users01.dbf
    5       Full 13802579   07-MAY-05 /u04/app/oracle/product/10.1.0/db_1/oradata/
➥TS10G/example01.dbf

BS Key  Type LV Size       Device Type Elapsed Time Completion Time
------- ---- -- ---------- ----------- ------------ ---------------
29    Full    2M        DISK        00:00:00    07-MAY-05
        BP Key: 29   Status: AVAILABLE  Compressed: NO  Tag: TAG20050507T154504
        Piece Name: /u04/app/oracle/product/10.1.0/db_1/flash_recovery_area/TS10
➥G/backupset/2005_05_07/o1_mf_ncsnf_TAG20050507T154504_17t714dq_.bkp
  Controlfile Included: Ckp SCN: 13802773    Ckp time: 07-MAY-05
  SPFILE Included: Modification time: 07-MAY-05

RMAN> sql 'alter system archive log current';

sql statement: alter system archive log current
```

In this case, we did not connect to a RMAN catalog database. Instead, we connected to the *target* database that needed to be backed up. You can connect to this database named TS10G using the CONNECT TARGET command from the RMAN utility, which was invoked from the operating-system command line using the *oracle* account. This special account owns the software and the database, and thus did not need a user name and password to be able to log in to RMAN. The TS10G database was run in ARCHIVELOG mode and was open and active during the backup. Note that we did not have to use the BEGIN BACKUP and END BACKUP commands to place the tablespaces in hot-backup mode. The simple RMAN BACKUP DATABASE command was sufficient to execute the backup. We followed this up with a LIST BACKUP command that listed the current backups available.

RMAN backs up all the files needed for recovery in the event of a failure. RMAN's BACKUP command supports backing up these types of files:

- Data files and image copies of data files

- Control files and image copies of control files

- Archived redo logs

- Server parameter files

- Backup pieces containing other backups created by RMAN

Other files needed for operation, such as network configuration files, password files, and the contents of the Oracle home, cannot be backed up with RMAN.

The backup can be stored as image copies as well as backup sets. Image copies are equivalent to operating-system copies of database and other files but are cataloged by RMAN and thus known to the system. A *backup set* is a *logical* structure that holds data from database files, control files, redologs, and archive files as well as system parameter files. A backup set consists of one or more physical files known as *backup pieces*. These files can be read only by RMAN and contain data multiplexed from one or more data files, control files, archivelog files, and redolog files. In Oracle Database 10g, all RMAN backup-related files are created in the flash recovery area by default. The backup set piece file created by the BACKUP DATABASE command can be seen in Listing 9.2.

LISTING 9.2   Listing of RMAN Backup Pieces and File Sizes

```
SQL> select file_name, bytes/1024/1024 size_mb
  2  from dba_data_files;


FILE_NAME                                                          SIZE_MB
---------------------------------------------------------------- ----------
/u04/app/oracle/product/10.1.0/db_1/oradata/TS10G/users01.dbf           5
/u04/app/oracle/product/10.1.0/db_1/oradata/TS10G/sysaux01.dbf       2690
/u04/app/oracle/product/10.1.0/db_1/oradata/TS10G/undotbs01.dbf        85
/u04/app/oracle/product/10.1.0/db_1/oradata/TS10G/system01.dbf        590
/u04/app/oracle/product/10.1.0/db_1/oradata/TS10G/example01.dbf       150
                                                                 ----------
sum                                                                  3520


$ pwd
/u04/app/oracle/product/10.1.0/db_1/flash_recovery_area/TS10G/backupset/2005_05_07
$ ls -lrt
total 6309424
-rw-rw---- 1 oracle dba 3227467776
➥May  7 15:50 o1_mf_nnndf_TAG20050507T154504_17t6p13k_.bkp
-rw-rw---- 1 oracle dba    2949120
➥May  7 15:51 o1_mf_ncsnf_TAG20050507T154504_17t714dq_.bkp
```

Implementing Recovery Manager

If you match the names of the files in Listing 9.2 to the descriptive lines in Listing 9.1 that list the backup set information, you will notice that backup set piece file o1_mf_nnndf_TAG20050507T154504_17t6p13k_.bkp contains the database files and the backup set piece file o1_mf_ncsnf_TAG20050507T154504_17t714dq_.bkp contains the control file and system parameter file (SPFILE). Note that the size of the former is approximately 3,077MB, which is less than the total of the individual database sizes amounting to 3,520MB, as seen in Listing 9.2. The files are created in a subdirectory under the flash recovery area, appropriately identified by the database name (TS10G), the nature of the contents (namely backupset), and the date of the backup. You will learn more about Flashback technologies in Chapter 17, "Effectively Using Flashback Technologies," but suffice it to say that you may need to adjust the size of this area using the DB_RECOVERY_FILE_DEST_SIZE initialization parameter to a size that is adequate for both the intended size of backups to be retained as well as other files such as archivelog and flashback information.

> If you intend to use RMAN for backup, you *will* have to configure an adequate value for the LARGE_POOL_SIZE initialization parameter. RMAN uses this area for its buffering. If this is not configured, RMAN uses the shared pool instead for buffers. This can result in pollution of the library and data dictionary caches, leading to ORA-4031 errors.

You will also notice the words *channel* and *tag*. An *RMAN channel* is a logical name for the backup to be placed in. In this case, the default channel was a disk area named ORA_DISK_1 that defaulted to the flash recovery area. You can configure multiple RMAN channels to either disk or tape devices enabled via the MML, and they can be used in parallel. The *tag* is a user- or system-defined handle for the backup. You can use this as a key to track and locate this particular backup. In this case, the system-defined tag was a string containing the date and time of backup; this is actually a good tag to use. Finally, notice that you can always execute SQL commands from within RMAN using the SQL 'Your_SQL_command' option as seen at the end of Listing 9.1.

RMAN Documentation

Documentation for RMAN has been strengthened in the documentation set for Oracle Database 10g. The following manuals should be perused for concepts, command references, and information about advanced topics:

- *Oracle Database 10g Recovery Manager Quick Start Guide*. Read this first if you want a quick synopsis of RMAN. It also has a quick reference and is task-oriented. At 28 pages, it is indeed a quick read!

- *Oracle Database 10g Backup and Recovery Basics*. This manual goes through the basics and concepts behind RMAN and is a prerequisite to the more advanced manuals noted next.

- *Oracle Database 10g Recovery Manager Reference*. This manual is the RMAN-equivalent of the SQL command reference.

- *Oracle Database 10g Backup and Recovery Advanced User's Guide*. This manual discusses in great detail concepts and advanced topics such as tuning and troubleshooting RMAN.

After you become familiar with the basics of RMAN, this is a must-read. If you are already familiar with older versions of RMAN, this manual has a section that covers new RMAN features in Oracle Database 10g.

Accessing RMAN

RMAN can be accessed via both the command line, as seen in Listing 9.1, as well as using OEM Database Control. The backup/recovery commands in OEM can be accessed via the Maintenance tab. Certain simple operations related to RMAN can be performed from the following OEM screens:

- **Schedule Backup.** In this screen, you can specify a backup strategy to use, the backup destination, and so on. You will have to specify operating-system credentials in order for the agent to log in and perform certain operations. Both an Oracle-suggested and a customized strategy can be chosen.

- **Perform Recovery.** Simple restores and recoveries can be performed from this screen, including block recovery as well as data file and database restore and recovery.

- **Manage Current Backups.** You can list, delete, delete obsolete, and perform various related operations for backup sets as well as image copies. In short, this screen can act as a GUI front end to many of the command-line actions required in RMAN.

- **Configure Backup Settings.** In this screen, you can set the parallism, configure a backup location different from the default flash recovery area, choose the backup type (backup set, compress backup set, or image copy), as well as establish tape settings specific to the MML.

- **Configure Recovery Settings.** This screen is not entirely connected to RMAN but is used for setting parameters that can affect RMAN. This includes the Mean Time To Recover (MTTR), archive log destinations, flash recovery area location and size, flashback logging, and flashback retention time. Note that you will have to be logged in as SYSDBA to perform these actions because the form needs to access and change the initialization parameters.

- **Configure Recovery Catalog Settings.** In this screen, you can specify the details of the recovery catalog to be used for RMAN backup including the database name, schema, and password, as well as register the target database in the RMAN catalog.

We suggest you use these screens to set up your database initially for RMAN backup. Most of the screens also have a button to generate the RMAN script or the corresponding SQL so you can log what commands were executed in order to be able to record and repeat the actions when necessary.

New Features of RMAN

As indicated before, RMAN was introduced in Oracle 8 and has grown in functionality and stability through Oracle 8i and Oracle 9i. Oracle Database 10g continues that tradition and provides a number of new, especially useful features. These are listed in the various sections that follow.

Use of Flash Recovery Area

The ability to flash back, or go back in time, was introduced in Oracle 9i. Oracle Database 10g has introduced a slew of new features in this area as detailed in Chapter 17. What is interesting is that a new command, FLASHBACK DATABASE, can be used to reset the whole database back in time without resorting to a Point-In-Time-Recovery (PITR) using a backup of the database. A particular table can also be restored to a previous point in time, even if it was dropped. Use of such features can sometimes obviate the need for a RMAN or user-managed recovery from backup. All this information is stored in the flash recovery area as determined by the DB_ RECOVERY_FILE_DEST parameter and bounded by both the DB_RECOVERY_FILE_DEST_SIZE and DB_FLASHBACK_RETENTION_TARGET parameters for size and retention time respectively. Notice that the latter is just a target; the size parameter along with other internal adjustments may decide the actual amount of data retained for flashback purposes. Note that flashback needs to be specifically enabled, and that you can use RMAN regardless of whether flashback is enabled or not.

Size of Flash Recovery Area

Note that the flash recovery area holds much more than just RMAN backups. By default, it also holds the archive logs and flashback logs. In addition, if so configured, it holds Oracle-managed files, multiplexed copies of the online redo logs, and control files. However, only the total size of this area can be defined, and when there is disk pressure on account of rapid generation of archivelogs and adequate disk is not available, RMAN backups will fail with messages such as ORA- 19809: limit exceeded for recovery files and ORA-19804: cannot reclaim 52428800 bytes disk space from 2147483648 limit. Be sure to calculate and set an adequate value for the DB_RECOVERY_FILE_DEST_SIZE parameter. Note that this is independent of the actual disk space available in that filesystem or ASM disk group; this value is simply a logical upper limit and exists to prevent some runaway job from filling up the disk space.

The flash recovery area is actually a directory or file system dedicated to storing all recovery-related data such as copies of multiplexed online redo logs and control files, archive logs, flashback logs, and finally RMAN backups as seen in Listing 9.2. In Oracle Database 10g, the flash recovery area can also be an Automatic Storage Management (ASM) disk group. Using a well-protected ASM disk group ensures that this important portion of the database is provided the right amount of protection from disaster. ASM was discussed in detail in Chapter 4, "Setting Up Automatic Storage Management."

RMAN can back up directly to the disk rather than to tape, specifically to the flash recovery area by default as you saw earlier. By configuring a large bunch of low-cost disks such as SATA (Serial ATA) to function as the flash recovery area, many organizations are trying to provide online backups using disk technology rather than tape technology. The advantages of using disk-based backup are many, including performance and shrinking time windows for backup and most importantly restoration, longevity of technology, avoidance of environmental issues that result in tape read and tape head problems, and so on. RMAN with Oracle Database 10g is poised to provide you with the ability to do this easily.

As with any other backup medium, you will have to define retention periods for backups, and RMAN will automatically manage the expiration of backups and files. This is another advantage of using the flash recovery area for backups.

Fast Incremental Backups

RMAN allows for incremental backups that can be used to back up only the blocks that were changed since the last full backup. Formerly, this was done by recording the SCN (System Change Number) at the last full backup and scanning all the data files for any block whose SCN was later than the previously recorded SCN. Although incremental backups saved backup storage space at the expense of some administrative work during a restore, all data files still had to be scanned, and this overhead made incremental backups impractical in most situations. Now, however, RMAN can perform incremental backups quickly using a new feature called *block change tracking*.

Block change tracking records the list of blocks in each data file that have changed in a change-tracking file. RMAN uses the change-tracking file to identify changed blocks for incremental backup quickly and directly, thus avoiding the need to scan every

> Because change tracking has some minimal performance overhead on your database during normal operations, it is disabled by default.

block in the data file during an incremental backup. After enabling change tracking, the first level 0 incremental backup still has to scan the entire data file, because the change-tracking file does not yet reflect the status of the blocks. Subsequent incremental backup that use this level 0 as parent will take advantage of the change-tracking file. There is no need to change any of the commands that were previously used to perform incremental backup; RMAN automatically uses the change-tracking files once this is configured.

One block change-tracking file is created for the whole database. By default, the block change-tracking file is created as an Oracle-managed file in DB_CREATE_FILE_DEST. Alternatively, you can specify the name and location of the block change-tracking file. The size of the change-tracking file is proportional to the size of the database and the number of enabled threads of redo, rather than to the amount or frequency of updates to the database. For databases up to 1TB, a 10MB change-tracking file is sufficient, with sizes doubling every TB. The command to create a change-tracking file is shown in Listing 9.3. Once created, the V$BLOCK_CHANGE_TRACKING view is populated as seen in Listing 9.3.

LISTING 9.3   Creating a Change-Tracking File

```
SQL> alter database enable block change tracking
  2;
SQL>
```

LISTING 9.3   Continued

```
SQL> alter database enable block change tracking using file
  2  '/u04/app/oracle/product/10.1.0/db_1/oradata/TS10G/rman_chg_track.f';


Database altered.


SQL> select status, bytes, filename from v$block_change_tracking;


STATUS          BYTES
---------- ----------
FILENAME
--------------------------------------------------------------------------
ENABLED      11599872
/u04/app/oracle/product/10.1.0/db_1/oradata/TS10G/rman_chg_track.f
```

When Should You Consider Incremental Backups?

If you are already using RMAN for your database backups, you should consider using incremental backups when the number of updates is minimal compared to the size of the database, regardless of the Oracle database version you are using. Incremental backup is especially useful for databases supporting Data WareHouse (DWH) applications, where the size of the database is large compared to the periodic updates, and you know the tablespaces or data files that would undergo changes during the data load. The use of block change tracking will further enhance the usefulness of incremental backup. Be aware, though, that recovery scenarios when incremental backups are used are slightly more complex than with full backups. This complexity can be reduced by scripting and preparing procedures for all possible recovery scenarios ahead of time.

MetaLink Note #262853.1, titled "10G RMAN Fast Incremental Backups," provides a quick overview of this useful feature.

Incrementally Updated Backups

Also known as *backup merging*, RMAN in Oracle Database 10g supports the merging of backup incrementals to previously created data file image copies so as to roll them forward to a specified point in time. Using these incrementally updated backups, you can reduce recovery time by applying incrementals specifically to data file image copies and avoid taking a full data file image copy. This backup method is possible only when using data file image copies, rather than backup sets, and these data file image copies are retained on disk rather than tape. This is an incredibly powerful feature that can drastically reduce backup and recovery times. The command to create and maintain such a backup is shown in Listing 9.4.

LISTING 9.4   Creating an Incrementally Updated Backup

```
RUN {

    RECOVER COPY OF DATABASE WITH TAG 'TS10G_INCR_UPDATE';
```

LISTING 9.4   Continued

```
        BACKUP INCREMENTAL LEVEL 1 FOR RECOVER OF COPY WITH TAG 'TS10G_INCR_UPDATE'
        DATABASE;
}
```

The simple example in Listing 9.4 shows how a RMAN command script can be created. Assuming this has not been run before, the first command, RECOVER COPY, will fail with error messages such as no copy of datafile 1 found to recover for those data file image copies that do not yet exist. However, the second BACKUP INCREMENTAL command with FOR RECOVER OF COPY would create a level 0 backup of all the data files in the database with the specified tag for such data files. In the second and all subsequent runs, it will produce level 1 incremental backups of all the data files in the database. If a cataloged data file image copy exists, all incremental data changes are placed in a separate backup set piece that can now be applied to the level 0 copy of the specific data file image copy.

This is clear from Listing 9.5, which is the output produced by the BACKUP command in Listing 9.4. You can see from the first set of bold lines that a level 0 image copy of data file 3 (sysaux01.dbf) was not present and hence it was created in the flash recovery area under the aptly named datafile directory. Similarly, an image copy for data file 1 (system01.dbf) was also not found and hence was created. A comparison of file sizes at the operating system showed that the sizes of the physical data files and their image copies are exactly the same. The next bold section shows that an incremental level 1 data file backup set was created for the example01.dbf, undotbs01.dbf, and users01.dbf files. This backup set piece file, of course, was created in the backupset/2005_05_09 subdirectory. Finally, the control file and SPFILE were backed up into a separate backup set piece.

LISTING 9.5   Log of Incrementally Updated Backup

```
Starting backup at 09-MAY-05
using channel ORA_DISK_1
no parent backup or copy of datafile 1 found
no parent backup or copy of datafile 3 found
channel ORA_DISK_1: starting datafile copy
input datafile fno=00003 name=/u04/app/oracle/product/10.1.0/db_1/oradata/TS10G/
➥sysaux01.dbf
output filename=/u04/app/oracle/product/10.1.0/db_1/flash_recovery_area/TS10G/
➥datafile/o1_mf_sysaux_1806hz6y_.dbf tag=TS10G_INCR_UPDATE recid=65 stamp=557879069
channel ORA_DISK_1: datafile copy complete, elapsed time: 00:05:55
channel ORA_DISK_1: starting datafile copy
input datafile fno=00001 name=/u04/app/oracle/product/10.1.0/db_1/oradata/TS10G/
➥system01.dbf
output filename=/u04/app/oracle/product/10.1.0/db_1/flash_recovery_area/TS10G/
➥datafile/o1_mf_system_1806v2bw_.dbf tag=TS10G_INCR_UPDATE recid=66 stamp=557879147
channel ORA_DISK_1: datafile copy complete, elapsed time: 00:01:15
channel ORA_DISK_1: starting incremental level 1 datafile backupset
```

LISTING 9.5   Continued

```
channel ORA_DISK_1: specifying datafile(s) in backupset
input datafile fno=00005 name=/u04/app/oracle/product/10.1.0/db_1/oradata/TS10G/
➥example01.dbf
input datafile fno=00002 name=/u04/app/oracle/product/10.1.0/db_1/oradata/TS10G/
➥undotbs01.dbf
input datafile fno=00004 name=/u04/app/oracle/product/10.1.0/db_1/oradata/TS10G/
➥users01.dbf
channel ORA_DISK_1: starting piece 1 at 09-MAY-05
channel ORA_DISK_1: finished piece 1 at 09-MAY-05
piece handle=/u04/app/oracle/product/10.1.0/db_1/flash_recovery_area/TS10G/
➥backupset/2005_05_09/o1_mf_nnnd1_TAG20050509T221838_1806xfjs_.bkp comment=NONE
channel ORA_DISK_1: backup set complete, elapsed time: 00:00:01
channel ORA_DISK_1: starting incremental level 1 datafile backupset
channel ORA_DISK_1: specifying datafile(s) in backupset
including current controlfile in backupset
including current SPFILE in backupset
channel ORA_DISK_1: starting piece 1 at 09-MAY-05
channel ORA_DISK_1: finished piece 1 at 09-MAY-05
piece handle=/u04/app/oracle/product/10.1.0/db_1/flash_recovery_area/TS10G/
➥backupset/2005_05_09/o1_mf_ncsn1_TAG20050509T221838_1806xgsf_.bkp comment=NONE
channel ORA_DISK_1: backup set complete, elapsed time: 00:00:01
Finished backup at 09-MAY-05
```

Subsequent incremental executions of the command script would create additional backup set pieces that contain changed blocks that can be used to roll forward the previous level 0 data file image copies. Note that this roll-forward recovery merging can be performed only via RMAN, because the changes are held in a backup set piece.

Recovery Through RESETLOGS

The loss of all control files, or the loss of all copies of an online redo log file, will always force incomplete recovery whether the database was recovered via RMAN or from the traditional hot backup. One of the prerequesites before the database is opened is to perform an ALTER DATABASE OPEN RESETLOGS. In this case, the online redo logs are reset by initialization of both contents and the numbering scheme. As a result, going forward from that point in time, you will not be able to use previous backup sets, also known to RMAN as *incarnations*. Hence, you will have to immediately create another full backup of the database after you have opened the database with the RESETLOGS operation. With RMAN in Oracle Database 10g, this is no longer required. The procedure to restore a database is as easy and transparent as recovering a backup from the same incarnation. Also, the ALTER DATABASE OPEN RESETLOGS statement has now been modified so that the database archives the current online redo logs (if possible) before clearing the logs. This is an unexpected but welcome side effect! The only caveat is that you cannot restore a data file from a previous incarnation; you will have to perform complete database recovery.

RMAN Tuning

Current enterprise-level databases are usually 24×7, and are employed throughout by users all around the globe. RMAN now allows for additional tuning via the use of the RATE parameter, which can be used to throttle down the I/O in case backup periods affect other online users. You can also use the COMPRESSED keyword with any BACKUP command to compress the backup. This can save backup I/O and disk space at the expense of some CPU on the backup client, and can also relieve network congestion by reducing the amount of backup traffic. The BACKUP command with the DURATION option lets you specify limited time windows for backup activities and minimize load imposed by backup activities during those backup windows. When a backup runs beyond the specified time, it is aborted. An optional PARTIAL parameter can be added to display which files could not be backed up. You can also use the MINIMIZE TIME or MINIMIZE LOAD parameters with the DURATION option to ensure that backups use all available resources in the first instance or throttle the resources so that the backup window is fully utilized in the latter instance.

As well, RMAN can adjust its backup parameters dynamically using the disk topology APIs. This can influence which files are multiplexed, the level of multiplexing, as well as the number and size of buffers used for input and output disk buffers. Note that these buffers are allocated out of the LARGE_POOL_SIZE and this parameter needs to be configured properly.

Other RMAN Improvements

RMAN has introduced a slew of new features too numerous to list in detail. Briefly, they include the following:

- **Automatic file creation.** Files are automatically created when data files are found missing during restore or recover operations.

- **Restore failover.** If a backup piece is not found or is corrupt, RMAN can automatically use other copies if present or previous backups sets.

- **Backup set creation.** The BACKUP command can now create backup sets as well as data file image copies through the use of the new BACKUP AS COPY command. The previous COPY DATAFILE command is now deprecated. Please note this change if you were backing up data file image copies.

- **Backup identification.** The RESTORE restore_level PREVIEW command can be used to identify the backups required to carry out a given restore operation, based on the information in the RMAN repository. This could be backup sets or image copies, on disk or on other media such as tapes. You can now use the PREVIEW option to ensure that all required backups are available or to identify situations in which you may want to direct RMAN to use or avoid specific backups. Note that this command is different from the RESTORE restore_level VALIDATE command, which physically checks the availability of the required files.

- **Cross-platform tablespace conversion.** The CONVERT TABLESPACE command performs tablespace transportation of a tablespace from a database running on one platform to a database running on a different platform. This conversion is required when the source and target's endian bytes are dissimilar. For more details, refer to MetaLink Note #243304.1.

- **Compressed backup.** When the COMPRESSED option is added to any BACKUP command, the data written into the backup set is compressed to reduce the overall size of the backup set using binary compression methods. All backups that create backup sets can create compressed backup sets. Restoring compressed backup sets is no different from restoring uncompressed backup sets. Note that this compression is more efficient than the hardware compression obtained at the tape-drive level.

- **New views.** The V$RMAN_OUTPUT and V$RMAN_STATUS views can now be used to view both messages and status from RMAN. Note that these are in-memory views.

There are many other small improvements that when considered together make a very strong case to move to the new version of RMAN.

Recovery Without Hurdles

A backup is no good if it cannot be restored. In fact, a backup cannot be considered successful if it cannot be restored. So how can you make sure that a backup can be restored? This question can be tackled by ensuring that you understand the various recovery scenarios ahead of time and document what steps you need to take to recover the object in question for that particular scenario. We do not list all the scenarios here; rather, we provide an overview of what needs to be done for backup as well as restore and recovery. Detailed information for backup strategies and recovery options is available in the *Oracle Database 10g Backup and Recovery Basics* manual, as well as in the *Oracle Database 10g Backup and Recovery Advanced User's Guide*.

Backup Strategies

The recovery and restore of databases is greatly influenced by the way you back up the database. Each type of data recovery will require that you take certain types of backup steps. You will need to cater to failures from user error, data file block corruption, and media failure, as well as plan for situations such as the complete loss of a data center. How quickly you can resume normal operation of your database is a function of what kinds of restore and recovery techniques you include in your planning. Each restore and recovery technique will impose requirements on your backup strategy, including which features of the Oracle database you use to take, store, and manage your backups.

We described a few features of RMAN such as fast incremental backups with block tracking, incrementally updated backups, and so on in the previous sections. These will help you decide which backup method is right for you. More information about the various types of backups is detailed in the manuals noted in the previous section. Overall, you will have to decide on issues such as the use of ARCHIVELOG mode, choosing a backup retention period, using the flash recovery area, archiving of older backups, establishing a backup period, and related tuning parameters. You can optionally implement backing up of often-used tablespaces versus entire databases, use of NOLOGGING, and related backups. If you were using RMAN previously and had not imple-mented incremental backups because such backups scanned the whole data file, you might want to reconsider using block tracking to mitigate this issue.

Additionally, when you want to use an MML, you will need to decide which software vendor to use and their relative merits, costs, and hardware support. When backing up directly to tape, note that tape drives are much slower than disk-based backups and hence require careful plan-ning and testing in order to meet backup and restore window requirements.

Recovery Scenarios

RMAN recovery consists of two operations: RESTORE, which retrieves files from RMAN backups based on the contents of the RMAN repository, and RECOVER, which performs complete or point-in-time media recovery using available data files and redo logs. Simple restore and recover oper-ations can be performed using the OEM Database Control. For more advanced scenarios, you should document the various recovery scenarios and the exact actions that need to be performed in each case. Optionally, you can prepare scripts that can be used from the command line in each of these cases. This preparation is wise considering that restores and recoveries are usually performed at unexpected times and under pressure.

The list of recovery scenarios and the overall actions are listed here. Note that before performing the actual recovery, you can use the RESTORE *restore_level* VALIDATE and PREVIEW commands to make sure that you have all the required files.

- **Whole database recovery.** Use the RESTORE DATABASE and RECOVER DATABASE commands on the whole database. Note that the database must not be open when restoring or recov-ering the entire database.

- **Recovering current tablespaces.** Use the RESTORE TABLESPACE and RECOVER TABLESPACE commands on individual tablespaces when the database is open. Only the tablespace that needs recovery should be taken offline. These operations restore and then recover the tablespace. You will need to bring the recovered tablespace online manually.

- **Recovering current data files.** Use the RESTORE DATAFILE and RECOVER DATAFILE commands on individual current data files when the database is open. Take the data file that needs recovery offline, restore and recover the data file, and bring the data file online.

- **Recovering individual data blocks.** RMAN can recover individual corrupted data file blocks. When RMAN performs a complete scan of a file for a backup, any corrupted blocks are listed in V$DATABASE_BLOCK_CORRUPTION. Corruption is usually reported in alert logs, trace files, or results of SQL queries. Use BLOCKRECOVER to repair all corrupted blocks using the BLOCKRECOVER CORRUPTION LIST command. You can also recover individual blocks using the BLOCKRECOVER DATAFILE *file#* BLOCK *block#* command.

- **Performing tablespace Point-In-Time Recovery (TSPITR).** You should first determine whether you can use the FLASHBACK TABLE or FLASHBACK DROP as described in Chapter 17 to revert the dropped or modified tables prior to considering TSPITR. If not, then you can use an RMAN-managed auxiliary database instance or another of your own database instances to perform this TSPITR.

- **Performing database Point-In-Time Recovery (DBPITR).** You should first determine whether you can use the FLASHBACK DATABASE as described in Chapter 17 to take the database back to the required time. If this is not possible, then you will have to use the SET UNTIL command followed by restore and recovery of all data files. You can also perform this recovery to a previous incarnation of the database.

- **Performing recovery with a backup control file.** RMAN can perform this recovery with and without a catalog, but note that you will have to perform a RESETLOGS operation as you would have to when all the control files are lost.

- **Restoring the database to a new host.** RMAN provides a DUPLICATE command to restore the database on another host for creating clones. Although this is not a strict recovery scenario, we mention this on account of its common occurrence.

- **Disaster recovery.** This operation is similar to restoring the database on a new host. However, you will not have any prior information about existing data files, tablespaces, and other files, or control information such as the catalog or OEM repositories. The key, of course, is having up-to-date documentation about the backups and databases themselves. Note that you can use the SET DBID *DB ID_number* command to set the DB ID back to the original one after you have performed recovery.

The exact commands and other information are available in the manuals mentioned in the previous section.

New Features in Oracle Database 10g Release 2

RMAN continues to improve in Oracle Database 10g Release 2, with the addition of the following features:

- **New views.** These views correlate and simplify the metadata of an RMAN backup job. This enhances the manageability of RMAN backups by providing a SQL interface to this data rather than relying on RMAN reports and commands. For example, V$BACKUP_ARCHIVELOG_DETAILS and V$BACKUP_ARCHIVELOG_SUMMARY provide details such as the name, compression ratio, and other details of archive logs in a backup set or proxy copy. Similar views display details for control file, system parameter (SPFILE), data file, and backup sets.

- **Temporary data files (TEMPFILE) re-creation.** TEMPFILEs that are part of the locally managed TEMPORARY tablespace are now recreated during recovery. Such TEMPFILE recreation, when forgotten during database cloning, used to result in errors when the process required space in the TEMPORARY tablespace.

- **OEM for RMAN.** OEM has been modified to use the built-in RMAN compression feature when used to clone databases, saving on both disk space and network usage at the expense of some CPU cycles for compression/decompression.

- **Dynamic channel allocation in RAC environments.** By configuring parallelism when backing up or recovering a RAC database, RMAN channels are dynamically allocated across all RAC instances. This is similar to dynamic RMAN channel allocation for a single instance. Channel failover allows a failed operation on one node to be continued on another node. This feature eliminates manual allocation of RMAN channels for each RAC node and provides better tolerace of media failures. In other words, when one node fails, another node can continue the backups.

Summary

This chapter demonstrated how RMAN has been improved in Oracle Database 10g. If you are new to RMAN or have not implemented it yet, we suggest you do so because the features and interface to RMAN have been greatly improved. If you are already using RMAN, you should reconsider the backup strategies that you had implemented previously in view of the new improvements such as incremental backups and incrementally updated backups.

PART III

Tuning Oracle Database 10g

10 Adopting a New Approach to Tuning

11 Effectively Using the Automatic Workload Repository

12 Effectively Using the Automatic Database Diagnostic Monitor

13 Effectively Using the SQL Advisors

14 Influencing the Cost Based Optimizer

10

Adopting a New Approach to Tuning

IN THIS CHAPTER

A New Performance Philosophy	175
New and Improved Views	180
Time and Wait Model	191
OEM and Tuning	194
New Features in Oracle Database 10g Release 2	205

A New Performance Philosophy

While Oracle Database 10g has introduced major changes in many areas, there has been significant improvement in the area of performance monitoring and tuning. Indeed, the philosophy in this RDBMS version has been one of automation, a philosophy that has been fully implemented in this important component.

Performance Analyst

"Performance analyst" is a special role that has the responsibility of tuning the database and the application code in order to obtain better performance from the system as a whole. In most cases, the Database Administrator (DBA) is tasked with this role, because this person usually deals with the internals of the database. It is not necessary, however, that the DBA alone should fill this role. It can be equally well handled by anyone who has adequate knowledge, the right privileges to get to the variety of performance statistics that the Oracle Database 10g can provide, and more importantly, the persistence to go after the problem at hand. Knowledge of SQL, PL/SQL, and the database is a must for this performance analyst. Some knowledge of operating-system performance characteristics and the underlying hardware, although not essential, can be of great help.

Traditionally, the Oracle RDBMS has not suffered from nonavailability of detailed performance statistics. Rather, users have lacked both a consistent method of easily exposing and using these performance statistics, as well as tools that analyzed these statistics and provided sane advice. Although the aptly named *Oracle Wait Interface* has existed since Oracle 7.0, only after the turn of the century has it become popular as a method used for tuning. Since then, however, a number of Oracle-provided and third party–developed tools have tried to fill the gaps and attempted to distill these statistics into meaningful information that can be used to tune the database.

We make constant reference to the Oracle Wait Interface and Wait events in this section, and hence it is necessary for you to understand what we are talking about. Essentially, the Oracle Wait Interface is a method of identifying database performance issues by viewing, monitoring, and analyzing Wait events, with the purpose of reducing or removing the waiting portion of an Oracle process. An active Oracle process moves through many stages in its life. At any point of time, it is in any one of the following states:

- Starting up or shutting down

- Executing on the CPU

- Waiting in the CPU queue to execute

- Waiting for an event external to the process to complete

It is this waiting for the external event that the Oracle Wait Interface describes. The Oracle kernel can expose the *event* for which a process is *waiting* at a point in time, and thus the term *Wait event*. These events include waiting for disk or network I/O to complete, waiting for a shared resource such as a lock or latch that is being used by another process to be released, and so on. Each of these Wait events is named, and the total time waited and number of times the process waited on that particular event is tracked and exposed via a variety of internal V$ views. Understanding and quantifying these Wait events thus becomes key to performance analysis and remediation.

In Oracle Database 10g, the Wait events are classified as well, which helps a performance analyst to quickly assess the significance of various events without knowing lower-level details. The number of Wait events has also grown significantly in Oracle Database 10g. Essentially, it means that more and more sections of the kernel code have been instrumented to record the event as the session passes through it. In fact, while Oracle Version 7.3.4 had about 100 Wait events, Oracle 8i recorded over 200 such events and Oracle 9i doubled that number to 400. Ultimately, Oracle Database 10g Release 1 records over 800 Wait events!

The Oracle Wait Interface has been the subject of many books, articles, and discussions. We will not go into details here. But as we said before, we will make reference to these events. A complete list of events is detailed in Appendix C, "Oracle Wait Events," of the *Oracle Database 10g Reference Manual*. This section of the manual is also not new; it has been available since Oracle Version 7.0.

> **What's in a Name?**
>
> The term *Oracle Wait Interface* has never been officially recognized by Oracle. It is, however, generally well known and widely accepted in the Oracle user community, and hence we will use it. A search of the technical notes at Oracle's MetaLink site throws up lots of links for the term "Wait event," but not a single reference to the "Wait Interface." The OWI, as it is affectionately known in its short form, actually evolved from another acronym, YAPP, which stands for "Yet Another Performance Profiling" methodology, but that is entirely another story! Whatever you call it, remember that it is based on analyzing the Oracle Wait events and using this information to detect and correct performance problems.

Performance-Management Tools

Before looking at what Oracle Database 10g provides, it is wise to look at what these Oracle-provided and third-party tools lacked so that you can understand why they did not fully serve their purpose. The Oracle-provided STATSPACK is one such tool. It is free and is relatively well documented. It is also widely used, and hence we have chosen this standard tool to critique the previous philosophy so that you can appreciate the new. In any case, most other tools provided a GUI-based view of the very same performance data that STATSPACK also used.

STATSPACK **Shortfalls**

First of all, STATSPACK had to be installed and configured manually. The DBA had to first install STATSPACK in the database and then set up scripts or jobs to collect *snapshots* of performance data at an appropriate interval. The DBA also had to manage the maintenance of STATSPACK data, performing purges to keep the amount of data in check. The DBA then had to manually generate reports using the Oracle-supplied SPREPORT script, which determined and listed the differences in statistics collected between two snapshots. A database restart between snapshots rendered the statistics for that pair meaningless, because they are essentially snapshots of counters that get reset during the restart event—and the DBA was supposed to keep track of this! The DBA then had the most difficult task of all: making sense of the reams of figures that this report generated.

As well, there was no standardization of the snapshot schedule, and this resulted in many DBAs performing snapshots for intervals that essentially rendered the information meaningless. For example, if snapshots were performed once in the morning at start of business day, and again at the end of the business day, peaks in usage during the day could not be determined from the collected snapshots—the peak values would be lost due to the law of averages, rendering the whole STATSPACK collection virtually useless. To top it all, there was no GUI interface to STATSPACK data—either for management or for interpretation.

STATSPACK also cannot determine the negative effects on the overall performance caused by a single offending session or even a small number of such sessions because the system statistics are collected globally and averaged out over both active and inactive sessions. For example, in a STATSPACK snapshot, a total wait time of 100 seconds accumulated by 100 connected sessions would be calculated to have an average wait time of 100 seconds /100 sessions = 1 second of wait time per session. This is obviously untrue and provides an incorrect picture of the problem. In fact, you may not even notice that there was a problem.

Although SQL statements that violated some preconfigured limits could be captured via STATSPACK, there were no in-built tools that connected them back to performance problems and issues. There was also no way to perform a comparison between multiple occurrences of a particular high-usage SQL so that you could determine what occurred between two snapshots. Thus, there was no way of tying a performance issue back to a particular SQL statement.

Extending STATSPACK

It is possible to extend STATSPACK to collect, store, and report additional information by adding to the various tables and SQL code. This is neither standardized nor documented, however, and hence adds to the confusion.

Finally, although no performance analysis can be considered complete without due consideration of operating-system performance statistics, STATSPACK does not collect or store this information.

Oracle Corporation seems to have recognized these shortfalls and prevented them by taking the following actions:

- Installing the Automatic Workload Repository (AWR) collector, the Automatic Database Diagnostic Monitor (ADDM), and other advisors by default during database installation

- Offloading collection, management, and processing of performance-related data to two separate Oracle background processes, named MMON and MMNL. This includes capturing both Oracle-related as well as operating-system performance statistics

- Providing the ability to capture performance baseline figures and alert against violations to these baselines

- Providing advisors, such as the SQL Tuning Advisor and SQL Access Advisor, that operate against this captured data

- Providing both a GUI interface from OEM as well as API calls from SQL to this data

Another major weakness in the previous versions was the lack of history information with regard to performance statistics. Apart from the STATSPACK snapshot information that was collected periodically, there was no way to determine what occurred in the immediate past. For example, suppose that a user is suddenly facing a performance issue in a form that normally performs well. She calls you to say that for the past five minutes, the response from this form has slowed considerably. In previous versions, there was no way for you to determine what occurred. To track down this issue, the DBA would have to either attempt to recreate it in a controlled environment with extended SQL tracing turned on or resort to high-overhead monitoring tools that sampled session information with very short time periods.

In Oracle Database 10g, however, this information is automatically available for all connected and active sessions in the Active Session History (ASH). The Oracle kernel snapshots session information, stores it in a temporary circular buffer within the System Global Area (SGA), and exposes this via the V$ACTIVE_SESSION_HISTORY and other views. Using ASH, a DBA can perform an on-the-spot analysis, without having to resort to the other complicated means described previously.

Another major change in Oracle Database 10g was the introduction of the Time and Wait model. The response time of a database action that produces meaningful work in the database consists of two components: service time and wait time. These can be summarized using the following formula:

Response Time = Service Time + Wait Time

Service time is the time spent by the process in the CPU, usually clocked as the *user time* from the operating system, and *wait time* is time spent by the process waiting for specific resources to be available before continuing its processing. Examples of wait time include the time spent waiting for I/O operations to complete, or even the time spent by one process waiting for a conflicting row lock to be released by another process. Thus, to reduce the response time and hence increase the performance of database actions, either the service time or the wait time (or a combination of both) must be reduced. In order to do this, you must be able to drill down into both the service and wait times and determine which components of these two has contributed most to the timings.

Service time is exposed in the V$SYSSTAT view at the database level and in the V$SESSTAT view at the individual session level. In a similar way, wait time is exposed in the V$SYSTEM_EVENT view at the database level and in the V$SESSION_EVENT view at the individual session level.

In earlier versions, the service and wait times were not classified; thus, it was not an easy task to determine what contributed most to the issue at hand. The Oracle Wait Interface

> **Service Time in** STATSPACK
> **Oracle Corporation seems to have recognized the importance of figuring the service time in** STATSPACK. **As compared to the Oracle 8i version or even the Oracle 9i Release 1 version, the Oracle 9i Release 2 version of a** STATSPACK **report includes DB Time in the renamed "Top 5 Timed Events" section. The earlier versions listed only the Wait events and titled the section "Top 5 Wait Events."**

was able to expose some of the components of the wait time, but the service time (or CPU time) was not well understood or exposed. Oracle rectified this problem with the introduction of the Time and Wait model, described in the "Time and Wait Model" section later in this chapter. Essentially, using this model, a performance analyst could easily classify and thus isolate the various components of service and wait time, leading to intuitive and quicker performance-problem diagnosis and rectification.

Thus, out of the box, Oracle Database 10g provides preconfigured, easily accessible tools and advisors that deal with all aspects of performance. When understood and used properly, they provide a well-structured and automated performance toolkit. Although we will discuss AWR, ADDM, and the advisors in great detail in subsequent chapters, we have mentioned them here so that we can provide an overall sense of where they fit and what they can contribute to the whole. In essence, Oracle Database 10g automates, standardizes, and simplifies many actions that were previously done manually for performance monitoring and tuning. This frees the performance analyst from carrying out mundane tasks, allowing them to instead concentrate on more complex ones, and enables the less skilled to come up to speed quickly on this important but often ill-understood area of database operations.

New and Improved Views

Views upon Views: The X$ Views

The V$ views are actually more readable and understandable representations of other internal views, known as the *X$ views*. If you are really curious, you can determine the definition of the V$ views using the V$FIXED_VIEW_DEFINTION view. Contrary to popular myth, all X$ views are actually SQL accessible structures in the SGA, and viewing them will not cause performance problems unless there is excessive access. Although you could write direct SQL against these views that are seen only from the SYS account, this is not encouraged because these X$ view definitions, column names, and meanings are subject to change without documentation or notice.

Setting the Right STATISTICS_LEVEL Parameter

You must set the STATISTICS_LEVEL initialization parameter to either TYPICAL or ALL for statistics to be collected and exposed in most of the views noted in the following sections. Setting this parameter to BASIC will disable collection of many of these statistics. The default value of TYPICAL ensures that the most relevant statistics required for database self-management functionality is collected and provides best overall performance. The default value should be adequate for most environments. Note that TIMED_STATISTICS is automatically set to TRUE if the STATISTICS_LEVEL parameter is set to at least TYPICAL. See Table 10.1 for what does and does not get collected or implemented for the various settings.

Before we get into details, we need to describe the new and modified sets of views that Oracle Database 10g provides for performance monitoring and tuning. The number of Dynamic performance views, also known as the *V$ views*, has steadily increased as the version levels increased. Oracle 8i provided 191, while Oracle 9i Release 2 provided 266. Oracle Database 10g has built on that with a massive count of 347! Although there are many new views that the larger Oracle community has not yet probed in depth, even in Oracle 9i, we need to only take note of a select number of these views.

The following section describes the performance-related V$ views in this version. It is important to know of these views because you might have to use them on occasion to detect current and past performance issues and to drill down into the details. Both the standalone Oracle Enterprise Manager (OEM) Database Control and Grid Control elements present the data from these views in easily accessible GUI screens. Knowledge of some of these views will help you to bypass these screens and get to the data quickly and to automate many of these tasks via scripts. As well, OEM does not view-enable all these views; hence, you need to get to the data in these views via the SQL interface alone.

When we describe these views, we will highlight only the relevant uses of the view, making mention of columns only when required. We will also present the views in a logical sequence rather than alphabetically.

Some of the views are exposed as DBA_ and ALL_ views and are not fully documented. However, we have chosen to detail them although they are "hidden" because they sometimes provide additional information. Detailed information for some of the views can be obtained from the *Oracle Database 10g Reference Manual*.

TABLE 10.1

Settings for STATISTICS_LEVEL **and the Effect on Advisors and Statistics Collections**

Advisor or Statistics	BASIC	TYPICAL	ALL
Buffer cache advice	None	X	X
MTTR advice	None	X	X
Shared pool advice	None	X	X
Segment-level statistics	None	X	X
PGA advice	None	X	X
Timed statistics	None	X	X
Timed OS statistics	None	None	X
Plan execution statistics	None	None	X

V$METRIC, V$METRIC_HISTORY, V$METRICNAME, **and** V$METRICGROUP

These views expose the individual and grouped sets of metrics that are used for Server Generated Alerts (SGAs). Before you look at these views, however, you need to understand what *metrics* are.

Most of the database statistics that you know of and use with other versions are essentially cumulative counters. For example, the V$SYSTEM_EVENT shows the cumulative value of various Wait events in the database that have accumulated from the time the database started until the time when you chose to view it. Similarly, the V$SYSSTAT view displays accumulated database statistics since database startup. When performing reactive real-time performance diagnosis, however, it is the *rate of change* of the counter that is important, rather than its absolute value since instance startup. Knowing that the system performed 2,000 I/Os per second or three I/Os per transaction during the last minute is rather more helpful than knowing that the database has performed 27,000,000 I/Os since it was started. As such, you can call the rate of change a metric because you know that when a particular rate is excessive as compared to a previous lower rate of change, you might expect to see some performance issue. In other words, thresholds for alerting can often be set based on rates. In Oracle Database 10g, metrics are available in a precalculated manner, normalized by both time and transaction. Most metrics are maintained at a one-minute interval and are also available in a historical fashion.

You can use these views to determine the units of various metrics that you will encounter and the OEM agent would use. V$METRIC displays metrics from the immediate past, while V$METRIC_HISTORY exposes the history. V$METRICNAME names and describes the units for these metrics, while V$METRICGROUP groups them. These views are not documented in the *Oracle Database 10g Reference Manual*. For more details on how these views matter in Server Generated Alerts, look at MetaLink Note #266970.1.

V$SERVICES, V$SERVICEMETRIC, **and** V$SERVICEMETRIC_HISTORY

These views expose the metrics mentioned in the previous section, broken down by services. *Services* are essentially classifications of layers where work is done. For example, for a database named TS10G, you would see services such as TS10G, TS10GXDB, SYS$USERS, and SYS$BACKGROUND. V$SERVICES displays the service names available, V$SERVICEMETRIC displays the metrics by service for the immediate past (usually one minute), while V$SERVICEMETRIC_HISTORY keeps a rolling history for about 10 minutes.

V$SERVICE_STATS

This view displays sets of performance statistics by service name. In most cases, these individual values will be rolled up into statistics otherwise seen via the well-known V$SYSSTAT view. These statistics can be used to determine the amount of work done by a specific service—for example, you can see the statistic db block changes broken down as shown in Listing 10.1.

LISTING 10.1   Snapshot of V$SERVICE_STATS

```
SQL> compute sum of value on report
SQL> break on report skip 1
SQL> select service_name, stat_name, value
  2  from v$service_stats where stat_name = 'db block changes';


SERVICE_NAME    STAT_NAME                       VALUE
--------------- ------------------------------- ----------
TS10GXDB        db block changes                         0
SYS$USERS       db block changes                    585733
SYS$BACKGROUND  db block changes                   1240945
TS10G           db block changes                         8
                                                ----------
sum                                                1826686


SQL> clear compute
SQL> select name, value from v$sysstat
  2  where name = 'db block changes';


NAME             VALUE
---------------- ----------
db block changes 1826686
```

Note that these queries were run on an inactive database. There were minimal, if any, changes between the queries; thus, the total value as shown by the SQL*Plus COMPUTE clause and the rolled-up value from V$SYSSTAT for this statistic have the same value from both views. Also, the history of this data is presented via DBA_HIST_SERVICE_STAT.

V$SERVICE_EVENT

This view displays sets of aggregated wait counts and wait times for each Wait event statistic, again by service name. As before, in most cases, these individual values will be rolled up into statistics seen via the well-known V$SYSTEM_EVENT view. Listing 10.2 shows an example for database reads and writes.

> **View and Column Naming Inconsistencies**
>
> You may have noticed that the S is missing at the end in the view DBA_HIST_SERVICE_STAT even though it is connected to the V$SERVICE_STATS view, which *does* have a S at the end. Although we wish that Oracle Corporation would be consistent in naming its views, we will doubtless have to live with such small inconsistencies. This is not new—many a DBA has been tripped up by the inconsistently named DBA_DATA_FILE.FILE_ID and V$FILESTAT.FILE# columns, both of which mean the same thing and participate often in joins!

LISTING 10.2 Snapshot of V$SERVICE_EVENT

```
SQL> compute sum of total_waits on report
SQL> compute sum of time_waited on report
SQL> break on report skip 1
SQL> select service_name, event, total_waits, time_waited
  2  from v$service_event
  3  where event in ('db file parallel write','db file scattered read')
  4  order by service_name, event;


SERVICE_NAME    EVENT                     TOTAL_WAITS TIME_WAITED
--------------- ------------------------- ----------- -----------
SYS$BACKGROUND  db file parallel write          52916        9698
SYS$BACKGROUND  db file scattered read           7279         585
SYS$USERS       db file scattered read           5462        1477
                                          ----------- -----------
sum                                             65657       11760


SQL> select event, total_waits, time_waited
  2  from v$system_event
  3  where event in ('db file parallel write','db file scattered read')
  4  order by event;


EVENT                     TOTAL_WAITS TIME_WAITED
------------------------- ----------- -----------
db file parallel write          52916        9698
db file scattered read          12741        2063
                          ----------- -----------
sum                             65657       11761
```

From Where do Database Writes Emanate?

The query of V$SERVICE_EVENT makes it clear that the db file parallel write event is associated only with background processes, while the db file scattered read event could originate from both background and foreground (or user) processes. In fact, by looking at V$SESSION_EVENT and V$SESSION, you can verify that the db file parallel write event, which is the Wait event signifying the writing to a database file, is present only in the DB writer processes. The only database writes that a user process is allowed are direct writes to the sort segments in the temporary tablespace.

As before, these queries were run on an inactive database, one after another, and the total waits and total time waited agree across these views. Expect some differences if you are running these queries on a busy system.

V$EVENTMETRIC

This view displays values of Wait event metrics for the most recent and active 60-second interval and can be used to take a quick look at what happened in the last *active* minute. These values are built on a circular buffer in memory and are thus overwritten every minute or so. Note that on a quiet system, these values will live on past the minute—the start and end times for this quick snapshot can be seen from the BEGIN_TIME and END_TIME columns.

V$EVENT_HISTOGRAM

This is a very interesting view that displays a histogram of the number of waits, the maximum wait, and total wait time on an event basis. The histogram has buckets of time intervals from < 1 millisecond, < 2 milliseconds, < 4 milliseconds, < 8 milliseconds, and so on, in increasing powers of 2 up to 2^22 milliseconds. Note that the values are cumulative and reflect the current state since the instance started up. The bucket values for the histograms cannot be changed and the view is populated only when TIMED_STATISTICS is set. This is an excellent view to use when you want to see the spread of wait times for certain events since database startup. Listing 10.3 illustrates this.

LISTING 10.3   Wait Event Histograms for Database Reads

```
SQL> break on event skip 1
SQL> select event, wait_time_milli, wait_count
  2  from v$event_histogram
  3  where event in
  4  ('db file sequential read','db file scattered read');


EVENT                          WAIT_TIME_MILLI WAIT_COUNT
------------------------------ --------------- ----------
db file sequential read                      1      19403
                                             2       6450
                                             4        411
                                             8       1853
                                            16       2091
```

LISTING 10.3   Continued

	32	381
	64	106
	128	10
	256	1
db file scattered read	1	11193
	2	451
	4	291
	8	184
	16	394
	32	218
	64	84
	128	24
	256	1

From Listing 10.3, one can conclude that a majority of single-block reads in the form of db file sequential read and multiblock reads in the form of db file scattered read events completed in 1 millisecond or less. You can see that during some unknown point of time, some indexed data-block reads (in the form of db file sequential read) took between 8 and 16 milliseconds. These values are acceptable if not excellent. Note the value 2091 for the 16-millisecond histogram; we will refer to this later in this chapter in the section titled "V$FILE_HISTOGRAM."

You can use this view to determine the existence of yet another issue. The SQL*Net message to client, SQL*Net more data to client, and SQL*Net break/reset to client events are normally considered idle events and are ignored. However, we have seen cases where these events have contributed significantly to performance issues, generally due to bad or misconfigured network hardware or saturated networks. In such cases, prior to Oracle Database 10g, there was no way to determine whether this was an issue by looking at the values from V$SYSTEM_EVENT, because the values there are averaged out. Now, with the V$EVENT_HISTOGRAM, you can look at the spread of wait times for these idle events. Recording these values before and after a problem occurs and looking at oddities can help point to the existence of network- and interface-related issues. Consider the example in Listing 10.4.

LISTING 10.4   Event Histogram for SQL*Net Events

```
SQL> column event format a30
SQL> select event, wait_time_milli, wait_count
  2  from v$event_histogram
  3  where event like 'SQL*Net %to client';


EVENT                          WAIT_TIME_MILLI WAIT_COUNT
------------------------------ --------------- ----------
```

LISTING 10.4   Continued

SQL*Net message to client	1	4866
SQL*Net more data to client	1	1582
SQL*Net break/reset to client	1	60

You can see from this snippet that most SQL*Net messages to the client completed within a millisecond, so this is not an issue.

Breaking Out Certain Wait Events

One of the shortcomings that we have noticed with both the V$EVENT_HISTOGRAM and V$SYSTEM_EVENT views is the fact that the latch free event is lumped into one counter, unlike with the V$SESSION_EVENT view, which breaks out the latch free event into classified events such as latch: cache buffers chains, latch: cache buffers lru chain, latch: library cache, and latch: shared pool to name a few. Such classification becomes important when trying to resolve latch-related issues, and we wish Oracle Corporation had carried this classification forward into all levels. If you are actively using the V$SESSION_WAIT view, then you will notice that even this view breaks out the latch free and enqueue events.

Note that we did not include SQL*Net message from client in this discussion because this event caters to both program response time as well as the idle time, or *think* time, awaiting user input at a keyboard. Thus, an interactive session with a long think time when the user is inactive at the keyboard would produce an event with a large wait time. This is not necessarily a problem, because the user is inactive. The values will be skewed, however, and hence cannot be considered at the aggregated system level. If you observe large counts and wait times for this supposedly idle event in a batch or non-interactive program, however, then you should investigate this further. In summary, not all idle events are actually idle and thus do deserve some attention. You will need to see such idle events in context.

V$FILEMETRIC and V$FILEMETRIC_HISTORY

These views expose file I/O metrics. The number and average duration of reads and writes to specific data files over the last 10 minutes is seen from V$FILEMETRIC, and V$FILEMETRIC_HISTORY stores these values for the past hour or so in an in-memory circular buffer.

V$FILE_HISTOGRAM

This is another interesting view that displays a histogram of single-block reads on a per-file basis. The histogram has buckets of time intervals from < 1 millisecond, < 2 milliseconds, < 4 milliseconds, < 8 milliseconds, and so on, in increasing powers of 2 up to 2^22 milliseconds. Note that the values are cumulative and reflect the current state since the instance started up. The bucket values for the histograms cannot be changed and the view is populated only when TIMED_STATISTICS is set. This is an excellent view to use when you want to see the spread of single-block read wait times by individual files since database startup. You will of course need to join this to DBA_DATA_FILES to get the filenames. Listing 10.5 provides an example.

LISTING 10.5   File-Wise Read Response Histogram

```
SQL> break on file_name skip 1
SQL> column file_name format a25 wrap
SQL> select file_name,
  2  singleblkrdtim_milli, singleblkrds
  3  from v$file_histogram v, dba_data_files d
  4  where v.file# = d.file_id
  5  and file# = 3;


FILE_NAME                 SINGLEBLKRDTIM_MILLI SINGLEBLKRDS
------------------------- -------------------- ------------

/u04/app/oracle/product/1                    1         7540
0.1.0/db_1/oradata/TS10G/
sysaux01.dbf


                                             2         2811
                                             4          196
                                             8         1221
                                            16         1449
                                            32          206
                                            64           51
                                           128            8
```

This example shows that most single-blocks read to file #3 (seen normally as db file sequential read events), which happen to be the SYSAUX01.DBF file, completed within 1 to 2 milliseconds. So what is the difference between this histogram and the previous one seen from V$EVENT_HISTOGRAM for db file sequential read? V$FILE_HISTOGRAM breaks out the histogram values for the db file sequential read alone into component values on a *per-file* basis. Thus, if you see odd patterns in the histogram values *specifically* for the db file sequential read event in the V$EVENT_HISTOGRAM, then you might be able to investigate further as to which file actually caused this skew in values. You saw in the earlier example that there were 2,091 single-block reads waits, each taking 16 milliseconds. The question as to which of these files contributed to this can be determined from the following query in Listing 10.6.

LISTING 10.6   Determine Which File Contributed to the 16-Millisecond Response

```
SQL> column file_name format a25 wrap
SQL> select file_name, singleblkrdtim_milli, singleblkrds
  2  from v$file_histogram v, dba_data_files d
  3  where v.file# = d.file_id
  4  and singleblkrdtim_milli = 16;


FILE_NAME                 SINGLEBLKRDTIM_MILLI SINGLEBLKRDS
------------------------- -------------------- ------------
/u04/app/oracle/product/1                   16          623
```

LISTING 10.6   Continued

0.1.0/db_1/oradata/TS10G/ system01.dbf		
/u04/app/oracle/product/1 0.1.0/db_1/oradata/TS10G/ undotbs01.dbf	16	3
/u04/app/oracle/product/1 0.1.0/db_1/oradata/TS10G/ sysaux01.dbf	16	1477
/u04/app/oracle/product/1 0.1.0/db_1/oradata/TS10G/ users01.dbf	16	8
/u04/app/oracle/product/1 0.1.0/db_1/oradata/TS10G/ example01.dbf	16	10

You can deduce from the numbers in the preceding code that the SYSAUX01.DBF file contributed most to the 16-millisecond read response time. You might use this route to investigate whether a particular data file is contributing to the high values, and decide to move it around to spread the I/O. As before, this was run on a quiet system; expect some difference if the system is active and busy. The principle in general will work, though.

V$TEMP_HISTOGRAM

This displays the same kind of histogram as V$FILE_HISTOGRAM, but specifically for TEMPFILE files, which are used for temporary tablespaces. This view can be used in the same way to locate TEMPFILE hot spots.

V$ENQUEUE_STATISTICS

This view displays statistics about the number and duration of enqueue (lock) requests for each type. The columns EQ_NAME, EQ_TYPE, and REQ_DESCRIPTION make for interesting reading. In prior versions, Oracle Corporation exposed the enqueue name in various views such as V$LOCK and V$SESSION_WAIT using bitmap values, and you had to translate them using CHR and BITAND functions. This new view provides the same information in clear text with good explanations and is worth looking at when you encounter locking issues. Interestingly enough, there is another view named V$ENQUEUE_STAT, which is a summarized, less-detailed version of this informative view. The latter view was available in Oracle 9i, and provides the same information as in Oracle Database 10g. We advise using V$ENQUEUE_STATISTICS in Oracle Database 10g instead, and recommend that you go directly to the internal X$KSQST view in older versions because this contains accurate numbers.

V$OSSTAT

This is a new, very useful view that displays the system-utilization statistics from the operating system. One row is returned for each system statistic, with statistics ranging from informational values such as NUM_CPUS (number of CPUs) as well as metrics such as number of bytes sent and received, CPU ticks used, and so on. These are shown in Listing 10.7.

LISTING 10.7   Snapshot of V$OSSTAT

```
SQL> set numwidth 12
SQL> column stat_name format a30
SQL> select * from v$osstat;

STAT_NAME                            VALUE     OSSTAT_ID
------------------------------ ------------ ------------

NUM_CPUS                                 2            0
IDLE_TICKS                        11884181            1
BUSY_TICKS                          632793            2
USER_TICKS                          455624            3
SYS_TICKS                           177169            4
IOWAIT_TICKS                        393176            5
AVG_IDLE_TICKS                     5941049            7
AVG_BUSY_TICKS                      315355            8
AVG_USER_TICKS                      226774            9
AVG_SYS_TICKS                        87511           10
AVG_IOWAIT_TICKS                    195516           11
OS_CPU_WAIT_TIME                   1985600           13
RSRC_MGR_CPU_WAIT_TIME                   0           14
IN_BYTES                         21408317440         1000
OUT_BYTES                         8398913536         1001
FS_IN_BYTES                      11696422912         1002
FS_OUT_BYTES                      4750868480         1003
AVG_IN_BYTES                     10704158720         1004
AVG_OUT_BYTES                     4199456768         1005
AVG_FS_IN_BYTES                   5848211456         1006
AVG_FS_OUT_BYTES                  2375434240         1007
```

Changes in Existing Views

In addition to introducing new views, Oracle Database 10g has also added or changed some existing ones, and we highlight the relevant ones here. You have seen that the size of some of the columns—such as those holding instance, user, and other names—have been increased in this version. Many RAW(4) columns have been expanded to RAW(8). Wait class information (columns WAIT_CLASS_ID, WAIT_CLASS, and WAIT_CLASS#) has been added to many views that describe events, such as V$EVENT_NAME, V$SESSION, and V$SESSION_WAIT.

Changes in V$SESSION

The very popular V$SESSION view has had a large number of columns added, essentially merging all the columns previously available in V$SESSION_WAIT, such as EVENT, P1, P2, P3, and their raw equivalents. As well, information about blocking sessions is made available within V$SESSION using the intuitively named BLOCKING_SESSION column. This will obviate the need to join the V$SESSION view to the V$SESSION_WAIT view to obtain current session-wait information or to the V$LOCK view to obtain blocking-session information. See the very simple SQL in Listing 10.8, which can detect the details of any session whose DML has been blocked by another.

LISTING 10.8   Blocked-Session Details

```
SQL> select sid, blocking_session, username, blocking_session_status,
  2  program, event, seconds_in_wait
  3  from v$session
  4  where blocking_session_status = 'VALID';


 SID BLOCKING_SESSION USERN BLOCKING_SE PROGRAM
 ---- ---------------- ----- ----------- -------------------
EVENT                            SECONDS_IN_WAIT
-------------------------------- ---------------
 146             134 HR    VALID     PLSQLDev.exe
enq: TX - row lock contention                132
```

The SQL detects that an Oracle login user, HR, whose session ID is 146 and who is executing using the PLSQLDev.exe program, has been blocked for row update by another session, 134, and that the session has been waiting for 132 seconds. The event that describes this waiting is enq: TX - row lock contention, which is a broken-out detail of the enqueue wait. In previous versions, you had to join V$LOCK, V$SESSION_WAIT, and V$SESSION to obtain the same information.

Changes in V$SQL and V$SQLAREA

Another major addition has been to the V$SQL and V$SQLAREA views; they now have additional columns named APPLICATION_WAIT_TIME, CONCURRENCY_WAIT_TIME, CLUSTER_WAIT_TIME, USER_IO_WAIT_TIME, PLSQL_EXEC_TIME, and JAVA_EXEC_TIME that denote time waited for these different classifications. This makes it easy to pick out the "Top-N" resource consumers by whatever class of resource required. If you have scripts that use these views, you should change them to take advantage of this bonus!

We will discuss a number of other performance-related views in detail in the subsequent section and chapters, depending on their relevance. We will continue to make reference to the views described in this section as required later on.

Changes in Other Views

You haven't even looked at the other views, such as DBA_ and ALL_ views, that matter for performance, except to mention a few in passing. You can always use SQL and your favorite operating-system text-processing utilities to draw up and compare lists of views for both an Oracle Database 10g instance and an older Oracle 9i instance. Look up the new views in the *Oracle Database 10g Reference Manual*. MetaLink is slowly introducing an in-depth analysis of a number of them online as well.

Time and Wait Model

We briefly mentioned the Time and Wait model earlier, while introducing the performance-reporting philosophy new to Oracle Database 10g. In essence, in this version, metrics and statistics are classified by type of usage of CPU for the Time component and by type of waiting for the Wait component. In other words, the previous equation for response time can now be restated in its two component forms as follows:

Response Time = Σ CPU Consumption by Class + Σ Wait Time by Class

The difference is that now you can determine CPU time spent in various subcomponents (class of consumption) as well as time spent waiting for various classes of events. A quick look at the V$SYS_TIME_MODEL and V$SYSTEM_WAIT_CLASS views helps explain this in Listing 10.9.

LISTING 10.9   Snapshot of V$SYS_TIME_MODEL

```
SQL> column STAT_NAME format a50
SQL> set numwidth 12
SQL> select stat_name, value
    from v$sys_time_model;


STAT_NAME                                                VALUE
-------------------------------------------------- ------------
DB time                                              635611982
DB CPU                                               485511901
background elapsed time                            28179121230
background cpu time                                  1785120249
sequence load elapsed time                               49429
parse time elapsed                                    90176368
hard parse elapsed time                               61418093
sql execute elapsed time                             544301874
connection management call elapsed time                 707888
failed parse elapsed time                               191650
failed parse (out of shared memory) elapsed time             0
hard parse (sharing criteria) elapsed time              478684
hard parse (bind mismatch) elapsed time                 295962
PL/SQL execution elapsed time                         93880446
inbound PL/SQL rpc elapsed time                              0
PL/SQL compilation elapsed time                        4219341
Java execution elapsed time                            8220017
```

We need to clarify at this time that some of the lines seen in V$SYS_TIME_MODEL are actually subcomponents of other lines. For example, the `background cpu time` is part of `background elapsed time` and can never be larger than the former. Similarly `parse time elapsed` is a rollup of the other parse components. The `DB Time` is the most valuable of these and is the total time spent by the foreground sessions performing useful work. In other words, it is a combination of CPU spent parsing and executing SQL, PL/SQL, and Java, as well other overheads such as process setup and management.

In many ways, this view is similar to the V$SYSSTAT view from earlier (as well as this) versions. This view displays some CPU-related statistics, among many others. However, this is presented in a classified and compact manner in this new view. And just as V$SESSTAT describes the same statistics at the session level, Oracle Database 10g provides the V$SESS_TIME_MODEL to determine the same components at a session level. Using the latter, you can quickly drill down to determine individual CPU consumption by session.

Having dealt with the service component, or time spent on CPU, we will now look at the wait component in the form of the V$SYSTEM_WAIT_CLASS view. A sample is shown in Listing 10.10.

LISTING 10.10 Wait Components from V$SYSTEM_WAIT_CLASS

```
SQL> column WAIT_CLASS format a30
SQL> select wait_class, total_waits, time_waited
     from v$system_wait_class;


WAIT_CLASS                     TOTAL_WAITS  TIME_WAITED
------------------------------ ------------ ------------

Other                                10959      2595609
Application                             82            3
Configuration                          317          340
Concurrency                             74           15
Commit                                9941         4224
Idle                              2122944    823048107
Network                               7988            9
User I/O                             82315        13057
System I/O                          356979        85897
```

This view breaks down exactly how much time was spent by all sessions waiting in different types of waits. For example, if you see a large number of waits and time spent waiting under Concurrency, you might want to consider redesigning your application to minimize the time that rows are kept locked because locking is detrimental to concurrency. And after performing I/O tuning, you might want to monitor the time waited under System I/O and User I/O to verify that you did the right thing.

Just as we compared V$SYSSTAT and V$SYS_TIME_MODEL, we can compare V$SYSTEM_WAIT_CLASS to the V$SYSTEM_EVENT view available in older versions.

The time components for all these views are always displayed in microseconds (1/1000th of a second), and the counters are large enough to hold 580,000 years worth of statistics!

Another view, V$SERVICE_WAIT_CLASS, breaks out waits by service and wait class within the service since database restart. A comparison of statistics from this view before and after a performance event of interest can reveal much. A sample snapshot is shown in Listing 10.11.

The Concurrency Wait Class

Although we seem to imply that concurrency has to do with row locking (which ensures transaction consistency and is seen via the enqueue event and its subevents, such as enq: TX row lock contention), it can also be caused by excessive latching. Transaction-type locks are placed on data elements to make sure that concurrent sessions don't change them simultaneously, but are performed in a serial (one after another) manner on a first-come, first-served basis. Latching, on the other hand, protects *internal* structures from being accessed or modified but does not generally follow the first-come, first-served rule. A simple example of latching is the holding of the shared pool latch by a process that wants to de-allocate some space from one element in the shared pool and allocate it to another element. Locks, latches, and handling of other internal structures are vast subjects by themselves, and hence, we can mention them here in passing only.

LISTING 10.11   Snapshot of V$SERVICE_WAIT_CLASS

```
SQL> set numwidth 12
SQL> column SERVICE_NAME format a20
SQL> column WAIT_CLASS format a20
SQL> select service_name, wait_class, total_waits, time_waited
  2  from v$service_wait_class
  3  order by service_name, time_waited desc;


SERVICE_NAME         WAIT_CLASS            TOTAL_WAITS  TIME_WAITED
-------------------- -------------------- ------------ ------------

SYS$BACKGROUND       System I/O               8103534  72417515074
SYS$BACKGROUND       Idle                     1459745    508654694
SYS$BACKGROUND       Other                       8999      2158769
SYS$BACKGROUND       User I/O                   26733         3790
SYS$BACKGROUND       Commit                       383          315
SYS$BACKGROUND       Configuration                254          224
SYS$BACKGROUND       Concurrency                   46            3
SYS$USERS            Idle                      300152     95045746
SYS$USERS            User I/O                   36505         6394
SYS$USERS            Commit                      7910         3178
```

LISTING 10.11   Continued

SYS$USERS	Other	16	443
SYS$USERS	Configuration	28	53
SYS$USERS	System I/O	2361	17
SYS$USERS	Network	6820	9
SYS$USERS	Concurrency	21	6
SYS$USERS	Application	64	2
TS10G	Idle	11	165
TS10G	User I/O	18	6
TS10G	Commit	2	0
TS10G	Network	11	0

Summarized this way, it is easy to see classified wait statistics for both system and user I/O load as well as any concurrency issues at the system level.

In summary, interpretation of statistics that was previously based on experience and specialized knowledge is now available in a very intuitive, easy-to-understand, and classified format.

OEM and Tuning

In previous chapters, you have seen how the Oracle Enterprise Manager (OEM) has helped administrators and developers obtain quick insights into and help manage the database via an easy-to-use graphical user interface. This section will show how OEM can help the performance analyst view and interpret performance statistics.

Simply stated, OEM is packaged in two forms:

■ **Oracle Enterprise Manager Database Control.** OEM Database Control is a Web-based tool that serves as the primary tool for administering, maintaining, and viewing the performance of a *single* database. The Database Control component is usually installed by default and is available on all Oracle Database 10g databases.

■ **Oracle Enterprise Manager Grid Control.** The Grid Control version is a Web-based tool that performs the same actions on a *group* of databases. In fact, the Grid Control tool is a replacement for the previous OEM Repository and Console and is used to centrally manage your entire Oracle environment.

The main difference between these as far as this section is concerned is in the login process. Assuming that both components are installed and configured, in order to manage a single database via Database Control, you would log in directly to the database using the correct URL. If you wanted to manage a single database that has been configured as part of a Grid Control environment, you would first log in to the OEM Grid Control console using the correct URL, and then choose the required target—in this case, a database. When this is complete, all actions are the same. Hence, for the purpose of this section, we will assume that you are logging into the `TS10G` database on a host named `test10g` using the Database Control via the following URL: `http://test10g:5550/em`.

This will bring up a login page, where you will first log in using the `SYS` or `SYSTEM` account. When this is done, depending on your requirement, you can create additional Database Control users that can be used by a designated set of other personnel.

We will concern ourselves only with the performance menus and functions at this time. There are numerous pages, menus, submenus, area graphs, drill-downs, and hyperlinks available for performance monitoring and reporting. Rather than detail all of them, we will highlight those that are most useful.

Navigating OEM Database Control

In OEM Database Control, you can get to the same information using a variety of paths.

> ### OEM Configuration Changes
>
> Changing the configuration of the database or listener may require changes in the OEM configuration files. Even a simple change, such as to the listener port, will require changes in these configuration files. This is because OEM Database Control is an Oracle Application Server container for J2EE-based Web applications. Further details may be seen in the
> `$ORACLE_HOME/Hostname_Db_SID` directory and its subdirectories, where *Hostname* is the database server host name and *Db_SID* is the database SID.
>
> The methodology and further details for such change is documented in Chapter 7, "Reconfiguring the Management Agent and Management Service," in *Oracle Enterprise Manager Advanced Configuration 10g Release 1*. You could also look at MetaLink Note #289966.1. We mention this here because later reconfigurations can suddenly make this very useful tool stop working and start throwing out errors such as "Database is down"!

For example, you can get to the Top Sessions detail page via either of the following routes:

- Database Control Home (page) -> Host (area graph) -> *Database SID* (drill-down) -> Top Sessions tab in the Top Consumers menu

- Database Control Home (page) -> Performance (menu) -> Top Sessions (hyperlink) in Additional Monitoring Links (collection of links)

General Database and Host Information

Analyzing database performance without considering the underlying operating system will result in both an incomplete and incorrect diagnosis. OEM in Oracle Database 10g provides lots of information about the database as well as the host operating system, as compared to earlier versions. Host information includes CPU statistics categorized by both database and other types of processes, CPU utilization, CPU I/O wait, CPU load, run queue length, paging rate, and so on, as well as session information such as CPU, I/O, and categorized waits. An incredible amount of drill-down information is available at all levels in both tabular and graphical form. These drill-downs are contextual and appropriate, providing for in-depth analysis without unnecessary clutter. Graphs include line and stacked charts for representing values against time scales, and pie charts when representing percentages of an entity.

> **OEM Imposed Load**
>
> Naturally, we question the load imposed on the system by this tool. OEM is a J2EE-based application execution, and can potentially be heavy on CPU usage. Thus, you need to consider both application server load as well as the database load imposed to collect these statistics. We saw that the Java process collected just 2.5 minutes of CPU time in about three hours of collection on a Sun Fire V240 Dual CPU server. The database sessions showed relatively low overheads, due to the fact that the performance-statistics collection is offloaded to two background processes, MMON and MMNL. As mentioned before, these background processes collect and expose some short-term historical statistics via a circular buffer and provide longer-term historical statistics via some of the WRH tables.

Most screens refresh themselves in real time and can thus impose an unnecessary load on the system. On a heavily loaded system, use the Interval drop-down menu to change the rate to Manual. When historical information is available, choosing this option brings up options to view successively larger intervals, usually for the past 24 hours, past seven days, and so on. The highlight, however, is the availability of a slider tool in many screens that can be used to drag a shaded box over to the selected interval.

A Quick Example

This section demonstrates the use of OEM Database Control for performance diagnosis and tuning quickly using a very simple example. We will use a few objects from the HR schema from the sample schemas that are shipped along with the Oracle Database 10g and are installed by the DBCA installation assistant. For further details, refer to the *Oracle Database 10g Sample Schema* manual.

The example shown here is a simple way of generating an enormous but controlled load on the system. You will notice that we used very simple techniques and tools already available in the UNIX operating system command-line commands. It could very well be generated using Windows command scripts with the FOR statement.

We used the SQL shown in Listing 10.12 to create a large number of rows in the EMPLOYEES table of the HR schema. No extra objects need to be created, although the widths of the FIRST_NAME, LAST_NAME, and EMAIL columns were increased to an even VARCHAR2(50) from their default.

LISTING 10.12 Script to Generate a Large Number of Rows in the EMPLOYEES Table

```
insert into employees (
employee_id, first_name, last_name, email, phone_number,
hire_date, job_id, salary, commission_pct, manager_id, department_id )
select
 employees_seq.nextval ,
 first_name || ' ' || employees_seq.currval ,
 last_name || ' ' || employees_seq.currval ,
 email || ' ' || employees_seq.currval ,
```

LISTING 10.12   Continued

```
phone_number, hire_date , job_id, salary, commission_pct,
manager_id, department_id
from employees;
```

This SQL copies the current set of rows in the EMPLOYEES table into itself, while generating new key values for the EMPLOYEE_ID as well as concatenating new numeric values to the employee details. This generates a fairly even spread of rows, each distinct from the others in some way. Executing this SQL a number of times will successively insert a larger and larger number of rows. For example, the first time this SQL is run in the HR schema, it doubles the 107 rows. Running this SQL again will double the result, with a final total of (107 + 107 + 314 = 628) rows. Run the SQL as many times as required—we tested this out with 14,000 rows in the EMPLOYEES table.

We then used the following embedded query to extract the employee data held in the sample HR schema. To complicate the SQL and provide many type of joins and opportunities for tuning, we joined the detail table, namely EMPLOYEES, to the other master tables such as REGIONS, DEPARTMENTS, LOCATIONS, and COUNTRIES as shown in the SQL statement in Listing 10.13. The following UNIX shell script segment was then used to generate a large but set number of executions by wrapping the SQL in a shell script named multi.ksh, shown in Listing 10.13.

LISTING 10.13   UNIX Script for Simulating a Large User Load

```
i=1
while [ $i -le 100 ]          # Control number of executions using this number
do
echo $i
sqlplus -silent hr/hr123 <<EOF > $i.out 2>&1 &  # Use the & to launch in the background
set termout off
select e.*
from hr.employees e, hr.departments d, hr.locations l,
hr.countries c, hr.regions r
where e.department_id = d.department_id
and d.location_id = l.location_id
and l.country_id = c.country_id
and c.region_id = r.region_id
and employee_id between substr(to_char(abs(dbms_random.random)),1,4)
and substr(to_char(abs(dbms_random.random)),1,4);
exit
EOF
sleep 1        # Sleep for a brief second
i=`expr $i + 1`
done
wait           # Wait after launching a number of SQLs in the background
echo All done!
```

The call DBMS_RANDOM.RANDOM generates a random number. You apply some transformations to obtain a starting and ending number, each of which could range from 0 to 9,999. When the first random number is larger than the second, no rows were selected, so some of the SQLs do not return any rows. On the other hand, some of the other SQLs select a lot of rows, all at random. This simply and perfectly simulates a live system with random queries and load.

Main OEM Performance-Related Screens

After the test started, we logged on to the Enterprise Manager Database Console using the SYSTEM account. You can also use another user with access to the Database Control to view the results. Snapshots of relevant portions are shown in subsequent paragraphs with explanations.

The Database Control home page is displayed upon successful login to OEM Database Control, as shown in Figure 10.1. This screen displays quite a handful of information, including the overall system health for all areas. We will zoom in only on the relevant areas, namely the graphs that show the operating system as well as the Session area.

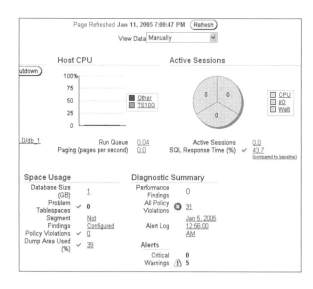

FIGURE 10.1

The OEM Database Control home page showing relevant performance areas.

When you click on the Wait link in the Session area, you will see the host and session information relevant to waiting, as shown in Figure 10.2. This shows the overall performance for the host, session, and throughput in real time. You can switch this to Historical view or to a Manual refresh view to enable going back to or stopping the screen for further drill-downs. Notice the line across Maximum CPU; we had two CPUs in this case.

Session waits are classified into many categories, such as User I/O and System I/O, Concurrency, Application, and so on. You can link this directly to the Wait class categories seen earlier. The host run queue length, which is a measure of "waiting for CPU" is also seen on this Wait page. This helps you appreciate how the designers of OEM have kept the related details together so a performance analyst can see both database *and* operating-system statistics together, helping to determine root causes and the relationships quickly and intuitively.

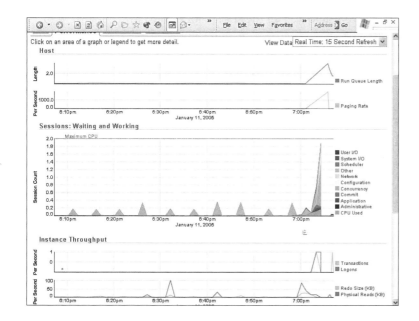

FIGURE 10.2
Performance page showing host and database wait information.

When you hover the cursor over the `Concurrency` section of the `Sessions: Waiting and Working` graph shown in Figure 10.2, the `Concurrency` portion of the graph is highlighted. As well, you can click and drill down to get the reasons for the concurrency issue for the selected period. This drill-down screen, shown in Figure 10.3, shows the waits related specifically to the `Concurrency` wait class. As mentioned previously, this can relate to latching or internal concurrency as well as to row or other resource locking, which is external concurrency.

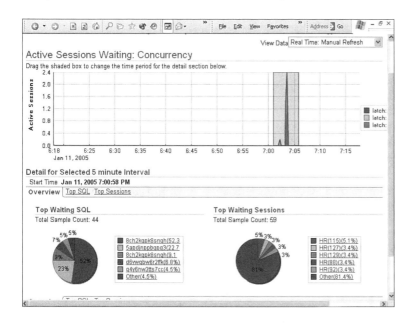

FIGURE 10.3
Page showing concurrency-related wait information.

This is a historical view; hence, we were able to drag the slider tool over to the time period of interest. This slider is shown with a darkened background, and can be set to a period of as little as five minutes and as large as a day.

Note that we have not drilled down into all the subsections in this page. You can determine Top SQL as well as Top Sessions in the lower part of the screen. You can see that there were about three active concurrent sessions out of 59 connected sessions, and that the SQL run by at least one of them contributed to 52% of the waits. Specifically, this was broken down into `latch: session allocation` and `latch free` (not shown in the figure due to screen-shot limitations). You can now drill down into the details of the top SQL statements that contributed to the majority of the waits. In this specific case, drill down into the SQL using the links shown against the SQL hash values. In particular, the screen shown in Figure 10.4 is displayed when you click on the top-most link that corresponds to the SQL statement emanating from the shell script shown in Listing 10.13.

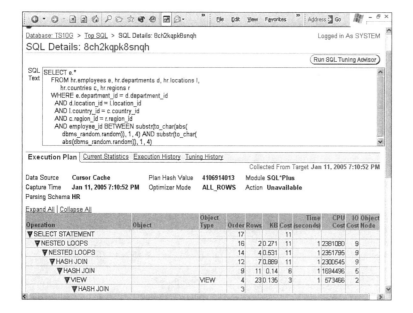

FIGURE 10.4
Details of the Top SQL, which contributed to 52% of the waits.

Figure 10.4 shows the SQL that contributed most to the waiting. As expected, it was the SQL that was executed simultaneously from many sessions. The SQL is shown along with the execution plan and other parameters. Because this was a Top SQL and is possibly worth tuning, OEM provides an easy link to the aptly named SQL Tuning Advisor, shown in Figure 10.5, via the Run SQL Tuning Advisor button.

The SQL Tuning Advisor can apply various tuning scenarios on the selected SQL and needs some scheduling parameters, as seen in Figure 10.5. Choosing the required parameters and allowing the advisor to operate results in the screen shown in Figure 10.6.

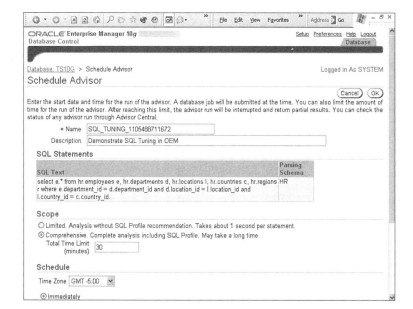

FIGURE 10.5
SQL Tuning Advisor
scheduling screen.

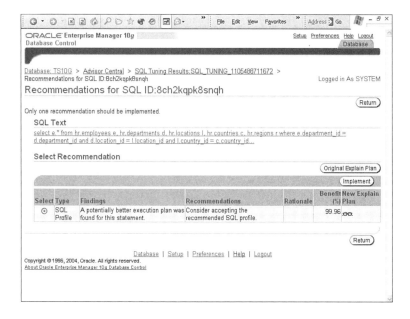

FIGURE 10.6
SQL Tuning Advisor
results, showing recom-
mendations.

As you can see, SQL Tuning Advisor recommends that this SQL be tuned using an *SQL profile*. We will look at this type of tuning in depth in Chapter 13, "Effectively Using the SQL Advisors," so we will not go into details now. In any case, you might want to view the changed execution plan before accepting it. To do so, click on the eyeglasses shown in Figure 10.6. This will result in the tuned execution plan for the same SQL, as shown in Figure 10.7.

Recommendations for SQL ID:8ch2kqpk8snqh > New Explain Plan

Logged in As SYSTEM

New Explain Plan

Expand All | Collapse All

Operation	Line ID	Order	Rows	KB	Cost	Time (seconds)	CPU Cost	IO Cost	Object	Object Type	Object Node
SELECT STATEMENT	0	18	1	0.136	11	1	3048466	9			
NESTED LOOPS	1	17	1	0.136	11	1	3048466	9			
HASH JOIN	2	15	1	0.133	11	1	3041145	9			
MERGE JOIN CARTESIAN	3	10	25	3.174	8	1	1923215	6			
HASH JOIN	4	7	1	0.121	7	1	1911093	5			
VIEW	5	4	27	0.185	3	1	576466	2	HR.index$_join$_002	VIEW	
HASH JOIN	6	3									
INDEX FAST FULL SCAN	7	1	27	0.185	1	1	15651	1	HR.DEPT_ID_PK	INDEX (UNIQUE)	
INDEX FAST FULL SCAN	8	2	27	0.185	1	1	15651	1	HR.DEPT_LOCATION_IX	INDEX	
TABLE ACCESS BY INDEX ROWID	9	6	7697	879.442	3	1	22464	3	HR.EMPLOYEES	TABLE	
INDEX RANGE SCAN	10	5	1		2	1	14642	2	HR.EMP_EMP_ID_PK	INDEX (UNIQUE)	
BUFFER SORT	11	9	25	0.146	5	1	1346748	4			
INDEX FULL SCAN	12	8	25	0.146	1	1	12121	1	HR.COUNTRY_C_ID_PK	INDEX (UNIQUE)	

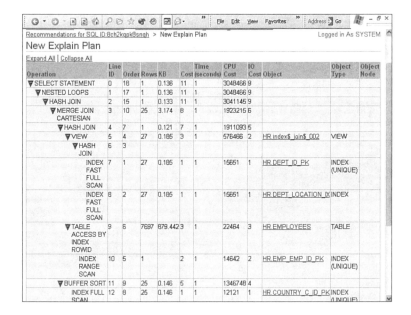

FIGURE 10.7
Details of the new explain plan.

You can then compare this to the older execution plan, as shown in Figure 10.8, by clicking the Original Explain Plan button in Figure 10.6.

Database: TS10G > Advisor Central > SQL Tuning Results:SQL_TUNING_1105488711672 >
Recommendations for SQL ID:8ch2kqpk8snqh > Original Explain Plan

Logged in As SYSTEM

Original Explain Plan

The following is the original explain plan for the SQL statement being tuned. The cost might be adjusted by the SQL Tuning Advisor to reflect the real cost.

Expand All | Collapse All

Operation	Line ID	Order	Rows	KB	Cost	Time (seconds)	CPU Cost	IO Cost	Object	Object Type
SELECT STATEMENT	0	17	996643	135,286.5	38500	463	41449218048	8		
NESTED LOOPS	1	16	996643	135,286.5	38500	463	41449218048	8		
NESTED LOOPS	2	14	1993287	264,733.438	24947	300	26855485440	8		
HASH JOIN	3	12	3667647	465,619.25	10	1	3028683	8		
HASH JOIN	4	9	27	0.343	6	1	1694496	5		
VIEW	5	4	23	0.135	3	1	573466	2	HR.index$_join$_003	VIEW
HASH JOIN	6	3								
INDEX FAST FULL SCAN	7	1	23	0.135	1	1	14651	1	HR.LOC_COUNTRY_IX	INDEX
INDEX FAST FULL SCAN	8	2	23	0.135	1	1	14651	1	HR.LOC_ID_PK	INDEX (UNIQUE
VIEW	9	8	27	0.185	3	1	576466	2	HR.index$_join$_002	VIEW
HASH JOIN	10	7								
INDEX FAST FULL SCAN	11	5	27	0.185	1	1	15651	1	HR.DEPT_ID_PK	INDEX (UNIQUE

FIGURE 10.8
Details of the original explain plan.

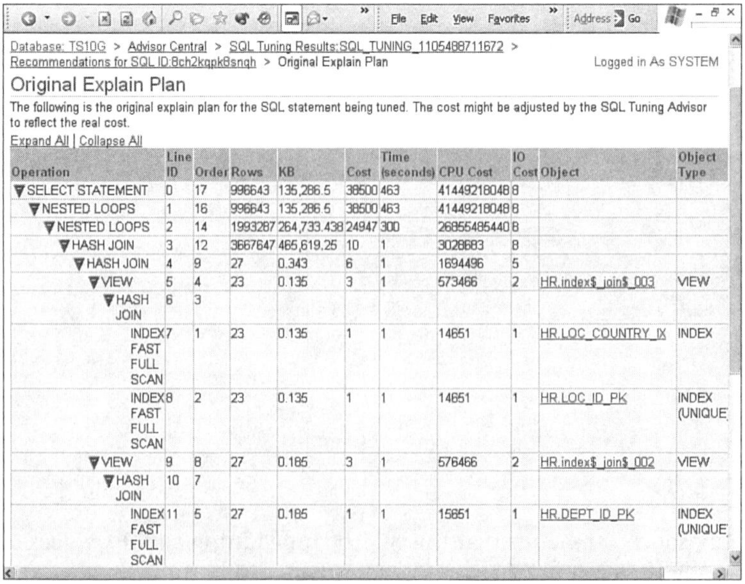

That is not all. Shown in Figure 10.9 are some other statistics obtained from the OEM Database Control. To access these, from the home page, click on the Other link in the Host graph.

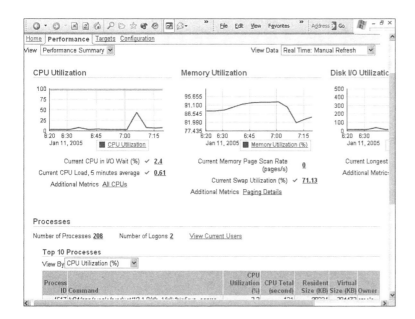

FIGURE 10.9
Host performance summary showing CPU, memory, and disk I/O utilization.

Notice the View drop-down menu at the top-left side of the screen. This shows the Performance Summary option by default, which includes utilization graphs for CPU, memory, and disk I/O. By default, the lower portion of the screen displays top processes by CPU consumption as well. This section can be changed via the View Data drop-down menu, found in the top-right corner of the screen. Use this menu to control the rate of refresh or to view the history for this statistic.

You can drill down further by choosing CPU Details or Memory Details from the View drop-down menu. This results in the screens displayed in Figure 10.10 for CPU details and Figure 10.11 for memory details.

Note that the bottom part of the screen automatically varies between the two figures, first to display the Top 10 Processes (ordered by CPU) and then to display the Top 10 Processes (ordered by Memory), keeping in sync with the type of statistics displayed above.

Alerts and Metrics

Not everything is displayed via graphs in OEM. A good example is the Metrics screen, which you access by clicking the All Metrics link that is available on all pages. A sample Metrics page is shown in Figure 10.12.

A large number of alerts, including performance alerts, are configured out of the box in OEM. These are available as links in the bottom of most pages. These screens display all alerts, including performance alerts such as Database Time spent Waiting. Use the Manage Metrics link on this page to view the details of these metrics and the Edit Thresholds button to enable/disable alerts and to change the various thresholds for the Warning and Critical levels. You can also specify response actions, which are triggered when these alerts are triggered, as well as multiple

Adopting a New Approach to Tuning

thresholds at which they trigger. This is a very powerful option that is sure to replace many other third-party and home-grown tools and scripts.

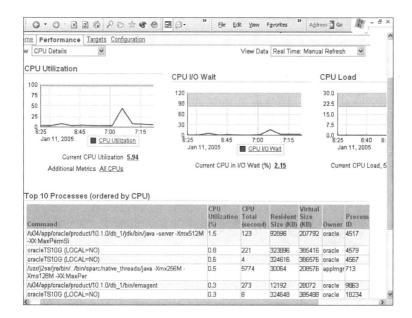

FIGURE 10.10
Host performance CPU drill-down details as well as top CPU processes.

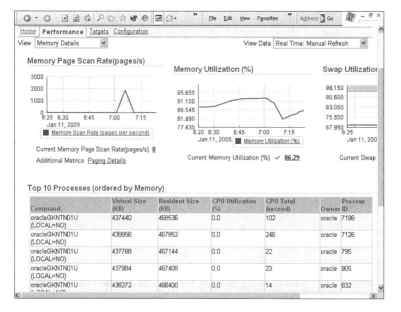

FIGURE 10.11
Host performance Memory drill-down details as well as top memory processes.

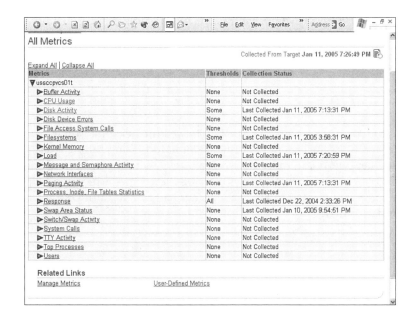

FIGURE 10.12
The All Metrics page.

Advisors

Numerous advisors can be accessed via the Advisor Central link in the Related Links section in most pages. They include the following:

- ADDM (Automatic Database Diagnostic Monitor)

- SQL Tuning Advisor

- SQL Access Advisor

- Memory Advisor

- MTTR (Mean Time To Recover) Advisor

- Segment Advisor

- Undo Management Advisor

We will look in greater detail at some of these advisors in later chapters.

New Features in Oracle Database 10g Release 2

Oracle Database 10g Release 2 promises to improve on the new direction in performance management set by the first release. For example, more statistics are now collected and analyzed in the advisors. We will deal with specifics in subsequent chapters; let us just mention that 48 new dynamic performance views and 60 new Wait events have been added in Oracle Database 10g Release 2 as compared to the previous release. This includes intriguing views named

V$PROCESS_MEMORY and V$PROCESS_MEMORY_DETAIL for monitoring and viewing process memory details as well as V$ASM_DISK_STAT and V$ASM_DISKGROUP_STAT for monitoring ASM disks and disk groups.

Summary

This chapter shows that Oracle Database 10g has consistently followed the new philosophy of automation and ease of management in the area of performance monitoring and tuning. You were introduced to some of the new views and tools that you can now use to detect, record, and fix performance issues. You also saw some innovative ways of using these views, which can help throw light on areas that you knew you wanted to know about, but had to wait until Oracle Database 10g rolled into your data center!

11

Effectively Using the Automatic Workload Repository

IN THIS CHAPTER

Introducing the AWR	207
Customizing the AWR	215
Performing Baselining	220
Active Session History	222
New Features in Oracle Database 10g Release 2	236

In this chapter, we will see in greater detail two of the components that were introduced in Chapter 10, "Adopting a New Approach to Tuning"—namely AWR and ASH. Both these components set the stage for the performance advisors that act on the data they collect. These performance advisors are detailed in the next two chapters, and you will need to understand the data that AWR and ASH collect in order to appreciate what the advisors do.

Introducing the AWR

The Automatic Workload Repository (AWR) is a new infrastructure component that is at the heart of the collection and processing of the vast amount of performance data in Oracle Database 10g. The data collected by AWR forms the basis for most of the problem-detection and self-tuning mechanisms that

Oracle Database 10g provides. In fact, the performance-alert mechanisms rely on this data, as do many of the performance advisors. The Automatic Database Diagnostic Monitor (ADDM) uses this data as well, performing scheduled analysis of the data collected by AWR.

AWR consists of two components: in-memory performance statistics, accessible through V$ views, and snapshots of these V$ views "persisted" in the database that record the historical values.

AWR **Collection**

AWR consists of the following collections:

- Active Session History (ASH)

- High-load SQL statements

- Time model statistics at the database level as well as at the session level for CPU usage and wait classifications

- Object statistics that record usage as well as access counts for segments such as tables, indexes, and other database objects

- Traditional V$SESSTAT, V$SYSSTAT, V$SYSTEM_EVENT, and V$SESSION_EVENT data

---

Licensing Information

As per the terms laid out in the *Oracle Database 10g Licensing Information* manual, AWR, ADDM, performance monitoring, and alerting are part of the Oracle Diagnostic Pack, which in itself is part of the Oracle Management Packs. Note that these management packs can be purchased only with the Enterprise Edition of the Oracle Database 10g software. Also note that AWR requires the use of the Partitioning option, which is also available only with the Enterprise Edition.

Unlike other Oracle background system processes such as SMON (System Monitor) or PMON (Process Monitor), the death of these performance-related background processes does not stop or abort the database. The health of these background processes does not affect the main system because these processes are not really deemed essential from an operational point of view. When these processes die, an appropriate message is posted in the alert.log and processing continues. Performance data, however, stops being collected when these processes die for any reason.

In this list, the collection for all but the last item is new.

So how does all of this happen? The Oracle kernel allocates a small but distinct portion of the System Global Area (SGA) to buffers that are dedicated to holding session history and other AWR-related information. These in-memory buffers are updated by the MMNL and MMON background processes via sampling of session information and counters. The Memory Monitor Light (MMNL) process, new to Oracle Database 10g, performs tasks such as session history capture and metrics computation and stores this information in these buffers. It also persists the statistics in these buffers to disk as needed in the form of AWR tables. The Memory Monitor (MMON) process performs various background tasks, such as issuing alerts whenever a given metric violates its threshold value and taking snapshots by spawning additional process (MMON slaves), among others. Together, they are responsible for the statistics, alerts, and other information maintained by AWR. These statistics are made permanent in the AWR, which consists of a number of tables.

By default, these background jobs automatically generate snapshots of the performance data once every hour and flush the statistics to the workload repository. The Automatic Database Diagnostic Monitor (ADDM) then kicks in to analyze the data from the immediately prior and current snapshots, and to highlight any performance issues or problems. You can perform all this manually as well, and you will see how to do that later in this chapter.

Ultimately, because SQL executing in a user or background session produces database work and hence load, AWR works to compare the difference between snapshots to determine which SQL statements should be captured based on their effect on the system load. You saw examples of such SQL in the previous chapter when looking at how OEM uses this data. This reduces the number of SQL statements that need to be captured over time, while still capturing the essential ones.

Out of the box, AWR serves as a performance warehouse for the Oracle Database 10g, generating, maintaining, and reporting these performance statistics. AWR purges its own data in a scheduled manner, thus self managing itself.

Comparison to STATSPACK

In many ways, AWR rose from the foundation laid by STATSPACK. The concepts are similar: Capture snapshots of required internal V$ views, store them, and analyze them. There are some major differences between AWR and STATSPACK, however. We hinted at this in the previous chapter, and it is worth looking at both the similarities and differences here:

> ### Memory Allocated to AWR Buffers
>
> **There is no clear documentation as to how much memory is used by** AWR. **There are some clues, however, that can be seen from the** V$SGASTAT **view, which lists the various subsections of memory used within the System Global Area** (SGA). **We were able to see two distinct areas, both within the** Shared Pool: event statistics per sess **and** ASH buffers. **Each consumed about 1.5% of the combined** SGA, **and seemed to be dependent on other parameters such as** sessions. **We will mention a MetaLink Note later on that lists how** ASH **buffers can be determined, but there is no information about sizing for the** AWR **buffers.**

- Both STATSPACK and AWR use snapshots to store current performance data exposed in selected V$ views. Both types of snapshots are uniquely identified via the SNAP_ID column. Similarly named tables store the same type of data in both environments.

- Both STATSPACK and AWR produce similar reports using packaged SQL*Plus scripts. STATSPACK uses spreport.sql, while AWR uses a number of AWR-specific scripts detailed later on in this chapter.

- While STATSPACK needs to be installed manually, AWR is installed, configured, and managed by default in a standardized manner.

- STATSPACK snapshots impose a reasonable load during collection. However, AWR collections occur continually and are offloaded to selected background processes, allowing for smoother, less perceptible, and less disruptive progress.

- STATSPACK analysis is complex and needs a skilled eye and an adequate level of experience to detect problems. AWR, along with ADDM, runs continually, generates alerts, and performs analysis automatically.

- STATSPACK is not accessible via a GUI such as OEM for viewing or management, whereas AWR is accessible both via the OEM GUI as well as via SQL and PL/SQL for viewing and management.

- The way high-impact or high-load SQL is captured in AWR is quite different from STATSPACK. While STATSPACK scans V$SQL for high-load SQL based on a certain set of defaulted lower limits, such as on number of logical and physical I/Os per stored SQL statement, AWR recognizes high-load SQL as it occurs. This enables accurate capture of the right SQL data as it occurs, rather than collecting high-load SQL from V$SQL, which may capture SQL that occurred prior to, and thus outside of, the snapshot period. This was a major weakness in STATSPACK.

- STATSPACK data is stored in the PERFSTAT schema in any designated tablespace, while AWR data is stored in the SYS schema in the new SYSAUX tablespace.

> **STATSPACK in Oracle Database 10g**
>
> Curiously enough, STATSPACK is also available for Oracle Database 10g! The PERFSTAT schema is installed by default, although no STATSPACK related objects are created. The standard sp*.sql scripts are available in the RDBMS\ADMIN directory.

These similarities have prompted the renaming of the AWR/ADDM combination to "STATSPACK on Steroids"—a steroid we would heartily recommend!

AWR **Storage and Reporting**

All the AWR objects (tables and their indexes) start with one of the following prefixes:

- WRH$ tables, which store workload repository history. Some of these tables are range-partitioned.

- WRI$ tables, which store workload repository internal details.

- WRM$ tables, which store workload repository metadata.

All these tables reside in the SYSAUX tablespace. In fact, in Oracle Database 10g Release 1, there are 140 of these tables, and many of the larger ones are range-partitioned by DB_ID and SNAP_ID along with their indexes, which helps during purging of older snapshot information. The table names have suffixes that are the same or similar to their equivalents in STATSPACK's PERFSTAT schema. For example, the statistical contents and use of the STATS$FILESTATXS table of STATSPACK and the WRH$FILESTATXS table of AWR are the same; they store snapshot detail information from V$FILESTAT. Hence, understanding their use is simpler if you already know of their use in STATSPACK.

A number of views can access some of these tables. Generally, these views start with the DBA_HIST prefix, and some of them are detailed in Table 11.1. You looked at some of the base views that are captured in the snapshot by AWR in the previous chapter. This list is not comprehensive, but is indicative of every type of view.

TABLE 11.1

Some AWR Views

View Name	Description
DBA_HIST_DATABASE_INSTANCE	Displays constant database instance information such as the database and instance ID and names as well as startup time and the last ASH sample ID. You can also use this view to determine shutdown/startup times.
DBA_HIST_SNAPSHOT	Displays the details of currently available AWR snapshot information, including the start/end time, the elapsed time for flushing the data to disk, the snap level, and the error count. For error details, see the DBA_HIST_SNAP_ERROR view.
DBA_HIST_WR_CONTROL	Displays the current snapshot interval and retention period.
DBA_HIGH_WATER_MARK_STATISTICS	Displays high water marks and last value for object statistics, such as the number of user tables, indexes and partitions, user sessions, and so on. Similar to the V$LICENSE view of previous versions.
DBA_HIST_SEG_STAT	Displays snapshot-wise object statistics including the number of logical and physical reads and writes, ITL waits, and so on. The current-at-snapshot value as well as the delta difference for the snapshot period is displayed as well.
DBA_HIST_JAVA_POOL_ADVICE	Displays the historical Java Pool advisory details and exposes the V$JAVA_POOL_ADVICE view.

The amount of space occupied by these AWR objects depends on the following:

■ The snapshot interval determines the frequency at which snapshots are captured and stored. A smaller snapshot interval increases the frequency, which in turn increases the volume of data collected and stored by AWR.

■ The historical data retention period determines how long AWR data is retained before being purged. Obviously, a longer retention period increases the space required by AWR.

■ Because ASH session information is also stored in the AWR, the number of active sessions in the system at any given time also determines the space required.

By default, snapshots are taken every hour and retained for a period of seven days. You will see later in this chapter, in the section titled "Customizing the AWR," how these intervals can be changed. The space usage can be seen using the query shown in Listing 11.1.

LISTING 11.1   AWR Data from the V$SYSAUX_OCCUPANTS View

```
SQL> select occupant_name, occupant_desc, space_usage_kbytes
  2  from v$sysaux_occupants
  3  where occupant_name like 'SM%';
```

Effectively Using the Automatic Workload Repository

LISTING 11.1   Continued

OCCUPANT_NAME	OCCUPANT_DESC	SPACE_KB
SM/AWR	Server Manageability - Automatic Workload Repository	83,072
SM/ADVISOR	Server Manageability - Advisor Framework	8,512
SM/OPTSTAT	Server Manageability - Optimizer Statistics History	21,120
SM/OTHER	Server Manageability - Other Components	8,704

V$SYSAUX_OCCUPANTS

This new view allows you to view the details of the special occupants of the new SYSAUX tablespace. The occupant name, a short description, the schema owner, the space used, as well the procedure that should be used to move this occupant out to another tablespace is listed. Note that the server manageability objects in Listing 11.1 *cannot* be moved to another tablespace. Only other objects such as those related to LogMiner, Oracle Spatial, and Oracle Text can be moved using the specified procedure listed under the MOVE_PROCE- DURE column. For more details, see MetaLink Note #243246.1, "10G: SYSAUX Tablespace."

A more detailed report of AWR objects, usage, and the like, along with information on Active Session History (ASH), can be produced using awrinfo.sql. This is found in the $ORACLE_HOME/rdbms/admin directory in UNIX or the equivalent %ORACLE_HOME%\RDBMS\ADMIN directory in Windows. A large amount of information is reported under the headings shown in Listing 11.2.

LISTING 11.2   Various Heads Under Which AWR Information Is Reported

```
(I) AWR Snapshots Information
(1a) SYSAUX usage - Schema breakdown
(1b) SYSAUX usage - SYS Schema
(2) Size estimates for AWR snapshots
(3a) Space usage by AWR components (per database)
(3b) Space usage within AWR Components (> 500K)
(4) Space usage by non-AWR components (> 500K)
(5a) AWR snapshots - last 50
(5b) AWR snapshots with errors or invalid
(5c) AWR snapshots -- OLDEST Non-Baselined snapshot
(6) AWR Control Settings - interval, retention
(7a) AWR Contents - row counts for each snapshot
(7b) AWR Contents - average row counts per snapshot
(7c) AWR total item counts - names, text, plan
(II) ASH Usage Info
(1a) ASH histogram (past 3 days)
(1b) ASH histogram (past 1 day)
(2a) ASH details (past 3 days)
(2b) ASH details (past 1 day)
(2c) ASH sessions (Fg Vs Bg) (past 1 day across all instances in RAC)
```

Of these, Size estimates for AWR snapshots is quite useful because it enables you to see the effects of increasing or decreasing the snapshot frequency or manipulating the retention periods.

Also note that storage of objects related to ASH is also detailed here. Of interest is the section ASH histogram (past 3 days) (or even ASH histogram past 1 day). This histogram gives a fair indication of the number of sessions active at any point of time during that period.

> **The SWRF Acronym**
>
> If you looked at some of the AWR statistics related control mechanisms such as latches and other elements, you will come across the acronym *SWRF*. There seem to be no direct published references, but it seems to expand into Statistics Workload Repository Facilities, as per a related MetaLink Note #240052.1. This was probably what AWR was called before the "A" (for Automatic) was prefixed to the name.

Accessing the AWR Snapshots

The AWR snapshots can be accessed using either the OEM screens or directly from a SQL aware tool such as SQL*Plus or iSQL*Plus. When using OEM, you can use either of the following routes:

■ Database Control Home (page) -> Administration (breadcrumb menu) -> Automatic Workload Repository (link) -> Snapshots (link)

■ Database Control Home (page) -> Performance (breadcrumb menu) -> Snapshots (link) in Additional Monitoring Links (collection of links)

Figure 11.1 shows the Snapshots page. Note that you can use the drop-down menu next to the Go button to perform any of the following tasks:

■ Create a preserved snapshot set (also known as a *baseline*)

■ Create an SQL tuning set

■ View a report

■ Create an ADDM task

■ Delete a snapshot range

■ Compare timelines

You can also use the Create button to create an on-demand snapshot.

The AWR can be accessed from SQL using calls to the DBMS_WORKLOAD_REPOSITORY built-in PL/SQL package to perform required processes. To generate reports, you can use the following SQLs found in the $ORACLE_HOME/rdbms/admin directory in UNIX (%ORACLE_HOME%\RDBMS\ADMIN directory in Windows):

■ **awrinfo.sql**. Displays general AWR information, as described earlier.

■ **awrinput.sql**. Sets up variable information for subsequent AWR reports.

- **awrrpt.sql**. Generates an AWR report in either HTML or plain text from the instance on which it is run and calls awrrpti.sql when input specification is complete.

- **awrrpti.sql**. Generates an AWR report in either HTML or plain text from any other instance for which the data is held in this instance. This script finally calls the DBMS_ WORKLOAD_REPOSITORY built-in PL/SQL package, whose source is wrapped and is thus hidden.

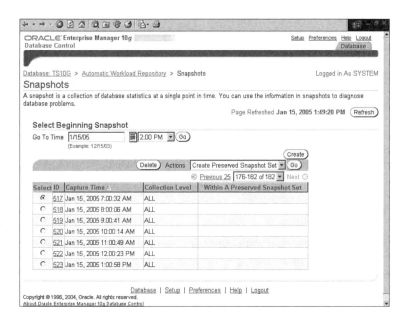

FIGURE 11.1
AWR snapshots and their details.

You will notice that awrrpt.sql produces a report that is similar to STATSPACK, but has more sections that cover the new views that Oracle Database 10g provides. Some of the new sections are shown in Listing 11.3.

LISTING 11.3   Various New Sections in the AWR Report

```
Time Model Statistics
Operating System Statistics
Service Statistics and Service Wait Class Stats
SQL ordered by Elapsed Time, CPU Time ( in addition to the SQL ordered
➥by Gets, Reads and Executions, Parse calls, Sharable Memory
➥and Version count that was previously available)
Instance Activity Stats – by Absolute values as well as Derived values
Instance Activity Stats - Thread Activity
Other advisories for the Buffer Pool, PGA Memory, Shared Pool,
➥Java Pool turned on by default
Enqueue Activity
Top Segments by Buffer Busy Waits, Row Lock Waits and ITL Waits
```

Note that if you don't specify otherwise, invoking the `awrrpt.sql` script displays only the last three days of snapshot settings. Use `awrinput.sql` followed by the `awrrpt.sql` script to report on previous snapshots. This is a little cumbersome, but it does avoid displaying the list of all the previous snapshots as is done with a `STATSPACK` report.

Customizing the AWR

The AWR and its collections can be customized to some extent. You can customize AWR in the following areas:

- Change the period between collections (also known as *snapshots*), even to the extent of switching off collection.

- Change the period of retention of data.

- Create on-demand snapshots.

- Create baselines for comparison.

With the exception of the last bullet point, you will see how these can be done in this chapter. Before you customize the AWR however, you need to understand the dependencies.

AWR **Dependencies**

Most of the downstream self-managing, proactive, reporting features of Oracle Database 10g depend on the AWR data collected periodically. You need to keep this in mind if you reduce or change the AWR collection and storage parameters. For example, if AWR was changed to collect snapshots once every eight hours, then it is possible that the subsequent ADDM run that analyzes this pair of snapshots might not detect peak usage and attendant issues that occurred during the first hour. On the other hand, not having enough data can affect the validity and accuracy of other components and features such as the SQL Tuning Advisor, the Undo Advisor, and Segment Advisors.

> **Overheads for AWR**
>
> Note that persisting of AWR information involves inserts to tables, while purging results in `DELETE` operations. These operations result in some overhead, albeit minimal and offloaded to the MMNL and MMON background processes. As well, they will generate redo and undo information, whose rate depends on the rate of the collection. If your databases are in `ARCHIVELOG` mode, you will notice a minimal but constant stream of archive-log generation even if there is no activity on the database. Under certain circumstances, it is possible that you'll encounter library cache contention due to MMON slave processes. This is due to a bug that has been corrected in later patchsets. Please refer to MetaLink Note #296765.1 for details.

Suggested AWR **Settings**

At the end of the day, you will need to remember that taking a snapshot, whether automatic or manual, involves a minimal amount of overhead in terms of CPU time, I/O operations, and database space. Our suggestion is to not go above the one-hour period for the AWR snapshot interval. A larger period will provide very coarse reporting, and you may miss catching peak workload within the hour. If you experience high periods of activity only during fixed office hours, you might choose to increase the frequency of the snapshots during such peak times and minimize snapshots during off hours using scheduled scripts that will automatically reduce and increase the snapshot frequency as required.

As for retention, our suggestion is to capture at least one or two periods more than the full workload cycle. For example, if you experience monthly peaks of usage, then to make effective comparisons, you will need to retain at least one month plus a few days' data. Use `awrinfo.sql` to estimate space requirements.

> **Emergency Purging**
>
> AWR purges its repository once a day, removing all snapshots that are past their retention period and that do not belong to a preserved set by value of being associated with a baseline. AWR, however, will automatically initiate an emergency purge if it determines that it is under space pressure. This "emergency purge" will not obey retention rules and it is possible that you will lose data that is not yet expired. In this case, an alert will be raised, and a record to this effect will be logged in the alert log. We suggest you monitor the alert log and add sufficient space in the SYSAUX tablespace when you see such messages in order to ensure that required data is not being inadvertently purged.

In the previous chapter, we indicated that the STATISTICS_LEVEL should be set to either TYPICAL or ALL for performance statistics to be collected. If this were set to BASIC, AWR snapshots would not be collected by default. You would however, be able to manually perform snapshots and ADDM runs.

Using the OEM to Customize the AWR

You can use the OEM as well as SQL commands to view the contents of AWR as well as to customize it. To use AWR within OEM, navigate the following path:

- Database Control Home (page) -> Administration (breadcrumb menu) -> Automatic Workload Repository (Page)

This displays the screen shown in Figure 11.2.

You will notice that the current number of snapshots is shown, along with the number of preserved snapshot sets (also known as *baselines*). Clicking the number of snapshots displays the screen shown in Figure 11.1. Click the Edit button to display the Edit Settings screen, shown in Figure 11.3.

Notice the Show SQL button on this page. You can click this button to preview the SQL that will be executed to change that setting. Notice also that you can choose to retain the snapshots forever as well as to turn off the snapshotting functionality. As well, the Collection Level parameter is set to the current value of STATISTICS_LEVEL. In this particular case, it is set to ALL. This value can be changed either in the OEM or using the SQL interface by setting the initialization parameters for STATISTICS LEVEL or using the ALTER SYSTEM SET STATISTICS_LEVEL command.

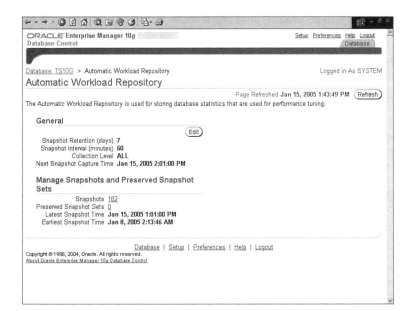

FIGURE 11.2
AWR main page (notice the current settings).

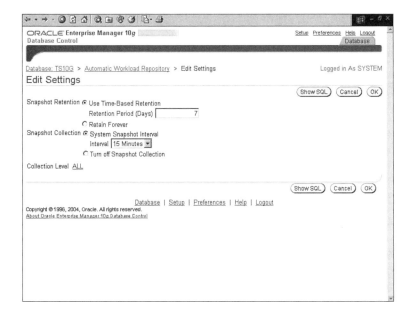

FIGURE 11.3
The Edit Settings screen.

Using the SQL Interface to AWR

The SQL interface can also be used to customize the AWR using the DBMS_WORKLOAD_REPOSITORY built-in PL/SQL package. This package provides the following procedures and functions to enable manual interaction with the AWR:

- The `AWR_REPORT_HTML` function can be used to display the `AWR` report in HTML, and returns a pipelined row of 150 characters.

- The `AWR_REPORT_TEXT` function can be used to display the `AWR` report in text, and returns a pipelined row of 80 characters.

- The `CREATE_BASELINE` function and procedure create a single named baseline for a given range of snapshots.

- The `CREATE_SNAPSHOT` function creates a manual snapshot immediately.

- The `DROP_BASELINE` procedure drops a named baseline and, optionally, the set of snapshots associated with it.

- The `DROP_SNAPSHOT_RANGE` procedure drops a range of snapshots.

- The `MODIFY_SNAPSHOT_SETTINGS` procedure modifies the snapshot settings.

Although the `AWR` report can be produced using the `AWR_REPORT_HTML` and `AWR_REPORT_TEXT` functions, we suggest you use `awrrpt.sql` or `awrrpti.sql` as required. In fact, these reports ultimately call these functions. You can find details of the variables required and other usage in the *Oracle Database 10g PL/SQL Packages and Types Reference Manual*. You will see some examples for creating and managing snapshots and look at baselining in the next section.

A common parameter in most of these procedures and functions is the database ID, or DBID, which is unique to every created database. This parameter will default to the DBID of the database on which it is running. This implies, of course, that you could import the `AWR` data from another instance into a master instance for reporting purposes.

Creating an AWR Snapshot

You can call the `CREATE_SNAPSHOT` object within the `DBMS_WORKLOAD_REPOSITORY` package either as a procedure or as a function to create an on-demand snapshot using the commands shown in Listing 11.4.

LISTING 11.4   Generating On-Demand Snapshots Using the `CREATE_SNAPSHOT` Procedure and Function

```
SQL> begin
  2          dbms_workload_repository.create_snapshot();
  3  end;
  4  /

PL/SQL procedure successfully completed.

SQL> select dbms_workload_repository.create_snapshot('ALL') from dual;

CREATE_SNAPSHOT
--------------
           603
```

Note that when invoked as a function, CREATE_SNAPSHOT returns the current snapshot number as its Return_Value, and this can be displayed. You can view all currently available AWR snapshots using the DBA_HIST_SNAPSHOT view.

When snapshots are taken using this procedure, the default flush level is TYPICAL. Because the flush level was not specified in this case when using the procedure, you will be able to observe in the DBA_HIST_SNAPSHOT view that the corresponding SNAP_LEVEL column shows a value of 1 for this snapshot. When invoking the snapshot using the function, we specified a flush level of ALL; hence the SNAP_LEVEL for this snapshot will be set to 2.

> **Effect of** STATISTICS_LEVEL **on** SNAP_LEVEL
>
> When the STATISTICS_LEVEL initialization parameter is changed, the snapshots taken automatically by the database default to ALL or TYPICAL depending on the current value of the initialization parameter. When a snapshot is taken manually, however, it always defaults to TYPICAL. Just note this as one more inconsistency, and move on!

Deleting an AWR Snapshot

You can use the DROP_SNAPSHOT_RANGE procedure within the DBMS_WORKLOAD_REPOSITORY package to drop one or more previously recorded snapshots. To perform this action, you will need to know the starting and ending snapshot IDs. An example is shown in Listing 11.5.

LISTING 11.5   Deleting One or More Snapshots Using the DROP_SNAPSHOT_RANGE Procedure

```
SQL> execute dbms_workload_repository.drop_snapshot_range -
> ( low_snap_id => 705, high_snap_id => 706 );

PL/SQL procedure successfully completed.
```

Modifying AWR Settings

You need to use the DBMS_WORKLOAD_REPOSITORY.MODIFY_SNAPSHOT_SETTINGS procedure to modify the AWR settings. This can be best explained using the example shown in Listing 11.6.

LISTING 11.6   Modifying AWR Settings Using the DBMS_WORKLOAD_REPOSITORY Package

```
SQL> execute dbms_workload_repository.modify_snapshot_settings -
> ( retention => 46080, interval => 15 );

PL/SQL procedure successfully completed.
```

Note that both the retention period and the default snapshot interval are specified in minutes. The specified retention value of 46,080 minutes equals 32 days. The retention value can be specified to a maximum of 100 years (52,560,000 minutes) and the snapshot interval can be a maximum of 525,600 minutes or one year. Specifying a special value of 0 minutes for the retention value will retain the AWR repository forever. In this case, a value of 40,150 days (equal to 110 years) is displayed in the OEM screen. The special value of 0 minutes for the interval will switch off automatic AWR collection. In this case, the OEM Workload Repository screen in Figure 11.3 will show a value of Not Collecting against the Interval parameter.

The SYS.WRM$WR_CONTROL table lists the retention, status, and purge details along with other AWR control details.

Performing Baselining

We alluded to a baseline before, and will define and detail it in this section. An AWR *baseline* is a collection of snapshots usually taken over a representative time period. For example, you might record a baseline where the system is performing well at peak load. You can then use this baseline as a way of comparing statistics captured during a period of bad performance. This baseline comparison can help pinpoint certain statistics that have changed significantly as compared to the period when the database was performing well. You can then analyze the statistics that differ vastly to determine the cause of the problem. Baselines can also be used with SQL tuning sets; we talk about this in detail in a Chapter 13, "Effectively Using the SQL Advisors."

AWR supports the capture of baseline data by allowing you to specify and preserve a range or even the minimum of a pair of AWR snapshots as a baseline. You should, however, carefully consider the time period you choose as a baseline. This period should be a good representation of the normal, expected load on the system. In the future, you can compare these baselines with snapshots captured during periods of poor performance for comparison purposes.

Note that the snapshots that are linked to baselines are never purged from the AWR repository even if they are past the purge period. For this reason, baselines are also known as preserved snapshot sets.

Current baselines can be viewed using the DBA_HIST_BASELINE view or the WRM$_BASELINE view at a lower level.

Capturing Baselines

Similar to the CREATE_SNAPSHOT object, the CREATE_BASELINE object can be called as a procedure or as a function from within the DBMS_WORKLOAD_REPOSITORY package to create a baseline. The required input parameters include a starting and ending SNAPSHOT_ID corresponding to the period of the baseline as well as a descriptive name for the baseline. The kernel internally assigns a baseline ID, which can be seen from the OEM Preserved Snapshot Set screen shown in Figure 11.4. The commands to create these baselines are shown in Listing 11.7.

LISTING 11.7   Using the DBMS_WORKLOAD_REPOSITORY Package to Create Baselines

```
SQL> begin
  2     dbms_workload_repository.create_baseline(start_snap_id=>715, -
  3     end_snap_id=>717, baseline_name=>'New Backup baseline' );
  4  end;
  5  /
```

LISTING 11.7   Continued

```
PL/SQL procedure successfully completed.

SQL> select
  2    dbms_workload_repository.create_baseline
  3    (703, 711, 'Good Batch baseline')
  4    from dual;


DBMS_WORKLOAD_REPOSITORY.CREATE_BASELINE(703,711,'GOODBATCHBASELINE')
------------------------------------------------------------------
                                                                  3
```

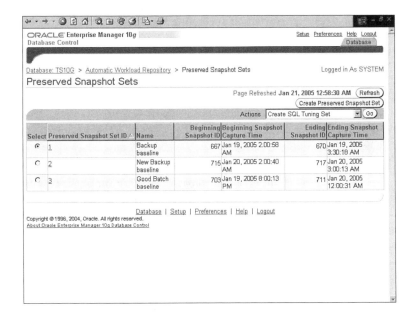

FIGURE 11.4
The Preserved Snapshot Sets screen.

Note that the snapshots associated with a baseline will not be purged even if they are past their retention time, as long as the baseline exists. They are purged only when the baseline is dropped.

Dropping Baselines

A previously captured baseline can be dropped using the DROP_BASELINE procedure, as shown in Listing 11.8.

LISTING 11.8   Using DROP_BASELINE to Drop Existing Baselines

```
SQL> begin
  2    dbms_workload_repository.drop_baseline(baseline_name =>, -
  3    'New Backup baseline', cascade=> TRUE );
```

LISTING 11.8   Continued

```
4  end;
5  /
```

PL/SQL procedure successfully completed.

Deleting Recent Baselines

When deleting baselines associated with snapshots that are still within the retention period—that is, a recent baseline—make sure you don't use the `cascade => TRUE` option to delete the baseline. This removes the associated snapshots even though they do not qualify for deletion!

Internal Documentation About ASH

Internal documentation about Active Session History is quite sparse. Minimal details about ASH are available in MetaLink Note #243132.1, last revised in August of 2004.

The `cascade` option is optional and defaults to `FALSE`. When defaulted, the underlying snapshots for that baseline will not be deleted. If, however, `cascade` is set to `TRUE`, the associated snapshots are dropped along with the baseline. When you drop a baseline without specifying the deletion of the associated snapshots, and the time period for the purging of the baseline has passed, the snapshots will not be deleted immediately, but will be purged in the next purge cycle.

Active Session History

Active Session History (ASH) is absolutely new in Oracle Database 10g. Very simply, it is both the recording and retention—short and long term—of crucial session-state information. The reasoning behind the provisioning of this very interesting data is to allow the performance analyst to perform on-the-spot analysis of a current session as well as to be able to look at the overall breakdown of session-related information in the short term.

Session-State Information

You saw an example of a session-related analysis in Chapter 10, which presented the details of current performance issue and drilled down into the details of a Top Session. This section illustrates how ASH helps collect this information. The Database Control in Oracle Database 10g is, of course, able to roll this up and present it graphically and easily.

The session-state information for active sessions is collected by a very low-overhead direct memory sampling of the session-state information that is held in the SGA for all sessions. The display of session-state information is not exactly new, however. Way back, Oracle 7 introduced the V$SESION and V$SESSION_WAIT views, which could be combined to provide many details of the state of a particular session from a snapshot of it. The information, of course, was current at the time these views were queried, and this information was not stored anywhere for later analysis. To analyze this, let's use an example. The query in Listing 11.9 shows how you can obtain these session details. We have listed the various column and other SQL*Plus settings in the query because they control the heading, formatting, and placement, and add value to the query.

LISTING 11.9   Query Against Views Showing Session-State Information

```
SQL> set linesize 80 verify off
SQL> column sid_serial heading "Sid,Ser#" format a10
SQL> column spid format a5 heading "OSPid"
SQL> column process format a6 heading "ClntPr"
SQL> column username format a17 heading "DB/OSUser"
SQL> column status heading "Status" format a8
SQL> column program heading "Program" format a31  trunc
SQL> column machine_prog heading "Machine/Program/Module" format a32  wrap
SQL> column last_call_et format 9999.99 heading "LastCallMn"
SQL> column logon_time format a18 heading "Logon Time"
SQL> column waiting_event format a47 heading "Waiting on event + p1/p2/p3" trunc
SQL> select s.sid || ',' || s.serial# sid_serial, p.spid, s.process,
  2  s.username || '/' || s.osuser username, s.status,
  3  to_char(s.logon_time, 'DD-MON-YY HH24:MI:SS') logon_time,
  4  s.last_call_et/60 last_call_et,
  5  w.event || ' / ' || w.p1 || ' / ' || w.p2 || ' / ' || w.p3 waiting_event,
  6  s.machine || '/' || s.program || '/' || s.module machine_prog
  7  from v$process p, v$session s, v$session_wait w
  8  where s.paddr=p.addr  and s.sid in (&List_of_Oracle_SIDs)
  9  and w.sid = s.sid
 10  order by s.logon_time;
Enter value for list_of_oracle_sids: 180,842


Sid,Ser#  OSPid ClntPr DB/OSUser        Status  Logon Time         LastCallMn
--------- ----- ------ ---------------- ------- ----------------- ----------
Waiting on event + p1/p2/p3               Machine/Program/Module
---------------------------------------   --------------------------------
180,8310  3156  2368   SYSTEM/oracle     ACTIVE  25-JAN-05 06:00:16       .38
db file scattered read / 12 / 75857 / 8   tst10gclnt/dbsnmp@tst10gclnt (TN
                                          S V1-V3)/VPXDBA


842,47516 17847 17846  SYS/oracle        INACTIVE 25-JAN-05 18:55:06    10.02
SQL*Net message from client / 1650815232 / 1 / tst10gclnt/sqlplus@tst10gclnt (T
                                          NS V1-V3)/
```

Using Session-State Information

The SQL in Listing 11.9 cleverly determines quite a lot of information from just the V$SESSION and V$SESSION_WAIT views; the V$PROCESS process is joined in order to provide operating-system process information (column OSPid) alone. Let's look in detail at what these columns are so that you can understand how ASH builds on this.

The Sid, Ser# (serial number), OSPid, ClntPr (client process ID, if available), Logon Time, and DB/OSUser (database and OS user) columns are pretty self-explanatory, and are available from the V$SESSION and V$PROCESS views. As well, the Machine/Program/Module column is taken directly from the corresponding V$SESSION columns. The MACHINE column is automatically populated and is a good one to look at when determining the source of the connection. The PROGRAM and MODULE columns are populated only when the DBMS_APPLICATION_INFO package is used within the program to record this information. For more details on usage of the DBMS_APPLICATION_INFO, refer to MetaLink Note #67549.1.

The V$SESSION.STATUS column shows whether the process was in the ACTIVE state within a database call or in the INACTIVE state after having completed it. A *database call* is an action being performed due to an SQL executed either directly by the session or indirectly due to a recursive SQL such as a trigger. Obviously, you would want to track all currently ACTIVE sessions.

In the case of an ACTIVE session, LastCallMn (V$SESSION.LAST_CALL_ET) shows how many minutes the session has clocked since the last *new* call the session issued directly or indirectly and is a good measure of long-running SQL queries. In the case of an INACTIVE session, this is a good indication of how long it has been since the client session interacted with the back-end process to make a new call.

Of course, the most interesting part is the detailed *event* information that is available in V$SESSION_WAIT. These columns are described in detail here so that you can understand them both in the context of older versions as well as within the context of Oracle Database 10g. Note that the meanings of these columns have not changed between versions. The columns of interest within V$SESSION_WAIT are listed in Table 11.2.

TABLE 11.2

Columns of Interest in V$SESSION_WAIT

Column Name	Meaning
EVENT	This VARCHAR2(64) column displays the current event on which the session is waiting or has last recorded. The contents are also known as the *Wait events* and form the basis for the Oracle Wait Interface tuning methodology.
P1, P2, and P3	These columns are basically parameters that can further describe the event. Their meaning changes with the event. These are discussed in great detail in the *Oracle Database 10g Reference Manual*, Appendix C. Also see the text columns P1TEXT, P2TEXT, and P3TEXT later in this table.
P1RAW, P2RAW, and P3RRAW	These columns expose the values of P1, P2, and P3 in a hexadecimal form. Generally not used.
P1TEXT, P2TEXT, and P2TEXT	These contain text that briefly describes the meaning of the P1, P2, and P3 columns.
WAIT_TIME	A non-zero value represents the session's last wait time in the unit shown here:
	0: The session is currently waiting.
	−2: The duration of last wait is unknown.
	−1: The last wait was < 1/100th of a second in duration.
	>0: The duration of the last wait in 1/100th second units (10 milliseconds).
	<−2: The internal time has probably wrapped.

TABLE 11.2

Continued

Column Name	Meaning
SECONDS_IN_WAIT	When WAIT_TIME = 0, then this shows the number of seconds spent in the current wait, generally updated every three seconds on most platforms and versions. This value will not be reset on events with timeouts, such as row lock enqueues.
	When WAIT_TIME != 0, this column shows the number of seconds since the start of the last wait.
STATE	This column interprets the value of WAIT_TIME and further describes the state that the session is in and takes any one of the following values:
	WAITING: The session is currently waiting.
	WAITED UNKNOWN TIME: The duration of the last wait is unknown (this normally appears when the TIMED_STATISTICS is defaulted to FALSE).
	WAITED SHORT TIME: The last wait was < 1/100th of a second.
	WAITED KNOWN TIME: WAIT_TIME equals the duration of last wait.
SEQ#	The sequence number that uniquely identifies one episode of the Wait event. This is incremented every time one Wait event completes and another is recorded. You can track the progress of a session from this column. More importantly, when this value does not increment even though the session consumes CPU, it is a sure indicator that the session is hanging. On the other hand, if the session is always ON CPU, but this value increments, it means that the session is performing some work and is probably spinning.
WAIT_CLASS	The classification text of the class of Wait event. For example, the wait could be classified as Idle, Configuration, Concurrency, User I/O, and so on. This helps to immediately identify the type of wait being suffered. This column is available in Oracle Database 10g only.

Hence, using this table, you can conclude that the session with SID 180 performed a db file scattered read event, which is another name for a multiblock read. For this event, the parameter P1 represents the file ID (12), P2 represents the starting block read (block #75857), and P3 represents the number of blocks read. In this case, you know that the DB_FILE_MULTIBLOCK_READ_COUNT parameter, which determines how many blocks should be read in a multiblock read, was set to 8, and hence eight blocks were read into the database buffer cache.

Similarly, the session with SID 842 is now inactive, waiting on the SQL*Net message from client, which normally represents a session waiting for input from a user.

The Connection to Active Session History

If a simple, static snapshot of the V$SESSION_WAIT and V$SESSION was able to provide so much information, would it not be beneficial to provide a set of snapshots of the session-state information so that a performance analyst could see what occurred within a session in terms of events? The obvious answer is a resounding yes, and this is exactly what Active Session History does.

ASH samples session-state information for active sessions once every second and exposes it via a number of views, the details of which you will see later in this section. ASH records these details in a circular memory buffer for quick access. CPU overheads associated with ASH have been claimed to be as low as 0.1% of 1 CPU. This sampling and recording is performed by the AWR-related processes, namely MMNL and MMON. This activity occurs without any latching and serialization, which results in the relatively low overhead for such collections at the expense of some accuracy.

As well, every 10th sample is also persisted to disk, effectively recording a snapshot of the session state for every 10th second in which the session was active. The persisted session-state history data is both timestamped and associated with the SNAP_ID of the corresponding AWR snapshot for that period. In fact, as noted before, ASH data is also collected via the same processes and stored within the same repository as AWR snapshots.

Thus, using ASH data, you can perform both on-the-spot analysis as well as look back into history and perform retroactive analysis because the ASH data is tied to a snapshot and a period. The advantage of immediate analysis is that you can obtain a larger number of samples directly from the memory buffer, while the data is coarser when viewed later using the persisted copy on disk.

> ### A Little History
>
> Sampling the SGA for performance statistics is not a new idea, although this is the first time such sampling is provided via the Oracle Database 10g kernel itself. The idea of sampling the SGA directly (Direct Memory Access, or DMA) probably evolved from a program named *m2*, which was the first program written by an Oracle Support analyst to determine V$SESSION_WAIT details in the early days of Oracle Version 7. Although it was never released or made available to Oracle users, m2 was probably the spark that ignited the concept of ASH.

ASH data is used in AWR snapshot and other collections as well. For example, we mentioned previously that AWR tracks and collects high-load SQL that occurs within the snapshot period rather than trolling through V$SQL for previously recorded SQL. It does this based on ASH data for SQL from sessions that either caused a majority of the waits during the period or consumed the most CPU. Other information collected directly from ASH includes "hot" files and segments as well as database metrics.

ASH data can be viewed both directly using the views as well as indirectly via OEM Database Control. We look at some of these views in greater detail next.

V$ACTIVE_SESSION_HISTORY

This view is the base ASH view that exposes the contents of the ASH buffers and in turn is based on the internal views, such as X$KEWASH and X$ASH. This view holds all the relevant details that both V$SESSION and V$SESSION_WAIT hold, along with some additional columns. Note that the column names for some of the common columns have changed. For example, the SID and SERIAL# columns are now known as SESSION_ID and SESSION_SERIAL# respectively. Table 11.3 describes only the new columns.

TABLE 11.3

Columns of Interest in V$ACTIVE_SESSION_HISTORY

Column Name	Meaning
SAMPLE_ID	The sample ID.
SAMPLE_TIME	The TIMESTAMP(3) column that describes the time at which that particular sample was captured.
SQL_ID	SQL identifier of the SQL statement that the session was executing at the time of sampling. This is a VARCHAR2(13) variable that has a more unusual footprint than the older SQL_HASH_VALUE from V$SESSION. This SQL_ID is used to search in V$SQL at the time of AWR snapshot collection for high-load SQL.
SQL_CHILD_NUMBER	Child number of the SQL statement that the session was executing at the time of sampling.
SQL_PLAN_HASH_VALUE	Hash value to get to the SQL plan that is stored in V$SQL_PLAN, matches with PLAN_HASH_VALUE. The information here may not always be available because it may be freed for other plans when the shared pool in the SGA is under memory pressure.
SQL_OPCODE	Indicates what phase of operation the SQL statement is in; maps to V$SESSION.COMMAND.
SERVICE_HASH	A hash that identifies the service; maps to V$ACTIVE_SERVICES.NAME_HASH.
SESSION_TYPE	Indicates the session type—that is, FOREGROUND or BACKGROUND.
SESSION_STATE	Indicates the session state—that is, whether the session is currently WAITING or ON CPU. This depends on the WAIT_TIME column. If it is 0, then the state is WAITING; if not, it is ON CPU. This column is actually a better representation of WAIT_TIME. If you see a nonblocking event such as db file sequential read, and the state is ON CPU, then it means that the process actually *completed* the last I/O and is currently not waiting. The event that is displayed is actually the *last recorded* Wait event.
QC_SESSION_ID and QC_SESSION_INSTANCE	Populated only when the session is a parallel query slave and indicates the query coordinator session and instance.
EVENT	The name of the event. If SESSION_STATE = WAITING, then it is the event for which the session was waiting at the time of sampling. If SESSION_STATE = ON CPU, then it is the event for which the session *last waited* before being sampled. EVENT_ID and EVENT# are also shown in this view and correspond to their equivalents in V$SESSION and V$SESSION_WAIT.
WAIT_TIME	The SESSION_STATE is derived from this column. It is 0 if the session was waiting at the time of sampling, and is the total wait time for the event for which the session last waited if the session was on the CPU when sampled. Whether or not WAIT_TIME = 0 is what is used to determine the SESSION_STATE at the time of sampling, rather than the actual value of WAIT_TIME itself. Maps to V$SESSION.WAIT_TIME.
TIME_WAITED	If SESSION_STATE = WAITING, then this is the amount of time that the session actually spent waiting for the event. This column is set for waits that were in progress at the time the sample was taken. If a Wait event lasted for more than a second and was caught waiting in more than one session sample row, then the actual time spent waiting for that Wait event will be populated in the last of those session sample rows. At any given time, this information will not be available for the latest session sample. TIME_WAITED is shown in number of microseconds (1,000th of a second). Note that this information is not recorded in the documentation.

TABLE 11.3

Continued

Column Name	Meaning
CURRENT_OBJ#, CURRENT_FILE#, and CURRENT_BLOCK#	Along with the CURRENT_FILE# and CURRENT_BLOCK#, the CURRENT_OBJ# column is populated only if the session is waiting for some I/O-related events or for some enqueue waits. They map to the V$SESSION.ROW_WAIT_OBJ#, ROW_WAIT_FILE#, and ROW_WAIT_BLOCK# columns.
P1, P2, and P3	These have the same meanings as in the V$SESSION_WAIT view. Note, however, that the P1TEXT, P2TEXT, and P3TEXT columns as well as the P1RAW, P2RAW, and P3RAW columns are *not* displayed. These columns are rarely used, if ever; hence, omitting them saves memory in the ASH buffers.
PROGRAM, MODULE, ACTION, and CLIENT_ID	Along with MODULE, ACTION and CLIENT_ID describe the current environment of the connecting session. These are set using the DBMS_APPLICATION_INFO package.

Inconsistencies in Column Names

There is one more example of inconsistency in column naming in the V$ACTIVE_SESSION_HISTORY view. The view uses the name SESSION_ID and SESSION_SERIAL# for the generally well known SID and SERIAL# equivalent columns from V$SESION and V$SESSION_WAIT. This particular inconsistency in naming seems prevalent in many other views related to session information.

V$SESSION_WAIT_HISTORY

This view shows the last 10 waits for any session from V$ACTIVE_SESSION_HISTORY. This view can be accessed only via the SID and does not contain the SERIAL#, which uniquely identifies a session. Thus, when multiple sessions connect and disconnect within a short period of time, you might be getting incorrect data—that is, data from a previous session that completed but whose SID is being reused by a later, newer connection. We suggest ignoring this view and looking up such data from V$ACTIVE_SESSION_HISTORY. Unfortunately, it seems that OEM uses this view, and incorrectly.

WRH$_ACTIVE_SESSION_HISTORY

This is the persisted version of the ASH data. As indicated before, the session-state information in V$ACTIVE_SESSION_HISTORY from every 10th sample is written out to disk into this table. Each of these samples is associated with the SNAP_ID of the current AWR snapshot. In fact, output from the query listed in Listing 11.10 will confirm that this is indeed the case.

LISTING 11.10   Query to Confirm AWR Snapshot Matches ASH Persisted Data

```
select s.snap_id, min(begin_interval_time), max(end_interval_time), min(sample_time),
➥max(sample_time)
from sys.wrm$_snapshot s, sys.wrh$_active_session_history h
where s.snap_id = h.snap_id
group by s.snap_id;
```

Size of Active Session History Buffers

As mentioned before, ASH maintains samples of the session-state information in its own buffers within the System Global Area (SGA). The amount of information that ASH maintains could quickly become substantial if not managed properly. Hence, ASH maintains a *fixed size circular buffer* that is allocated in the SGA at system startup using the formula:

ASH_Buffer_Size = Max (Min(No.of CPUs * 2 Mb, 5% of Shared Pool size, 30 MB), 1 Mb)

In other words, it is at least 1MB and goes up to a maximum of 30MB. In between these extremes, the size is determined by the number of CPUs (No. of CPUs * 2) or by the size of the shared pool (5% of the shared Pool size). Because ASH collects session-state information for *active* sessions only, it is obvious that the buffer will become full more quickly when there are more active sessions in the database. By default, this persistence, or writing out to disk, is set to occur when the buffers are 66% full. When this occurs, every 10th ASH record for each session is associated with the current snapshot and written out to disk as the rows in the WRH$_ACTIVE_SESSION_HISTORY table. This occurs in the same manner of persisting AWR data to disk. The ASH buffer space is then released for capturing newer session-state information.

> **Hidden Parameters for** ASH
>
> It seems that there are a few hidden parameters—those that start with _ (underscore) and should NOT be changed except under Oracle Support's direction—related to ASH. This includes _ash_enable, which by default is set to TRUE and seems to allow ASH to be switched off. Other parameters include _ash_disk_filter_ratio, the ratio of in-memory sample to flush (every 10th by default); _ash_eflush_trigger, the percentage at which an emergency disk flush should occur (66% by default); and _ash_sampling_interval, the time interval between ASH samples (1,000 milliseconds or 1 second by default). Changing these values may adversely affect the behavior of ASH. As the TV commercial says, "Don't try this at home" (or on your production instance)!

An Example of Spot Analysis Using ASH

To showcase how you can use ASH from SQL, let's use the same example of high-load SQL that we used in Chapter 10. The SQL query runs against the HR schema and joins EMPLOYEES and its related tables. In this example, the query was run simultaneously from two SQL*Plus sessions. The result was that both sessions contended on the cache buffer chain latch because they were trying to access the same blocks in memory while performing occasional physical reads. Listing 11.11 shows the query used to display the ASH data. The session and serial numbers of the sessions as they occurred in the tests are shown. Listing 11.12 shows the output of the query, partially snipped showing a time of interest in which this contention could be seen. Lines in this listing are numbered and these line numbers are used in the explanation that follows.

LISTING 11.11   Query to Show Many Details from V$ACTIVE_SESSION_HISTORY for Two Known Contending Sessions

```
column time format a8
column sid format a9
column event format a25 trunc
column wt_time format 999999
column tm_waitd format 99999
column seq# format 9999
select to_char(sample_time,'HH24:MI:SS') time,
session_id ||','|| session_serial# sid,
session_state s_state,event,seq#,
wait_time wt_time,time_waited tm_waitd
from v$active_session_history where session_id in (136,158)
and session_serial# in (67,11953)
order by session_id,sample_time;
```

LISTING 11.12   Output of Query in Listing 11.11

```
 1  TIME      SID        S_STATE EVENT                      SEQ# WT_TIME TM_WAITD
 2  -------- ---------- ------- ------------------------- ----- ------- --------
 3  <snip - First session>
 4  23:53:09 136,67     ON CPU  SQL*Net message from clie    34    1134        0
 5  23:53:10 136,67     ON CPU  SQL*Net message from clie    34    1134        0
 6  23:53:11 136,67     ON CPU  latch: cache buffers chai    35    1949        0
 7  23:53:12 136,67     ON CPU  latch: cache buffers chai    36       4        0
 8  23:53:13 136,67     ON CPU  latch: cache buffers chai    36       4        0
 9  23:53:14 136,67     ON CPU  latch: cache buffers chai    38   19462        0
10  23:53:15 136,67     WAITING latch: cache buffers chai    40       0    19506
11  23:53:16 136,67     ON CPU  latch: cache buffers chai    40   19506        0
12  <snip>
13  23:53:25 136,67     ON CPU  latch: cache buffers chai    49   19502        0
14  23:53:26 136,67     ON CPU  latch: cache buffers chai    49   19502        0
15  23:53:27 136,67     ON CPU  db file sequential read       51      84        0
16  23:53:28 136,67     ON CPU  latch: cache buffers chai    52       5        0
17  23:53:29 136,67     ON CPU  latch: cache buffers chai    54   19445        0
18  23:53:30 136,67     ON CPU  latch: cache buffers chai    54   19445        0
19  23:53:31 136,67     ON CPU  latch: cache buffers chai    56   19468        0
20  23:53:32 136,67     ON CPU  latch: cache buffers chai    58       2        0
21  23:53:33 136,67     ON CPU  latch: cache buffers chai    58       2        0
22  <snip - Second session>
23  23:53:08 158,11953 ON CPU  db file sequential read      206      26        0
24  23:53:09 158,11953 ON CPU  db file sequential read      206      26        0
25  23:53:10 158,11953 ON CPU  latch: cache buffers chai    216   19485        0
26  <snip>
27  23:53:25 158,11953 WAITING latch: cache buffers chai    253       0    13112
```

LISTING 11.12   Continued

```
28  23:53:26 158,11953 ON CPU  latch: cache buffers chai  257  19642   0
29  23:53:27 158,11953 ON CPU  latch: cache buffers chai  262  19493   0
30  23:53:28 158,11953 ON CPU  latch: cache buffers chai  264      4   0
31  23:53:29 158,11953 ON CPU  latch: cache buffers chai  266  19583   0
32  23:53:30 158,11953 ON CPU  latch: cache buffers chai  267      4   0
```

Let us now analyze the output shown in Listing 11.12. You can arrive at a number of conclusions from this data.

The Wait event in lines 4 and 5 show that the session was waiting on SQL*Net message from client. Although this event is classified as an idle event, you know that the session was active because ASH data would not have otherwise been collected! This is clarified by the STATE column, which shows ON CPU for these two lines. You can thus understand that between 23:59:09 and 23:59:10, the session was actually consuming CPU waiting on the client (the SQL*Plus session in this case), which in turn was processing—probably formatting the data sent across, which consumes some CPU.

In lines 7–10, you see that the session was waiting on the latch: cache buffer chain event. Lines 7 and 8 look the same, so you can conclude that the session was using CPU but never posted a Wait event during this period. In fact, from the nature and operation of a latch, you can conclude that the process was spinning on the latch. This is a basic operating system call where you can perform a set-and-test operation, where the process idly spins for a short period and tests for the latch before yielding the CPU. Although this spinning reduces operating-system process context switching (which is expensive in itself), it does consume some CPU. Monitoring of this process from the operating system supported the conclusion that a significant amount of user CPU was consumed by this process.

You see a state change between lines 8 and 9; the event is the same, but the SEQ# column has moved from 36 to 38. What happened to 37? Actually, ASH missed recording the event; the sampling period wasn't small enough to catch all the events. This looks like a weakness in ASH, and we will deal with this later. Line 10 implies some waiting on the same latch, probably for a latch sleep. The TIME_WAITED is now posted and is taken into account in other counters, such as V$SESSION_EVENT and V$SYSTEM_EVENT, as well as in V$LATCH and V$LATCH_CHILDREN. We hope you are now able to see how this information is rolled up from ASH into higher levels.

Note that in the definition of TIME_WAITED, we stated that "If a Wait event lasted for more than a second and was caught waiting in more than one session sample row, then the actual time spent waiting for that Wait event will be populated in the last of those session sample rows." You can see this occur in line 10.

Let us now look at lines 15, 23, 24, and 29. Except line 15, all are from the second session. And although you do see file I/O in the form of db file sequential read events from both sessions, you also see the contention on the cache buffer chain latch. Further analysis of other data, such as P1, P2, and P3 (not shown due to size and formatting limitations) helped you understand that these two sessions may be contending for the same blocks, and the solution may be to schedule them to run one after another.

You can also summarize information from V$ACTIVE_SESSION_HISTORY to obtain summary counts that will help you quickly get to the main bottleneck at hand, and support the conclusion arrived at here. This is made clear in the query and output shown in Listing 11.13.

LISTING 11.13   Query to Confirm Conclusions Using Summaries on V$ACTIVE_SESSION_HISTORY

```
SQL> column event format a35 trunc
SQL> select session_id sid, event, session_state state,
  2  count(*) times, sum(time_waited) tm_waited
  3  from v$active_session_history
  4  where program like 'sqlplus%'
  5  group by session_id, event, session_state;


    SID EVENT                                STATE      TIMES  TM_WAITED
 ------- ---------------------------------  -------  --------- ----------
     136 db file sequential read             ON CPU        32          0
     136 SQL*Net message from client         ON CPU         9          0
     136 latch: cache buffers chains         ON CPU       426          0
     136 latch: cache buffers chains         WAITING       15     430403
     158 db file sequential read             ON CPU         2          0
     158 SQL*Net message from client         ON CPU        17          0
     158 latch: cache buffers chains         ON CPU       466          0
     158 latch: cache buffers chains         WAITING       16     718216
```

It is clear from this listing that the most waiting was on the latch: cache buffer chains event. In fact, you can conclude that both sessions spent almost 100% of their time on this latch, and were in fact contending for the same buffers in memory. This becomes apparent when the session is run alone. The output from the same query when run alone is shown in Listing 11.14.

LISTING 11.14   Query to Show Wait Events When Run Alone

```
SQL> column event format a35 trunc
SQL> select session_id sid, event, session_state state,
  2  count(*) times, sum(time_waited) tm_waited
  3  from v$active_session_history
  4  where session_id = 151 and session_serial# = 365
  5  group by session_id, event, session_state;

Sid EVENT                                STATE      TIMES   TM_WAITED
---- ---------------------------------  -------  ---------- ------------
 151 db file sequential read             ON CPU       105            0
 151 SQL*Net message from client         ON CPU       107            0
```

This query shows that minimal if no waiting was recorded in the wait history for that session, and most work was only on the CPU—probably due to formatting and displaying the data when run alone by itself.

You should be able to cross-check these findings using the Time and Wait model views at the session level, namely the V$SESSION_WAIT_CLASS view using the SESSION and SERIAL# values. Note, however, that the data for that session in this view exists only as long as the said session is connected and alive. In contrast, the ASH data is available even after the session has disconnected.

Using OEM to Obtain Active Session History

You can use OEM Database Control to obtain session statistics from ASH. There are available from the Top Sessions link in the Performance screen or from any session-related drill-down. Figure 11.5 shows the Session Details screen for one session numbered 150.

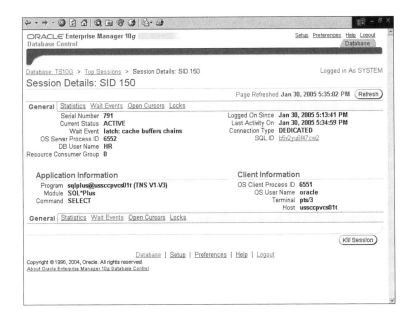

FIGURE 11.5
The Session Details screen.

Note that the status, current SQL, and so on are obtained and displayed from the V$SESSION view. The menu includes the following:

- **Statistics.** These are the session statistics available from the V$SESSTAT view. The names of the various statistics are derived from V$STATNAME.

- **Wait Events.** This is the session wait history.

- **Open Cursors.** This is a list of currently open cursors obtained from the V$OPEN_CURSORS view. It can be instrumental in figuring out the various activities completed by this session, when such cursor information is available.

■ **Locks.** This is a list of locks currently being faced by the session, and derived from the blocking session details available in V$SESSION.

Upon clicking the Wait Events link in the menu, the last 10 waits suffered by the session are displayed, as shown in Figure 11.6. Note, however, that these waits are shown regardless of whether the session was active. As well, this information is not from V$ACTIVE_SESSION_HISTORY, but from V$SESSION_WAIT_HISTORY; hence, you might be looking at incorrect data as explained when we discussed the latter view.

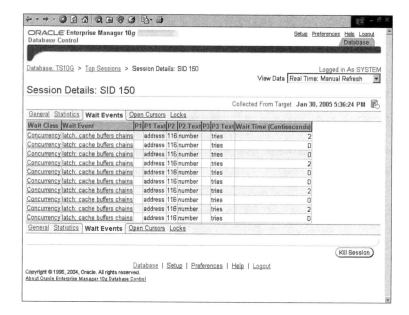

FIGURE 11.6
The Wait Events screen.

Dumping ASH Buffer Contents

As per the previously mentioned MetaLink Note #243132.1, it is possible to dump the contents of the ASH buffers. The command does not work as stated, however. The difference is minor and has to do with the statement in the MetaLink Note that the number specified in the command is the number of *minutes*, when it seems to be the number of seconds instead. To dump the contents of the ASH buffers, obtain a login as SYS. Then run the commands as shown in Listing 11.15.

LISTING 11.15   Dumping Contents of the ASH Buffers to Trace

```
SQL> oradebug setmypid
Statement processed.
SQL> oradebug dump ashdump 10000
Statement processed.
```

The trace file can be found in the UDUMP directory. The file is named according to the convention of your platform, as with any other user trace file. Although the MetaLink Note suggests that the number specified is the number of minutes of historical data, it seems that only a large number produces all the output. ORADEBUG is a special command available in the SYS login to produce a variety of dumps and other traces. The file that is produced, after some header information is removed, is a comma-separated value (CSV) file that can be loaded into a Microsoft Excel spreadsheet or even another database table using SQL*Loader for analysis. The partial contents are shown in Listing 11.16. You will notice that there is a header line that specifies the full column list of V$ACTIVE_SESSION_HISTORY.

LISTING 11.16   Partial Contents of the ASH Dump

```
*** 2005-01-30 23:22:37.981
*** SERVICE NAME:(SYS$USERS) 2005-01-30 23:22:37.979
*** SESSION ID:(140.360) 2005-01-30 23:22:37.979
<<<ACTIVE SESSION HISTORY - PROCESS TRACE DUMP HEADER BEGIN>>>
DBID, INSTANCE_NUMBER, SAMPLE_ID, SAMPLE_TIME, SESSION_ID, SESSION_SERIAL#, USER
_ID, SQL_ID, SQL_CHILD_NUMBER, SQL_PLAN_HASH_VALUE, SERVICE_HASH, SESSION_TYPE,
SQL_OPCODE, QC_SESSION_ID, QC_INSTANCE_ID, CURRENT_OBJ#, CURRENT_FILE#, CURRENT_
BLOCK#, EVENT_ID, SEQ#, P1, P2, P3, WAIT_TIME, TIME_WAITED, PROGRAM, MODULE, ACT
ION, CLIENT_ID
<<<ACTIVE SESSION HISTORY - PROCESS TRACE DUMP HEADER END>>>
<<<ACTIVE SESSION HISTORY - PROCESS TRACE DUMP BEGIN>>>
845721274,1,3064021,"01-30-2005 23:22:35.178099000",166,1,0,"",0,0,165959219,2,0
,0,0,4294967295,0,0,866018717,536,300,0,0,3004674,0,"oracle@ussccpvcs01t (CKPT)"
,"","",""
<snipped>
845721274,1,3063605,"01-30-2005 23:15:26.638099000",170,1,0,"",0,0,165959219,2,0
,0,0,4294967295,0,0,3539483025,7,300,0,0,2936573,0,"oracle@ussccpvcs01t (PMON)",
"","",""
845721274,1,3063597,"01-30-2005 23:15:18.398099000",152,1,22,"c1599tjmzu1fc",0,0
,3427055676,1,0,0,0,8548,3,34825,1148964757,1500,8552,2429532560,5,5008574,0,"em
agent@ussccpvcs01t (TNS V1-V3)","emagent@ussccpvcs01t (TNS V1-V3)","",""
<snipped>
845721274,1,3063515,"01-30-2005 23:13:53.928099000",145,9,54,"2b064ybzkwf1y",0,0
,1594506128,1,47,0,0,47741,3,19916,218649935,295,2432172472,2432129528,0,1005847
,0,"OMS","OEM.SystemPool","",""
845721274,1,3063453,"01-30-2005 23:12:50.068099000",150,19,58,"b5v2yu6f47cw2",0,
4106914013,3427055676,1,3,0,0,49788,5,10659,2652584166,252,5,10659,1,63,0,"sqlpl
us@ussccpvcs01t (TNS V1-V3)","SQL*Plus","",""
845721274,1,3063452,"01-30-2005 23:12:49.038099000",150,19,58,"b5v2yu6f47cw2",0,
4106914013,3427055676,1,3,0,0,49788,5,10659,2652584166,252,5,10659,1,63,0,"sqlpl
us@ussccpvcs01t (TNS V1-V3)","SQL*Plus","",""
```

The Downside of ASH

Although the overhead for collection of ASH data is minimal, access to the ASH data in human-readable format, either via the OEM interface or the more traditional SQL access, is not without the normal overhead of SQL processing, including the need for a connection, some latching, as well as associated CPU usage. On a badly overloaded system, you may not be able to obtain a *new* SQL*Plus or OEM session in order to get to ASH data.

As well, when the system is heavily contending on the shared pool and library cache latches, your query may take a long time to parse and execute. Indeed, frequent queries to ASH data may impose additional waits for these latches. This is not the case with an *external* program that reads SGA directly. ASH, however, needs to run within the context of Oracle and hence will have to follow all the rules of the Oracle kernel as far as a normal process is concerned.

A workaround is to maintain a perpetual connection to the database using an account that has privileges to query ASH data. If you used precompiled code in a PL/SQL package that is pinned in the SGA and can produce canned ASH queries, then you can even get around the parsing issues.

It is very possible, indeed probable, to lose some wait information because the sampling rate is only once a second by default. You saw an example of this issue in the previous example. So how can this be countered? The answer lies in using Extended SQL Trace, better known as 10046 trace. Using this method, all the Wait events as well as the SQL executed by the session are dumped directly to the trace file, which can later be viewed and processed. These trace files are cumbersome to track and process, however. As well, you can only perform such a trace as the problem is occurring, not in a retrospective manner as with ASH.

New Features in Oracle Database 10g Release 2

Oracle Database 10g Release 2 collects additional statistics as compared to Release 1. AWR now includes a collection of streams-specific performance data in a set of tables prefixed by WRH$STREAMS_ to assist in detecting streams-related issues. As well, additional information is collected in order to determine the efficacy and usage of SQL tuning sets. Other changes include a new AWR table named WRH$_COMP_IOSTAT that seems to catergorize and record different types of I/O.

Changes have also been made in the area of metrics reporting. OEM now computes statistical alert thresholds using either static (user-defined) or dynamic (self-adjusting) baselines. Dynamic baselining can significantly improve the accuracy of performance alerting while reducing false positives that commonly occur when fixed thresholds are in effect. A new AWR Diff-Diff report allows users to generate AWR reports identifying differences between two pairs of snapshots. This report will help users better understand changes in workload, correlate it to performance problems pointed to by other advisors such as ADDM, or validate tuning actions implemented based on such advisors. This feature enhances manageability by enabling simpler and more accurate performance diagnosis.

AWR can now be customized to set the thresholds for collecting top resource-consuming SQLs. OEM now displays ASH information for both recent as well as past sessions from historical ASH tables. This was identified and noted earlier as lacking in the current version of ASH.

Summary

In this chapter, you saw AWR and ASH in great detail. These two tools can and should be your first line of defense in tracking, viewing, and diagnosing performance issues with an Oracle Database 10g instance. Knowing and understanding the views behind AWR and ASH as well as the SQL and PL/SQL interface to these tools will enable you to get to the root of the problem quickly and efficiently.

12

Effectively Using the Automatic Database Diagnostic Monitor

IN THIS CHAPTER

Introduction to ADDM	239
Interfacing to ADDM	244
Making Sense of ADDM Data	254
New Features in Oracle Database 10g Release 2	262

Introduction to ADDM

As mentioned in previous chapters, Oracle Database 10g comes with a number of advisors built in. For the performance analyst, the Automatic Database Diagnostic Monitor (ADDM) is the most important of the advisors and is indeed the starting point in the investigation of any performance issue. Affectionately called "ADDuM" or "ADAM," this component of the Database Diagnostic Pack is a powerful aide to the performance analyst when it is understood and used carefully. Simply stated, it is a self-diagnostic mechanism built into the kernel that automatically examines and analyzes the AWR snapshots at the end of every snapshot with

Effectively Using the Automatic Database Diagnostic Monitor

the objective of determining any performance-affecting issue. It is then able to recommend corrective action; these recommendations come with an expected benefit.

ADDM does not stop with these recommendations. Just as a general practitioner examines a patient in an initial investigation and recommends further examination in particular areas by other specialists, ADDM can direct the performance analyst to other advisors such as the SQL Tuning Advisor or the SQL Access Advisor when it determines that a problem exists. By default, ADDM executes at the end of every scheduled snapshot, performing a scheduled "database performance health checkup" using the captured AWR snapshots. In effect, it is casting an expert eye on the AWR report in a scheduled manner, every time, all the time. This is equivalent to an unpaid expert DBA performing analysis of these snapshots 24/7/365! These recommendations and findings are stored in the database so that you can analyze and report on them later on, at a convenient time.

The Goal of ADDM

Ultimately, the goal of ADDM is to reduce the DB Time component generated by any load on the database. As you saw in Chapter 10, "Adopting a New Approach to Tuning," the DB Time is the total time spent by the foreground sessions performing useful work. In other words, it is a combination of CPU spent parsing and executing SQL, PL/SQL, and Java as well other overheads such as process setup and management. When triggered, ADDM drills down into the performance statistics to identify the root cause of problems rather than just the symptoms, and reports the overall impact of the issue on the system as a whole. In making a recommendation, it reports the benefits that can be expected, again in terms of this DB Time. The use of this common currency allows the impact of several problems or recommendations to be compared effectively.

Inside Scoop on ADDM **Rules**

Because the Time and Wait model helps greatly in summarizing and classifying the various performance statistics, ADDM can quickly focus on where time is spent by using a set of top-down tree-structured rules. These rules are based on decades of collective experience of performance experts in a dedicated Oracle Server Technologies Performance group at Oracle HQ. Apparently, these rules have been validated by applying them on a number of STATSPACK reports and comparing the results with conclusions arrived via experience. We understand that the same personnel who created STATSPACK in Oracle 8i and improved it in Oracle 9i were behind ADDM, so that certainly explains both the similarities as well as the improvements.

Using such a well-understood and easily identifiable set of components to quantify the impact also prevents judgments based on experience rather than hard figures. For example, a rule of thumb, based on experience, might have said that an IOPS (the number of I/O operations per second) should not exceed the rate of, say, 1,000 per second. Anything more than this rate was classified as a problem that should be fixed. That said, we are aware of many systems that can run significantly higher IOPS rates without noticeably affecting performance. Using the new Time and Wait model data in AWR, ADDM can now report quantitatively that such I/O operations are, say, taking 30% of time spent in the database during that period. This quantified value makes it much easier to understand the problem and help determine the *effect* of fixing the issue, rather than just making a judgmental statement such as "The database is performing too much I/O." Better still, it helps the performance analyst concentrate on what is important to tune so that the fix has the most effect.

Problem Areas Handled by ADDM

ADDM handles the most frequently observed performance problems and drills down to the root cause rather than taking the easier approach of just reporting symptoms. This reporting includes but is not limited to problems seen in the following areas:

- **CPU bottlenecks.** Is the system CPU bound by Oracle processes or by some other applications?

- **Excessive parsing.** Is there too much parsing due to use of short SQLs that do not use bind variables?

- **Lock contention.** Is there application-level lock contention?

- **Concurrency.** Is there an excessive number of buffer busy waits, latching, and the like, which reduce concurrency and thus prevent the application from scaling effectively?

- **I/O capacity.** Is the I/O subsystem performing as required, as compared to a set of expected I/O throughput figures?

- **Incorrect sizing of Oracle memory and file structures.** Are Oracle memory structures, such as the buffer cache and redo log buffer, adequate? Are Oracle's file structures, such as the size of redo logs, adequate? Are Oracle settings, such as an aggressive MTTR (mean time to recover), stressing the system?

- **High-load SQL statements.** Are any SQL statements consuming excessive system resources?

- **High-load Java and PL/SQL time.** Are Java and PL/SQL statements consuming a large amount of resources?

- **Poor connection management.** Are there excessive logon/logoff rates?

- **Hot objects.** Are any "hot" objects assessed repeatedly and needing investigation?

- **RAC-specific issues.** Are there any hot blocks in the global cache that result in inter instance contention? Is the interconnect behaving properly, without any latency issues?

ADDM reports these problems as "findings," but does not stop with the diagnosis; it recommends possible solutions, based on the detected problem areas. When appropriate, ADDM recommends multiple solutions for the performance analyst to choose from. These are in the form of recommendations, and include the following:

- **Hardware changes.** This includes increasing the CPU capacity or changing the I/O subsystem configuration.

- **Database-configuration changes.** This includes changing initialization parameter settings, such as those for session caching of cursors, sort area size, and so on.

■ **Schema-level changes.** ADDM may recommend partitioning a table or index, using automatic segment-space management (ASSM) for certain segments, and so on.

■ **Application changes.** ADDM may recommend using the cache option for sequences when it encounters high access rates for SEQ$, and recommend using bind variables when it observes short SQLs that have hard-coded values.

■ **Using other advisors.** ADDM may recommend running the SQL Tuning Advisor on high-load SQL or running the Segment Advisor on hot objects.

Using ADDM with ASH

When ADDM is combined with ASH data, it is possible to quickly determine the root cause as well as to drill down to the depths of session details to document what exactly transpired. It is thus possible to even determine what occurred a while ago without having to resort to setting up a replay of the workload in a test environment. Even if ASH data is flushed from the buffers, keep in mind that every 10th sample is retained, and this provides at least a coarse drill down. In comparison, STATSPACK and most other tools do not store session-level data that could assist in such drill downs. As mentioned previously, the extended SQL trace cannot be used in this case because trace needs to be switched on prior to the occurrence of the problem.

Nonproblematic Areas

ADDM highlights nonproblematic areas in addition to the problem areas. This is based on wait classes that have been determined as not affecting the result significantly, but are nevertheless listed. A performance analyst can then quickly see that these wait classes were eliminated and hence not spend time and effort working on something that will not produce significant improvement. This is akin to a general practitioner assuring a patient that an otherwise worrying symptom is not the cause of a deeper issue, helping the patient concentrate on battling what is more important to his or her health. Sometimes, large values in STATSPACK reports that actually do not pose a problem seem alarming. Many a performance analyst has wasted time and resources trying to chase and fix such issues. This is almost entirely avoided in Oracle Database 10g as you'll see later.

Helpful ADDM **Views**

It pays to be aware of a number of views that ADDM uses. You can use these views in many innovative ways. For example, you can use them to help preserve interesting scenarios and findings before the data is purged by AWR. A small number of these views is listed in Table 12.1. More details can be found in the *Oracle Database 10g Reference Manual* as well as in the *Oracle Database 10g Performance Guide.*

TABLE 12.1

Some ADDM **Views**

View Name	Description
DBA_ADVISOR_LOG	This view shows the state of all tasks from all advisors, including ADDM. A scheduled check of the STATUS and ERROR columns is advised to make sure that nothing amiss is occurring on these scheduled tasks. Scheduled ADDM runs are stamped as ADDM:*DBID_Instance_Snapshot_ID* for easy identification, while manually scheduled ADDM runs are named TASK_*Task_ID*. This can help differentiate between manual and automated runs.
DBA_ADVISOR_FINDINGS	This view exposes the findings of the various advisors. Both the type of finding and the expected impact is shown. See Listing 12.1 for an example of how this view can be used. When no significant activity occurs between two snapshots, the MESSAGE column in this view records the message There was no significant database activity to run the ADDM. Thus you can use this as a criterion for discarding any ADDM tasks that need not be considered.
DBA_ADVISOR_RECOMMENDATIONS	This view details the advisor recommendations that follow the findings. The recommendations are tied to the findings. As well, the BENEFIT_TYPE and BENEFIT columns display the type and amount of expected benefit by following that recommendation.
DBA_ADVISOR_ACTIONS	This view exposes the actions required by the recommendations of the aforementioned advisors. Of particular interest is the MESSAGE column.
DBA_ADVISOR_RATIONALE	This view lists the rationale behind the recommendations from the aforementioned advisors. It identifies the impact of each recommendation. Look at the MESSAGE, IMPACT, and IMPACT_TYPE columns for more information.

Before you move to the next section, let's look at a brief example of how one of the views can be used. A performance analyst has many other tasks, so rather than expecting him or her to review all the ADDM reports that are automatically produced by the system throughout the day and night, the DBA_ADVISOR_FINDINGS view can be used to summarize this information. The query and output are shown in Listing 12.1.

LISTING 12.1   Determining Whether ADDM Found Problems in the Past 24 Hours

```
SQL> select type, count(*) from dba_advisor_findings
  2   where task_id in
  3   (select task_id from dba_advisor_log where execution_start > sysdate - 1)
  4   group by type;
```

LISTING 12.1 Continued

```
TYPE         COUNT(*)
...........  ..........
INFORMATION        40
PROBLEM            31
SYMPTOM            18
```

From the result, you can see that there were at least 31 problems detected by ADDM during the past 24 hours. This will warrant more research and analysis of individual ADDM tasks. You can use the query shown in Listing 12.2 to determine which ADDM task IDs to query on.

LISTING 12.2 Determining the ADDM Task IDs with Problems in the Past 24 Hours

```
SQL> select distinct f.task_id, f.task_name, l.execution_start
  2  from dba_advisor_findings f, dba_advisor_log l
  3  where f.type in ('PROBLEM', 'SYMPTOM')
  4  and f.task_id = l.task_id
  5  and l.execution_start > sysdate - 1;

   TASK_ID TASK_NAME                        EXECUTION
.......... ...............................  ..........
      1490 TASK_1490                        05-FEB-05
      1493 ADDM:845721274_1_1522            05-FEB-05
      1494 TASK_1494                        05-FEB-05
      1495 ADDM:845721274_1_1523            05-FEB-05
```

You can then use this output to produce a detailed ADDM report, given the task IDs. You also notice that tasks 1490 and 1494 were probably manually performed, while ADDM automatically produced tasks 1493 and 1495.

Interfacing to ADDM

You can interface to the ADDM using either the Oracle Enterprise Monitor (OEM) or the advisor APIs described in this section. First, you will look at how you can use OEM Database Control to get to ADDM. For the purpose of generating load on the database, we used a variation of the example in previous chapters. This is based on the HR Demo schema, and the code can be seen in the various listings in this chapter.

Using OEM for ADDM

ADDM can be accessed from OEM in a variety of ways:

■ **Advisor Central.** Access the Advisor Central page using the link at the bottom of all the database pages and click the ADDM link therein.

- **Database Performance page.** This page displays a number of clipboard icons just below the Sessions: Waiting and Working area. Click on this icon to display the ADDM analysis for that period.

- **AWR Snapshot Page.** ADDM tasks can be run on selected snapshots or on a set of preserved snapshots from the AWR Snapshots page, described in the previous chapter. On the Snapshots page, select Create ADDM Task from the Actions pull-down menu, and then select the beginning and ending snapshots corresponding to the time period that you want to analyze. Note that you can also create an ADDM report from the preserved snapshot set corresponding to the time period that you want to analyze.

Figure 12.1 shows the Advisor Central screen. This is the launching point for most of the advisors. The last ADDM task is always displayed. You can use the Search facility to obtain previous ADDM tasks based on a time period under Advisor Runs or use the search to specify a required name. You can also click the ADDM link in the top of the page to create a new ADDM task.

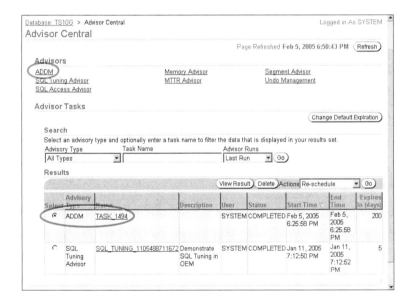

FIGURE 12.1
Advisor Central page: Launch point for all advisors.

This now displays the ADDM main page with camera icons denoting currently available snapshots and ADDM reports as well as a graph showing the number of sessions waiting, performing I/O, and so on. This will enable you to quickly identify a period of interest. You can also use the arrow keys to move back and forth to the correct period. Hovering the cursor over any of the camera icons will display the actual snapshot time period. You can now select the starting and ending snapshot using these icons, which will create an ADDM task that is automatically named and results in producing an ADDM report that lists the findings. Alternatively, you can choose the currently listed ADDM snapshot. In both cases, OEM will display a screen similar to that shown in Figures 12.2 and 12.3. (This screen is shown in two figures because there is a wealth of information displayed, which you must scroll down to access.)

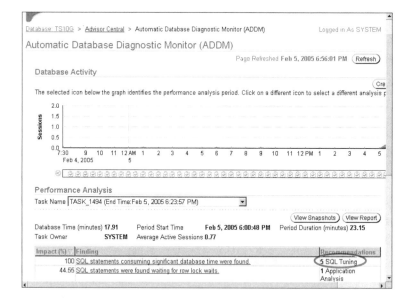

FIGURE 12.2
Top half of the ADDM Main page, showing database activity, recent snapshots, and the ADDM task name.

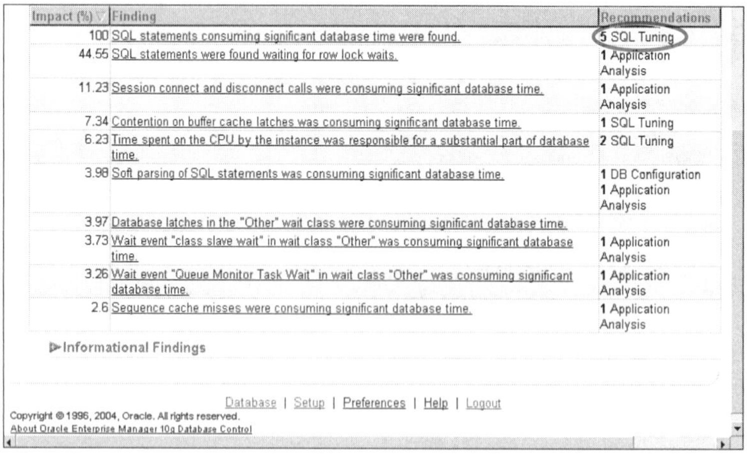

FIGURE 12.3
Bottom half of the ADDM Main page, showing the findings and recommendations.

The findings shown in Figure 12.3 are the heart of the matter, and are discussed in detail in the next section. First, however, you need to look at the various drill-downs available in this screen. Notice that each finding, which is actually text with links, has an impact denoted as a percentage. For example, clicking the link for the statement "SQL statements consuming significant database time were found" opens the Performance Finding Details screen, shown in Figure 12.4.

If applicable, the ability to link to an advisor also appears. As well, each finding has a benefit percentage attached to it. This denotes the expected benefit that could be obtained by tuning this SQL. In this particular case, because you clicked on a finding involving SQL, the Run SQL Tuning Advisor button is shown. Notice also that there were five findings for the SQL statements, as seen in the Recommendation column, which shows the text "5 SQL Tuning" for this finding. Thus, you will notice that the details of five separate SQL statements are shown in this screen. You will also notice that further drill-down is enabled for each of SQL statement, and you can choose to hide or display these details. If the link is clicked, these details will be shown in a separate drill-down screen. Short SQLs will be shown where possible; for larger PL/SQL blocks, the link is shown with the SQL ID as the text. Clicking on this link will take you to the screen shown in Figure 12.5.

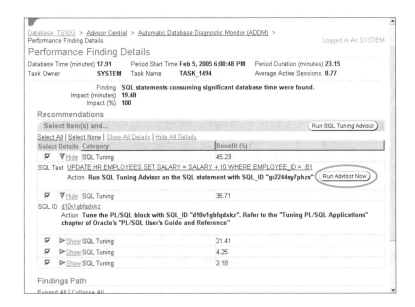

FIGURE 12.4
The Performance Finding Details screen for the first finding.

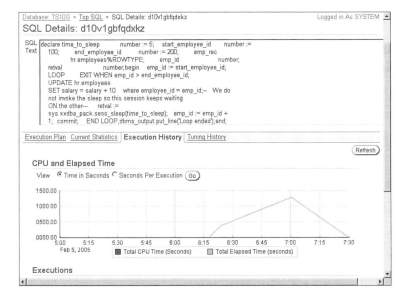

FIGURE 12.5
SQL details for the PL/SQL block.

Transitory Details for SQL and PL/SQL

Some of the details shown in the **SQL and PL/SQL details are transitory in nature because they are fetched directly from the** V$SQL_PLAN and V$SQL_PLAN_STATISTICS **views if available. Because these views fetch current data from the shared pool, these statistics are not available for statements that were aged out of the shared pool because of memory pressure, time elapsed since occurrence, or loss via a database restart. Note that some part of the** V$SQL_PLAN **is being stored for snapshots in the** WRH$_SQL_PLAN **table in** AWR**, presumably for high-load SQL, although there is no equivalent for** V$SQL_PLAN_STATISTICS**. Although Oracle Database 10 Release 1 does not store the details of** V$SQL_PLAN_STATISTICS **in the Workload Repository, the newer Oracle Database 10g Release 2 is able to do so.**

In this screen, you can view the details of the PL/SQL block as well as its execution details, such as the number of times the block was executed, a graph showing both the CPU and elapsed time as total seconds or as seconds per execution, as well as other transitory details such as the execution plan and other statistics. Note that these details are available for both SQL and PL/SQL blocks—we chose to expose just the PL/SQL block because we are aware that the SQL is actually part of the PL/SQL block and is thus considered recursive.

Just to create a complete picture, let's see what happens for other types of findings. Clicking the finding labeled "SQL statements were found waiting for row lock waits" on the ADDM main page shown in Figure 12.3 will take you to the screen shown in Figure 12.6.

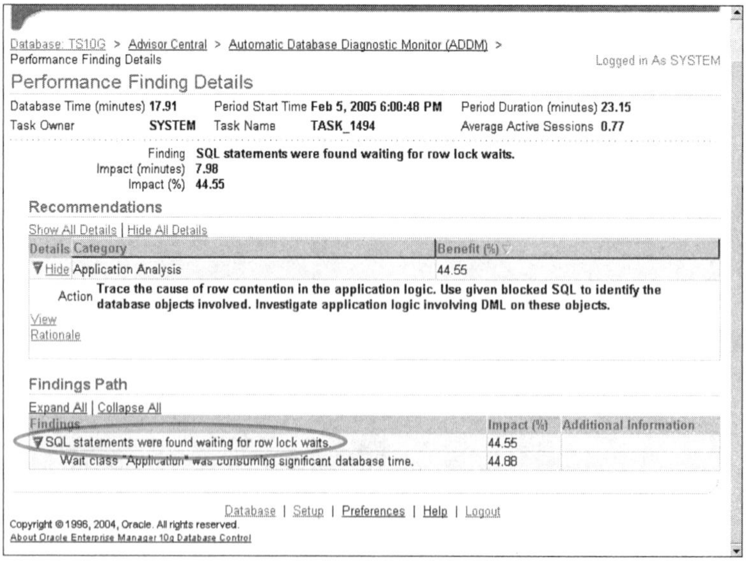

FIGURE 12.6
Performance finding details.

This screen does not show any advisors or other details, but instead states the following: "Trace the cause of row contention in the application logic. Use given blocked SQL to identify the database objects involved. Investigate application logic involving DML on these objects." This does not really state what caused the row locking, although there is a clue in the form of the SQL that was blocked. This is shown in the View Rationale link when available. Clicking this link opens the window shown in Figure 12.7.

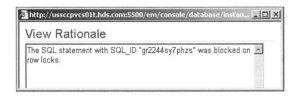

FIGURE 12.7   Details of blocked SQL.

Notice that just the SQL ID is provided, although it may have been a simple matter to fetch the accompanying SQL. You will need to fetch this SQL from the AWR tables by yourself. The query is shown in Listing 12.3.

LISTING 12.3   SQL to Obtain the Blocked SQL from the Rationale Screen

```
SQL> set long 1000
SQL> select snap_id, sql_text
  2  from sys.wrh$_sqltext where sql_id = 'gr2244sy7phzs';

   SNAP_ID
----------
SQL_TEXT
-------------------------------------------------------------------------
      1571
UPDATE HR.EMPLOYEES SET SALARY = SALARY + 10 WHERE EMPLOYEE_ID = :B1
```

That you need to perform additional analysis was actually evident from the category of the recommendation, namely "Application Analysis." Clearly, the performance analyst is expected to perform more application tracing to determine the root cause. ADDM was kind enough to highlight the problem and provide an impact analysis, however.

Before moving on, let us look at just one other high-impact finding. This is shown in Figure 12.8, and is an example of a recommendation to change the environment external to the database.

In this case, the recommendation text is "Investigate application logic for possible reduction of connect and disconnect calls. For example, you might use a connection pool scheme in the middle tier." This implies that you might be able to use a web server that supports connection pooling to mitigate this issue.

You may have noticed in all these screens that both the impact of the finding as well as the benefit of implementing the recommendation are expressed as a percentage. Actually, these values are calculated using the DB Time value accumulated against that particular activity using an internal algorithm. The point is that using this common currency, ADDM can assign a number that can be used to compare problems and alternatives, rather than just stating that a problem exists.

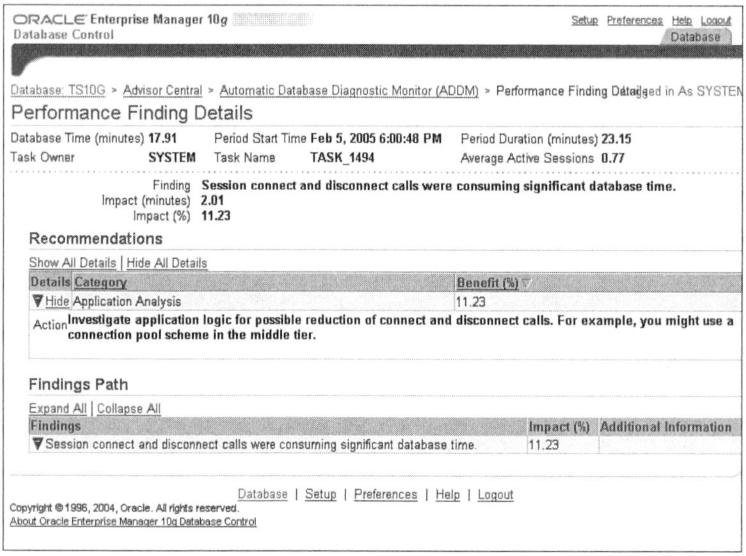

FIGURE 12.8
Performance finding
details recommendation
for an external environ-
ment.

Using SQL to Get to ADDM

Oracle has provided a number of application program interfaces (APIs) to get to ADDM data. In fact, OEM uses them in the background to obtain and display the information. The simplest way to generate an ADDM report is to use the addmrpt.sql script. This script, along with addmrpti.sql, is stored in the $ORACLE_HOME/rdbms/admin directory for UNIX servers and the %ORACLE_HOME%\RDBMS\ADMIN directory for Windows servers. Similar to the AWR scripts that are named in the same fashion, the addmrpt.sql script is a wrapper that invokes the addmrpti.sql script, which in turn sets up and invokes various procedures in the DBMS_ADVISOR PL/SQL built-in package.

Invoking the addmrpt.sql Script

To invoke the addmrpt.sql script, go to the $ORACLE_HOME/rdbms/admin directory and log in using an account that has privileges to access ADDM. This could be the SYSTEM account or any other account that has the DBA privilege. Alternatively, it must be a user that has both the SELECT_CATALOG_ROLE as well as the EXECUTE privilege assigned directly to the DBMS_ADVISOR package. An example of the partial dialogue for invoking this script and the resulting output, again partial, is shown in Listing 12.4.

LISTING 12.4   Running an ADDM Report Using SQL*Plus

```
SQL> @addmrpt

Current Instance
~~~~~~~~~~~~~~~~

   DB Id    DB Name      Inst Num Instance
```

LISTING 12.4   Continued

```
.......... ............ ........ ...........
  845721274 TS10G              1 TS10G


Instances in this Workload Repository schema
~~~~~~~~~~~~~~~~~~~~~~~~~~~~~~~~~~~~~~~~~~~~~~
  DB Id     Inst Num DB Name     Instance     Host
.......... ........ ............ ............ ...........
* 845721274        1 TS10G        TS10G        test10g


Using  845721274 for database Id
Using          1 for instance number


Specify the number of days of snapshots to choose from
~~~~~~~~~~~~~~~~~~~~~~~~~~~~~~~~~~~~~~~~~~~~~~~~~~~~~~~~~
Entering the number of days (n) will result in the most recent
(n) days of snapshots being listed.  Pressing <return> without
specifying a number lists all completed snapshots.


Listing the last 3 days of Completed Snapshots
                                                   Snap
Instance      DB Name        Snap Id    Snap Started    Level
.......... ............ .......... ................. .....
TS10G         TS10G            1629 08 Feb 2005 00:00     2
                               1630 08 Feb 2005 00:30     2
                               1631 08 Feb 2005 01:00     2
<snipped to reduce space>
                               1771 10 Feb 2005 23:00     2
                               1772 10 Feb 2005 23:30     2


Specify the Begin and End Snapshot Ids
~~~~~~~~~~~~~~~~~~~~~~~~~~~~~~~~~~~~~~~~
Enter value for begin_snap: 1515
Begin Snapshot Id specified: 1515


Enter value for end_snap: 1524
End   Snapshot Id specified: 1524


Specify the Report Name
~~~~~~~~~~~~~~~~~~~~~~~~~
The default report file name is addmrpt_1_1515_1524.txt.  To use this name,
press <return> to continue, otherwise enter an alternative.


Enter value for report_name: addmrpt_task1494
```

LISTING 12.4   Continued

```
Using the report name addmrpt_task1494
Running the ADDM analysis on the specified pair of snapshots ...
Generating the ADDM report for this analysis ...


             DETAILED ADDM REPORT FOR TASK 'TASK_1750' WITH ID 1750

             -------------------------------------------------------
             Analysis Period: 05-FEB-2005 from 17:00:13 to 19:30:07
         Database ID/Instance: 845721274/1
       Database/Instance Names: TS10G/TS10G
                    Host Name: test10g
             Database Version: 10.1.0.2.0
               Snapshot Range: from 1515 to 1524
                Database Time: 3037 seconds
       Average Database Load: .3 active sessions
<Rest of the output snipped>
```

All that you will have to input to this report is the starting and ending snapshot IDs covering the time period of choice; the listing of the snapshots in Listing 12.4 will help you choose the right snapshot IDs. It goes without saying that there should not have been a database restart between these snapshots, as with the AWR snapshots. Note that we used the same starting and ending snapshots that were used in the OEM screens. We will look at the rest of the report while discussing the details in the next section. For now, note the Database Time value, which is 3,037 seconds. This denotes the DB Time value as deduced from the AWR data for these two snapshots.

While using the addmrpti.sql script instead of the addmrpt.sql script, you will be able to specify the database ID as well as the instance ID, and be able to list all the existing snapshots as well. As stated before, addmrpt.sql sets up all the variables before invoking addmrpti.sql.

Using the DBMS_ADVISOR API

The DBMS_ADVISOR built-in PL/SQL package is the main API for most of the advisors. This package contains interfaces to access and use most of the advisors. In this section, you will look only at those that pertain specifically to the ADDM. Of course, the source code for the DBMS_ADVISOR package is wrapped and hence cannot be viewed. There are general advisor parameters and procedure/function calls as well as advisor-specific parameters and related calls. Details of these procedures and calls can be found in the *Oracle Database 10g PL/SQL Packages and Types Reference Manual* as well as in the *Oracle Database 10g Performance Tuning Guide*. Only some of the relevant and specific procedures are listed here, in Table 12.2.

TABLE 12.2

ADDM-**specific** DBMS_ADVISOR **Procedures and Functions**

Procedure Name	Details
CREATE_TASK, DELETE_TASK	These procedures create or delete a new advisor task in the repository. The first parameter is the advisor name; a valid list can be seen in the DBA_ADVISOR_DEFINTIONS view. In this case, this essential parameter should be ADDM. All other parameters can be defaulted, although we suggest using a known string for the task name.
SET_TASK_PARAMETER	This procedure sets up the parameters for the task to later work on, and is essentially the setup of a simple variable specific to the advisor. In this case, calls to this procedure set the starting and ending snapshot IDs. Note that this part is not well documented because a list of valid parameters is not provided. A related SET_DEFAULT_TASK_PARAMETER procedure sets up the default parameter for some of the advisors. The list of current per-task and system-level default parameters and their values can be seen in the DBA_ADVISOR_PARAMETERS and DBA_ADVISOR_DEF_PARAMETERS views, respectively.
EXECUTE_TASK	This procedure should be called when the tasks are set up. In this case, the task is executed using its name.
GET_TASK_REPORT	This function returns a CLOB that details the ADDM report (or any other advisor task generated as explained before) in detail. You can choose TEXT, HTML, or XML as the output format. You can also specify a report level—BASIC, TYPICAL, or ALL. Set other values to NULL in the case of ADDM reports.
CANCEL_TASK, RESET_TASK	Use these procedures to cancel or reset a currently running or previously failed task.

The PL/SQL segment shown in Listing 12.5 is taken from a relevant portion of the extended SQL trace file that is generated when the addmrpt.sql script is executed.

LISTING 12.5   PL/SQL Section Showing How the ADDM API Is Invoked

```
begin
  declare
    id number;
    name varchar2(100);
    descr varchar2(500);
  BEGIN
    name := '';
    descr := 'ADDM run: snapshots [' || :bid || ', '
             || :eid || '], instance ' || :inst_num
             || ', database id ' || :dbid;
    dbms_advisor.create_task('ADDM',id,name,descr,null);
    :task_name := name;
    -- set time window
    dbms_advisor.set_task_parameter(name, 'START_SNAPSHOT', :bid);
    dbms_advisor.set_task_parameter(name, 'END_SNAPSHOT', :eid);
    -- set instance number
```

LISTING 12.5   Continued

```
    dbms_advisor.set_task_parameter(name, 'INSTANCE', :inst_num);
    -- set dbid
    dbms_advisor.set_task_parameter(name, 'DB_ID', :dbid);
    -- execute task
    dbms_advisor.execute_task(name);
  end;
end;
```

The CREATE_TASK procedure sets up the task to be performed, while the task parameters
START_SNAPSHOT, END_SNAPSHOT, INSTANCE, and DB ID are later set up. The final procedure,
EXECUTE_TASK, performs the actual task of generating the ADDM report. Once this is done, the
GET_TASK_REPORT function is executed, as shown in Listing 12.6, to print the report.

LISTING 12.6   Print the ADDM Task Report

```
set long 10000 longchunksize 10000
select dbms_advisor.get_task_report('TASK_1494', 'TEXT', 'TYPICAL')
from   sys.dual;
```

The task name was TASK_1494 in this case.
For an excellent example of determining the
snapshots and task name directly from the
DBA_HIST_SNAPSHOT view given a start and
end time, and displaying the results, have a
look at Example 6-2 in the *Oracle Database
10g Performance Tuning Guide*.

Even though the ADDM task was created manually, this fact is still recorded in
DBA_ADVISOR_TASKS. Note that the
GET_TASK_REPORT function returns a CLOB
and hence has to be handled accordingly. For
example, if executed within SQL*Plus, you
will have to use SET LONG *No_of_bytes* and
SET LONGCHUNKSIZE *No_of_bytes* to be able
to view the output.

Making Sense of ADDM Data

The best way to make sense of ADDM data is to look at the details of the ADDM report that we
generated as shown in Listing 12.4. We will use portions of the report and comment on how it
can be interpreted and used. This example showed many types of findings, typical in such
tuning scenarios.

Finding 1: SQL Statements Consuming Significant Time

As stated previously, application-generated SQL statements are the cause of most of the issues.
After all, what use would a database (and hence a database administrator!) be without users and
the SQLs that they execute? Listing 12.7 shows one such section. It is, in fact, the first of the
various findings.

LISTING 12.7   Details of Finding 1 from the ADDM Report

```
FINDING 1: 100% impact (3872 seconds)
------------------------------------
SQL statements consuming significant database time were found.

    RECOMMENDATION 1: SQL Tuning, 56% benefit (1695 seconds)
        ACTION: Run SQL Tuning Advisor on the SQL statement with SQL_ID
            "gr2244sy7phzs".
            RELEVANT OBJECT: SQL statement with SQL_ID gr2244sy7phzs and
            PLAN_HASH 2585813084
            UPDATE HR.EMPLOYEES SET SALARY = SALARY + 10 WHERE EMPLOYEE_ID = :B1

    RECOMMENDATION 2: SQL Tuning, 55% benefit (1677 seconds)
        ACTION: Tune the PL/SQL block with SQL_ID "d10v1gbfqdxkz". Refer to the
            "Tuning PL/SQL Applications" chapter of Oracle's "PL/SQL User's Guide
            and Reference"
            RELEVANT OBJECT: SQL statement with SQL_ID d10v1gbfqdxkz
            declare
            time_to_sleep          number := 5;
            start_employee_id        number := 100;
            end_employee_id        number := 200;
            emp_rec          hr.employees%ROWTYPE;
            emp_id          number;
            retval          number;
            begin
            emp_id := start_employee_id;
            LOOP
            EXIT WHEN emp_id > end_employee_id;
            update hr.employees set salary = salary + 10
            where employee_id = emp_id;
            --
            We do not invoke the sleep so this session keeps waiting on the other
            ---
            retval := sys.xxdba_pack.sess_sleep(time_to_sleep);
            emp_id := emp_id + 1;
            commit;
            END LOOP;
            dbms_output.put_line('Loop ended');
            end;
    RECOMMENDATION 3: SQL Tuning, 9.2% benefit (280 seconds)
        ACTION: Run SQL Tuning Advisor on the SQL statement with SQL_ID
            "8ch2kqpk8snqh".
            RELEVANT OBJECT: SQL statement with SQL_ID 8ch2kqpk8snqh and
            PLAN_HASH 4106914013
            select e.*
```

LISTING 12.7   Continued

```
    from hr.employees e, hr.departments d, hr.locations l,
    hr.countries c, hr.regions r
    where e.department_id = d.department_id
    and d.location_id = l.location_id
    and l.country_id = c.country_id
    and c.region_id = r.region_id
    and employee_id between substr(to_char(abs(dbms_random.random)),1,4)
    and substr(to_char(abs(dbms_random.random)),1,4)


RECOMMENDATION 4: SQL Tuning, 4.2% benefit (129 seconds)
    ACTION: Run SQL Tuning Advisor on the SQL statement with SQL_ID
        "5apdjnppbgpg3".
        RELEVANT OBJECT: SQL statement with SQL_ID 5apdjnppbgpg3 and
        PLAN_HASH 272231759
        SELECT NULL FROM DUAL FOR UPDATE NOWAIT


RECOMMENDATION 5: SQL Tuning, 3% benefit (92 seconds)
    ACTION: Run SQL Tuning Advisor on the SQL statement with SQL_ID
        "ft4twdjk99kxb".
        RELEVANT OBJECT: SQL statement with SQL_ID ft4twdjk99kxb and
        PLAN_HASH 645813381
        select sn.snap_id, sn.instance_number, sn.end_interval_time,
        sn.snap_level, (select unique 1 from dba_hist_baseline b where
        (sn.snap_id >= b.start_snap_id) and b.dbid = :1 and (sn.snap_id <=
        b.end_snap_id)) within_baseline_range, startup_time from
        dba_hist_snapshot sn where sn.dbid = :2 and sn.instance_number = :3
```

We need to point out a few things here. First, note that in each case, the findings are listed first, and the recommendations, actions, and rationale for each of these findings is listed next. We have considered the first of the findings in Listing 12.7, and this finding is considered to have an impact of 100%. This is listed along with the CPU time consumed in seconds. This value is the total number of CPU seconds consumed by each of the SQL statements that prompted this finding as recorded in each of the recommendations, and is actually the DB Time as seen from the Time and Wait model views. As noted before, ADDM uses this model to look at the resource-intensive pieces of the workload.

That said, one of the issues is apparent if you look closely at the SQLs for the first and second recommendation. The second SQL is actually a PL/SQL procedure that contains the first SQL. The variable emp_id is replaced by the bind variable :B1 and the SQL translated into upper case. Further, you may note that the second SQL took 1,677 seconds, while the previous one took 1,695 seconds. The problem is that in the case of PL/SQL blocks that execute SQL statements inside, the SQL statement is shown and considered separately, and not as part of the PL/SQL procedure. In other words, the first SQL statement was actually part of the second block—namely, the PL/SQL block. Thus you can see that ADDM *double counted* the impact as well as other related statistics. Keep this in mind when looking at PL/SQL-based problems; the figures in the findings and recommendations may not exactly mean what they state, and you may have to manually inspect and adjust the values for SQL that originates from within PL/SQL. Such SQL is considered recursive in nature.

In Listing 12.4, we noted that the total database time spent was 3,037 seconds. This contrasts with the summary of 3,872 seconds in finding 1, which is substantially more than the listed total. Having explained the recursive SQL double counting, we can now exclude this value and recalculate the adjusted impact to be (1,677 + 280 + 129 + 92) seconds divided by the total of 3,037 seconds. This works out to about 72%, which is an understandable figure.

Another caveat is that ADDM will consider *all* SQL that is running in the database during the investigation period. Thus, recommendations 4 and 5 denote recursive and other performance management–related SQL. This is actually a good thing when comparing overall performance of the database as a whole, because you will need to include the load imposed by the internal operations of the database as well.

Note the text in the recommendations. They clearly indicate what the next step in the tuning exercise should be. For example, the action for recommendation 2 is to tune the PL/SQL block with the SQL ID d10v1gbfqdxkz.

Recursive SQL

Recursive SQL is generally meant to be SQL executed by the SYS user to perform some internal action on behalf of normal users. Prime examples of this are SQLs for space management and extent allocation. Specifically, when a row is inserted into a table and no free block is found for that insert, the Oracle kernel automatically allocates the next free extent and records this in the internal data dictionary using SQL statements that are called *recursive SQL*. That said, recursive SQL is also SQL that is executed from within PL/SQL or from cascading actions such as triggers and constraints.

An easy method of identifying such occurrences is to look at the user ID executing this recursive SQL; this should not have a user ID of 0, meaning that it belongs to a non SYS user. This double counting of recursive SQL is not new in ADDM alone, but is spread throughout other utilities such as TKPROF. While SYS-generated recursive SQL in TKPROF can be specifically avoided using the SYS=NO option, SQL statements within PL/SQL are still counted under the Recursive SQL section of the output in TKPROF.

This topic is not well explained in the manuals and as a result has generated a lot of myths. You can determine the recursive level of SQL only in the raw form in extended SQL trace files. For further details, refer to MetaLink Note #39817.1, "Interpreting Raw SQL_TRACE and DBMS_SUPPORT.START_TRACE Output."

(Refer to the "Tuning PL/SQL Applications" chapter of Oracle's PL/SQL User's Guide and Reference.) In the other cases, you are advised to run the SQL advisors on the noted SQL. You will find that such clear actions are a common theme in the ADDM report. ADDM thus not only helps you, the performance analyst, with capturing the workload with the most impact, it also tells you what to do next.

Finding 2: SQL Statements Waiting for Locks

A good example of a finding that uses the Wait portion of the Time and Wait model used by ADDM is shown in Listing 12.8. You are aware that in order to be able to perform DML, the Oracle kernel must place exclusive row locks on the required rows, and that these locks will not be released until either a COMMIT or a ROLLBACK is executed. When another process wants to place the same type of lock on this row, you then have a locking conflict. This results in the blocked session posting an enqueue wait in the form of the event enq: TX - row lock contention and waiting indefinitely for the blocking session to release the lock. This is deemed to be due to application logic, and the performance analyst is required to perform further analysis as seen in the Action section of this finding.

LISTING 12.8   Details of Finding 2 from the ADDM Report

```
FINDING 2: 55% impact (1676 seconds)
-----------------------------------
SQL statements were found waiting for row lock waits.

    RECOMMENDATION 1: Application Analysis, 55% benefit (1676 seconds)
        ACTION: Trace the cause of row contention in the application logic. Use
            given blocked SQL to identify the database objects involved.
            Investigate application logic involving DML on these objects.
        RATIONALE: The SQL statement with SQL_ID "gr2244sy7phzs" was blocked on
            row locks.
            RELEVANT OBJECT: SQL statement with SQL_ID gr2244sy7phzs
            UPDATE HR.EMPLOYEES SET SALARY = SALARY + 10 WHERE EMPLOYEE_ID = :B1

    SYMPTOMS THAT LED TO THE FINDING:
        Wait class "Application" was consuming significant database time. (56%
        impact [1688 seconds])
```

Finding 3: Session Management

Not only can ADDM point to problems observed within the database, it can suggest seeking an external solution to the problem. In Listing 12.9, you see such a case. ADDM has determined that the rate of session connection and disconnection is high, and thus suggests using a middle tier with a connection-pool mechanism to reduce this rate. Essentially, connection pooling allows user sessions to be serviced by a number of pre-established connections. User sessions connect and disconnect to the connection pool rather than directly to the database, thus overcoming this high-impact finding. As noted in Chapter 10, rates of an activity are actually determined and recorded in the V$SYSMETRIC view; ADDM checks these to determine whether these rates are being exceeded.

LISTING 12.9   Details of Finding 3 from the ADDM Report

```
FINDING 3: 12% impact (369 seconds)
-----------------------------------
Session connect and disconnect calls were consuming significant database time.
```

LISTING 12.9   Continued

```
RECOMMENDATION 1: Application Analysis, 12% benefit (369 seconds)
   ACTION: Investigate application logic for possible reduction of connect
      and disconnect calls. For example, you might use a connection pool
      scheme in the middle tier.
```

In reality, you see from Listing 12.10 that there was another knock-on effect of this high rate of session connection/disconnection. In finding 6 shown in Listing 12.10, ADDM noticed and recorded high activity in the session-allocation latch (appropriately named latch: session allocation).

LISTING 12.10   Details of Finding 6 from the ADDM Report

```
FINDING 6: 3.7% impact (111 seconds)
------------------------------------
Wait event "latch: session allocation" in wait class "Other" was consuming
significant database time.

   RECOMMENDATION 1: Application Analysis, 3.7% benefit (111 seconds)
      ACTION: Investigate the cause for high "latch: session allocation"
         waits. Refer to Oracle's "Database Reference" for the description of
         this wait event. Use given SQL for further investigation.
      RATIONALE: The SQL statement with SQL_ID "NULL-SQLID" was found waiting
         for "latch: session allocation" wait event.
         RELEVANT OBJECT: SQL statement with SQL_ID NULL-SQLID
```

Other Findings

Everything is not yet perfect with the findings of ADDM. This is evident in Listing 12.11.

LISTING 12.11   Details of Other Findings from the ADDM Report

```
FINDING 4: 7.3% impact (220 seconds)
------------------------------------
Wait event "class slave wait" in wait class "Other" was consuming significant
database time.
<snipped>
FINDING 5: 6.3% impact (190 seconds)
------------------------------------
Wait event "Queue Monitor Task Wait" in wait class "Other" was consuming
significant database time.
<snipped>
FINDING 8: 3.4% impact (104 seconds)
```

LISTING 12.11   Continued

```
------------------------------------
Wait class "Configuration" was consuming significant database time.

    NO RECOMMENDATIONS AVAILABLE
    ADDITIONAL INFORMATION: Waits for free buffers were not consuming
        significant database time.
        Waits for archiver processes were not consuming significant database
        time.
        Log file switch operations were not consuming significant database time
        while waiting for checkpoint completion.
        Log buffer space waits were not consuming significant database time.
        High watermark (HW) enqueue waits were not consuming significant
        database time.
        Space Transaction (ST) enqueue waits were not consuming significant
        database time.
        ITL enqueue waits were not consuming significant database time.
```

Exclusion of Idle Events

STATSPACK in Oracle 9i and earlier can recognize and exclude the impact of a number of Wait events that are deemed to be idle. These are generally events where the back-end shadow process is waiting for a message or request for action either from the foreground client process or from another coordinator process. Such idle events are recorded in the STATS$IDLE_EVENT table in the STATSPACK schema and are used during STATSPACK reporting as a filter for exclusion. Note that the idle nature of these idle events to some extent depends on context; this topic generates a lot of debate in the Oracle user community.

Findings 4 and 5 show that ADDM still does not properly consider idle events. The class slave wait and Queue Monitor Task Wait events are actually considered idle because they are "wait-for-work" type events. It seems that an exclusion of this type of event is not catered to; indications are that this will be fixed in Oracle Database 10g Release 2 as per MetaLink Note #3876475.8. This fix is also present in the 10.1.0.4 patch set.

As well, notice in finding 8 that the Configuration wait class was consuming some time, but no recommendations were available. To ADDM's credit, it did mention those configuration items that were *not* a problem, so you could pursue reasons other than those mentioned.

We saw other findings as well. For example, you saw that there was some contention for sequences, resulting in the recommendation of sequence caching, as well as a call for further investigation when using the ORDER setting in a RAC environment. As well, there is a separate section titled "Additional Information," as shown in Listing 12.12.

LISTING 12.12   Additional Information in the ADDM Report

```
          ADDITIONAL INFORMATION
          ----------------------


Wait class "Administrative" was not consuming significant database time.
Wait class "Cluster" was not consuming significant database time.
Wait class "Commit" was not consuming significant database time.
Wait class "Network" was not consuming significant database time.
Wait class "Scheduler" was not consuming significant database time.
Wait class "User I/O" was not consuming significant database time.


The analysis of I/O performance is based on the default assumption that the
average read time for one database block is 10000 micro-seconds.
```

This listing shows what you will not need to consider in your tuning efforts, thereby preventing wasted time.

Expected I/O Response Time

Note the last sentence in Listing 12.12. This assumption is hard-coded as a default value, as seen in the `DBA_ADVISOR_DEF_PARAMETERS` view. Listed as the `DBIO_EXPECTED` parameter for the ADDM Advisor Type, this is a seeded value and denotes that it takes 10,000 microseconds (10 milliseconds) for a single block read. If your I/O subsystem can provide better performance than this, then you should change this value. Note that this is used in the calculation of impact; hence, you should exercise caution. This value can be changed using the `DBMS_ADVISOR.SET_DEFAULT_PARAMETER` procedure for this parameter.

Cross-Verification from the Advisor Views

You can use some of the advisor views listed in Table 12.1 to cross-verify these findings, recommendations, and actions. Listing 12.13 shows an example of the findings.

LISTING 12.13   Cross-Verify Findings from Advisor Views

```
SQL> column task_name format a10
SQL> select task_name, finding_id, type, impact, message
  2  from dba_advisor_findings
  3  where task_id = 1494;


TASK_NAME  FINDING_ID TYPE          IMPACT
---------- ---------- ------------- ----------
MESSAGE
------------------------------------------------------------------------
TASK_1494           1 PROBLEM       478647593
SQL statements were found waiting for row lock waits.
```

LISTING 12.13   Continued

```
TASK_1494          2 SYMPTOM      482166171
Wait class "Application" was consuming significant database time.


TASK_1494          3 PROBLEM      42730598
Soft parsing of SQL statements was consuming significant database time.


TASK_1494          4 SYMPTOM      30738791
Contention for latches related to the shared pool was consuming significant data
base time.
<output snipped>
```

> ADDM **is still governed by a set of rules that were formed after observation of perform-ance problems in a variety of environments. That does not necessarily mean that these** ADDM **rules are 100% perfect or that the recommendations that it presents for what it observes in your environment are always correct. You should exercise your judgement in following or implementing the advice provided by** ADDM.

Similar verifications can be obtained via the DBA_ADVISOR_RECOMMENDATIONS, DBA_ADVISOR_RATIONALE, and DBA_ADVISOR_ACTIONS views.

New Features in Oracle Database 10g Release 2

In Oracle Database 10g Release 2, ADDM has been enhanced to make its analysis more accurate in the areas related to CPU, paging, and the cache areas of the database. As well, the scope of ADDM has itself been broadened to include more server components such as streams, AQ, RMAN, and RAC. The Resource Manager also has some hooks into ADDM and is expected to benefit from the self-management capability of these advisors. An AWR difference report is available that can be used to compare two pairs of snapshots so that the performance analyst can have a better understanding of what ADDM now shows and correlate the changes. AWR snapshots are also transportable between databases so you can run ADDM reports against the statistics from two different environments—say, Development and Production—in order to perform quick comparisons.

Summary

In this chapter, you saw how ADDM can be used as the first stop in detecting, diagnosing, and solving a performance problem. Although OEM hides a lot of the complexity of obtaining this information from the performance analyst, you can still get to this data quickly using the advisor views and the APIs. You also saw some of the shortfalls of ADDM, which you need to keep in mind while performing deeper analysis, and had a foretaste of what is to come yet in Oracle Database 10g Release 2.

13

Effectively Using the SQL Advisors

IN THIS CHAPTER

Automating the SQL Advisors	263
Using the Advisors for Tuning	268
Avoiding Advisor Pitfalls	284
New Features in Oracle 10g Release 2	285

Automating the SQL Advisors

Oracle Database 10g comes bundled with a number of advisors, a few of which you have already seen in previous chapters. This chapter discusses the SQL advisors—namely, the *SQL Tuning Advisor* and the *SQL Access Advisor*. We have combined the coverage of both these advisors into one chapter because they are somewhat related and operate exclusively on SQL statements.

Before launching into the details, it is wise to have some background information about these advisors as well as about SQL tuning in general so that you can keep everything in perspective.

The SQL Tuning Advisor

The SQL Tuning Advisor is actually a front-end interface to the deeper *Automatic SQL Tuning* capability of the query optimizer. The main objective of the SQL Tuning

Advisor (STA in its short form) is to automate the entire process of tuning SQL. Along with the SQL Access Advisor, it tries to automate one of the hardest and most complex tasks of a performance analyst—that of changing the SQL or the environment in which it works so that the SQL statement runs more efficiently.

> **Difference Between** EXPLAIN PLAN **and Automatic SQL Tuning**
>
> You are likely aware of the EXPLAIN PLAN statement in current and previous versions of Oracle. Although both the EXPLAIN PLAN command and automatic tuning determine the execution plan and do not actually execute the SQL, the similarity stops there. EXPLAIN PLAN works in normal mode and simply exposes the plan that the query optimizer would take if the SQL was executed at that point of time. The automatic tuning mode, however, does much more than just generate an execution plan, as you will see. Be aware that the execution plan shown by EXPLAIN PLAN may not always be the way it would execute. These plans are influenced by the environment in which they operate, which may not be the same as the actual execution environment. The actual execution plan can be seen only via the V$SQL_PLAN view.

The query optimizer actually operates in two modes: normal and tuning. In normal mode, the optimizer parses and executes a SQL without spending too much time generating the execution plan, which may hence be suboptimal. In tuning mode, the optimizer performs additional analysis to check whether the execution plan previously produced under the normal mode can be further improved. In this mode, however, the query optimizer does not execute the SQL, but similarly to ADDM produces a series of recommendations along with their rationale and the expected benefit for producing a significantly superior plan. When called under tuning mode, the optimizer is referred to as the *Automatic Tuning Optimizer* and the tuning performed therein is called *Automatic SQL Tuning*. The SQL Tuning Advisor simply exposes these recommendations and provides an interface to perform such tuning. All this is again possible via the use of an advisor framework in which advisor specific tasks are created and submitted to the advisors for processing.

Automatic SQL Tuning

We mentioned the two modes in which the query optimizer executes. Let's now look in detail at the tuning mode, because this is the mode that is involved with the SQL Tuning Advisor. This kernel code component is also known as the Automatic Tuning Optimizer, and is an integral part of the query optimizer. This integration provides several advantages:

- Because the query optimizer is ultimately responsible for execution plans and, hence, the SQL performance, it is expedient to extend the optimizer itself to perform more than just the run-time parsing and execution-plan generation. Oracle kernel code relating to the optimizer, internal rules, and the prior, deep knowledge about the optimizer can thus be reused when creating this extension.

- Enhancements to the query optimizer that are an ongoing exercise are passed on to the Automatic Tuning Optimizer component.

- This component can access the past execution statistics of a SQL statement and thus can customize the optimizer settings for that statement. This is critical because mistakes of the past can be used to avoid choosing a wrong path.

- In addition to the regular object statistics used by the query optimizer, the Automatic Tuning Optimizer collects auxiliary information that can be used in conjunction with the former.

In fact, you can consider the Automatic Tuning Optimizer as an extension and improvement to the runtime query optimizer that is available on call when required. This way, the overhead associated with in-depth analysis is not imposed on the normal, everyday SQL statements during parsing, but is reserved for invocation on high-load SQLs only, aiding efficient use of computing resources.

In normal mode, during the parse phase, the query optimizer generates an execution plan for a given SQL statement within a short amount of time, usually less than a second and at worst no more than few seconds. Because of this self-imposed stringent require-ment, the optimizer performs a limited plan search by using built-in heuristics to pare down the optimization phase of parsing. As well, there is no investigation and verification of objects and their statistics during the plan-generation process. On the other hand, the Automatic Tuning Optimizer is typically given much more time, usually in minutes, to perform the necessary investigation and veri-fication steps as part of the tuning process. Thus, the Automatic Tuning Optimizer has a much higher probability of generating a well-tuned plan. Because it is given sufficient time, the Automatic Tuning Optimizer uses dynamic sampling and partial execution tech-niques (that is, execution of fragments of a SQL statement) to verify its own estimates of cost, selectivity, and cardinality. It also uses the past execution history of the SQL state-ment to determine optimal settings when such history is available. For example, if it determines that a small number of rows will be returned by the SQL, then it may switch the OPTIMIZER_MODE from the default ALL_ROWS (which works toward higher throughput) to FIRST_ROWS (which works toward higher initial response).

> ### Parameters Controlling the Optimizer Permutations
>
> Most time and resources spent during the parsing of SQL is during the preparation of the execution plan. When an SQL is complex and has a large number of table joins, it is possible for the optimizer to consume a lot of CPU cycles, data dictionary I/O, and shared pool space computing the estimated cost of access for many thousands of permutations. Until the last release of Oracle 9i R2, the Cost Based Optimizer was restricted to calculating a specific number of such permutations using the OPTIMIZER_MAX_PERMUTATIONS and the related but hidden OPTIMIZER_SEARCH_LIMIT initialization parameters. The original default value of 80,000 in Oracle 8i for OPTIMIZER_MAX_PERMUTATIONS was scaled down to a reasonable value of 2000 in Oracle 9i R2. Ultimately, both these parameters are now hidden in Oracle Database 10g. The default value of 2000, however, has been retained, and it is assumed that this is the restricting factor for the normal mode of the optimizer. For more details, read MetaLink Notes #66030.1 and #62284.1.

When invoked, the Automatic Tuning Optimizer performs four types of analyses during the plan-generation phase:

1. **Statistics analysis.** This is the most basic of checks, something that a performance analyst would do when tuning a poorly performing SQL statement. The Automatic Tuning Optimizer checks each object involved in the query for missing or stale statistics, and makes recommendation to gather relevant statistics. This may be a moot point because optimizer statistics are normally automatically collected and refreshed. You need to keep in mind that this problem may be encountered only when automatic optimizer statistics collection has been turned off or tables or indexes have been created and populated, and the statistics have not yet collected because of the schedule. The Automatic Tuning Optimizer also collects auxiliary information to supply missing statistics or correct stale statistics in case recommendations are not implemented.

2. **SQL profiling.** The Automatic Tuning Optimizer uses the auxiliary information collected in step 1 to mitigate estimation errors as well as build an entity referred to as an *SQL profile*. This SQL profile enables the query optimizer to generate a well-tuned plan when executing later in the normal mode, as it forms a template for the better plan. This is in some ways similar to the use of Outlines to force SQL to behave in a certain way. SQL profiling allows ill-written SQL to execute efficiently without having to change the original code, and is thus ideal for use in tuning third-party applications. We will look at SQL profiles in detail in the next chapter.

3. **Access path analysis.** This is another one of the basic steps that a performance analyst would normally perform when tuning an SQL statement. The Automatic Tuning Optimizer explores whether a new index can be used to significantly improve access to each table in the query and, when appropriate, makes recommendations to create such indexes. At this point in time, such information can prompt the SQL Tuning Advisor layer that overlays the Automatic Tuning Optimizer to invoke another advisor, namely the SQL Access Advisor.

4. **SQL structure analysis.** This is the final step that a performance analyst would normally perform during SQL tuning. In this phase, the Automatic Tuning Optimizer identifies SQL statements that are prone to generate poor plans, and makes relevant suggestions to restructure them. This restructuring can involve syntactic as well as semantic changes to the SQL code.

As you may have noticed, these steps are similar in both sequence and nature to those used during manual SQL tuning. Automatic SQL tuning just performs this for you on demand, tirelessly, automatically, and free of charge! The SQL Tuning Advisor makes this wealth of tuning information available in an understandable and usable form.

The SQL Tuning Advisor is available for access both via OEM as well as via the advisor and SQL tuning API, described later in this chapter.

Inputs to the SQL Tuning Advisor

The SQL Tuning Advisor takes inputs from multiple sources. The SQL Tuning Advisor can deal with more than one SQL statement at a time, so you can submit a composite SQL workload for analysis. As you saw in previous chapters, high-load SQL statements identified by the ADDM form the main input for the SQL Tuning Advisor, which now plays the role of the Specialist in the

Patient-General Practitioner-Specialist story. Equally well, these statements could have also been identified by the AWR or even by a manual process. The manual process could include the testing of a set of SQL statements that are yet to be deployed, tuning individual performance as well as a collection of SQL statements. This collection is now turned into a persistent tuning object called the SQL tuning set (STS), which is described in detail later in this chapter.

The SQL Access Advisor

The SQL Access Advisor works alongside the SQL Tuning Advisor and could be called by the former when appropriate. It is a tuning tool that provides advice *specifically* on materialized views, indexes, and materialized view logs. Given a specified workload in the form of a SQL tuning set or even individual SQL statements, the SQL Access Advisor recommends the creation of materialized views, materialized view logs, and indexes for a given workload. In general, as the number of materialized views and indexes and the space allocated to them is increased, query performance improves. The SQL Access Advisor considers the tradeoffs between space usage and query performance and recommends the most cost-effective configuration of new and existing materialized views and indexes. The SQL Access Advisor is actually based on and builds upon the Oracle 9i Summary Advisor.

The SQL Access Advisor interfaces to generate SQL when requested. You can get to this tool both via the OEM as well as via the advisor and SQL tuning API.

Inputs to the SQL Access Advisor

The SQL Access Advisor can use the following inputs in order to operate on and produce recommendations:

- Current contents of the SQL cache
- Current object in a specified schema
- User-defined tables
- Additional SQL statements in a workload
- SQL tuning set

> **Materialized Views (MV) and MV Logs**
>
> A *materialized view* is like a query with a result that is materialized and stored in a table. When a user query is found compatible with the query associated with a materialized view, the user query can be rewritten in terms of the materialized view. This technique improves the execution of the user query, because most of the query result has been precomputed. The query transformer looks for any materialized views that are compatible with the user query and selects one or more materialized views to rewrite the user query. The use of materialized views to rewrite a query is cost-based. That is, the query is not rewritten if the plan generated without the materialized views has a lower cost than the plan generated with the materialized views. Note that the term *snapshot* was used for materialized views in Oracle Version 7.
>
> On the other hand, a materialized view log is a shadow table that stores a record for every change made to its master or source table. Essentially, it is used to perform refreshes of the corresponding materialized views. For more details, refer to the *Oracle Database 10g Administrator's Guide* and the *Oracle Database 10g Advanced Replication* manual.

The steps to use the SQL Access Advisor are as follows:

1. Create a task and optionally define parameters.

2. Create or specify a workload using any of the aforementioned input methods listed. Optionally define workload parameters.

3. Generate recommendations using either the OEM or the APIs.

4. Review and implement the recommendations as appropriate.

As with all other advisors, the option is left to the performance analyst or DBA to implement the recommendations.

Using the Advisors for Tuning

Let's now look at how to use the SQL advisors for tuning by taking a tour using OEM. As indicated before, the advisors are available from a variety of sources including the Advisor Central link in most OEM screens.

OEM Interface to the SQL Tuning Advisor

Launch the SQL Tuning Advisor from its link on the Advisor Central page. This displays a screen that lists all the possible inputs to this advisor. The links are as follows:

- **Top SQL.** Useful for obtaining tuning advice for either Spot SQL or Period SQL. The former shows all the Top SQL executed in a five-minute period in the immediate past, while the latter shows all the Top SQL for the past 24 hours or so. These SQLs are sorted by some criteria—in this case, activity percentage—so it is easy to pick out the top few. Note that you can sort them by other criteria and use the slider to select a specific time period. An example is shown in Figure 13.1. Note that you can select a number of SQL statements after viewing their details by clicking on the SQL ID link.

- **SQL Tuning Sets.** Click this link to view and create SQL tuning sets. In fact, the screen that is displayed allows you to create such sets from Spot SQL, Period SQL, or from high-load SQL seen either in previous snapshots or even in preserved snapshot sets. As shown in Figure 13.2, we created a SQL tuning set named SQL Tuning Set 2 with the description "Problematic period" from a few statements in the Top Spot SQL shown in Figure 13.1. Note that the details of the selected SQLs in SQL Tuning Set 2 are shown in a separate screen, as seen in Figure 13.3.

- **Snapshots.** Clicking this link takes you to the AWR Snapshots page shown in Chapter 11, "Effectively Using the Automatic Workload Repository." You can use the Snapshots page to select a pair or a set of snapshots that can be used to generate a SQL tuning set that will then be submitted to the SQL Tuning Advisor.

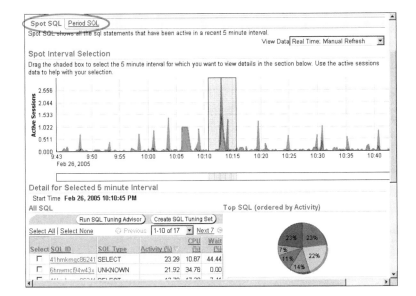

FIGURE 13.1
Spot SQL details seen when the Top SQL link in the SQL Tuning Advisor main page is clicked.

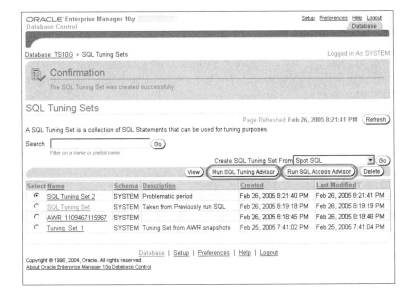

FIGURE 13.2
SQL tuning set screen showing a freshly created tuning set from the Top SQL screen (note the launch buttons for further advisors).

■ **Preserved Snapshot sets.** This link is similar to the links in the snapshots page in Chapter 11, "Effectively Using the Automatic Workload Repository," where you can use a preserved snapshot set to generate a SQL tuning set.

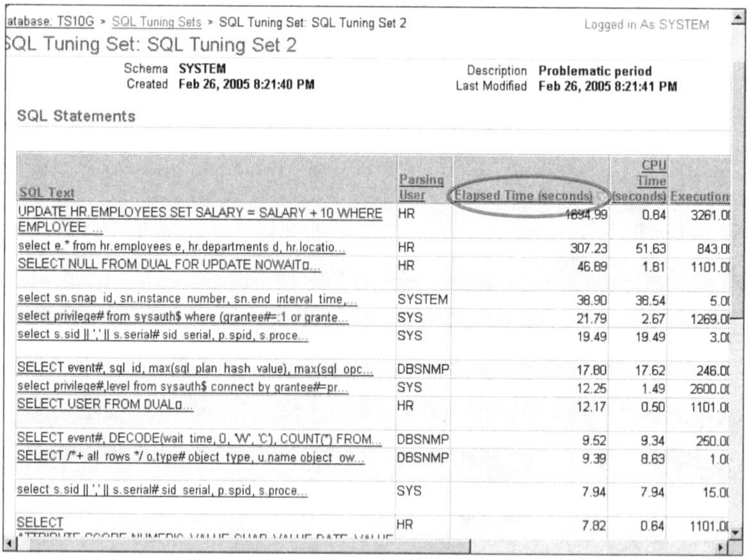

FIGURE 13.3
Details of the SQLs
within SQL Tuning Set
2, sorted by elapsed
time.

When an SQL or a set of SQL statements is ready for submission, you can launch the SQL advisor from the launch points. This will bring you to the Schedule Advisor screen shown in Figure 13.4, which can be used to determine both the scope and schedule for that run. Note that two modes, limited and comprehensive, are available. In limited mode, analysis is conducted without the long-running SQL profile option. The comprehensive mode takes longer, but generates an SQL profile if appropriate.

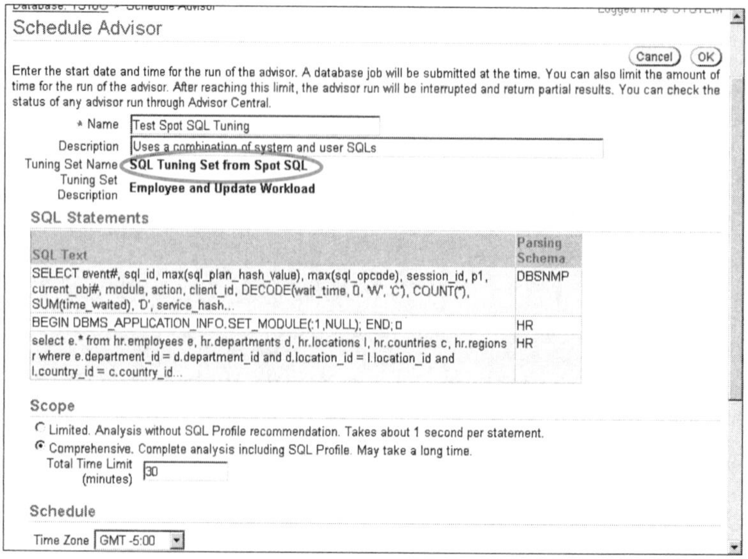

FIGURE 13.4
Schedule Advisor screen.

Executing this schedule advisor for a SQL tuning set named "SQL Tuning Set from Spot SQL" displays the screen shown in Figure 13.5.

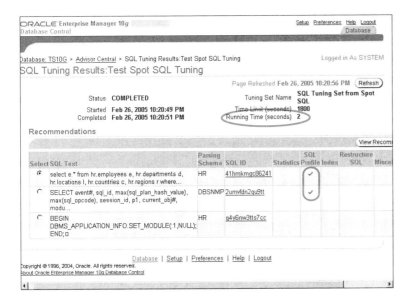

FIGURE 13.5
SQL Tuning Advisor results screen.

Note that the running of the analysis actually took only about two seconds, and a set of recommendations are shown. These recommendations are based on one or more of the four different areas of analysis mentioned before, namely statistics analysis, SQL profiling, access path analysis (indexing), and SQL structural analysis. When a recommendation is available for one of these areas, this is indicated by a check mark. For example, you see that the first and second queries could possibly be improved via the use of a SQL profile. A miscellaneous section as well as errors encountered are displayed (not shown in the figure). Clicking the View Recommendation button would show a screen that asks you to accept the SQL profile after viewing the old and new explain plans. An example of this was shown in detail in Chapter 10, "Adopting a New Approach to Tuning."

OEM Interface to the SQL Access Advisor

The SQL Access Advisor can be launched from a variety of screens, but we will consider the link from the Advisor Central screen. Clicking the SQL Access Advisor link found there opens the screen shown in Figure 13.6.

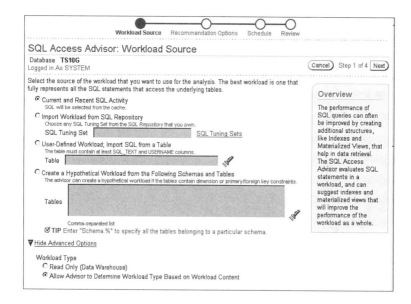

FIGURE 13.6
SQL Access Advisor input
screen.

This screen is arranged into four distinct steps, where input and various options can be entered. These steps can be seen in the form of a workflow on top of the screen and involve specifying the workload source, recommendation options, and scheduling parameters, and finally viewing a review screen. All the options are not shown in the figures, but in this first screen, you can specify the source of the workload, along with some options. The source can be from a variety of inputs:

- **SQL tuning set.** The SQL Tuning set link in the second option in Figure 13.6 can be used to return to the screen shown in Figure 13.2, where you can select a SQL tuning set that is already stored and available or create a new input set using the procedure described previously.

- **User-defined workload.** In this source, you use the Torch icon to choose a table in a schema that contains at least the SQL_TEXT and a USERNAME column. You can use this option to run the advisor on a prepopulated set of SQL statements.

- **Hypothetical load.** This is the most intriguing of the choices. Basically, it enables a performance analyst to choose a schema or a set of tables that contain dimensions or primary and foreign key constraints. SQL Access Advisor can then generate recommendations for indexes and materialized views based on these relationships.

An advanced set of options is available; access them by clicking the + sign. These allow for the following options and filters:

- **Choose the workload type.** Opt for read-only, as in a data warehouse, or allow the advisor to determine the type depending on the SQL content of the workload.

- **Include recommendations for dropping unused indexes.** The default is no, assuming that other statements not in the workload may be affected by dropping the indexes.

■ **Filters.** You can either evaluate the entire workload or use filters to reduce and focus the workload. These filters are in the form of *Top N* consumers on various criteria including optimizer cost, buffer gets, CPU time, physical reads, elapsed time, and execution count (SQL executed by a set of selected users, or those that access a set of tables). If you use the MODULE_ID and ACTION fields set by the DBMS_APPLICATION_INFO package to identify the source and current status of SQLs, these can be used in the filter as well.

When this is specified, you can move forward to the second page of inputs.

In the second page, you can specify the following. The last three options are available when you click the + arrow for Show Advanced Options:

■ **Recommendation types.** Specify whether the advisor should consider just indexes, just materialized views, or both.

■ **Advisor mode.** The choices are Limited and Comprehensive. When the former is chosen, the workload will be processed quickly, potentially ignoring statements with an estimated cost below a threshold. In comprehensive mode, a complete and exhaustive analysis will be performed.

■ **Space restrictions.** Because indexes and materialized views take up database space, you can specify an upper limit to the estimated space that may be used if the recommendations are implemented. We suggest that all recommendations be shown and that a performance analyst be allowed to make the choice later on.

■ **Tuning options.** You can choose the criteria by which SQL statements will be prioritized for tuning. This is the same list as for the selection criteria. When a sort order other than the default, optimizer cost, is chosen, this becomes a secondary sort order.

■ **Default storage locations.** You can choose the default locations and schemas where the recommended indexes and materialized views could be created.

When this is complete, move on to the third page of inputs, where you can schedule the advisor run. First, you must specify a task name (to override the default name) and a description, and then use one of the

> **Identifying Unused Indexes**
>
> We recommend using index monitoring in order to identify unused indexes rather than allowing the SQL Access Advisor to identify them for you. Index monitoring was made available in Oracle 9i, and is enabled by default in Oracle Database 10g. We will deal with this topic in Chapter 14, but keep in mind that you should monitor the index usage over a sufficient period—preferably over one or two complete business-cycle periods and events, such as month-end, quarter, or yearly closes—before deciding to drop them.

> **Bug in the Name Used for Submission**
>
> It seems that the default advisor task name used in creating the submitted job is prefixed with the text ADV_. When a long name is used, the additional prefix overflows the available column space used for the job name in the DBMS_SCHEDULER call and an error, Failed to COMMIT, is displayed with message ORA-27452, ADV_Your_chosen_Advisor_task_name is an invalid name for a database object. For this reason, we suggest using a short but meaningful name rather than the default.

following schedules. By default, the advisor is run immediately. If scheduled to run later, a database job is created and submitted to the database scheduler using the DBMS_SCHEDULE built-in PL/SQL package.

When a schedule is chosen, the scheduling parameters change as well in the input screen:

- **Standard.** You can choose to run the advisor immediately or at a later time using a calendar. You can also choose to repeat the analysis on a periodic basis, with periodicity ranging from minutes to years.

- **Standard using PL/SQL for repeated intervals.** This is similar to the Standard schedule, with the only difference being that you can use a PL/SQL expression to calculate the schedule.

- **Predefined schedule.** You can choose a predefined schedule that is available in the system.

- **Predefined window.** You can choose a predefined time period that is defined as a relatively inactive window in the system.

Scheduling Constraints

When you schedule a resource-intensive analysis such as analyzing a hypothetical workload or generating advice for materialized views, you will not be able to schedule them immediately, even if the choice is allowed. Such analysis will always be scheduled during a time that the database determines is off hours based on AWR data.

Once this entry is complete, you can move to the final submission page, which simply confirms all the inputs. Clicking the Submit button will create the task and set it up for execution as per the schedule.

When the SQL Access Advisor analysis is complete, you can view the results using links from the Advisor Central screen; select the completed run for the SQL Access Advisor using the drop-down list. Figure 13.7 shows a sample screen with the results of one such run.

You will be able to see the impact of each of the recommendations in a graphical form, so you can immediately zero in on the most effective ones. Below this graph, each of the recommendations and related actions are shown, along with a benefit percentage, estimated space used (if the option is selected), and any SQL that has been generated. In this case, we clicked on the first recommendation, which brought up the screen shown in Figure 13.8. You can also select the recommendations to be implemented and schedule them to be run at a later time. To view the complete SQL, click the Show SQL button. You can also change the view to see the SQL statements affected by the recommendations. The advanced options display the details of the run such as the source, limits, filters, and so on.

A table lists the actions that are needed to implement the selected recommendation. Certain fields such as the name, schema, and tablespace name in the case of indexes and materialized views to be created can be changed. Dependent names will be changed as required. If the Tablespace field is left blank, the default tablespace of the schema will be used. When you click OK, the SQL script is modified, but it is not actually executed until you select Schedule Implementation on the Recommendations page.

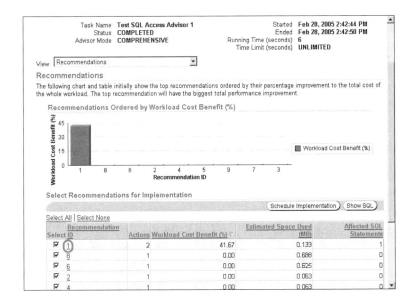

FIGURE 13.7
SQL Access Advisor
results screen.

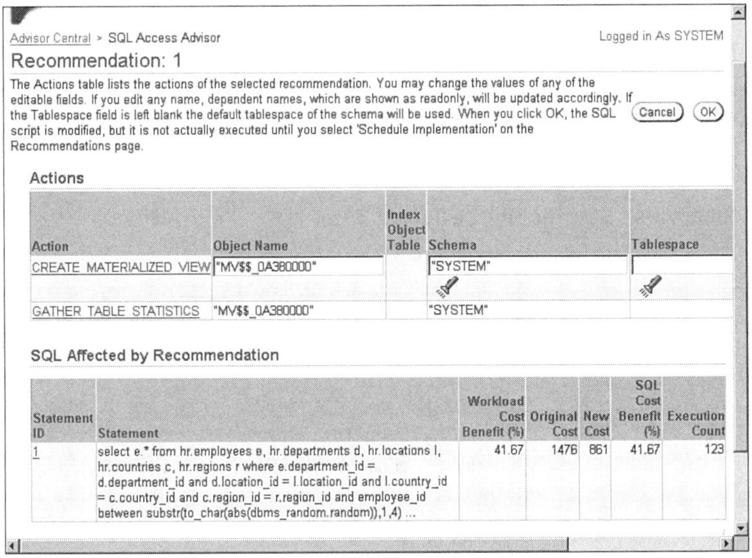

FIGURE 13.8
SQL Access Advisor
recommendation details.

APIs to the SQL Tuning Advisor

Just as with all the advisors described previously, the SQL Tuning Advisor and the SQL Access Advisor can be viewed and manipulated using APIs in the DBMS_SQLTUNE and the now-familiar DBMS_ADVISOR built-in PL/SQL packages. The framework and general methodology is the same for both types of advisors in the sense that you will need to create tasks, set up parameters for executing them, schedule the execution, and view the results, all using specific calls in these PL/SQL packages. Additionally, the SQL tuning sets can be manipulated using the DBMS_SQLTUNE

Package Usage Inconsistency

It seems that there is some inconsistency in grouping and naming the PL/SQL packages used as APIs to the advisors. While the DBMS_ADVISOR package is used for both the ADDM and the SQL Access Advisor, the DBMS_SQLTUNE is a separate package specifically for the SQL Tuning Advisor and for manipulating SQL tuning sets. Because the framework and general methodology of creating, submitting, and viewing advisor tasks remain the same, we hope there is a good reason for this deviation.

package. Because this could be used as an input to both the SQL Access Advisor as well as the SQL Tuning Advisor, you will need to understand both packages together in this context.

Setting Up and Using SQL Tunings Sets

As stated previously, an SQL tuning set (STS) is a new object for capturing SQL workload information. SQL tuning sets provide a common infrastructure for dealing with SQL workloads and enable tuning of a large number of SQL statements as a collective, related unit. SQL tuning sets store SQL statements along with the execution context, such as the parsing schema name and bind values, as well as execution statistics such as average elapsed time and execution count.

SQL tuning sets can be created by filtering or ranking SQL statements from several sources including the cursor cache (Spot SQL), Top SQL statements executed during some prior interval from AWR snapshots, a user-defined workload, or even other SQL tuning sets.

You first need to understand how SQL tuning sets can be manipulated using the DBMS_SQLTUNE package because they can be used as input to both the SQL Tuning Advisor and the SQL Access Advisor. You can use the functions and procedures in Table 13.1 to manipulate SQL tuning sets.

TABLE 13.1

DBMS_SQLTUNE **Functions and Procedures Specific to SQL Tuning Sets**

Function/Procedure	Description
CREATE_SQLSET, DROP_SQLSET	These procedures create/drop a SqlSet object in the database by name. They are exposed via the view DBA_SQLSET. The STATEMENT_COUNT column shows the number of statements in the STS.
LOAD_SQLSET	This procedure populates the STS with a set of selected SQLs using the Sqlset_Cursor type.
SELECT_SQLSET	This function collects SQL statements from the cursor cache.
SELECT_WORKLOAD_REPOSITORY	This function collects SQL statements from the workload repository.
UPDATE_SQLSET	This procedure updates selected string fields such as MODULE and ACTION or updates numerical attributes of a SQL in a SQL set.
ADD_SQLSET_REFERENCE, DROP_SQLSET_REFERENCE	These functions add/drop a reference to/from an existing SqlSet to indicate its use (or lack thereof) by a client. They are recorded in the DBA_SQLSET_REFERENCES view.

Accessing the SQL Tuning Advisor APIs

The SQL Tuning Advisor uses the DBMS_SQLTUNE built-in PL/SQL package to perform its tuning activities. The relevant procedures and functions can be seen in Table 13.2.

> More details about DBMS_SQLTUNE functions and procedures specific to SQL tuning sets are available in the *Oracle Database 10g PL/SQL Packages and Types Reference*. An example can be seen in MetaLink Note #259188.1.

TABLE 13.2

DBMS_SQLTUNE **Functions and Procedures Specific to SQL Tuning Advisor**

Function/Procedure	Description
CREATE_TUNING_TASK, DROP_TUNING_TASK	These functions create/drop a SQL Tuning Advisor task in the database by name. CREATE_TUNING_TASK is an overloaded function that can take in a variety of inputs including a single SQL statement to tune either by specifying its text or the IDs of a statement in the cursor cache, a SQL set, or a range of snapshot IDs from AWR. Other inputs include bind variables, scope, and time limit, as well as SQL-statement ranking parameters.
EXECUTE_TUNING_TASK, INTERRUPT_TUNING_TASK, CANCEL_TUNING_TASK, RESUME_TUNING_TASK	These procedures execute/interrupt/resume/cancel a named tuning task, respectively.
REPORT_TUNING_TASK	This function displays the result of a tuning task given a task (by default the last task for that user). Optionally, an object within an SQL set and limits of reporting can be specified.
ACCEPT_SQL_PROFILE, ALTER_SQL_PROFILE, DROP_SQL_PROFILE	These procedures create/alter/drop SQL profiles for the specified SQL tuning task, respectively. An SQL profile can be enabled or disabled.

A simple example of setting up and executing an SQL tuning task for a single SQL statement is shown in Listing 13.1. The same SQL statement discussed in Listing 10.13 of Chapter 10 is listed. In order to force a problem, we dropped both an index as well as the statistics.

LISTING 13.1   Use of the DBMS_SQLTUNE Package

```
SQL> drop index HR.EMP_DEPARTMENT_IX;
Index dropped

SQL> execute dbms_stats.delete_table_stats('HR','EMPLOYEES');

PL/SQL procedure successfully completed.

SQL> execute dbms_sqltune.drop_tuning_task('STA Tuning task 2');
```

LISTING 13.1   Continued

```
PL/SQL procedure successfully completed.

SQL> declare
  2          sql_tuning_task VARCHAR2(30);
  3          sql_to_tune     CLOB;
  4  begin
  5          sql_to_tune := 'select e.* ' ||
  6          'from hr.employees e, hr.departments d, hr.locations l, ' ||
  7          'hr.countries c, hr.regions r ' ||
  8          'where e.department_id = d.department_id ' ||
  9          'and d.location_id = l.location_id ' ||
 10          'and l.country_id = c.country_id ' ||
 11          'and c.region_id = r.region_id ' ||
 12          'and employee_id = ' ||
 13          'substr(to_char(abs(dbms_random.random)),1,4)';
 14          sql_tuning_task := DBMS_SQLTUNE.CREATE_TUNING_TASK (
 15                  sql_text        => sql_to_tune,
 16                  scope           => 'COMPREHENSIVE',
 17                  time_limit      => 30,
 18                  task_name       => 'STA Tuning task 2',
 19                  description     => 'STA Tuning task desc');
 20          DBMS_SQLTUNE.EXECUTE_TUNING_TASK(task_name => 'STA Tuning task 2');
 21  end;
 22  /

PL/SQL procedure successfully completed.

SQL> select dbms_sqltune.report_tuning_task('STA Tuning task 2')
  2  from dual;

DBMS_SQLTUNE.REPORT_TUNING_TASK('STATUNINGTASK2')
-------------------------------------------------------------------------------
GENERAL INFORMATION SECTION
-------------------------------------------------------------------------------
Tuning Task Name   : STA Tuning task 2
Scope              : COMPREHENSIVE
Time Limit(seconds): 30
Completion Status  : COMPLETED
Started at          : 03/05/2005 18:09:14
Completed at        : 03/05/2005 18:09:16


-------------------------------------------------------------------------------
SQL ID  : c3zbnzmnart60
SQL Text: select e.* from hr.employees e, hr.departments d, hr.locations l,
```

LISTING 13.1   Continued

```
         hr.countries c, hr.regions r where e.department_id =
         d.department_id and d.location_id = l.location_id and l.country_id
         = c.country_id and c.region_id = r.region_id and employee_id =
         substr(to_char(abs(dbms_random.random)),1,4)


--------------------------------------------------------------------------
FINDINGS SECTION (1 finding)
--------------------------------------------------------------------------


1- Statistics Finding
----------------
```

The Finding section correctly identifies the problem and states that statistics need to be gathered for the objects involved. When this is performed and the tuning task is rerun, the finding There are no recommendations to improve the statement is displayed.

Please note that the SQL statement should be syntactically and semantically correct. If not, an Errors section with the relevant error is displayed instead of the Findings section. An example is shown in Listing 13.2. This is a snippet of the code shown in Listing 13.1, but with some subtle syntactical errors deliberately introduced.

LISTING 13.2   Snippets Showing Errors

```
 7          'hr.countries c, hr.regions r' ||
 8          'where e.department_id = d.department_id' ||
 9          'and d.location_id = l.location_id' ||
10          'and l.country_id = c.country_id' ||
11          'and c.region_id = r.region_id' ||
12          'and employee_id = ' ||
<snipped to reduce space>

SQL ID  : a75nmwywsu87r
SQL Text: select e.* from hr.employees e, hr.departments d, hr.locations l,
          hr.countries c, hr.regions rwhere e.department_id =
          d.department_idand d.location_id = l.location_idand l.country_id =
          c.country_idand c.region_id = r.region_idand employee_id =
          substr(to_char(abs(dbms_random.random)),1,4)


--------------------------------------------------------------------------
ERRORS SECTION
--------------------------------------------------------------------------
- ORA-00933: SQL command not properly ended
```

Can you spot the errors in the bold-faced text? There was no space after the id terms at the end of every line, and the concatenation produced incorrect SQL. Keep in mind that such simple mistakes will produce errors when the advisor is run.

When appropriate, additional information such as rationales and execution plans may be displayed. As well, when a tuning task is set up using the CREATE_TUNING_TASK function, but never executed using the EXECUTE_TUNING_TASK procedure, you will get the Error: task *Your tuning task* needs to be executed first message if you try to use the REPORT_TUNING_TASK function on it.

Accessing the SQL Access Advisor APIs

The SQL Access Advisor uses certain procedures and functions from the DBMS_ADVISOR built-in PL/SQL package. You already saw some of its functions and procedures in the previous chapter, so keeping those in mind, we've listed only those that are relevant to the SQL Access Advisor in Table 13.3.

TABLE 13.3

DBMS_ADVISOR **Functions and Procedures Specific to SQL Access Advisor**

Function/Procedure	Description
CREATE_SQLWKLD, DELETE_SQLWKLD	These procedures create/delete an SQL workload object to hold all the relevant details of a set of SQL statements.
ADD_SQLWKLD_STATEMENT, DELETE_SQLWKLD_STATEMENT	These procedures add/delete a single SQL statement along with required workload parameters to/from a previously defined workload.
ADD_SQLWKLD_REF, DELETE_SQLWKLD_REF	These procedures establish/remove the link between the SQL workload object and an advisor task, thus setting up/removing the task to be executed later using the EXECUTE_TASK procedure common to advisors.
IMPORT_SQLWKLD_SCHEMA, IMPORT_SQLWKLD_SQLCACHE, IMPORT_SQLWKLD_STS, IMPORT_SQLWKLD_SUMADV, IMPORT_SQLWKLD_USER	These procedures import SQL statements from a variety of sources including the SQL cache, a SQL tuning set, a Summary Advisor workload (from Oracle 9i), or a specified user table, respectively. This mirrors the input sources explained earlier.
GET_TASK_SCRIPT, CREATE_FILE	The GET_TASK_SCRIPT function and the CREATE_FILE procedure can be used in a combination to create a script that will implement the recommendations as seen in Listing 13.5.

Note that you will use some of the previously defined procedures and functions such as the CREATE_TASK and EXECUTE_TASK calls that are common to all the advisors. These were listed in the previous chapter. Listing 13.3 shows procedures that can be used to help tune a summary SQL. In this case, we chose the SH schema from the sample schemas and created an SQL that performed a summary of sales as shown in the SQL. Because a summary is being performed, you might expect that one of the recommendations would be to create a materialized view.

LISTING 13.3   Use of the `DBMS_ADVISOR` Package for the SQL Access Advisor

```
SQL> DECLARE
  2  workload_name VARCHAR2(30);
  3  task_id        VARCHAR2(30);
  4  task_name      VARCHAR2(30);
  5  BEGIN
  6  workload_name := 'SAA Workload';
  7  task_id       := 'SAA Task';
  8  task_name     := 'Generate Access Advice Task';
  9  -- Create the SQL Access Advisor workload
 10  dbms_advisor.create_sqlwkld(workload_name, 'Test SQL Access Adv Workload');
 11  -- Setup the SQL Access Advisor , including cost of access and SQL
 12  dbms_advisor.add_sqlwkld_statement(workload_name, 'Reporting', 'Rollup',
 13  200,420,3424,4203,640445,680000,2,1,SYSDATE,1,'SH',
 14  'select p.prod_category, t.week_ending_day, s.cust_id, ' ||
 15  'sum(s.amount_sold) from sh.sales s, sh.products p, sh.times t ' ||
 16  'where s.time_id = t.time_id and s.prod_id = p.prod_id ' ||
 17  'group by p.prod_category, t.week_ending_day, s.cust_id');
 18  -- Now create an Advisor task for the SQL Access Advisor
 19  dbms_advisor.create_task ('SQL Access Advisor', task_id, task_name);
 20  -- Associate the Workload to the Advisor task
 21  dbms_advisor.add_sqlwkld_ref(task_id, workload_name);
 22  -- Execute the Advisor task
 23  dbms_advisor.execute_task(task_id);
 24  END;
 25  /

PL/SQL procedure successfully completed.
```

The calls to the specific `DBMS_ADVISOR` package are in bold, and the SQL statement itself is in italics. The workload `SAA Workload` is first created and a particular SQL statement attached to it. The SQL statement needs certain other inputs such as module, action, CPU and elapsed time, disk reads, buffer gets, rows processed, optimizer cost, number of executions, priority, execution date, user name, and so on, in addition to the actual SQL statement. These values are required in order to provide a cost to the query so that an internal comparison to the initially supplied values can be made once tuning is complete. Similar to the input specified to the SQL Tuning Advisor, this SQL needs to be syntactically and semantically correct. When this is done, a task named `SAA Task` is created with the named advisor (in this case, SQL Access Advisor) and associated with the workload. It is then executed via the previously explained `EXECUTE_TASK` call just like other advisors.

The processed results are exposed through a number of `DBA_ADVISOR_` tables. The SQLs against these specific tables and outputs shown in Listing 13.4 show the end result.

LISTING 13.4   Cross-Check the Results

```
SQL> select sql_id, rec_id, precost, postcost,
  2  (precost-postcost)*100/precost pct_benefit, importance
  3  from dba_advisor_sqla_wk_stmts
  4  where task_name = 'SAA Task';

    SQL_ID     REC_ID    PRECOST    POSTCOST PCT_BENEFIT IMPORTANCE
---------- ---------- ---------- ---------- ----------- ----------
        42          1      43138        4020  90.6810701        100

SQL> column command format a30
SQL> select rec_id, action_id, substr(command,1,30) command
  2  from dba_advisor_actions
  3  where task_name = 'SAA Task' order by rec_id, action_id;

    REC_ID  ACTION_ID COMMAND
---------- ---------- ------------------------------
         1          1 CREATE MATERIALIZED VIEW LOG
         1          3 CREATE MATERIALIZED VIEW LOG
         1          5 CREATE MATERIALIZED VIEW LOG
         1          7 CREATE MATERIALIZED VIEW
         1          8 GATHER TABLE STATISTICS
```

The PRECOST and POSTCOST columns show the actual estimated cost of access for the original SQL as well as the estimated cost of the rewritten SQL that would now execute using the materialized view on behalf of the user. Now that the results are in, you can use the code shown in Listing 13.5 to obtain a physical script that can be used for implementation later. The resultant script that was produced is also shown.

LISTING 13.5   Creating the Implementation Scripts

```
SQL> create directory advisor_results as '/tmp/adv_results';

Directory created.

SQL> exec dbms_advisor.create_file (dbms_advisor.get_task_script('SAA Task')
> , 'ADVISOR_RESULTS','saa_task_cr_script.sql');

PL/SQL procedure successfully completed.

$ cat /tmp/adv_results/saa_task_cr_script.sql
Rem  SQL Access Advisor: Version 10.1.0.1 - Production
Rem
Rem  Username:       SYS
Rem  Task:           SAA Task
```

LISTING 13.5   Continued

```
Rem   Execution date:   07/03/2005 18:53
Rem

set feedback 1
set linesize 80
set trimspool on
set tab off
set pagesize 60

whenever sqlerror CONTINUE

CREATE MATERIALIZED VIEW LOG ON
    "SH"."PRODUCTS"
    WITH ROWID, SEQUENCE("PROD_ID","PROD_CATEGORY")
    INCLUDING NEW VALUES;

CREATE MATERIALIZED VIEW LOG ON
    "SH"."TIMES"
    WITH ROWID, SEQUENCE("TIME_ID","WEEK_ENDING_DAY")
    INCLUDING NEW VALUES;

CREATE MATERIALIZED VIEW LOG ON
    "SH"."SALES"
    WITH ROWID, SEQUENCE("PROD_ID","CUST_ID","TIME_ID","AMOUNT_SOLD")
    INCLUDING NEW VALUES;

CREATE MATERIALIZED VIEW "SYS"."MV$$_0BBF0002"
    REFRESH FAST WITH ROWID
    ENABLE QUERY REWRITE
    AS SELECT SH.PRODUCTS.PROD_CATEGORY C1, SH.TIMES.WEEK_ENDING_DAY C2,
    SH.SALES.CUST_ID C3,
    SUM("SH"."SALES"."AMOUNT_SOLD") M1, COUNT("SH"."SALES"."AMOUNT_SOLD") M2,
    COUNT(*) M3 FROM SH.PRODUCTS, SH.TIMES, SH.SALES WHERE SH.SALES.TIME_ID
        = SH.TIMES.TIME_ID AND SH.SALES.PROD_ID = SH.PRODUCTS.PROD_ID GROUP BY
        SH.PRODUCTS.PROD_CATEGORY, SH.TIMES.WEEK_ENDING_DAY, SH.SALES.CUST_ID;

begin
  dbms_stats.gather_table_stats('"SYS"','"MV$$_0BBF0002"',NULL,dbms_stats.auto_s
ample_size);
end;
/

whenever sqlerror EXIT SQL.SQLCODE
```

LISTING 13.5 Continued

```
begin
  dbms_advisor.mark_recommendation('SAA Task',1,'IMPLEMENTED');
end;
/
```

Note that the system generated its own names for the objects. You have the choice of changing them prior to implementation.

Avoiding Advisor Pitfalls

You may have noticed that the approach taken by the advisors is very similar to that used by a performance analyst. For example, when the SQL Tuning Advisor is invoked, it checks for the presence of valid and up-to-date object statistics. It then performs access path analysis such as checking for the presence of appropriate indexes. The SQL Access Advisor performs a similar task while looking for opportunities to create materialized views and to utilize the query-rewrite facility. In other words, the advisors automate what a human would do. Hence, when used incorrectly or without a complete understanding of the application and environment, the advisors suffer from the same shortfalls and mistakes that a human would be expected to commit. Some of these possible stumbling blocks and how to guard against them include the following:

- **Out-of-the-box thinking.** Sometimes, the solution to a perplexing performance issue is not the standard one, such as addition of an index or creation of a materialized view. The solution may instead be to redesign a part or even the whole application, or even something as simple as parallelizing the effort via the Parallel Query (PQ) or Parallel DML (PDML) facilities. Obviously, the advisors currently do not have the capability to think along these terms, while a human could. What you will need to do is to use the advice generated by the advisors as just that, and look beyond the obvious.

- **False positives.** In certain situations, a piece of advice that is currently valid may become invalid during another period. For example, the advice to drop certain unused indexes may be valid during normal days, but implementation (that is, the removal of these indexes) may result in performance issues during period-end reporting. In this case, the out-of-the-box solution may be to drop the indexes during the normal days and create them prior to such reporting requirements.

- **Changing workload or environment.** It is a given that an application's code, usage, data size, and execution environment change constantly. Thus, the performance analyst must continually look for tuning opportunities and keep track of what was done prior. For example, you may need to regenerate an SQL tuning set because of the increased and changed code base. You might also have to keep regenerating SQL profiles for a set of Top SQL in a scheduled manner so that the profiles can accommodate changes in data and execution pattern.

In short, the performance analyst should consider the SQL advisors as just one more, albeit important, set of tools in the quest to keep the application and database performing well.

New Features in Oracle Database 10g Release 2

Oracle Database 10g Release 2 promises quite a few additions for SQL tuning. For example, the OEM has been enhanced to provide a better user experience and to expose more powerful features of the SQL Access Advisor. Recommendation and action implementation statuses are now available. In addition, SQL Access Advisor will be able to recommend function-based indexes. SQL profiles have also been enhanced to match SQL text with literal values by normalizing them into bind variables. As well, SQL profiles and SQL tuning sets are transportable across databases so you can easily test production scenarios in development instances.

Summary

In this chapter, you saw how Oracle Database 10g was able to assist the performance analyst in capturing, tuning, and implementing changes that can improve the performance of the database as a whole using the SQL Tuning Advisor and the SQL Access Advisor. The OEM interface as well as the APIs were described. We also listed some of the possible pitfalls of using these advisors and how to avoid these while still making use of the advice provided by these advisors.

14

Influencing the Cost Based Optimizer

IN THIS CHAPTER

New Optimizer Improvements	287
SQL Profiles	304
Effective Use of Histograms	307
New Features in Oracle Database 10g Release 2	309

New Optimizer Improvements

The Cost Based Optimizer is at the heart of the Oracle kernel and plays a large part in the efficient execution of SQL statements in Oracle Database 10g. This is a very complex and involved topic; at the very least, however, you need to know about some of the new features in the optimizer that is now available in Oracle Database 10g. This chapter discusses the most important set of changes, along with some conceptual information that will help you keep your database running efficiently. We can promise you that the going will be heavy in this chapter, but reading it is well worth it because of the useful nuggets of information about the optimizer it contains.

As you saw in previous chapters, the Optimizer in Oracle Database 10g has been substantially improved—so much so that

When we use the term *Optimizer* when discussing Oracle Database 10g, we mean the *Cost Based Optimizer*, or CBO. Oracle Corporation, in fact, is proposing to refer to the CBO as the *Oracle Query Optimizer* (OQO) in future versions.

the familiar but staid Rule Based Optimizer (RBO) has finally been placed to rest. Although the official de-support of the RBO is probably the most visible improvement in this area, there are a number of other improvements, as well as documented pitfalls of which you need to be aware.

Before you launch into the changes to the Optimizer in Oracle Database 10g, however, you'll need some basic understanding of the terms that we will use later on, as well as an overview of how the Optimizer works. As we describe some of these elements, we will also mention how certain aspects have been changed in the Optimizer in Oracle Database 10g.

RBO and CBO: A Comparison

What Does Cost Mean?

The CBO uses cost as a basis for all its decisions. So what exactly does this cost mean? There have been (and will certainly continue to be) various arguments about what cost means within the Oracle user community. A precise explanation that everyone agrees on does not really exist. The cost has no relation to the run time of the query; a query with higher cost may complete sooner than a query with lower cost. The cost is, however, closely related to the estimated number of I/O operations. In fact, in some cases, the cost is a function of the number of I/O requests. Whatever the case may be, it is a fact that cost is the currency used by the Optimizer to compare two or more competing execution paths. More on this later!

The Optimizer is at the heart of the Oracle kernel's access layer and determines how the required data should be accessed. Until Oracle 7, the Rule Based Optimizer (RBO) was the only optimizer in use. In Oracle 7 and onward, Oracle Corporation made the Cost Based Optimizer (CBO) available in the database. The difference between the two optimizers is simple: The RBO instructs the Oracle Kernel to get to the data based on a set of rules, while the CBO performs this action using the estimated cost of access. It does this by performing calculations based on statistics about objects such as tables, indexes, columns, and histograms, and choosing the best access route or execution plan among the many available paths that have the lowest cost of access. (The CBO, in fact, was turned on by the CHOOSE keyword in the OPTIMIZER_MODE initialization parameter's value in previous versions of the software.) This possible execution plan can be determined using the EXPLAIN PLAN statement. When the SQL is traced, the actual execution plan can also be seen in raw form in the trace file or in a processed form in the TKPROF output after the trace file is processed. The plan that was used for the actual execution can also be seen via the V$SQL_PLAN view on Oracle 9i databases and above immediately after the SQL statement completes executing.

Both the CBO and the RBO produce execution plans. The RBO cannot, however, use statistical information about the object when generating an execution plan. The CBO, on the other hand, is flexible enough to adapt its access path according to this information. Thus, if the size and nature of the objects varies, the CBO can adapt and adjust its execution plan accordingly. The CBO can also cater to new types of objects such as function-based indexes, partitioned tables, bitmap indexes, and so on, as well as perform new methods of access such as hash joins, while the RBO does not. For these reasons, Oracle has been discouraging the use of the RBO and has in fact fully de-supported its use with Oracle Database 10g onward. This is one of the major changes in the Optimizer. Indeed, it forces all users to use the Cost Based Optimizer, because that is the only optimizer that Oracle Database 10g supported. In fact, Oracle manuals and other documents use the words *Optimizer* or *Query Optimizer* instead of the term *CBO*. We use the same terminology here; hence, all references to the Optimizer specifically mean the CBO unless otherwise stated. For more details on the obsolescence of the RBO, see MetaLink Note #189702.1.

> **Moving to the Cost Based Optimizer**
> Even though the CBO has been around for more than a decade, many applications continue to use the RBO. If you are responsible for one such RBO-based application, you might want to read a paper titled "Safely Navigating the RBO to CBO Minefield," written by one of the authors of this book and available on the Internet at `http://www.geocties.com/john_sharmila/links.htm`. This paper, although written for Oracle 8i, espouses practical principles that are applicable to the Optimizer of today, and points out pitfalls that you should avoid and myths that still abound.

What the Optimizer Does

A SQL statement can be executed in many different ways, such as using full table scans, index scans in certain cases, and join methods such as nested loops and hash joins when one table is joined to one or more others. The Query Optimizer determines the most efficient way to execute a SQL statement after considering many factors related to the objects referenced and the conditions specified in the query. This determination is an important step in the processing of any SQL statement and can greatly affect execution time. Thus, improvements in the Optimizer greatly improve the holistic performance of the databases based on Oracle Database 10g, as you will see later in this chapter.

We will now look at how the Optimizer works. The various operations of the Optimizer include:

- **Evaluation of expressions and conditions.** First, the Optimizer must evaluate all expressions and conditions in the specified SQL statements and simplify these conditions and expressions as much as possible.

- **Statement transformation.** For complex statements involving correlated subqueries or views, the optimizer transforms the original statement into an equivalent join statement. In other circumstances, the Optimizer can break up a complex query into smaller chunks. After this is done, the Optimizer may merge views, push predicates, and perform query rewrites if supporting structures such as materialized views are available. These actions are controlled to some extent by certain Optimizer parameters, including the hidden `COMPLEX_VIEW_MERGING` initialization parameter.

- **Choice of optimizer goals.** The Optimizer determines the goal of optimization. The default goal, or mode, is `ALL_ROWS`. This optimizes for throughput and is best suited for batch and OLAP processing, which requires *all* the selected rows to be returned as quickly as possible. The other goal, or mode, is `FIRST_ROWS`, which optimizes for best response, where the *first* set of rows is returned as quickly as possible. This goal mostly influences the join method. Note that the default value of the OPTIMIZER_MODE parameter in Oracle Database 10g is ALL_ROWS rather than CHOOSE, as in previous versions. In fact, because there is no choice, the CHOOSE as well as the RULE values for the OPTIMIZER_MODE parameter have been made obsolete in Oracle Database 10g. The functionalities for these hints remain, but Oracle Corporation does not support their use, and promises to remove even these functionalities in a future release.

- **Choice of access paths.** For each table accessed by the statement, the Optimizer chooses one or more of the available access paths to obtain table data. This includes full table scans; row ID scans; various types of index scans including index unique scans, index range scans, index skips scans, and fast full index scans; and cluster and hash access.

- **Choice of join orders.** When parsing a join statement that joins more than two tables, the Optimizer chooses the first pair of tables to join, and then the next table that is joined to the result, and so on. For the best run times, it is important that the first join produces the smallest *result set* (or number of rows returned from the join) and increases in number as the join progresses. A large number of join methods is available, including nested loop, hash, sort merge, Cartesian, and outer joins. The Optimizer must pick the type of join that is appropriate for the intended Optimizer goal, objects involved, and execution environment for that SQL.

Full Table Scans—Good or Bad?

Full table scans (FTSes) have historically been considered evil. Indeed, performance analysts have always been advised to avoid FTS. That said, there are cases when an FTS may actually result in less I/O and, with fewer computing resources being consumed. Without going into details, keep in mind that the DB_FILE_MULTIBLOCK_READ_COUNT (MBRC) parameter kicks in to enable reading of MBRC-number of blocks in a single I/O. In a simple example, suppose a table consists of 16 blocks and the MBRC is set to 16, then the entire table could be read into the buffer cache in just one I/O operation, even if just one row was actually required. In comparison, an indexed read may have required at least two or even three reads—first the root block, next, a leaf block if present, and finally the actual data block, all of these operations using a single I/O each. In many cases, the operating system performs its own read improvements, such as read ahead and track caching, and can satisfy the I/O requirement of an FTS with far less actual I/O.

Throughout these operations, the estimated cost of access for each of these paths is continually calculated and evaluated, and the best plan chosen on the basis of lowest cost.

So how does the Optimizer make all these decisions? The answer to this is the key to this entire chapter. Simply put, the Optimizer estimates the cost of each plan based on statistics in the data dictionary for the data distribution and storage characteristics of the tables, indexes, and partitions accessed by the statement. The cost is an *estimated* value that is proportional to the expected resource use needed to execute the statement with a particular plan. In Oracle Database 10g, the Optimizer calculates the cost of access paths and join orders based on the estimated computer resources, which now include I/O and CPU. The key word here is *estimated*. In other words, the Optimizer applies certain calculations using internal algorithms to the statistics stored in the data dictionary for the involved objects. Expressed in another way, the cost of a query is arrived at in the following manner:

Cost = (Costing Algorithms, Influenced by Optimizer Settings and System Statistics) -> (Operating on Object Statistics)

When the object statistics are incorrect, do not exist, or do not reflect the current state of the object, or when the Optimizer settings are incorrectly configured, the Optimizer may arrive at the wrong cost values for various alternatives. As a result, the query chooses an inefficient path, resulting in poor performance. These two sets of inputs—namely, object statistics and Optimizer settings—are under the direct control of the performance analyst. It is obvious that you should have the proper set of up-to-date object statistics as well as the correct values for the Optimizer settings in order for the Optimizer to perform optimally.

What is more subtle, though, is that the algorithms themselves can have a major influence on the cost calculations. As well, the Oracle kernel must make some assumptions about the environment in the form of the cost of I/O and the availability of CPU resources. If the parameters of the environment are not known or if a bug is present in the algorithms, then the cost model could again go wrong. In Oracle Database 10g, most of these risks have been mitigated in some form or other, as discussed in the next few sections.

> It is important to note that the Oracle Database 10g Optimizer can operate in an Advanced Automatic Tuning mode, which it does when invoked by the SQL Tuning Advisor. You saw details of how this is done and what it entails in Chapter 13, "Effectively Using the SQL Advisors."

The Relevance of Object Statistics

As you saw before, the Optimizer is very dependent on correct and up-to-date object statistics. These statistics include the following:

- Table statistics, including the number of rows, number of blocks both used and empty, average row length, and so on. This is exposed via the DBA_TABLES view. When table statistics are not present, the Optimizer assumes some internal default values for number of blocks, average row length, and so on in order to proceed.

- Column statistics, including the number of distinct values (NDV) in a column, low and high values, the number of nulls, and density. This is exposed via the DBA_TAB_COL_STATISTICS view, as well as through the more familiar DBA_TAB_COLUMNS view. Data distribution for columns is available in a separate structure known as a *histogram*. This is exposed via the DBA_HISTOGRAMS view.

- Index statistics, including the number of leaf blocks, the index level, the clustering factor, and so on. This is exposed via the DBA_INDEXES or the DBA_IND_STATISTICS view. As with table statistics, when index statistics are

> The default values for missing table and index statistics is detailed in the *Oracle Database 10g Performance Tuning Guide* in Chapter 15, "Managing Optimizer Statistics," in the section titled "Handling Missing Statistics."

missing, the Optimizer assumes some default values for level, number of leaf blocks, number of distinct keys and so on.

COMPUTE **Versus** ESTIMATE

Oracle Database 10g collects object statistics by scanning the table or index to obtain values such as the average row size, the number of distinct values, the clustering factor, and so on. Oracle allows you to estimate these values using a sample number of table or index blocks or compute these values accurately using a full scan. When the objects are large, a proportionally larger amount of I/O, and thus time and CPU resources, is spent collecting these statistics. Hence, practical issues of time and resources, especially on today's large databases, mandate that a sample set of blocks from the object be scanned and the statistics estimated using the ESTIMATE option rather than computed via the COMPUTE option. Note, though, that there are cases when the use of the ESTIMATE option would automatically upgrade into a COMPUTE option—when the SAMPLE_SIZE is greater than 50% or the object being sampled is less than 100 blocks.

Even if the matter of using ESTIMATE or COMPUTE is settled, the argument about what percentage of data should be used for estimation continues. Oracle Database 10g (and even Oracle 9i) allows you to specify a parameter DBMS_STATS.AUTO_SAMPLE_SIZE in the statistics-gathering routines that can be used to automatically estimate the best value for the estimate percentage. We suggest using this parameter, especially for very large objects, as the Optimizer scales down the amount of I/O used for the sample while ensuring that accuracy is not lost. The downside is some extra I/O sampling for probes as the Optimizer works with smaller or larger samples, going in either direction until it gets the right level. The initial sample takes into account the original size estimate from the object data size available in the DBA_EXTENTS view.

- System statistics, including I/O performance and utilization as well as CPU performance and utilization. This is stored in the undocumented AUX_STATS$ table in the SYS schema. Although, in a strict sense, system statistics are not really object statistics, we will discuss them within the context of this topic for the sake of continuity.

All these object and system statistics are maintained by the built-in DBMS_STATS PL/SQL package, a well-known package that has existed since Oracle 8i and needs no explanation. The various procedures, including GATHER_TABLE_STATS, GATHER_INDEX_STATS, and GATHER_SYSTEM_STATS, can be used to gather and store the aforementioned object and system statistics. Object statistics can also be manually set, exported to and imported from specially created statistics tables, and manipulated in many other ways using other procedures in DBMS_STATS.

New in Oracle Database 10g is the capability to lock down object statistics at the table or the schema level using the LOCK_TABLE_STATS or the LOCK_SCHEMA_STATS. When this is done, procedures such as GATHER, SET, and so on cannot be used to change the statistics; in fact, an error will be raised in the event an attempt is made to perform this action. Many other new procedures and functions are now available in Oracle Database 10g, and details about them can be found in the *Oracle Database 10g PL/SQL Packages and Types Reference*.

The Relevance of System Statistics

System statistics are different from object statistics in that they quantify the capability of the environment in which the database operates. In other words, system statistics can be used to describe the performance characteristics of the hardware platform including the CPU and I/O. The Optimizer can then compare the CPU costs and I/O costs. Because the speed of the CPU, as well as I/O performance, varies widely between different configurations, it is essential that the optimizer be able to factor these values into its cost calculation model. Rather than relying on a fixed formula for combining CPU and I/O costs, Oracle provides a facility for gathering information about the characteristics of an individual system during a typical workload in order to determine the CPU speed and the performance of the various types of I/O including single-block, multi-block, and direct-disk I/Os. By tailoring the system statistics for each hardware environment, Oracle's cost model can be very accurate on any configuration from any combination of hardware vendors.

> **DBMS_STATS Versus ANALYZE**
>
> Prior to the arrival of DBMS_STATS in Oracle 8i, the ANALYZE command was used to collect object statistics. Although the ANALYZE command was deprecated in Oracle 9i, many sites continue to use this command to collect such statistics. Be aware that ANALYZE does *not* collect certain important sets of statistics related to partitions as well as some of the newer objects in Oracle 8i and above, and hence should not be used to collect object statistics. It is, however, still present as a valid command and should be used *only* to collect non–Optimizer related information, such as information about chained rows and freelist blocks, as well as to perform the VALIDATE function on tables and indexes. For more details, refer to MetaLink Note #236935.1.

Although the concept of system statistics was introduced in Oracle 9i, these statistics were not gathered or used by default. In Oracle Database 10g, system statistics are collected by default, and the costing model uses them automatically. In addition, a number of additional parameters such as I/O seek time and I/O transfer speed are collected and used in cost calculations.

The DBMS_STATS.GATHER_SYSTEM_STATS procedure can be used for gathering system statistics. The data thus collected can be stored in a user-defined statistics table under a named category. Later, you can use the DBMS_STATS.IMPORT_SYSTEM_STATS procedure to make these values active. This can be used to set, for example, the appropriate values for I/O during a batch-processing period favoring multi-block I/O and later changed during an

> The collection of object statistics invalidates the currently cached SQL cursors that refer to those objects whose statistics were collected. Collection of system statistics, on the other hand, does not invalidate current SQL cursors. However, only new SQL statements being parsed after the collection completes will use the latest system statistics for cost calculation.

OLTP period to favor single-block I/O. For details on how this can be done, see MetaLink Note #149560.1.

You should be very careful how and when these statistics are collected, because they exert a powerful influence on cost calculations. Although the CPU speed remains constant, the estimated I/O figures could be unnaturally skewed because of unusual activity taking place during collection. In case you want to play safe, we recommend that you do *not* collect system statistics at random, but instead set these values once and for all by using values specified by the vendor of the hardware configuration in use. You could also use an I/O benchmarking tool such as IOZone (http://www.iozone.org) to determine the values for multiple types of reads, and use that benchmark to set the values for the system statistics.

The current, live system statistics are stored in the AUX_STATS$ table in the SYS schema. Listing 14.1 shows a sample of the contents of this table.

LISTING 14.1   Sample System Statistics in AUX_STATS$

```
SQL> column sname format a20
SQL> column pname format a15
SQL> column pval1 format 999999.999
SQL> column pval2 format a20
SQL> column status format a15
SQL> select * from sys.aux_stats$;


SNAME                 PNAME               PVAL1 PVAL2
-------------------   ---------------  -------- --------------------
SYSSTATS_INFO         STATUS                    COMPLETED
SYSSTATS_INFO         DSTART                    04-18-2005 01:40
SYSSTATS_INFO         DSTOP                     04-18-2005 02:40
SYSSTATS_INFO         FLAGS               1.000
SYSSTATS_MAIN         CPUSPEEDNW        584.441
SYSSTATS_MAIN         IOSEEKTIM           4.573
SYSSTATS_MAIN         IOTFRSPEED      11554.658
SYSSTATS_MAIN         SREADTIM            4.576
SYSSTATS_MAIN         MREADTIM            5.644
SYSSTATS_MAIN         CPUSPEED          580.000
SYSSTATS_MAIN         MBRC               11.000
SYSSTATS_MAIN         MAXTHR
SYSSTATS_MAIN         SLAVETHR
```

System Statistics in a RAC Environment

The AUX_STATS$ view does not have the INST_ID column that can be used to identify the instance in a Real Application Cluster (RAC). Thus, the statistics apply globally across all nodes. If you use different nodes in a RAC cluster for different purposes—say, one for reporting and one for OLTP type of application—then the system stats will not provide the true picture for any one node, and the CPU costing may not be accurate for that type of workload.

You can see from Listing 14.1 that the system statistics were collected in the space of an hour (DSTART/DSTOP). The CPU speed for both *at workload* (CPUSPEED) and *no workload* (CPUSPEEDNW) is shown in million cycles per second. The single-/multi-block I/O (SREADTIM/MREADTIM) values are the wait time, in milliseconds, to read single- and multi-block reads. MBRC is the estimated best value for DB_FILE_MULTIBLOCK_READ_COUNT. The I/O seek time (IOSEEKTIM) is the seek time in milliseconds influenced by both the disk latency and operating system buffering overhead. The I/O transfer speed (IOTFRSPEED) is the number of bytes transferred from the disk each millisecond. These values were collected to show actual values; hence, we recommend that you use the DBMS_STATS.SET_SYSTEM_STATS procedure to set predetermined values in the system statistics tables.

The Relevance of Dictionary Statistics

The conventional wisdom has always been that statistics on data dictionary objects—that is, on objects owned and used by SYS and SYSTEM schemas for internal operations—should never be collected. Although this restriction was removed starting in Oracle 9i, it is still common to find that object statistics do not exist for the SYS, SYSTEM, and other system-related schemas such as MDSYS and CTXSYS. Starting in Oracle Database 10g, however, object statistics on these data dictionary objects are collected and used. The DBMS_STATS.GATHER_DICTIONARY_STATS procedure is used for this purpose, and you are encouraged to keep the dictionary statistics up to date.

Dynamic Sampling

One of the most important new features in the Optimizer is the automatic collection of these object statistics using what is called *dynamic sampling*. When the Optimizer determines that either the required object statistics are stale or, worse still, that tables or indexes involved in the query do not have statistics at all, estimated values of object statistics are automatically collected for these objects. Although dynamic sampling was introduced in Oracle 9i Release 2 using the OPTIMIZER_DYNAMIC_SAMPLING initialization parameter with a default value of 1, the default level of this parameter was increased to 2 in Oracle Database 10g.

The value of this level can range from 0 to 10, with a value of 0 effectively disabling dynamic sampling and increasing levels taking more aggressive estimates for collections of statistics. For example, at level 1, the optimizer samples all tables that do not have statistics if the following criteria are met:

- There is at least one table with no statistics in the query.

- This table is joined to another table or appears in a subquery or non-mergeable view.

- This table has no indexes.

- This unanalyzed table has more blocks than the number of blocks that would be used for dynamic sampling of this table. An undocumented parameter OPTIMIZER_DYN_SMP_BLKS controls the number of blocks used for sampling and is set at 32 by default.

At level 2, all tables and objects that are not analyzed will be sampled regardless of the exclusions at level 1, and the number of blocks sampled doubles to 64. At level 3, all objects at level 2, as well as analyzed tables where a guess at selectivity was made, are sampled. At level 4, all objects at level 3 along with tables that have single-table predicates that reference two or more columns are sampled.

At levels 5 through 9, the criteria for previous levels are applied, but the number of blocks sampled doubles at every level. At level 10, all tables that meet the criteria for level 9 are selected, but the whole table is sampled. Although the default value of 2 is sufficient in most cases, you can easily go up to a value of 4 or more in order to fully equip the Optimizer with correct statistics in DSS types of applications. The end result is that having missing statistics is no longer a major concern.

> ### Downside of Dynamic Sampling
>
> Dynamic sampling occurs at parse time, when the cost calculation is performed, so be prepared to suffer longer parse times and increased resources allocated and recorded under the `parse time elapsed` values in the Time and Wait model statistics (`V$SYS_TIME_MODEL` view) discussed in Chapter 10, "Adopting a New Approach to Tuning." Because this is performed using recursive SQL, the counts in `V$SYSSTAT` for recursive calls will go up as well. Depending on the level that has been set, some amount of I/O and CPU is used to perform sampling and related calculations. As well, dynamic sampling occurs only when the `OPTIMIZER_FEATURES_ENABLE` initialization parameter is set to at least 9.2.0 or higher. Dynamic sampling also cannot be performed on external tables or on remote tables in other databases accessed via database links.

Dynamic sampling is very useful when using temporary tables and staging tables in your application. The nature of these tables is such that the volume of data varies significantly during the course of a day, but the object statistics may not reflect this correctly depending on what time they were collected. For example, staging tables may be purged at the end of the day, but may have millions of rows during the processing part of the day. If object statistics were collected at the end of the day, these tables would be empty, and the statistics would not accurately reflect the picture that evolves during the day. In the case of temporary tables that exist for the duration of the transaction or session only, dynamic sampling will provide an accurate picture during the time when a query is executed against such a temporary table.

When dynamic sampling is not set or enabled, or if object statistics cannot be collected because the objects are either remote or in external tables, the Optimizer is forced to assume certain fixed values. This includes an almost ridiculous assumption of 2,000 rows for remote tables and a row length of 100 bytes. Both dynamic sampling and the details of these assumptions are discussed in the *Oracle Database 10g Performance Tuning Guide*. Note that dynamic sampling can also be forced by the new `DYNAMIC_SAMPLING` hint in a SQL statement.

Table and Index Monitoring

As mentioned previously, one of the main factors influencing the Optimizer is the presence (or absence, or staleness, as the case may be) of up-to date object statistics, not to mention whether those object statistics are the correct set. The amount of data stored in tables (and in their indexes by extension) varies depending on the level of DML activity on the tables. Although DBAs schedule periodic collection of statistics for all objects in their databases, the blind collection of object statistics may result in wasted I/O and computing resources as well as varying performance when the statistics collection window spills over into an active period. This is where table and index monitoring comes in.

Table monitoring was introduced in Oracle 8i, and index monitoring in Oracle 9i. When monitoring is switched on for selected tables, counts for DML activity on those tables, through execution of `INSERT`, `DELETE`, and `UPDATE` statements, are recorded and exposed via the `DBA_TAB_MODIFICATIONS` view. Depending on the level of DML activity on these tables, a DBA could schedule selective collection of object statistics so that only the very active tables are analyzed—this, too, according to the volume of DML. In Oracle Database 10g, table monitoring is switched on by default when the STATISTICS_LEVEL is set to TYPICAL or ALL. SMON collects the information by scanning V$SQL; the information is updated periodically. This is a very useful tool in helping to reduce the cost, resource, and time window for collection of object statistics while keeping the statistics up to date. Any object missed here would then be caught by dynamic sampling.

Index monitoring exposes the use of indexes in the V$OBJECT_USAGE view, specifically in the USED column, and can be used to ascertain the presence of unused indexes. Note that this information can be picked up in the SQL Access Advisor, as shown in Chapter 13. MetaLink Note #144070.1 has more details on this topic.

Parameters Influencing the Optimizer

Certain Optimizer-related initialization parameters, both well-known and hidden, influence the costing algorithms and hence the cost calculations and, ultimately, the efficient execution of the query. Many books, websites, and even MetaLink Notes refer to these parameters; these should be read and understood. In addition, these parameters should not be changed without a complete understanding as well as Oracle support's advice.

> For further details on usage, please refer to MetaLink Note #102334.1. Although this note was written for Oracle 8i, the contents are applicable even in Oracle Database 10g with the only caveat being that monitoring is now automatically enabled.

How Often Should You Collect Object Statistics?

The frequency of collection of object statistics has been a source of contention for many DBAs. Many sites resort to a daily or weekly collection of statistics on all objects. This is usually counterproductive, however, because such collections, when not completed in time, can actually result in sudden variations in performance as statistics are incompletely collected. As well, they impose a regular— often unnecessary—load on the system when the statistics are collected. Table monitoring, available from Oracle 8i onward, should always be used to determine only those objects that merit such collection. We recommend setting up a process whereby only those objects that undergo a change in 10% of the total rows should be included in a round of object statistics collection.

Note that the counters for a table in the DBA_TAB_MODIFICATIONS view are reset when object statistics is collected for that table. That way, the most active tables bubble up for collection again and again and always have fresh statistics. Inactive tables, which do not need object statistics to be collected as often, would still have up-to date statistics as the contents are determined not to have changed as per the DBA_TAB_MODIFICATIONS view.

You saw two of these initialization parameters—namely OPTIMIZER_MAX_PERMUTATIONS and OPTIMIZER_SEARCH_LIMIT—in earlier chapters. A complete list of parameters that can directly influence the Optimizer is shown in Listing 14.2. This can be obtained fairly easily using a little-known trace event numbered 10053. You will see how to use this trace later; suffice it to say that it can reveal a lot about what is happening under the surface.

Influencing the Cost Based Optimizer

LISTING 14.2   Initialization Parameters

```
*************************************
PARAMETERS WITH ALTERED VALUES
*******************************
db_file_multiblock_read_count    = 16
sqlstat_enabled                  = true
statistics_level                 = all
*************************************
PARAMETERS WITH DEFAULT VALUES
*******************************
optimizer_mode_hinted            = false
optimizer_features_hinted        = 0.0.0
parallel_execution_enabled       = true
parallel_query_forced_dop        = 0
parallel_dml_forced_dop          = 0
parallel_ddl_forced_degree       = 0
parallel_ddl_forced_instances    = 0
_query_rewrite_fudge             = 90
optimizer_features_enable        = 10.1.0
_optimizer_search_limit          = 5
cpu_count                        = 2
active_instance_count            = 1
parallel_threads_per_cpu         = 2
hash_area_size                   = 131072
bitmap_merge_area_size           = 1048576
sort_area_size                   = 65536
sort_area_retained_size          = 0
_sort_elimination_cost_ratio     = 0
_optimizer_block_size            = 8192
_sort_multiblock_read_count      = 2
_optimizer_max_permutations      = 2000
pga_aggregate_target             = 24576 KB
_pga_max_size                    = 204800 KB
_sort_space_for_write_buffers    = 1
_query_rewrite_maxdisjunct       = 257
_smm_auto_min_io_size            = 56 KB
_smm_auto_max_io_size            = 248 KB
_smm_min_size                    = 128 KB
_smm_max_size                    = 1228 KB
_smm_px_max_size                 = 7371 KB
_cpu_to_io                       = 0
_optimizer_undo_cost_change      = 10.1.0
parallel_query_mode              = enabled
parallel_dml_mode                = disabled
parallel_ddl_mode                = enabled
```

LISTING 14.2   Continued

```
optimizer_mode                     = all_rows
_optimizer_percent_parallel        = 101
_always_anti_join                  = choose
_always_semi_join                  = choose
_optimizer_mode_force              = true
_partition_view_enabled            = true
_always_star_transformation        = false
_query_rewrite_or_error            = false
_hash_join_enabled                 = true
cursor_sharing                     = exact
_b_tree_bitmap_plans               = true
star_transformation_enabled        = false
_optimizer_cost_model              = choose
_new_sort_cost_estimate            = true
_complex_view_merging              = true
_unnest_subquery                   = true
_eliminate_common_subexpr          = true
_pred_move_around                  = true
_convert_set_to_join               = false
_push_join_predicate               = true
_push_join_union_view              = true
_fast_full_scan_enabled            = true
_optim_enhance_nnull_detection     = true
_parallel_broadcast_enabled        = true
_px_broadcast_fudge_factor         = 100
_ordered_nested_loop               = true
_no_or_expansion                   = false
optimizer_index_cost_adj           = 100
optimizer_index_caching            = 0
_system_index_caching              = 0
_disable_datalayer_sampling        = false
query_rewrite_enabled              = true
query_rewrite_integrity            = enforced
_query_cost_rewrite                = true
_query_rewrite_2                   = true
_query_rewrite_1                   = true
_query_rewrite_expression          = true
_query_rewrite_jgmigrate           = true
_query_rewrite_fpc                 = true
_query_rewrite_drj                 = true
_full_pwise_join_enabled           = true
_partial_pwise_join_enabled        = true
_left_nested_loops_random          = true
_improved_row_length_enabled       = true
```

LISTING 14.2   Continued

```
_index_join_enabled                     = true
_enable_type_dep_selectivity            = true
_improved_outerjoin_card                = true
_optimizer_adjust_for_nulls             = true
_optimizer_degree                       = 0
_use_column_stats_for_function          = true
_subquery_pruning_enabled               = true
_subquery_pruning_mv_enabled            = false
_or_expand_nvl_predicate                = true
_like_with_bind_as_equality             = false
_table_scan_cost_plus_one               = true
_cost_equality_semi_join                = true
_default_non_equality_sel_check         = true
_new_initial_join_orders                = true
_oneside_colstat_for_equijoins          = true
_optim_peek_user_binds                  = true
_minimal_stats_aggregation              = true
_force_temptables_for_gsets             = false
workarea_size_policy                    = auto
_smm_auto_cost_enabled                  = true
_gs_anti_semi_join_allowed              = true
_optim_new_default_join_sel             = true
optimizer_dynamic_sampling              = 2
_pre_rewrite_push_pred                  = true
_optimizer_new_join_card_computation = true
_union_rewrite_for_gs                   = yes_gset_mvs
_generalized_pruning_enabled            = true
_optim_adjust_for_part_skews            = true
_force_datefold_trunc                   = false
_optimizer_system_stats_usage           = true
skip_unusable_indexes                   = true
_remove_aggr_subquery                   = true
_optimizer_push_down_distinct           = 0
_dml_monitoring_enabled                 = true
_optimizer_undo_changes                 = false
_predicate_elimination_enabled          = true
_nested_loop_fudge                      = 100
_project_view_columns                   = true
_local_communication_costing_enabled = true
_local_communication_ratio              = 50
_query_rewrite_vop_cleanup              = true
_slave_mapping_enabled                  = true
_optimizer_cost_based_transformation = linear
_optimizer_mjc_enabled                  = true
```

LISTING 14.2   Continued

```
_right_outer_hash_enable               = true
_spr_push_pred_refspr                  = true
_optimizer_cache_stats                 = false
_optimizer_cbqt_factor                 = 50
_optimizer_squ_bottomup                = true
_fic_area_size                         = 131072
_optimizer_skip_scan_enabled           = true
_optimizer_cost_filter_pred            = false
_optimizer_sortmerge_join_enabled      = true
_optimizer_join_sel_sanity_check       = true
_mmv_query_rewrite_enabled             = false
_bt_mmv_query_rewrite_enabled          = true
_add_stale_mv_to_dependency_list       = true
_distinct_view_unnesting               = false
_optimizer_dim_subq_join_sel           = true
_optimizer_disable_strans_sanity_checks = 0
_optimizer_compute_index_stats         = true
_push_join_union_view2                 = true
_optimizer_ignore_hints                = false
_optimizer_random_plan                 = 0
_query_rewrite_setopgrw_enable         = true
_optimizer_correct_sq_selectivity      = true
_disable_function_based_index          = false
_optimizer_join_order_control          = 3
```

The new parameters that appear in Oracle Database 10g and that are now acknowledged as influencing the Optimizer have been highlighted in bold in Listing 14.2. As you can see, numerous hidden parameters influence the Optimizer. Interestingly enough, a number of parameters, including CPU_COUNT, now play a part in describing the environment. As well, you may also note that parameters that were previously exposed, such as HASH_JOIN_ENABLED, HASH_MULTIBLOCK_IO_COUNT, and the previously discussed OPTIMIZER_SEARCH_LIMIT, are now hidden. Indeed, Oracle Database 10g Release 1 has 151 parameters, both hidden and exposed, that influence the Optimizer, while Oracle 9i Release 2 has just 62 parameters of this nature, revealing the extent of internal algorithmic changes in the Optimizer.

Oracle Database 10g has reduced the number of exposed parameters that influence the Optimizer while at the same time increasing the number of hidden parameters in this genre. This enables simplification from a user's point of view while providing greater

Hidden Parameters

Note that there are no "silver bullet" hidden parameters, such as MAKE_SQL_GO_FASTER, in Oracle Database 10g. Even so, Oracle Database 10g continues to depend on these initialization parameters, and has in fact increased the number of hidden parameters from 588 in Oracle 9i Release 2 to a humungous 912 in Oracle Database 10g Release 1. As before, these parameters should not be changed without Oracle Support's advice.

control of the Optimizer to both the internal algorithms as well as Advanced Oracle Support for tuning purposes.

Cardinality, Selectivity, and Column Usage

Cardinality is the number of rows expected to be returned by the query or the row set. The Optimizer needs to have some mechanism to compute the cardinality of the query. *Selectivity*, on the other hand, is a factor with a value between 0 and 1 and is a measure of the percentage of rows from the table that are estimated to be selected by the query. The cardinality can be seen in the output of an EXPLAIN PLAN command in the CARD or CARDINALITY column. Both these values depend heavily on column statistics; hence, it is important that these statistics be kept up to date. When column statistics do not reflect the current data distribution, the Optimizer may choose an inefficient execution path.

The availability of additional structures such as histograms and indexes on columns can greatly help in providing good selectivity for queries involving these columns. So how do you decide which columns need these supporting structures? The answer lies in a little-known feature called *column usage tracking*, which was actually introduced in Oracle 9i itself. In Oracle Database 10g, it is turned on by default and hence collects information about how a particular column is used.

In Oracle Database 10g, the Oracle SMON (System Monitor) process regularly gathers information on columns that are used in query predicates and updates them automatically into a table named COL_USAGE$ in the SYS schema. Unlike the MON_MODS table, also in the SYS schema, which records table-level DML activity such as the number of rows changed by INSERT, DELETE, and UPDATE operations, and exposes them via the DBA_TAB_MODIFICATIONS view, the COL_USAGE$ view is neither documented nor wrapped by a legible view. The column names, however, are very revealing; these are detailed in Table 14.1.

TABLE 14.1
Description of Columns in the COL_USAGE$ **View**

Column Name	Description
OBJ#	Object number. Corresponds directly to the OBJ# column in the SYS.OBJ$ table. You can use this to determine the name of the table containing that column.
INTCOL#	Column number. Corresponds directly to the COL# column in the SYS.COL$ table. You can use this to determine the name of the column involved.
EQUALITY_PREDS	Number of times this column uses an equality predicate of the form table.column = *constant*.
EQUIJOIN_PREDS	Number of times this column was used in an equijoin using a predicate of the form table1.column1 = table2.column2.
NONEQUIJOIN_PREDS	Number of times this column was used in an nonequijoin using a predicate of the form table1.column1 != table2.column2.
RANGE_PREDS	Number of times this column was used as a predicate of the form table1.column1 BETWEEN *constant1* AND *constant2*.

TABLE 14.1

Continued

Column Name	Description
LIKE_PREDS	Number of times this column was used as a predicate of the form `table1.column1 LIKE like_constant`.
NULL_PREDS	Number of times this column was used as a predicate of the form `table1.column1 IS NULL`.
TIMESTAMP	The timestamp when the column was last recorded as having been used as a predicate in any query. This is updated by SMON once every 15 minutes.

Using the values in this table, you can determine whether additional indexes and histograms can be created on these columns based on how the columns are referred and by what type of predicates.

As usual, there are some caveats. Be aware that SMON obtains this information by scanning the library cache in the shared pool and updating this table once every 15 minutes or so. In an active database with memory pressure on the shared pool, this information may be lost. This information may also be lost when the database is shut down unless you invoke the DBMS_STATS.FLUSH_DATABASE_MONITORING_INFO procedure beforehand.

> **Other Apparent Uses of** COL_USAGE$
>
> The Oracle kernel seems to utilize the information stored in the COL_USAGE$ table to determine which columns should have histograms when the options => GATHER AUTO parameter is specified during object statistics-gathering at all levels. As well, it seems that this information is being used to recommend creating (and dropping) additional indexes in the various advisors.

Tracing the Optimizer

No account of the Optimizer would be complete without mention of the 10053 event. Just as the 10046 event produces a detailed trace of the execution of SQL, the 10053 event produces a detailed trace of the inner workings of the Optimizer. In fact, the

> You can look at MetaLink Note #225598.1, titled "How to Obtain Tracing of Optimizer Computations (EVENT 10053)," if you are interested in further details.

list of initialization parameters affecting the Optimizer was determined using such a trace. This trace is very cryptic and hard to read, but if understood, produces a wealth of information about the Optimizer—including how the final cost was arrived at as well as the various alternate routes (and their costs) considered. Listing 14.3 shows a snippet of the 10053 trace file. You can see the various objects and their statistics being considered. For example, CDN is the estimated cardinality for the table, NBLKS is the number of blocks in the table, and LVLS and CLUF are the number of levels and clustering factor of the named index. You can also see the effects of CPU and I/O costing in the calculations.

LISTING 14.3   Snippet of 10053 Event Trace File

```
QUERY BLOCK SIGNATURE
*********************
qb name was generated
signature (optimizer): qb_name=SEL$1 nbfros=1 flg=0
  fro(0): flg=0 objn=49788 hint_alias="EMPLOYEES"@"SEL$1"
*****************************************
BASE STATISTICAL INFORMATION
***********************
Table stats    Table: EMPLOYEES   Alias: EMPLOYEES
  TOTAL :: CDN: 13696  NBLKS:  496  AVG_ROW_LEN:  117
Index stats
  Index: EMP_EMAIL_UK  COL#: 4
    TOTAL :: LVLS: 1   #LB: 136  #DK: 13696  LB/K: 1  DB/K: 1  CLUF: 13696
  Index: EMP_EMP_ID_PK  COL#: 1

    TOTAL :: LVLS: 1   #LB: 136  #DK: 13696  LB/K: 1  DB/K: 1  CLUF: 13696
  Index: EMP_EMP_ID_PK  COL#: 1
    TOTAL :: LVLS: 1   #LB: 26  #DK: 13696  LB/K: 1  DB/K: 1  CLUF: 235
  Index: EMP_JOB_IX  COL#: 7
    TOTAL :: LVLS: 1   #LB: 37  #DK: 19  LB/K: 1  DB/K: 120  CLUF: 2285
  Index: EMP_MANAGER_IX  COL#: 10
    TOTAL :: LVLS: 1   #LB: 67  #DK: 18  LB/K: 3  DB/K: 148  CLUF: 2675
  Index: EMP_NAME_IX  COL#: 3 2
    TOTAL :: LVLS: 1   #LB: 256  #DK: 13696  LB/K: 1  DB/K: 1  CLUF: 13689
_OPTIMIZER_PERCENT_PARALLEL = 0
*****************************************
SINGLE TABLE ACCESS PATH
  TABLE: EMPLOYEES  Alias: EMPLOYEES
    Original Card: 13696  Rounded Card: 13696  Computed Card: 13696.00
  Access Path: table-scan  Resc:  97  Resp:  97
  Access Path: index (index-ffs)
    Index: EMP_EMAIL_UK
    rsc_cpu: 968516   rsc_io: 27
    ix_sel:  0.0000e+00   ix_sel_with_filters:  1.0000e+00
  Access Path: index-ffs  Resc:  27  Resp:  27
  Access Path: index (index-ffs)
    Index: EMP_EMP_ID_PK
```

SQL Profiles

We mentioned SQL profiles in Chapter 13 when discussing the SQL Tuning Advisor. SQL profiles come into play when the Optimizer operates in the Automatic Tuning mode. In this mode, the

Optimizer collects and uses auxiliary information to both mitigate estimation errors as well as build an SQL profile. When available, the Optimizer also uses the SQL execution plan history stored in AWR's WRH$_SQL_PLAN table. The SQL profile also changes the Optimizer settings as required—for example, it may change the OPTIMIZER_MODE setting from ALL_ROWS to FIRST_ROWS to see if this will generate a more efficient plan. SQL profiling is invoked via the SQL Tuning Advisor information, and this is then presented as a recommendation to accept the profile. You saw an example of how this was done in Chapter 13. Once accepted, the additional costing information in the SQL profile takes effect when the same SQL is run in the normal mode.

This SQL profile enables the Query Optimizer to generate a well-tuned plan when executing later in the normal mode. This is in some ways similar to the use of outlines to force SQL to behave in a certain way. SQL profiling allows ill-written SQL to execute efficiently without having to change the original code, and is thus ideal for use in tuning third-party applications. A brief comparison of SQL profiles and outlines is in order. This is shown in Table 14.2.

TABLE 14.2

Comparison of Outlines and SQL Profiles

Feature	Outlines	SQL Profile
First appeared	Oracle 8i, improved in Oracle 9i with editing of stored outlines	Oracle Database 10g
Method	Uses hints to force a fixed SQL to behave in a certain way	Provides additional information at parse time to enable accurate costing
Flexibility	Once an outline is fixed, the plan is also fixed	Flexible because the additional information only helps in cost calculation and does not fix any execution path
Objects	Exposed via DBA_OUTLINES and DBA_OUTLINE_HINTS; manipulated via CREATE/DROP OUTLINE statement	Exposed via a number of SQL set–related objects including DBA_SQL_PROFILES and DBA_SQLTUNE_PLANS; managed via the DBMS_SQLTUNE package
Monitoring usage	Via the contents of the V$SQL.OUTLINE_SID column in Oracle 9i and the V$SQL.OUTLINE_CATEGORY column in Oracle 8i	Via the contents of the V$SQL.SQL_PROFILE column

SQL profiles are also grouped under categories and thus can be used to limit the scope of the profile. A DEFAULT category exists as a catch-all for unnamed SQL profiles and it matches the SQLTUNE_CATEGORY initialization profile. Particular sessions that change their SQLTUNE_CATEGORY event value at the session level will enable use of a previously named category of SQL profiles. This way, you can provide limited SQL profile–based tuning for testing purposes even on a production system with other live SQL queries. SQL profiles can be used for SELECT, INSERT, UPDATE, DELETE, CREATE TABLE AS SELECT (CTAS), and MERGE statements only.

SQL profiles run into the same issues that outlines face—the SQL statement that needs to use the profile has to hash exactly to the same value generated previously. This means that SQLs that contain literal values that change cannot use previously stored SQL profiles. SQL profiles also cannot be moved across databases because there is no way to export or import them as is done with object statistics.

The creation and use of an SQL profile can be determined using a little-known hidden parameter named _STN_TRACE. A relevant snippet from this trace is shown in Listing 14.4. Notice the different operations that the Optimizer attempts and the explanation of terms, which you can use elsewhere to determine their meaning in other types of traces, notably the 10053 trace!

LISTING 14.4   Snippet of the SQL Profile Trace

```
Registered qb: SEL$1 0x7b65a0b8 (PARSER)
  signature (): qb_name=SEL$1 nbfros=1 flg=0
    fro(0): flg=4 objn=51338 hint_alias="EMPLOYEES"@"SEL$1"
***************************
Predicate Move-Around (PM)
***************************
PM: Considering predicate move-around in SEL$1 (#0).
PM:   Checking validity of predicate move-around in SEL$1 (#0).
CBQT: Validity checks failed for 3ghpkw4yp4dzm.
CVM: Considering view merge in query block SEL$1 (#0)
CBQT: Validity checks failed for 3ghpkw4yp4dzm.
***************
Subquery Unnest
***************
SU: Considering subquery unnesting in query block SEL$1 (#0)
*************************
Set-Join Conversion (SJC)
*************************
SJC: Considering set-join conversion in SEL$1 (#0).
***************************
Predicate Move-Around (PM)
***************************
PM: Considering predicate move-around in SEL$1 (#0).
PM:   Checking validity of predicate move-around in SEL$1 (#0).
PM:     PM bypassed: Outer query contains no views.
apadrv-start: call(in-use=352, alloc=1048), compile(in-use=26960, alloc=29832)
kkoqbc-start
            : call(in-use=408, alloc=1048), compile(in-use=27720, alloc=29832)
********************************************
Current SQL statement for this session:
select count(*) from hr.employees
********************************************
Legend
The following abbreviations are used by optimizer trace.
CBQT - cost-based query transformation
```

LISTING 14.4   Continued

```
JPPD - join predicate push-down
PM - predicate move-around
CVM - complex view merging
SPJ - select-project-join
SJC - set join conversion
SU - subquery unnesting
qb - query block
LB - leaf blocks
DK - distinct keys
LB/K - average number of leaf blocks per key
DB/K - average number of data blocks per key
CLUF - clustering factor
NDV - number of distinct values
Resp - response cost
Card - cardinality
Resc - resource cost
NL - nested loops (join)
SM - sort merge (join)
HA - hash (join)
dmeth - distribution method
  1: no partitioning required
  2: value partitioned
  4: right is random (round-robin)
  512: left is random (round-robin)
  8: broadcast right and partition left
  16: broadcast left and partition right
  32: partition left using partitioning of right
  64: partition right using partitioning of left
  128: use hash partitioning dimension
  256: use range partitioning dimension
  2048: use list partitioning dimension
  1024: run the join in serial
  0: invalid distribution method
sel - selectivity
ptn - partition
```

Effective Use of Histograms

Essentially, a *histogram* is information about the values in a selected column. Histograms are used in Oracle to describe the skew in the distribution of data in columns that hold non-unique, repeating values. In other words, when a few distinct values in that column form a sizeable portion of the row count, and this count is not uniformly distributed, then histograms can describe this distribution mathematically. Thus, when histograms are created on key columns like those that contain a set of repeating values, such as the state ID in a national cell phone company's customer table, they can quantify the spread of distinct values. Histograms exert a great influence on the Optimizer and are essentially "buckets" that specify a range of values in a column. The Oracle kernel sorts the non-null values in the column and groups them into the specified number of these buckets so that each bucket holds the same number of data points, bounded by the end-point value of the previous bucket. Histograms can be either height balanced or width balanced. In other words, if the distinct sets of values are less than the number of histograms that are required to be collected, a width-balanced histogram is created, otherwise, a height-balanced histogram is collected. Histograms can be created and used on numeric, character, and date columns.

In the simplest case, when the Optimizer considers the value of the predicate in a WHERE clause, and histograms are available for that key column, the Optimizer calculates the "cost" of access for both an indexed read as well as a full table scan (FTS), based on the frequency of occurrence of that key value. Depending on the frequency of occurrence of the value, the Optimizer may decide to use an FTS rather than an indexed read for popular values that occur frequently, because this option may be less costly in terms of total I/O. On the other hand, the Optimizer may decide to use indexed reads for less-popular keys, again based on the total I/O. In a slightly more complex setting, the Optimizer considers histograms while determining the optimal order in which tables should be joined. For example, when presented with the need to join multiple tables using join conditions on columns that contain histograms, the Optimizer can determine the order in which the tables should be joined, executing the join that is expected to produce the least number of rows first, followed by joins that produce successively larger numbers of rows. All this occurs without the programmer manipulating the SQL, and this concept thus lends itself to reduced program "tuning fixes" as data patterns change. This is a key strength of the Optimizer and is an important reason for considering histograms in your database.

There is a caveat, though. Until Oracle 9i, the Optimizer considered histograms during the SQL parse phase only if literal values (of the form WHERE PREDICATE = '123') rather than bind variables (of the form WHERE PREDICATE = :key_value) were used in SQL conditional clauses. From Oracle 9i Release 9.0.1 on, the Optimizer could "peek" at the value of the bind variable prior to the parse, and use histograms when available. The downside, though, in both Oracle 9i and Oracle Database 10g, is that the execution plan is generated based on the current value of the bind variable at the time of parsing and is thus "fixed" during the first parse. Hence, subsequent changes in the value of the bind variable do not change the path. This has resulted in a number of performance issues, so you need to keep this information in mind. This functionality is turned on by default in both Oracle 9i and Oracle Database 10g, but can be manually disabled via the undocumented and hidden parameter _OPTIM_PEEK_USER_BINDS. Of course, changes should be done only under Oracle Support's direction!

In Oracle Database 10g, histograms are not automatically created on all key columns, nor should they be. Histograms are collected using the very same built-in DBMS_STATS PL/SQL package, which collects object statistics for tables, indexes, and columns for use by the Optimizer. They are collected based on the METHOD_OPT parameter of any of the DBMS_STATS.GATHER_*object*_STATS procedures. Histograms are collected only when the clause FOR ALL [INDEXED ¦ HIDDEN] COLUMNS *size_clause* is set and the *size_clause* is set to a value more than 1. The number specifies the number of buckets that the histogram should have; the maximum is 254.

Both Oracle Database 10g and Oracle 9i allow histograms to be selectively created only for those columns that are determined to have a skew. This is done at the time of sampling when METHOD_OPT is set to FOR ALL COLUMNS SIZE AUTO. In this case, Oracle automatically determines which columns require histograms and the number of buckets (size) of each histogram by considering both the data distribution in the column as well as the usage from COL_USAGE$. The SKEWONLY option does not consider column usage and hence should not be used. Another option, new in Oracle Database 10g, is the REPEAT keyword, which collects histograms only for those columns that already have them—in effect refreshing the values. You can also manually specify which columns should have histograms and the size of each histogram individually. For further details and examples of how this is done, refer to the *Oracle Database 10g PL/SQL Package and Types Reference* as well as the *Oracle Database 10g Performance Tuning Guide*.

Histograms can be viewed using ALL_HISTOGRAMS, ALL_PART_HISTOGRAMS, ALL_TAB_HISTOGRAMS, and their DBA_% equivalents. Columns containing histograms can be determined from the NUM_BUCKETS column in the ALL_TAB_COLUMNS; this value should be greater than 1 for histograms to exist. Note that all columns that have statistics attached to them by virtue of being analyzed will have at least two entries in the ALL_TAB_COLUMNS view, with these entries containing the low and high values for the column. Histogram information for those columns that have more than two rows is available in the ALL_HISTOGRAMS view.

There are some downsides to collecting and using histograms:

- They take up space in the data-dictionary portion of the shared pool and use additional resources and storage space during statistics collection.

- They add some minimal overhead during SQL parse time because the Optimizer now must compute additional paths.

- As with any other object statistics, they can become stale, and their staleness can produce a greater impact than with some of the other object statistics.

New Features in Oracle Database 10g Release 2

Oracle Database 10g Release 2 provides a number of enhancements to the Optimizer. Notable among them is the capability to transport SQL profiles between databases. This allows you to generate a SQL profile and SQL tuning sets in the production environment and transport them to the development and user acceptance database, just as you would transfer object statistics. SQL profiles can now be matched to SQL text with literals after they have been normalized into bind variables (somewhat similar to the effects of the CURSOR_SHARING initialization parameter). A new view, V_$SQL_STATS, can display, among other interesting tidbits, a LAST_ACTIVE_TIME column. SQL statistics are also updated once every five seconds for a SQL that is still in progress.

As well, it is evident from the increase in the number of hidden parameters (1,047 in Release 2 versus the 911 in Release 1) that a number of these new parameters will continue to influence the Optimizer, making it even better.

Summary

In this chapter, you saw how the Optimizer in Oracle Database 10g helps enhance overall performance by using innovative ways of making sure that the best execution paths are chosen. Along the way, you delved into details about the Optimizer including histograms, dynamic sampling, and SQL profiles. We discussed some tips—as well as potential traps—for using the Optimizer in Oracle Database 10g.

PART IV

Scaling and Availability with Oracle Database 10g

15 Utilizing Oracle Database 10g Real Applications Clusters

16 Utilizing 10g Physical and Logical Standby with Data Guard

17 Effectively Using Flashback Technologies

18 Leveraging Grid Technology Features

15

Utilizing Oracle Database 10g Real Applications Clusters

IN THIS CHAPTER

Oracle 10g RAC Overview	313
Cluster Ready Services	314
Service Workload Management	323
10g RAC Installation and Migration Enhancements	324
10g RAC Manageability Enhancements	326
Automatic Storage Management for Cluster Management	331
Third-Party Cluster Management Support	333
Limited Rolling Upgrade with OPATCH	334
10g RAC Tips for Better Use	335
Advanced RAC Features in Oracle Database 10g Release 2	337

Oracle 10g RAC Overview

Oracle continues to redefine its high-availability solution by expanding the solid footprint achieved with Oracle 9i Real Application Clusters (RAC) and previously introduced with Oracle 6.2 Oracle Parallel Server (OPS). Oracle 10g RAC takes the 9i RAC technology to the next level by providing a complete clustering solution on all supported platforms. Oracle 10g RAC now offers its own portable clusterware and volume-management solutions with the introduction of Cluster Ready Services (CRS) and Automatic Storage Management (ASM),

10g RAC Standard Edition

Previously, you needed Oracle Enterprise Edition to install and configure Oracle RAC. Starting with Oracle 10g, however, any customer who has purchased the 10g Standard Edition, not Standard Edition One, is allowed to use the RAC option under the specific license limitations within the Standard Edition. If you use 10g Standard Edition RAC, the use of ASM is mandatory. All other third-party clusterware is prohibited. Also, 10g Standard Edition RAC users have a maximum of four CPUs within the entire cluster.

as detailed in Chapter 4, "Setting Up Automatic Storage Management." With the combination of CRS and ASM, there is no need to purchase any third-party cluster-management software for your RAC environment. Oracle 10g RAC also provides many enhancements for the Oracle database, such as improved installation process via the Oracle Universal Installer (OUI), improved cluster-migration support via the Database Upgrade Assistant (DBUA), improved rolling patch upgrade support with OPATCH, workload management via the 10g Service Management framework, and greater flexibility for adding and removing the number of nodes within a predefined cluster via the Database Configuration Assistant (DBCA). This chapter reviews the latest clustering features that have been introduced specifically for 10g Release 1 RAC, as well as previews what's to come with Oracle 10g Release 2.

Cluster Ready Services

Prior to Oracle 10g RAC, customers who purchased the RAC option had to depend on third-party vendors—such as Veritas, Sun, HP, and IBM—for cluster communication and management support. Depending on what flavor of cluster support you selected, your install and management responsibilities could differ from one to the other. Having different vendors for cluster management and the database was problematic and introduced many obstacles for administrators, such as multiple vendors to contact for support and licensing management. This, as you can imagine, could lead to finger-pointing among vendors if serious problems occurred. Oracle 10g RAC now eliminates these issues with the introduction of Cluster Ready Services.

Cluster Ready Services is a new feature, introduced with Oracle 10g RAC that provides high-availability services for cluster communication and management. CRS is the first true portable clusterware that is integrated within the 10g RDBMS kernel and offers all the features of traditional operating-system cluster-management support such as node connectivity, membership, messaging, and recovery. With CRS, users can expect quick, consistent, and reliable clusterware support with no dependencies on any platform-specific clusterware. Starting with Oracle 10g, CRS is required to be installed and running prior to installing Oracle 10g RAC.

Because CRS is tightly integrated with 10g RAC, there is no need to purchase additional cluster-management support from third-party vendors, making Oracle support your one-stop shop for cluster support. However, users who wish to continue using third-party clusterware for cluster support will still be able to utilize all the benefits of CRS. When enabled, CRS can interact and coordinate cluster-management services with vendor clusterware. Likewise, CRS also supports third-party cluster file system support for physical file storage as well as generic raw devices or Automatic Storage Management (ASM), as discussed in Chapter 4.

Cluster Ready Services Architecture

The incorporation of CRS and 10g RAC provides high-availability support for the instances in the cluster as well as any supporting applications. CRS enables this support by defining individual resources to monitor. A CRS resource is a named process or entity whose availability is maintained and monitored by the CRS clusterware. Each resource is automatically created and registered to CRS either during installation or manually by a standard command line interface. Each defined resource within CRS has a profile built in, which includes metadata about the specific resource. This resource metadata is stored in the Oracle Cluster Registry (OCR) and describes management information for CRS such as how to start, stop, and check the health of the resource.

Out of the box, CRS automatically manages the following resources across each node of a cluster:

- The Global Services daemon (GSD)

- The Oracle Notification Services daemon (ONS)

- Virtual IPs (VIPs)

- RAC Database

- RAC instances

- RAC Database Listeners

- RAC Database Services

Within this group, CRS classifies each resource into one of two distinct subgroups to manage: nodeapps and database-related resources. Nodeapps are specific resources that pertain to the individual node within the cluster; each node will have its own set of the resources. Nodeapps include the Global Services Daemon (GSD), Oracle Notification Services Daemon (ONS), virtual IPs (VIPs), and the RAC Database Listeners. The second group, database-specific resources, pertains to the resources that are shared among all nodes in the cluster. The database-specific resources include the database, instances, and any services that are configured for the specific instances. The GSD, ONS, and VIP nodeapps are created and registered with OCR during the installation of RAC. The database listener, database, instance, and service CRS resources can be created either during the RAC installation process or afterward by using manual tools such as SRVCTL, DBCA, and NETCA.

The heart of the CRS technology relies on three main components that run as daemons on UNIX platforms or as services in Windows environments:

- **The CRSD daemon.** CRSD is the main engine for all high-availability operations and provides management for application resources. CRSD will start, stop, and fail over application resources as well as spawn separate processes to check the application resource health if

Running OCSSD in Single-Instance Mode with ASM

The OCSSD is also used in single-instance environments to fully utilize Automatic Storage Management (when used). Failure of the OCSSD in a single-instance environment will not cause a full system reboot as noted with a RAC environment.

As reported in metalink note: 277274.1, if the CRSD daemon detects any failure with the VIP (Virtual IP) and the VIP can not be restarted, CRSD will stop all dependent resources, including the listener, the ASM instance (if it exists), and the database instance. Because CRS will gracefully stop all dependent resources, no errors will be evident in the ASM or database alert log. To verify whether the VIP experienced an error, review the CRSD log files within the $CRS_HOME/crs/log directory for the following message:

```
ora.nodename.vip on nodename went OFFLINE
unexpectedly
```

To resolve this issue (logged as BUG #3718601), the root cause of the failure of the VIP must be uncovered. The trace file for the VIP will be found in the ORA_CRS_HOME/racg/dump directory—the file will be named ora.*nodename*.vip.trc—where *nodename* is the name of the node. The problem is very likely to be due to current known issues with timeouts of the VIP under a high load. A possible workaround for this timeout issue is to increase the timeout values for the VIP from its default setting of 60 seconds to 120 seconds. This can be accomplished by the following:

1. `cd $CRS_HOME/bin`

2. Create a .cap file for each .vip resource on each node, such as:

   ```
   ./crs_stat -p ora.ccpfna.vip >
   /tmp/ora.ccpfna.vip.cap
   ```

3. Update the .cap file using the following syntax and values:

   ```
   ./crs_profile -update ora.ccpfna.vip
   -dir /tmp -o ci=120,st=120
   ```

   (Where `ci` = the `CHECK_INTERVAL` and `st` = the `SCRIPT_TIMEOUT` value.)

4. Finally, re-register the new file using the `-u` option:

   ```
   ./crs_register ora.ccpfna.vip -dir
   /tmp -u
   ```

needed. It maintains its configuration data within the OCR.

- **The OCSSD daemon.** OCSSD facilitates cluster communication among all nodes within the cluster. It provides basic node-management services such as node membership, cluster locking, and split brain protection. If third-party cluster-ware is installed, OCSSD can integrate to provide the same services for cluster management.

- **The EVMD daemon.** EVMD provides event notification in case CRS detects any errors that have occurred. It will create another process, EVMLOGGER, to facilitate any event-logging activities if needed.

Of these processes, OCSSD and EVMD (like-wise for EVMLOGGER) run as the `oracle` user ID, while CRSD runs as `root`. If for some reason the CRSD or the EVMD processes experience any failure, they will restart automatically. However, any failure with OCSSD will lead to a full system reboot.

Installing Cluster Ready Services

Before installing CRS and 10g RAC, DBAs and system administrators must familiarize themselves with the capabilities of CRS. Following are a few key items to consider prior to installing 10g CRS:

- CRS is shipped on a separate CD-ROM within your 10g CD pack. You must use this CD to install CRS, not the 10g Database CD.

- Installing CRS is mandatory prior to installing 10g RAC. CRS is not required and cannot work with any release prior to Oracle 10g. CRS should never be disabled with 10g RAC.

- CRS must be installed in its own unique location (for example, CRS_HOME), not within any existing ORACLE_HOME.

- CRS can run either on top of third-party clusterware or without any third-party clusterware.

- Shared disk or raw file locations for the Oracle Cluster Registry (OCR) and voting file must be configured prior to installing CRS. Due to the nature of these files, they must be placed on shared devices, either on cluster file systems or shared raw devices. As part of the CRS install, you will be prompted to provide two locations for these files. On average, both files should grow to about 100MB each. Note that in 10g Release 1, neither the OCR nor the voting file for Oracle clusterware can be stored in ASM.

- Ensure that user equivalence has been established on all nodes within the cluster. Within the Oracle 10g OUI (which actually first appeared with 9.2.0.5), Oracle will first attempt to use SSH and SCP. If these two are detected then the OUI will use these for all user equivalence needs. If SSH and SCP are not detected, then the OUI will revert back to RSH and RCP as used in previous versions of the OUI. For proper user equivalence, the oracle user should be able to perform a remote login to each node in the cluster (including node connections to itself) without the need for a password.

- Once CRS has been installed, the OCR location is referenced in /var/opt/oracle/ocr.loc using the ocrconfig_loc parameter for UNIX environments and in HKEY_LOCAL_MACHINE\Software\Oracle\OCR\ using the ocrconfig_loc parameter for Windows environments.

> **Moving the OCR Location After Installation**
>
> If you ever run into the situation that you need to move your OCR location, stop your CRS stack on all nodes (using init.crs stop), edit your ocr.loc with the new setting for ocrconfig_loc, restore your OCR from one of the automated backups using ocrconfig -restore, use ocrcheck to verify your new environment, and then reboot your server to restart the CRS stack.

- The following network interfaces must also be configured prior to installing CRS:

- Public Interface

- Private Interface

- Virtual Interface (must be Public)

These network interfaces must also be configured within your /etc/hosts file on each node with unique names that are easy to remember for each. During the install, you will be prompted for these entries:

- The CRS stack is started by running the root.sh file at the end of the CRS install. This step must be executed successfully on each node of your cluster.

- Only one CRS stack (CRS daemons) can be running per node of your RAC cluster.

- The supported method to stop the CRS stack is to shut down the node or use the /etc/inittab/init.crs stop command.

■ The only supported method to restart the CRS daemons is a complete server reboot. The manual method to start the CRS stack, `/etc/inittab/init.crs start`, has caused some abnormal behavior that leads to bug #3214576. Manual CRS restart is not supported until 10.1.0.4 or higher.

After you have configured all necessary components for your cluster (namely shared storage, network, and interconnect components), you can begin the CRS install. Again, CRS is shipped on a separate CD-ROM. You will need to mount this CD, run runInstaller, and follow the prompts from the OUI. You will find the CRS install to be fairly straightforward and error-free, assuming that all components are configured properly.

The following is a brief example of correctly installing the new 10g CRS:

1. After starting runInstaller, the CRS install main page appears, as shown in Figure 15.1. Specify the unique `CRS_HOME` for the CRS install.

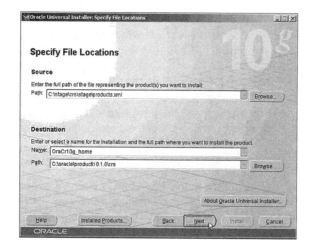

FIGURE 15.1
Initial screen for the 10g CRS install.

2. After specifying the `CRS_HOME`, choose the language desired, as shown in Figure 15.2.

3. On the Cluster Configuration page, specify the cluster name and your public and private node names for both nodes, as shown in Figure 15.3.

4. On the Specify Network Interface Usage page, you will see a list of clusterwide interfaces (see Figure 15.4). Select the correct public and private interface and click next.

5. If using Oracle Cluster File System (OCFS), you can format specified files for data and software storage. For ASM storage, do not format any logical drives, as shown in Figure 15.5.

6. On the Disk Configuration page, select the location for the OCR and voting disk, as shown with Figures 15.6 and 15.7.

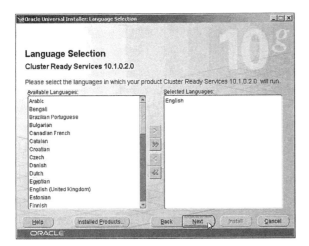

FIGURE 15.2
Language selection for the 10g CRS install.

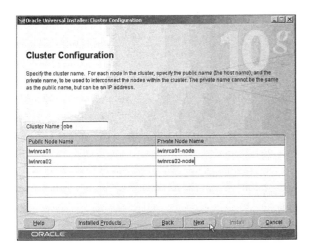

FIGURE 15.3
Cluster configuration for the 10g CRS install.

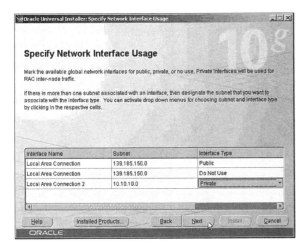

FIGURE 15.4
Network interface configuration for the 10g CRS install.

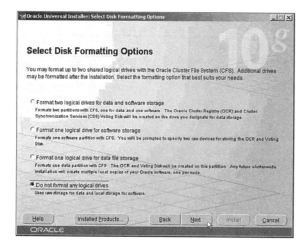

FIGURE 15.5
Disk-formatting options for the 10g CRS install.

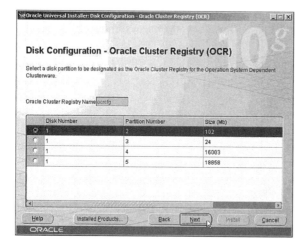

FIGURE 15.6
OCR configuration for the 10g CRS install.

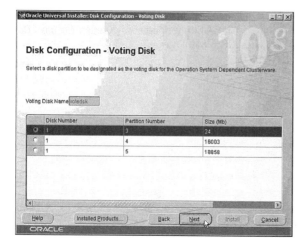

FIGURE 15.7
Voting-disk configuration for the 10g CRS install.

7. On the Summary page, shown in Figure 15.8, review the options you chose in the previous steps and then click the Install button to run the installer.

Starting with 10g Release 1, Oracle does not support the use of third-party clusterware for failover and restart of Oracle resources. When running 10g RAC, CRS should never be disabled.

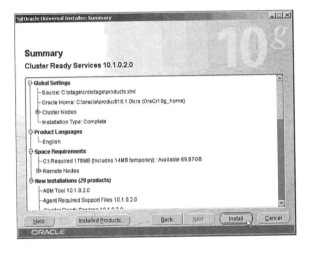

FIGURE 15.8
Overall summary for the 10g CRS install.

Depending on your cluster file system of choice, you will have the option of installing the CRS_HOME in a local or shared environment. Installing in a shared environment is very much like installing in a single environment where you have several shared mounts on which to install your files. These shared mounts can be accessed from all nodes in your cluster. However, you also can install locally on one node. If installing locally, you will be pleasantly surprised to learn that the 10g OUI will actually push the new CRS_HOME files to all other nodes in your cluster. This new method eliminates the need for separate installs on each node. If installing locally, be sure to note the location of all CRS_HOME log files for future reference. All CRS-related error and diagnostic files will be generated and stored locally on each node.

To verify that your CRS_HOME install was successful, you can use a few utilities from the CRS_HOME/bin directory. The first utility,

Installing CRS with a 10g Database Already in Place Using ASM

If you are trying to install CRS with a single-instance 10g database already in place using the new Automatic Storage Management feature, you will notice that an OCSSD daemon will already exist, running out of the pre-existing ORACLE_HOME. The OCSSD is needed for communications between the database and the ASM instance. With CRS, however, there should be only one OCSSD process, which will manage both RAC and non-RAC instances running out of the new CRS_HOME. Due to this, you will need to stop and remove the pre-existing OCSSD process by running the $ORACLE_HOME/bin/localconfig.sh script (for Windows, it's localconfig.bat). This script should be executed on all nodes that will become cluster members and also have a pre-existing non-RAC ORACLE_HOME using ASM. Stop all databases and ASM instances, log in as root, and run localconfig.sh. This will remove the entry from inittab and OCR. After you complete the script, you will be able to complete the new CRS install.

Re-running The CRS Root.sh

If you experience any issue while running the CRS root.sh, there is no need to de-install and re-install CRS. Once the problem affecting the execution of the `CRS root.sh` has been fixed, `root.sh` can be executed again.

Installing 10g CRS With Veritas or Fujitsu Cluster File System

Currently when installing 10g CRS on a Solaris cluster that does not have Sun Cluster installed, but has Veritas or Fujitsu clustering, you could hit a possible bug (3412743) in which the CRS daemons never start on the node. Basically, Veritas and Fujitsu clusters are incorrectly identified as a nonclustered Sun Cluster boot which prevents the CRS daemons from starting. The workaround is to modify the `$CRS_HOME/css/admin/init.cssd` before running the CRS `root.sh`:

[before SunOS definition]

```
VENDOR_CLUSTER_DAEMON_CHECK="PSEF ¦
$GREP 'dlmn[o]n' 1>$NULL 2>$NULL
```

[after SunOS definition]

```
VENDOR_CLUSTER_DAEMON_CHECK="null_
command"
```

This bug and workaround is also pointed out in the Veritas Storage Foundation 4.1 for Oracle RAC Installation guide. Before running the CRS `root.sh` you need to perform the following steps:

Log in as root user

Navigate to `$CRS_HOME/css/admin`

Run the following command:

```
        # patch init.cssd <
/opt/VRTSvcs/rac/patch/init.cssd.
patch
```

Once either one of these steps has been completed you can then run the CRS `root.sh` to start the CRS daemons.

olsnodes, will display each node name in your cluster on which CRS is currently running. Here's an example:

```
oracle@ccpfna> $CRS_HOME/bin/olsnodes
ccpfna
ccpfnb
ccpfnc
ccpfnd
```

When you have verified that CRS has been successfully installed and started on all nodes, you can proceed with the RDBMS install.

Troubleshooting the CRS Install

While running `root.sh`, you may experience errors if you do not have the proper environment configured. If you run into any errors during your CRS install, you will need to review the following directories under your CRS_HOME for trace file information:

- **$CRS_HOME/css/log.** Includes log and trace files for the OCSSD resources.

- **$CRS_HOME/css/init.** Includes core dumps for OCSSD.

- **$CRS_HOME/crs/log.** Includes log and trace files for CRSD resources.

- **$CRS_HOME/crs/init.** Includes core dumps for CRSD.

- **$CRS_HOME/evm/log.** Includes log and trace files for the EVMD and EMVLOGGER resources.

- **$CRS_HOME/evm/init.** Includes core dumps for EVMD.

- **$CRS_HOME/srvm/log.** Includes log and trace files for the OCR.

Oracle support has also published a MetaLink document that details the process of properly cleaning up from a failed CRS install: Note

#239998.1, "10g RAC: How to Clean Up After a Failed CRS Install." After you identify the issues to be resolved and follow the steps described in this MetaLink Note, you will be able to correct the problem and restart the install process.

Service Workload Management

Oracle 10g has expanded the usage of database services by offering enhanced support for workload management. The idea behind the 10g service-management framework is to improve the manageability and increase the availability, recoverability, and performance of resources that share the same functionality and/or expectations and are grouped as one logical unit of work. Although service management can be used in both single-instance and RAC databases, 10g RAC service management can span one or more instances within a cluster. This capability provides a single system image for competing resources running within a single instance or across multiple instances in a cluster. Now with 10g RAC, services running in a failed node can be automatically routed to a surviving node without users experiencing any noticeable outage. 10g CRS takes this a step further by restarting the failed node when available and relocating the misplaced services back to their original locations.

Within the new 10g service-management framework, two types of services can be utilized: application services and internal services. Application services are used to support business logic and/or requirements that you may have with your application or data. Within application services, the workload-management capabilities are further broken down into three separate categories:

- **Functional services.** Resources working together for a common business function or requirement.

- **Data-dependent services.** Resources that utilize services based on data key values.

- **Pre-connect services.** Resources that span a set of clustered instances to maximize availability requirements.

In addition to application services, Oracle 10g also offers two internal services for workload management:

- **SYS$BACKGROUND.** Used by related background processes for workload-management support.

- **SYS$USER.** Default service for user sessions not assigned with any application service.

Application services can be created, stopped, and even disabled, but internal services can never be stopped or disabled.

> **10g Service Management Limitations**
> Currently in 10g Release 1, you can only have 64 services per database—two internal services and 62 application services.

With Oracle 10g, anyone can create a new service by using the Database Configuration Assistant (DBCA), Server Control (SRVCTL), or manually with the DBMS_SERVICE package. For backward compatibility, services can also be created and started by using the SERVICE_NAMES initialization parameter.

10g RAC Installation and Migration Enhancements

Oracle 10g offers several exciting enhancements for RAC installation and migration. First, as mentioned earlier in this chapter, 10g introduces Cluster Ready Services (CRS). Because CRS provides the needed clusterware for the 10g RAC environment, you must install CRS before installing the RAC database. After you have verified that the CRS stack has been successfully installed and is operational on each node, you are ready for the RDBMS install.

Local Versus Shared Install

As you noticed while installing the CRS_HOME, you also have the option to install the RDBMS or ORACLE_HOME in a shared or local environment. Again, installing in a shared environment is very much like installing in a single environment. When installing in a shared environment, all ORACLE_HOME and ORACLE_BASE files can be accessed from any node within the cluster. For more information about managing RAC in a shared environment, please reference the section "Third-Party Cluster Management Support" later in this chapter.

Installing in a local environment is also the same as with your previous CRS install, but the files will be pushed to each remote node via the new 10g OUI. If installing locally, all ORACLE_BASE alert, trace, and diagnostic files will be generated locally on each node. Therefore, you will also need to reference the location of ORACLE_BASE for future reference. Local installs are actually preferred over shared installs, mainly to support the new rolling patch upgrades now available with 10g (actually, they've been available since 9.2.0.2). For more detail about rolling patch support, please reference the "Limited Rolling Upgrade with OPATCH" section later in this chapter.

Installing the 10g ORACLE_HOME

As pointed out in Chapter 2, "Installing Oracle Database 10g," the new installation method for Oracle 10g is much faster than ever before. The fact that the installation media are now distributed on one CD-ROM is an added bonus. Gone are the days of having to swap and/or stage disks in order to install the RDBMS. It's worth noting, however, that many items that were previously part of the database installation media have been relocated to another CD-ROM known as the "companion CD." Please check with your install documentation to determine whether you need anything from the companion CD after you install the RDBMS media.

> During the RAC install process, the 10g OUI will actually use SSH (Secure Shell) or RSH (Remote Shell) to perform tests on the nodes of your cluster. Be sure you have one of these utilities correctly configured (that is, without promoting for a password) before starting any installation.

The overall installation process for 10g RAC has been improved to provide a single-install image. This single-install image has been added to improve the experience of installing a RAC database as well as to support any future node additions if you choose to add any future nodes to your environment. With previous RAC installs, DBAs had the option of installing the RDBMS on all available nodes in a single operation, but because only one installation could be run at a time, all cluster nodes had to be consistent with the location of the ORACLE_HOME and installed products, and the installer could not detect any violations with the install process. The Oracle 10g OUI now ensures that the RAC installation proceeds after several prerequisite node checks. If any of your nodes are not correctly configured, the installation process will fail and display the necessary error message for correction.

Adding a Node to or Removing a Node from an Existing ORACLE_HOME

Another new feature with the 10g OUI is the ability to add a new node to an existing Oracle binary install. In this case, you have either added a new node to your RAC environment or you previously installed the product in a subset selection of nodes within the cluster. In any case, the 10g OUI will be able to successfully clone an existing product installation to the new node.

To perform the clone process, you must begin the installation process on a node where the ORACLE_HOME is currently located. When the Welcome screen appears, you have the choice to install from a stage location or install from an existing Oracle Home. In this case, you

> After you have a successful node list from the selected node page, your installation will continue in the same way as your previous install did.

will need to select to install from an existing Oracle Home and provide the correct name for the Oracle Home (source) for the cloning process. When you click the Next button, you will see the Add Node page. Here you can select the nodes (target) that you wish to add the previously selected Oracle Home. When you click the Next button, the 10g OUI will perform the same checks as before. Again, these checks are needed to ensure that the node will be a successful addition into the cluster installation. If any errors exist, the installation process will fail, and you will see the specific error message for you to correct. After clicking Next, you will see an informational page of selected nodes from which you can clone the source Oracle Home. From this page, if you see a node that is no longer part of the installation cluster, it will have a Not Available message. Before proceeding with this installation, you must remove or correct the inventory information for the missing node. If this is not corrected or if the node is not removed, the installation process will fail when you try to update the inventory on the selected nodes. To remove any unwanted nodes from your environment, use the Inventory Dialog page discussed in a moment.

To remove or detach a node from an existing Oracle Home, you must use the Inventory Dialog page. To access this page, click the Installed Products link on one of the early install screens or click Detach Nodes on the Selected Node Informational page as described previously. The Inventory Dialog page displays a list of nodes, and a list of products installed on each node. To remove a node, select the target node from the list, and then click Remove Nodes at the bottom of the page. Detaching a node using the Inventory Dialog page does not remove the entire ORACLE_HOME contents from the target node, but simply relinks the target node without the RAC option. Actually, you could still use the ORACLE_HOME in a single-node environment; in order to completely remove the ORACLE_HOME contents, however, you will need to access the Deinstall Products page from the Welcome page.

Migrating from a Previous Release

The 10g Database Upgrade Assistant (DBUA) has been updated to provide support for migrating previous versions of RAC databases to a 10g RAC environment. Specifically, 10g DBUA can now upgrade Oracle 8 and Oracle 8i Oracle Parallel Server (OPS) databases to 10g RAC, as well as support Oracle 9i RAC–to–10g RAC. Upon successful completion of the 10g DBUA migration, all necessary CRS resources are created and started. DBAU actually ensures that the required CRS nodeapps (GSD, VIP, ONS, and listeners) exist on each node within the cluster. Overall, DBUA has the same functionality as it did in Oracle 9i; you will, however, notice additional wizard pages specifically designed for detecting errors for cluster migrations.

10g RAC Manageability Enhancements

Oracle 10g offers a more mature framework for managing a RAC environment. With the introduction of the new Oracle Cluster Registry to the enhanced RAC support for commonly used database utilities, 10g RAC now supports clusters of up to 64 nodes on all certified platforms.

Oracle Cluster Registry

Starting with Oracle 10g, the Oracle 8i and 9i Server Manageability Repository (SRVM) has been redesigned and is referred to as the Oracle Cluster Registry (OCR). The OCR, like its predecessor, is used to maintain the necessary information about the high-availability components in your RAC environment, such as databases, instances, and node information. With the introduction of CRS, the OCR also maintains the information for the required resources defined within CRS such as node applications, services, instances, and databases. During the install of CRS, you are prompted for the location of the OCR and voting disk. If migrating from a previous release, the SRVM will be converted to the OCR. You can place the OCR either on raw devices or shared storage that is managed by a certified cluster file system. Note that in 10g Release 1 neither the OCR nor the voting file for Oracle Clusterware can be stored in ASM. During system startup, CRS will read the contents of the OCR to determine the necessary resources to bring up. Also, due to the redesign and introduction of OCR, the `srvConfig.loc` configuration file has been renamed the `ocr.loc` file.

Although the OCR primarily manages RAC environments, if you use Automatic Storage Management (ASM) for a single-instance environment, the OCR is also created to serve as a configuration file for ASM. In a RAC environment, there is only one OCR for the entire cluster For a single-instance environment using ASM, however, the OCR is shared for all databases per server.

Considered the backbone for RAC manageability, the OCR should always be protected in case of media failure. In 10g Release 1, the OCR and voting disks are not mirrored and rely on protection from third-party redundancy support. You can, however, use a set of new commands that will allow you to back up, restore, export, import, and perform integrity checks against the OCR. Three commands that you can use for cluster repository maintenance include `ocrconfig`, `ocrdump`, and `ocrcheck`.

For `ocrconfig`, you can use the following options for repository maintenance:

- **backuploc.** This option enables you to change the default location where OCR backups are stored. The default location is under the directory $CRS_HOME/cdata/*cluster_name* where *cluster_name* is the unique name you will assign to the cluster configuration. Also, Oracle automatically takes backups of the OCR every four hours to this location. For recovery purposes, Oracle will always keep the last three backups, a day-old backup, as well as a week-old backup in this location.

- **showbackup.** This option details the location of backups, with timestamp and node name.

- **restore** *filename*. This option restores an OCR backup identified by the *filename* parameter, which you provide.

- **export** *filename*. This option exports the OCR to the *filename* parameter, which you provide.

- **import** *filename*. This option imports the OCR with the *filename* parameter, which you provide.

> By using the export and import options with ocrconfig, you can copy your OCR contents across different platforms and even to different storage devices (for example, from CFS to raw partitions).

- **upgrade.** This option, which is called automatically by OUI as part of the CRS installation, upgrades your OCR from a previous release.

- **downgrade.** This option allows you to revert your OCR to a previous release. All instances within the cluster must be down if this option is used.

- **help.** This option displays the help for the various options.

The ocrdump command allows you to view the contents of the OCR. ocrdump only has one option, *filename*, which represents the location and name of the ASCII dump file. The ocrcheck command performs block integrity checks on the OCR and displays valuable information such as the total space used, total space available, and current version.

Most of the administration on the OCR is handled implicitly by most of the 10g utilities such as DBCA, EM, and so on during installation and/or configuration. Before modifying the OCR with any of these commands, it is recommended that you review the latest information regarding these utilities from MetaLink and the latest version of the *Oracle Real Application Clusters Administrators Guide*. Also, if you ever experience a condition wherein you need to repair or restore the OCR, Oracle support has published a very detailed MetaLink note about this process: Note #268937.1, "Repairing or Restoring an Inconsistent OCR in RAC."

New Support for 10g Utilities

New 10g RAC high-availability (HA) support has been added to many commonly used database utilities. The Server Control (SRVCTL) utility retained all its functionality from 9i Release 2, but now has new commands to support 10g-specific items. SRVCRL is now fully integrated with 10g CRS because the objects managed with SRVCTL are now administrated by CRS. With 10g

SRVCTL, you can manage ASM instances, services, and nodeapps. Three new commands provide you the capabilities to manage these new objects with SRVCTL: `enable`, `disable`, and `relocate`. The `enable` and `disable` commands record the persistent state in OCR that is used to decide whether the specific resource can run under CRS. The resources used by these commands include services, databases, and instances. The `relocate` command can be used with services only when moving a workload to another instance within your cluster.

The 10g Database Configuration Assistant (DBCA) also has been improved by providing more support for RAC databases. When using 10g DBCA, the first screen will prompt you to choose between creating an Oracle RAC database or an Oracle single-instance database if the CRS stack is properly configured and running (as shown in Figure 15.9).

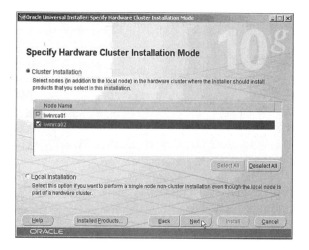

FIGURE 15.9
Installation method using 10g DBCA.

If you do not receive the Oracle RAC option via DBCA, you will need to ensure that CRS is up and running. The next few screens allow you to choose the database options and the nodes to which instances will be created. Also, as shown in Figure 15.10, 10g DBCA gives you three choices for shared storage of your database files: file system (cluster file system for RAC environments), Automatic Storage Management (ASM), or raw devices.

At the end of database creation, DBCA adds the necessary configuration to CRS and the OCR, and configures the listener and VIP end points if they are not present via the VIP configuration assistant (VIPCA). VIPCA is called when you execute `root.sh` at the end of the database installation (only on the first node; all other nodes will not call VIPCA). You need to enter your virtual IP information via VIPCA, as shown in Figure 15.11.

Upon successful installation of VIPCA, the necessary services are started on all available nodes within the cluster (as shown in Figure 15.12).

Finally, DBCA now has support to create and manage 10g services, add and remove RAC instances from preconfigured databases, and establish a transparent application failover (TAF) policy for your RAC environment.

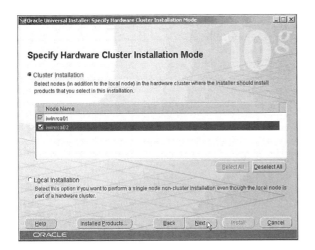

FIGURE 15.10
File-storage options using 10g DBCA.

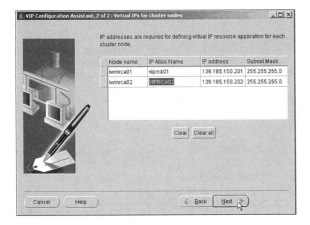

FIGURE 15.11
Configuring virtual IPs using the 10g VIPCA.

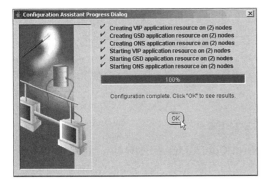

FIGURE 15.12   10g VIPCA configuration
summary.

After using DBCA to create your RAC database, you can verify your install was correct by using the crs_stat utility from the $CRS_HOME/bin directory. You can use crs_stat to confirm that all VIP, GSD, and ONS resources were configured correctly, as well as any database, listener, and instance information for your entire RAC environment. Usually, the naming method for crs_stat uses the ora.*hostname*.service format—for example:

```
oracle@ccpfna> $CRS_HOME/bin/crs_stat

NAME=ora.ccpfna.gsd
TYPE=application
TARGET=ONLINE
STATE=ONLINE on ccpfna

NAME=ora.ccpfna.ons
TYPE=application
TARGET=ONLINE
STATE=ONLINE on ccpfna

NAME=ora.ccpfna.vip
TYPE=application
TARGET=ONLINE
STATE=ONLINE on ccpfna
...

NAME=ora.ccpfnb.gsd
TYPE=application
TARGET=ONLINE
STATE=ONLINE on ccpfnb

NAME=ora.ccpfnb.ons
TYPE=application
TARGET=ONLINE
STATE=ONLINE on ccpfnb

NAME=ora.ccpfnb.vip
TYPE=application
TARGET=ONLINE
STATE=ONLINE on ccpfnb
...
```

Managing RAC with 10g Enterprise Manager

10g Enterprise Manager (EM) Database Control and Grid Control have been enhanced for better manageability for RAC environments. 10g EM provides consolidated views for monitoring and managing cluster databases at the cluster level. The addition of the new consolidated views provides a better, more manageable environment for DBAs to support Oracle 10g RAC. 10g EM is also intelligent enough to manage node membership, meaning that if nodes are added or removed, 10g EM will update accordingly. In addition to supporting RAC-specific metrics, 10g EM also supports configuration of 10g services and jobs for high availability within a RAC environment. To access the 10g EM Cluster home page, click the Targets tab, click All Targets, and then click the link that represents your cluster name. For more information about 10g EM Database Control or Grid Control, please reference the *Oracle 10g Enterprise Manager Concepts* guide.

Automatic Storage Management for Cluster Management

As you learned in Chapter 4, Oracle 10g now ships its own volume manager with the introduction of Automatic Storage Management, or ASM. ASM was designed to ease the tasks associated with database administration by automatically distributing and rebalancing files across all available raw devices within the ASM disk group. ASM offers a unique alternative for supporting the physical requirements of RAC by combining Oracle-managed files and volume-management technology, all within a shared cluster environment. This new concept offers RAC DBAs the opportunity to create Oracle data files in a self-managing and automatically stripped and mirrored clustered environment. By using ASM with RAC, DBAs can eliminate the manageability issues that come with raw devices as well as the extra layer of software required for a cluster file system.

Managing ASM with 10g RAC

In order to utilize ASM volume management for 10g RAC, each node within your cluster must have its own ASM instance. If you use the 10g DBCA utility to create your RAC database, DBCA will also provide you the opportunity to create your ASM instance.

Because ASM is designed specially for the Oracle database, only Oracle-specific files are supported. All other files can only be utilized locally on each node. Files supported with ASM include the following:

- Database files
- Control files
- Online redo log files
- Archived redo log files
- Flash recovery area files
- RMAN image copy and backupset files

Files not supported with ASM include the following:

- `ORACLE_HOME` install files
- `CRS_HOME` install files
- `ORACLE_BASE` files, including alert log, trace files, and so on
- CRS voting disk and OCR files

- Oracle 9i external table files

- Output data from UTL_FILE

- Any user application–specific files, such as XML or Java files

ASM Maximum File Size Limitation with 10g RAC

For files that are supported on ASM disk groups, Oracle does impose specific maximum file sizes depending on the redundancy level of each ASM disk group. These maximum file sizes are enforced regardless of whether you create your 10g tablespaces with the small file or BigFile syntax. Because the data file size limit essentially depends on the DB_BLOCK_SIZE of your database, the ASM limitations would only affect 32KB block size for small file tablespaces and all block sizes using BigFile tablespaces.

The maximum file sizes per redundancy level are as follows:

- External redundancy: 300GB

- Normal redundancy: 150GB

- High redundancy: 100GB

If you created your tablespace data files using normal syntax or specifically using the small file syntax, the maximum file sizes on ASM disk groups would be as follows:

- 4KB block size: 16GB

- 8KB block size: 32GB

- 16KB block size: 64GB

- 32KB block size: 100GB if on high redundancy. However, if on normal or external redundancy, the normal limit of 128GB will apply.

If you created your tablespace data files using the new BigFile syntax, then the ASM maximum file limits will apply to all block sizes:

- 2KB block size: Normally 8TB, but restricted by ASM limits

- 4KB block size: Normally 16TB, but restricted by ASM limits

- 8KB block size: Normally 32TB, but restricted by ASM limits

- 16KB block size: Normally 64TB, but restricted by ASM limits

- 32KB block size: Normally 128TB, but restricted by ASM limits

Because ASM is the new volume management/file system solution that is designed specifically for Oracle database files, it is now the recommended shared storage environment for all 10g RAC environments. Also, ASM does not require any additional license fee as you would find with third-party cluster vendors. If you are interested in migrating your clustered environment to ASM, please refer to the section "Non-ASM to ASM Migration" in Chapter 4.

Third-Party Cluster Management Support

As an alternative to regular raw devices or the new Automatic Storage Management feature, Oracle 10g also supports third-party cluster file–management software in a RAC environment. Third-party cluster-file management, referred to as "Cluster File System" (CFS), provides a shared environment where node members within a predefined cluster can access the same files. Third-party CFS not only supports the Oracle-specific files that are supported on ASM, but also supports the file types that are not supported by ASM, such as ORACLE_HOME and ORACLE_BASE files, CRS voting and OCR files, and any other relevant files needed to support your application.

Currently with Oracle 10g, only certified third-party cluster-management software may be used to support RAC. You can find a complete certification matrix of all certified platforms and third-party CFS providers by accessing MetaLink Note #184875.1, "How to Check the Certification Matrix for RAC," or via OTN at http://www.oracle.com/technology/support/metalink/index.html. If you click View Certifications by Product and then click Real Application Clusters, you can choose whatever platform you wish. Unlike ASM, customers who choose to use third-party cluster support must also purchase separate software licenses, additional to any Oracle licenses already purchased.

Possible Veritas Library Issue for 10g

As noted on MetaLink, Veritas 3.5 and 4.0 are certified with 9iR2 32bit RAC and Veritas 4.1 is certified with 9i and 10g 64bit RAC. However, during RAC installation, the Veritas library file called `libskgxp9.so` is overwritten with Oracle's `libskgxpu.so` library file, which is not the correct library file for Veritas CFS support. Proof of this can be found in your alert log if you see a message that reads `cluster interconnect IPC version: Oracle UPD/IP`. To properly link the correct library files, you will need to perform the following steps:

For Veritas 3.5 or 4.0 using 32bit 9i RAC:

1. `cd /opt/ORCLcluster/lib/9iR2`

2. `cp libskgxn2_32.so ../libskgxn2.so`

3. `cp /opt/ORCLcluster/lib/9iR2/ libskgxp92_32.so $ORACLE_HOME/ lib/libskgxp9.so`

4. `cp /opt/ORCLcluster/lib/9iR2/ libskgxp92_32.so $ORACLE_HOME/ lib/libskgxpu.so`

5. `cd $ORACLE_HOME/lib`

6. `ln -s /usr/lib/libodm.so libodm9.so`

7. `$ORACLE_HOME/rdbms/lib/make -f ins_rdbms.mk rac_on ioracle or run 'relink all' to relink the oracle libraries`

For Veritas 4.1 using 64bit 10g and 9i RAC:

1. `cd /opt/VRTSvcs/rac/lib`

2. `cp libskgxp10_64.so $ORACLE_HOME/lib/libskgxp10.so`

3. `cd $ORACLE_HOME/lib`

4. `mv libodm10.so libodm10.so.old`

5. `ln -s /usr/lib/sparcv9/libodm.so libodm10.so`

6. `relink libraries if necessary`

If the correct library is linked with Veritas, you should see the following from your alert log: `cluster interconnect IPC version: Veritas IPC 4.1.`

> ### Installing Oracle UDLM
>
> If you are using Sun Cluster 3.1, then you must install the Oracle-provided UDLM (UNIX Distributed Lock Manager or Cluster Membership Monitor) patch on each node that is part of your cluster installation. Even if you have a previous version of UDLM, you must install the Oracle 10g–provided UDLM before you install 10g CRS. To install the UDLM patch, review the procedures in the README file located under the /racpatch directory on the 10g CRS CD.

Limited Rolling Upgrade with OPATCH

Prior to Oracle 9i Release 2, whenever you were required to apply a patch to your RAC environment, you had to shut down all instances on each node under the specific ORACLE_HOME to be patched. As you can imagine, this did not sit well with programs that have high availability requirements. Starting with 9.2.0.2, and further enhanced in Oracle 10g, the server now supports the application of patches to nodes of a RAC cluster in a rolling manner with zero down time. Eligible patches can be applied using the opatch utility one node at a time, while the other active nodes in the cluster remain up and operational. Currently, only individual patches—that is, one-off patches, not complete patch sets—may be classified by Oracle support as rolling upgradeable. Usually, patches that have the highest probability of becoming rolling upgradeable have the following characteristics:

- They are unrelated to the RAC internode communication infrastructure.

- They have no effect on database contents.

- They do not modify shared database components such as file headers, kernel modules, and control files.

> ### Is Your One-Off Patch Rolling Upgradable?
>
> Starting with 9.2.0.4, all one-off patches released by Oracle support will be classified as either rolling or not rolling. One-off patches prior to 9.2.0.4 were originally classified as not rolling, but could become eligible for re-release as rolling upon analysis from Oracle support. If you would like to see whether a specific one-off patch could become eligible for re-release as rolling upgradeable, contact Oracle support to reopen the bug. If approved, the current patch will become obsolete and a new patch will be released as rolling upgradeable.

You can check to see whether a patch has been marked rolling upgradeable by running $opatch query –is_rolling or by checking the online_rac_installable flag for a value of TRUE within etc/config/inventory directory. Usually, the patch README file should detail whether the patch is rolling upgradeable, but when in doubt, you can use one of the aforementioned methods.

Also, rolling patch upgrades are not supported if your Oracle Home exists on a shared cluster file system. Rolling patch upgrades are only supported on clusters where each node has its own local copy of the Oracle binaries.

It is still possible to maintain high-availability requirements in your RAC environment in case your patch is not rolling upgradeable. For patches that do not qualify for this new feature, you can configure your RAC environment with 10g SQL Apply support via logical standby database. Before and after you complete the patch process, you can perform a scheduled switchover to ensure your user community does not experience any extended downtime. For more information about configuring 10g SQL Apply support for your RAC environment, please review the section titled "Applying Patch sets with Data Guard in Place" in Chapter 16, "Utilizing 10g Physical and Logical Standby with Data Guard."

10g RAC Tips for Better Use

This section discusses several best-practice tips and techniques for managing your 10g RAC environment. This section is not intended to serve as a "RAC how-to," but rather to document several operational essentials we have experienced for ourselves at various customer sites.

Cluster Interconnect

The cluster interconnect is the backbone of RAC performance. Having a poorly performing interconnect would cause many problems in any 9i or 10g RAC environment. Two main RAC components use the cluster interconnect for traffic between the nodes: Global Enqueue Service (GES) and Global Cache Service (GCS). Although the GES is used to synchronize access for various database resources, the GCS serves as the primary component of Cache Fusion. Cache Fusion, as you probably know from Oracle 9i, is used to eliminate the need for disk I/O (known as a *disk ping* in 8i) by allowing nodes to share contents of their buffer cache through the interconnect. Knowing this, DBAs must ensure that all GES and GCS traffic and block transfers are using the correct dedicated private interconnect and not being inadvertently routed over a public network. To check the current IP address assigned to your interconnect, you can run the following SQL*PLUS commands to generate a trace file in your udump directory, located via the USER_DUMP_DEST initialization parameter:

```
SQL> oradebug setmypid
SQL> oradebug ipc
SQL> oradebug tracefile_name
```

Generally, the use of gigabit ethernet with UDP (unreliable datagram protocol) has proven to be very solid in most RAC environments, but depending on the cluster file system used, we have learned that the use of low-latency or user-mode IPC protocol (such as Veritas LLT) rather than UDP is not preferred wherever possible. Your interconnect interface should use at the very least a 1GB transmission rate.

SGA Components

In most RAC environments, you want to increase your default buffer cache and share pool sizes more than you did as a single-node database. A good rule of thumb is to increase both pools by 15% due to the extra overhead associated with Oracle RAC. Because Cache Fusion is the fundamental component of RAC, you need to make more room for past image buffers (PI). A past image version of a block is generated before the current block is shipped via Cache Fusion. Accessing data that is already in cache is always more efficient.

Also, you must avoid unnecessary parsing where necessary. Library cache and row cache operations are globally coordinated, so excessive parsing means additional interconnect traffic.

Tablespaces

If you aren't already doing so, you need to use local managed tablespaces. Introduced with Oracle 8i and now enforced with Oracle 10g, using LMTs will save you the data dictionary hits on the UET$ and FET$ tables. You should also be using the 9i feature, automatic segment-space management (ASSM), in conjunction with LMTs. ASSM removes the overhead of dealing with freelists and freelist groups and uses bitmaps, similar to LMTs. Also, read-only tablespaces should be used to hold all read-only tables for your environment. Moving these tables to read-only tablespaces reduces interconnect traffic because reading from disk does not result in global cache gets.

Tables and Indexes

Nonselective index blocks can be subject to inter-instance contention, which leads to increased cache transfers and degrading DML performance. When necessary, use the 9i Alter Index Monitoring Usage feature to monitor the usage of any target indexes and remove any that are not being used.

If you are using sequences to populate table values, it is recommended that you cache your sequences using the CACHE keyword and increase the default cache value (which is currently 20).

Function-Dependent Routing

Eliminate disk hot spots and contention by manually routing specific users or functions to specific nodes within the clusters. Known as *application partitioning*, this procedure may save you from performance hits during peak times and overall interconnect traffic contention. This method does not require any application and/or code changes.

Object Partitioning

You can reduce contention on heavily used blocks on tables and indexes by using range, list, or hash partitioning. Range or list partitioning would be effective in conjunction with function-dependent routing. Hash partitioning may help to reduce buffer-busy contention by spreading out the buffer access distribution patters.

Running 10g RAC with 9i RAC in Same Environment

Oracle support does not recommend (but will support) running 9i RAC and 10g RAC in the same production environment due to high availability issues. Basically, this recommendation is due to how the 10g CRS algorithm (managed by the OCSSD daemon) handles split brain conditions. When a split brain occurs, the cluster is reconfigured into multiple partitions with each partition forming its own subcluster without the knowledge of each other existing. This would lead to corruption of the shared OCR, as each subcluster would race to assume ownership of the OCR. 10g CRS is designed to prevent split brain conditions by rebooting one or more nodes automatically to prevent OCR corruption, thereby affecting any critical applications that are running under Oracle 9i RAC on the same node.

CRS and ASM

Because CRS creates only one copy of the OCR and voting file, we recommend using third-party mirroring software to protect these files with 10g Release 1. 10g Release 2, as discussed in the next section, eliminates the need of third-party mirroring support by supporting multiple copies of these files.

Now that Oracle 10g ships with its own version of volume manager and file system, ASM is now considered the new best practice for cluster storage management.

Advanced RAC Features in Oracle Database 10g Release 2

The major focus for Oracle 10g Release 2 RAC is to increase the availability and support for Cluster Ready Services (renamed *Oracle Clusterware*) and to improve the availability, integrity, and performance for the overall 10g RAC environment. Following is a brief summary of what's with Oracle 10g Release 2 RAC support:

- Starting with Oracle Database 10g Release 2, Cluster Ready Services has been improved and renamed *Oracle Clusterware*. Oracle Clusterware can be implemented independently of Oracle RAC.

- Oracle Clusterware provides automatic clusterware file redundancy by maintaining two copies of the Oracle Cluster Registry (OCR) and three or more copies of the voting disk files. This extends the availability of Oracle Clusterware and eliminates the 10g Release 1 single point of failure and the need for third-party redundancy support.

- Oracle Clusterware provides an open API to extend support for third-party components running on the server.

- Oracle 10g Release 2 provides a new validation tool named *Cluster Verification Utility* (CVU) to ensure that all necessary components are correctly installed and configured during the initial deployment of a new RAC environment. CVU divides its deployment checks into the following stages: hardware and O/S setup, Cluster File System setup, Oracle Clusterware setup, RDBMS installation and configuration, node setup and addition, storage addition, and network modification.

- Oracle 10g Release 2 extends the support for connection load balancing by offering a new RAC load balancing advisory. This new advisory monitors the RAC workload activity across all instances in the cluster as well as analyzes the service level for each instance based on service time or throughput.

- Oracle 10g Release 2 provides new tracing and diagnostic services for the RAC environment. This support improves the diagnostics of cluster wait/hang conditions as well as provides more effective logging of Oracle Clusterware error and alert messages.

- Oracle 10g Release 2 supports clusters of up to 100 nodes on all certified platforms. In 10g Release 1, Oracle supported clusters of up to only 64 nodes.

- Oracle 10g Release 2 allows dynamic RMAN channel allocation for RAC environments.

Summary

This chapter reviewed the latest features of Oracle Database 10g Real Application Clusters, including new clusterware support offered by Cluster Ready Services; new enhancements with the 10g service management framework; new volume management support offered by Automatic Storage Management; new enhancements for RAC installation, migration, and manageability; extended support for rolling patch upgrades; and the major RAC features for 10g Release 2 10.2.0. This chapter also reviewed some best practices for running RAC with Oracle 10g. These new features and enhancements create a very solid high-availability framework for running Oracle 10g RAC in all supported environments.

16

Utilizing 10g Physical and Logical Standby with Data Guard

IN THIS CHAPTER

Oracle 10g Data Guard Overview   339

General Improvements with Oracle 10g Data Guard   340

Logical Standby Improvements   346

Data Guard Broker Improvements   351

Applying Patch Sets with Data Guard in Place   361

New Features in Oracle Database 10g Release 2   367

Oracle 10g Data Guard Overview

Up to this point, you have learned about the many new features with Oracle Database 10g. Although many of these major changes provide you with a new way of managing your data, the new features of Oracle 10g Data Guard will change the way you protect your data from events ranging from unplanned outages to major catastrophes.

> **Post 9/11**
>
> The events of September 11, 2001, have proved to the world that major catastrophes can happen at any time without warning. Database administrators tasked with architecting a disaster-recovery plan will need to understand how to reconstitute their production application at a remote site. Any event that will render your system useless should be included in your disaster-recovery plan.

Overall, the latest improvements to 10g Data Guard can be broken down into three separate categories:

- General improvements
- Logical standby improvements
- Data Guard Broker improvements

This chapter dissects the latest features within each of these categories.

General Improvements with Oracle 10g Data Guard

The new features of Oracle 10g Data Guard were developed with the following goals in mind:

- Ease of use
- Improved manageability and flexibility
- Improved degree of high availability
- Tight integration of other 10g high-availability features such as Flashback
- Low infrastructure cost

The general improvements to the Data Guard environment include the introduction of Real Time Apply, integration of the latest flashback support, advanced security support with authentication and encryption, specifying role-based destinations, and improved Data Guard configuration management. New features with 10g Release 2 include Automatic Failover Flashback Database support across switchovers, and improved asynchronous redo transmission support.

Real Time Apply

Real Time Apply is a new optional feature that automatically applies redo information from the primary database's redo log files to the standby database in real time (at the same time the redo log files are being written to) by the remote file server (RFS) process. With Real Time Apply enabled, redo information from standby redo log files can be recovered at the same time the log files are being written to, as opposed to when a log switch occurs. Prior releases of Data Guard required this redo data to be fully archived at the standby site via archive logs prior to being applied. Real Time Apply, however, allows your standby databases to be closely synchronized with your primary databases, which increases the speed of switchover and failover times and in turn reduces your downtime impact. If for any reason the apply service is unable to process the redo data in a timely fashion, the apply service will automatically go to the archive log files as needed. Also, if you define a delay on a destination and use Real Time Apply, the delay is ignored. Using Real Time Apply in conjunction with Maximum Protection, programs get the benefits of both zero data loss as well as minimal downtime in the event of a planned or unplanned outage. The benefits of using Real Time Apply include the following:

- Faster switchover/failover operations
- Up-to-date results when switching over to read-only
- Up-to-date reporting from a logical standby database
- The ability to leverage larger log files

Real Time Apply is also supported by the Data Guard Broker, so you can utilize this feature via the Enterprise Manager GUI or via the command-line interface.

Figure 16.1 details the overall process for the 10g Real Time Apply architecture.

> **Real Time Apply Log Size File**
> Having larger redo log files with Real Time Apply is very helpful because the apply service will stay in a log longer, thereby reducing the overhead associated with log switches on Real Time Apply processing.

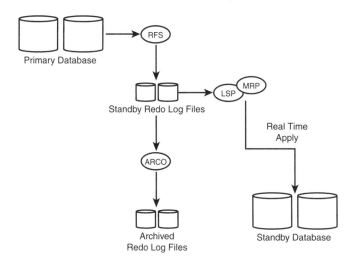

FIGURE 16.1
Oracle 10g Real Time Apply architecture.

Standby redo log files are required for Real Time Apply processing. It is recommended that you have one more standby redo log group than your primary database redo log group for Real Time Apply.

For physical standby databases, the managed recovery process (MRP) will apply the redo information from the standby redo logs as soon as the remote file server (RFS) process finishes writing. To enable Real Time Apply for your physical standby database environment, issue the following statement:

```
SQL> ALTER DATABASE RECOVER MANAGED STANDBY DATABASE USING CURRENT LOGFILE;
```

For logical standby databases, the logical standby process (LSP) will apply the redo information from the standby redo logs as soon as the remote file server (RFS) process finishes writing. To enable Real Time Apply for your logical standby database environment, issue the following statement:

```
SQL> ALTER DATABASE START LOGICAL STANDBY APPLY IMMEDIATE;
```

To verify that Real Time Apply is enabled, you can query the RECOVERY_MODE column of the V$ARCHIVE_DEST_STATUS view. When Real Time Apply is enabled, the column will display the MANAGED_REAL_TIME_APPLY value.

```
SQL> select recovery_mode from v$archive_dest_status;


RECOVERY_MODE
---------------------
MANAGED REAL TIME APPLY
```

Flashback Database Support

> **10g Behavior Changes for**
> LOG_ARCHIVE_FORMAT
>
> When you set the COMPATIBLE initialization parameter to 10.0.0 or higher, it is mandatory that all archive log file names contain the following elements: %s (sequence), %t (thread) and %r (resetlogs ID). This new naming convention ensures that all archive log file names are unique if recovery past resetlogs is ever used.

In prior releases of Oracle Data Guard, any failover operation required you to re-instantiate the old primary database so it could be re-established into the Data Guard environment. Also, any time you had to perform a RESETLOGS operation on your primary database, it invalidated your standby database and required a full rebuild of your standby. Re-instantiation of the standby database often took a long time because you had to restore from a remote or local backup copy, which often included copying large files

across a network. In Oracle 10g, however, Data Guard can utilize the benefits of Flashback Database to mitigate these problems.

> You must have the Flashback Database feature enabled on the old primary database prior to using this feature.

When using the new 10g Flashback Database technology in your Data Guard environment, the need to rebuild your standby from a past failover or RESETLOGS is a thing of the past. Now when you experience a failover, you can convert the old primary database into a new standby database without doing a complete rebuild from a previous backup. You can flashback the old primary database so that it only contains the changes already applied to the old standby database. Also, any RESETLOGS operation can be resolved by invoking Flashback Database on your standby to ensure that your standby contains only the changes that are represented in your primary database.

Using Flashback Database on your standby database also eliminates the need for any delay of redo data. Previously, some shops purposely delayed the application of redo data to add a layer of protection against user or logical corruption on the standby. Also, using the 10g Real Time Apply feature along with Flashback Database enables the standby database to be more closely synchronized with the primary database, thereby reducing failover and switchover times, while not promoting user or logical corruption.

Using Flashback Database to aid in the rebuild and recovery efforts of standby re-instantiation is well worth the price to upgrade to Oracle 10g. This feature alone will save DBAs valuable time because they will no longer need to copy or restore from a previous backup to enable the standby database. A detailed step-by-step configuration of 10g Flashback Database with a physical and logical standby database is discussed later in this chapter.

Redo Transmission Authentication and Encryption

Authentication is now required for all redo shipments in Oracle 10g Data Guard. You must set the REMOTE_LOGIN_PASSWORDFILE parameter to SHARED or EXCLUSIVE at all sites in your Data Guard environment. Also, the password for SYS must be the same at all databases within your Data Guard environment, but it is noted that the password can be changed. This password check is only performed once, when a connection is established for the redo shipment.

Also in 10g, you now have the option to utilize redo encryption during the redo shipment. To enable encryption of the redo transfer, do the following:

1. Install the Oracle Advanced Security option at both the primary and standby Oracle Home.

2. Configure the appropriate SQLNET.ORA parameters as documented in the *Oracle Advanced Security Guide*.

When you set the necessary parameters in the SQLNET.ORA file, Oracle Net will be allowed to encrypt and integrity-checksum all redo traffic shipped to the standby database.

Role-Based Destinations

New in Oracle 10g, the LOG_ARCHIVE_DEST_n initialization parameter introduces a new attribute, VALID_FOR, which allows you to identify exactly when the archived destination will be used as well as for what type of log file. This new attribute allows you to set up specific archive log destinations to be used only under specific standby database roles. Now, when you experience a switchover or failover, there is no need to enable or disable role-specific archive destinations after performing a role switch.

The VALID_FOR attribute accepts two parameters, archive_source and database_role. The archive_source keywords are as follows:

- **ONLINE_LOGFILE.** Used only when archiving online redo log files.

- **STANDBY_LOGFILE.** Used only when archiving standby redo log files or receiving archive logs from another database.

- **ALL_LOGFILES.** Used when archiving either online or standby redo log files.

The `database_role` keywords are as follows:

- **PRIMARY_ROLE.** Used only when the database is in the primary database role.

- **STANDBY_ROLE.** Used only when the database is in the standby role (works for both physical and logical standby).

- **ALL_ROLES.** Used when the database is in either primary or standby role (works for both physical and logical standby).

Almost all possible combinations for `archive_source` and `database_role` **are accepted. One combination, however, returns an error:** STANDBY_LOGFILE, PRIMARY_ROLE. **If this is specified, it will cause the** ORA-16026 **error for all database roles:** The parameter LOG_ARCHIVE_DEST_n contains an invalid attribute value. **Although it is valid to configure standby redo log files on a primary database, a database that is running in the primary role cannot use standby redo log files.**

Because the keywords are unique, the `archive_source` and `database_role` values can be specified in any order. Following are a few examples of how you can use the new attribute `VALID_FOR`:

```
LOG_ARCHIVE_DEST_3= 'SERVICE=DRZEUS
VALID_FOR= (STANDBY_LOGFILE,STANDBY_ROLE)'

LOG_ARCHIVE_DEST_1= 'LOCATION=/ora_log/ZEUS
VALID_FOR= (ALL_LOGFILES,ALL_ROLES)'
```

To identify all destination settings that are currently configured in your Data Guard environment, you will need to review the new `VALID_NOW` column in the `V$ARCHIVE_DEST` view. This column indicates whether the archive log destination will be used.

```
SQL> select valid_type, valid_role, valid_now from v$archive_dest;

VALID_TYPE        VALID_ROLE      VALID_NOW
---------------   -------------   ---------------
ALL_LOGFILES      ALL_ROLES       YES
STANDBY_LOGFILE   STANDBY_ROLE    WRONG VALID_TYPE
ONLINE_LOGFILE    STANDBY_ROLE    WRONG VALID_ROLE
ALL_LOGFILES      ALL_ROLES       UNKNOWN
ALL_LOGFILES      ALL_ROLES       UNKNOWN
ALL_LOGFILES      ALL_ROLES       UNKNOWN
```

The column values for `VALID_NOW` are as follows:

- **YES.** Indicates that the archive log destination is appropriately defined for the current database role.

- **WRONG VALID_TYPE.** Indicates that the archive destination is appropriately defined for the current database role but cannot be used.

- **WRONG VALID_ROLE.** Indicates that the archive log destination is not appropriately defined for the current database role.

- **UNKNOWN.** Indicates that the archive log destination is not defined.

Improved Data Guard Configuration Management

10g Data Guard identifies all the databases in its configuration using the new initialization parameter DB_UNIQUE_NAME. When assigning database identifiers with this new parameter, you must choose names that are unique for each database. When you have chosen your unique value for DB_UNIQUE_NAME, the value must remain constant for the given database,

> DB_UNIQUE_NAME **replaces** LOCK_NAME_SPACE, **which is now deprecated in 10g. You can still use** LOCK_NAME_SPACE **in 10g and it will not halt the startup of your instance, but** DB_UNIQUE_NAME **takes precedence over** LOCK_NAME_SPACE.

so please choose names that are easy for you to remember and identify.

The default value for DB_UNIQUE_NAME is the database name, so if you use the Data Guard Manager GUI to create a standby, it will set this to a unique value for your new standby. Each DB_UNIQUE_NAME value can be as many as 30 characters long and must be the same for all instances in a RAC database environment. In prior versions of Oracle Data Guard, this process was also achieved by using the LOCK_NAME_SPACE initialization parameter.

Oracle 10g Database Release 2 expands the usage of DB_UNIQUE_NAME by reassigning the default value of SERVICE_NAMES to DB_UNIQUE_NAME.DB_DOMAIN rather than DB_NAME.DB_DOMAIN.

Improved Data Guard STARTUP Command

Starting with 10g, the STARTUP command now evaluates the database's control file to determine what type of database it is. Now, issuing STARTUP or STARTUP MOUNT brings the standby database up to the appropriate state without requiring the explicit use of the terms STANDBY DATABASE or READ ONLY. In prior versions, you needed to explicitly issue three statements to start, mount, and open a physical standby in read only mode. The STARTUP statement starts, mounts, and opens a physical standby database in read-only mode, all in one step.

In prior versions, you had to issue two commands to start and then mount your physical standby. Now, however, the STARTUP MOUNT statement both starts and mounts a physical standby database. You will still need to start the managed recovery process via the ALTER DATABASE RECOVER MANAGED STANDBY DATABASE DISCONNECT FROM SESSION command, however.

Improved Data Guard Archiving

Now with 10g, the ALTER DATABASE ARCHIVELOG command enables automatic archiving by default, thus eliminating the need to issue a separate LOG ARCHIVE START command. If needed, a new MANUAL parameter on the ALTER DATABASE ARCHIVELOG statement overrides automatic archiving and allows manual archiving.

To check which archive log mode your database is in, query the LOG_MODE column of the V$DATABASE view like so:

```
SQL> select log_mode from v$database;

LOG_MODE
----------
AUTOMATIC
```

Also with 10g, the archive process can now archive to remote standby redo logs directly. Previously, only the log writer (LGWR) process could archive remotely to standby redo log files. This feature eliminates the need to register partial archived redo logs in case your standby database crashes.

Logical Standby Improvements

10g introduces many new enhancements to logical standby databases. New features discussed in this chapter include the following:

- Zero downtime for instantiation
- Support for redo log files
- The PREPARE TO SWITCHOVER command
- Support for SQL Apply services
- Rolling database upgrades using SQL Apply
- Enhanced commands and views that support logical standby database management

Zero Outage for Instantiation

> In 10g Release 1 RMAN does not support the new logical standby control file.

Prior to Oracle 10g, the major limitation with logical standby was that DBAs had to accept some type of outage in order to complete the build. The creation of the logical standby required the primary database to be shut down completely or required a quiesce of the database via Resource Manager. A clean shutdown was necessary to ensure that there were no in-flight transactions running during the time of the dictionary build on the primary; however, any downtime on your primary is not the best case. The alternative, a quiesce of the database via Resource Manager, required your instance to have an active Resource Manager in place, and then required the database to be placed in quiesce mode. Due to the load on some systems, quiescing a primary database could run for days without completion, and could cause errors. Now, with 10g, DBAs are not required to shut down the primary or use the quiesce command. DBAs can now use the new logical standby control file without having to experience any downtime to build the logical standby.

Following are the steps DBAs should take in Oracle 10g to build a logical standby:

1. Create an online (hot) backup of your primary database and ensure you have all archive logs from all threads through the end of the backup process.

2. Create a logical standby control file on your primary database. (A logical standby control file is like a physical standby control file, with the key difference that `database guard` is set to `ALL` by default. This prevents anyone from making changes that might corrupt the logical standby.)

> In previous versions, you were required to do a quiesce of the database at the end of a hot backup to record the SCN (system change number). This was necessary because you needed to have the recovery portion end during a time when the database was not active. Then you would start the SQL Apply service. With the new 10g logical standby control file, however, the quiesce and SCN snapshot are no longer needed.

```
SQL> alter database create logical standby control file as 'LOGICAL_STDBY.ctl';
```

3. Copy all necessary files—including the backup, archive log files, and logical standby control file—to the standby host.

4. Restore your backup database to mount stage using the logical standby control file. Do not open the database.

5. On the primary database, set up Log Transport services.

6. Place the standby database in recover managed mode. The recovery is the same as it would be for a physical standby. The recovery end point is governed by the information in the logical standby control file.

```
SQL> alter database recover managed standby database
```

7. When the recovery is complete, activate the logical standby database. When you activate the database, it is a new database.

```
SQL> alter database activate standby database
```

8. On the logical standby, use `DBNEWID` to change the `DBNAME` and `DBID`. To begin, shut down the database using the `IMMEDIATE` option; then, start up and mount the database.

9. Run NID (New Database ID utility introduced in Oracle 9.2) to change your `DBNAME` and `DBID` settings. When you're finished, shut down the database, restart it, and open the database with reset logs again.

> When using the NID utility in a RAC environment, the database must be mounted in `NOPARALLEL` mode—that is, set the initialization parameter `CLUSTER_DATABASE=FALSE`.

```
$> nid target=sys/password@standby_db
```

10. On the logical standby, add the necessary temporary tablespaces, and start the SQL Apply services:

```
SQL> alter database start logical standby apply immediate
```

> As a review, the Oracle Data Guard configuration has three specific data-protection modes to meet your business needs: Maximum Protection, Maximum Availability, or Maximum Performance. Maximum Protection mode guarantees that no data loss will occur if the primary database fails by committing data on the primary only after it is committed on the standby. Maximum Availability mode provides the same protection as Maximum Protection, but the primary will not shut down if communications with the standby are lost. Instead, the communications will operate in a Resync mode until all gaps are corrected. Maximum Performance mode uses the online or archive redo log files to propagate changes from the primary to the standby asynchronously. For more information about the Data Guard protection modes, please review the *Data Guard Concepts and Administration* documentation.

You now have a fully functioning logical standby database. By default, the logical standby is in maximum performance mode.

Support for Redo Log Files

Oracle 10g introduces new standby redo log support for logical standby databases. With this support, it is possible for a logical standby database to support the Maximum Protection and Maximum Availability modes. Because standby redo logs survive failures, it is no longer necessary to register partial archive log files if a failure occurs. Logical standby redo logs use the RFS process for redo shipment.

The PREPARE TO SWITCHOVER Command

Starting with 10g, you now have the ability to build the LogMiner dictionary before you need to perform a switchover operation. The new PREPARE TO SWITCHOVER TO [PRIMARY | LOGICAL STANDBY] command optimizes the switchover operations to enable this new behavior. After the LogMiner dictionary build has completed, you can use the COMMIT TO SWITCHOVER statement to switch the roles of the primary and logical standby databases. Here's how it's done:

1. Execute the PREPARE TO SWITCHOVER command on the primary database. This command enables the primary database to accept redo information from one of its logical standby members; that said, the primary will not yet *apply* the redo information. When this command is executed, you can observe the value of PREPARING SWITCHOVER in the SWITCHOVER_STATUS column in V$DATABASE view:

```
SQL> alter database prepare to switchover to logical standby;
```

2. Execute the PREPARE TO SWITCHOVER command on the logical standby database. This will build and send the LogMiner dictionary to the primary.

```
SQL> alter database prepare to switchover to primary;
```

3. Execute the COMMIT TO SWITCHOVER command on the primary database:

```
SQL> alter database commit to switchover to logical standby;
```

4. Execute the `COMMIT TO SWITCHOVER` command on the logical standby database.

```
SQL> alter database commit to switchover to primary;
```

5. When the commit is complete, start the SQL Apply services on the new logical standby (the original primary is the new logical standby):

```
SQL> alter system archivelog current;
SQL> alter database start logical standby apply;
```

Support for SQL Apply Services

Oracle 10g expands the benefits of using SQL Apply services on your logical standby database. For one, SQL Apply now supports multibyte `CLOB`, `NCLOB`, `LONG`, `LONG_RAW`, `BINARY_FLOAT`, and `BINARY_DOUBLE` data types. This new datatype support allows the logical standby database to process a wider variety of data. SQL Apply also supports indexed organized tables (IOTs), although these IOTs cannot contain overflow segments of LOB columns. Also, tables with unused columns are now supported with the new 10g SQL Apply.

Rolling Database Upgrades with SQL Apply

Oracle 10g introduces the foundation for rolling upgrades within the SQL Apply services to eliminate any downtime previously associated with this maintenance operation. For example, using SQL Apply and logical standby databases, you can upgrade the Oracle Database software from patch set release 10.1.0.n to the next database 10.1.0.(n+1) patch set release. With 10.1.0.2, this process cannot be invoked, but you can still apply patches with a logical or physical standby in place following the steps outlined later in this chapter in the section titled "Applying Patch Sets with Data Guard in Place." Only specific patch sets can be used with this online patching method, so you will need to check the patch README file to see whether your patch is a valid candidate.

Enhanced Logical Standby Commands and Views

In prior versions of Data Guard, you needed to explicitly skip the transaction and then restart the SQL Apply service. Now starting with Oracle 10g, the updated `ALTER DATABASE START LOGICAL STANDBY APPLY` command offers the `SKIP FAILED TRANSACTION` clause to automatically skip any failed transactions to start the SQL Apply service.

> DBAs should use the new `SKIP FAILED TRANSACTION` clause with caution. Skipping DDL operations is fine as long as you are able to reproduce it manually and all dependencies are not affected. If you ever skip a DML operation, however, you may make your logical standby unusable.

```
SQL> alter database start logical standby apply skip failed transaction;
```

If you do have to make any change on the logical standby, such as adding indexes or modifying tables that are not maintained by SQL Apply, 10g allows you to enable or disable the Data Guard process at the session level.

To disable the Data Guard process, issue this command:

```
SQL> alter session disable guard;
```

To enable the process, issue this command:

```
SQL> alter session enable guard;
```

10g offers several new updates to its Data Dictionary tables and views to support logical standby processing. Following is a summary of a few of the changes:

- You can now view all unsupported storage attributes with the new column ATTRIBUTES in DBA_LOGSTDBY_UNSUPPORTED:

  ```
  SQL> select distinct table_name, attributes from dba_logstdby_unsupported where owner =
  'TSDATA';
  ```

TABLE_NAME	ATTRIBUTES
USERS	Segment Compression
DOCUEMNTS	Segment Compression
DOC_COMPONENTS	Index Organized Table

- Several new columns in DBA_LOGSTDBY_PROGRESS reveal details on the progress of the SQL Apply service in your standby database:

  ```
  SQL> select applied_scn, applied_thread#, newest_scn, newest_thread# from
  dba_logstdby_progress;
  ```

APPLIED_SCN	APPLIED_THREAD#	NEWEST_SCN	NEWEST_THREAD#
34872	2	34872	2

- Using the new APPLIED column in the DBA_LOGSTDBY_LOG view, you can now easily see which logs have been applied to your logical standby database:

  ```
  SQL> select thread#, sequence#, applied from dba_logstdby_log order by sequence;
  ```

THREAD#	SEQUENCE#	APPLIED
1	51	YES
1	52	YES
1	53	YES
1	54	CURRENT
1	55	CURRENT

Data Guard Broker Improvements

The Oracle 10g Data Guard also has its share of improvements, including the following, which are discussed in more detail next:

- Broker support for RAC databases

- Enhancements to the 10g Enterprise Manager Data Guard GUI

- New Data Guard Broker commands

Broker Support for RAC Databases

Starting in 10g, the Data Guard Broker has added support for a RAC database environment. This means that DBAs who run a RAC environment can now configure and support Data Guard configurations using the Broker GUI or the command-line interface. You can use the same Broker commands and GUI pages you used for a single instance, now for a RAC instance. It is important to understand, however, that the Broker only supports sending redo to one instance of the standby database. The standby database can be either a single instance or a RAC-enabled instance, but in either case, only one instance would act as the receiving instance and apply the redo information. It would be convenient to have a standby RAC database apply redo information in case of standby instance failure. If the receiving instance fails, the Broker automatically detects the failure, selects a new receiving instance on the RAC standby, redirects redo shipment to the new receiving instance, and starts log apply on the instance. Just as in prior releases, to perform any switchover with a RAC database in place, all instances except one must be shut down. Because Data Guard and RAC are integrated, however, the Broker will invoke the shutdown commands and perform all necessary work for the switchover.

> If you use the GUI interface to create a standby from a RAC database, the standby will be created as a single-instance database.

Enhancements to the Enterprise Manager Data Guard GUI

The 10g Enterprise Manager has updated the interface for the Data Guard Broker GUI. From the Data Guard home page, shown in Figure 16.2, you can now see an overview of the configuration, a summary of the amount of data shipping and applied to each standby, and the status of the standby databases. As a result, DBAs can now easily manage the Data Guard environment.

The Performance Overview page, which you access by clicking the Performance Overview link in the Performance section of the Data Guard home page, consists of four new charts:

- **Data Archived (MB).** This chart indicates the amount of redo generated on the primary over time.

- **Standby Progress Summary.** This chart includes Data Not Applied and Data Not Received statistics.

- **Data Applied.** This chart conveys the amount of redo being applied on each standby over time.

- **Log Services Summary.** This chart includes detailed information about the current log file being used by each database.

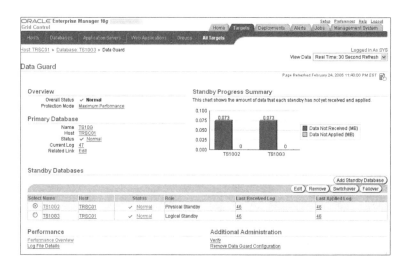

FIGURE 16.2
The Data Guard home page via 10g EM Grid Control.

This page, shown in Figure 16.3, is monitored in real-time, manually or automatically (every 30 or 60 seconds). There is no difference in the appearance if the databases are RAC or single-instance. If the primary database is a RAC database, each chart will aggregate the information across all necessary threads.

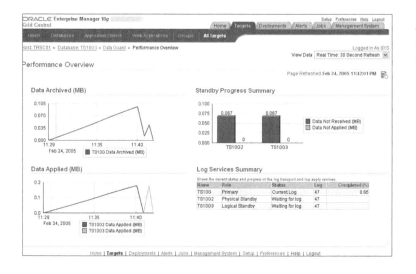

FIGURE 16.3
The 10g Data Guard Performance Overview page.

Also new in 10g Enterprise Manager is the Add Standby Database wizard, which you access by clicking the Add Standby Database button in the Standby Databases section of the Data Guard home page. Using the Add Standby Database wizard enables individuals who previously did not have an advanced understanding of Data Guard to quickly and easily build and run standby databases in any environment.

Building a standby database with the Standby Database Creation Wizard is as easy as providing a few bits of information about your configuration. Figure 16.4 displays the first screen of the Add Standby Database wizard.

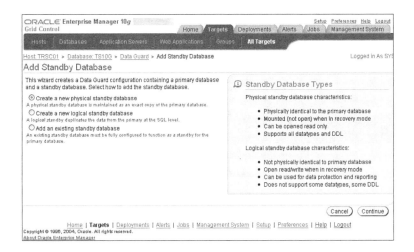

FIGURE 16.4
The new 10g Standby Database Creation wizard.

When you use the wizard to build a new standby database, the wizard will first display a window to allow you to choose your backup method. Because a hot or cold backup is needed to begin the process, Data Guard Manager utilizes RMAN to perform this backup process (see Figure 16.5). You may also receive a warning at this point if your

> To use the new 10g Standby Database Creation wizard to build your new standby environment, your primary database must be in archive log mode. If it is not, you will receive an error message about the NOARCHIVELOG MODE status.

database is not in force-logging mode. Force logging is not required, but Oracle recommends that your primary database be placed in force-logging mode to ensure that no no-logging operations can be executed at the primary.

Next, as shown in Figure 16.6, the wizard will prompt you for a working directory and the user admin credentials of the Oracle Home owner. The working directory will be used to house the primary database backup files during the standby build process. You can also choose to delete or retain the working directory for future builds.

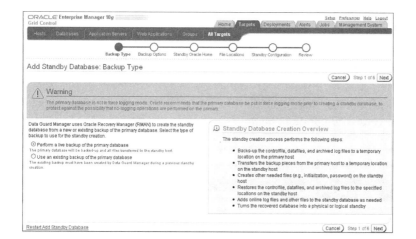

FIGURE 16.5
Choosing a backup method for the 10g Standby Database Creation wizard.

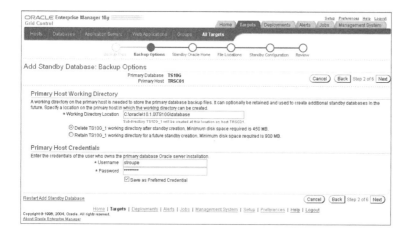

FIGURE 16.6
Providing the backup options for the 10g Standby Database Creation wizard.

The wizard's third step, shown in Figure 16.7, prompts you for the standby instance name as well as the user admin credentials over the standby Oracle Home. In this example we used the same Oracle Home for the primary and standby; note, however, that the primary and standby Oracle Homes could have different user admin credentials.

Next, the wizard verifies the standby file locations as well as the network configuration file location, as shown in Figure 16.8. Because our sample standby database uses the same host as the primary, Data Guard Manager automatically uses the OFA (Oracle Flexible Architecture) file structure.

The next screen, shown in Figure 16.9, prompts you for the specific information about your standby configuration. Here you will need your database unique name, target name, and standby archive location.

FIGURE 16.7
Providing the necessary instance name and host credentials for the 10g Standby Database Creation wizard.

FIGURE 16.8
Verifying the standby database and network file locations for the 10g Standby Database Creation wizard.

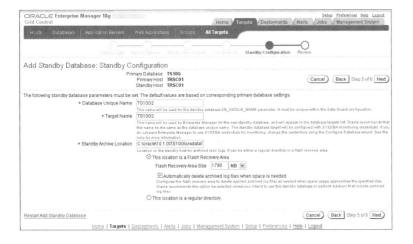

FIGURE 16.9
Configuring the new standby database using the 10g Standby Database Creation wizard.

Possible Error with Standby Filenames

When using the wizard to build your logical or physical standby database, it is possible that you may run into bug 3655231 if you are using Version 10.1.0.3 or below. If you receive the `Can't find unicode character property definition via main->r or r.pl at unicode/Is/r.pl line 0` error message during your standby build you have hit this bug. The workaround is to remove any standby data file and/or log file names that contain \p. If this exists, either rename the directory or choose a different directory to house the files. Then, rename the files accordingly using the Customize button in the screen shown in Figure 16.8. You could also avoid this issue by applying the 10.1.0.4 patch set or oneoff patch 4039195 to version 10.1.0.2.

Finally, the wizard displays a summary of your standby build options, as shown in Figure 16.10. Review your choices. If any are incorrect, click the Back button repeatedly until you reach the relevant screen to correct them. When you're satisfied with your selections, click the Finish button.

Data Guard Manager proceeds with the build by creating your configuration (see Figure 16.11), preparing and submitting the build job (see Figure 16.12), and adding your standby target to Enterprise Manager Grid Control (see Figure 16.13).

When the target is complete, Enterprise Manager redirects you to the Data Guard home page so you can monitor the standby database build (see Figure 16.14).

FIGURE 16.10
Overall summary for new target standby database using the 10g Standby Database Creation wizard.

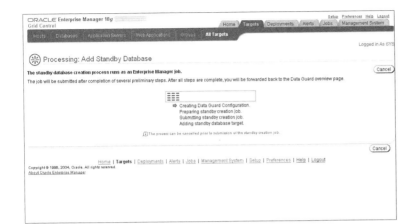

FIGURE 16.11
Process screen showing the creation of the new standby database environment.

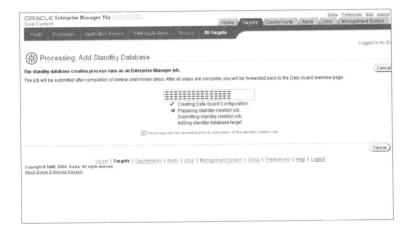

FIGURE 16.12
Process screen showing the necessary jobs submitted to build the new standby database.

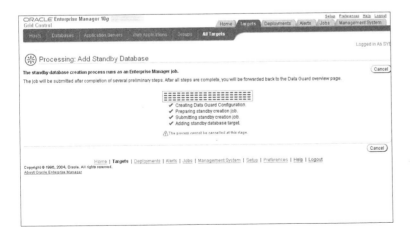

FIGURE 16.13
Process screen showing the necessary jobs submitted to build the new standby database.

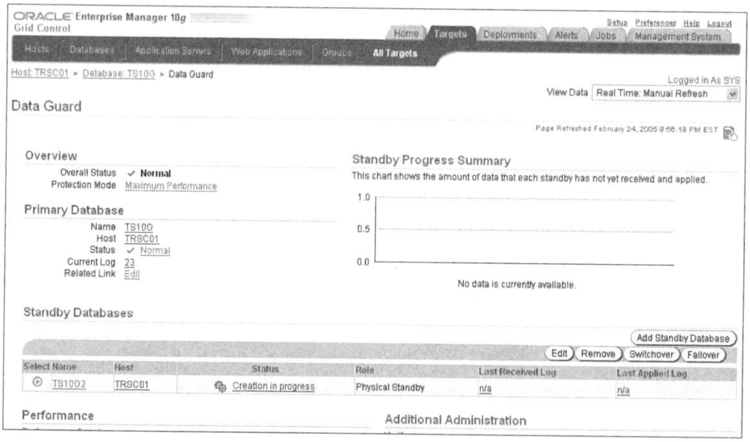

FIGURE 16.14
The 10g Data Guard home page showing the new standby database in process.

New 10g Broker Commands

With Oracle 10g, most `DGMGRL` commands have changed. Many have been improved with simplified meanings; others are just brand new due to the changes with the 10g Data Guard Broker configuration model. Following are the more notable changes with the 10g Broker command line syntax.

CREATE CONFIGURATION

One command that has become highly simplified with 10g is the `CREATE CONFIGURATION` command. In previous releases, the `CREATE CONFIGURATION` command was highly complex; with 10g, however, all you need to supply is three arguments to create your new configuration—configuration name, database name, and connect identifier—as shown here:

```
DGMGRL> create configuration 'DR_CONFIG' as primary database is 'PROD'
connect identifier is 'RAC_PROD';
```

- The *configuration name* is a name you provide for the Broker configuration. The name, like most names in Oracle, must be made up of alphanumeric characters and can only consist of 30 characters. The preceding example shows `DR_CONFIG` as the configuration name.

- The *database name* is the name that will be used by the Broker to refer to the primary database object. The name must match that value of the corresponding database `DB_UNIQUE_NAME` parameter. In the preceding example, `PROD` is the database name.

- The *connect identifier* can be a fully specified connect descriptor or name that is reprehensive in an Oracle Net environment (a `tnsnames.ora` entry) to the primary database. In a RAC environment, you must make sure your connect identifier can be used to address at least one instance of the primary database. In the preceding example, `RAC_PROD` is the connect identifier.

When your configuration is set, you can then use the new `ADD DATABASE` command to add standby databases to the configuration.

ADD DATABASE

This new Broker command is used to add databases to a configuration. The database name is the DB_UNIQUE_NAME of the standby and the connect identifier must resolve to the standby database. The type of standby (physical or logical) can be interchangeable with this command.

```
DGMGRL> add database 'DRPROD' as connect identifier is 'RAC_DRPROD' maintained as physical;
```

REMOVE DATABASE

The REMOVE DATABASE command is used to remove a standby database from your configuration. The database name is the DB_QUIQUE_NAME of the standby you want removed.

```
DGMGRL> remove database 'DRPROD';
```

DISABLE DATABASE (Replaces DISABLE_RESOURCE)

The DISABLE DATABASE command is used to disable Broker management of a standby database within a configuration. This means that all Broker-directed modifications will be ignored for this specific standby database. Also, the Broker will no longer monitor the specified database for health-status checks. The database name is the DB_UNIQUE_NAME of the standby you want to disable.

```
DGMGRL> disable database 'DRPROD';
```

ENABLE DATABASE (Replaces ENABLE_RESOURCE)

The ENABLE DATABASE command is used to restore Broker management of a standby database that was previously disabled. The database name is the DB_UNIQUE_NAME of the standby you want to disable.

```
DGMGRL> enable database 'DRPROD';
```

EDIT DATABASE (Replaces ALTER_RESOURCE)

The EDIT DATABASE command is used to set a new property value to your specified database, rename your database, or modify the state of the database. The database name is the DB_UNIQUE_NAME of the standby you want to disable.

```
DGMGRL> edit database 'DRPROD' set property 'logarchivetrace'='127';
DGMGRL> edit database 'DRPROD' set state='read-only';
DGMGRL> edit database 'DRPROD' rename to  'DRPROD_STDBY';
```

EDIT CONFIGURATION (Replaces ALTER_CONFIGURATION)

The EDIT CONFIGURATION command is used to modify the current protection mode setting for a predefined configuration.

```
DGMGRL> edit configuration set protection mode as maxprotection;
```

Valid protection modes for a configuration are MAXPROTECTION, MAXAVAILABILITY, and MAXPERFORMANCE. The default is MAXPERFORMANCE.

EDIT INSTANCE

The EDIT INSTANCE command is used to modify the value of a property for a specified instance. For these commands, if your instance name is unique across the configuration, then the database name is not required.

```
DGMGRL> edit instance 'DRPROD_N1' on database 'DRPROD' set property lsbymaxservers = '4';
```

Properties that can be modified with the EDIT INSTANCE command include the following:

- **StandbyArchiveLocation.** Location of archived redo logs arriving from a primary database.

- **AlternateLocation.** Alternate location to be used if the standby can no longer archive to StandbyArchiveLocation.

- **LogArchiveTrace.** Integer value to denote the progression of the archiving of redo logs on the primary and standby databases.

- **LogArchiveFormat.** Format for filenames of archived redo log files.

- **LsbyMaxSga.** Number of megabytes allocated from the System Global Area (SGA) for the log apply services cache. The default value is one quarter (1/4) of the value set for SHARED_POOL_SIZE parameter.

- **LsbyMaxServers.** Number of parallel query servers specifically reserved for log apply services.

FAILOVER

The new FAILOVER command specifies that a standby database will take on the role of a primary database.

```
DGMGRL> failover to DRPROD_STDBY;
```

If the Data Guard Broker configuration is in Maximum Protection or Maximum Availability mode, a failover will force the protection mode to be MAXIMUM PERFORMANCE. After the failover has occurred, the DBA can change this mode if needed.

SHOW

The new SHOW command displays the current settings of your configuration model. The SHOW command can be used at the configuration, database, or instance level.

```
DGMGRL> show configuration;
DGMGRL> show database 'DRPROD';
DGMGRL> show instance 'RAC_DRPROD';
```

SWITCHOVER

The new SWITCHOVER command performs a switchover operation to the database object corresponding to the named site.

```
DGMGRL> switchover to DRPROD_STDBY;
```

Applying Patch Sets with Data Guard in Place

Starting in Oracle 9i, DBAs had the option to apply major patch sets to an existing configuration that may include one or more physical and logical standby database environments (9.0.1 for physical standby and 9.2.0 for logical standby). Although the methods remain the same, the steps have evolved with the new features and commands.

The steps that follow only apply to 10.1.0.2 and higher installations. As with all patch sets, these steps should be used to supplement the latest edition of the patch set README file. For the latest patch set README, please visit MetaLink or OTN.

If your Data Guard environment also uses Real Application Clusters (RAC), the following procedures should be performed on only one node of the system unless otherwise noted in a particular step.

If you are using the Data Guard Broker, you will have to disable the Broker prior to running these procedures. You can disable the Broker via the command line utility dgmgrl or by changing the db_broker parameter to FALSE.

Patching a Physical Database

Following are the steps required to apply any necessary patches if you are using a physical standby database in your Data Guard environment:

1. Log in to the Oracle account on both the primary and standby hosts. Ensure that you have your ORACLE_HOME and ORACLE_SID environment variables set properly.

2. On both the primary and standby hosts, uncompress and untar the patch set in your new patch directory.

3. Perform a clean shutdown of the existing primary instance (normal or immediate) and stop all listeners, agents, and processes running under the ORACLE_HOME.

```
SQL> shutdown immediate
$ lsnrctl stop
$ emctl stopall
```

If running RAC, perform these steps on all nodes. If running Automatic Storage Management (ASM), shut down all databases that run on ASM and then shut down the ASM instance:

   a. Shut down all RAC instances.

   b. Shut down ASM instances.

   c. Shut down all processes running the ORACLE_HOME on each node.

   d. Shut down CRS processes on all nodes under the CRS_HOME.

```
$ /etc/init.d/init.crs stop
```

4. Cancel managed recovery on the standby database:

```
SQL> recover managed standby database cancel;
```

5. Shut down the standby instance on the standby host. Stop all instances, listeners, agents, and other processes by following the instructions in step 3.

> It's a good idea to review the patch set's known-issues document from MetaLink. The known-issues document details information that was not included or was missed in the patch set README or instructions document. The known-issues document also includes bugs that are introduced in the specific patch.

6. Install the patch set on both the primary and standby host using the installer. Be sure to read the patch set instructions and README prior to installing the patch.

```
$ ./runInstaller
```

7. When the patch set has been completed on all hosts and nodes, start up the standby listener and mount the standby database:

```
$ lsnrctl start
$ sqlplus /nolog
SQL> connect / as sysdba
SQL> startup mount
```

8. Place the standby database in managed recover mode:

```
SQL> recover managed standby database nodelay disconnect;
```

9. Start up the primary listener and instance in upgrade mode on the primary host:

```
$ lsnrctl start
$ sqlplus /nolog
SQL> connect / as sysdba
SQL> startup upgrade
```

10. Verify that remote archiving to the standby database is functioning correctly by checking the STATUS column from V$ARCHIVE_DEST view. You may also want to switch the log files on the primary database in case you notice any discrepancy.

```
SQL> alter system archive log current
SQL> select dest_id, status from v$archive_dest
```

11. On the primary instance, run catpatch.sql to update the metadata from the patch install:

```
SQL> spool catpatch_10.1.0.3.log
SQL> @?/rdbms/admin/catpatch.sql
SQL> spool off
```

12. Review the catpatch spool log and check for errors. If needed, correct any errors and execute catpatch.sql again.

13. When `catpatch.sql` completes, make note of the log sequence number and issue the following:

```
SQL> alter system archive log current
```

14. Restart the primary database:

```
SQL> shutdown immediate
SQL> startup
```

15. Verify that the standby database has been recovered to the log sequence number from step 13:

```
SQL> select max(sequence#) from v$log_history;
```

From this point on, you should complete any remaining tasks from the post install actions from the patch set instructions or known-issues document. Understand that it is not necessary to shut down the standby database in conjunction with the primary during any post install action task.

If needed, you can check the max log sequence number to ensure that the standby has been recovered to the last archive log produced by the primary. From the primary, run the following command:

```
SQL> select max(sequence#) from v$archived_log;
```

From the standby, run the following command:

```
SQL> select max(sequence#) from v$log_history;
```

Patching a Logical Database

Until a new Oracle patch is made available that will allow you to use the new 10g SQL Apply features to apply the patch without any downtime, the following steps need to be taken to patch your database with a logical standby in place:

1. Log in to the Oracle account on both the primary and standby hosts. Ensure that you have your `ORACLE_HOME` and `ORACLE_SID` environment variables set properly.

2. On both the primary and standby hosts, uncompress and untar the patch set in your new patch directory.

3. On your primary host, stop all user activity on the primary database. If you are running RAC, shut down all but one instance (normal or immediate). On your remaining instance, identify and record the current log thread and sequence number, and then archive the current log to ensure that all available redo data from your primary is shipped over to the standby database:

```
SQL> select thread#, sequence# from v$log where status = 'CURRENT';
SQL> alter system archive log current;
```

4. On both standby hosts, if you are using RAC, shut down all but one instance (normal or immediate). On your remaining instance, verify that you have received the redo log from step 3 by querying DBA_LOGSTDBY_LOG view. Use the thread and sequence numbers to qualify your command.

```
SQL> select file_name from dba_logstdby_log where thread#=5 and sequence#=51;
```

5. Verify that all remaining redo logs have been applied by querying the DBA_LOGSTDBY_PROGRESS view. When the values in the applied_scn and newest_scn columns are equal, all available data from the primary has been received by the standby.

```
SQL> select applied_scn, newest_scn from dba_logstdby_progress;
```

6. Stop SQL Apply operations on the standby database:

```
SQL> alter database stop logical standby apply;
```

7. Perform a clean shutdown of the standby instance (normal or immediate) and stop all listeners, agents, and processes running under the ORACLE_HOME.

```
SQL> shutdown immediate
$ lsnrctl stop
$ emctl stopall
```

   If running RAC on your standby, then do the following:

   a. Shut down all RAC instances.

   b. Shut down ASM instances.

   c. Shut down all processes running the ORACLE_HOME.

   d. Shut down CRS processes on all nodes under the CRS_HOME.

```
$ /etc/init.d/init.crs stop
```

8. On your primary host, perform a clean shutdown of the primary instance (normal or immediate) and stop all listeners, agents, and processes running under the ORACLE_HOME.

```
SQL> shutdown immediate
$ lsnrctl stop
$ emctl stopall
```

   If running RAC on your standby:

   a. Shut down all RAC instances.

   b. Shut down ASM instances.

   c. Shut down all processes running the `ORACLE_HOME`.

   d. Shut down CRS processes on all nodes under the `CRS_HOME`.

```
$ /etc/init.d/init.crs stop
```

9. Install the patch set on the primary database as outlined in the patch set instructions. Follow any post-install steps if required by Oracle support.

10. After the patch set has been installed, start up the primary database in upgrade mode, disable remote archiving, and run `catpatch.sql`:

```
$ sqlplus /nolog
SQL> connect / as sysdba
SQL> startup upgrade
SQL> alter system set log_archive_dest_state_2=DEFER;

SQL> spool catpatch_10.1.0.3.log
SQL> @?/rdbms/admin/catpatch.sql
SQL> spool off
```

11. Review the catpatch spool log and check for errors. If needed, correct any errors and execute `catpatch.sql` again.

12. Shut down the primary database instance and restart the listener and agent:

```
SQL> shutdown immediate
$ lsnrctl start
$ emctl start
```

13. Start up the primary instance in restricted session mode to restrict any user DML/DDL:

```
SQL> startup mount
SQL> alter system enable restricted session
```

14. Open the primary database and build the LogMiner dictionary:

```
SQL> alter database open
SQL> exec dbms_logstdby.build;
```

15. Disable restricted session mode on the primary instance and archive the current log file. Then capture the latest dictionary build log:

```
SQL> alter system disable restricted session;
SQL> alter system archive log current;
SQL> select name from v$archived_log where (sequence#=(select max(sequence#) from
v$archived_log
2>  where dictionary_begin='YES' and standby_dest='NO'));
```

16. On the standby host, install the patch set on the standby database as outlined in the patch set instructions. Follow any post-install steps if required by Oracle support.

17. After the patch set has been installed, start up the standby database in migrate mode, activate the standby database, disable remote archiving, and run `catpatch.sql`:

```
$ sqlplus /nolog
SQL> connect / as sysdba
SQL> startup migrate
SQL> alter database activate logical standby database;
SQL> alter system set log_archive_dest_state_2=DEFER;

SQL> spool catpatch_10.1.0.3.log
SQL> @?/rdbms/admin/catpatch.sql
SQL> spool off
```

18. Review the catpatch spool log and check for errors. If needed, correct any errors and execute catpatch.sql again.

19. Shut down the standby database instance and restart the listener and agent:

```
SQL> shutdown immediate
$ lsnrctl start
$ emctl start
```

20. Copy the latest dictionary build log, identified in step 15, from the primary host to the standby host.

21. Start up the standby database instance and turn on database guard to restrict users from updating any objects:

```
SQL> startup mount
SQL> alter database guard all
SQL> alter database open
```

22. Register the copied log file from step 20 on the standby database:

```
SQL> alter database register logical logfile '/ora1/drprod/standby/arc2_51.log';
```

23. Begin SQL Apply operations on the standby database:

```
SQL> alter database start logical standby apply initial;
```

If you were using RAC on your standby host, start up the other standby instances.

24. Begin remote archiving to the standby database:

```
SQL> alter system set log_archive_dest_state_2=ENABLE;
```

If you were using RAC on your primary host, start up the other primary instances.

To minimize the total downtime for the patch process, you can optionally perform steps 9–11 (install the patch on the primary) in parallel with steps 16–18 (install the patch on the standby). If you choose to run these steps in parallel, however, you must complete steps 12–15 on the primary host before you can run step 20 on the standby host.

New Features in Oracle Database 10g Release 2

Following is a brief summary of the Data Guard features that will be introduced in Oracle 10g Release 2.

Automatic Failover

New with Oracle 10g Database Release 2, you can invoke fast-start failover to automatically failover to a designated synchronized standby database in the event of loss of the primary database. In previous versions (including 10g Release 1), manual commands were still needed to complete the failover process to a standby database. Now there is no need for manual intervention in case of a major catastrophe.

Also, after a fast-start failover occurs, the old primary database is automatically reconfigured as a new standby database upon reconnection to the configuration. Keep in mind, however, that you still may need the use of Flashback Database to get your old primary in sync with the new primary; those steps are the same as in 10g Release 1.

Faster Redo Apply Failover

Oracle 10g Release 2 allows you to failover a physical standby database to the primary database role without doing a database restart, as long as the physical standby database has never been opened as read-only.

Flashback Database Across Switchovers

Oracle 10g Release 2 allows you to flashback the primary and standby databases to a point in time or System Change Number (SCN) prior to a switchover operation using Flashback Database. When you use this feature of Flashback Database on a physical standby, the standby role is preserved; when used on a logical standby, however, the role is changed to what it was at the target time or SCN. This feature extends the protection against user or logical errors.

Asynchronous Redo Transmission

Asynchronous redo transmission using the log writer process (LGWR ASYNC) has been improved to reduce the performance effect on the primary database. During asynchronous redo transmission, the network server (LNS) process transmits redo data out of the online redo log files on the primary database and no longer interacts directly with the log writer process. This change in behavior allows the log writer process to archive redo data to the current online redo log file and continue processing the next request without waiting for network I/O to complete.

SQL Apply

Oracle 10g Release 2 also introduces even more useful new features with SQL Apply. Here is a short summary of these upcoming changes:

- **Faster failover with SQL Apply.** Failover operations to a logical standby will be much faster because it will be no longer necessary to restart the SQL Apply service as part of the failover operation.

- **Optimized creation of logical standby database.** The creation of logical standby databases no longer requires the creation of the logical standby control file, which could not be used by RMAN. With 10g Release 2, logical standby databases cannot be easily created from a physical standby database. This reduces the manual operations required for creating a logical standby database.

- **Automatic deletion of applied archived redo logs.** All archived redo log files that are applied on the logical standby database will be automatically removed by the SQL Apply service.

- **Expanded IOT support.** IOTs that contain LOB columns and overflow segments will be supported with SQL Apply.

Summary

This chapter reviewed the latest features of 10g Data Guard, including the major features for 10g Release 2 10.2.0. These new features should be used to minimize downtime for all maintenance activities with both physical and logical standby databases. Learning and understanding the latest features of Oracle Data Guard should motivate any team to implement its features to provide higher availability for your production environment.

17

Effectively Using Flashback Technologies

IN THIS CHAPTER

Brief Overview of Flashback Technology   369

Flashback Database   370

Flashback Table   385

Flashback Drop with Recycle Bin   392

Flashback Versions Query   399

Flashback Transaction Query   405

Advanced Flashback Features in Oracle Database 10g Release 2   409

Brief Overview of Flashback Technology

The term *flashback* was first introduced with Oracle 9i in the form of the new technology known as flashback query. When enabled, flashback query provided a new alternative to correcting user errors, recovering lost or corrupted data, or even performing historical analysis without all the hassle of point-in-time recovery.

The new flashback technology was a wonderful addition to Oracle 9i, but it still had several dependencies and limitations. First, flashback forced you to use Automatic Undo Management (AUM) and to set the UNDO_RETENTION parameter. Second, you needed to make sure your flashback users had the proper privileges on the

> Oracle 9i offers an unsupported method for extending the five-day limit of UNDO_RETENTION.
>
> Basically, the SCN and timestamp are stored in SYS.SMON_SCN_TIME, which has only 1,440 rows by default (5 days×24 hours×12 months = 1,440).
>
> At each five-minute interval, the current SCN is inserted into SMON_SCN_TIME, while the oldest SCN is removed, keeping the record count at 1,440 at all times.
>
> To extend the five-day limit, all you need to do is insert new rows to the SMON_SCN_TIME table.
>
> Oracle 10g extends this limit to eight days by extending the default record count of SMON_SCN_TIME to 2,304 (8 days×24 hours×12 months = 2,304).

DBMS_FLASHBACK package. After these prerequisite steps were completed, users were able to use the flashback technology based on the SCN (system change number) or by time. However it's important to note that regardless of whether users used the time or SCN method to enable flashback, Oracle would only find the flashback copy to the nearest five-minute internal. Furthermore, when using the flashback time method in a database that had been running continuously, you could never flashback more than five days, irrespective of your UNDO_RETENTION setting. Also, flashback query did not support DDL operations that modified any columns or even any drop or truncate commands on any tables.

Oracle 10g has evolved the flashback technology to cover every spectrum of the database. Following is a short summary of the new flashback technology that is available with Oracle 10g:

- **Flashback Database.** Now you can set your entire database to a previous point in time by undoing all modifications that occurred since that time without the need to restore from a backup.

- **Flashback Table.** This feature allows you to recover an entire table to a point in time without having to restore from a backup.

- **Flashback Drop.** This feature allows you to restore any accidentally dropped tables.

- **Flashback Versions Query.** This feature allows you to retrieve a history of changes for a specified set of rows within a table.

- **Flashback Transaction Query.** This feature allows users to review and/or recover modifications made to the database at the transaction level.

Flashback Database

> Unlike standard point-in-time recovery methods, the time required to invoke Flashback Database for a specific time in the past is directly proportional to the number of changes made, not on the size of the database.

Oracle Flashback Database can be used to undo the following:

- Changes that have resulted in logical data corruption

- Changes that are a result of user error

Flashback Database Architecture

Flashback Database utilizes a new type of log file called *flashback logs*. These files are created in the flash recovery area by the Oracle server

> **If you have experienced physical corruption or media failure in your database, then you must use traditional recovery methods.**

and contain data block images for changed blocks, which are recorded at a timed interval. When invoked by the Flashback Database operation, these data block images are used to quickly back out any changes to the database that you specify with the FLASHBACK DATABASE command. You do not have to create or manage the flashback logs, nor do you have to explicitly size the flashback logs; you must, however, decide how much space is allocated to the flash recovery area, as well as manage it. Depending on the activity of your database, the flashback logs could accumulate very quickly within your flash recovery area; for this reason, having the right flash recovery area size is critical. Because the flashback logs must be created in the flash recovery area, you must have a flash recovery area initialized prior to running Flashback Database.

Flashback Database also utilizes a new background process called recover writer (RVWR). When Flashback Database is enabled, RVWR is responsible for writing flashback data to the flashback logs. RVWR is very similar to the log writer, LGWR, however RVWR only writes to the flashback logs.

Following are the initialization parameters that are needed to configure Flashback Database and the flash recovery area:

- **DB_RECOVERY_FILE_DEST (dynamic).** This parameter specifies the physical location for the flash recovery area. The RVWR background process will create and write the flashback logs in this location. The specified location can be defined as a directory, file system, or ASM disk group. Flash recovery area cannot be stored on a raw file system. There is no default setting.

- **DB_RECOVERY_FILE_DEST_SIZE (dynamic).** This parameter specifies the amount of total space used in the flash recovery area. The size you set depends on the activity of your database. If you do not allocate enough space, you will limit your flashback time table. There is no default setting.

> **Possible Flashback Error**
>
> Specifying DB_RECOVERY_FILE_DEST without also specifying the DB_RECOVERY_FILE_DEST_SIZE parameter is not allowed. You will receive an ORA-19801 and/or ORA-19802 error if you do. DB_RECOVERY_FILE_DEST_SIZE must be set before setting DB_RECOVERY_FILE_DEST.

> **Possible Error When Deleting Flashback Logs**
>
> Because the flashback logs are stored in the flash recovery area, you should use RMAN to back up and manage the retention policy for space requirements. If someone happened to manually remove a flashback log from the flash recovery area, the database will continue to function normally as long as the delete file was not the current flashback log. However once you shut down your database and try to start up the instance, you will receive ORA-38701 and ORA-27041 unable to open file errors. To fix the problem, clear out the flash recovery area by mounting the database, turn off flash recovery, and then turn on flash recovery. After you do this you can open your database again. If you remove the current flashback log or kill the RVWR process, however, the instance will crash and you will have to follow the aforementioned re-initialization steps.

■ **DB_FLASHBACK_RETENTION_TARGET** (**dynamic**). This parameter specifies the limit (in minutes) of flashback data that Oracle should retain. This limit is contingent upon sufficient space within the flash recovery area. The default setting is 1,440 minutes (24 hours).

When running Oracle RAC, each instance must have all three parameters set with the same setting.

> A clean shutdown via SHUTDOWN NORMAL, IMMEDIATE, or TRANSACTIONAL is mandatory before starting the initial configuration of Flashback Database

Configuring Flashback Database

Before you can start enjoying the benefits of Flashback Database, you must make sure you follow the necessary steps to properly configure your instance to use flashback logging.

1. Start your instance in MOUNT EXCLUSIVE mode. The database must be mounted but not open.

   ```
   SQL> startup mount;

   SQL> select status from v$instance;

   STATUS
   -------
   MOUNTED
   ```

2. If it's not already enabled, enable archivelog mode:

   ```
   SQL> alter database archivelog;

   SQL> select log_mode from v$database;

   LOG_MODE
   -------
   ARCHIVELOG
   ```

3. Configure the flash recovery area by setting the DB_RECOVERY_FILE_DEST and DB_RECOVERY_FILE_DEST_SIZE parameters:

   ```
   SQL> alter system set db_recovery_file_dest_size = 4G;
   SQL> alter system set db_recovery_file_dest = 'C:\oracle\10.1.0\flash_recovery_area';
   ```

4. Set the flashback retention target by using the DB_FLASHBACK_RETENTION_TARGET parameter:

   ```
   SQL> alter system set db_flashback_retention_target = 1440;
   ```

5. Enable flashback logging. (Note: The database must be in mount exclusive mode and in archivelog mode to issue this command; otherwise you will receive an error message.)

   ```
   SQL> alter database flashback on;
   ```

6. Verify your Flashback Database settings:

```
SQL> show parameter recovery

NAME                                    TYPE          VALUE
------------------------------------ ------------  --------------------------------------
db_recovery_file_dest                   string        C:\oracle\10.1.0\flash_
➡recovery_area
db_recovery_file_dest_size              big integer   4G


SQL> sho parameter db_flashback

NAME                                    TYPE          VALUE
------------------------------------ ------------  --------------------------------
db_flashback_retention_target           integer       1440


SQL> select flashback_on, current_scn from v$database;

FLA CURRENT_SCN
--- -----------
YES           0
```

7. Optionally, disable flashback logging for any nonessential tablespaces:

```
SQL> alter tablespace stroupe flashback off;
```

8. Open the database:

```
SQL> alter database open;
```

Managing Flashback Database

Now that you have properly configured Flashback Database, let us focus on the available techniques and methods to manage and monitor its capabilities. Once Flashback Database is up and running, you will need to make sure that you have enough space to store the flashback logs based on your current workload as well as to monitor the overhead associated with the flashback logging.

When Flashback Database is enabled, Oracle starts tracking the amount of flashback logging that is occurring and stores it in the view V$FLASHBACK_DATABASE_LOG. DBAs will want to query this view throughout the day to monitor the flashback retention target and the flashback recovery size that was previously set.

The column values for V$FLASHBACK_DATABASE_LOG are as follows:

- **OLDEST_FLASHBACK_SCN.** Indicates the lowest system change number (SCN) in the flashback data.

- **OLDEST_FLASHBACK_TIME.** Indicates the time of the lowest SCN in the flashback data (oldest time you can flashback the database to, given the size of your flash recovery area).

- **RETENTION_TARGET.** Indicates the target retention time (in minutes).

- **FLASHBACK_SIZE.** Indicates the current size of the flashback data (in bytes).

- **ESTIMATED_FLASHBACK_SIZE.** Indicates the estimated size of flashback data needed for the current target retention.

You can actually use V$FLASHBACK_DATABASE_LOG to estimate the amount of flashback space required based on your current workload:

```
SQL> select * from v$flashback_database_log;

OLDEST_FLASHBACK_SCN OLDEST_FLASHBACK_T RETENTION_TARGET FLASHBACK_SIZE
➥ESTIMATED_FLASHBACK_SIZE
-------------------- ------------------ ---------------- -------------- --------------------
--
            685607 21:33:42 10-MAR-05             1440       36175872
25165824
```

> Unlike redo log files, flashback logs are not
> archived.

The estimate is based on the workload since the instance was started or during the most recent time interval equal to the flashback retention target, whichever is shorter.

Depending on your result from V$FLASHBACK_DATABASE_LOG, you should adjust the database retention target as needed.

To monitor the overhead with flashback logging, Oracle stores all logging activity statistics in the V$FLASHBACK_DATABASE_STAT view. Using this view, you can review the estimated flashback size based on previous workloads (usually within the last 24 hours). Each row represents data based over a one-hour window. Along with flashback logging, V$FLASHBACK_DATABASE_STAT also displays redo and actual database data generated over the same time frame.

```
SQL> select * from v$flashback_database_stat

BEGIN_TIME          END_TIME          FLASHBACK_DATA    DB_DATA   REDO_DATA
➥ESTIMATED_FLASHBACK_SIZE
-----------------   ----------------- -------------- ---------- ---------- --------------------
-----
22:56:35 11-MAR-05 23:20:22 11-MAR-05         3293184    4284416    2502144
0
21:56:26 11-MAR-05 22:56:35 11-MAR-05         4374528    7086080    2852352
25288704
20:56:16 11-MAR-05 21:56:26 11-MAR-05         4202496    7028736    2916352
23568384
19:56:06 11-MAR-05 20:56:16 11-MAR-05         4046848    6717440    2916352
21897216
```

```
18:55:56 11-MAR-05 19:56:06 11-MAR-05        4300800    6799360    2755584
20201472
17:55:46 11-MAR-05 18:55:56 11-MAR-05        4046848    6668288    2836480
18309120
16:55:39 11-MAR-05 17:55:46 11-MAR-05        1990656    4562944    1176064
16465920
...
```

You can use V$FLASHBACK_DATABASE_STAT to determine how the rate of generation of flashback data has changed over a 24-hour period. Based on this information, you may need to adjust the retention time or the overall size of the flash recovery area.

Flashback Database in Action

The best way to truly understand Flashback Database is to see the technology in action. You can use any of the following tools to flashback the database to a point in time or a specific SCN:

- FLASHBACK DATABASE SQL command
- FLASHBACK DATABASE RMAN command
- Enterprise Manager 10g Recovery wizard

As discussed previously, the database must be in a mounted state. When Flashback Database is invoked, the server uses the flashback logs to back out of all modifications during the specified time frame. In addition, redo log entries may be applied to ensure consistency. After the flashback operation has been completed, you can open the database in read-only mode to verify that you have corrected the problem. If not, you can continue the flashback operation or perform additional recovery to roll the database forward to a different point in time.

Following is a brief example of using the Flashback Database command via SQL:

1. Verify your Flashback Database settings (if you haven't already, make sure you properly configure Flashback Database by following the steps listed in the section titled "Configuring Flashback Database"):

   ```
   SQL> select flashback_on, current_scn from v$database;

   FLA CURRENT_SCN
   --- -----------
   YES           0
   ```

2. Capture the current SCN number from the database:

   ```
   SQL> select current_scn from v$database;

   CURRENT_SCN
   -----------
       703327
   ```

3. We introduce logical errors to our example:

```
SQL> select count(*) from emp;

  COUNT(*)
----------
       107

SQL> truncate table emp;

Table truncated.

SQL> select count(*) from emp;

  COUNT(*)
----------
         0

SQL> drop table dept;

Table dropped.

SQL> desc dept
ERROR:
ORA-04043: object dept does not exist
```

4. Perform a clean shutdown and mount the database:

```
SQL> conn / as sysdba
Connected.
SQL> shutdown immediate
Database closed.
Database dismounted.
ORACLE instance shut down.
SQL> startup mount;
ORACLE instance started.

Total System Global Area  171966464 bytes
Fixed Size                   787988 bytes
Variable Size             145750508 bytes
Database Buffers           25165824 bytes
Redo Buffers                 262144 bytes
Database mounted.
```

5. Issue the FLASHBACK DATABASE SQL command:

```
SQL> flashback database to scn 703327;
Flashback complete.
```

You can also use the FLASHBACK DATABASE SQL command using a timestamp:

```
SQL> flashback database to timestamp(SYSDATE - 1/24);
Flashback complete.
```

6. Open the database in read-only mode and verify that you corrected the problem:

```
SQL> alter database open read only;

Database altered.

SQL> conn stroupe/gwu
Connected.
SQL> select count(*) from emp;

  COUNT(*)
----------
       107

SQL> select count(*) from dept;

  COUNT(*)
----------
        27
```

7. Perform a clean shutdown and open the database with the RESETLOGS command:

```
SQL> conn / as sysdba
Connected.
SQL> shutdown immediate
Database closed.
Database dismounted.
ORACLE instance shut down.
SQL> startup mount
ORACLE instance started.

Total System Global Area  171966464 bytes
Fixed Size                   787988 bytes
Variable Size             145750508 bytes
Database Buffers           25165824 bytes
Redo Buffers                 262144 bytes
```

```
Database mounted.
SQL> alter database open resetlogs;

Database altered.
```

Along with the SQL, you can also use the FLASHBACK DATABASE command via Oracle RMAN. The syntax is very similar to what you can use with SQL. Using the V$FLASHBACK_DATABASE_LOG view, you can retrieve the OLDEST_FLASHBACK_SCN and OLDEST_FLASHBACK_TIME (same as before) and use the following RMAN commands to invoke Flashback Database:

SCN-based FLASHBACK DATABASE command:

```
RMAN> FLASHBACK DATABASE TO SCN=703327;
```

Time-based FLASHBACK DATABASE command:

```
RMAN> FLASHBACK DATABASE TO TIME = TO_DATE('2005-03-12 01:00:00',
➡'YYYY-MM-DD HH24:MI:SS');
```

As noted previously, you can use the Flashback Database feature with SQL, RMAN, and Enterprise Manager via the Recovery wizard. Following is a small example of using Flashback Database via 10g OEM—a.k.a., Database Control:

1. From the Maintenance tab, click Perform Recovery.

2. On the Perform Recovery Page: Type page, shown in Figure 17.1, choose Whole Database from the Object Type drop-down list and then choose your recovery type. If your database is open, you will be notified that the database needs to be in mount stage. Here, you will need to enter the O/S login credentials so OEM can restart your instance and place it in the mount stage.

3. Recovery wizard shuts down your database and restarts it in the mount stage. Click the Refresh button, as shown in Figure 17.2, when the database has been placed in mount stage.

4. After the database is placed in mount stage, the Recovery wizard will prompt you with several options for recovery, as shown in Figure 17.3. You can either recover by date, SCN, or sequence. Recovery wizard will also provide you with the oldest SCN and time to which you can flashback.

5. After you have chosen the best recovery time, the Recovery wizard will prompt you for the recovery method—either flashback or traditional point-in-time recovery (see Figure 17.4).

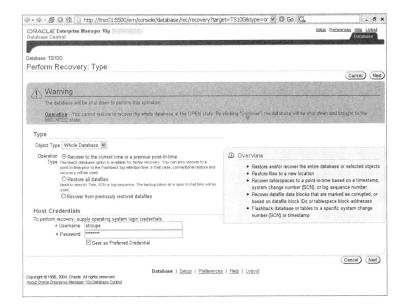

FIGURE 17.1
The Enterprise Manager 10g Perform Recovery home page.

FIGURE 17.2
Shutting down the database with the Enterprise Manager 10g Recovery wizard.

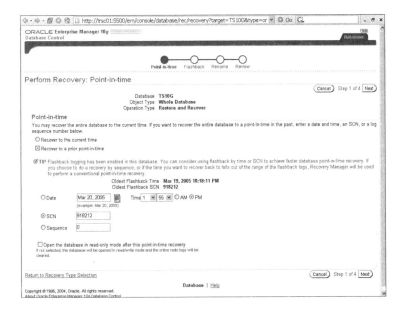

FIGURE 17.3
Specifying the point in time recovery options using the 10g Recovery wizard.

FIGURE 17.4
Specifying Flashback
options using the 10g
Recovery wizard.

6. Review your selections for the recovery operation, as shown in Figure 17.5. Here, because
   OEM will use RMAN to perform the recovery, you can also choose to edit the RMAM
   script that OEM will use if you wish. Once you click Submit, the job will be processed via
   the scheduler. When complete, OEM will provide you a success message along with the
   output from the RMAN script that was used (see Figure 17.6).

FIGURE 17.5
10g Recovery wizard
Summary page.

Using Flashback Database with Data Guard

> You must have Flashback Database enabled
> on both the primary and the standby data-
> base to utilize its features in a Data Guard
> environment.

As mentioned in Chapter 16, "Utilizing 10g
Physical and Logical Standby with Data
Guard," Oracle 10g provides the ability to
fully utilize the benefits of Flashback
Database in your Data Guard environment. In
earlier releases of Oracle, your old primary
database was removed from the Data Guard environment after a failover operation occurred.
The only way to reinstantiate the old primary database back into the Data Guard environment
involved restoring a previous backup of the new primary and then resynchronizing any missing
archive logs. This process was very cumbersome, especially if you had a large database. Now,
with 10g, you can use the Flashback Database feature to convert the old primary database into a
new standby database without performing this time-consuming reinstantiation process.

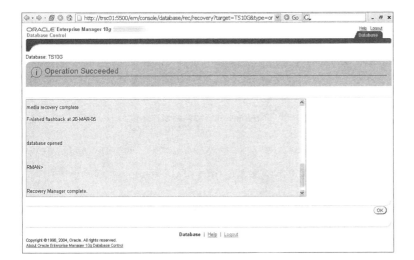

FIGURE 17.6
Successful results using
10g Recovery wizard.

After a failover has occurred, you can perform the following steps to utilize the Flashback Database feature for your new standby database.

In a physical standby configuration, do the following:

1. On the new primary database, capture the SCN at the time of the database role reversal with the following query:

   ```
   SQL> select standby_became_primary_scn from v$database;
   ```

2. After the old primary database site becomes available, start the old primary database in the mount stage.

3. Use the FLASHBACK DATABASE command with the SCN number you determined in step 1 on the old primary database:

   ```
   SQL> flashback database to scn <scn>;
   ```

4. Disable the Flashback Database feature on the old primary database:

   ```
   SQL> alter database flashback database off;
   ```

5. Create a new standby control file on the old primary database and then issue the shutdown command:

   ```
   SQL> alter database create standby controlfile as 'C:\oracle\physical_std.ctl';
   ```

6. Replace the old primary control file with the new standby control file from step 5 and start the old primary database in the mount stage.

7. On the new standby (old primary), enable the Flashback Database feature:

   ```
   SQL> alter database flashback database on;
   ```

8. On the new primary database (old standby), enable log transport services to the new standby database (old primary) and manually archive a new log:

```
SQL> alter system archive log current;
```

9. On the new standby database (old primary), start the managed recovery service:

```
SQL> alter database recover managed standby database disconnect;
```

In a logical standby configuration, do the following:

1. On the new primary database, capture the SCN at the time of the database role reversal with the following query:

```
SQL> select value from dba_logstdby_parameters where name = 'END_PRIMARY_SCN';
```

2. After the old primary database site becomes available, start the old primary database in the mount stage.

3. Use the FLASHBACK DATABASE command with the SCN number you determined in step 1 on the old primary database:

```
SQL> flashback database to scn <scn>;
```

4. Use the security_clause (GUARD) to protect data in the database from being changed:

```
SQL> alter database guard all;
```

5. Open the database with the RESETLOGS command:

```
SQL> alter database open resetlogs;
```

6. On the new primary database, find the redo log file where the data dictionary dump begins:

```
SQL> select name from v$archive_log where (sequence# =
        (select max(sequence# from v$archived_log
            where dictionary_begin= 'YES' and standby_dest = 'NO'));
```

7. Copy the redo log file identified in step 6 to the standby site and register it in the new standby database:

```
SQL> alter database register logical logfile <logfile>;
```

8. Start the SQL Apply services on the new logical standby database:

```
SQL> alter database start logical standby apply initial;
```

Along with the failover operation, the Flashback Database feature can also be used when a RESETLOGS command has been issued in your Data Guard environment. Previously, anytime you issued a RESETLOGS command to your primary database, your standby database became invalidated and had to be re-created. Perform the following steps to avoid having to rebuild your standby database after a RESETLOGS command has been issued.

In a physical standby configuration, do the following:

1. On the primary database, capture the SCN that was used before the RESETLOGS command was issued:

   ```
   SQL> select (resetlogs_change# - 2) from v$database;
   ```

2. On the standby database, capture the current SCN number:

   ```
   SQL> select current_scn from v$database;
   ```

3. Issue the FLASHBACK DATABASE command on the standby database to the SCN number you ascertained in step 1:

   ```
   SQL> flashback standby database to scn <before RESETLOGS scn>;
   ```

4. Restart the managed recovery services on the standby database:

   ```
   SQL> alter database recover managed standby database disconnect;
   ```

In a logical standby configuration, do the following:

1. On the primary database, capture the SCN that was used before the RESETLOGS command was issued:

   ```
   SQL> select (resetlogs_change# - 2) from v$database;
   ```

2. On the standby database, capture the current SCN number:

   ```
   SQL> select current_scn from v$database;
   ```

SQL Apply After RESETLOGS

It is possible that the SQL Apply service does not halt when the RESETLOGS command is issued on the primary database. If the logical standby's SCN is far behind the primary's SCN, then the SQL Apply service can interpret the OPEN RESETLOGS command without stopping. Only use the following steps below if you have made sure that your SQL Apply process has halted on the logical standby.

3. Issue the FLASHBACK DATABASE command on the standby database to the SCN number you ascertained in step 1:

   ```
   SQL> flashback standby database to scn <before RESETLOGS scn>;
   ```

4. Restart SQL Apply on the standby database:

   ```
   SQL> alter database start logical standby apply immediate;
   ```

Troubleshooting Flashback Database

Although the Flashback Database feature does offer significant benefits to your 10g environment, it is important to understand the limitations that exist with Oracle 10g Release 1 as well as some common errors you may receive when using its syntax.

Currently in Oracle 10g Release 1, you cannot use the Flashback Database feature if:

- Any condition exists where you must use media recovery.

- The control file has been restored or re-created.

- Any data file has been dropped or shrunk.

- A tablespace has been dropped.

Flashback Database Using Automatic Extension

You can use the Flashback Database feature with data files that you have configured for automatic extension. Only files that have been shrunk, not expanded, lose support for Flashback Database.

Flashback Database supports all datatypes in the database, but all data files must remain online during the time in which Flashback Database is enabled. Dropped data files will not be recovered with Flashback Database. After the flashback operation is completed, you can restore and recover any dropped data files to the same point in time as the rest of your database if needed. If you have a data file that has been resized (shrunk) during the flashback span, you should take the file offline before issuing the FLASHBACK DATABASE command. After the flashback operation is completed, you can restore and recover any resized data files to the same point in time if needed.

It is possible that you could receive failures during your Flashback Database operation. In normal operation, there are two types of errors that can occur when there is not enough flashback data to process the command:

- `ORA-38729: Not enough flashback database log data to do FLASHBACK.` This error indicates that your time or SCN did not have enough flashback data to process the command. You must change the time or SCN to an appropriate time that would remain valid in your flash recovery area.

- `ORA-38753: Cannot flashback data file #; no flashback log data.` This error indicates that these specific files did not have enough flashback data to process the command. You can take these files offline and continue the flashback operation if you like. If you do, the offline files can be recovered to the same point in time by using traditional point-in-time recovery methods.

If you do receive any of these errors, you should consider increasing your flashback retention period to a higher value. Because these errors are happening while your database is mounted, you can simply reissue the FLASHBACK DATABASE command after you take appropriate measures if needed. If you even experience an instance crash during a Flashback Database operation, simply restart and mount your database and reissue the FLASHBACK DATABASE command to resume the recovery operation.

Flashback Table

Another new flashback feature introduced with the Oracle 10g database is Flashback Table. Flashback Table, much like Flashback Database, allows you to recover data to a specific point in time without restoring from a backup; however, the recovery is handled at the table level. When the Flashback Table feature is invoked, the data stored in the tables and all objects that are related to the table (indexes, constraints, triggers, and so on) are also restored. This new feature is extremely useful when a user accidentally inserts, updates, or deletes the wrong rows in a table or even accidentally drops a table if he or she has the proper privileges to do so.

In previous versions of the database, the recovery operation for a single table or multiple tables involved a full point-in-time recovery, restoring specific tables from a clone, importing from a previous table-level export, utilizing Oracle LogMiner to extract the SQL from the undo column to "rewind" the table to a specific point, or in some cases utilizing the 9i flashback query operation to capture the previous version of the target data in a user-defined cursor and then correcting any errors as needed. Depending on your specific situation, any of the recovery tasks listed could become a long and labor-intensive operation. Now, with the 10g Flashback Table feature, you can easily and quickly recover any database table from accidental drops or modifications, and in some cases without the involvement of a DBA.

Configuring Flashback Table

To perform its necessary operations, Flashback Table utilizes the data from your undo segments. The undo tablespace (as you may have learned from Oracle 9i) utilizes the UNDO_RETENTION initialization parameter to specify the amount of committed undo data that should be retained in the database. Because UNDO_RETENTION determines the recovery window of the Flashback Table feature, you should set this parameter based on your flashback requirements or user needs.

> **Flashback Table Using Automatic Undo**
>
> Remember, if an active transaction needs undo space and the undo space does not have any free space available, then the system starts reusing undo space as needed. If needed, use the RETENTION GUARANTEE clause to specify that all unexpired undo data will be preserved.

In addition to setting the correct undo parameters, the Flashback Table feature also requires you to enable row movement on each target table. In previous versions, row movement was used to enable or disable the migration of a row to a new partition if its key was updated. Flashback Table utilizes row movement to aid in the recovery of table data from the defined undo segments.

When you have configured your undo settings properly and enabled row management for your target table, the last prerequisite for using Flashback Table is to grant the necessary privileges.

You must grant the FLASHBACK object privilege or FLASHBACK ANY TABLE system privilege to any user who wants to utilize the Flashback Table feature. In addition, the flashback user must also have the SELECT, INSERT, DELETE, and ALTER TABLE object privileges on the target table.

Flashback Table in Action

You can use one of the following tools to flashback the table to a point in time or a specific SCN:

- FLASHBACK TABLE SQL command

- Enterprise Manager 10g Flashback Table wizard

As stated previously, you must enable automatic undo management, set your UNDO_RETENTION parameter to a reasonable setting, enable row management on your target tables, and grant the necessary FLASHBACK privileges. Depending on your recovery condition, you will need to choose either an SCN or time-based flashback time. To determine the appropriate flashback time for your operation, you can use flashback versions query and flashback transaction query. Both of these new flashback features are discussed later in this chapter in the sections "Flashback Versions Query" and "Flashback Transaction Query" respectively.

Row Movement with Flashback Table

Oracle does not allow you to enable row movement on a table and then flashback a table to a time prior to issuing the enabling row-movement command. If you plan to use Flashback Table, you need to make sure to enable row movement on your target tables as early as possible. If you ever hit this limitation, you will need to use the flashback transaction query command, covered later in the Flashback Transaction Query section.

Following is a brief example of using the FLASHBACK TABLE command via SQL:

1. Grant the necessary privileges for flashback (if needed).

   ```
   SQL> grant flashback, select, insert,
   delete, alter on flashtest to stroupe;
   ```

   or

   ```
   SQL> grant flashback any table to
   stroupe;
   ```

2. Enable row movement on any candidate tables:

   ```
   SQL> alter table flashtest enable row movement;
   ```

3. Gather necessary information for flashback operation

   ```
   SQL> select * from flashtest;

           ID
   ----------
         1000
         2000
         3000
         4000
   ```

```
SQL> select current_scn from v$database;

CURRENT_SCN
-----------
     771390
```

4. Introduce table-level errors:

```
SQL> delete from flashtest where id in (2000,4000);
SQL> commit;
SQL> select * from flashtest;

        ID
----------
      1000
      3000
```

5. Invoke Flashback Table to correct these user errors:

```
SQL> flashback table flashtest to scn 771390;

Flashback complete.

SQL> select * from flashtest;

        ID
----------
      1000
      2000
      3000
      4000
```

Alternatively, you could also use the time-based FLASHBACK TABLE command:

```
SQL> flashback table flashtest to
timestamp to_
⮩timestamp('2005-03-15 11:05:01','YYYY-
MM-DD HH:MI:SS');
```

You can also use the Flashback Table feature via Enterprise Manager. Following is a step-by-step example of how to use Flashback Table with OEM:

What Is SYS_TEMP_FBT**?**

When using the Flashback Table feature, a global temporary table called SYS_TEMP_FBT is created in your schema unconditionally. This required table is used to track internal flashback information. To remove this table, simply truncate, and then drop the table when you are finished with your flashback operation. Currently in 10g Release 1, Oracle support is tracking this issue as bug 3076151, which is fixed with 10g Release 2.

1. From the OEM home page, choose the Maintenance tab, and then click the Perform Recovery link under Backup/Recovery.

2. The Perform Recovery page opens, as shown in Figure 17.7. From the Object Type drop-down menu, select Tables.

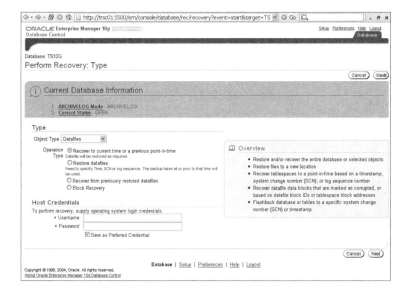

FIGURE 17.7
The 10g OEM Perform Recovery home page.

3. When the page is refreshed, you will need to choose between flashing back existing tables or dropped tables, as shown in Figure 17.8. Click on the Flashback Existing Tables option, and click Next.

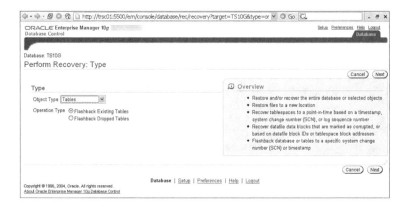

FIGURE 17.8
Specifying table recovery type from the 10g OEM Recovery wizard.

4. When the Perform Recovery: Point-in-time page appears (see Figure 17.9), you will need to specify the point in time to which to recover. You can enter in a table so Oracle can evaluate row changes and decide the best point in time to recover to, or you can enter in a known time or SCN. For the purpose of this example, we will choose a time to recover.

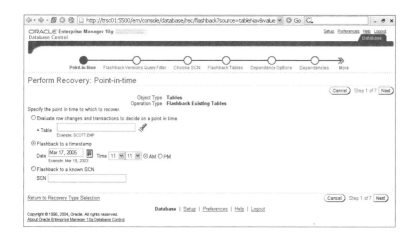

FIGURE 17.9
Specifying table recovery options from the 10g OEM Recovery wizard.

5. The Perform Recovery: Flashback Tables page opens, as shown in Figure 17.10. Choose the table you wish to flashback and click Next.

FIGURE 17.10
Specifying tables to use flashback table recovery from the 10g OEM Recovery wizard.

6. If any dependencies exist, you will be prompted with the Dependencies Option page. Choose the best option for managing your table dependencies. If you do not have any dependencies with your table, you will bypass this page, and the Perform Recovery: Review page will appear (see Figure 17.11). From here, you can review the changes you are about to enter. Also from this page you can click the Show Row Changes button to see what you are about to recover as well as the SQL that OEM will use to perform the recovery for you. When confirmed, click Submit to invoke Flashback Table recovery.

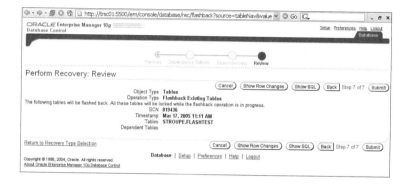

FIGURE 17.11
Flashback Table Summary from the 10g OEM Recovery wizard.

7. After the recovery is complete, a confirmation page will appear, telling you that the specified table was recovered (see Figure 17.12). From here, click OK to return to the Maintenance window.

FIGURE 17.12
Confirmation page for Flashback Table Recovery.

Troubleshooting Flashback Table

Even though the Flashback Table feature is fairly straightforward, there are a few limitations worth noting. Currently in Oracle 10g Release 1, you cannot use the Flashback Table feature for the following:

- Any table in the SYS schema
- Tables that are part of a cluster
- Materialized views
- Advanced Queuing (AQ) tables
- Static data dictionary Tables
- System tables
- Nested tables
- Remote tables via database links
- Partitions of a table
- Temporary tables

Most commands are supported by Flashback Table. That said, if the following DDL commands are issued on supported tables, the Flashback Table command does not work:

- ALTER TABLE .. DROP COLUMN

- ALTER TABLE .. DROP PARTITION

- CREATE CLUSTER

- TRUNCATE TABLE

- ALTER TABLE .. MOVE

If you do run into this limitation, you will receive the ORA-01455 error message: Unable to read data – table definition has changed:

```
SQL> select current_scn from v$database;

CURRENT_SCN
-----------
     816801

SQL> truncate table flashtest;

Table truncated.

SQL> flashback table flashtest to scn 816801;
flashback table flashtest to scn 816801
              *
ERROR at line 1:
ORA-01466: unable to read data - table definition has changed
```

As previously noted, when you use Flashback Table to recover a table or tables to a specific point in time, all associated objects with the table data are also restored, such as indexes, constraints, triggers, and so on. There are, however, a few gotchas with associated table objects when using the Flashback Table feature:

- The FLASHBACK TABLE command will fail if one of your referential integrity constraints is violated. Because your FLASHBACK TABLE command did fail, the table remains as it was prior to your issuing the command.

- By default, all triggers are disabled for the duration of the Flashback Table operation. After the operation has completed, all triggers are returned to the state they were in prior to the flashback. You can, however, use the ENABLE TRIGGERS option of the FLASHBACK TABLE command to override this default behavior.

  ```
  SQL> flashback table flashtest to scn 816851 enable triggers;
  ```

Flashback Drop with Recycle Bin

In previous releases of the database, when you issued the DROP command to drop a table, all contents of that table were permanently removed from the database. Now, with Oracle 10g Flashback Drop, a dropped table and its dependent objects (such as indexes, constraints, and triggers) are renamed to a system-generated string and logically placed in the *recycle bin*. Each recycle bin object will physically reside in the same tablespace and schema from which it was dropped. For example, if the DOCUMENTS table was created in the HIGH_GROWTH tablespace, then the dropped DOCUMENTS table will remain in the HIGH_GROWTH tablespace as long as the table remains in the recycle bin.

> ### Using Flashback Table with Table-Dependent Objects
>
> Usually, table-dependent objects such as indexes, triggers, and constraints should retain the original name after a dropped table has been recovered. However, the FLASHBACK TABLE ..BEFORE DROP command is used to recover a dropped table, all the indexes associated with the recovered table are recovered with a new system-generated name, not the original index name. Oracle is tracking this limitation as bug 3422568.

Once a table is logically placed in the recycle bin, a user or DBA can recover it at a later time in case the table was dropped in error. This new flashback feature eliminates the need to perform a point-in-time recovery to recover a table that has been dropped, which would affect all database users. Flashback Drop is actually an extension of the Flashback Table command. Now you can issue the FLASHBACK TABLE .. TO BEFORE DROP command to recover the table from the recycle bin. You can also recover the dropped table from the recycle bin and provide a new name using the TABLE .. TO BEFORE DROP RENAME TO command. The Flashback Drop feature only supports tables and their dependent objects. Flashback Drop does not support data from the DROP TABLESPACE or DROP USER commands.

Oracle Recycle Bin

The recycle bin is actually a new data dictionary table (SYS.RECYCLEBIN$) that records information about dropped objects from your database. When objects are dropped, Oracle records all associated information needed to possibly recover the object at a later time in the recycle bin table. Tables and all depend objects are given a system-generated name with the prefix of BIN$. Users can also continue to access the data in the recycle bin and even perform actions with flashback query, but you must use the new system-generated name when accessing the data. Users will retain all writes and privileges to the recycle bin objects, just as they had prior to the DROP command. The recycle bin does not have any special storage requirements because all dropped objects will remain in the same tablespace they were dropped from, but it's worth noting that dropped objects still count against a user's quota. You can access the new recycle bin from the following data dictionary views:

- `RECYCLEBIN`

- `USER_RECYCLEBIN`

- `DBA_RECYCLEBIN`

> **The** `RECYCLEBIN` **Data Dictionary View**
> `RECYCLEBIN` **is actually a public synonym that is based on the view** `USER_RECYCLEBIN`. `USER_RECYCLE` **is a view that is based on the** `SYS.RECYCLEBIN$` **table.**

Dropped objects will not be logically removed from the recycle bin unless

- The object is manually purged from the recycle bin using the `PURGE` command.

- The tablespace that contains the dropped object runs out of space.

- A user's quota has been met.

- The tablespace that contains the dropped object needs to perform the autoextend operation.

Any tablespace that encounters space limitations will automatically purge recycle bin objects from oldest to newest. If required, Oracle will actually try to remove all table-dependent objects before removing the table itself. Also, if any tablespace has the autoextend option turned on, all recycle bin objects will be removed before the tablespace autoextends. To manually purge objects from the recycle bin, you can use the new `PURGE` command. The `PURGE` command can be used to manually remove one or all objects from the recycle bin, as well as recycle bin objects from specific tablespaces.

```
SQL> purge recyclebin;
SQL> purge dba_recyclebin;   (Must by executed by SYSDBA)
SQL> purge table hr.sales;;
SQL> purge tablespace users;
```

You can also use the new `PURGE` command to drop tables and bypass the recycle bin all together. By using the following command, the table that is referenced is not entered into the recycle bin, and hence reverts back to pre-10g behavior:

```
SQL> drop table emp purge;
```

Flashback Drop in Action

You can use one of the following tools to flashback a table prior to the `DROP` command:

- `FLASHBACK TABLE .. TO BEFORE DROP` SQL command

- Enterprise Manager 10g Flashback Table wizard

Following is a brief example of using the `FLASHBACK TABLE .. TO BEFORE DROP` command via SQL:

1. Detail the target table contents and drop the table:

```
SQL> select * from flashtest;

        ID
----------
      1000
      2000
      3000
      4000


SQL> drop table flashtest;

Table dropped.

SQL> select * from flashtest;
select * from flashtest
              *
ERROR at line 1:
ORA-00942: table or view does not exist
```

2. Review the new entry in the recycle bin:

```
SQL> select object_name, original_name, ts_name, droptime from recyclebin;

OBJECT_NAME                      ORIGINAL_NAME        TS_NAME              DROP_TIME
-------------------------------- -------------------- -------------------- ----------
BIN$yPOGdfEpQSqPLOx/PD260A==$0 FLASHTEST              USERS
➥2005-03-17:22:10:42
```

You can also use the show recyclebin command as follows:

```
SQL> show recyclebin

ORIGINAL NAME   RECYCLEBIN NAME                 OBJECT TYPE  DROP TIME
--------------- ------------------------------- ------------ --------------------


FLASHTEST       BIN$yPOGdfEpQSqPLOx/PD260A==$0 TABLE        2005-03-17:22:10:42
```

3. If needed, query the contents of the dropped table in the recycle bin:

```
SQL> select * from "BIN$yPOGdfEpQSqPLOx/PD260A==$0";

        ID
----------
      1000
```

```
        2000
        3000
        4000
```

4. Recover the dropped table:

```
SQL> flashback table flashtest to
before drop;

Flashback complete.

SQL> select * from flashtest;

        ID
- - - - - - - - - -
      1000
      2000
      3000
      4000

SQL> select * from recyclebin;

no rows selected
```

5. Recover the dropped table with the RENAME option:

```
SQL> select * from flashtest;

        ID
- - - - - - - - - -
      1000
      2000
      3000
      4000

SQL> drop table flashtest;

Table dropped.

SQL> select * from flashtest;
select * from flashtest
              *
ERROR at line 1:
ORA-00942: table or view does not exist

SQL> flashback table flashtest to before drop rename to flashtest1;
```

Querying Recycle Bin Objects

It is required that you place quotes around the recycle bin object name because special symbols are used to rename the dropped object.

Using Flashback Table for Dropped Tables

You may experience a time when you have multiple copies of the same table in the recycle bin. When using the FLASHBACK TABLE command-line syntax to retrieve a dropped table, make sure that the server retrieves the table that was dropped most recently from the recycle bin. If you needed to retrieve a table other than the most recently dropped table, you can use Enterprise Manager to select the appropriate table from the complete history.

```
Flashback complete.

SQL> select * from flashtest1;

        ID
----------
      1000
      2000
      3000
      4000
```

Along with SQL, you can also utilize the Flashback Drop feature via 10g Enterprise Manager. Following is a brief example using Enterprise Manager Flashback Drop:

1. Under the Maintenance tab, select Perform Recovery under Backup/Recovery.

2. Select Tables from the Object Type drop-down menu (see Figure 17.13).

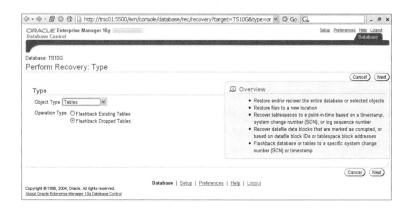

FIGURE 17.13
Specifying recovery type from the 10g OEM Recovery wizard.

3. Select Flashback Dropped Tables as the operation type, and click Next.

4. Enter the schema name and click Go. Under the Results heading, you will see all the tables listed in the recycle bin (see Figure 17.14). As you can see, there are multiple copies of the same table; you can choose to view the contents of and retrieve a specific table.

5. If you like, you can view the contents of each table in the recycle bin, as shown in Figure 17.15.

6. Click the check box next to the table you want to recover from the recycle bin, and then click Next. On the Rename page, shown in Figure 17.16, rename the table as desired.

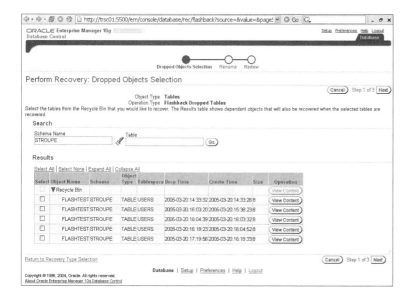

FIGURE 17.14
Specifying the correct
table from the recycle
bin from the 10g OEM
Recovery wizard.

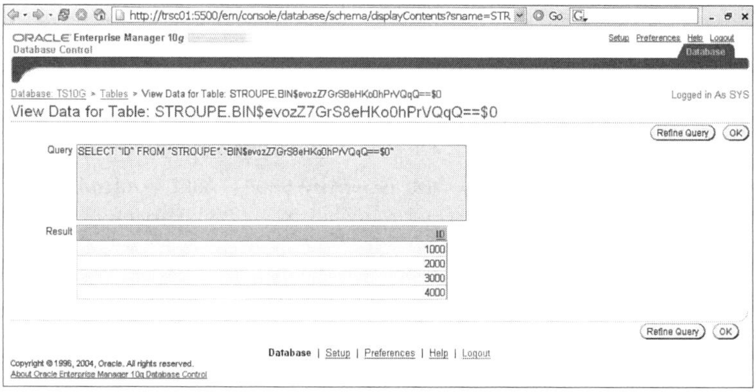

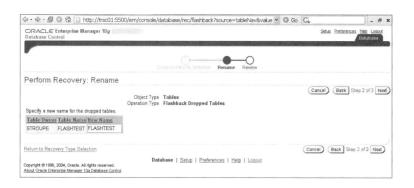

FIGURE 17.15
Viewing the contents
from the recycle bin from
the 10g OEM Recovery
wizard.

FIGURE 17.16
Renaming the dropped
table within the recycle
bin from the 10g OEM
Recovery wizard.

7. After you enter the correct name for the table, click Next to go to the Review page, shown in Figure 17.17. Here you can review and submit your changes. When your changes are successfully made, a confirmation page will appear; click OK to return to the Maintenance page.

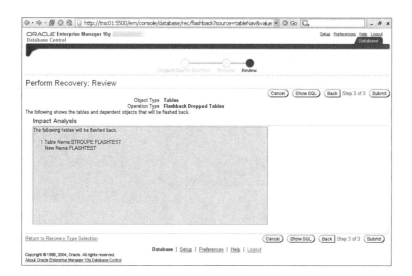

FIGURE 17.17
Table Recovery Summary from the 10g OEM Recovery wizard.

Troubleshooting Flashback Drop

The Flashback Drop feature works only for tables where you issue the DROP TABLE command and when its corresponding information is registered in the recycle bin. The Flashback Drop feature is not supported in the following situations:

- When you issue the DROP TABLE .. PURGE command. Here, the data will bypass the recycle bin and will be permanently removed.

  ```
  SQL> drop table flashtest purge;

  Table dropped.

  SQL> select * from recyclebin;

  no rows selected
  ```

- When you issue the DROP TABLESPACE .. INCLUDING CONTENTS command. All data will bypass the recycle bin and will be permanently removed. Any recycle bin objects belonging to the tablespace are also purged.

- When you issue the DROP TABLESPACE command with active recycle bin objects. All recycle bin objects will be purged when this command is issued.

■ When you issue the DROP USER .. CASCADE command with or without active recycle bin objects. With this command, all objects owned by this user will bypass the recycle bin and be permanently removed. Any recycle bin objects belonging to the user are also purged.

Disabling Flashback Drop

Flashback Drop requires the functionality of the recycle bin to perform its work. In the event you ever want to disable the behavior of recycling, there is an undocumented parameter that you can set to disable it. The parameter _recyclebin controls the behavior of the database recycle bin. The default setting is TRUE, so setting its value to FALSE will disable the feature.

```
SQL> alter system set "_recyclebin"=FALSE;

System altered.

SQL> conn stroupe/gwu
Connected.
SQL> create table flash as select * from sys.flashtest;

Table created.

SQL> drop table flash;

Table dropped.

SQL> sho recyclebin
SQL> select * from recyclebin;

no rows selected
```

Flashback Versions Query

The flashback versions query is another new feature introduced with the 10g Database that will allow you to retrieve a history of changes for a specified set of rows within a table. This new feature expands the flashback query technology first introduced in Oracle 9i. Instead of specifying a time or SCN to enable flashback query for analysis, you can now use the VERSIONS_BETWEEN clause to retrieve all the versions of a specified set of rows that exist or ever existed between the time the query was issued and a point back in time that you must specify. The VERSIONS_BETWEEN clause eliminates the need to flashback in time to review historical row modifications over time.

The flashback versions query feature, like Flashback Table, utilizes data from the undo segments, so you must configure your instance to use automatic undo management. The amount of data that you can retrieve with the VERSIONS_BETWEEN clause is limited by the setting of the

UNDO_RETENTION initialization parameter. Because the UNDO_RETENTION parameter determines your row history, you should set this parameter based on your needed timeline to utilize flashback versions query. Also, you can use the RETENTION GUARANTEE clause to ensure that you will retain all critical undo data when using flashback versions query.

Along with the row history, the flashback versions query feature also returns specific data about each transaction using its own pseudocolumns. You can include these pseudocolumns with your query to provide a greater level of validity for the row history. The new pseudocolumns that flashback versions query can use include the following:

- **VERSIONS_STARTTIME.** Starting timestamp of the row version.

- **VERSIONS_ENDTIME.** Timestamp when the row version expired.

- **VERSIONS_STARTSCN.** Starting SCN of the row version.

- **VERSIONS_ENDSCN.** SCN when the row version expired.

- **VERSIONS_XID.** Identifier of the transaction that created the row version.

- **VERSIONS_OPERATION.** Row operation used (I for insert, U for update, and D for delete).

Flashback Versions Query in Action

Using the flashback versions query is simple, but any user who uses it will require the SELECT and FLASHBACK object privileges.

You can use one of the following tools to retrieve row history using flashback versions query:

- VERSION_BETWEEN SQL command

- Enterprise Manager 10g Flashback Query wizard

Following is a brief example of using the VERSION_BETWEEN command via SQL:

1. Create your sample data and grant necessary privileges:

```
SQL> create table flashtest as select * from hr.employees;
Table created.
SQL> grant select, flashback on flashtest to stroupe;
```

2. Initiate modifications to rows in the table:

```
SQL> select first_name, email from flashtest where department_id = 30;

FIRST_NAME          EMAIL
------------------- -------------------------
Den                 DRAPHEAL
Alexander           AKHOO
Shelli              SBAIDA
Sigal               STOBIAS
```

```
Guy                 GHIMURO
Karen               KCOLMENA

SQL> update flashtest set email = EMAIL¦¦'@HRDEPT' where department_id = 30;
commit.

SQL> select first_name, email from flashtest where department_id = 30;


FIRST_NAME          EMAIL
------------------- ------------------------
Den                 DRAPHEAL@HRDEPT
Alexander           AKHOO@HRDEPT
Shelli              SBAIDA@HRDEPT
Sigal               STOBIAS@HRDEPT
Guy                 GHIMURO@HRDEPT
Karen               KCOLMENA@HRDEPT


SQL> delete flashtest where department_id = 30;


6 rows deleted.


SQL> commit;
```

3. Review the row history using the VERSIONS_BETWEEN clause:

   ```
   SQL> select versions_startscn, versions_endscn, versions_xid, versions_operation,
   first_name, email from flashtest VERSIONS BETWEEN SCN MINVALUE and MAXVALUE
   where department_id = 30;
   ```

VERSIONS_STARTSCN	VERSIONS_ENDSCN	VERSIONS_XID	V	FIRST_NAME	EMAIL
929764		05002300BF000000	D	Karen	KCOLMENA@HRDEPT
929764		05002300BF000000	D	Guy	GHIMURO@HRDEPT
929764		05002300BF000000	D	Sigal	STOBIAS@HRDEPT
929764		05002300BF000000	D	Shelli	SBAIDA@HRDEPT
929764		05002300BF000000	D	Alexander	AKHOO@HRDEPT
929764		05002300BF000000	D	Den	DRAPHEAL@HRDEPT
929683	929764	0A002E0076000000	U	Karen	KCOLMENA@HRDEPT
929683	929764	0A002E0076000000	U	Guy	GHIMURO@HRDEPT
929683	929764	0A002E0076000000	U	Sigal	STOBIAS@HRDEPT
929683	929764	0A002E0076000000	U	Shelli	SBAIDA@HRDEPT

```
       929683        929764 0A002E0076000000 U Alexander        AKHOO@HRDEPT
       929683        929764 0A002E0076000000 U Den              DRAPHEAL@HRDEPT
                     929683                    Den              DRAPHEAL
                     929683                    Alexander        AKHOO
                     929683                    Shelli           SBAIDA
                     929683                    Sigal            STOBIAS
                     929683                    Guy              GHIMURO
                     929683                    Karen            KCOLMENA

18 rows selected.
```

You can also easily use Enterprise Manager to display the row history using flashback versions query. Following is a brief example of flashback versions query using OEM:

1. After you have created your table and initiated changes on the rows (as shown in steps 1 and 2 of the SQL flashback versions query), review your table via OEM by selecting from the OEM home page (choose Administration and Tables under the Schema subheading). After you enter your schema name, select the correct table name and then select the View Data action in the Actions drop-down list and click Go. Here, you can click the Refine Query button to return a specific result set (see Figure 17.18).

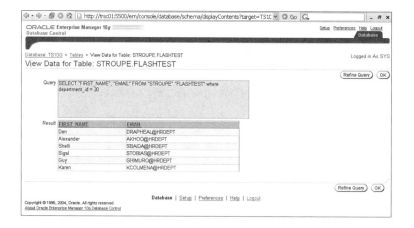

FIGURE 17.18
Viewing table data from 10g OEM.

2. Choose your recovery method by selecting the Maintenance tab and choosing Perform Recovery under the Backup/Recovery subheading.

3. Via the Recovery wizard, select Tables as the object type, select Flashback Existing Tables from the Recovery Type page, and then click next.

4. To evaluate the row history, select the schema and table name to evaluate. See Figure 17.19.

FIGURE 17.19
Specifying a table for
flashback versions query
from 10g OEM Recovery
wizard.

FIGURE 17.19
Specifying a table for
flashback versions query
from 10g OEM Recovery
wizard.

5. Using the flashback query filter, select the table columns and the correct predicate value for your analysis (see Figure 17.20).

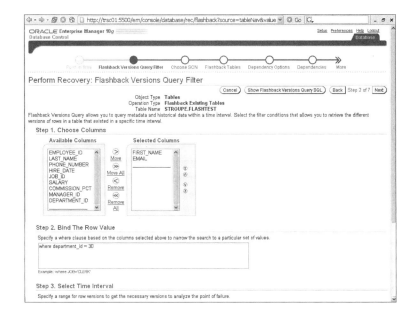

FIGURE 17.20
Specifying filter condi-
tions for flashback
versions query from 10g
OEM Recovery wizard.

6. When you have the correct filter information, you will see the OEM flashback versions query result set, as shown in Figure 17.21. From here you can choose the row or rows if you wish to use the Flashback Table option for point-in-time recovery.

7. To ensure that OEM is using the correct flashback versions query information, click the Show Flashback Versions Query SQL button in the screen shown in Figure 17.20 (refer to step 5). This displays the screen shown in Figure 17.22.

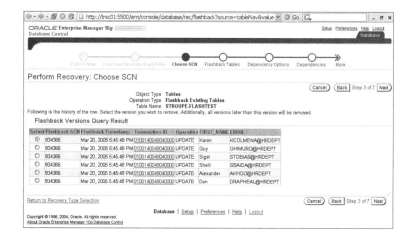

FIGURE 17.21
Reviewing the Flashback Versions Query Result Set from 10g OEM Recovery wizard.

FIGURE 17.22
Flashback Versions Query SQL from 10g OEM Recovery wizard.

Troubleshooting Flashback Versions Query

The only major requirement to utilizing the flashback versions query feature is to set up and configure automatic undo management to the appropriate size for UNDO_RETENTION. That said, there are a few specific limitations for 10g Release 1, outlined here:

- The flashback versions query feature only retrieves committed modifications of the rows. Any row modifications that are not committed, including current active transactions, are not supported by the flashback versions query.

- You cannot use the flashback versions query feature to retrieve data from a view, but you can use the VERSIONS_BETWEEN clause in a view definition.

- You cannot use the flashback versions query feature to retrieve data across certain DDL commands. The VERSIONS_BETWEEN clause will not show row history after it reaches a time in the past when the table specification was changed.

- Currently in 10g Release 1, you cannot use the flashback versions query on any table that has a block size higher than 8KB. If you have a table that uses 16KB or 32KB block sizes, you will receive an ORA-600 error message when using flashback versions query. Oracle support is tracking this issue as bug 3469992.

- If you migrate your 9i database to 10g (even using the Migration Assistant), you will need to run the following SQL to fully utilize 10g flashback versions query:

```
SQL>  delete from smon_scn_time where orig_thread <> 0;
```

After migration to 10g, you cannot fully utilize flashback up to the UNDO_RETENTION setting. See MetaLink Note #301502.1 for more information about this limitation.

Flashback Transaction Query

Another new flashback query feature introduced with Oracle 10g is flashback transaction query. The new flashback transaction query feature allows users to review and/or recover modifications made to the database at the transaction level—meaning that users can use this new feature to diagnose and resolve logical problems, perform historical analysis, or even audit transactions from a single transaction or by all the transactions during a period of time. Prior to 10g, DBAs had to mine redo logs with LogMiner to extract specific transactional information to possibly correct or audit SQL statements. Now, with flashback transaction query, you can undo the effects of a bad transaction much more quickly than before by querying FLASHBACK_ TRANSACTION_QUERY. The undo SQL generated by this new feature can be used to roll back changes made by a transaction. Flashback transaction query can be used to retrieve historical transaction data over a certain time frame via SCN or a time value.

Like other flashback features, flashback transaction query utilizes undo data to retrieve the modification history for quick retrieval performance. Flashback transaction query is also limited by the setting of UNDO_RETENTION, so you should set this parameter based on your needed time-line.

Flashback transaction query also requires the database to have supplemental logging enabled. When you enable supplemental logging, additional information is logged in the undo segments and redo log files. To enable supplemental logging, issue the following SQL command:

```
SQL> alter database add supplemental log data;
```

You can also query V$DATABASE to ensure that supplemental logging is enabled:

```
SQL> select supplemental_log_data_min from v$database;

SUPPLEME
--------
YES
```

Flashback Transaction Query in Action

Before you can start using the flashback transaction query feature, you must grant the SELECT
ANY TRANSACTION and FLASHBACK ANY TABLE system privileges in order to be able to issue queries
against the FLASHBACK_TRANSACTION_QUERY table.

You can use one of the following tools to retrieve transaction history using flashback transaction
query:

- FLASHBACK_TRANSACTION_QUERY table

- Enterprise Manager 10g Flashback Query wizard

Following is a brief example of using FLASHBACK_TRANSACTION_QUERY via SQL:

1. Create your sample data and grant necessary privileges:

   ```
   SQL> create table flashtest as select * from hr.employees;
   Table created.
   SQL> grant flashback any table, select any transaction to stroupe;
   ```

2. Initiate modifications to rows in the table:

   ```
   SQL> select first_name, email from flashtest where department_id = 20;


   FIRST_NAME          EMAIL
   ------------------- ------------------------
   Michael             MHARTSTE
   Pat                 PFAY


   SQL> delete from flashtest where department_id = 20;


   2 rows deleted.


   SQL> commit;
   ```

3. Review the transaction history from FLASHBACK_TRANSACTION_QUERY:

   ```
   SQL> select max(start_scn), max(commit_scn) from flashback_
   ➡transaction_query where logon_user = 'STROUPE';


   MAX(START_SCN) MAX(COMMIT_SCN)
   -------------- ---------------
           955272          955280


   SQL> select operation, table_name, undo_sql from flashback_transaction_query
   where start_scn = 955272 and commit_scn = 955280;
   ```

```
OPERATION       TABLE_NAME     UNDO_SQL
--------------- -------------- -----------------------------------------------------
DELETE          FLASHTEST      insert into "STROUPE"."FLASHTEST"
➥("EMPLOYEE_ID","FIRST_NAME",
 "LAST_NAME","EMAIL","PHONE_NUMBER","HIRE_DATE","JOB_ID",
 "SALARY","COMMISSION_PCT","MANAGER_ID","DEPARTMENT_ID") values
 ('202','Pat','Fay','PFAY@FINDEPT','603.123.6666',TO_DATE('17
 -AUG-97', 'DD-MON-RR'),'MK_REP','6000',NULL,'201','20');

DELETE          FLASHTEST      insert into "STROUPE"."FLASHTEST"
➥("EMPLOYEE_ID","FIRST_NAME",
 "LAST_NAME","EMAIL","PHONE_NUMBER","HIRE_DATE","JOB_ID",
 "SALARY","COMMISSION_PCT","MANAGER_ID","DEPARTMENT_ID") values ('201','Michael','Hart-
 stein','MHARTSTE@FINDEPT','515.123.555
 5',TO_DATE('17-FEB-96', 'DD-MON-RR'),'MK_MAN','13000',NULL,'100','20');
```

Flashback transaction query can also be used in conjunction with flashback versions query to provide a higher level of detail, as detailed in the following example. The VERSIONS_XID value from a flashback versions query can be used to retrieve additional information about a transaction with flashback transaction query.

```
SQL> select versions_startscn, versions_endscn, versions_xid, versions_operation,
  2  first_name, email from flashtest VERSIONS BETWEEN SCN MINVALUE and MAXVALUE
  3  where department_id = 30;

VERSIONS_STARTSCN VERSIONS_ENDSCN VERSIONS_XID     V FIRST_NAME           EMAIL
----------------- --------------- ---------------- - -------------------- --------------------
-----
          982338                  07002C00A1000000 D Karen                KCOLMENA
          982338                  07002C00A1000000 D Guy                  GHIMURO
          982338                  07002C00A1000000 D Sigal                STOBIAS
          982338                  07002C00A1000000 D Shelli               SBAIDA
          982338                  07002C00A1000000 D Alexander            AKHOO
          982338                  07002C00A1000000 D Den                  DRAPHEAL
                           982338                    Den                  DRAPHEAL
                           982338                    Alexander            AKHOO
                           982338                    Shelli               SBAIDA
                           982338                    Sigal                STOBIAS
                           982338                    Guy                  GHIMURO
                           982338                    Karen                KCOLMENA

12 rows selected.

SQL> select operation, table_name, undo_sql from flashback_transaction_query where xid =
'07002C00A1000000';
```

```
OPERATION        TABLE_NAME     UNDO_SQL
...............  .............  ......................................................

DELETE           FLASHTEST      insert into "STROUPE"."FLASHTEST"("EMPLOYEE_ID","F
                                IRST_NAME","LAST_NAME","EMAIL","PHONE_NUMBER","HIR
                                E_DATE","JOB_ID","SALARY","COMMISSION_PCT","MANAGE
                                R_ID","DEPARTMENT_ID") values ('119','Karen','Colm
                                enares','KCOLMENA','515.127.4566',TO_DATE('10-AUG-
                                99', 'DD-MON-RR'),'PU_CLERK','2500',NULL,'114','30
                                ');

DELETE           FLASHTEST      insert into "STROUPE"."FLASHTEST"("EMPLOYEE_ID","F
                                IRST_NAME","LAST_NAME","EMAIL","PHONE_NUMBER","HIR
                                E_DATE","JOB_ID","SALARY","COMMISSION_PCT","MANAGE
                                R_ID","DEPARTMENT_ID") values ('118','Guy','Himuro
                                ','GHIMURO','515.127.4565',TO_DATE('15-NOV-98', 'D
                                D-MON-RR'),'PU_CLERK','2600',NULL,'114','30');

...
```

Enterprise Manager also provides the capability to easily find detailed information using flashback transaction query, as detailed the following steps:

1. Using the table from the previous example, introduce a bad transaction:

   ```
   SQL> delete from flashtest where department_id = 30;
   ```

2. Use OEM to review the changes by clicking on the Administration tab and the table's link under the Schema subheading.

3. When you select your target table, choose the Flashback Table action from the Actions drop-down list, then click Go.

4. Choose any columns you wish, add the bind row value to set the query limit, and click Next.

5. On the Choose SCN page, shown in Figure 17.23, you can see the entire row history (the same information you reviewed for flashback versions query). To review the transaction information, click on a specific transaction ID.

6. After you click on the transaction ID, you can review the operation, table owner, table name, and undo SQL (the same information you can select manually from FLASHBACK_TRANSACTION_QUERY), as shown in Figure 17.24.

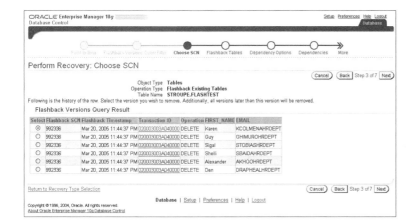

FIGURE 17.23
Reviewing the Flashback
Versions Query Result
Set from 10g OEM
Recovery wizard.

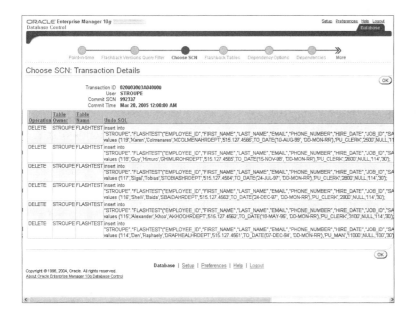

FIGURE 17.24
Transaction ID Details
from 10g OEM Recovery
wizard.

Advanced Flashback Features in Oracle Database 10g Release 2

In Oracle Database 10g Release 2, the flashback technology has been enhanced to provide greater flexibility with your recovery options. 10g Release 2 introduces two new features with Flashback Database and Flashback Table: flashback restore points and flashback across global database changes.

Flashback Restore Points

Flashback restore points are associated names that you define for a given point in time. Restore points, much like a transaction savepoint, allow you to flashback to a defined alias within your flashback history. By creating save points, users no longer have to investigate the SCN or time-stamp of a specific operation before using the Flashback Table or Flashback Database feature. With restore points, you can create a custom snapshot of the database and later flashback to that specific point in time.

Restore points are maintained in the database control file for at least the number of days speci-fied by the CONTROL_FILE_RECORD_KEEP_TIME setting, which has a default setting of seven days. When the number of restore points reaches the maximum value, the oldest restore points will simply age out.

If age is an issue for your restore points, you can elect to use a guaranteed restore point. *Guaranteed restore points* provide a guaranteed flashback point, never age out of the control file, and must be dropped explicitly when not needed. Keep in mind, however, that once a guaran-teed restore point is created, all associated flashback logs that are needed to flashback to that specific point will be retained in the flash recovery area until you delete the guaranteed restore point.

To support the flashback restore points, 10g R2 introduced the CREATE ¦ DROP RESTORE POINT commands, as well as new functionality within 10g Enterprise Manager (as showed here):

- To create new restore points (with or without the guarantee clause), do the following:

```
SQL> create restore point before_patch_apply;
SQL> create restore point before_patch_apply guarantee flashback database;
```

- To use Flashback Database with restore points, do the following:

```
SQL> flashback database to restore point before_patch_apply;
```

- To use Flashback Table with restore points, do the following:

```
SQL> flashback table flashtest to restore point before_patch_apply;
```

- To drop restore points, do the following:

```
SQL> drop restore point before_patch_apply;
```

Flashback Across Global Database Changes

The second major new flashback feature with 10g Release 2 is the ability to flashback across global database changes. With this new functionality, you can use the Flashback Database feature to flashback through a database RESETLOGS operation, after a switchover/failover opera-tion with your physical or logical standby database or even after physical standby database acti-vation. Previously, when any of these global database changes occurred, all flashback log data was discarded and subsequently removed. With 10g Release 2, the flashback across global change support extends the functionality of the Flashback Database feature.

To flashback through RESETLOGS, do the following:

```
SQL> shutdown immediate;
SQL> startup mount;
SQL> flashback database to before resetlogs;
SQL> alter database open;
```

Additional 10g R2 Views

Also with 10g Release 2, two new V$ views are introduced to provide greater manageability with your flashback environment:

- **V$RESTORE_POINT.** Details the specifics of user-defined database restore points such as SCN, incarnation, storage, time, name, and so on.

- **V$FLASH_RECOVERY_AREA_USAGE.** Details the specifics on flash recovery area disk space used.

Summary

This chapter reviewed the latest suite of new 10g flashback technologies including Flashback Database, Flashback Table, Flashback Drop, flashback versions query, and flashback transaction query, as well as the major flashback features for 10g Release 2.10 via the improved Enterprise Manager or manually from enhanced command-line syntax. These new features offer users and DBAs alike greater flexibility to correct user-based and logical errors as well as enhanced commands to increase overall availability with your production environment.

18

Leveraging Grid Technology Features

IN THIS CHAPTER

What Exactly Is the Grid?	413
Oracle's Version of the Grid	418
Managing the Grid	420

What Exactly Is the Grid?

The term *grid* is very much a part of Oracle Database 10g. In fact, the "g" in "10g" comes from the word "grid," just as the "i" in "8i" was derived from "Internet." And just as Oracle 8i heralded the arrival of Oracle Corporation's flagship RDBMS as a major player in shaping the Internet—something it accomplished by hosting the massive databases behind the various websites—so too does Oracle hope that Oracle Database 10g will help shape the notion of the computing grid in today's IT world.

So what exactly is the grid? And a deeper question: Why do we need a grid? The answer lies in looking at a familiar example, and considering how we can adapt and use that model in computing.

A Familiar Example: The Electricity Grid

The electricity grid has been around for such a long time that we do not even consider its existence as a grid. However, this grid exhibits most of the characteristics that we would like to have in a computing grid. Some of the characteristics of an electricity grid are noted next.

The Electricity Grid from a Consumer's Point of View

First, we will consider the electricity grid from a user or consumer's point of view:

- Electricity is available any time you need it. When you come home in the evening and switch on the light, you expect it to work—not to have to wait for the system to "boot."

- Electricity is available at the right levels of voltage and frequency. Whether it is at 110 volts and 60Hz or 220 volts and 50Hz (as it is outside the United States), you are pretty much guaranteed the right level of voltage, except when the load becomes high and slight variations creep in.

- Consumers pay for electricity using a "pay-per-use" model. In other words, you pay for what you use, not for the excess capacity that is available in the system. On the other hand, there are some limits on usage, and you may be charged higher rates if you use more than the norm. Rates may also vary by season.

- Consumers don't have to manage or worry about the availability of electricity in built-up areas. Electric connections are part of every developed location. As a consumer, you just have to purchase the appliance of your choice and plug it in. The choice or brand of appliance does not matter. That said, the appliance does have to conform to certain specifications of voltage and power consumption.

- Modern life, as we know it, comes to a standstill if this crucial component fails. This became vastly clear on August 14, 2003, when a massive blackout swept across the Eastern United States and parts of Canada. Although individual consumers can protect themselves to some extent, the majority of everyday appliances and systems that are taken for granted simply stopped working. Extended outages, both in terms of time and geographies, will result in massive losses to an individual's, organization's, and even a country's economy.

The Electricity Grid from a Producer's Point of View

From an electricity producer's or distributor's point of view, the following characteristics apply:

- Individual producers and distributors must agree on and abide by some standards, and know each other's production and distribution capacities and capabilities. The producers and distributors may be entirely different organizations, but have to work together as a cohesive unit.

- Both producers and distributors do not really care about end-use, but do care about short-term and long-term demand. They are responsible for day-to-day operations as well as forecasting and planning. Most of all, they are responsible for keeping the grid available at all times.

- To enable this, producers and distributors use sophisticated monitoring tools that can track usage and respond to fluctuations in demand. For example, when demand increases in the evening, additional generators may be started up and placed online; when demand decreases, these same generators may be taken offline. At times, this excess generation capacity might be used to feed growing demand in another time zone.

- Most of these actions happen automatically, but are overseen and monitored by skilled human operators. Usually they are managed using a central monitoring facility that can look at the entire electricity grid using a single, consistent, up-to-date view.

- Although glitches and hitches in electricity generation and distribution are day-to-day events, most of these can be smoothed out. Only when a massive power outage occurs, such as the one described previously, does the consumer even become aware of such control centers. Again, when events occur, the operators and planners are ultimately held responsible.

- Although it is expedient to keep a grid as well connected as possible, the failure of one component could bring down the whole grid as occurred in the massive blackout noted previously. As the grid evolves, disaster-recovery and backup planning as well as forecasting and constant checking and testing needs to keep in sync with these changes.

We have described this familiar grid in detail so that you have an idea of the kind of commodity that computing should become. We are already seeing this in some aspects on the consumer side of computing. For example, specifically in the area of availability and accessibility, anytime-anywhere Web access from mobile devices and always-on wireless PCs at home or work are common in most developed nations.

Similarities in the Computing Grid

A computing grid aims to have similar characteristics to an electricity grid. In short, the following should be possible in a computing grid:

- Computing power should be available at all times to all users, regardless of geography and time zone. High-availability systems enable such computing power.

- Applications should be able to run regardless of the platform on which they are located, and be able to access data stored anywhere in the grid. There has to be a high level of interoperability at all levels: hardware, software, middleware, and ultimately data.

- Applications should respond in the same fashion and level of response, regardless of current load and location of use. Additional computing resources should be brought online as required and also taken off as required.

- The costing model should be of the "pay-per-use" variety. Users should not have to pay for excess capacity that is held in reserve.

- From an administrative and operational point of view, the computing grid should automatically adjust and heal itself, and be available for both monitoring and control from a single, consistent tool.

- When a computer system is down, depending on the use of that system, it might spell doom for the organization. For example, when a development server goes down, your internal programmers are unproductive. But if the server that is your online store and your only source of revenue goes down during a peak sales period, your organization may not be able to recover from lost customers who moved their accounts and allegiance to a competitor. Connected computing systems in the grid are so complex that they will become extremely difficult to manage. Complexities also multiply exposure to mismanaged changes as well as extend recovery periods due to complexities. The requirement, however, is that recovery should be quick, with as little impact as possible, and as simple to perform as possible.

Virtualization and Provisioning

Just as with any new technology, buzzwords abound in grid computing. We will define two of them here in plain English: virtualization and provisioning.

Virtualization refers to the methods and tools used to expose the services of every physical and logical entity in a grid. For example, a four-node Oracle Database 10g RAC is *virtualized* using a service name. A user connects to the virtual service, but any one of the four instances virtualized by the service name could be serving the user.

Provisioning is the controlled allocation of resources or privileges when required. For example, in disk provisioning, ASM disk groups can be used to provide storage space for specific types of files with specific protection. For computing-resource provisioning, policies can be used to provide controlled resources at the right time using the Oracle Scheduler and the Database Resource Manager.

In short, the basic idea of grid computing is the notion of computing as a utility, analogous to the electricity grid described previously. A user in the grid does not care where the data is present or where computation is done, as long as it is done and information is delivered whenever required. From the provider's side, the grid is about virtualization and provisioning. All your resources are pooled together and provisioned dynamically based on the needs of the business, thus simultaneously achieving better resource utilization.

A number of recent industry trends helped shape the growing presence of the computing grid. Hardware trends include low-cost, high-volume processors that power server blades with low power and size footprints that reduce cost and increase the density of servers. This in turn ultimately leads to lower costs in running IT services and data-center operations. Network attached storage (NAS) and storage area networks (SANs) provide terabyte-sized storage, while gigabit ethernet and infiniband networks connect them all. Software trends include the availability of open-source software such as the Linux operating system and the Apache Web server, both of which can run on these inexpensive boxes. As a result, an increase in the number of servers does not necessarily mean an increase in software license costs. Both these downward trends, combined with the rapidly changing and increasing computing requirements, have necessitated and enabled the computing grid.

Simply put, *grid computing* can be defined as applying resources from many computers in a network to a single problem, usually one that requires a large number of processing cycles or access to large amounts of data. As you saw in previous sections, the computational power grid is analogous to the electric power grid. Basically, grid computing allows the coupling of geographically distributed resources to offer consistent and inexpensive access to resources irrespective of their physical location or access point. A wide variety of distributed computational resources varying from supercomputers, computer clusters, storage systems, and data sources can be connected via the Internet or dedicated networks and presented to the user community as a single, unified resource.

In other words, grid computing enables devices, regardless of their operating characteristics, to be virtually shared, managed, and accessed across an enterprise, industry, or workgroup. The keyword here is *virtualization*, which means that these resources will appear as a single, virtual piece of computing equipment. This virtualization of resources places all the necessary access, data, and processing power at the fingertips of those who need to rapidly solve complex business problems, conduct computation-intensive research and data analysis, and operate in real time. For example, through grid computing a company with about 2,000 desktop computers can use those computers to harvest nearly one teraflop (one trillion floating-point operations per second) of computing capacity. Thus, grid computing promises to consolidate, simplify, and fully utilize the available computing resources.

Now that we have defined what a computing grid should have, let us see how Oracle Database 10g fits into the picture. Before that, however, let's look at a little history of grid computing.

Grid Computing: A Little History

Grid computing is not a new concept. Universities and research institutions have been using grid-computing technology for decades. This concept has recently started making inroads into the business market, however. When applied to an enterprise, this kind of computing is specifically known as *enterprise grid computing*, in order to clarify that it supports the IT requirements of an enterprise.

According to a recent survey conducted by Insight Research, awareness of grid computing in the business domain is rapidly growing, with 37% of respondents saying they are now evaluating the case for grid computing. Insight Research expects global enterprises to spend $4.9 billion (U.S. dollars) on grid computing in 2008, which is nearly 20 times higher than the 2003 spending level of $250 million (U.S. dollars). By 2007, market researcher International Data Corp expects the world to spend $3 billion (U.S. dollars) on the software needed to virtualize grid components such as storage, security, and applications. That's a doubling of the $1.5 billion (U.S. dollars) spent globally in 2002. This translates to sales on the horizon for providers and early implementers of this technology, including Oracle Corporation. Hence the suffix change from "i" to "g" in the RDBMS versioning.

Oracle, along with a few other organizations in the computing world, have formed a consortium named the Enterprise Grid Alliance (EGA). The EGA is an open, nonprofit, vendor-neutral organization formed to develop enterprise grid solutions and accelerate the deployment of grid computing in enterprises. The other organizations in the consortium include EMC, Fujitsu-Siemens, HP, Intel, Sun Microsystems, NetApp, and NEC. Hopefully, the EGA will develop and implement standards that are beneficial to the user community rather than to themselves.

Oracle's Version of the Grid

Now that we have defined the characteristics of a computing grid, let us list the essential components of such a grid—specifically, Oracle's version of such as grid. In no particular order, the components of such a grid are as follows:

- Computing resources such as servers, including their components such as CPUs, memory, and self-contained internal hard disks containing the operating system and swap.

- Storage resources such as SANs, NAS, and even simple disk farms in some form of RAID (Redundant Array of Inexpensive Disks). It is important to note that these storage resources should be exposed to and be seen by all the servers.

- Networks connecting servers. Usually, these are high speed, geographically clustered networks with servers connected to each other in a local enterprise grid. There are also cases where a grid consists of servers connected over long distances, but they usually do not access *shared* storage components.

- Clustering software that allows these computing resources to work together, see the same storage devices, and access them simultaneously. Clustering software also includes the capability to provide high availability by enabling server failover.

- Application software that is cluster or grid aware. This includes software at the application front end such as Web servers and J2EE containers as well the database back end.

The way these components fit together is shown in Figure 18.1. The highlighted portions show where technology and components from Oracle Corporation fit into the computing grid. First come the load-balanced and clustered application servers, which may include Oracle's Application Server 10g (previously Oracle iAS). The applications themselves could include enterprise resource planning (ERP) applications such as the Oracle E-Business Suite (also known as Oracle Applications 11i). At the next level are the highly available clustered servers that run Oracle Database 10g RAC. Included in the services at this layer is Oracle Database 10g Cluster Ready Services (CRS). These servers in turn are back-ended by storage area networks accessed via dual-network storage switches. The disks themselves are presented to the Oracle Database 10g RAC instances as many Oracle Database 10g ASM disk groups. From this figure, it is obvious that Oracle Corporation can provide software components at almost all levels of the grid.

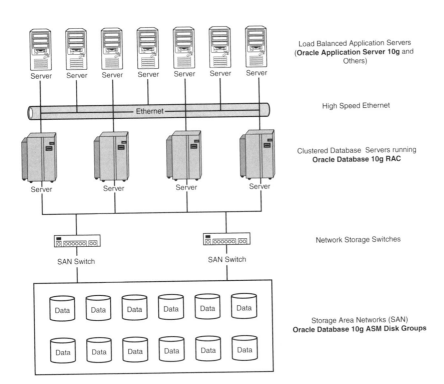

FIGURE 18.1
A typical computing grid.

This architecture is actually familiar in most enterprises. So how is this picture different, and in what way is it a grid? The answer lies in the capability of each of these Oracle components to enable one or more requirements of the computing grid, as explained in the previous section:

■ **High availability.** Oracle Database 10g RAC provides high availability by presenting multiple database instances that can access the same set of data and in turn present this data to a pool of application servers running Oracle Application Server 10g. Failovers are automatic and can occur at the instance level or application server level. These failovers could be caused by both hardware and software components. Technologies such as Transparent Application Failover (TAF) can make such failovers transparent to users. You saw in detail how this is made possible in Part IV, "Scaling and Availability with Oracle Database 10g."

■ **High performance.** Although individual Oracle Database 10g instances can provide high throughput and performance by themselves, there is still a point in the curve when even the best server cannot provide the level of performance required for a very large number of users. Oracle Database 10g RAC enables horizontal scalability by adding computing nodes or instances that access a common database. When combined with remote terminal services such as Citrix, these instances can provide the same kind of rich-client performance, even for remote locations and individuals that use dial-up lines. You saw how Oracle Database 10g could provide this in Part III, "Tuning Oracle Database 10g," as well as in Part IV, "Scaling and Availability with Oracle Database 10g."

- **High resiliency.** The capability to quickly recover from natural, technical, and man-made disasters is provided by the various components of Oracle Database 10g. For example, ASM has built-in disk protection that can enable a database to continue functioning despite disk failures. Oracle flashback features protect from user and administrator errors. Oracle Data Guard provides for setting up physical and logical standby copies of the primary database at an alternate, geographically remote site. Oracle RMAN simplifies recovery by automating the process and thus preventing lag due to administrators working out manual procedures. As well, RMAN can stage the recovery directly from the flash recovery area so that tape restoration time is saved as well. You saw details of how this is made possible in various parts of this book.

- **Hardware independence.** The provision of transportable tablespaces provides for hardware vendor independence. For example, you might front-end the grid with smaller independent Oracle databases on Linux servers, consolidating data via transportable tablespaces to a larger Sun or HP box.

- **Virtualization at all layers.** Rather than make static ties that determine and isolate where an application and its corresponding data resides, Oracle Database 10g's grid-aware products, including ASM, RAC, and application layers, virtualize all the resources shown in Figure 18.1.

- **Profiled resource usage.** At almost all levels in the technology stack, Oracle Database 10g and its related products in the grid arena can provide the required quality of service (QoS) for the user or type of application. For example, an Oracle Database 10g instance can be configured to provide the right level of computing resources such as CPU and I/O limits to identified sets of users or processing via the Resource Manager. Although not fully enabling "pay-per-use," this does lay the framework for presenting user communities with a means of paying for and obtaining the right levels of service.

- **Self managing and self healing.** Due to the sheer number of components and the complexities involved in connecting all of them together, the grid should have some self-managing and self-healing capabilities. We have seen in various places in this book how Oracle Database 10g can diagnose, alert, and optionally heal itself of issues, thus drastically reducing the administrative burden of managing very large numbers of instances.

Managing the Grid

It is always a given that when the user side of the story is simplified, the administrative side of story becomes much more complex. This is true of the computing grid as well. Therefore, being able to monitor and manage the grid becomes very important. Oracle Database 10g solves this problem via the provision of the Oracle Enterprise Manager Grid Control utility. Listed here are some of the challenges associated with managing a grid, and how Oracle Grid Control solves them:

- **Managing a large number of components.** In an enterprise grid, the number of components can be quite large, as implied in Figure 18.1. They include Oracle management-related components such as agents and repositories, application servers, databases, database groups, HTTP servers, hosts, LDAP servers, and so on, with each performing various functions. Oracle Database 10g Grid Control can define and manage them as groups, and can apply a defined set of policies against such groups. Groups can be database-specific, host-specific, application server–specific, or heterogenous. You can then assign specific groups to specific administrators so that the administrative load is shared.

- **Unified management interface.** In an enterprise grid, the presence of many different components from different vendors creates a management nightmare, because various tools will have to be procured and installed with the administrators trained on all of them. In the case of Oracle Database 10g Grid Control, however, management is enabled via a Web browser, so administrators with the right permissions can manage them from anywhere within the organization as well from outside via the use of wireless-enabled personal digital assistants (PDAs). This offers a single, unified view of all the components, including servers, databases, application servers, and so on. Hence, the grid administrator does not have to use different tools for the many components.

- **Centralized job control.** Administrators have to run a variety of jobs in managing a grid. Scheduled backups, periodical data movement and data loads, and purge routines, not to mention monitoring these jobs, presents many challenges. Oracle Database 10g Grid Control automates many of these functions by providing graphical front-ends and integrated database features such as RMAN, Data Pump, Resource Manager, and transportable tablespaces. Using these, administrators can schedule, monitor, troubleshoot, and fix problems associated with multiple jobs in the enterprise Oracle grid without much effort.

- **Patch management.** Newly discovered security vulnerabilities, software failures and bugs, new features, and so on result in a constant stream of software updates and patches. Administrators find it extremely difficult to stay on top of these patches, let alone apply them to all the components. Oracle Database 10g Grid Control enables automated patch downloads and updates. In fact, it allows you to define policies about software levels and check for and warn about violations against these policies.

- **Managing user security.** One of the major headaches, especially in the current days of government-regulated compliance requirements, is enabling and maintaining adequate security for user accounts across the enterprise. Oracle Database 10g, along with Oracle intenet Directory (OiD) and Oracle Label Security, centralizes the management of user credentials and privileges in a secure directory. This avoids the need to create the same user in multiple databases across a grid. A directory-based user can authenticate and access all the databases that are within an enterprise domain based on the credentials and privileges specified in the directory. With Oracle Database 10g, grid users also have the ability to store an SSL certificate in a smart card for roaming access to the grid. Oracle Database 10g also comes with Oracle Certificate Authority, which simplifies the provisioning of certificates to grid users.

> The specifics of how each of these activities is done is outside the scope of this book. This is detailed in two separate manuals, namely the *Oracle Database 10g Enterprise Manager Concepts* and *Oracle Database 10g Enterprise Manager Advanced Configuration* manuals.

Summary

This chapter defined what grid computing is by comparing it to another very familiar grid. It then outlined what Oracle provides by way of grid-enabling computing resources, and finally how Oracle Database 10g Grid Control lays the framework for such a grid. Although the computing industry has quite a way to go before grid computing becomes an everyday affair, it is clear from this chapter that Oracle Database 10g is indeed poised to make that leap.

PART V

Using Oracle Database 10g Utilities and Other Advanced Features

19 Maximizing Data Movement with Oracle Data Pump

20 Using 10g SQL*Plus and iSQL*Plus

21 Making the Most of Oracle Database 10g

19

Maximizing Data Movement with Oracle Data Pump

IN THIS CHAPTER

Oracle 10g Data Pump Enhancements   425

External Table Enhancements   443

Advanced Data Pump Features in Oracle Database 10g Release 2   444

Oracle 10g Data Pump Enhancements

Starting with 10g, Oracle now provides new infrastructure support for high-speed data movement in and out of the database. The foundation for this support is referred to as *Oracle Data Pump*. This chapter details the new features of Oracle Data Pump and how to effectively utilize its capabilities and features to dramatically increase data movement performance compared to previous releases of the Oracle database.

Oracle 10g Data Pump Concepts

Data Pump is a new feature offered with Oracle Database 10g that enables high-speed data and metadata movement for the Oracle database. The primary goal of Data Pump is to provide a dramatic increase in performance and manageability compared to the original export and import utilities as well as to add high-speed data load and unload capabilities for existing tables. Oracle 10g Data Pump provides this new technology by extracting data at the block level into platform-independent flat files using an efficient proprietary format via the new PL/SQL package DBMS_DATAPUMP. The DBMS_DATAPUMP PL/SQL package serves as the core application program interface (API) for high-speed data and metadata movement within the Oracle server. Oracle Data Pump is also the cornerstone for other key 10g database features such as transportable tablespace, logical standby database, and Oracle streams.

> Oracle 10g Data Pump is available in all versions of the database, but parallelism with a degree greater than one is available only in the Enterprise Edition.

Data Pump has the same look and feel as the original export (EXP) and import (IMP) utilities, however is completely different. Dump files created by the new Data Pump technology are not compatible with the dump files created by EXP. Therefore, dump files created by the EXP utility cannot be used with Data Pump.

Data Pump Architecture

The diagram in Figure 19.1 details the major components for 10g Data Pump.

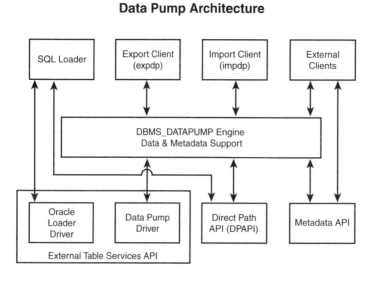

Data Pump Architecture

FIGURE 19.1
Oracle 10g Data Pump architecture overview.

In basic terms, the Data Pump architecture consists of the following:

- **DBMS_DATAPUMP engine.** This is the PL/SQL package that provides the necessary API for high-speed import and export utilities for bulk data and metadata movement.

- **External Table Services API.** Data Pump uses external tables by the following drivers:

    - **Oracle Loader driver.** This provides external table read-only access to SQL Loader compatible files (debuted with Oracle 9i).

    - **Oracle Data Pump driver.** This is a new access driver that provides external tables with read and write access using Direct Path API (DPAPI).

- **Direct Path API (DPAPI).** This is a new stream interface that serves in addition to the already existing column array interface. Basically, row data is read or written to dump file sets with DPAPI, which minimizes the necessary data parsing and conversion during load and unload time.

- **Metadata API.** Metadata support is offered via the DBMS_METADATA package, which debuted with Oracle 9i. This package provides database object definition support to Data Pump worker processes.

- **Export and import Data Pump clients.** New import (impdp) and export (expdp) clients make thin layer connections to the DBMS_DATAPUMP package to initiate and monitor Data Pump operations. While the impdp and expdp clients do offer several new capabilities, they remain compatible with the original import and export clients IMP and EXP, which are also still available in Oracle 10g.

> Oracle 10g Data Pump does not the support the export and import of XML schemas and XML schema–based tables. If you need export and import support for XML schemas, you will need to use the original EXP and IMP utilities.

- **SQL Loader client.** The original SQL Loader client has been integrated with 10g external table support to provide automatic migration of loader control files to external table access parameters.

- **External clients.** Oracle technologies such as transportable tablespaces, logical standby databases, streams-based replication, and Enterprise Manager can also benefit from the Data Pump infrastructure. SQL*Plus may also be used as a client for operational query support against the DBMS_DATAPUMP package.

As noted, 10g Data Pump offers two access methods to table data: Direct Path API (DPAPI) and External Table Services API. Because both methods support the same external data representation, data that is unloaded with one method can be loaded by using the other method. When invoked, Data Pump will automatically select the most appropriate access method for each operation. By default, Data Pump will use the Direct Path API (DPAPI) when a table's structure allows it and when maximum performance is desired. If, however, any of the following conditions exist with your operation, Data Pump will automatically use external table support rather than direct path API support:

- Clustered tables

- Tables with valid triggers

- Tables with FGAC (fine grain access control) enabled for selects and inserts

- Tables with RI (referential integrity) constraints

- Tables with BFILE or opaque-type columns

- Tables with a VARRAY column with an embedded opaque-type column

- Partitioned tables where a global index exists during a single-partition load

- A domain index for a LOB column

Because Data Pump is server based, all Data Pump operations, regardless of where the command is started, are handled in the database server. Because Data Pump is server based and not client based, dump-file sets and log files are written on the server specified by server-based directory paths. When using Data Pump, the following order of precedence is employed to define directory structure paths and to locate the necessary dump files for the operation:

- **Per-file directory path.** Per-file directory paths may be specified for each dump file, log file, or SQL file per operation. If specified, they must be separated by a colon (:). When used, per-file directory objects have the highest precedence, even if other methods are presented at the time of the operation.

- **Data Pump client `DIRECTORY` parameter.** Data Pump import and export operations can provide a value for the `DIRECTORY` parameter, which specifies the name of a directory object. These directory objects detail the location in which the files are accessed. These directories must have been created in the database by a DBA and the appropriate read and write privileges must be granted to the necessary users prior to running a Data Pump operation.

- **`DATA_PUMP_DIR` client environment variable.** You can alternatively specify the environment variable `DATA_PUMP_DIR` on the client rather than creating the `DIRECTORY` client parameter for your Data Pump operation. If no explicit directory objects are specified, the Data Pump operation will attempt to use this environment variable.

> In Oracle 10g Release 1, there is no default `DATA_PUMP_DIR`, so you must specify a valid directory object for your operation using one of the valid methods. If you do not specify a valid directory object for your operation, your operation will fail.

If none of the previous three conditions returns a directory object and you are a privileged user (that is, a user who has been granted `EXP_FULL_DATABASE` and `IMP_FULL_DATABASE` roles), then Data Pump will attempt to use the value for the server-based `DATA_PUMP_DIR` environment variable. It's important to note that Data Pump does not create the `DATA_PUMP_DIR` directory object; it only attempts to use its value when a privileged user has not provided a valid directory object using any methods previously described. This default directory object must first be created by a DBA with 10g Release 1.

Oracle 10g Data Pump offers support for command-line and GUI interfaces as well as API support via `DBMS_DATAPUMP`. Command-line support is offered by the new expdp and impdp utilities found in the `$ORACLE_HOME/bin` directory. GUI support is offered by the new Web-based

Enterprise Manager, a.k.a. Database Control. Database Control provides an interface to create and manage Data Pump import and export jobs within the EM environment. Starting with 10g Release 2, you can use the EM GUI interface to monitor all Data Pump jobs including those created by the expdp and impdp command-line utilities or by using the DBMS_DATAPUMP package.

Data Pump Process Flow

Once a Data Pump process has been initiated from an import, export, or external client connection, a shadow process is created on the server to act in its behalf. The Data Pump client will also make a call to DBMS_

> A Data Pump operation executes in the schema of the job creator with that user's rights and privileges.

DATAPUMP.OPEN to establish the specifics of the operation. When the call is established on the server, a new service called the *Master Control Process* (MCP) is started and returns a handle identifying the specific session's access to the Data Pump operation. Along with the creation of the MCP, two queues are established. The first queue, the Status queue, is used to send status and error messages to any client connection that is interested in this operation. Basically, this queue is populated by the MCP, is consumed by any client queries, and carries the name KUPC$S_<job_timestamp_identifier>. The second queue, the Command and Control queue, is used as management control for the worker processes that are established by the MCP. The Command and Control queue is also used by the client's shadow process executing dynamic commands to the MCP via DBMS_DATAPUMP and carries the name KUPC$C_<job_timestamp_identifier>. After the queues are created, the client establishes the session parameters to DBMS_DATAPUMP using various methods such as SET_PARAMETER and ADD_FILE. Data Pump uses Advanced Queuing (AQ) to facilitate the communication between these two queues and the various Data Pump processes.

After all the parameters are set, the client calls DBMS_DATAPUMP.START_JOB to start the actual Data Pump job. If requested, the MCP will create any necessary parallel streams via the worker processes. After the worker processes have initialized and instructed the MCP to perform the specific action, the MCP will detail another worker process to extract the necessary database object metadata via DBMS_METADATA. Depending on whether your operation performs an export, all metadata is written to a new dump file set in XML format. If your operation is an import, the target dump file will be processed.

During a data dump operation, a master table is created and maintained in the schema of the user initiating the Data Pump operation. The master table is used by the Data Pump process to track the health of the Data Pump

> During a Data Pump operation, more than one client process may be attached to a job to monitor its progress.

job as well as to control the ability of both import and export operations to restart. At any point in time during the operation, the client process can detach from the job without having to abort the job. Basically, when metadata is retrieved from the Data Pump job, location and size information about each object is written to the master table. When the entire Data Pump operation is complete, the master table is loaded in its entirety into the dump-file set. While the master table serves as a recorder for export operations, an import operation will actually read, load, and process the master table from the dump-file set to complete the operation. If the operation is killed or if the MCP process is terminated, the master table will be dropped from the requester's schema.

Data Pump Export and Import Utilities

Data Pump export (expdp) and Data Pump import (impdp) are the new high-speed export and import utilities offered with Oracle 10g. These essentially replace the previous version of export (EXP) and import (IMP). While Data Pump export unloads data and metadata into a set of operation system files called *dump-file sets*, Data Pump import is used to load data and metadata from these files into any 10g target database. Data Pump export can be used to export data and metadata from both local and remote databases directly to a local dump-file set. Data Pump import can also be used to load data into a target system directly from a remote source system without any configuration files needed. These types of remote operations are known as *network-mode operations* and can be processed over predefined database link connections.

Although the new Data Pump export and import clients do offer the same benefits as their predecessors, several new features are also introduced with their addition:

- The opportunity to detach from and reattach to long-running jobs without affecting the job itself through the use of the new ATTACH parameter. This allows you to monitor jobs from multiple locations as well as to stop and restart a job at a later time.

- Support for fine-grain object selection through the use of the CONTENT, INCLUDE, and EXCLUDE parameters.

- Support for two different access methods: direct path and external tables. Each operation automatically determines what access method can be used.

- Support for parallelism through the use of the PARALLEL parameter.

- The capability to estimate how much space an export or import job would need without actually performing the operation through the use of the ESTIMATE_ONLY parameter.

- Support for network export mode to allow export of remote databases directly to local dump-file sets or import of data directly to a local system without any necessary configuration files.

The Data Pump export and import clients provide three separate modes for user interaction: command line, parameter file, and interactive command mode. The command-line interface can be used to specify most of the Data Pump parameters directly on the command line. With the parameter-file interface, you can list all necessary command-line parameters in a parameter file called PARFILE. Interactive command interface stops logging to a terminal session and allows you to perform various commands while the operation continues to run in the background. To start interactive command mode, you will need to perform one of the following tasks:

- At the terminal where the user started the Data Pump job, press and hold down the Ctrl+C keys to interrupt the job and place the client in interactive mode.

- From a terminal other than the one where the job is currently running, use the ATTACH parameter to attach to the operation.

The Data Pump import and export clients also provide five different modes that can define the scope of the operation. For Data Pump export, the following modes can be used for unloading different portions of the database:

- **Full export.** In full-export mode, the entire database is unloaded. Full-export mode requires the user to have the EXP_FULL_DATABASE role and is specified through the use of the FULL parameter.

- **Tablespace export.** In tablespace-export mode, objects that are contained in a specified set of tablespaces are unloaded. Tablespace-export mode requires the user to have the EXP_FULL_DATABASE role and is specified through the use of the TABLESPACES parameter.

- **Transportable tablespace export.** In transportable tablespace–export mode, only the metadata for the tables (and any dependent objects from these tables) from a specified set of tablespaces is unloaded. Transportable tablespace–export mode requires that the user have the EXP_FULL_DATABASE role and is specified through the use of the TRANSPORTABLE_TABLESPACES parameter.

- **Schema export.** In schema-export mode, only the objects belonging to a specified set of schemas are unloaded. Schema-export mode requires that the user have the EXP_FULL_DATABASE role and is specified through the use of the SCHEMAS parameter.

- **Table export.** In table-export mode, only a specified list of tables, any partitions, and any dependent objects are unloaded. Table-export mode requires that the list of tables be from the same schema, and is specified through the use of the TABLES parameter.

For Data Pump import, the specified mode actually applies to the source of the operation: either a dump-file set or a remote database if the NETWORK_LINK parameter is used. When the import source is a local dump-file set, specifying a mode is actually optional. If no mode is specified, the import operation attempts to load the entire dump-file set in the mode in which the export operation was executed.

For Data Pump import, the following modes can be used for loading data and metadata from either a valid dump-file set or a remote database:

- **Full import.** In full-import mode, the entire contents of the source (be it a dump-file set or a remote database) are loaded into the target database. If no mode is specified, this is the default import mode. Full-import mode requires the user to have the IMP_FULL_DATABASE privilege. The EXP_FULL_DATABASE privilege is also required if the source is a remote database.

- **Tablespace import.** In tablespace-import mode, objects that are contained in a specified set of tablespaces are loaded. The source can be a full-mode, schema-mode, tablespace-mode, or table-mode export dump-file set or a remote database. Tablespace-import mode requires the user to have the IMP_FULL_DATABASE role and is specified through the use of the TABLESPACES parameter.

- **Transportable tablespace import.** In transportable tablespace–import mode, only the metadata from a transportable tablespace export dump file set or from a remote database is loaded. The data files specified by the `TRANSPORT_DATAFILES` parameter must be made available from the source system for use in the target database. Transportable tablespace–import mode requires that the user have the `IMP_FULL_DATABASE` role and is specified through the use of the `TRANSPORTABLE_TABLESPACES` parameter.

- **Schema import.** In schema-import mode, only the specified schema or schemas are loaded. The source can be a full-mode or schema-mode dump-file set or a remote database. Schema-import mode requires that the user have the `IMP_FULL_DATABASE` role and is specified through the use of the `SCHEMAS` parameter.

> When using table-import mode, specifying tables that are not in your own schema requires the `IMP_FULL_DATABASE` privilege.

- **Table import.** In table-import mode, only a specified list of tables, any partitions, and any dependent objects are loaded. The source can be a full-mode, schema-mode, tablespace-mode, or table-mode dump-file set or a remote database. Table-import mode requires that specified tables be from the same schema and is specified through the use of the `TABLES` parameter.

Following is an example of how one would use the Data Pump feature to run a full export of a user's schema and then use the import feature to import the data:

1. Create the necessary directory for Data Pump processing and grant the necessary permissions:

```
SQL> create directory DP as 'C:\temp';
Directory created.
SQL> grant read, write on directory DP to public;
Grant succeeded.
```

2. Create the Data Pump job at the command line prompt:

```
C:\>expdp stroupe/gwu job_name=DP directory=DP

Export: Release 10.1.0.3.0 - Production on Thursday, 26 May, 2005 22:19

Copyright (c) 2003, Oracle.  All rights reserved.

Connected to: Oracle Database 10g Enterprise Edition Release 10.1.0.3.0 - Production
With the Partitioning, OLAP and Data Mining options
FLASHBACK automatically enabled to preserve database integrity.
Starting "STROUPE"."DP":  stroupe/******** job_name=DP directory=DP
...
```

3. To attach to the job from another location and check the status, use the ATTACH keyword:

```
C:\>expdp stroupe/gwu attach=DP

Export: Release 10.1.0.3.0 - Production on Thursday, 26 May, 2005 22:20

Copyright (c) 2003, Oracle.  All rights reserved.

Connected to: Oracle Database 10g Enterprise Edition Release 10.1.0.3.0 - Production
With the Partitioning, OLAP and Data Mining options

Job: DP
  Owner: STROUPE
  Operation: EXPORT
  Creator Privs: FALSE
  GUID: 070003D3031D4B608BE0296E9439C4DF
  Start Time: Thursday, 26 May, 2005 22:20
  Mode: SCHEMA
  Instance: ts10g
  Max Parallelism: 1
  EXPORT Job Parameters:
  Parameter Name      Parameter Value:
     CLIENT_COMMAND        stroupe/******** job_name=DP directory=DP
     DATA_ACCESS_METHOD    AUTOMATIC
     ESTIMATE              BLOCKS
     INCLUDE_METADATA      1
     LOG_FILE_DIRECTORY    DP
     LOG_FILE_NAME         export.log
     TABLE_CONSISTENCY     0
     USER_METADATA         1
  State: EXECUTING
  Bytes Processed: 0
  Current Parallelism: 1
  Job Error Count: 0
  Dump File: C:\TEMP\EXPDAT.DMP
    bytes written: 4,096

Worker 1 Status:
  State: EXECUTING

Export>
```

4. You can also check the DBA_DATAPUMP_JOBS data dictionary table for updates on all current running jobs. As soon as all jobs are completed or if the job is terminated, entries to this table are also removed.

```
SQL> select * from dba_datapump_jobs;


OWNER_NAME JOB_NAME    OPERATION   JOB_MODE    STATE        DEGREE  ATTACHED_SESSIONS
---------- ----------- ----------- ----------- ----------- ------- -----------------
STROUPE    DP          EXPORT      SCHEMA      COMPLETING  1       1
```

5. When your job completes, Data Pump will detail what objects have been processed:

```
C:\>expdp stroupe/gwu job_name=DP directory=DP


Export: Release 10.1.0.3.0 - Production on Thursday, 26 May, 2005 22:19


Copyright (c) 2003, Oracle.  All rights reserved.


Connected to: Oracle Database 10g Enterprise Edition Release 10.1.0.3.0 - Production
With the Partitioning, OLAP and Data Mining options
FLASHBACK automatically enabled to preserve database integrity.
Starting "STROUPE"."DP":  stroupe/******** job_name=DP directory=DP
Estimate in progress using BLOCKS method...
Processing object type SCHEMA_EXPORT/TABLE/TABLE_DATA
Total estimation using BLOCKS method: 192 KB
Processing object type SCHEMA_EXPORT/USER
Processing object type SCHEMA_EXPORT/SYSTEM_GRANT
Processing object type SCHEMA_EXPORT/ROLE_GRANT
Processing object type SCHEMA_EXPORT/DEFAULT_ROLE
Processing object type SCHEMA_EXPORT/SE_PRE_SCHEMA_PROCOBJECT/PROCACT_SCHEMA
Processing object type SCHEMA_EXPORT/TABLE/TABLE
Processing object type SCHEMA_EXPORT/TABLE/INDEX/INDEX
Processing object type SCHEMA_EXPORT/TABLE/CONSTRAINT/CONSTRAINT
Processing object type SCHEMA_EXPORT/TABLE/INDEX/STATISTICS/INDEX_STATISTICS
Processing object type SCHEMA_EXPORT/TABLE/STATISTICS/TABLE_STATISTICS
Processing object type SCHEMA_EXPORT/TABLE/COMMENT
. . exported "STROUPE"."DEPT"                     6.632 KB     27 rows
. . exported "STROUPE"."EMP"                      15.77 KB    107 rows
. . exported "STROUPE"."FLASHTEST"               15.36 KB    101 rows
Master table "STROUPE"."DP" successfully loaded/unloaded
******************************************************************************
Dump file set for STROUPE.DP is:
  C:\TEMP\EXPDAT.DMP
Job "STROUPE"."DP" successfully completed at 22:22
```

6. If you attempt to attach to a job that has already completed or was aborted, you will discover that the master table has already been dropped when you receive the following error message:

```
C:\>expdp stroupe/gwu attach=DP

Export: Release 10.1.0.3.0 - Production on Thursday, 26 May, 2005 22:39

Copyright (c) 2003, Oracle.  All rights reserved.

Connected to: Oracle Database 10g Enterprise Edition Release 10.1.0.3.0 - Production
With the Partitioning, OLAP and Data Mining options
ORA-31626: job does not exist
ORA-06512: at "SYS.DBMS_SYS_ERROR", line 79
ORA-06512: at "SYS.KUPV$FT", line 330
ORA-31638: cannot attach to job DP for user STROUPE
ORA-31632: master table "STROUPE.DP" not found, invalid, or inaccessible
ORA-00942: table or view does not exist
```

7. After the export completes, run the import to import the data:

```
C:\>impdp testuser/asu full=y directory=DP job_name=DP2

Import: Release 10.1.0.3.0 - Production on Thursday, 26 May, 2005 22:55

Copyright (c) 2003, Oracle.  All rights reserved.

Connected to: Oracle Database 10g Enterprise Edition Release 10.1.0.3.0 - Production
With the Partitioning, OLAP and Data Mining options
Master table "TESTUSER"."DP2" successfully loaded/unloaded
Starting "TESTUSER"."DP2":  testuser/******** full=y directory=DP job_name=DP2
Processing object type SCHEMA_EXPORT/USER
Processing object type SCHEMA_EXPORT/SYSTEM_GRANT
Processing object type SCHEMA_EXPORT/ROLE_GRANT
Processing object type SCHEMA_EXPORT/DEFAULT_ROLE
Processing object type SCHEMA_EXPORT/SE_PRE_SCHEMA_PROCOBJACT/PROCACT_SCHEMA
Processing object type SCHEMA_EXPORT/TABLE/TABLE
Processing object type SCHEMA_EXPORT/TABLE/TABLE_DATA
. . imported "STROUPE"."DEPT"                         6.632 KB      27 rows
. . imported "STROUPE"."EMP"                         15.77 KB     107 rows
. . imported "STROUPE"."FLASHTEST"                   15.36 KB     101 rows
Processing object type SCHEMA_EXPORT/TABLE/STATISTICS/TABLE_STATISTICS
Job "TESTUSER"."DP2" successfully completed at 22:55
```

You can also use 10g Enterprise Manager (EM) Database Control to perform Data Pump export and import operations. 10g EM offers both the Data Pump Export wizard and Data Pump Import wizard to provide the necessary GUI for Data Pump responsibilities and tasks. To access the Data Pump Export wizard, click the Export to Files link in the Utilities section of the Maintenance tab.

When the Data Pump Export wizard launches, the Export: Export Type page is displayed. It offers you three choices for your export operation: Database, Schemas, or Tables, as shown in Figure 19.2.

FIGURE 19.2
Choosing the export type from the Data Pump Export wizard.

After you choose your selection, enter the necessary host credentials for the user name and password to process the export request, and click Next. If you selected Schemas or Tables, then the next page will be the Export: Select Users page, followed by the Export: Options page. If you chose Database as your export operation, you'll skip the Select Users page and land directly on the Export: Options page, shown in Figure 19.3. Here, you can set thread options, estimate disk space, specify optional files for the export operation, as well as use advanced options such as content exclusion or inclusion, flashback, and even predicate options for your export operation. Make your selections and click Next.

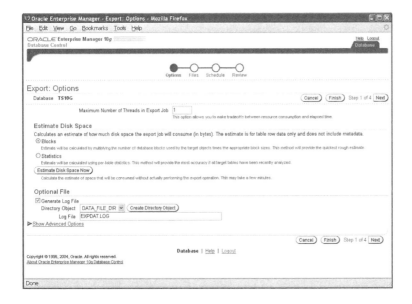

FIGURE 19.3
Listing of the export options from the Data Pump Export wizard.

You will see the Export: Files page, shown in Figure 19.4. Here you can set the path, name, and maximum size for the Data Pump export files. You can also add multiple files to meet your needs. Make your selections and click Next.

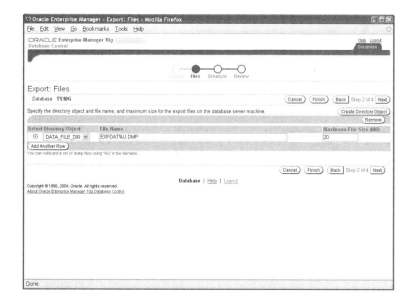

FIGURE 19.4
Specifying additional export files from the Data Pump Export wizard.

Next up is the Export: Schedule page, shown in Figure 19.5. Here you can schedule to run your export job immediately or at a later time, depending on your business needs. Usually you will want to schedule long-running jobs during off peak hours. Make your selections and click Next.

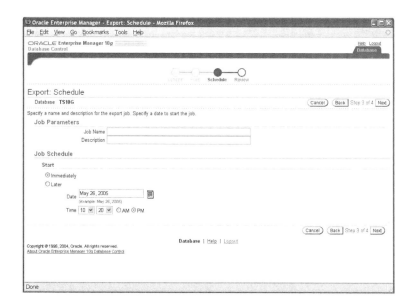

FIGURE 19.5
Specifying any scheduling options for your export job.

The Export: Review page is displayed, as shown in Figure 19.6. Here you will see the PL/SQL command-line interface code for the Data Pump operation, which was generated by your selections in the preceding screens. You can copy this code into a text editor to save it as a script, as well as click the Submit Job button to start the export operation.

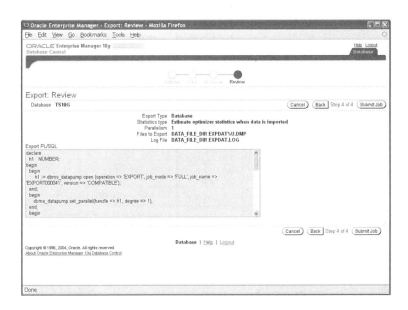

FIGURE 19.6
Data Pump Export wizard Summary page.

The Data Pump Import wizard has the same look and feel as the Data Pump Export wizard. To access the Data Pump Import wizard, click the Import from Files link or the Import from Database link in the Utilities section of the Maintenance tab.

The first screen of the Data Pump Import wizard, shown in Figure 19.7, prompts you to choose your import method: entire files, schemas, or tables. You also need to select the correct directory object and file name so EM can process the file for the import operation.

After the file is processed, the import operation displays the valid options for processing. In the example shown in Figure 19.8, the entire file was processed and only one schema was available for the import operation.

If needed, you can re-map schemas, tablespaces, or data files from the import file. Use the screen shown in Figure 19.9 to designate whether to import each user's schema into the same schema or to import into a different schema, import each object into the same or different tablespace, or change the data-file names of specific tablespaces. The remap keyword is the same as the original import/export keywords fromuser and touser.

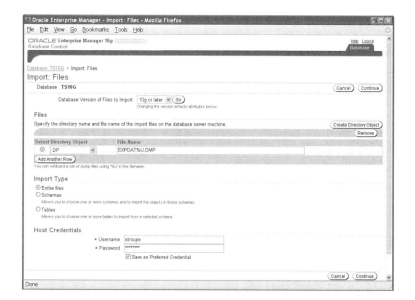

FIGURE 19.7
Specifying the import
type and import files
from the Data Pump
Import wizard.

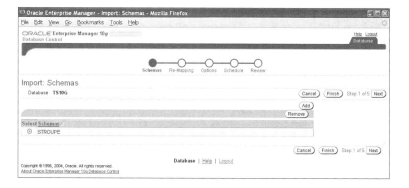

FIGURE 19.8
Listing of valid schemas
from target import file.

Next is the Import: Options screen, as shown in Figure 19.10. Here you can select a nondefault log file as well as parallelism and other advanced options. When you click Next, you will see the Import: Scheduling page. Its features are the same as the Data Pump Export wizard's Scheduling page. Here you can schedule to run your import job immediately or at another time.

The last page is the Import: Review page, as shown in Figure 19.11. Here you can review the PL/SQL command line–interface code for the import operation that was generated by the selections made from this wizard. You can copy this code into a text editor to save as a script as well as click the Submit Job button to start the import operation.

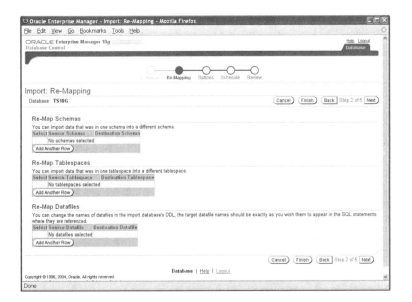

FIGURE 19.9
Import re-mapping
options from the Data
Pump Import wizard.

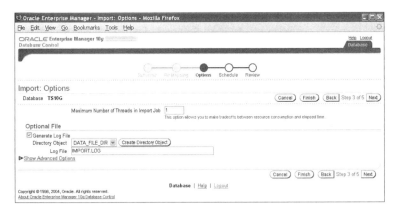

FIGURE 19.10
The Import: Options
screen.

Along with export and import support, Data Pump also provides DDL transformation support. When using impdp to import data from a dump-file set, you can use the REMAP_SCHEMA parameter to provide the same support as the fromuser/touser capability from the original IMP and EXP utilities. You can also move objects from one tablespace to another using the REMAP_TABLESPACE parameter as well as move data files across platforms using the REMAP_DATAFILE parameter.

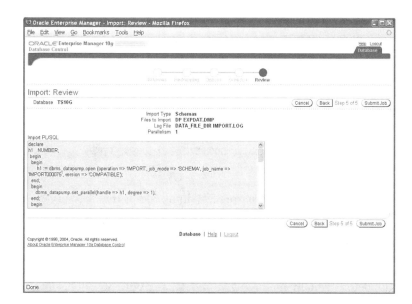

FIGURE 19.11
Data Pump Import wizard
Summary page.

Diagnosing Data Pump Issues with TRACE

Oracle 10g Data Pump also provides the capability to diagnose and troubleshoot any issue or abnormal behavior with the Data Pump operation. The undocumented parameter TRACE can be used to trace specific Data Pump components to assist in any troubleshoot needed. You can enable tracing when you initially create your Data Pump job or by temporarily stopping your current job and then restarting the job with the TRACE parameter defined. To invoke tracing, the TRACE parameter is initialized by a pre-defined hex value that will detail what specific subcomponent you wish to trace. All Data Pump components such as MCP, worker processes, fixed views, and even the underlying API are eligible for tracing. Following are a few of the possible combinations for Data Pump component tracing:

- Master Control Process (MCP): TRACE=80300

- Fixed views: TRACE=20300

- Worker process: TRACE=400300

- MCP + worker process: TRACE=480300

- MCP + worker + fixed view: TRACE=4A0300

- Full Data Pump tracing: TRACE=1FF0300

The majority of errors from Data Pump can be diagnosed by using 480300 MCP + worker process tracing only. Before tracing any other component, start with this trace value first.

Along with these values, you can also specify tracing for the Data Pump API calls. This must be set at the system level with event 39089, but you must restart your instance for this to take effect:

```
SQL>  alter system set event='39089 trace name context forever, level 0x300' scope=spfile;
```

Following is an example showing how to invoke tracing with the Data Pump export utility (expdp):

```
$ expdp stroupe/asu directory=DP dumpfile=DUMP.dmp tables=DOCUMENTS, DOCUMENT_TYPES,
PRODUCT_TYPES logfile=EXP_LOG.log trace=480300
```

The default location for the Data Pump MCP and worker process dump files is the directory specified by BACKGROUND_DUMP_DEST. The Data Pump component trace files will be written to the directory specified by USER_DUMP_DEST. If one of these directories is not specified in your instance, Oracle will send the trace files to $ORACLE_HOME/rdbms/log.

Along with tracing, you can also use the SQLFILE parameter to test the validity of your Data Pump import operation (impdp) before actually modifying your database. With SQLFILE, all the SQL DDL that impdp would have executed is written to a file for review. The output file is written to the directory object specified in the DIRECTORY parameter. An example of this feature is listed here:

```
$ impdp stroupe/asu directory=DP dumpfile=DUMP.dmp logfile=IMP_LOG.log
SQLFILE=IMP_SQL_TEST.sql
```

You can even expand this feature to generate the XML code from the export file by specifying TRACE=2:

```
$ impdp stroupe/asu directory=DP dumpfile=DUMP.dmp logfile=IMP_LOG.log
SQLFILE=IMP_SQL_TEST.sql TRACE=2
```

Managing Data Pump Jobs

Oracle Data Pump maintains several DBA and USER views to allow users to monitor the overall progress and health of Data Pump jobs running within the server. Data Pump users should use this to also investigate and/or troubleshoot issues that may arise from using Oracle Data Pump in their environment. Following is a short summary of a few views available to Data Pump users in Oracle 10g:

- **DBA_DATAPUMP_JOBS and V$DATAPUMP_JOB.** These detail an overall summary of all active Data Pump jobs running from the database.

- **DBA_DATAPUMP_SESSIONS and V$DATAPUMP_SESSION.** These display all sessions attached to actively running Data Pump jobs.

- **USER_DATAPUMP_JOBS.** This details an overall summary of the current user's Data Pump jobs running from the database.

- **V$SESSION_LONGOPS.** This details the health and progress for each active Data Pump job within the database. The OPNAME (operation name) column displays the Data Pump job name for each Data Pump operation.

- **SYS.KUPC$DATAPUMP_QUETAB and SYS.AQ$KUPC$DATAPUMP_QUETAB.** These display the necessary queuing information from the Data Pump operation and the two queue tables, Command and control queue and Status queue.

There are other DATAPUMP-type views in Oracle 10g, such as DATAPUMP_REMAP_OBJECTS, DATAPUMP_DDL_TRANSFORM_PARAMS, and DATAPUMP_OBJECT_CONNECT. These serve only as static parameter settings for the Data Pump feature.

External Table Enhancements

Along with the introduction of Oracle 10g Data Pump, the external table feature, which was introduced with Oracle 9i, also offers new improvements for data movement within the Oracle server. Prior to Oracle 10g, external table support was limited to only read-only access. This limitation meant you could load data only from a properly formatted external table.

With Oracle 10g, external tables can now be also written to through the use of the new ORACLE_DATAPUMP access driver. The major benefit of this new functionality is that it allows you to unload and transform large volumes of data into platform-independent flat files and use them for either data propagation or storage.

> Because the SQL data is the only part of the external table data set, you can optionally use the DBMS_METADATA package to extract any necessary metadata information for your external table.

Although neither DML (data manipulation language) operations nor index creation are allowed on an external table, you can use the CREATE TABLE AS SELECT... command to populate the external table. When populating an external table using the Data Pump access driver, the data is converted from its Oracle internal representation into an equivalent proprietary format using the Direct Path API (DPAPI). Because of this new DPAPI proprietary format, you cannot use the new external table population operation with any external table created using the ORACLE_LOADER access driver. Although the Data Pump export and import utilities support the new external table access driver, using this technology for complex ETL (extract, transform, and load) purposes should be handled manually with external table commands.

When running large external operations, you can use a parallel-population operation to unload your data. You can initiate parallelism on your external table operation by using the PARALLEL parameter. Unlike with a parallel query from an external table, the DOP (degree of parallelism) of a parallel-population operation is constrained by the number of concurrent files that can be written to by the access driver. Therefore, there is no longer the one parallel-execution server writing to one file any one point during your parallel-population operation.

Following is an example of using the new external table–population operation. In this example, an external table (TS_DOC_EXT) is created using the new external table–population operation (in parallel) from a join between the DOCUMENTS and DOCUMENT_COMPONENTS tables.

```
create table TS_DOC_EXT (doc_id, doc_title, doc_slug, doc_date)
ORGANIZATION EXTERNAL (
                type ORACLE_DATAPUMP
                default directory ts_dir
                location ('ts01.exp','ts02.exp', 'ts03.exp', 'ts04.exp')
            )
PARALLEL
as
select d.document_id, d.document_title, c.document_slug, d.create_date
from documents d, document_components c
where d.document_id = c.doc_document_id
and d.create_date > sysdate - 14;
```

Advanced Data Pump Features in Oracle Database 10g Release 2

In Oracle Database 10g Release 2, the Data Pump technology has been enhanced to provide greater manageability and flexibility with your export and import options. Following is a short summary of the new 10g Release 2 features with Oracle Data Pump:

- **Default Data Pump directory object.** Starting with 10g Release 2, you no longer have to manually create the directory object prior to using Data Pump. 10g Release 2 will create a default Data Pump directory object (DATA_PUMP_DIR) in $ORACLE_BASE/admin/DB_UNIQUE_NAME as long as ORACLE_BASE is defined during the 10g Release 2 database creation or upgrade. If for some reason ORACLE_BASE is not found, the default directory object will be created in $ORACLE_HOME/admin/DB_UNIQUE_NAME. If there is a problem with both of these locations, then Oracle will create the default directory object in $ORACLE_HOME/rdbms/log. In any case, all Data Pump users must have the appropriate permissions to the default directory object that Data Pump uses. Access to the default DATA_PUMP_DIR is granted automatically to the EXP_FULL_DATABASE and IMP_FULL_DATABASE roles.

- **Expanded support for 10g Enterprise Manager.** Starting with 10g Release 2, you can use the EM Database Control GUI to monitor all Data Pump jobs, including those created by the expdp and impdp utilities as well as the DBMS_DATAPUMP package. Within the 10g Release 2 EM, you can view the current status of the job and also change the status to EXECUTE, SUSPEND, or STOP.

- **New export command-line parameters.** Starting with 10g Release 2, you can use the COMPRESSION parameter to indicate whether the metadata should be compressed in the export dump file to reduce space consumption. The possible values are METADATA_ONLY (default) or NONE. If this parameter is used, the metadata is automatically uncompressed during the import operation. Also new with 10g Release 2 is your ability to use the SAMPLE parameter to specify a percentage of data to be sampled and unloaded from the source database. You can indicate the chosen percentage (.000001 to 100) by adding the number preceding the schema and table, such as SAMPLE="PROXY"."USERS":51. If you specify a schema, you must also specify a table, but you can specify a table without a schema because Data Pump will assume the table is part of the current user's schema. If no table is specified with the SAMPLE parameter, then the percentage will apply to the entire export operation.

- **New export interactive-mode parameters.** Starting with 10g Release 2, you can use the FILESIZE parameter to set the default file size (in bytes) for subsequent ADD_FILE commands. In 10g Release 1, the size of files added using ADD_FILE was unlimited.

- **New import command-line parameters.** Starting with 10g Release 2, you can use the ENCRYPTION_PASSWORD parameter to specify a password key for accessing encrypted column data from a dump file. ENCRYPTION_PASSWORD cannot be used in conjunction with the NETWORK_LINK parameter

- **New DBMS_DATAPUMP API calls.** Starting with 10g Release 2, you can use the WAIT_FOR_JOB API to provide specifics for completion time for Data Pump operations as well as the GET_DUMPFILE_INFO API to provide more detail on dump-file sets such as version, creation date, and character set.

Summary

This chapter reviewed the new Oracle 10g Data Pump feature, the new enhancements for 10g external tables, and the major Data Pump features for 10g Release 2 10.2.0. Oracle 10g Data Pump not only supports all the functionality of the original export and import clients, but also supports many new features such as stop and restart support, remote operations from other databases, and job-size estimation. These new features and enhancements enable high-speed data and metadata movement within the Oracle 10g Database server, providing a dramatic increase in performance and manageability.

20

Using 10g SQL*Plus and iSQL*Plus

IN THIS CHAPTER

10g SQL*Plus Enhancements 447

10g iSQL*Plus Enhancements 450

Advanced iSQL*Plus and SQL*Plus Features in Oracle Database 10g Release 2 453

10g SQL*Plus Enhancements

The Oracle 10g Database offers several new features for SQL*Plus. The two main new features introduced with 10g are the new DEFINE variables and the enhanced SPOOL command.

DEFINE Enhancements

Starting with Oracle 10g, the DEFINE command has three new predefined variables:

- **_USER.** This Contains the user name that is supplied by the user to make the current connection. The result here is the same as the output from the SHOW USER command.

- **_DATE.** This contains the current date or a user-defined fixed string. By default, _DATE displays the current date and is dynamic. _DATE uses the date format as shown with NLS_DATE_FORMAT.

- **_PRIVILEGE.** This contains the privilege level of the current connection. The value for _PRIVILEGE will be AS SYSDBA, AS SYSOPER, or blank to indicate a normal connection.

You can access and redefine the new variables just as with the original DEFINE variables, as well as use them for TTITLE SQL*Plus reporting, & substitution variables, and with SQL*Plus prompts using the SET SQLROMPT command.

To display the current DEFINE values, you can issue the DEFINE command at the SQL prompt as follows:

```
SQL> DEFINE
DEFINE _DATE           = "28-MAY-05" (CHAR)
DEFINE _CONNECT_IDENTIFIER = "TS10G" (CHAR)
DEFINE _USER           = "STROUPE" (CHAR)
DEFINE _PRIVILEGE      = "" (CHAR)
DEFINE _SQLPLUS_RELEASE = "1001000300" (CHAR)
DEFINE _EDITOR         = "Notepad" (CHAR)
DEFINE _O_VERSION      = "Oracle Database 10g Enterprise Edition
➥Release 10.1.0.3.0 - Production
With the Partitioning, OLAP and Data Mining options" (CHAR)
DEFINE _O_RELEASE      = "1001000300" (CHAR)
```

> SET SQLPROMPT **is not supported with Oracle 10g iSQL*Plus.**

> **Starting with Oracle 10g, the site profile files** glogin.sql **and** login.sql **are executed after each successful database connection from a SQL*Plus or** CONNECT **command.**

As noted, you can now use any of the DEFINE variables with SQL prompt variable substitution. To reset the SQL*Plus prompt with any DEFINE variable setting, you will need to use the SET SQLPROMPT command or add the entries in the glogin.sql or local login.sql profile files. Following are examples showing how one can use the DEFINE variable values for this purpose:

- To set the SQL*Plus command prompt to show the current user, use the following:

```
SQL> SET SQLPROMPT "_USER > "
STROUPE >
```

- To set the SQL*Plus command prompt to display the current user, the current date, and the user's privilege level, use the following:

```
SQL> SET SQLPROMPT "_USER _DATE _PRIVILEGE> "
STROUPE 28-MAY-05 >
STROUPE 28-MAY-05 > conn / as sysdba
Connected.
SYS 28-MAY-05 AS SYSDBA>
```

- You can also use user-defined variables with the SQL*Plus prompt. To set the SQL*Plus prompt to display a user-defined variable, use the following:

```
SQL>DEFINE INSTANCE=ZEUS
SQL>SET SQLPROMPT"INSTANCE> "
ZEUS>
```

- You can also use custom text with the SQL*Plus prompt. Because text in nested quotes is not parsed, to have a SQL*Plus prompt of your user name, followed by @ and then your connection identifier, you can use the following:

```
SQL>SET SQLPROMPT "_USER'@'_CONNECT_IDENTIFIER > "
SYS@TS10G >
```

SPOOL **Enhancements**

Prior to Oracle 10g, when you invoked the SQL*Plus SPOOL command, the spool file was either created or replaced depending on the file name you used. If the file did not exist, then a new file was created for you. If the file did exist, then SPOOL would automatically overwrite the existing file and replace it with the new file. This limitation was very troublesome for anyone who inadvertently overwrote files in the working directory.

Oracle 10g has removed this limitation by allowing users to either append or replace existing files when using the SPOOL command. Replacing a file is still the default behavior, however. To append an existing file you must use the new APPEND key word. Here is a small example showing how this new feature can be used:

```
SQL> spool asu.txt
SQL> select name from v$database;

NAME
----------
TS10G

SQL> spool off
SQL> spool asu.txt append
SQL> select sys_context ('USERENV', 'SESSION_USER') from dual;

SYS_CONTEXT('USERENV','SESSION_USER')
------------------------------------
STROUPE

SQL> spool off
SQL> ! cat asu.txt

SQL> select name from v$database;
```

```
NAME
----------
TS10G

SQL> spool off
SQL> select sys_context ('USERENV', 'SESSION_USER') from dual;

SYS_CONTEXT('USERENV','SESSION_USER')
------------------------------------
STROUPE

SQL> spool off
```

10g iSQL*Plus Enhancements

Oracle 10g iSQL*Plus has been enhanced to provide greater flexibility and manageability for end-user support. Following is a short summary of the new features that are now available for 10g iSQL*Plus.

iSQL*Plus Environment

Oracle Database 10g introduces major changes to the underlying iSQL*Plus infrastructure environment. Prior to Oracle 10g, iSQL*Plus used the Oracle HTTP server to enable communication and authentication between the client and the database layers, respectively. With Oracle 10g, the iSQL*Plus middle tier consists of a Java2 Enterprise Edition (J2EE) compliant application server and uses Oracle Containers for Java (OC4J) as the server engine. Along with these changes, there are also notable changes with the iSQL*Plus URL and the iSQL*Plus configuration files. When accessing iSQL*Plus, users will need to use the following URL: `http://`*hostname*`.`*domainname*`:`*port*`/isqlplus`. With Oracle 9i, the port had a default value of 80. Any time you wanted to check the configuration files for errors or change the default port number, you had to review `$ORACLE_HOME/Apache/Apache/conf/httpd.conf`, `$ORACLE_HOME/Apache/Apache/conf/oracle_apache.conf`, and the `$ORACLE_HOME/sqlplus/admin/isqlplus.conf` files. With Oracle 10g, the default port value is 5560 and users will need to review the `$ORACLE_HOME/oc4j/j2ee/isqlplus/config/http-web-site.xml` file for any port changes or errors.

iSQL*Plus Workspace

The iSQL*Plus workspace, formerly called the Work Screen, has been enhanced to provide a more robust working environment. The 10g iSQL*Plus workspace consist of the SQL Workspace, SQL History, and Load Script screens. From the main workspace screen, shown in Figure 20.1, you can enter and execute SQL scripts, load and save SQL scripts, view SQL output, access preferences, view the SQL history, and access the iSQL*Plus help files.

FIGURE 20.1
10g iSQL*Plus Workspace overview.

When entering SQL from the main workspace screen, you can specify the number of lines of data returned from your query by using the SET PAGESIZE command. After the initial result set is displayed, you can click the Next Page button to view the next result set. By default, the page size is set to 24. You can change the settings by accessing the preferences, modifying the glogin.sql file, or using the SET PAGESIZE command before you issue your query in the iSQL*Plus input window (shown in Figure 20.2).

FIGURE 20.2
Specifying page size limits in the 10g iSQL*Plus Workspace.

From the History screen, shown in Figure 20.3, you can access a list of scripts that you previously executed during your session. You can either load scripts from the History screen to the Workspace Input screen or delete scripts from the History screen. If you select multiple scripts from the History screen, the scripts are loaded into the Workspace Input screen in the order they were displayed in the History list. It's also important to note that the script history is only available for the current session. The history is not saved over multiple sessions, nor can it be exported for future use.

FIGURE 20.3
List of previous scripts from the iSQL*Plus History screen.

When you click on the Preferences link in the top-right corner, you can access the Interface Configuration screen, shown in Figure 20.4, to control the look and feel of the iSQL*Plus interface. Starting with 10g Release 1 you can set number of scripts within the script history, set the size of the script input area, set the location where the output should be displayed (below the input area or in an HTML file), and specify whether output is displayed on a single page or spread over multiple pages. From here you can also set the number of rows on each page as well as customize text to be displayed at each page break.

FIGURE 20.4
Interface configuration options from 10g iSQL*Plus.

You can also access the System Configuration screen from the Preferences link. The System Configuration screen replaces the System Variables screen in the previous release of iSQL*Plus. It contains three links to configure script formatting, script executing, and database administration. The Script Formatting screen lists the configuration options that affect the way the report is displayed. The Script Execution screen lists the configuration options that affect the way scripts are executed. The Database Administration screen, shown in Figure 20.5, lists configuration options that affect database administration. The options include specifying whether to use default archive log file names during recovery as well as the archive log location for recovery.

FIGURE 20.5
Database administration options from 10g iSQL*Plus.

You can also access the Change Password screen from the preferences link, as shown in Figure 20.6. From the Change Password screen, you can change your iSQL*Plus password in the same fashion as you can by issuing the PASSWORD clause from the original SQL*Plus screen.

> **Privileged users can change the password for other users from the iSQL*Pluspassword screen.**

FIGURE 20.6
Change Password screen from 10g iSQL*Plus.

Advanced iSQL*Plus and SQL*Plus Features in Oracle Database 10g Release 2

Oracle 10g Release 2 offers several new features with SQL*Plus and iSQL*Plus. Following is a short overview of the new features that will be included in the upcoming release:

■ 10g Release 2 offers the new XQUERY SQL*Plus command and iSQL*Plus support. XQUERY allows you to enter XQuery statements and retrieve results in SQL*Plus. Following is an example of this new feature:

```
SQL> XQUERY for $i in ora:view("documents")
2 return $i
3 /

Result Sequence
---------------------------------------------------------------------------
<ROW><DOC_ID>69923</DOC_ID><DOC_TITLE> Earthquake triggers deadly tsunami </DOC_TITLE>
<DOC_DATE>20-MAY-2005</DOC_DATE> …
```

■ Along with the new support for XQUERY, 10g Release 2 also introduces the SET XQUERY command to declare options used in XQuery statements. Following is a short summary of each option used with SET XQUERY:

  ■ **BASEURI.** This defines the base URL to use for the doc() and collection() functions. The default value is an empty string.

  ■ **ORDERING.** This allows you to specify whether the ordering mode used with XQuery statements is enabled. The default value is DEFAULT.

  ■ **NODE.** This allows you to specify the node identify preservation mode used with XQuery statements. The default value is DEFAULT.

  ■ **CONTEXT.** This allows you to set the default document context to be passed with XQuery statements. The default value is an empty string.

With Oracle 10g Release 2, the syntax for the SET SERVEROUTPUT command has been enhanced to allow a SIZE specification of UNLIMITED. The existing range of values for the SET SERVEROUTPUT command remains unchanged, but if no value is specified it will default to UNLIMITED. This new feature works in conjunction with the new maximum line size for DBMS_OUTPUT, which has been enhanced from 255 to 32,767 bytes.

Summary

This chapter reviewed the latest features for Oracle Database 10g SQL*Plus and iSQL*Plus as well as the new features introduced with Oracle 10g Release 2. These new features and enhancements add greater manageability and flexibility to the SQL environment by adding new DEFINE variables as well as the ability to append to existing SPOOL files.

21

Making the Most of Oracle Database 10g

IN THIS CHAPTER

A Collection of Useful Features   455

DML/DDL Features   455

Network Features   456

Security Features   458

Resource Manager and Scheduler   459

New Database Initialization
Parameters   461

Oracle Streams Enhancements   462

MetaLink Integration with Oracle
Database 10g   465

Oracle Database 10g EM Patch Cache   466

Oracle Applications 11i with Oracle
Database 10g   467

A Collection of Useful Features

Oracle Database 10g comes with a slew of new features too numerous to list. Chapter 1, "Exploring Oracle Database 10g Architecture," dealt with some of the new features from an architectural point of view. This chapter discusses some of the most useful features with a short explanation and usage where warranted. Many of the new features add new functionality, while others remove minor limitations that used to exist before or change the way a particular action was done.

DML/DDL Features

In SQL*Plus, you can use the `DBMS_OUTPUT` information from a nested PL/SQL procedure or trigger in a `SELECT` statement to improve PL/SQL debugging and reporting.

The improved functionality of transparent gateways in Oracle Database 10g allows the use of remote stored functions in database `SELECT` statements. This will help you to query data and use remote functions stored in a non-Oracle database with `SELECT` statements. This feature helps to improve the local processing of non-Oracle data and helps the gateway deal with a reduced amount of data processing.

Data Manipulation Language (DML) statements are part of all databases. DML statements query or manipulate the data in schema objects such as tables. In Oracle Database 10g, you can use single-set aggregates in `RETURNING` clauses of DML statements. This helps to improve the performance in transactions involving many rows of the same table as in batch jobs. Similarly, the new SQL DML Web Services allows the implementation of Web services as a single or group `INSERT`, `UPDATE`, and `DELETE` operation.

In Oracle Database 10g Release 2, DML is supported in the `RETURNING` clause of JDBC operations. This will increase database query performance by saving on a client-to-database roundtrip access. Also, intra-partition DML is now possible with bitmap indexes.

A DML error-logging table is a new feature in Oracle Database 10g Release 2. It allows bulk DML operations to continue processing even when an error occurs. When a DML error occurs, the statement continues after recording the errors in a DML error-logging table. This helps in the functionality of row-level error handling in bulk data processing. The database user can specify whether or not errors should be logged at the DML statement level. Similarly, the user can control the level of details and maximum error threshold as in SQL*Loader and external tables.

Network Features

The improved network-management features in Oracle Database 10g eliminate the manual steps required to configure the Oracle networking environment. Oracle automatically configures many of the shared server parameters. You can connect to a database from a client machine without creating the client configuration files. You can also switch back and forth between dedicated and shared server mode while you remain connected.

Another important feature enables you to back up directory naming entries into a local `tnsnames.ora` file. Using this feature, database clients can use the local copies of the saved file when a directory server is unavailable or when not upgraded to use directory naming.

The dynamic Connection Manager (CMAN) allows you to easily change the Connection Manager parameters without shutting down the CMAN process. The easy connect naming method enables a database connection without configuring a net service name at the client. This also helps to connect to different databases or instances running on the same server. You can also create access rules for Connection Manager to filter traffic for CMAN based on subnet mask, timeout, idle timeout, and other rule-level controls.

With Oracle Database 10g LDAP, a client Oracle home does not require the directory usage configuration file (`ldap.ora`) to use the directory. Only the Oracle internet Directory (OiD) Server needs to be registered with the Domain Name System (DNS) for clients to automatically connect to the directory server. If the `ldap.ora` file is configured, it will supercede the auto-discovery mechanism.

Oracle Database 10g includes protocol support for the Sockets Direct Protocol (SDP) for Infiniband high-speed networks. This is a new protocol for a high-speed communication for better performance of client/server and server/server connections. Currently, SDP is not available on all platforms. Refer to your platform-specific Oracle manual for more details.

> **The Demise of Oracle Name Server**
>
> Oracle Database 10g has finally laid the Oracle Name Server to rest. Clients based on Oracle Database 10g cannot use Oracle Name Services; you will have to use local naming methods (tnsnames.ora) or implement Oracle internet Directory (OiD). Note that this affects even the Oracle Database 10g client software installed on desktop PCs. Keep this in mind before rolling out updated client versions, even if these clients connect to databases that are still in lower versions.

New Features in Oracle Database 10g Release 2

In Oracle Database 10g Release 2, you can simplify client configuration by using the easy connect naming method with TCP/IP environments as well. The easy connect naming method eliminates the need for service name lookup in the `tnsnames.ora` files for TCP/IP environments and provides instant TCP/IP connectivity to databases. Clients can connect to a database server with an optional port and service name along with the host name of the database as shown here:

```
CONNECT username/password@[//]host[:port][/service_name]
```

`//` specifies an optional URL, while `host` specifies the host name or IP address of the database server. The listening port (`port`) is optional, while the default is 1521. The `service_name` of the database is also optional. If the host name does not match the database service name, then enter a valid service name value rather than accepting the default. A typical service name description will be as follows:

```
(DESCRIPTION=
  (ADDRESS=(PROTOCOL=tcp)(HOST=host)(PORT=port))
  (CONNECT_DATA=
    (SERVICE_NAME=service_name)))
```

The following example gives a database CONNECT string and its corresponding `tnsnames.ora` entry:

```
CONNECT user/password@QLAB10G:1521/QLAB10G.US.ACME.COM

(DESCRIPTION=
  (ADDRESS=(PROTOCOL=tcp)(HOST=QLAB10G)(PORT=1521))
  (CONNECT_DATA=
    (SERVICE_NAME=QLAB10G.US.ACME.COM)))
```

If you wish to make URL or JDBC connections to the database, prefix the connect identifier with a double-slash (//) like so:

```
CONNECT user/password@[//][host][:port][/service_name]
```

> This type of connection specification is reminiscent of SQL*Net Version 1 that was available in Oracle V5 and V6.

In Oracle Database 10g Release 2, the DISPATCHERS parameter need not be specified to enable shared servers. If the DISPATCHERS parameter is not configured and the shared server is configured, then a dispatcher listening on TCP/IP port 1521 is started automatically. Configuration of the DISPATCHERS parameter is required for dispatchers that do not listen on the TCP/IP protocol.

Security Features

Oracle Corporation has improved the security features in Oracle Database 10g over previous versions to provide better data security, integrity, authentication, auditing, and access control based on industry standards. Oracle Advanced Security provides these features along with strong authentication methods such as Kerberos, smart cards, and digital certificates.

Fine-grained auditing (FGA) has been updated to enable queries for granular auditing along with INSERT, UPDATE, and DELETE operations. Also, bind variable information is now captured in both DBA_AUDIT_TRAIL and DBA_FGA_AUDIT_TRAIL via the new SQL_BIND column.

Sensitive enterprise data should always be encrypted to prevent illegal viewing or tampering by malicious users and external hackers. Corporate databases should be set up in a way to detect, block, and log the illegal attempts to get to the data. Oracle protects the sensitive data traveling over enterprise networks and the Internet using encryption algorithms like RC4 encryption, DES and Triple-DES (3DES) encryptions, and Advanced Encryption Standard (AES). For RC4 encryption, a secret, randomly generated key that is unique to each session is created by the encryption module with encryption key lengths of 40 bits, 56 bits, 128 bits, and 256 bits. Oracle Advanced Security implements the U.S. Data Encryption Standard algorithm (DES) with a standard 56-bit key encryption algorithm, and provides DES40 with 40-bit keys for backward compatibility to older applications. The Triple-DES encryption encrypts data with three passes of the DES algorithm for higher security at lower performance rates. 3DES is available in two-key (112 bits) and three-key (168 bits) formats. For more details on Oracle security packages, refer to *Oracle Database 10g Security Guide*.

Oracle Advanced Security ensures data integrity over the network by generating a cryptographically secure message using a Message Digest 5 (MD5) algorithm or a Secure Hash Algorithm (SHA-1) and including it with the data (message). The integrity algorithm protects against data modification, data deletion, and replay attacks on a network.

User authentication in distributed environments is usually provided by means of passwords. Oracle Advanced Security supports various third-party authentication services including Secure

Sockets Layer (SSL with digital certificates), DCE (Distributed Computing Environment), Kerberos (authentication server), RADIUS (Remote Authentication Dial-In User Service), and Entrust/PKI. Oracle Connection Manager makes secure data transfer across network protocols such as LU6.2, TCP/IP, and DECnet by passing encrypted data between protocols without additional costs of repeated encryption and decryption.

Access Control Features

Now that you have reviewed the encryption, integrity, and authentication parts of database security, let's focus on access control features for the enterprise. Oracle internet Directory (OiD) is an LDAP-compliant directory service that helps to manage the security privileges for users at the attribute level in a database. Other database-security features are Virtual Private Database (VPD) and Oracle Label Security.

Virtual Private Database enforces security at a lower level of granularity on database tables, views, and synonyms, preventing any ways to bypass security. When a user accesses a database object protected by a VPD policy, the server will dynamically add predicates to the user's SQL statement in accordance with the security policy. Thus, VPD policies restrict access to the database tables, can be easily changed as necessary, and do not require modifications to application code. This is especially useful in enterprise resource planning (ERP) applications, where database objects are highly customized for a variety of users.

Oracle Label Security controls user access to a data record (row) by comparing that row's label with a user's label and privileges. Database administrators can easily add selective row-restrictive policies to existing databases' Oracle Policy Manager GUI and fortify their existing applications without changing any application code.

Oracle Java Virtual Machine (OracleJVM) can be used to run Java objects inside the database in tandem with the database-security features. The Oracle Advanced Security User Migration utility helps to migrate users from existing databases to OiD. For existing applications with several hundred users, the users can be ported over using the migration utility and authenticated through OiD for new applications.

Resource Manager and Scheduler

Oracle Database 10g enables enterprise-level databases to perform efficiently via a variety of methods. Two of those involve both scheduling the resource usage via a database scheduler and controlling usage via a database

> Note that both these tasks can be performed using the OEM Database Control screens.

resource manager. This requires the use of the Oracle-supplied DBMS_SCHEDULER, DBMS_RESOURCE_MANAGER, and DBMS_RESOURCE_MANAGER_PRIVS built-in PL/SQL packages. We will deal with them briefly here.

Job Management Using the Scheduler

Jobs and programs that execute in the database can be scheduled via a variety of means. Traditionally, these were scheduled using operating-system utilities such as cron in UNIX/Linux environments or the AT utility in Windows or the DBMS_JOB built-in PL/SQL package inside the Oracle database. The new DBMS_SCHEDULER takes that a large step forward. The new scheduler enables the following functions:

- **Schedule job execution based on time.** This is the same as the functionality provided by DBMS_JOB or cron.

- **Reuse existing programs and schedules.** Programs are a collection of metadata about what will be run by the scheduler, and schedules specify when jobs should be run. For example, you can create one program that takes the schema name as a parameter to analyze objects in a schema and reuse that program for different schedules to analyze different schemas.

- **Schedule job processing according to your business model.** The scheduler enables plan-limited computing resources to be allocated appropriately among competing jobs, thus aligning job processing with your business needs. You can group jobs into job classes according to their business characteristics and priorities and then prioritize these jobs within themselves and according to a larger schedule.

- **Manage and monitor jobs.** Scheduling activity is logged and can be monitored via SQL or even from OEM.

- **Execute and manage jobs in a clustered environment.** The scheduler supports job scheduling in a clustered environment and enables load balancing by assigning jobs to be run against specific service names.

Detailed information is available in the *Oracle Database 10g Administrators Guide* and the *Oracle Database 10g PL/SQL Packages and Types Reference*.

Overview of the Resource Manager

The resource manager was introduced in Oracle 8i as a way of controlling resource usage by individual sessions and users. Oracle has been adding functionality in various versions to this often underutilized feature. Adaptive consumer group mapping is a new feature added in Oracle Database 10g. This feature makes it easier to use the database resource manager without requiring any application changes, which removes one of the main stumbling blocks to its usage. You can configure the database resource manager to automatically assign consumer groups to sessions by providing mappings between session attributes and consumer groups. Further, you can prioritize the mappings to indicate which mapping has precedence in case of conflicts. You use the SET_CONSUMER_GROUP_MAPPING and SET_CONSUMER_MAPPING_PRI procedures in the DBMS_RESOURCE_MANAGER built-in PL/SQL package to configure the automatic assigning of sessions to consumer groups.

New Database Initialization Parameters

Oracle Database 10g has introduced a large number of new initialization parameters, many of which have been covered in previous chapters. This section covers some of the interesting ones that have not yet been mentioned:

- `DDL_WAIT_FOR_LOCKS` specifies whether DDL statements such as `ALTER TABLE ... ADD COLUMN` wait and complete instead of timing out if the statement is not able to acquire all required locks. The default value is `FALSE` and hence DDL statements time out if the statement cannot obtain all required locks.

- `LDAP_DIRECTORY_ACCESS` specifies whether Oracle refers to the Oracle internet Directory (OiD) for user-authentication information. If directory access is turned on, then this parameter also specifies how users are authenticated. The default is `NONE`.

- `LOG_ARCHIVE_LOCAL_FIRST` specifies when the archiver processes (ARC*n*) transmit redo data to remote standby database destinations. The default value is `TRUE`, which directs the ARC*n* process to transmit redo data *after* the online redo log file has been completely and successfully archived to at least one local destination. Because the online redo log files are archived locally first, the LGWR process reuses the online redo log files much earlier than would be possible if the ARC*n* processes archived to the standby database concurrently with the local destination. This behavior is useful when archiving to remote destinations that use a slow network connection, such as a long-distance wide area network (WAN).

- `PLSQL_CODE_TYPE` specifies the compilation mode for PL/SQL library units in order to support native compilation when set to `NATIVE`. The default value is `INTERPRETED`, which is the old method in order to keep applications from breaking unexpectedly. Native compilation will enable faster execution. The new `PLSQL_OPTIMIZE_LEVEL` parameter further defines the level used to compile these library units.

- `PLSQL_DEBUG` specifies whether or not PL/SQL library units will be compiled for debugging. The default value is `FALSE`. When `PLSQL_DEBUG` is set to `TRUE`, PL/SQL library units are always compiled `INTERPRETED` in order to support debugging. Note that the `PLSQL_COMPILER_FLAGS` parameter has been deprecated in favor of this and the `PLSQL_CODE_TYPE`-parameters.

- `PLSQL_WARNINGS` enables or disables the reporting of warning messages by the PL/SQL compiler and specifies which warning messages to show as errors. The default value is `DISABLE:ALL`.

- `RESUMABLE_TIMEOUT` enables or disables resumable statements and specifies resumable timeout at the system level. The *Oracle Database Administrator's Guide* specifies how to enable resumable space allocation, what conditions are correctable, what statements can be made resumable, and so on. The default value is 0 seconds and can go up to $2^{31}-1$.

Oracle Streams Enhancements

Previously introduced with Oracle 9.2, Oracle Streams is a lightweight replication feature that enables the sharing of data and events via a data stream within a database or from one database to another. Oracle Database 10g has taken the initial baseline of this technology and greatly enhanced its footprint in the latest version of the database. Following is a short summary of these features now available with Oracle Database 10g.

Streams Architecture

Starting with Oracle Database 10g, you can specify a new SGA pool for Oracle streams memory allocation called the *streams pool*. This new pool is created by specifying a value for the new dynamic initialization parameter STREAMS_POOL_SIZE. Prior to Oracle Database 10g, memory allocation for Oracle streams was taken from the shared pool and therefore DBAs who used Oracle streams had to provide extra space for this type of processing.

At instance startup, if the size of the streams pool is 0, then the memory used by Oracle streams is allocated from the shared pool. Even knowing that the STREAMS_POOL_SIZE parameter is dynamic, increasing it beyond 0 after the instance has already started has no effect on the current instance. Also, if the STREAMS_POOL_SIZE parameter is set to a value greater than 0 when the instance starts and then is reduced to 0 while the instance is already running, Oracle streams will not allocate any additional memory from the shared pool, thus not allowing streams to properly run in your environment.

When specifying the size for the STREAMS_POOL_SIZE, you should consider the following factors:

- 10MB for each capture process parallelism

- 1MB for each apply process parallelism

- 10MB or more for each queue staging captured events

Along with the new streams pool, Oracle 10g also provides a new dynamic performance view called V$STREAMS_POOL_ADVICE that can help determine the best size for optimal performance.

Along with the SGA changes, Oracle Database 10g has also moved the necessary streams and LogMiner tables out of the SYSTEM tablespace over to the new SYSAUX tablespace. For more information about the new SYSAUX tablespace, refer to Chapter 1.

Streams Administrator

Prior to Oracle 10g, the DBA had to create a user and grant the necessary privileges to connect and manage the various objects for streams. Missing any of these privileges would have caused a loss of functionality for your environment. To address this limitation, Oracle Database 10g introduces a new streams administrator package called DBMS_STREAMS_AUTH to assist with this effort. DBMS_STREAMS_AUTH can be used to grant and revoke the necessary privileges that are needed to manage streams. This new package enables a user to perform all the steps in the streams process such as capture, apply, propagate, queue, rule, and so on for the streams environment. For example, to assign someone the streams administrator privilege, you will need to use the GRANT_ADMIN_PRIVILEGE procedure:

```
SQL> conn / as sysdba
Connected.
SQL> begin
  2  dbms_streams_auth.grant_admin_privilege (
  3  grantee => 'STROUPE',
  4  grant_privileges => TRUE);
  5  end;
  6  /

PL/SQL procedure successfully completed.
```

You can also optionally assign someone the streams administrator privilege as well as generate a script to manually assign the necessary privileges for future users. The generated script will have the same benefit as running the GRANT_ADMIN_PRIVILEGE procedure.

```
SQL> create directory TEMP as 'C:\temp';

Directory created.

SQL> begin
  2  dbms_streams_auth.grant_admin_privilege(
  3  grantee => 'STROUPE',
  4  grant_privileges => TRUE,
  5  file_name => 'gen_streams_admin.sql',
  6  directory_name => 'TEMP');
  7  end;
  8  /

PL/SQL procedure successfully completed.
```

To monitor the current streams administrators for your environment, query the new DBA view DBA_STREAMS_ADMINISTRATOR like so:

```
SQL> select * from dba_streams_administrator;

USERNAME                        LOC ACC
------------------------------- --- ---
STROUPE                         YES YES
```

To remove the streams administrator privilege, use the REVOKE_ADMIN_PRIVILEGE procedure. When removed, the user is also removed from the DBA_STREAMS_ADMINISTRATOR view.

```
SQL> begin
  2  dbms_streams_auth.revoke_admin_privilege (
  3  grantee => 'STROUPE');
  4  end;
  5  /

PL/SQL procedure successfully completed.

SQL> select * from dba_streams_administrator;

no rows selected
```

Streams Downstream Capture

Streams capture involves a rigorous process of relaying changes from the redo logs over to a staging queue. This process requires extra resource overhead at the source database, which could have a negative impact for overall performance. Starting with Oracle Database 10g, you can shift this work to an alternative database to eliminate this overhead. This new process, known as *downstream capture*, creates the related database objects such as the LogMiner session, queues, rules, and necessary streams processes on another database for processing. The redo logs generated at the source database can be transported to the downstream database using generic log transport services, File Transfer Protocol (FTP), or the DBMS_FILE_TRANSFER package. Creating a database link from the downstream site to the source database is optional; however, it will greatly simplify the management between the two. If you do not use log transport services for the redo log copy, you must register the log file to the capture process by using the following command:

```
SQL> alter database register logical logfile <FILENAME> for <CAPTURE_PROCESS>;
```

Because the source and downstream databases use the same archive log files, both databases must run Oracle Database 10g on the same operating system. If, however, the downstream database is set up to send event messaging to another destination with streams, the remote destination is not required to be on the same operation system, although it must use Oracle Database 10g.

Streams-Enhanced RAC Support

To increase performance of streams in a RAC environment, a capture process can now capture changes propagated via archive redo log files or from the online redo log files. Modifications using streams can now be captured more closely to the time they were executed, thereby reducing the capture latency between the environments.

Also with Oracle Database 10g, RAC instance failover has been enhanced to provide greater support for streams capture and propagation. Now when there is a RAC failover, each queue used by the capture or apply from the failed instance is automatically assigned to a new instance in the cluster; the capture and apply processes follow their queues to the new instance, and all propagation jobs also automatically migrate over to the new instance. Please note, however, that for any propagations that were configured with the failed instance as the destination using database links, you must drop and re-create the database link using the same global name but point it to the new instance that owns the queue.

Other Streams Enhancements

Oracle Database 10g also offers the following enhancements for stream propagation:

- Enhanced message propagation and notification.

- Manageability improvements such as a new streams queue purging API, the capability to remove unnecessary archive log files, a new Point-In-Time Recovery API with flashback support, delete cascade constraints across databases, the capability to drop an unused streams rule set, subset rules for capture and propagation, replication support for a single tablespace or set of tablespaces, the capability to configure a capture user, support for negative rule sets, user-defined pre-commit handlers, enhanced DBMS_STREAMS_ADM methods to remove a streams queue or the entire streams environment, and enhancements to many existing and new streams-monitoring and performance views.

- Enhanced data type support for LONG, LONG RAW, CLOB, NCLOB, BINARY_FLOAT, BINARY_DOUBLE, and UROWID columns.

> Streams cannot support IOTs that contain LOB columns, cannot support overflow segments, and cannot have row movement enabled.

- New support for index-organized tables (IOTs) as well as tables with function-based and descending indexes.

- New streams-instantiation support for RMAN and Data Pump, or manually with SET_SCHEMA_INSTANTIATION_SCN and SET_GLOBAL_INSTANTIATION_SCN procedures in the DBMS_APPLY_ADM built-in PL/SQL package.

- Migration support from advanced replication to streams using the DBMS_REPCAT.STREAMS_MIGRATION procedure.

MetaLink Integration with Oracle Database 10g

Starting with Oracle Database 10g, Enterprise Manager (EM) has integrated the Oracle MetaLink support vehicle for up-to-date patch advisories and notifications. From the EM home page, under the Critical Patch Advisories subheading, you can access and configure the Oracle MetaLink Credentials link to register your environment for this service. In order to register your environment, you will need a valid CSI (customer support identifier) with MetaLink. Log in as SYSDBA to perform the registration. When you click the Not Configured link, you will be directed to the Patching Setup screen, shown in Figure 21.1, to enter your MetaLink user ID and password.

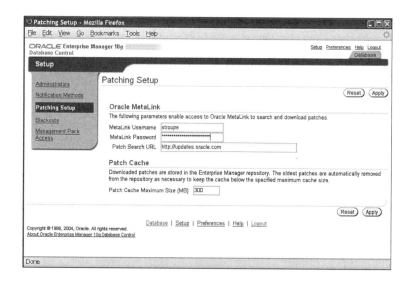

FIGURE 21.1
Configuring MetaLink
credentials via 10g EM.

The patch search URL is already predefined as `http://updates.oracle.com`, which is a redirect to `http://metalink.oracle.com/`, so there is no need for any change. You can optionally change the size of your patch cache (described later in this chapter). After you properly register, you can access the Refresh from MetaLink link under Critical Patch Advisory to download the latest patch advisories and patch sets for your environment. You will notice when you click this link that a job called `REFRESH_FROM_METALINK_JOB` is executed from the EM job scheduler. This is a predefined job and should never be removed from your system.

Oracle Database 10g EM Patch Cache

Along with the new 10g EM integration for Oracle MetaLink, users can now manually or automatically upload patches downloaded from MetaLink to the EM patch cache. The patch cache can be accessed from the Maintenance tab under the Deployments subheading. Clicking the View Patch Cache link will direct you to the Patch Cache screen. The patch cache contains patches that have been downloaded from Oracle MetaLink to your Enterprise Manager repository either manually or automatically. Automatic patch downloads are performed for you via the `REFRESH_FROM_METALINK_JOB` that is executed when you properly register your MetaLink credentials as described in the previous section. To manually upload a patch to the patch cache, click the Upload Patch File button; this will direct you to the Add Patch File to Patch Cache screen, shown in Figure 21.2.

When using the Patch Cache wizard to manually upload a large patch (larger then **128MB**) into the patch cache, a "Failed to Upload File Uploaded file of length *xxxx* bytes exceeded maximum allowed length (**134217728**)" error can occur. This bug (**#3719280**) is fixed with **10.1.0.4** and **10.2.0**.

To manually add a patch, you first must download the patch and have it available on your system. Then, fill in all the corresponding patch attributes. When you are ready to proceed, click the Upload button. Manually adding a patch to the cache is only necessary if you have not properly registered your MetaLink credentials, you do not have an Internet connection at the time of patching, or the patch is not yet available from MetaLink.

FIGURE 21.2
Manually uploading a patch to the 10g EM Patch Cache.

Oracle Applications 11i with Oracle Database 10g

Oracle Applications 11i, also known as the Oracle E-Business Suite, has recently been certified with Oracle Database 10g. Specifically, Oracle Applications Release 11.5.9 and Oracle Applications Release 11.5.10 have been certified to work with Oracle Database 10g Release 10.1.0.4 on a number of UNIX and Windows platforms. A number of prerequisites will have to be met; these are detailed in the Certification Matrix for your platform of choice. A special patch known as the interoperability patch for that platform and that application version must also be applied. For more details, refer to MetaLink Note #282038.1 Oracle Applications Release 11i with Oracle Database 10g Release 1 (10.1.0). With this version of the database stack, a number of initialization parameters should be removed, and the COMPATIBLE parameter should be set to 10.1.0. As well, the automatic SGA tuning should be enabled by setting the SGA_TARGET parameter. Further details can be obtained from MetaLink Note #216205.1, "Database Initialization Parameters for Oracle Applications 11i."

Summary

This chapter looked at some of the new features of Oracle Database 10g that weren't mentioned elsewhere. The complete set of new features is covered in the *Oracle Database 10g Release 1 New Features* manual and its equivalent for Release 2. Product-specific changes are also available in the first chapter of most manuals, such as the *Oracle Database 10g Concepts* manual and the *Oracle Database 10g Administrators Guide*.

Index

Symbols

+ (plus) sign, 83

/ (forward slash), 83

10053 event trace file, 303-304

A

ACCEPT_SQL_PROFILE function, 277

Access Advisor. *See* SQL Access Advisor

access control, 459

access path analysis, 266

ACTION column (V$ACTIVE_SESSION_HISTORY), 228

Active Session History. *See* ASH

ADD ALIAS clause (ALTER DISKGROUP command), 84

ADD DATABASE command, 359

ADD DIRECTORY clause (ALTER DISKGROUP command), 83

ADD DISK clause (ALTER DISKGROUP command), 80

Add Standby Database wizard, 353

ADD_SQLSET_REFERENCE function, 276

ADD_SQLWKLD_REF function, 280

ADD_SQLWKLD_STATEMENT function, 280

ADDM (Automatic Database Diagnostic Monitor), 12-13, 239-240

    accessing from OEM, 244-249

        ADDM Main page, 246

        Advisor Central, 244-245

        AWR Snapshot page, 245

        Database Performance page, 245

        performance finding details, 248-249

        SQL details for PL/SQL block, 247-248

Additional Information findings (ADDM), 260-261

addmrpt.sql script, 250-252

ASH data, 242

cases when ADDM analysis is not done, 242

DBMS_ADVISOR package, 252-254

goal of, 240-241

new features, 262

nonproblematic areas, 242

problem areas handled by, 241

recommendations, 241-242

reports, analyzing

    Additional Information findings, 260-261

    cross-verification from advisor views, 261-262

    expected I/O response time, 261

    idle events, 259-260

    session management, 258-259

    SQL statements consuming significant time, 254-257

    SQL statements waiting for locks, 257-258

rules, 240

views, 243-244

ADDM Main page (OEM), 246

administrator privileges, 463

addmrpt.sql script, 250-252

Advanced Queuing (AQ), 429

Advisor Central, 244-245

advisors, 19, 205

    ADDM (Automatic Database Diagnostic Monitor), 12-13, 239-240

      accessing from OEM, 244-249

      addmrpt.sql script, 250-252

      ASH data, 242

      cases when ADDM analysis is not done, 242

      DBMS_ADVISOR package, 252-254

      goal of, 240-241

      new features, 262

      nonproblematic areas, 242

      problem areas handled by, 241

      recommendations, 241-242

      reports, analyzing, 254-262

rules, 240

views, 243-244

Segment Advisor, 143-144

    invoking from OEM, 144-145

    invoking from PL/SQL, 145-146

    reviewing results of, 146-147

SQL Access Advisor, 19

    APIs, 280-284

    DBMS_ADVISOR package, 280-284

    inputs, 267-268

    materialized views, 267

    new features, 285

    OEM interface, 271-274

    potential pitfalls, 284-285

    steps for use, 268

SQL Tuning Advisor, 19, 200-201, 263-264

    access path analysis, 266

    APIs, 275-280

    Automatic Tuning Optimizer, 264-266

    DBMS_SQLTUNE package, 277-280

    inputs, 266-267

    OEM interface, 268-271

    potential pitfalls, 284-285

    SQL profiling, 266

    SQL structure analysis, 266

    statistics analysis, 266

    STS (SQL tuning sets), 276

Undo Advisor, 134-137

alerts, 58, 203-204

    clearing, 60

    metrics, 126-127

    setup, 60

aliases, 83-84

ALL_ views, 190

ALL_LOGFILES keyword, 343

ALL_ROLES keyword, 344

allocation of resources, 147-148

ALTER DATABASE ARCHIVELOG command, 345

ALTER DATABASE BEGIN BACKUP command, 156

ALTER DATABASE END BACKUP command, 156

ALTER DATABASE START LOGICAL STANDBY APPLY command, 349

ALTER DISKGROUP command, 76, 82-83

    ADD ALIAS clause, 84

    ADD DIRECTORY clause, 83

    ADD DISK clause, 80

    ALL clause (ALTER DISKGROUP command), 82

    ALTER TEMPLATE clause, 83

    CHECK clause, 85

    DELETE ALIAS clause, 84

    DISMOUNT clause, 82

    DROP DIRECTORY clause, 83

    DROP DISK clause, 80-81

    DROP FILE clause, 84

    DROP TEMPLATE clause, 83

    MOUNT clause, 82

    NOREPAIR clause, 85

    REBALANCE clause, 81-82

    RENAME ALIAS clause, 84

    RENAME DIRECTORY clause, 83

    RESIZE clause, 81-82

ALTER TEMPLATE clause (ALTER DISKGROUP command), 83

ALTER_SQL_PROFILE function, 277

ANALYZE command, 111, 293

application partitioning, 336

AQ (Advanced Queuing), 429

archive logs, 154

archive_source keywords, 343

Archiver processes (ARCn), 15

archiving, 345-346

ARCn (Archiver processes), 15

ASH (Active Session History), 179. *See also* ADDM (Automatic Database Diagnostic Monitor)

    buffer contents, dumping, 234-235

    displaying, 222-223

    documentation, 222

    fixed-size circular buffers, 229

    hidden parameters, 229

    limitations, 236

    OEM Database Control, 233-234

    session-state information, 222-226

    spot analysis example, 229-233

    V$ACTIVE_SESSION_HISTORY, 226-228

    V$ACTIVE_WAIT_HISTORY, 228

    V$SESSION_WAIT, 224-225

    WRH$_ACTIVE_SESSION_HISTORY, 228

ASM (Automatic Storage Management), 73-74, 337

    ASMCMD (ASM command-line interface), 9

    configuration

        DBCA (Database Configuration Assistance), 76

        initialization parameters, 78

        remote connections, 77

        startup/shutdown commands, 79

    disk groups

        adding disks to, 80

        checking internal consistency of, 84-85

        creating, 79-80

        definition of, 75

        directory structure, 83

        disk-group templates, 76, 82-83

        dropping, 84

        dropping disks from, 80-81

        failure groups, 75

        mounting, 82

        rebalancing, 81-82

        redundancy, 75

        resizing disks in, 81-82

    failure groups, 75

    files

        aliases, 83-84

        definition of, 76

        filenames, 76

    improvements and new features, 89-90

    installations on Linux, 77

    managing with RAC, 331-332

    maximum file size, 332-333

migration

ASM to non-ASM migration, 87-88

non-ASM to ASM migration, 86-87

multiple Oracle instances, 74

operational limits, 77

prerequisites, 74-75

RAC environments, 85, 88-89

startup/shutdown commands, 79

troubleshooting connections, 85

when to use, 89

ASM_DISKGROUPS (NULL) parameter, 78

ASM_DISKSTRING (NULL) parameter, 78

ASM_POWER_LIMIT (1) parameter, 78

ASMB process, 16

ASMCMD (ASM command-line interface), 9

ASMM (Automatic Shared Memory Management), 93-96

auto-tuned SGA parameters, 94

automated maintenance tasks, 100

converting manual memory-managed databases to, 101-102

initialization parameters, 94-96

Memory Advisor, 97-99

memory management tips, 100-101

new features, 104

scaling for database expansion, 103-104

SGA sizing, 96-97, 102-103

SGA_TARGET, 102-103

ASSM (automatic segment-space management)

data blocks, 142

data segments, 142

dictionary-managed tablespaces, 150

disabling, 143

enabling, 143

extents, 141

HWM (high-water mark), 148

index segments, 142

LMT (locally managed tablespaces), 148

new features, 150

Segment Advisor, 143-144

invoking from OEM, 144-145

invoking from PL/SQL, 145-146

reviewing results of, 146-147

segment resource allocation, 147-148

segment-shrink operations, 149-150

temporary segments, 142-143

asynchronous redo transmission, 367

ATTACH keyword, 433

auditing, fine-grained (FGA), 458

authentication, 343

AUTO EXTEND initialization parameter, 132

auto-tuned SGA parameters, 94

automated maintenance tasks, 100

automatic alerts, 58, 60

Automatic Database Diagnostic Monitor. See ADDM

automatic extension, 384

automatic failover, 367

Automatic Shared Memory Management. See ASMM

automatic SQL tuning, 264-266

automatic statistics collection, 105-106

AWR snapshots, 109-110

base statistics, 108

baselines, 109-110

metrics, 108

operating-system statistics, 108

session statistics, 107-108

statistics levels, 108-109

system statistics, 107-108

time-model statistics, 107

wait events, 106-107

Automatic Storage Management. See ASM

Automatic Tuning Optimizer, 264-266

automatic undo management, 18

advantages of, 132

AUTO EXTEND initialization parameter, 132

Flashback Table, 385

guaranteeing undo availability, 137-138

new features, 139

OEM (Oracle Enterprise Manager), 135-136

RAC (real application clusters), 134

redo log file sizings, 134

resumable space allocation, 133

tips, 138-139

Undo Advisor, 134-137

undo data, 131-132

UNDO_MANAGEMENT initialization parameter, 131

UNDO_RETENTION initialization parameter, 133

Automatic Workload Repository. *See* AWR

AUX_STATS$ table, 294

AWR (Automatic Workload Repository), 11-12, 207-208.
 See also ASH (Active Session History)

 baselines

  capturing, 220-221

  dropping, 221-222

 buffers, 208

 collections, 208-209

 compared to STATSPACK, 209-210

 customizing with OEM, 216

 DBMS_WORKLOAD_REPOSITORY package, 217-218

  creating snapshots, 218-219

  deleting snapshots, 219

  modifying AWR settings, 219-220

 dependencies, 215-216

 emergency purging, 216

 licensing information, 208

 memory requirements, 209

 new features, 236-237

 overheads, 215

 reports, generating

  awrddrpt.sql script, 120-122

  awrrpt.sql script, 113-117

  awrrpti.sql script, 117-119

  awrsqrpi.sql script, 123-124

 snapshots

  accessing, 213, 215

  creating, 109, 218-219

  deleting, 110, 219

 frequency of, 109-110

 retention period, 110

 storage and reporting, 210-213

 suggested settings, 215-216

 views, 211-212

 WRH$ tables, 210

 WRI$ tables, 210

 WRM$ tables, 210

AWR Snapshot page (OEM), 245

AWR_REPORT_HTML function, 218

AWR_REPORT_TEXT function, 218

awrddrpt.sql script, 120-122

awrinfo.sql script, 213

awrinput.sql script, 213

awrrpt.sql script, 113-117, 214-215

awrrpti.sql script, 117-119, 214

B

backdoor installation techniques, 24

background processes

 Archiver processes (ARC*n*), 15

 ASMB, 16

 Change Tracking Writer processes (CTWR), 16

 Checkpoint process (CKPT), 15

 Database Writer process (DBW*n*), 14

 Job Queue processes (J*nnn*), 15

 Log Writer process (LGWR), 15

 Memory Monitor Light process (MMNL), 16

 Memory Monitor processes (MMON), 15

 ORB*n*, 16

 Process Monitor process (PMON), 15

 Queue Monitor processes (QMN*n*), 15

 RBAL, 16

 Recovery Writer process (RVWR), 16

 System Monitor process (SMON), 15

BACKUP command, 159, 167

BACKUP DATABASE command, 158

How can we make this index more useful? Email us at indexes@samspublishing.com

BACKUP INCREMENTAL command, 165

backuploc option (ocrconfig command), 327

backups

    archive logs, 154

    cold backup, 156

    hot backup, 154-156

    RMAN (Recovery Manager)

        accessing, 161

        advantages of, 154-156

        automatic file creation, 167

        backup identification, 167

        backup pieces, 159-160

        backup set creation, 167

        backup sets, 159

        backup strategies, 168-169

        block change tracking, 163-164

        CATALOG mode, 155

        channels, 160

        compared to hot backup, 154-156

        compressed backups, 168

        cross-platform tablespace conversion, 167

        documentation, 160-161

        fast incremental backups, 163-164

        flash recovery area, 162-163

        incrementally updated backups, 164-166

        new features, 170-171

        NOCATALOG mode, 155

        performance tuning, 167

        recovery scenarios, 169-170

        restore failover, 167

        RESETLOGS operation, 166

        sample backup session, 156-158

        tags, 160

    strategies, 168-169

base statistics, 108

baselines, 109

    capturing, 220-221

    creating, 110

    dropping, 110, 221-222

BASEURI option (SET XQUERY command), 454

BEGIN BACKUP command, 158

BFTs (BigFile tablespaces), 9-10

big-endian format, 11

BigFile tablespaces (BFTs), 9-10

binary cloning, 36-39

    common steps, 37-38

    OEM (Oracle Enterprise Manager), 38-39

bitmap tablespaces, 148

block change tracking, 163

BLOCKRECOVER CORRUPTION LIST command, 169

Broker (Data Guard)

    commands

        ADD DATABASE, 359

        CREATE CONFIGURATION, 358

        DISABLE DATABASE, 359

        EDIT CONFIGURATION, 359

        EDIT DATABASE, 359

        EDIT INSTANCE, 360

        ENABLE DATABASE, 359

        FAILOVER, 360

        REMOVE DATABASE, 359

        SHOW, 360

        SWITCHOVER, 360

    GUI enhancements, 351-356

    RAC database support, 351

Buffer Cache Advisor, 19

buffers

    ASH (Active Session History)

        buffer contents, dumping, 234-235

        fixed-size circular buffers, 229

    AWR (Automatic Workload Repository), 208

    Buffer Cache Advisor, 19

C

cache, data dictionary cache, 17

CANCEL_TASK function, 253

CANCEL_TUNING_TASK function, 277

Cannot flashback data file # (error), 384

capturing baselines, 220-221

CATALOG mode (RMAN), 155

catnoqm.sql script, 62

catqm.sql script, 62

CBO (Cost Based Optimizer), 287-288

    capabilities, 289-291

    cardinality, 302-303

    COL_USAGE$ view, 302-303

    column statistics, 291

    column usage, 302-303

    compared to RBO (Rule Based Optimizer), 288-289

    COMPUTE versus ESTIMATE, 292

    cost, 288, 291

    dictionary statistics, 295

    dynamic sampling, 295-296

    frequency of statistic collection, 297

    histograms, 307-309

    initialization parameters, 297-301

    new features, 309-310

    result sets, 290

    selectivity, 302-303

    SQL profiles, 304-307

        compared to outlines, 305

        tracing, 306-307

    system statistics, 292-295

    table and index monitoring, 296-297

    table statistics, 291

    tracing, 303-304

centralized job control, 421

Change Password screen (10g iSQL*Plus workspace), 453

Change Tracking Writer processes (CTWR), 16

change-tracking files, 163-164

channels (RMAN), 160

CHECK clause (ALTER DISKGROUP command), 85

checklists, installation, 36

CKPT (Checkpoint process), 15

clearing alerts, 60

client processes, 14

CLIENT_ID column (V$ACTIVE_SESSION_HISTORY), 228

cloning databases, 36-39

    common steps, 37-38

    OEM (Oracle Enterprise Manager), 38-39

cluster interconnect, 335

Cluster Ready Services. *See* CLS

Cluster Verification Utility (CVU), 337

clusters. *See* RAC (Real Application Clusters)

CMAN (Connection Manager), 456

code listings

    ADDM (Automatic Database Diagnostic Monitor)

        accessing from OEM, 249

        additional information, 261

        ADDM rask reports, printing, 254

        cross-verification from advisor views, 261-262

        DBA_ADVISOR_FINDINGS view, 243-244

        idle events, 259-260

        PL/SQL section, 253-254

        running reports with SQL*Plus, 250-252

        session management, 258-259

        SQL statements consuming significant time, 255-256

        SQL statements waiting for locks, 258

    ASH (Active Session History)

        buffers, dumping, 234-235

        session-state information, 223

        spot analysis, 230-232

    AWR (Automatic Workload Repository)

        awrddrpi.sql script, 123-124

        awrddrpt.sql script, 120-122

        awrrpt.sql script, 115, 214

        awrrpti.sql script, 118-119

        CREATE_BASELINE function, 220

        CREATE_SNAPSHOT function, 218

        DROP_BASELINE function, 221

        DROP_SNAPSHOT_RANGE function, 219

        MODIFY_SNAPSHOT_SETTINGS function, 219

        report headings, 212

        V$SYSAUX_OCCUPANTS view, 211

How can we make this index more useful? Email us at indexes@samspublishing.com

code listings

CBO (Cost Based Optimizer)

  10052 event trace file, 304

  AUX_STATS$ system statistics, 294

  initialization parameters, 298-301

  SQL profile trace, 306-307

DBMS_ADVISOR package, 146

  cross-checking results, 282

  example, 281

  implementation scripts, 282-284

DBMS_SQLTUNE package

  errors, 279

  example, 277-279

OEM installation

  EMCA installation script, 56

  emctl command, 57

  OEM control, checking status of, 57

performance tuning

  event histogram for SQL*Net events, 185

  file-wise read response histogram, 187

  OEM Database Control, 196-197

  SGA_TARGET tuning, 102

  V$FILE_HISTOGRAM view, 187-188

  V$OSSTAT snapshot, 189

  V$SERVICE_EVENT snapshot, 183

  V$SERVICE_STATS snapshot, 182

  V$SERVICE_WAIT_CLASS snapshot, 193-194

  V$SESSION view, 190

  V$SYS_TIME_MODEL snapshot, 191

  V$SYSTEM_WAIT_CLASS snapshot, 192

  Wait event histograms for database reads, 184-185

RMAN (Recovery Manager)

  backup pieces, 159

  change-tracking files, 163-164

  incrementally updated backup, 164-166

  sample backup session, 156-158

SNAP_IDs, 117

statistics, 148

COL_USAGE$ view, 302-303

cold backups, 156

column statistics, 291

commands. *See also* functions and procedures

  ADD DATABASE, 359

  ALTER DATABASE ARCHIVELOG, 345

  ALTER DATABASE START LOGICAL STANDBY APPLY, 349

  ALTER DISKGROUP, 76, 80-83

    ADD ALIAS clause, 84

    ADD DIRECTORY clause, 83

    ADD DISK clause, 80

    ALL clause, 82

    ALTER TEMPLATE clause, 83

    CHECK clause, 85

    DELETE ALIAS clause, 84

    DISMOUNT clause, 82

    DROP DIRECTORY clause, 83

    DROP DISK clause, 80-81

    DROP FILE clause, 84

    DROP TEMPLATE clause, 83

    MOUNT clause, 82

    NOREPAIR clause, 85

    REBALANCE clause, 81-82

    RENAME ALIAS clause, 84

    RENAME DIRECTORY clause, 83

    RESIZE clause, 81-82

  ANALYZE, 293

  COMMIT TO SWITCHOVER, 348-349

  CREATE CONFIGURATION, 358

  CREATE DISK GROUP, 79-80

  CREATE TABLESPACE, 8

  CREATE TABLESPACE SYSAUX , 8

  DBMS_STATS, 293

  DEFINE, 447-449

  disable, 328

  DISABLE DATABASE, 359

  dpexp (Data Pump Export), 13

  dpimp (Data Pump Import), 13

  DROP DATABASE, 13

  DROP TABLE, 398

  DROP TABLESPACE, 398

DROP USER, 399

EDIT CONFIGURATION, 359

EDIT DATABASE, 359

EDIT INSTANCE, 360

emctl, 57

enable, 328

ENABLE DATABASE, 359

EXPLAIN PLAN, 264, 302

FAILOVER, 360

FLASHBACK DATABASE, 371, 378, 381

FLASHBACK TABLE, 386-387, 391-393

FLASHBACK_TRANSACTION_QUERY, 406-408

LOCK_SCHEMA_STATS, 292

LOCK_TABLE_STATS, 292

lsnrctl, 61

ocrcheck, 327

ocrconfig, 327

ocrdump, 327

ORADEBUG, 235

PREPARE TO SWITCHOVER, 348-349

PURGE, 393

relocate, 328

REMOVE DATABASE, 359

RESETLOGS, 377, 382-383, 411

SET SERVEROUTPUT, 454

SET SQLROMPT, 448

SET XQUERY, 454

SHOW, 360

SHUTDOWN ABORT, 79

SHUTDOWN IMMEDIATE, 79

SHUTDOWN NORMAL, 79

SHUTDOWN TRANSACTIONAL, 79

SPOOL, 449-450

STARTUP, 345

STARTUP FORCE, 79

STARTUP MOUNT, 79, 345

STARTUP NOMOUNT, 79

STARTUP OPEN, 79

SWITCHOVER, 360

UPGRADE CATALOG, 70

VERSION_BETWEEN, 400

VERSIONS_BETWEEN, 399-401

XQUERY, 454

COMMIT TO SWITCHOVER command, 348-349

companion CD installation, 35

COMPLEX_VIEW_MERGING initialization parameter, 289

compressed backups, 168

COMPRESSED keyword (BACKUP command), 167

COMPRESSION initialization parameter, 444

COMPUTE option (object statistics), 292

COMPUTE STATISTICS option (ANALYZE command), 111

computing grid, 413

    characteristics of, 415-416

    compared to electricity grid, 414415

    components of, 418

    definition of, 416-417

    EGA (Enterprise Grid Alliance), 417

    enterprise grid computing, 417

    hardware independence, 420

    high availability, 419

    history of, 417-418

    managing, 420-421

    performance, 419

    profiled resource usage, 420

    provisioning, 416

    resiliency, 420

    self-healing, 420

    virtualization, 416-417, 420

configuration. See installation

Configure Backup Settings screen (OEM), 161

Configure Recovery Catalog Settings (OEM), 161

Configure Recovery Settings screen (OEM), 161

CONNECT TARGET command, 158

Connection Manager (CMAN), 456

consistency of disk groups, checking, 84-85

ConText. See Oracle Text

CONTEXT option (SET XQUERY command), 454

COPY command, 154

Cost Based Optimizer. *See* CBO

crawlers, 64

CREATE CONFIGURATION command, 358

CREATE DISK GROUP command, 79-80

CREATE TABLE AS SELECT, command, 443

CREATE TABLE command, 112

CREATE TABLESPACE command, 8

CREATE TABLESPACE SYSAUX command, 8

CREATE_BASELINE function, 109-110, 218, 220-221

CREATE_FILE function, 280

CREATE_SNAPSHOT function, 218-219

CREATE_SQLSET function, 276

CREATE_SQLWKLD function, 280

CREATE_TASK function, 253-254

CREATE_TUNING_TASK function, 277

cross-checking statistics, 112-113

cross-platform transportable tablespaces, 10-11

cross-verifying ADDM reports, 261-262

CRS (Cluster Ready Services), 75, 314. *See also* RAC
(Real Application Clusters)

  CRSD daemon, 315

  database-specific resources, 315

  EVMD daemon, 316

  Fujitsu clustering, 322

  installing, 316-318, 321-322

  nodeapp resources, 315

  OCR (Oracle Cluster Registry), 315

  OCSSD daemon, 315-316

  troubleshooting, 322-323

  Veritas, 322

CRSD daemon, 315

CSS (Cluster Synchronization Services), 49-50, 75

CTWR (Change Tracking Writer) processes, 16

CURRENT_BLOCK# column
(V$ACTIVE_SESSION_HISTORY), 228

CURRENT_FILE# column (V$ACTIVE_SESSION_HISTORY),
228

CURRENT_OBJ# column (V$ACTIVE_SESSION_HISTORY),
228

custom installations. *See* installation/configuration

CVU (Cluster Verification Utility), 337

D

daemons

  CRSD, 315

  CSS, 75

  EVMD, 316

  OCSSD, 315-316

data blocks, 142

Data Definition Language (DDL), 455-456

data dictionary cache, 17

Data Encryption Standard algorithm (DES), 458

Data Guard, 339-340

  archiving, 345-346

  Broker improvements

    ADD DATABASE command, 359

    CREATE CONFIGURATION command, 358

    DISABLE DATABASE command, 359

    EDIT CONFIGURATION command, 359

    EDIT DATABASE command, 359

    EDIT INSTANCE command, 360

    ENABLE DATABASE command, 359

    FAILOVER command, 360

    GUI enhancements, 351-354, 356

    RAC database support, 351

    REMOVE DATABASE command, 359

    SHOW command, 360

    SWITCHOVER command, 360

  configuration management, 345

  DB_UNIQUE_NAME initialization parameter, 345

  Flashback Database, 342-343, 380-383

  goals of, 340

  logical databases, patching, 363-367

  logical standby improvements

    commands and views, 349-350

    PREPARE TO SWITCHOVER command, 348-349

redo log file support, 348

SQL Apply rolling database upgrades, 349

SQL Apply service support, 349

zero outage for instantiation, 346-348

new features, 367-368

physical databases, patching, 361-363

RAC (Real Application Clusters) installation, 68

Real Time Apply, 340-342

redo transmission authentication and encryption, 343

role-based destinations, 343-344

STARTUP command, 345

Data Manipulation Language (DML), 455-456

Data Pump, 13-14, 425-426

AQ (Advanced Queuing), 429

command-line parameters, 444-445

command-line support, 428

DATA_PUMP_DIR directory object, 444

DBMS_DATAPUMP engine, 426

DPAPI (Direct Path API), 427

dump-file sets, 430

Enterprise Manager support, 444

expdp (export) client, 427

full-export mode, 431

new features, 430

sample application, 432-440

schema-export mode, 431

table-export mode, 431

tablespace-export mode, 431

transportable-tablespace-export mode, 431

external clients, 427

External Table Services API, 427

external table support, 427-428, 443-444

impdp (import) client, 427

full-import mode, 431

new features, 430

sample application, 432-440

schema-import mode, 432

table-import mode, 432

tablespace-import mode, 431

transportable-tablespace-import mode, 432

interactive-mode parameters, 445

Metadata API, 427

new features/enhancements, 444-445

operation precedence, 428

process flow, 429-430

SQL Loader client, 427

tracing, 441-442

views, 442-443

data segments, 142

DATA_PUMP_DIR environment variable, 13, 428, 444

Database Administration screen (10g iSQL*Plus workspace), 453

Database Configuration Assistant. See DBCA

Database Control (OEM)

concurrency-related wait information, 199

example, 196-198

general database and host information, 195-196

home page, 198

host and database wait information, 198-199

host performance CPU drill-down details, 203-204

host performance memory drill-down details, 204

host performance summary, 202-203

SQL Tuning Advisor, 200-201

Top SQL, 200

tuned execution plans, 201

Database Performance page (OEM), 245

Database Point-In-Time Recovery (DBPITR), 170

database scheduler, 460

database statistics. See statistics

Database Upgrade Assistant. See DBUA

Database Writer process (DBWn), 14

database_role keywords, 344

databases

blocks, 142

buffer cache, 17

database and binary cloning, 36-39

common steps, 37-38

OEM (Oracle Enterprise Manager), 38-39

Flashback Database, 20, 342-343, 370
    automatic extension, 384
    configuring, 372-373
    Data Guard, 380-383
    flashback logs, 371
    initialization parameters, 371-372
    managing, 373-375
    RVWR (recover writer), 371
    sample flashback operation, 375-380
    troubleshooting, 384-385
    V$FLASHBACK_DATABASE_LOG, 373-374
    V$FLASHBACK_DATABASE_STAT, 374-375
global database changes, 410-411
instances, identifying, 48
logical standby databases
    commands and views, 349-350
    PREPARE TO SWITCHOVER command, 348-349
    redo log file support, 348
    SQL Apply rolling database upgrades, 349
    SQL Apply service support, 349
    zero outage for instantiation, 346-348
migrating from 8i or 9i, 39-40
patching, 46-47
    logical databases, 363-367
    physical databases, 361-363
removing, 48-49
resources, 315
scaling for expansion, 103-104
target databases, unregistering, 71
upgrading
    RMAN (Recovery Manager), 70
    rolling database upgrades, 349
    statistics collection, 128
DB_CACHE_SIZE initialization parameter, 18
DB_FLASHBACK_RETENTION_TARGET initialization parameter, 372
DB_nK_CACHE_SIZE initialization parameter, 18
DB_RECOVERY_FILE_DEST initialization parameter, 20, 371

DB_RECOVERY_FILE_DEST_SIZE initialization parameter, 20, 371
DB_UNIQUE_NAME initialization parameter, 78, 345
DBA_ views, 190
    DBA_ADVISOR_ACTIONS, 243
    DBA_ADVISOR_FINDINGS, 243
    DBA_ADVISOR_LOG, 243
    DBA_ADVISOR_RATIONALE, 243
    DBA_ADVISOR_RECOMMENDATIONS, 243
    DBA_DATAPUMP_JOBS, 442
    DBA_DATAPUMP_SESSIONS, 442
    DBA_HIGH_WATER_MARK_STATISTICS, 211
    DBA_HIST_DATABASE_INSTANCE, 211
    DBA_HIST_JAVA_POOL_ADVICE, 211
    DBA_HIST_SEG_STAT, 211
    DBA_HIST_SNAPSHOT, 211
    DBA_HIST_WR_CONTROL, 211
    DBA_STREAMS_ADMINISTRATOR, 463
DBCA (Database Configuration Assistant), 328-330
    ASM (Automatic Storage Management) configuration, 76
    creation options, 33
    database content, 33
    database credentials, 33
    database file options, 33
    database identification, 32
    database storage, 33
    database templates, 32
    initialization parameters, 33
    management options, 32
    recovery configuration, 33
    storage options, 33
    tracing, 33-34
    XML DB installation, 61-62
DBMS_ADVISOR package, 145-146, 280-284
    ADDM-specific functions and procedures, 252-254
    cross-checking results, 282
    functions and procedures, 280
    implementation scripts, 282-284
    sample code listing, 281

DBMS_DATAPUMP engine, 426

DBMS_DATAPUMP package. *See* Data Pump

DBMS_FILE_TRANSFER package, 464

DBMS_RESOURCE_MANAGER, 460

DBMS_SCHEDULER, 460

DBMS_SQLTUNE package, 277-280

    errors, 279

    functions and procedures, 277

    sample code listing, 277-279

DBMS_STATS command, 293

DBMS_STREAMS_AUTH package, 462-463

DBMS_WORKLOAD_REPOSITORY package, 109-110, 217-218

    creating snapshots, 218-219

    deleting snapshots, 219

    modifying AWR settings, 219-220

DBPITR (database Point-In-Time Recovery), 170

DBUA (Database Upgrade Assistant), 40-41

    Oracle 9i physical logical configuration, 44-46

    Oracle 9i physical standby configuration, 42-44

    silent mode, 42

    upgrade paths for standby environments, 41

DBW*n* (Database Writer process), 14

DDL (Data Definition Language), 455-456

DDL_WAIT_FOR_LOCKS initialization parameter, 461

DEFINE command, 447-449

DELETE ALIAS clause (ALTER DISKGROUP command), 84

DELETE_SQLWKLD function, 280

DELETE_SQLWKLD_REF function, 280

DELETE_SQLWKLD_STATEMENT function, 280

DELETE_TASK function, 253

deleting. *See* dropping

dependencies (AWR), 215-216

DES (Data Encryption Standard algorithm), 458

destinations, role-based, 343-344

dictionary statistics, 295

dictionary-managed tablespaces, 150

Direct Path API (DPAPI), 427

directories

    disk groups, 83

    ORACLE_HOME/bin, 55

    ORACLE_HOME/hostname_sid, 55

    ORACLE_HOME/sysman, 55

DIRECTORY parameter, 428

disable command, 328

DISABLE DATABASE command, 359

disabling

    ASSM (automatic segment-space management), 143

    Flashback Drop, 399

disaster recovery, 170

disk groups

    adding disks to, 80

    checking internal consistency of, 84-85

    creating, 79-80

    definition of, 75

    directory structure, 83

    disk-group templates

        adding, 82

        definition of, 76

        dropping, 83

    dropping, 84

    dropping disks from, 80-81

    failure groups, 75

    mounting, 82

    rebalancing, 81-82

    redundancy, 75

    resizing disks in, 81-82

disk-space management. *See* ASM (Automatic Storage Management)

DISMOUNT clause (ALTER DISKGROUP command), 82

DML (Data Manipulation Language), 455-456

documentation (RMAN), 160-161

downgrade option (ocrconfig command), 327

downstream capture (streams), 464

DPAPI (Direct Path API), 427

dpexp (Data Pump Export), 13

dpimp (Data Pump Import), 13

dr0inst.sql script, 64

drivers, 427

DROP DATABASE command, 13

DROP DIRECTORY clause (ALTER DISKGROUP command), 83

DROP DISK clause (ALTER DISKGROUP command), 80-81

DROP DISKGROUP command, 84

DROP FILE clause (ALTER DISKGROUP command), 84

DROP TABLE command, 398

DROP TABLESPACE command, 398

DROP TEMPLATE clause (ALTER DISKGROUP command), 83

DROP USER command, 399

DROP_BASELINE function, 110, 218, 221-222

DROP_SNAPSHOT_RANGE function, 110, 218-219

DROP_SQLSET function, 276

DROP_SQLSET_REFERENCE function, 276

DROP_SQL_PROFILE function, 277

DROP_TUNING_TASK function, 277

dropping

    ASM file aliases, 84

    AWR (Automatic Workload Repository) snapshots, 219

    baselines, 110, 221-222

    disk groups, 84

    disk-group templates, 83

    disks from disk groups, 80-81

    files, 84

    flashback logs, 371

    snapshots, 110

    tables, 392-399

dump-file sets, 430

dumping ASH buffer contents, 234-235

DUPLICATE command, 170

DURATION keyword (BACKUP command), 167

Dynamic performance views. See V$ views

dynamic sampling, 295-296

E

E-Business Suite, 467

EDIT CONFIGURATION command, 359

EDIT DATABASE command, 359

EDIT INSTANCE command, 360

EGA (Enterprise Grid Alliance), 417

electricity grid, 414-415

EM (Enterprise Manager). See OEM (Oracle Enterprise Manager)

EM2Go, 60-61

EMCA (Enterprise Manager Configuration Assistant) installation script, 55-56

emctl command, 57

enable command, 328

ENABLE DATABASE command, 359

enabling

    ASSM (automatic segment-space management), 143

    tracing, 30

encryption, 343, 458

ENCRYPTION_PASSWORD initialization parameter, 445

END BACKUP command, 158

endianness, 11

Enterprise Grid Alliance (EGA), 417

enterprise grid computing, 417

Enterprise Manager. See OEM (Oracle Enterprise Manager)

Enterprise Manager Concepts Guide and Enterprise Manager Advanced Configuration Guide, 21

Enterprise Manager Configuration Assistant (EMCA) installation script, 55-56

EQUALITY_PREDS column (COL_USAGE$), 302

EQUIJOIN_PREDS column (COL_USAGE$), 302

errors

    ORA-01455, 391

    ORA-15021 error, 78

    ORA-15055 error, 85

    ORA-17203 error, 85

    ORA-27041, 371

    ORA-38701, 371

ORA-38729, 384

ORA-38753, 384

ESTIMATE option (object statistics), 292

EVENT column

    V$ACTIVE_SESSION_HISTORY, 227

    V$SESSION_WAIT, 224

events

    idle events, 259-260

    wait events, 106-107, 176

EVMD daemon, 316

EXECUTE_TASK function, 253-254

EXECUTE_TUNING_TASK function, 277

expdp (export) client, 427

    full-export mode, 431

    new features, 430

    sample application, 432-440

    schema-export mode, 431

    table-export mode, 431

    tablespace-export mode, 431

    transportable-tablespace-export mode, 431

expected I/O response time (ADDM), 261

EXPLAIN PLAN command, 264, 302

export client. See expdp client

export option (ocrconfig command), 327

extending STATSPACK, 178

extents, 141

external redundancy (disk groups), 75

External Table Services API, 427

external table support (Data Pump), 443-444

F

failed installations, uninstalling from, 47-48

    CSS (Cluster Synchronization Services), 49-50

    databases, removing, 48-49

    databases instances, identifying, 48

    Oracle software, removing, 50-51

failover, 367

FAILOVER command, 360

failure groups, 75

fast incremental backups, 163-164

FAST_START_MTTR_TARGET initialization parameter, 134

FGA (fine-grained auditing), 458

files

    10052 event trace file, 304

    ASM files

        aliases, 83-84

        definition of, 76

        filenames, 76

    change-tracking files, 163-164

    flashback logs, 371

    MV (materialized views) logs, 267

    redo log files, 134, 348

    tnsnames.ora, 456-458

FILESIZE initialization parameter, 445

fine-grained auditing (FGA), 458

fixed-size circular buffers, 229

flash recovery area, 19-20, 162-163

Flashback Database, 20, 342-343, 370

    across switchovers, 367

    automatic extension, 384

    configuring, 372-373

    Data Guard, 380-383

    flashback logs, 371

    initialization parameters, 371-372

    managing, 373-375

    RVWR (recover writer), 371

    sample flashback operation, 375-380

    troubleshooting, 384-385

    V$FLASHBACK_DATABASE_LOG, 373-374

    V$FLASHBACK_DATABASE_STAT, 374-375

FLASHBACK DATABASE command, 162, 371, 378, 381

Flashback Drop

    disabling, 399

    Oracle recycle bin, 392-393

    sample flashback operation, 393-398

    troubleshooting, 398-399

FLASHBACK DROP command, 169

flashback logs, 371

flashback restore points, 410

Flashback Table

    automatic undo, 385

    configuring, 385-386

    dropped tables, 395

    sample flashback operation, 386-387, 389-390

    SYS_TEMP_FBT, 387

    table-dependent objects, 392

    troubleshooting, 390-391

FLASHBACK TABLE command, 169, 386-387, 391-393

flashback technology, 369-370

    flashback across global database changes, 410-411

    Flashback Database, 20, 342-343, 370

        across switchovers, 367

        automatic extension, 384

        configuring, 372-373

        Data Guard, 380-383

        flashback logs, 371

        initialization parameters, 371-372

        managing, 373-375

        RVWR (recover writer), 371

        sample flashback operation, 375-380

        troubleshooting, 384-385

        V$FLASHBACK_DATABASE_LOG, 373-374

        V$FLASHBACK_DATABASE_STAT, 374-375

    Flashback Drop

        disabling, 399

        Oracle recycle bin, 392-393

        sample flashback operation, 393-398

        troubleshooting, 398-399

    flashback restore points, 410

    Flashback Table

        automatic undo, 385

        configuring, 385-386

        dropped tables, 395

        sample flashback operation, 386-390

        SYS_TEMP_FBT, 387

    table-dependent objects, 392

    troubleshooting, 390-391

flashback transaction query, 405-408

flashback versions query, 399-400

    sample flashback operation, 400-403

    troubleshooting, 404-405

V$FLASH_RECOVERY_AREA_USAGE view, 411

V$RESTORE_POINT view, 411

FLASHBACK_TRANSACTION_QUERY command, 406-408

FLUSH_DATABASE_MONITORING_INFO function, 303

fractured block reads, 154

free lists, 150

FREELIST GROUPS initialization parameters, 150

FTSes (full table scans), 290

Fujitsu clustering, 322

full table scans (FTSes), 290

full-export mode (expdp), 431

full-import mode (impdp), 431

function-dependent routing, 336

functions and procedures

    ACCEPT_SQL_PROFILE, 277

    ADD_SQLSET_REFERENCE, 276

    ADD_SQLWKLD_REF, 280

    ADD_SQLWKLD_STATEMENT, 280

    ALTER_SQL_PROFILE, 277

    AWR_REPORT_HTML, 218

    AWR_REPORT_TEXT, 218

    CANCEL_TASK, 253

    CANCEL_TUNING_TASK, 277

    CREATE_BASELINE, 218-221

    CREATE_FILE, 280

    CREATE_SNAPSHOT, 218-219

    CREATE_SQLSET, 276

    CREATE_SQLWKLD, 280

    CREATE_TASK, 253-254

    CREATE_TUNING_TASK, 277

    DELETE_SQLWKLD, 280

    DELETE_SQLWKLD_REF, 280

DELETE_SQLWKLD_STATEMENT, 280

DROP_BASELINE, 218, 221-222

DROP_SNAPSHOT_RANGE, 218-219

DROP_SQL_PROFILE, 277

DROP_SQLSET, 276

DROP_SQLSET_REFERENCE, 276

DROP_TUNING_TASK, 277

EXECUTE_TASK, 253-254

EXECUTE_TUNING_TASK, 277

FLUSH_DATABASE_MONITORING_INFO, 303

GATHER_DICTIONARY_STATS, 295

GATHER_SYSTEM_STATS, 293

GET_TASK_REPORT, 253-254

GET_TASK_SCRIPT, 280

IMPORT_SQLWKLD_SCHEMA, 280

IMPORT_SQLWKLD_SQLCACHE, 280

IMPORT_SQLWKLD_STS, 280

IMPORT_SQLWKLD_SUMADV, 280

IMPORT_SQLWKLD_USER, 280

IMPORT_SYSTEM_STATS, 293

INTERRUPT_TUNING_TASK, 277

LOAD_SQLSET, 276

MODIFY_SNAPSHOT_SETTINGS, 218-219

REPORT_TUNING_TASK, 277

RESET_TASK, 253

RESUME_TUNING_TASK, 277

SELECT_SQLSET, 276

SELECT_WORKLOAD_REPOSITORY, 276

SET_TASK_PARAMETER, 253

UPDATE_SQLSET, 276

G

GATHER_DATABASE_STATS_JOB_PROC command, 112

GATHER_DICTIONARY_STATS command, 111

GATHER_DICTIONARY_STATS function, 295

GATHER_STATS_JOB command, 112

GATHER_SYSTEM_STATS function, 293

GET_DUMPFILE_INFO API, 445

GET_TASK_REPORT function, 253-254

GET_TASK_SCRIPT function, 280

global database changes, 410-411

GRANT_ADMIN_PRIVILEGE command, 463

granting administrator privileges, 463

granules, 18

grid (computing), 21, 413

    characteristics of, 415-416

    compared to electricity grid, 414-415

    components of, 418

    definition of, 416-417

    EGA (Enterprise Grid Alliance), 417

    enterprise grid computing, 417

    hardware independence, 420

    high availability, 419

    history of, 417-418

    managing, 420-421

    performance, 419

    profiled resource usage, 420

    provisioning, 416

    resiliency, 420

    self-healing, 420

    virtualization, 416-417, 420

guaranteed restore points, 410

guaranteeing undo availability, 137-138

GUI (Data Guard Broker), 351-356

H

HA (high availability), 327, 419

hardware independence, 420

help option (ocrconfig command), 327

HHWM (High High Water Mark), 149

hidden parameters, 301

high availability (HA), 327, 419

HIGH REDUNDANCY (disk groups), 75

histograms, 307-309

How can we make this index more useful? Email us at indexes@samspublishing.com

History screen (10g iSQL*Plus workspace), 451

hot backup, 154-156

HWM (high-water mark), 148

I

I/O response time (ADDM), 261

idle events, 259-260

impdp (import) client, 427

    full-import mode, 431

    new features, 430

    sample application, 432-440

    schema-import mode, 432

    table-import mode, 432

    tablespace-import mode, 431

    transportable-tablespace-import mode, 432

import client. See impdp

import option (ocrconfig command), 327

IMPORT_SQLWKLD_SCHEMA function, 280

IMPORT_SQLWKLD_SQLCACHE function, 280

IMPORT_SQLWKLD_STS function, 280

IMPORT_SQLWKLD_SUMADV function, 280

IMPORT_SQLWKLD_USER function, 280

IMPORT_SYSTEM_STATS function, 293

in-memory statistics collection (AWR), 12

incarnations, 166

incremental backups, 163-164

incrementally updated backups, 164-166

indexes

    index segments, 142

    monitoring, 273, 296-297

    RAC (Real Application Clusters), 336

individual session tuning, 242

initialization parameters

    ASM_DISKGROUPS (NULL), 78

    ASM_DISKSTRING (NULL), 78

    ASM_POWER_LIMIT (1), 78

    CBO (Cost Based Optimizer), 298-301

    COMPLEX_VIEW_MERGING, 289

    DB_CACHE_SIZE, 18

    DB_FLASHBACK_RETENTION_TARGET, 372

    DB_nK_CACHE_SIZE, 18

    DB_RECOVERY_FILE_DEST, 20, 371

    DB_RECOVERY_FILE_DEST_SIZE, 20, 371

    DB_UNIQUE_NAME, 345

    DB_UNIQUE_NAME (+ASM), 78

    DDL_WAIT_FOR_LOCKS, 461

    ENCRYPTION_PASSWORD, 445

    FAST_START_MTTR_TARGET, 134

    hidden parameters, 301

    INSTANCE_TYPE (ASM), 78

    JAVA_POOL_SIZE, 18

    LARGE_POOL_SIZE, 18, 78

    LDAP_DIRECTORY_ACCESS, 461

    LOG_ARCHIVE_DEST_n, 343

    LOG_ARCHIVE_LOCAL_FIRST, 461

    LOG_BUFFER, 18

    OPTIMIZER_DYN_SMP_BLKS, 295

    OPTIMIZER_DYNAMIC_SAMPLING, 295

    OPTIMIZER_MAX_PERMUTATIONS, 265, 297

    OPTIMIZER_MODE, 290

    OPTIMIZER_SEARCH_LIMIT, 265, 297

    PLSQL_CODE_TYPE, 461

    PLSQL_DEBUG, 461

    PLSQL_WARNINGS, 461

    REMOTE_LOGIN_PASSWORDFILE, 343

    RESUMABLE_TIMEOUT, 133, 461

    RETENTION, 109

    SGA_TARGET, 94-96

    SHARED_POOL_SIZE, 18

    STATISTICS_LEVEL, 95, 100-101, 108-109, 180-181

    STREAMS_POOL_SIZE, 462

    TRACE, 441-442

UNDO_MANAGEMENT, 18, 131

UNDO_RETENTION, 133, 369-370

initxqry.sql script, 63

installation, 23-24

    ASM (Automatic Storage Management)

        DBCA (Database Configuration Assistance), 76

        initialization parameters, 78

        remote connections, 77

        startup/shutdown commands, 79

    backdoor installation techniques, 24

    common steps for installation, 30-32

    companion CD installation and patches, 35

    CRS (Cluster Ready Services), 316-318, 321-322

    database and binary cloning, 36-39

        common steps, 37-38

        OEM (Oracle Enterprise Manager), 38-39

    database management options, 29

    database storage options, 28-29

    DBCA (Database Configuration Assistant)

        creation options, 33

        database content, 33

        database credentials, 33

        database file options, 33

        database identification, 32

        database storage, 33

        database templates, 32

        initialization parameters, 33

        management options, 32

        recovery configuration, 33

        storage options, 33

        tracing, 33-34

    DBUA (Database Upgrade Assistant), 40-41

        Oracle 9i logical standby configuration, 44-46

        Oracle 9i physical standby configuration, 42-44

        silent mode, 42

        upgrade paths for standby environments, 41

    failed installations, uninstalling from, 47-48

        CSS (Cluster Synchronization Services), 49-50

        databases, removing, 48-49

        databases instances, identifying, 48

        Oracle software, removing, 50-51

    Flashback Database, 372-373

    Flashback Table, 385-386

    installation checklists, 36

    manual database installation, 36

    memory requirements, 35

    migration from 8i or 9i, 39-40

    OEM (Oracle Enterprise Manager), 53-54

        alerts, 58-60

        EM2Go, 60-61

        installation process, 55-57

        metric-thresholds management, 59

        Oracle management agents, controlling, 58

        preinstallation requirements, 54-55

    Oracle Text, 63-64

        manual installation, 64-65

        Oracle Spatial installation, 65

        Oracle UltraSearch installation, 65-66

        search issues, 65

    ORACLE_HOME, 324-325

    patches, 46-47

    platform-independent database installation questions, 27-29

    prerequisites, 24-25

    RAC (Real Application Clusters), 66-68

    RMAN (Recovery Manager), 68-70

        backup pieces, 69

        database upgrades, 70

        target databases, unregistering, 71

        unused block compression, 69

    silent installation, 25

    on UNIX/Linux platforms, 25-26

        components to access other databases/applications, 32

        hardware requirements, 26

        installation steps, 27

        OFA (Optimal Flexible Architecture), 29-30

    on Windows platforms, 34-35

How can we make this index more useful? Email us at indexes@samspublishing.com

XML DB

   DBCA, 61-62

   listener configuration on nonstandard ports, 62

   manual installation, 62

   removing, 62-63

   timeout levels, 63

   XQuery support, 63

INSTANCE_TYPE (ASM) parameter, 78

INTCOL# column (COL_USAGE$), 302

Interface Configuration screen (10g iSQL*Plus workspace), 452

interMedia Text. See Oracle Text

internal consistency of disk groups, checking, 84-85

INTERRUPT_TUNING_TASK function, 277

iSQL*Plus enhancements

  infrastructure environment, 450

  SET SERVEROUTPUT command, 454

  SET XQUERY command, 454

  workspace, 450-453

   Change Password screen, 453

   Database Administration screen, 453

   History screen, 451

   Interface Configuration screen, 452

   System Configuration screen, 453

  XQUERY command, 454

J-K-L

Java pool, 17

JAVA_POOL_SIZE parameter, 18

Jnnn (Job Queue processes), 15

Job Queue processes (Jnnn), 15

jobs, scheduling, 460

Label Security, 459

large pool, 17

LARGE_POOL_SIZE parameter, 18, 78

LDAP_DIRECTORY_ACCESS initialization parameter, 461

LGWR (Log Writer process), 15

LHWM (Low High Water Mark), 149

libraries, Veritas, 333

Library Cache Advisor, 19

LIKE_PREDS column (COL_USAGE$), 303

Linux

  ASM (Automatic Storage Management) installation, 77

  Oracle Database 10g installation, 25-26

   common steps for installation, 30-32

   companion CD installation and patches, 35

   components to access other databases/applications, 32

   database and binary cloning, 36-39

   database management options, 29

   database storage options, 28-29

   DBCA (Database Configuration Assistant), 32-34

   DBUA (Database Upgrade Assistant), 40-46

   failed installations, uninstalling from, 47-51

   hardware requirements, 26

   installation checklists, 36

   installation steps, 27

   manual database installation, 36

   migration from 8i or 9i, 39-40

   OEM (Oracle Enterprise Manager), 38-39

   OFA (Optimal Flexible Architecture), 29-30

   patches, 46-47

   platform-independent database installation questions, 27-29

LIST BACKUP command, 158

listeners, configuring on nonstandard ports, 62

little-endian format, 11

LMT (locally managed tablespaces), 36, 148

LOAD_SQLSET function, 276

local versus shared install (RAC), 324

LOCK_SCHEMA_STATS command, 292

LOCK_TABLE_STATS command, 292

locking down object statistics, 292

log files

  archive logs, 154

  flashback logs, 371

MV (materialized views) logs, 267

redo log files, 134, 348

Log Writer process (LGWR), 15

LOG_ARCHIVE_DEST_*n* initialization parameter, 343

LOG_ARCHIVE_LOCAL_FIRST initialization parameter, 461

LOG_BUFFER initialization parameter, 18

LOG_MODE column (V$DATABASE view), 345

logical databases

logical standby databases

commands and views, 349-350

redo log file support, 348

SQL Apply rolling database upgrades, 349

SQL Apply service support, 349

zero outage for instantiation, 346-348

patching, 363-367

Low High Water Mark (LHWM), 149

lsnrctl command, 61

M

Manage Current Backups screen (OEM), 161

manual memory-managed databases, converting to ASMM, 101-102

materialized views (MV), 267

MCP (Master Control Process), 429

memory, 16

ASMM (Automatic Shared Memory Management), 93-96

auto-tuned SGA parameters, 94

automated maintenance tasks, 100

converting manual memory-managed databases to, 101-102

initialization parameters, 94-96

Memory Advisor, 97-99

memory management tips, 100-101

new features, 104

scaling for database expansion, 103-104

SGA sizing, 96-97, 102-103

SGA_TARGET, 102-103

buffers

ASH (Active Session History), 229, 234-235

AWR (Automatic Workload Repository), 208

Buffer Cache Advisor, 19

flash recovery area, 19-20

granules, 18

Memory Advisor, 97-99

MMAN (Memory Manager), 18

MMNL (Memory Monitor Light), 16, 208

MMON (Memory Monitor), 15, 208

PGA (Program Global Area), 18

SGA (System Global Area), 17-18

Memory Advisor, 97-99

Memory Manager (MMAN), 18

Memory Monitor (MMON), 15, 208

Memory Monitor Light (MMNL), 16, 208

Metadata API, 427

MetaLink, 35, 465-466

metric-thresholds management, 59

metrics, 108, 203-204

alerts, 126-127

collecting, 127-128

definition of, 58

metric-thresholds management, 59

monitoring and customization, 125-126

thresholds, 108

migrating

ASM (Automatic Storage Management)

ASM to non-ASM migration, 87-88

non-ASM to ASM migration, 86-87

databases from 8i or 9i, 39-40

MMAN (Memory Manager), 18

MMNL (Memory Monitor Light), 16, 208

MMON (Memory Monitor), 15, 208

mobile management, EM2Go, 60-61

MODIFY_SNAPSHOT_SETTINGS function, 109, 218-219

MODULE column (V$ACTIVE_SESSION_HISTORY), 228

How can we make this index more useful? Email us at indexes@samspublishing.com

monitoring

    indexes, 273, 296-297

    metrics, 125-126

    tables, 296-297

MONITORING keyword (CREATE TABLE command), 112

MOUNT clause (ALTER DISKGROUP command), 82

mounting disk groups, 82

multiple Oracle instances, 74

MV (materialized views), 267

N

Name Server, 457

network-mode operations, 430

networking, 456-458

new features/improvements, 8, 367

    access control, 459

    ADDM (Automatic Database Diagnostic Monitor), 12-13, 262

    ASM (Automatic Storage Management), 9, 89-90

    ASMM (Automatic Shared Memory Management), 104, 150

    automatic undo management, 18, 139

    AWR (Automatic Workload Repository), 11-12, 236-237

    BFTs (BigFile tablespaces), 9-10

    CBO (Cost Based Optimizer), 309-310

    cross-platform transportable tablespaces, 10-11

    Data Guard, 367-368

    Data Pump, 13-14

    DML/DDL features, 455-456

    DROP DATABASE, 13

    flash recovery area, 19-20

    Flashback Database, 20

    flashback operations, 20

    flashback restore points, 410

    grid technology, 21

    initialization parameters, 461

    iSQL*Plus enhancements

        infrastructure environment, 450

        SET SERVEROUTPUT command, 454

        SET XQUERY command, 454

        workspace, 450-453

        XQUERY command, 454

    MetaLink integration, 465-466

    network features, 456-458

    OEM (Oracle Enterprise Manager), 20-21

    Oracle Applications 11i, 467

    Oracle Streams

        architecture, 462

        DBMS_STREAMS_AUTH package, 462-463

        downstream capture, 464

        stream propagation enhancements, 465

        streams administrator, 462-463

        streams pool, 462

        streams-enhanced RAC support, 464-465

    Patch Cache, 466-467

    performance tuning, 205-206

    RAC (Real Application Clusters), 337-338

    Rename Tablespace feature, 8

    resource manager, 460

    RMAN (Recovery Manager), 170-171

    scheduler, 460

    security, 458-459

    SQL Access Advisor, 19

    SQL Advisors, 285

    SQL Tuning Advisor, 19

    SQL*Plus enhancements

        DEFINE command, 447-449

        SET SERVEROUTPUT command, 454

        SET XQUERY command, 454

        SPOOL command, 449-450

        XQUERY command, 454

    statistics, 128-130

    SYSAUX tablespace, 8

    TTGs (temporary tablespace groups), 9

NOCATALOG mode (RMAN), 155

NODE option (SET XQUERY command), 454

nodeapps, 315

nodes, adding/removing from ORACLE_HOME, 325-326

non-ASM to ASM migration, 86-87

non-threshold alerts, 127

NONEQUIJOIN_PREDS column (COL_USAGE$), 302

NOREPAIR clause (ALTER DISKGROUP command), 85

NORMAL REDUNDANCY (disk groups), 75

Not enough flashback database log data to do FLASH-BACK (error), 384

NULL_PREDS column (COL_USAGE$), 303

O

OBJ# column (COL_USAGE$), 302

object partitioning, 336

object statistics. *See also* system statistics

    column statistics, 291

    COMPUTE option, 292

    dictionary statistics, 295

    dynamic sampling, 295-296

    ESTIMATE option, 292

    frequency of collection, 297

    locking down, 292

    table statistics, 291

OCOPY command, 154

OCR (Oracle Cluster Registry), 315, 326-327

ocrcheck command, 327

ocrconfig command, 327

ocrdump command, 327

OCSSD daemon, 315-316

OEM (Oracle Enterprise Manager), 20-21, 53-54

    accessing ADDM (Automatic Database Diagnostic Monitor) from, 244-249

        ADDM Main page, 246

        Advisor Central, 244-245

        AWR Snapshot page, 245

        Database Performance page, 245

        performance finding details, 248-249

        SQL details for PL/SQL block, 247-248

    alerts, 58-60

    ASH (Active Session History), obtaining, 233-234

    automatic undo management, 135-136

    AWR (Automatic Workload Repository), customizing, 216

    checking status of, 56-57

    database cloning, 38-39

    Database Control

        concurrency-related wait information, 199

        example, 196-198

        general database and host information, 195-196

        home page, 198

        host and database wait information, 198-199

        host performance CPU drill-down details, 203-204

        host performance memory drill-down details, 204

        host performance summary, 202-203

        SQL Tuning Advisor, 200-201

        Top SQL, 200

        tuned execution plans, 201

    EM2Go, 60-61

    installation process

        emctl command, 57

        Enterprise Manager Configuration Assistant (EMCA) installation script, 55-56

        OEM control, checking status of, 56-57

    Memory Advisor, 97-99

    metrics, 58-59

    Oracle management agents, controlling, 58

    performance tuning, 194-195

        advisors, 205

        alerts, 203-204

        configuration changes, 195

        metrics, 203-204

        OEM Database Control, 195-204

    preinstallation requirements, 54-55

    RAC (Real Application Clusters), managing, 330-331

Segment Advisor, invoking, 144-145

SQL Access Advisor OEM interface

    input screen, 271-274

    recommendation details, 274-275

    results screen, 274-275

SQL Tuning Advisor OEM interface

    Preserved Snapshot Sets, 269

    results screen, 271

    Schedule Advisor, 270

    Snapshots, 268

    SQL Tuning Sets, 268

    Top SQL, 268

OFA (Optimal Flexible Architecture), 29-30

offline backups, 156

OiD (Oracle internet Directory) Server, 456

ONLINE_LOGFILE keyword, 343

opatch utility, 334-335

operating-system statistics, 108

Optimal Flexible Architecture (OFA), 29-30

Optimizer. See CBO (Cost Based Optimizer)

OPTIMIZER_DYN_SMP_BLKS initialization parameter, 295

OPTIMIZER_DYNAMIC_SAMPLING initialization parameter, 295

OPTIMIZER_MAX_PERMUTATIONS initialization parameter, 265, 297

OPTIMIZER_MODE initialization parameter, 288, 290

OPTIMIZER_SEARCH_LIMIT initialization parameter, 265, 297

OQO (Oracle Query Optimizer). See CBO (Cost Based Optimizer)

ORA-01455 error, 391

ORA-15021 error, 78

ORA-15055 error, 85

ORA-17203 error, 85

ORA-27041 error, 371

ORA-38701 error, 371

ORA-38729 error, 384

ORA-38753 error, 384

Oracle 8i, migrating databases from, 39-40

Oracle 9i

    logical standby configuration, 44-46

    migrating databases from, 39-40

    physical standby configuration, 42-44

Oracle Applications 11i, 467

Oracle Cluster Registry (OCR), 315, 326-327

Oracle Clusterware, 337

Oracle Data Pump. See Data Pump

Oracle Database 10g Backup and Recovery Advanced User's Guide, 160

Oracle Database 10g Backup and Recovery Basics, 160

Oracle Database 10g Licensing, 208

Oracle Database 10g Recovery Manager Quick Start Guide, 160

Oracle Database 10g Recovery Manager Reference, 160

Oracle Database 10g Security Guide, 458

Oracle E-Business Suite, 467

Oracle Enterprise Manager. See OEM

Oracle Enterprise Manager Grid Control Installation and Basic Configuration 10g, 55

Oracle Internet Directory (OiD) Server, 456

Oracle Java Virtual Machine (OracleJVM), 459

Oracle Label Security, 459

Oracle Loader driver, 427

Oracle management agents, controlling, 58

Oracle MetaLink, 35

Oracle Name Server, 457

Oracle Query Optimizer (OQO). See CBO (Cost Based Optimizer)

Oracle software, removing, 50-51

Oracle Spatial, 65

Oracle Streams

    architecture, 462

    DBMS_STREAMS_AUTH package, 462-463

    downstream capture, 464

    stream propagation enhancements, 465

    streams administrator, 462-463

    streams pool, 462

    streams-enhanced RAC support, 464-465

Oracle Text, 63-64

    manual installation, 64-65

    Oracle Spatial installation, 65

    Oracle UltraSearch installation, 65-66

    search issues, 65

Oracle UltraSearch, 65-66

Oracle Universal Installer (OUI). *See* installation

Oracle Wait Interface, 176-177

ORACLE_HOME

    adding nodes to, 325-326

    /bin directory, 55

    /hostname_sid directory, 55

    installing, 324-325

    removing nodes from, 325-326

    /sysman directory, 55

OracleJVM (Oracle Java Virtual Machine), 459

ORADEBUG command, 235

ORB*n* processes, 16

ORDERING option (SET XQUERY command), 454

ordinst.sql script, 65

OUI (Oracle Universal Installer). *See* installation

outlines, 305

P

P1-P3 column (V$ACTIVE_SESSION_HISTORY), 228

P1-P3 columns (V$SESSION_WAIT), 224

P1RAW column (V$SESSION_WAIT), 224

P1TEXT column (V$SESSION_WAIT), 224

P2RAW column (V$SESSION_WAIT), 224

P2TEXT column (V$SESSION_WAIT), 224

P3RRAW column (V$SESSION_WAIT), 224

partitioning, 336

patches

    logical databases, 363-367

    Patch Cache, 466-467

    patch management, 421

patch sets

    applying, 46-47, 361-367

    obtaining, 35

    physical databases, 361-363

PENDING OFFLINE mode (tablespaces), 138

Perform Recovery screen (OEM), 161

performance analysts, 176

performance tuning, 175. *See also* V$ views

    ADDM (Automatic Database Diagnostic Monitor), 239-240

        accessing from OEM, 244-249

        Additional Information findings, 260-261

        addmrpt.sql script, 250-252

        ASH data, 242

        cases when ADDM analysis is not done, 242

        cross-verification from advisor views, 261-262

        DBMS_ADVISOR package, 252-254

        expected I/O response time, 261

        goal of, 240-241

        idle events, 259-260

        new features, 262

        nonproblematic areas, 242

        problem areas handled by, 241

        recommendations, 241-242

        rules, 240

        session management, 258-259

        SQL statements consuming significant time, 254-257

        SQL statements waiting for locks, 257-258

        views, 243-244

    ASH (Active Session History)

        buffer contents, dumping, 234-235

        documentation, 222

        fixed-size circular buffers, 229

        hidden parameters, 229

        limitations, 236

        OEM Database Control, 233-234

        session-state information, 222-226

        spot analysis example, 229-233

V$ACTIVE_SESSION_HISTORY, 226-228

V$ACTIVE_WAIT_HISTORY, 228

V$SESSION_WAIT, 224-225

WRH$_ACTIVE_SESSION_HISTORY, 228

AWR (Automatic Workload Repository), 11-12, 207

baselines, 220-222

buffers, 208

collections, 208-209

compared to STATSPACK, 209-210

customizing with OEM, 216

DBMS_WORKLOAD_REPOSITORY package, 217-220

dependencies, 215-216

emergency purging, 216

licensing information, 208

memory requirements, 209

new features, 236-237

overheads, 215

snapshots, 213-215, 218-219

storage and reporting, 210-213

suggested settings, 215-216

views, 211-212

WRH$ tables, 210

WRI$ tables, 210

WRM$ tables, 210

computing grid, 419

EXPLAIN PLAN command, 264

individual session tuning, 242

new features, 205-206

OEM (Oracle Enterprise Manager), 194-195

advisors, 205

alerts, 203-204

configuration changes, 195

metrics, 203-204

OEM Database Control, 195-204

Oracle Wait Interface, 176-177

performance analysts, 176

RMAN (Recovery Manager), 167

SQL Access Advisor

APIs, 280-284

DBMS_ADVISOR package, 280-284

inputs, 267-268

materialized views, 267

new features, 285

OEM interface, 271-274

potential pitfalls, 284-285

steps for use, 268

SQL Tuning Advisor, 263-264

access path analysis, 266

APIs, 275-280

Automatic Tuning Optimizer, 264-266

DBMS_SQLTUNE package, 277-280

inputs, 266-267

OEM interface, 268-271

potential pitfalls, 284-285

SQL profiling, 266

SQL structure analysis, 266

statistics analysis, 266

STS (SQL tuning sets), 276

STATSPACK, 177-180

extending, 178

limitations of, 177-178

service time, 179

snapshots, 177

wait time, 179

Time and Wait model, 179, 191-194

PGA (Program Global Area), 18

PGA Advisor, 19

physical backups. See backups

physical databases, patching, 361-363

PL/SQL, 145-146

PLSQL_CODE_TYPE initialization parameter, 461

PLSQL_DEBUG initialization parameter, 461

PLSQL_WARNINGS initialization parameter, 461

PMON (Process Monitor process), 15

pools, 17

PREPARE TO SWITCHOVER command, 348-349

PRIMARY_ROLE keyword, 344

Process Monitor (PMON), 15

processes

background processes

Archiver processes (ARCn), 15

ASMB, 16

Change Tracking Writer processes (CTWR), 16

Checkpoint process (CKPT), 15

Database Writer process (DBWn), 14

Job Queue processes (Jnnn), 15

Log Writer process (LGWR), 15

Memory Monitor Light process (MMNL), 16

Memory Monitor processes (MMON), 15

ORBn, 16

Process Monitor process (PMON), 15

Queue Monitor processes (QMNn), 15

RBAL, 16

Recovery Writer process (RVWR), 16

System Monitor process (SMON), 15

centralized job control, 421

definition of, 14

Oracle processes, 14

scheduling, 460

user processes, 14

profiles, 304-307

compared to outlines, 305

resource usage, 420

SQL Tuning Advisor, 266

tracing, 306-307

Program Global Area (PGA), 18

PROGRAM column (V$ACTIVE_SESSION_HISTORY), 228

provisioning, 416

PURGE command, 393

purging recycle bin, 393

Q-R

QC_SESSION_ID column (V$ACTIVE_SESSION_HISTORY), 227

QC_SESSION_INSTANCE column (V$ACTIVE_SESSION_HISTORY), 227

QMNn (Queue Monitor processes), 15

queries

flashback versions query, 399-400

sample flashback operation, 400-403

troubleshooting, 404-405

recycle bin objects, 395

Query Optimizer. See CBO (Cost Based Optimizer)

Queue Monitor processes (QMNn), 15

RAC (Real Application Clusters), 66, 313-314

10g Standard Edition RAC, 314

application partitioning, 336

ASM (Automatic Storage Management), 85, 337

discovering ASM instances, 88

managing, 331-332

maximum file size, 332-333

streams-enhanced RAC support, 464-465

VIP timeouts and VIP failure, 88-89

automatic undo management, 134

Broker support for RAC databases, 351

CBO (Cost Based Optimizer), 294

cluster interconnect, 335

CRS (Cluster Ready Services), 314

CRSD daemon, 315

database-specific resources, 315

EVMD daemon, 316

Fujitsu clustering, 322

installing, 316-318, 321-322

nodeapp resources, 315

OCR (Oracle Cluster Registry), 315

OCSSD daemon, 315-316

troubleshooting, 322-323

Veritas, 322

CVU (Cluster Verification Utility), 337

DBCA (Database Configuration Assistant), 328-330

HA (high availability) support, 327

installing with Data Guard, 68

local versus shared install, 324

managing with EM (Enterprise Manager), 330-331

manual installation, 66-68

new features, 337-338

object partitioning, 336

OCR (Oracle Cluster Registry), 326-327

opatch utility, 334-335

Oracle Clusterware, 337

ORACLE_HOME

    adding nodes to, 325-326

    installing, 324-325

    removing nodes from, 325-326

running 10g RAC and 9i RAC in same environment, 336

service workload management, 323

SGA components, 335

SRVCTL (Server Control), 327

table and indexes, 336

tablespaces, 336

third-party cluster management, 333

UDLM (UNIX Distributed Lock Manager), 334

Veritas, 333

VIPCA (VIP configuration assistant), 328

RANGE_PREDS column (COL_USAGE$), 302

RBAL process, 16

RBO (Rule Based Optimizer), 288-289

Real Application Clusters. See RAC

Real Time Apply, 340-342

REBALANCE clause (ALTER DISKGROUP command), 81-82

rebalancing disk groups, 81-82

RECOVER command, 169

RECOVER COPY command, 165

RECOVER DATABASE command, 169

RECOVER DATAFILE command, 169

RECOVER TABLESPACE command, 169

recovery. See flashback technology; RMAN (Recovery Manager)

Recovery Manager. See RMAN

Recovery Writer (RVWR), 16, 371

recursive SQL, 257

recycle bin, 392-393

redo apply failover, 367

redo log files

    buffer, 17

    sizing, 134

    support for, 348

redo transmission authentication and encryption, 343

redundancy, 75

REFRESH_FROM_METALINK_JOB command, 466

relocate command, 328

REMOTE_LOGIN_PASSWORDFILE initialization parameter, 343

REMOVE DATABASE command, 359

removing

    databases, 48-49

    Oracle software, 50-51

    XML DB, 62-63

RENAME ALIAS clause (ALTER DISKGROUP command), 84

RENAME DIRECTORY clause (ALTER DISKGROUP command), 83

Rename Tablespace feature, 8

renaming

    ASM file aliases, 84

    tablespaces, 8

REPORT_TUNING_TASK function, 277

reports

    ADDM (Automatic Database Diagnostic Monitor)

        Additional Information findings, 260-261

        cross-verification from advisor views, 261-262

        expected I/O response time, 261

        idle events, 259-260

        session management, 258-259

        SQL statements consuming significant time, 254-257

        SQL statements waiting for locks, 257-258

AWR (Automatic Workload Repository), 210-213

    awrddrpt.sql script, 120-122

    awrrpt.sql script, 113-117

    awrrpti.sql script, 117-119

    awrsqrpi.sql script, 123-124

RESET_TASK function, 253

RESETLOGS command, 377, 382-383, 411

RESETLOGS operations, 166, 342

RESIZE clause (ALTER DISKGROUP command), 81-82

resizing disks, 81-82

resource allocation, 147-148

resource manager, 460

RESTORE command, 169

RESTORE DATABASE command, 169

RESTORE DATAFILE command, 169

restore option (ocrconfig command), 327

restore points, 410

RESTORE TABLESPACE command, 169

result sets, 290

resumable space allocation, 133

RESUMABLE_TIMEOUT initialization parameter, 133, 461

RESUME_TUNING_TASK function, 277

RETENTION initialization parameter, 109

retention period (snapshots), 110

RETURNING clause, 456

REVOKE_ADMIN_PRIVILEGE command, 463

revoking administrator privileges, 463

RMAN (Recovery Manager), 68-70, 153-154

    accessing, 161

    advantages of, 154-156

    automatic file creation, 167

    backup identification, 167

    backup pieces, 69, 159-160

    backup sets, 159, 167

    backup strategies, 168-169

    block change tracking, 163-164

    CATALOG mode, 155

    channels, 160

    compared to hot backup, 154-156

    compressed backups, 168

    cross-platform tablespace conversion, 167

    database upgrades, 70

    documentation, 160-161

    fast incremental backups, 163-164

    flash recovery area, 162-163

    incrementally updated backups, 164-166

    new features, 170-171

    NOCATALOG mode, 155

    performance tuning, 167

    recovery scenarios, 169-170

    restore failover, 167

    RESETLOGS operation, 166

    sample backup session, 156-158

    tags, 160

    target databases, unregistering, 71

    unused block compression, 69

role-based destinations, 343-344

rolling database upgrades, 334-335, 349

routing, function-dependent, 336

row cache, 17

RESETLOGS operation, 166

Rule Based Optimizer (RBO), 288-289

RVWR (Recovery Writer), 16, 371

S

"Safely Navigating the RBO to CBO Minefield" (paper), 289

SAMPLE_ID column (V$ACTIVE_SESSION_HISTORY), 227

SAMPLE_TIME column (V$ACTIVE_SESSION_HISTORY), 227

sampling, dynamic, 295-296

scaling for database expansion, 103-104

Schedule Backup screen (OEM), 161

scheduler, 460

scheduling constraints, 274

scheduling jobs, 460

How can we make this index more useful? Email us at indexes@samspublishing.com

schema-export mode (expdp), 431

schema-import mode (impdp), 432

scripts

    addmrpt.sql, 250-252

    awrddrpt.sql, 120-122

    awrinfo.sql, 213

    awrinput.sql, 213

    awrrpt.sql, 113-117, 214-215

    awrrpti.sql, 117-119, 214

    awrsqrpi.sql, 123-124

    catnoqm.sql, 62

    catqm.sql, 62

    dr0inst.sql, 64

    EMCA (Enterprise Manager Configuration Assistant), 55-56

    initxqry.sql, 63

    ordinst.sql, 65

    wk0deinst.sql, 66

    wk0install.sql, 65

SDP (Sockets Direct Protocol), 457

searching Oracle Text, 65

SECONDS_IN_WAIT column (V$SESSION_WAIT), 225

security. See also backups

    access control, 459

    administrator privileges, 463

    Data Guard, 339-340

        archiving, 345-346

        Broker improvements, 351-360

        configuration management, 345

        DB_UNIQUE_NAME initialization parameter, 345

        Flashback Database, 380-383

        flashback database support, 342-343

        goals of, 340

        logical databases, patching, 363-367

        logical standby improvements, 346-350

        new features, 367-368

        physical databases, patching, 361-363

        Real Time Apply, 340-342

        redo transmission authentication and encryption, 343

        role-based destinations, 343-344

        STARTUP command, 345

    encryption, 458

    FGA (fine-grained auditing), 458

    managing, 421

    new features, 458-459

    Oracle Label Security, 459

    user authentication, 458

    Virtual Private Database, 459

Segment Advisor, 19, 143-144

    invoking from OEM, 144-145

    invoking from PL/SQL, 145-146

    reviewing results of, 146-147

segment management

    data blocks, 142

    data segments, 142

    dictionary-managed tablespaces, 150

    disabling, 143

    enabling, 143

    extents, 141

    HWM (high-water mark), 148

    index segments, 142

    LMT (locally managed tablespaces), 148

    new features, 150

    Segment Advisor, 143-144

        invoking from OEM, 144-145

        invoking from PL/SQL, 145-146

        reviewing results of, 146-147

    segment resource allocation, 147-148

    segment-shrink operations, 149-150

    temporary segments, 142-143

SEGMENT SPACE MANAGEMENT AUTO clause, 143

SEGMENT SPACE MANAGEMENT MANUAL clause, 143

SELECT statements, 456

SELECT_SQLSET function, 276

SELECT_WORKLOAD_REPOSITORY function, 276

self-healing (computing grid), 420

sending metrics to third-party tools, 127

SEQ# column (V$SESSION_WAIT), 225

Server Control (SRVCTL), 327

server-generated alerts, 126

servers

OiD (Oracle internet Directory) Server, 456

Oracle Name Server, 457

SERVICE_HASH column (V$ACTIVE_SESSION_HISTORY), 227

services

CRS (Cluster Ready Services), 75, 314

CRSD daemon, 315

database-specific resources, 315

EVMD daemon, 316

Fujitsu clustering, 322

installing, 316-318, 321-322

nodeapp resources, 315

OCR (Oracle Cluster Registry), 315

OCSSD daemon, 315-316

troubleshooting, 322-323

Veritas, 322

service time, 179

service workload management, 323

session management, 258-259

session statistics, 107-108

SESSION_STATE column (V$ACTIVE_SESSION_HISTORY), 227

session-state information

displaying, 222-223

V$ACTIVE_SESSION_HISTORY, 226-228

V$ACTIVE_WAIT_HISTORY, 228

V$SESSION_WAIT, 224-225

WRH$_ACTIVE_SESSION_HISTORY, 228

SESSION_TYPE column (V$ACTIVE_SESSION_HISTORY), 227

SET DBID command, 170

SET SERVEROUTPUT command, 454

SET SQLROMPT command, 448

SET UNTIL command, 170

SET XQUERY command, 454

SET_TASK_PARAMETER function, 253

SGA (System Global Area), 179, 335

auto-tuned SGA parameters, 94

data dictionary cache, 17

database buffer cache, 17

Java pool, 17

large pool, 17

redo log buffer, 17

SGA Advisor, 19

shared pool, 17

size of, 18, 96-97

Streams pool, 17

SGA_MAX_SIZE initialization parameter, 102-103

SGA_TARGET initialization parameter, 94-96, 102-103

shared pool, 17

shared versus local install (RAC), 324

SHARED_POOL_SIZE initialization parameter, 18

SHOW command, 360

showbackup option (ocrconfig command), 327

shrink operations (segments), 149-150

SHUTDOWN ABORT command, 79

SHUTDOWN IMMEDIATE command, 79

SHUTDOWN NORMAL command, 79

SHUTDOWN TRANSACTIONAL command, 79

shutting down ASM (Automatic Storage Management), 79

silent installation, 25

silent mode (DBUA), 42

sizing

redo log files, 134

SGA, 96-97

SKIP FAILED TRANSACTION clause (ALTER DATABASE command), 349

SMON (System Monitor), 15

SNAP_IDs, 117

snapshots, 12, 177, 209-210

accessing, 213, 215

creating, 109, 218-219

deleting, 219

dropping, 110

frequency of, 109-110

retention period, 110

Sockets Direct Protocol (SDP), 457

Spatial option (Oracle), 65

SPOOL command, 449-450

spot analysis with ASH (Active Session History), 229-233

SQL (Standard Query Language). See also specific SQL statements

Access Advisor, 19, 267

APIs, 280-282, 284

DBMS_ADVISOR package, 280-284

inputs, 267-268

materialized views, 267

new features, 285

OEM interface, 271-275

potential pitfalls, 284-285

steps for use, 268

ADDM (Automatic Database Diagnostic Monitor) reports

addmrpt.sql script, 250-252

DBMS_ADVISOR package, 252-254

SQL statements consuming significant time, 254-257

SQL statements waiting for locks, 257-258

Apply

new features, 368

RESETLOGS command, 383

rolling database upgrades, 349

support for, 349

Loader client, 427

profiles, 304-307

compared to outlines, 305

tracing, 306-307

recursive SQL, 257

SQL*Plus enhancements

DEFINE command, 447-449

SET SERVEROUTPUT command, 454

SET XQUERY command, 454

SPOOL command, 449-450

XQUERY command, 454

STS (SQL tuning sets), 276

Tuning Advisor, 19, 200-201, 263-266

access path analysis, 266

APIs, 275-280

Automatic Tuning Optimizer, 264-266

DBMS_SQLTUNE package, 277-280

inputs, 266-267

OEM interface, 268-271

potential pitfalls, 284-285

SQL profiling, 266

SQL structure analysis, 266

statistics analysis, 266

STS (SQL tuning sets), 276

SQL_CHILD_NUMBER column (V$ACTIVE_SESSION_HISTORY), 227

SQL_ID column (V$ACTIVE_SESSION_HISTORY), 227

SQL_OPCODE column (V$ACTIVE_SESSION_HISTORY), 227

SQL_PLAN_HASH_VALUE column (V$ACTIVE_SESSION_HISTORY), 227

SQL*Plus enhancements

DEFINE command, 447-449

SET SERVEROUTPUT command, 454

SET XQUERY command, 454

SPOOL command, 449-450

XQUERY command, 454

SRVCTL (Server Control), 327

Standard Edition RAC (Real Application Clusters), 314

Standby Database Creation Wizard, 353-358

standby database upgrade paths, 41

STANDBY_LOGFILE keyword, 343

STANDBY_ROLE keyword, 344

START_JOB method, 429

STARTUP command, 345

STARTUP FORCE command, 79

STARTUP MOUNT command, 79, 345

STARTUP NOMOUNT command, 79

STARTUP OPEN command, 79

state, session-state information

displaying, 222-223

V$ACTIVE_SESSION_HISTORY, 226-228

V$ACTIVE_WAIT_HISTORY, 228

V$SESSION_WAIT, 224-225

WRH$_ACTIVE_SESSION_HISTORY, 228

STATE column (V$SESSION_WAIT), 225

stateless alerts, 127

statistics, 105-106

    analyzing, 111-112

    AWR reports, 12

        awrddrpt.sql script, 120-122

        awrrpt.sql script, 113-117

        awrrpti.sql script, 117-119

        awrsqrpi.sql script, 123-124

        creating, 109

        dropping, 110

        frequency of, 109-110

        retention period, 110

    base statistics, 108

    baselines, 109-110

    collecting, 12, 111-112

        during database upgrades, 128

        recommendations, 127-128

        timeouts, preventing, 112

    column statistics, 291

    COMPUTE option, 292

    cross-checking, 112-113

    dictionary statistics, 295

    dynamic sampling, 295-296

    ESTIMATE option, 292

    frequency of collection, 297

    locking down, 292

    metrics

        alerts, 126-127

        monitoring and customization, 125-126

        thresholds, 108

    new features, 128-130

    operating-system statistics, 108

    session statistics, 107-108

    statistics levels, 108-109

    system statistics, 107-108, 292-295

table statistics, 291

time-model statistics, 107

wait events, 106-107

Statistics Workload Repository Facilities (SWRF), 213

STATISTICS_LEVEL initialization parameter, 95, 100-101, 108-109, 180-181

STATSPACK, 177-180

    compared to AWR (Automatic Workload Repository), 209-210

    extending, 178

    limitations of, 177-178

    service time, 179

    snapshots, 177

    wait time, 179

STOP_ON_WINDOW_CLOSE parameter (GATHER_STATS_JOB command), 112

streams

    architecture, 462

    DBMS_STREAMS_AUTH package, 462-463

    downstream capture, 464

    stream propagation enhancements, 465

    streams administrator, 462-463

    Streams pool, 17, 462

    streams-enhanced RAC support, 464-465

Streams pool, 17, 462

STREAMS_POOL_SIZE initialization parameter, 462

STS (SQL tuning sets), 276

SWITCHOVER command, 360

switchovers, Flashback Database across, 367

SWRF (Statistics Workload Repository Facilities), 213

SYS.AQ$KUPC$DATAPUMP_QUETAB view, 443

SYS.KUPC$DATAPUMP_QUETAB view, 443

SYS_TEMP_FBT table, 387

SYSAUX tablespace, 8

System Configuration screen (10g iSQL*Plus workspace), 453

System Global Area. See SGA

System Monitor (SMON), 15

system statistics, 107-108, 292-295

T

table-export mode (expdp), 431

table-import mode (impdp), 432

tables

    AUX_STATS$, 294

    dropping, 392-399

    external table support (Data Pump), 443-444

    Flashback Table

        automatic undo, 385

        configuring, 385-386

        dropped tables, 395

        sample flashback operation, 386-390

        SYS_TEMP_FBT, 387

        table-dependent objects, 392

        troubleshooting, 390-391

    FTSes (full table scans), 290

    monitoring, 296-297

    RAC (Real Application Clusters), 336

    statistics, 291

    SYS_TEMP_FBT, 387

    WRH$ tables, 210

    WRI$ tables, 210

    WRM$ tables, 210

Tablespace Point-In-Time Recovery (TSPITR), 169

tablespace-export mode (expdp), 431

tablespace-import mode (impdp), 431

tablespaces

    ASSM (automatic segment-space management)

        dictionary-managed tablespaces, 150

        locally managed tablespaces, 148

    BFTs (BigFile tablespaces), 9-10

    cross-platform transportable tablespaces, 10-11

    locally managed, 36

    PENDING OFFLINE mode, 138

    RAC (Real Application Clusters), 336

    renaming, 8

    switching, 138

    SYSAUX, 8

TSPITR (Tablespace Point-In-Time Recovery), 169

TTGs (temporary tablespace groups), 9

tags (RMAN), 160

target databases, unregistering, 71

templates, disk-group

    adding, 82

    definition of, 76

    dropping, 83

temporary segments, 142-143

temporary tablespace groups (TTGs), 9

third-party cluster management, 333

threshold alerts, 126

thresholds, 108

Time and Wait model, 179, 191-194

time-model statistics, 107

TIME_WAITED column (V$ACTIVE_SESSION_HISTORY), 227

timeout levels, 63

TIMESTAMP column (COL_USAGE$), 303

tnsnames.ora file, 456-458

TRACE initialization parameter, 441-442

tracing

    CBO (Cost Based Optimizer), 303-304

    Data Pump, 441-442

    DBCA (Database Configuration Assistant), 33-34

    enabling, 30

    SQL profiles, 306-307

transactions, flashback transaction query, 405-408

transportable-tablespace-export mode (expdp), 431

transportable-tablespace-import mode (impdp), 432

Triple-DES encryption, 458

troubleshooting

    ASM (Automatic Storage Management) connections, 85

    CRS (Cluster Ready Services), 322-323

    Flashback Database, 384-385

    Flashback Drop, 398-399

    Flashback Table, 390-391

    flashback versions query, 404-405

TSPITR (tablespace Point-In-Time Recovery), 169

TTGs (temporary tablespace groups), 9

tuning. *See performance tuning*

Tuning Advisor. *See SQL Tuning Advisor*

U

UDLM (UNIX Distributed Lock Manager), 334

UltraSearch (Oracle), 65-66

Unable to read data – table definition has changed (errors), 391

Undo Advisor, 19, 134-137

undo management

    advantages of, 132

    AUTO EXTEND initialization parameter, 132

    guaranteeing undo availability, 137-138

    new features, 139

    OEM (Oracle Enterprise Manager), 135-136

    RAC (real application clusters), 134

    redo log file sizings, 134

    resumable space allocation, 133

    tips, 138-139

    Undo Advisor, 134-137

    undo data, 131-132

    UNDO_MANAGEMENT initialization parameter, 18, 131

    UNDO_RETENTION initialization parameter, 133, 369-370

uninstalling from failed installations, 47-48

    CSS (Cluster Synchronization Services), 49-50

    databases instances, identifying, 48

    databases, removing, 48-49

    Oracle software, removing, 50-51

UNIX Distributed Lock Manager (UDLM), 334

UNIX, installing Oracle Database 10g on, 25-26

    common steps for installation, 30-32

    companion CD installation and patches, 35

    components to access other databases/applications, 32

    database and binary cloning, 36-39

    database management options, 29

    database storage options, 28-29

    DBCA (Database Configuration Assistant), 32-34

    DBUA (Database Upgrade Assistant), 40-46

    failed installations, uninstalling from, 47-51

    hardware requirements, 26

    installation checklists, 36

    installation steps, 27

    manual database installation, 36

    migration from 8i or 9i, 39-40

    OEM (Oracle Enterprise Manager), 38-39

    OFA (Optimal Flexible Architecture), 29-30

    patches, 46-47

    platform-independent database installation questions, 27-29

unregistering target databases, 71

unused block compression, 69

UNUSED_SPACE procedure, 149

UPDATE_SQLSET function, 276

UPGRADE CATALOG command, 70

upgrade option (ocrconfig command), 327

upgrades

    RMAN (Recovery Manager), 70

    rolling database upgrades, 349

    statistics collection, 128

    upgrade paths for standby environments, 41

user authentication, 458

user processes, 14

user time, 179

USER_DATAPUMP_JOBS view, 442

V

V$ views, 180-181

    STATISTICS_LEVEL initialization parameter, 180-181

    V$ACTIVE_SESSION_HISTORY, 106-107, 226-228

    V$ACTIVE_WAIT_HISTORY, 228

V$ views

V$ARCHIVE_DEST, 344

V$DATABASE, 345

V$DATAPUMP_JOB, 442

V$DATAPUMP_SESSION, 442

V$ENQUEUE_STAT, 107

V$ENQUEUE_STATISTICS, 188

V$EVENT_HISTOGRAM, 107, 184-186

V$EVENTMETRIC, 184

V$FILE_HISTOGRAM, 107, 186-188

V$FILEMETRIC, 186

V$FILEMETRIC_HISTORY, 186

V$FILESTAT, 107

V$FLASH_RECOVERY_AREA_USAGE, 411

V$FLASHBACK_DATABASE_LOG, 373-374

V$FLASHBACK_DATABASE_STAT, 374-375

V$LATCH, 107

V$METRIC, 181

V$METRIC_HISTORY, 181

V$METRICGROUP, 181

V$METRICNAME, 181

V$OSSTAT, 189

V$RESTORE_POINT, 411

V$ROLLSTAT, 107

V$SEGMENT_STATISTICS, 147

V$SEGSTAT, 147

V$SEGSTAT_NAME, 147

V$SERVICE_EVENT, 183-184

V$SERVICE_STATS, 182-183

V$SERVICE_WAIT_CLASS, 193-194

V$SERVICEMETRIC, 182

V$SERVICEMETRIC_HISTORY, 182

V$SERVICES, 182

V$SESS_TIME_MODEL, 107

V$SESSION, 106, 190

V$SESSION_EVENT, 106, 179

V$SESSION_LONGOPS, 443

V$SESSION_WAIT, 106, 224-225

V$SESSION_WAIT_CLASS, 106

V$SESSION_WAIT_HISTORY, 107

V$SESSTAT, 179

V$SGA, 96

V$SGA_CURRENT_RESIZE_OPS, 97

V$SGA_DYNAMIC_COMPONENTS, 96

V$SGA_DYNAMIC_FREE_MEMORY, 96

V$SGA_RESIZE_OPS, 97

V$SGA_TARGET_ADVICE, 97

V$SGAINFO, 96

V$SGASTAT, 96

V$SQL, 190

V$SQLAREA, 190

V$STREAMS_POOL_ADVICE, 462

V$SYS_TIME_MODEL, 107, 191

V$SYSAUX_OCCUPANTS, 211-212

V$SYSSTAT, 107, 179

V$SYSTEM_EVENT, 107, 179

V$SYSTEM_WAIT_CLASS, 107, 192

V$TEMP_HISTOGRAM, 107, 188

V$UNDOSTAT, 107, 135

VALID_FOR attribute (LOG_ARCHIVE_DEST_n parameter), 343-344

VALID_NOW column (V$ARCHIVE_DEST view), 344

Veritas, 322, 333

VERSION_BETWEEN command, 400

VERSIONS_BETWEEN command, 399, 401

views, 180-181

    ALL_ views, 190

    AUX_STATS$, 294

    COL_USAGE$, 302-303

    DBA_ views, 190

        DBA_ADVISOR_ACTIONS, 243

        DBA_ADVISOR_FINDINGS, 243

        DBA_ADVISOR_LOG, 243

        DBA_ADVISOR_RATIONALE, 243

        DBA_ADVISOR_RECOMMENDATIONS, 243

        DBA_DATAPUMP_JOBS, 442

        DBA_DATAPUMP_SESSIONS, 442

        DBA_HIGH_WATER_MARK_STATISTICS, 211

        DBA_HIST_DATABASE_INSTANCE, 211

DBA_HIST_JAVA_POOL_ADVICE, 211

DBA_HIST_SEG_STAT, 211

DBA_HIST_SNAPSHOT, 211

DBA_HIST_WR_CONTROL, 211

DBA_STREAMS_ADMINISTRATOR, 463

MV (materialized views), 267

SYS.AQ$KUPC$DATAPUMP_QUETAB, 443

SYS.KUPC$DATAPUMP_QUETAB, 443

USER_DATAPUMP_JOBS, 442

See V$ views individual entry

VIP

VIP failure, 88-89

VIP timeouts, 88-89

VIPCA (VIP configuration assistant), 328

Virtual Private Database, 459

virtualization, 416-417, 420

W

wait events, 106-107, 176

wait time, 179

V$ACTIVE_SESSION_HISTORY view, 227

V$SESSION_WAIT view, 224

WAIT_CLASS column (V$SESSION_WAIT), 225

WAIT_FOR_JOB API, 445

whole database recovery, 169

Windows, installing Oracle Database 10g on, 34-35

companion CD installation and patches, 35

database and binary cloning, 36-39

DBUA (Database Upgrade Assistant), 40-46

failed installations, uninstalling from, 47-51

installation checklists, 36

manual database installation, 36

migration from 8i or 9i, 39-40

OEM (Oracle Enterprise Manager), 38-39

patches, 46-47

platform-independent database installation questions, 27-29

wizards

Add Standby Database, 353

Standby Database Creation Wizard, 353-356

wk0deinst.sql script, 66

wk0install.sql script, 65

workspace (iSQL*Plus), 450-453

Change Password screen, 453

Database Administration screen, 453

History screen, 451

Interface Configuration screen, 452

System Configuration screen, 453

WRH$ tables, 210

WRI$ tables, 210

WRM$ tables, 210

X-Y-Z

XML DB

installing manually, 62

installing with DBCA, 61-62

listener configuration on nonstandard ports, 62

removing, 62-63

timeout levels, 63

XQuery support, 63

XQuery, 63

XQUERY command, 454

zero outage for instantiation, 346-348

How can we make this index more useful? Email us at indexes@samspublishing.com